INDIGENOUS PEOPLES OF ASIA

INDIGENOUS PEOPLES OF ASIA

Edited by R. H. Barnes,
Andrew Gray,
and Benedict Kingsbury

Published by the Association for Asian Studies, Inc.
Monograph and Occasional Paper Series, Number 48

Published by The Association for Asian Studies, Inc.
1 Lane Hall, University of Michigan, Ann Arbor, Michigan 48109

This book is printed on acid-free, archival quality paper.
Printed in the United States of America.

Library of Congress Cataloging-in-Publication Data

Indigenous peoples of Asia/edited by R. H. Barnes, Andrew Gray, and Benedict
Kingsbury
p. cm.—(Association for Asian Studies monograph; no. 48)
Includes bibliographical references and index.
ISBN 0-924304-14-6 (cloth).—ISBN 0-924304-15-4 (paper)

1. Indigenous peoples—Asia.   I. Barnes, R. H. (Robert Harrison), 1944–
II. Gray, Andrew, 1955– .   III. Kingsbury, Benedict, 1961– . IV. Series: Monographs of the Association for Asian Studies; no. 48.

GN625.I53   1993   93-10487
305' .08'-95—dc20   CIP

The publication of this volume has been financed from a revolving fund,
supported in part by the Luce Foundation. A full listing of the Association for
Asian Studies Monograph Series appears at the end of this volume.

Contents

Tables

Maps

Plates

Preface

The core of this collection is formed by papers first given in the Colloquium on Indigenous Peoples of Asia at St. Antony's College, Oxford, on 25 November 1989, and in the Asian Studies Centre Seminar on Indigenous Peoples of Asia held at St. Antony's College in Hilary Term, 1990. Authors were invited to extensively revise and update their papers, while other articles were commissioned. There followed the long process of editing and conferring with authors.

In the best of circumstances it would be impossible to put together a completely representative book about the indigenous peoples of Asia given the uncertainties about who is or is not an indigenous person. In some cases we have regrettably been unable to identify anyone willing or able to contribute for a given region. In others, promised chapters never materialized. For this reason we have been unable to include planned chapters on Thailand and on the Nagas of the India-Burma border.

We have been sensitive to the problem of appearing to speak for, that is to say, in place of, indigenous peoples. Although we have not completely overcome this problem, we never had any such intention, and this book is less guilty of doing so than it would have been had we not made an effort to avoid this pitfall. Some chapters give extensive attention to the statements made by indigenous persons and movements. One example of such a statement by the Alliance of Taiwanese Aborigines, I Chiang, Lava Kau, is reproduced as chapter 18.

As the authors in this volume are of diverse backgrounds and hold differing views, the book has no main editorial line. It also makes no claim to providing a definitive statement about a movement that, by virtue of being relatively new, has much of its history ahead of it. The present situation is very fluid, and it can be anticipated that the future will harbor many surprises.

Willem van Schendel's article, "The Invention of the 'Jummas', State Formation and Ethnicity in Southeastern Bangladesh," first appeared in *Modern Asian Studies* 26, no. 1 (1991): 95–128. A version of Hélène Vacher's "Ethnicity and the National Question in Pakistan: The Example of Baluchistan" appeared in the *IWGIA Newsletter*, no. 57 (1989): 87–112. The "Report on the Human Rights Situation of Taiwan's Indigenous Peoples," by the Alliance of Taiwan Aborigines, I Chiang, Lava Kau, was first published in the *IWGIA Newsletter*, no. 2 (1991): 17–18. In each case we express our gratitude for permission to republish them.

We should also like to thank the Warden and Fellows of St. Antony's College for their hospitality.

CHAPTER 1

Introduction

R. H. BARNES

    This volume addresses an issue of novel and increasing concern in Asia, namely, the question of which groups regard themselves as indigenous peoples, which groups are permitted to regard themselves as indigenous peoples, and which groups succeed in being regarded by governments and international agencies as indigenous peoples. As Kingsbury notes in his opening article on "'Indigenous Peoples' as an International Legal Concept," the appeal of the term *indigenous peoples* as a self-chosen form of identity is largely the result of its currency in contemporary international legal and institutional activities. Large issues of personal and group identity, access to and control of resources, self-determination, political freedom, and relations to the state motivate diverse attitudes toward the indigenous-peoples question. Expanding involvement in issues related to the human rights of indigenous peoples has been fostered by agencies such as the International Labour Organisation (ILO), the United Nations Working Group on Indigenous Populations, and the World Council of Indigenous Peoples.

    As Kingsbury and other authors note, *indigenous peoples* is a vexed term with no fixed or generally accepted definition. It is a political category whose definition is in the making, and it will probably continue to change. Gray observes that indigenous movements sprang up throughout the Americas in the late 1960s, while in the 1980s indigenous affairs moved onto the international agenda. Participants in the Working Group on Indigenous Populations in 1985 were predominantly from North America and Australia, with some attendance from Central

1

and South America. By 1987, there was much broader participation from Asia. Meanwhile, with the collapse of the Soviet Union and the weakening of communist and statist governments elsewhere, room has been created for dramatic transformations in relations between states and in a state's relations with its constituent populations.

As even the boundaries of states become contested, different groups struggle to tailor them to their own advantage. In this process, once-dominated indigenous peoples may hope to become dominant in some areas, while dominant peoples run the risk of subjugation to others. Groups in some countries are effectively denied access to international fora in which to express their claims to recognition. However, for differing reasons, some peoples do not find self-identification as indigenous peoples the most advantageous way of furthering their interests. Others, such as the China-dominated Tibetans, anxious to form or reestablish a state in their own image, resist such categorization since they do not wish to be seen as a minority population of a larger state entity.

"Indigenous peoples," a category that first came into existence as a reaction to the legacy of Western European colonialism, has proven especially problematic in postcolonial Asia, where many governments refuse to recognize the distinction sometimes advanced by dissident ethnic groups between indigenous and nonindigenous populations. Gray's experience in Bangladesh provides an example of this reaction. There a government official told him that there were no indigenous peoples in the country, whereas the tribal peoples insisted that they were, of course, indigenous. Contrasting approaches to this dilemma were demonstrated by the delegations of Myanmar (Burma) and Indonesia to the ninth session of the Working Group on Indigenous Populations convened on 31 July 1991. Both congratulated the chairman for not permitting the Working Group to serve as a "chamber of complaints" and deplored the use of the forum by groups making claims for self-determination. Burma then stated that "in the Union of Myanmar there are no indigenous populations in its true sense of the word as there are no distinctly early comers or late comers among the national races of Myanmar." Indonesia, on the other hand, effectively argued that all of the country's three-hundred-odd ethnic groups are indigenous peoples, by implication even the Javanese, who number more than 100 million.

The purpose of this book is to assist in initiating a general understanding of the Asian indigenous-peoples movement or movements. The authors include sociologists, anthropologists, scholars of international law, and journalists. All have had direct experience with Asian peoples and take a professional interest in indigenous issues. Common themes addressed are the idea and definition (or lack of definition) of the term *indigenous peoples*, the question of ethnic identity, historical priority, the critical issue of self-determination, ownership and control of land and resources, ecological exploitation and protection, the colonial heritage, and relations to (usually domination by) the state. The authors explore these and other issues from their various points of view, and no claim can be made that their attitudes are uniform or that there is unanimity in their conclusions.

In chapter 2, Benedict Kingsbury surveys definitional issues relating to the position of indigenous peoples in international law. He considers that it is neither possible nor desirable to formulate a rigid list of requirements for determining which groups are indigenous. Nevertheless, he offers a list of indicia. Some, such as self-identification and vulnerability, are essential requirements, while others, such as nondominance and distinctive language, are relevant factors to be considered in cases of doubt or disagreement. There has been a remarkable increase in international awareness of issues relating to the well-being of indigenous peoples. Nevertheless, for many international purposes a precise definition is not necessary, and as a matter of law many claims do not depend for their legal validity upon the group being considered indigenous.

Andrew Gray follows with a general discussion of "The Indigenous Movement in Asia." Whether or not peoples call themselves indigenous, he argues, the phenomenon only makes sense in contexts in which there are human-rights interests opposed to those of the state. As an analytic category, "indigenous peoples" does not much help in understanding the diverse groups who apply the term to themselves. On the political level it is more an imperative than a descriptive category.

Marcus Colchester presents an overview for South and Southeast Asia in "Indigenous Peoples' Rights and Sustainable Resource Use in South and Southeast Asia." Indigenous peoples' struggle for rights and the sustainability of their resources has been expressed in opposition to socially and environmentally destructive developments coming from outside. Examples show that these peoples have created innovative approaches to the social and environmental problems brought about by development programs.

"Indigenous People of Asian Russia," by Jens Dahl, surveys the vastly transformed situation since the collapse of the Soviet Union. The new focus of concern is on the disastrous erosion of indigenous cultures.

The first indigenous-peoples meeting took place in March 1990. Out of a registered list of 180 speakers, 96 were able to speak before time ran out. A common theme was the social problems confronting various communities, among them alcoholism, illness, environmental destruction, unemployment, and poverty. In October 1990, an Association of Small Peoples of the Soviet North agreed upon a political platform calling for the establishment of legal and political rights. They chose to publish it in English rather than Russian.

Crispin Bates looks into the paradoxical situation of the *adivasi* movements of South Asia. He argues that these movements may depend on the prejudices associated with the term *tribal* for their survival, and that the *adivasi* may be seen as an invention rather than as victims of modernity. There is nothing indigenous, he says, about the term *adivasi* or the peoples it is supposed to describe. Claims that they are the original inhabitants are used by the *adivasi* to legitimize demands for the redress of present-day economic and political inequalities. Despite claims of a past golden age, their identity has a recent origin. Rather than being the original inhabitants, they are the recently dispossessed. Recognizing this may allow consideration of policy options more likely to serve their interests than do current policies based on misconceptions as to their identity and past.

In "The Invention of the '*Jummas*': State Formation and Ethnicity in Southeastern Bangladesh," Willem van Schendel describes an attempt to develop an indigenous model of state society and culture in the Chittagong Hills in opposition to the Bengali majority. The precolonial forebears of the Jumma felt no particular closeness deriving from occupation of a shared region. Today they identify strongly with, and only with, the Chittagong Hill Tracts. They are pursuing their aims through contacts with international organizations, seeking isolation from the dominant culture and state.

The Baluch represent a potentially dominant people now existing as ethnic minorities in three separate states: Pakistan, Iran, and Afghanistan. Hélène Vacher's "Ethnicity and the National Question in Pakistan: The Example of Baluchistan" recounts the history of their struggle for autonomy and resistance to the central government of Pakistan. Government and commercial life in Baluchistan is in the hands of non-Baluch. Although it produces two-thirds of Pakistan's natural gas, only minimal royalties are returned to the province. Despite dislocation caused by economic pressures and wars, the Baluch tribal system has remained the core of their society. The present picture is a contrasting one combining continuity of political efforts to secure the autonomy of the province and political fragmentation that might impede the Baluch movement. The risk exists that it will degenerate into forms of aggressive "little nationalism."

The Rana Tharu occupy the Nepali rain-forest area known as the Tarai. They are the subject of "Nepal, Indigenous Issues, and Civil Rights: The Plight of the Rana Tharu" by Harald O. Skar. These people have suffered land loss, increasing deforestation, and slavery. Today the indigenous peoples are becoming aware of their common problems and are moving toward the formation of a political platform. Awareness of fundamental rights is being transmitted through schools and adult education. Few regard themselves as indigenous but there are signs that a Pan-Tharu movement is beginning to develop.

Nicholas Tapp offers the first thorough review of minority peoples in the Peoples Republic of China in his "Minority Nationality in China: Policy and Practice." The "nationalities question" is directly relevant to the issues of international borders and the definition of the Chinese state but Chinese research into minorities has been confined to their classification in terms of evolutionary stages. An arbitrary classification of fifty-six nationalities (including the majority Han) had led to many misidentifications and the failure to recognize the separate existence of many smaller groups. Nevertheless, the recognized fifty-five minority nationalities number more than 80 million and make up 8.14 percent of the population. Most of the genuinely indigenous peoples are largely unheard of outside China owing to their small size, lack of power, lack of access to international organizations, and extensive assimilation into Han culture. The nationalities category includes an extremely diverse collection of peoples ranging from national groups whose territories have been annexed through acculturated groups, religious minorities, and immigrant or migrant populations. There are only a few properly indigenous groups. The national minority policy favors concessions to those populations and has resulted in benefits sufficient to produce a preference for official minority status.

Nevertheless, Han settlement in minority areas has created tensions. In practice, minority autonomy has been limited in several ways, illiteracy remains high, religious freedom is severely restricted, health care remains rudimentary, and minorities remain exposed to Han chauvinism. Minorities suffered atrocities during the Great Leap

Forward when the official policy was in effective abeyance. Han immigration and widening economic disparities have led to increased unrest in Tibet, Xinjiang, and Inner Mongolia.

In "A State of Strife: The Indigenous Peoples of Burma," Martin Smith surveys the ethnic diversity of a state at war with peoples it claims as its own. Burma has suffered nearly continuous ethnic conflict since independence in 1948, and it is the minorities who have suffered the most. Its experience of "the dilemma of national unity" has been particularly acute. There is an increasing refugee problem, growing prostitution and semislavery, ecological decline, a spreading narcotics problem, and a collapse of higher education.

The "Central Highlanders of Vietnam" described by Grant Evans lack the freedom to organize and establish contacts with other indigenous peoples for solidarity. The communists have broken their promises to the Central Highlanders to create autonomous zones and have carried forward a policy of Vietnamization and colonization. The Vietnamese migrants, however, are suffering from poorly prepared programs. One consequence is that they are resorting to slash-and-burn farming, illegal timber gathering and logging, and hunting of endangered species, leading to environmental destruction. Vietnam regards itself as a developmental state and is openly hostile to what it regards as the evolutionarily backward practices of highland cultures. These peoples were devastated during the Vietnam War, and subsequently by tensions with China and Cambodia that led the government to strive for stronger control over border areas where minorities overlapped.

The "original people," or Orang Asli, of Malaysia preceded the Malays, having entered the peninsula between three and eight thousand years ago. They make up only 1 percent of the present national population. The Malays advance their own claims to being indigenous, while using the state to try to limit the immigrant Chinese and Indian populations. Despite constitutional guarantees, the Malays are attempting to assimilate the Orang Asli. Since 1980, the government has ceased to list them separately from Malays in the census. They have not yet participated in Fourth World fora but in "Indigenous People of Peninsular Malaysia: It's Now or Too Late," Signe Howell writes that this situation is about to change.

After the Malays came to the region, about 2,000 years ago, the Orang Asli were forced further and further inland. After World War II they were caught in the conflicts between insurgents and colonial forces that arose during the Emergency (1948–60). In the past the Malays have regarded them as legitimate objects to hunt and enslave. Efforts to resettle them in the 1950s for national security purposes led to many deaths. The Department of Aboriginal Affairs has failed to protect their economic interests, to provide adequate health care and education, and to protect their religious freedom. Lacking legal title to their land, they have been unable to prevent Chinese and Malays from exploiting their fruit trees, fish, and game. They are also being pushed aside by logging companies and given no compensation. They strongly believe that the main aim of the government is to solve the "Orang Asli problem" by transforming them into settled peasants and converting them to Islam. A pressure group founded to further their interests now claims ten thousand members and publishes a newsletter. Efforts have been made to secure land titles, to demand effective representation in Parliament, and to place the administration of the Department of Aboriginal Affairs in their own hands. Encouragingly, a recent High Court ruling found that the State of Perak violated Orang Asli land rights by approving logging in an Aboriginal Reserve, offering hope of some effective legal protection.

The dilemma of whether or not to become Malay (*bumiputra*) is also faced by the indigenous peoples of Sarawak. This is explored by Victor T. King in "Indigenous Peoples and Land Rights in Sarawak, Malaysia: To Be or Not To Be a *Bumiputra*." As he writes, it is the nonindigenous groups who have suffered constitutional discrimination. The revised Federal Constitution of 1971 extended to the native peoples of Borneo all the special rights and privileges accorded to Malays. But despite this position they remain politically and economically subordinate to the Peninsular Malays, to such an extent that they can be spoken of as "second-class *bumiputra*." Sarawak natives are not, however, short of land, and many communities have remained in close contact with it. They have demonstrated marked resilience in the face of dramatic changes in their social, economic, and cultural lives. Nevertheless, there is still much poverty and economic deprivation. Recent publicly managed estates intended to modernize native farmers have failed. This failure has wasted large amounts of money and has led to increased marginalization and discontent. Longer term, market forces will continue to undermine native land rights. King recommends a gradualist policy of *in situ* development, coordinating the efforts of small landholders. He argues against a reservation policy, suggesting instead that Sarawak natives need to obtain a stronger political voice, and gain control of economic and political forces, so that they can select new opportunities on their own terms.

In "Being Indigenous in Eastern Indonesia," R. H. Barnes argues that the question of who is indigenous is both interesting and complex. The issue of whether indigenous peoples exist in the special sense of international law and politics is even more complex. The recent conquest of East Timor by the Indonesian army and the continued resistance by the East Timorese, coupled with their representations to international organizations, place them clearly in that class *in so far as* they do not choose instead to identify themselves as a separate nation temporarily under occupation. Their culturally and linguistically related neighbors do not in general regard themselves as being in the same position, and many express strong national feeling in relation to the Republic of Indonesia.

Several commonly mentioned criteria of indigenous peoples are surveyed and found to be imperfectly relevant to eastern Indonesian populations. These include nomadism, community-based political organization, Earth Mother beliefs, and a custodial attitude toward the land. As for the important criterion of self-definition, only the independence movements of Irian Jaya, the South Moluccas, and East Timor meet it, to the extent that they take this path among the alternatives open to them. In the case of preexistence, the peoples of eastern Indonesia, who are racially and linguistically mixed, have diverse explanations of their origins. Some claim to have had ancestors who emerged from the earth, from trees or rocks, or who descended from the heavens. Others regard themselves as descendants of immigrants, many of whom arrived in ancient times. These contrasting accounts often occur within the same community. In the end, excluding East Timor, none of the criteria reviewed fit very well. The cultural, linguistic, and racial differences do not coincide and do not permit a distinction between indigenous peoples and dominant intruders. What distinguishes East Timor is its separate history and the fact that it is dominated by a foreign army.

John G. Taylor looks specifically at East Timor in "The Emergence of a Nationalist Movement in East Timor." He reviews a series of historical and cultural factors in an attempt to explain why resistance to Indonesian occupation has proved to be so strong. The political group Fretilin led (and still leads) the resistance, and it has developed a high degree of support among the population. It moved (or was forced to move) increasingly into remote regions, where it worked with existing alliances based on kinship. It took traditional concepts and ideas as the bases for development programs. The military has been unable to fully control territory or to establish enthusiasm for annexation. Now a generation raised under Indonesian rule is expressing its opposition.

Charles Macdonald describes the position of the some fifty or more "Indigenous Cultural Communities" of the Philippines in "Indigenous Peoples of the Philippines: Between Segregation and Integration." As he says, in a country in which the concept of the nation has only recently emerged, one could argue that every ethnic group, even dominant ones, forms a separate minority with a sense of self-identity. The Indigenous Cultural Communities are too diverse to fit a single category but they have in common the fact that they are ostracized by the wider society. Macdonald describes how they are both rejected and included in the development of the nation. As elsewhere, the major problem confronting them is the loss of land. Lacking a traditional concept of individual land ownership, they are exposed to the legal and illegal land-grabbing activities of settlers from other areas. Nevertheless, although timber concessions, water projects, plantations, mining, and cattle ranching are destroying their natural environment, in a number of cases migrants and native peoples have found mutually beneficial ways of coexisting.

Indigenous peoples have been caught in the crossfire of insurgents and counterinsurgents. In addition, they lack access to health and sanitation services, and are exposed to a foreign, coercive, and authoritarian educational system. In response to their plight, numerous nongovernmental organizations (NGOs) have taken up their cause. The new attention they enjoy has had both beneficial and adverse effects, and the various organizations struggling to give them leadership are factionally split, threatening in some cases to divert the struggle into political channels of little relevance to them. In the end, Macdonald takes the mildly optimistic view that a number of these groups will survive in one form or another, provided that they are able to adapt and do not choose to adopt a different way of life.

The "Report on the Human Rights Situation of Taiwan's Indigenous Peoples," by the Alliance of Taiwan Aborigines, I Chiang, Lava Kau, is a statement by a group seeking international recognition. It is one of several such statements presented to the ninth session of the United Nations Working Group on Indigenous Populations in Geneva in 1991. Following a review of Taiwan's varied colonial history and its impact on the Aborigines, the report considers the present situation. The Aborigines complain that they not only share the political repression experienced by the dominant Han but they also suffer from the government's Han cultural chauvinism. The Kuomintang (KMT) Constitution contains no laws that specifically describe or protect the indigenous peoples of Taiwan, so they have no right to self-determination and no collective rights. The government's policy is one of assimilation. It has rejected demands that the indigenous peoples be given an autonomous region. They are subjected to unequal laws concerning the ethnic identities of mixed-group couples and their children. Regulations relating to land expose them to the loss of rights and control over their own territory. Furthermore, they are forbidden traditional uses of their land such as hunting and fishing. Driven into the cities, they are forced into low-status and poorly paid employment and must live in illegal constructions. Many are in debt. They are denied the right to register their traditional names, and children are forbidden to speak their own language in schools. Education for them is substandard and the educational system tends to discriminate against them. Many indigenous girls and young women are bought and sold as child prostitutes. Although Taiwan is no longer a member of the United Nations, the Alliance of Taiwan Aborigines welcomed the opportunity to make this presentation and thus to draw the attention of concerned international organizations to their human-rights problems.

The final chapter, "Practicing Ethnicity in a Hierarchical Culture: The Ainu Case," by Katarina Sjöberg, looks at the rather different position of the Ainu of Japan. The population of Japan consists of several peoples who differ culturally, linguistically, and biologically from the dominant Wajin. Japan recognizes the Ainu as a religious and cultural minority but Ainu efforts to celebrate, revive, and preserve the customs of the past are severely circumscribed. Japan argues that the Ainu have lost most of their cultural distinctiveness through assimilation, and that Ainu customs have only a touristic interest. Previously the Ainu did not object to regarding themselves as Japanese and devoted much effort to becoming assimilated. Recently they have begun to reconsider this approach. Despite the official position that the Ainu are also Wajin, the Wajin are reluctant to marry them and they remain outcastes.

Some Ainu place strong emphasis on their distinct cultural identity. Others identify themselves as Japanese in a national context and as Japanese of Ainu descent in local contexts. Others overtly reject their Ainu identity but reveal it in practice. Ainu regard themselves as neither marginal nor indigenous.

Production and display of cultural objects for tourists now play a large role in the Ainus' conscious reconstruction of their identity. This fact is ironic, since the Japanese authorities initiated tourist centers for reasons having little to do with Ainu customs, which they misrepresented. When Japanese journalists and students indulged in arson, bombings, and attempted murder in alleged sympathy with them, the result was temporary imprisonment of many innocent Ainu. They reacted by studying their culture and attempting to present a more accurate view of themselves in the tourist centers. Since Ainu from all over Hokkaido work in these centers, they provide the context for developing a network among Ainu communities. Japan's recent and belated recognition of the Ainu as a religious and cultural minority is unlikely to lead to much change, for the Japanese government would have to double or triple its financial support if it took recognition seriously. More likely the Ainu will continue to be slighted by the Wajin, while receiving only token recognition of their ethnic distinctiveness.

References to the situation in Pakistan, India, Bangladesh, Tibet, China, Japan, Burma, Thailand, Laos, Cambodia, Vietnam, Malaysia, Indonesia, East Timor, West Papua, and the Philippines are made in the chapters by Gray and Colchester. In addition, the yearbooks of the International Work Group for Indigenous Affairs (IWGIA) carry reports on Sri Lanka, Afghanistan, Europe and North Asia, Mongolia, Siberia, Iraq, Iran, and Turkey. These yearbooks provide summaries culled from such sources as the *TAPOL Bulletin*, *Survival International News*, *Tibetan Review*, *Timor Link*, Amnesty International, *Cultural Survival Quarterly*, and so on. IWGIA documents and newsletters provide further information. Debates over ILO Conventions 107 and 169 and the UN Working Group's Draft Declaration on the Rights of Indigenous Peoples (to which Kingsbury refers) can be followed in the relevant sections of the IWGIA yearbooks. For Southeast Asia, in particular, recent collections such as those edited by Wijeyewardene (1990), Lim and Gomes (1990), and the anonymously edited *Southeast Asian Tribal Groups and Ethnic Minorities* (1987) permit further exploration of these and related issues.

The concerns of indigenous peoples often are similar throughout Asia, and indeed throughout the world. They are also shared, as several of our authors report, by groups or populations which for one reason or another cannot be described as indigenous. It may be expected that the movement to define and protect the rights of indigenous peoples will have manifold consequences for other Asian populations, and may in the long run have general implications for the relations between states and the people living within them. Another foreseeable development is that more and more groups will decide to, and in some cases force their governments to permit them to, participate in international fora. No doubt many will explore alternative routes to recognition. These developments will have effects not only within states but also on relationships between states. It is hoped, therefore, that this book will contribute to scholarship on a subject of increasing salience. No doubt the indigenous peoples will themselves take control of much of the further scholarship and debate.

CHAPTER 2

"Indigenous Peoples" as an International Legal Concept

BENEDICT KINGSBURY

The fact that *indigenous peoples* has become an appealing term which many groups (or individuals speaking for them) choose to apply to themselves is largely a result of the currency given to the category by the international activities of nonstate and interstate organizations. The purpose of this paper is to examine definitional aspects of the use of "indigenous peoples" and related categories in contemporary international legal and institutional practice. It addresses the international-law aspects of a subject that recurs throughout this volume, that of the meaning of *indigenous peoples*. As the discussion of international practice will indicate, the term has two rather different functions in international legal materials. One function is to delimit the precise scope of international instruments, especially when an instrument proclaims rights of indigenous peoples or duties of states in relation to indigenous peoples. A second function is to indicate in broad terms the groups with whom a general and diffuse body of practice (such as that of the United Nations Working Group on Indigenous Populations when it engages annually in a "review of developments") is principally concerned.

The paper is organized as follows. The first section, by way of orientation, briefly outlines international activity concerning indigenous peoples. Subsequent sections examine the classifications used by the major international institutions concerned with such groups and consider the problems of definition faced by the UN Working Group in preparing a draft Declaration on the Rights of Indigenous Peoples. Based on international practice, a list of essential requirements and other indicia will be suggested. The conclusion summarizes the findings of the paper, and makes the point that much of the international law bearing upon claims by indigenous peoples does not depend directly on use of the category "indigenous peoples."

A Brief Overview of Interstate Activity Concerning Indigenous Peoples

The International Labour Organisation (ILO), an intergovernmental body with an unusual tripartite structure comprising representatives of governments, national employers, and trade-union groups, has been concerned with "indigenous" workers since the 1920s. In 1957, it adopted the first treaty of general application dealing with indigenous and tribal populations, ILO Convention 107. Following criticism of assimilationist provisions and other features of Convention 107, a revised version, Convention 169, was concluded in 1989. The new Convention entered into force in September 1991. Only four states (Bolivia, Mexico, Norway, and Venezuela) had ratified the Convention by that time, whereas twenty-five states (including three Asian states—Bangladesh, India, and Pakistan) remain parties to Convention 107. Although in the longer term it is possible that some Asian states will ratify Convention 169, no such ratifications are expected in the near future.

The United Nations Sub-Commission on Prevention of Discrimination and Protection of Minorities is a relatively low-level body in the institutional hierarchy of the UN human-rights system but it is energetic and somewhat independent of governments. In the 1970s, it appointed a Special Rapporteur on Indigenous Populations and established the Working Group on Indigenous Populations, which has met annually (except during a 1986 budget crisis) since 1982. The Working Group has only five official members but it hosts an annual gathering of up to four hundred persons who regard themselves as members of indigenous peoples' groups,[1] along with representatives of several dozen UN governments, including in 1993 those of Bangladesh, Bhutan, India, Indonesia, Japan, Myanmar, the Philippines, and the Russian Federation.[2] The Working Group has several aims. It provides a forum in which specific developments concerning indigenous peoples can be discussed and in which indigenous peoples can build coalitions and engage in dialogue with states. Issues of fundamental interest such as self-determination, land rights, or cultural property can be addressed. A major function of the Working Group has been to prepare a Draft Declaration on the Rights of Indigenous Peoples, adopted on its second reading in 1993. The UN General Assembly had proclaimed 1993 the International Year of the World's Indigenous People. The Draft Declaration is intended for eventual consideration by the General Assembly.[3]

The World Bank is the most prominent of several intergovernmental finance and aid institutions that have become concerned about the impact of their policies and project financing on particular groups. In 1982, the bank adopted an Operational Manual Statement concerning "tribal peoples" but this was broadened and enhanced in 1991 to apply also to groups that the bank characterizes as "indigenous peoples."[4]

In addition to these global institutions, regional or subregional intergovernmental activities concerning indigenous peoples have become increasingly significant in the Americas and in Northern Europe but there has been little such activity in Asia. The Inter-American Indian Institute, established by treaty in 1940, continues to operate under the auspices of periodic intergovernmental Inter-American Indian conferences.[5] A Special Commission on Indigenous Affairs was established by the Amazonian Pact countries in 1989, and the Nordic governments have promoted a Nordic Sami Parliament among other initiatives.[6] A great many nonstate organizations concerned with indigenous peoples' issues have been established, including the World Council of Indigenous Peoples, which has an Asia-Pacific regional division, the Pacific-Asia Council of Indigenous Peoples.

This international activity has contributed to—and has been influenced by—developments in domestic political organization and discourse. The language of indigenous rights has become increasingly popular for the expression of rights claims in national and international contexts.[7]

Defining "Indigenous Peoples"

The use and definition of the term *peoples* has proved sensitive in international practice, principally because it has been employed to designate a category of nonstate groups holding particular international-law rights, most notably the right of "all peoples" to self-determination. For that reason states have been reticent about use of the term *indigenous peoples* at the international level, even when they were willing to use such terms as *people* or *nation* domestically. The name of the UN Working Group on Indigenous Populations has not been changed because of the possibility of objections by some governments in higher-level bodies in the UN system but for most purposes the international institutions have accepted the term *indigenous peoples* as standard. One qualification is that the Commission on Human Rights and higher-level UN bodies, including the General Assembly when it proclaimed the 1993 International Year, continue to finesse the issue of collective rights (principally the right to self-determination) by referring to indigenous people rather than "indigenous peoples." A different approach was taken in ILO Convention 169, which expressly refers to "indigenous and tribal peoples" but stipulates in Article 1(3): "The use of the term 'peoples' in this Convention shall not be construed as having any implications as regards the rights which may attach to the term under international law." As a matter of international law this fixation with terminology is misconceived: right holders and the actual application of rights are both determined by substantive legal analysis rather than by terminology, and the logic of the principle of self-determination extends beyond the question of independent statehood to political and cultural options exercisable within the established state.[8]

The term *indigenous peoples* is used frequently in international organizations and by nongovernmental organizations (NGOs) and governments. While it has been used in a number of legal instruments to describe the scope of their application, these uses generally have not been accompanied by precise definitions. In treaty and policy instruments, as in international practice more generally, it is used primarily as a political and sociological term to denote in general terms a range of groups whose shared interests and concerns have been recognized internationally as warranting particular and distinct investigation and action. In some respects it has become advantageous for groups to characterize themselves as indigenous peoples, both because of the benefits of solidarity with other groups and because of the international political recognition of this category of claimant. Participation in meetings of or concerning indigenous peoples, and the international visibility of this category of issues, has increased steadily since the mid-1970s. Not surprisingly, the political category of "indigenous peoples" is largely undefined, and its existence provides little direct assistance in legal analysis.[9]

The following sections will set out the principal categories and definitions used by the ILO, the World Bank, and the UN. One basic terminological difference is that ILO Convention 169 expressly applies to both "indigenous peoples" and "tribal peoples," while the definition of the UN Special Rapporteur refers only to the former. The World Bank policy, which previously applied only to "tribal peoples," was recast in 1990–91 to apply to "indigenous peoples," a label the bank regards as extending to and including tribal peoples and other ethnic minorities. Other terminology is used also. In the Americas, the Inter-American Indian Institute and Congresses, the Inter-American Commission on Human Rights, and subregional bodies such as the Amazonia Special Commission on Indigenous Affairs appear to treat "Indian" and "indigenous" as interchangeable in their own practice. Asian governments and national legal systems use a range of terms in their domestic practice (discussed in subsequent chapters of this volume) but there does not appear to be any pertinent intergovernmental practice in Asia.

The UN Working Group on Indigenous Populations has proposed a Draft Declaration on the Rights of Indigenous Peoples, which does not contain an explicit statement as to the meaning of the term *indigenous peoples*. A limited degree of clarification may be derived from the practice of the Working Group and from statements of its members, particularly Chairperson-Rapporteur Erica-Irene Daes, but fundamental questions concerning definitions have not been resolved by the Working Group. In light of the international practice and other relevant considerations discussed in this chapter, an attempt is made below to identify some general indicia of the sort that might be used if it is eventually decided to include definitional provisions in the proposed Declaration or if the UN Working Group decides in the future that it needs a definition to guide its own practice.

The International Labour Organisation Conventions

The ILO governing body established a Committee of Experts on Native Labour in 1926, following earlier studies on the position of indigenous workers. Four conventions in this field were adopted by the ILO: the Forced Labour Convention of 1930, the Recruiting of Indigenous Workers Convention of 1936, the Contracts of Employment (Indigenous Workers) Convention of 1939, and the Penal Sanctions (Indigenous Workers) Convention of 1939. The latter three used a definition applicable in both dependent territories and independent countries.

> The term "indigenous workers" includes workers belonging to or assimilated to the indigenous populations of the dependent territories of Members of the Organisation and workers belonging to or assimilated to the dependent indigenous populations of the home territories of Members of the Organisation.

This identification of overlapping legal duties toward colonial populations and indigenous peoples in independent countries has continued in
some academic literature and in the statements of indigenous-peoples
groups but a sharp distinction was quickly drawn in international practice after 1944. Within the ILO, it appeared in the division of work
between the Committee of Experts on Social Policy in Non-Metropoli-
tan Territories, founded in 1945, and the Committee of Experts on
Indigenous Labour, which met in 1951 and 1954.[10]

The main impetus for ILO activity concerning indigenous peoples
during the period from 1945 until the adoption of ILO Convention 107
and Recommendation 104 in 1957 came from the Americas. A series of
conferences of the American states members of the ILO called for
specific measures to protect and assist indigenous workers, and for more
general action by the ILO concerning indigenous peoples worldwide.[11]
Several important development programs concerned with American
Indians were undertaken by the ILO and other international agencies,
and the Inter-American Indian Institute and some national institutes
actively coordinated practical and theoretical work. The meaning of
terms such as *indigenous peoples* or *Indians*, in the context of national and
international policies for their "protection" or "advancement," generated
debate in the Americas. One approach laid stress on evaluating the
cultural traits of each group, and treating as Indian those groups in
which pre-Columbian elements predominated.[12] This might involve
deciding, for instance, whether to classify as pre-Columbian a stick used
for planting seed corn that before European colonization was tipped
with copper or hardened wood but by the twentieth century had
acquired a wrought iron point.[13] Another approach, much closer to the
view currently favored by indigenous peoples' representatives, regarded
"Indianness" as an expression of group consciousness, itself molded by
language, tradition, economy, and labor patterns.[14]

Definitions embodying these and other approaches were put
forward by states during the drafting of ILO Convention 107. In the
matter of definition, at least, the latter approach was exemplified by
Brazil, which proposed inclusion of a clause stating that

> The term "indigenous" refers to the descendants of populations which
> existed prior to conquest or colonisation who retain socio-cultural institu-
> tions different from those of the nation on whose territory they live and
> to which they belong, and who are conscious of the ethnic features that
> distinguish them from the other communities with which they live and
> which shall be termed "national and non-indigenous" communities.[15]

Honduras went somewhat further, suggesting that

> a detailed definition of the indigenous peoples of independent countries is
> not needed. It would be sufficient to refer to the less favourable living
> conditions and the lower social, economic and cultural status of such
> peoples as compared with the remainder of the population, without neces-
> sarily speaking of conditions existing prior to conquest or colonisation.[16]

On the other hand, the major International Labour Office study
(1953) concentrated on indigeneity defined in terms of continuity from
precolonial or preinvasion structures and culture, using a working definition of *indigenous* that emphasized biological, social, cultural, and
economic continuity from the aboriginal population predating settlement or conquest.[17] Several states supported this approach, and it was
incorporated into the Convention 107 definition. In 1956, however, the
Office argued that international protection should apply to tribal or
semitribal peoples whether or not they could be regarded as indigenous
in this sense.[18] This view was reflected in the drafting of Convention 107
and in the subsequent publications of the ILO. As the Office later put it,

> The practical effect was a considerable increase in the kinds and numbers
> of groups considered potentially to fall within the scope of an international
> instrument. The [1956] report listed a large number of tribal populations
> in the Near and Middle East, including such groups as the Kurds, Bakhtiari
> and Baluchi who had tended traditionally to cross national frontiers.
> African tribal groups were also included, with specific mention of tribal
> populations in such countries as Ethiopia, Somalia, Liberia, Libya and
> South Africa.[19]

Another contentious issue was whether Convention 107 should
apply to individuals or to entire groups. Drawing on its own national
experience, Mexico had argued in 1956 that

> The practical difficulties involved in limiting Indian policy exclusively to
> persons who could be defined as Indians were so great that personal defi-
> nitions, such as those used in societies which have a high regard for
> individual rights, had to be abandoned in favour of a social definition
> stressing the concept of the organised group.[20]

The solution finally adopted in Convention 107, however, was a
compromise similar to that employed in other international human-
rights instruments (for example, the minority-rights provision of the
1966 International Covenant on Civil and Political Rights): to apply the
Convention to "members of tribal or semi-tribal populations." Thus, the

test of indigeneity or tribal status is applied to a particular population, while the test applied to individuals is that of membership. Article 1 provides that Convention 107 shall apply to

(a) members of tribal or semi-tribal populations in independent countries whose social and economic conditions are at a less advanced stage than the stage reached by the other sections of the national community, and whose status is regulated wholly or partially by their own customs or traditions or by special laws or regulations;

(b) members of tribal or semi-tribal populations in independent countries which are regarded as indigenous on account of their descent from the populations which inhabited the country, or a geographical region to which the country belongs, at the time of conquest or colonisation and which, irrespective of their legal status, live more in conformity with the social, economic and cultural institutions of that time than with the institutions of the nation to which they belong.[21]

While this provision recognizes that the Convention should apply to tribal peoples who cannot necessarily be regarded as indigenous, it assumes that all indigenous peoples requiring the protection of the Convention are tribal or semitribal. By the 1980s, the ILO recognized that this assumption was unwarranted and it was abandoned in Convention 169 along with the references to semitribal populations. Convention 169 expressly applies to "peoples"; the qualifier "members of" is not included in the definition provisions, nor does it appear in a number of the substantive articles. Article 1(1) of Convention 169 stipulates that the Convention applies to

(a) tribal peoples in independent countries whose social, cultural and economic conditions distinguish them from other sections of the national community, and whose status is regulated wholly or partially by their own customs or traditions or by special laws or regulations;

(b) peoples in independent countries who are regarded as indigenous on account of their descent from the populations which inhabited the country, or a geographical region to which the country belongs, at the time of conquest or colonisation or the establishment of present state boundaries and who, irrespective of their legal status, retain some or all of their own social, economic, cultural and political institutions.[22]

States parties have taken divergent approaches in interpreting the scope of Convention 107.[23] The ILO Committee of Experts on the Application of Conventions and Recommendations (the body that

monitors compliance with ILO conventions) has taken a relatively wide
view of the scope of Article 1. Of the twenty-seven states that became
parties to the Convention prior to the entry into force of Convention
169, the committee has accepted that Belgium, Cuba, the Dominican
Republic, Haiti, Portugal, and Tunisia do not have populations to whom
the convention applies.[24] In view of the breadth of the definition, the
inclusion of Tunisia on this list is surprising. There has been little
comment in the Committee of Experts on the application of the
Convention to indigenous and tribal populations in African states.
During a meeting convened at the beginning of the revision process, the
permanent secretary of the Botswana Department of Lands indicated
that his government accepted that the San were within the range of
appropriate beneficiaries of international instruments for the protection
of indigenous and tribal peoples,[25] but the ILO is unlikely to raise politically sensitive matters concerning the application of the Convention
with such sub-Saharan African states parties as Angola, Ghana, and
Guinea-Bissau except when particular states appear receptive or seek
technical assistance.

The applicability of Convention 107 to the three Asian states
parties, by contrast, has not raised great definitional difficulties. India,
Pakistan, and Bangladesh each distinguish particular tribal groups in
their national legal and policy arrangements, and they have not
contested the applicability of the Convention to these groups. While
differences could arise—for instance when a group appearing to be
within the scope of the Convention has not been classified as a "scheduled tribe" under the Constitution of India—in practice the concerns
expressed by the Committee of Experts have related only to the observance of the substantive provisions of the Convention.

One drawback of the scope of application clauses in Conventions
107 and 169 is the failure to indicate what is meant by the term *tribal.*
As Béteille pointed out in 1960,

> In the beginning, nobody bothered to give a precise meaning to the
> term tribe. This did not create very much confusion so long as the groups
> that were dealt with could be easily located and differentiated from groups
> of other types. By and large, this was the case in Australia, in Melanesia
> and in North America, the regions which were first studied by the
> anthropologists.
>
> In India, and also to a certain extent in Africa, the situation is *conspicu-
> ously* different....Except in a few areas, it is very difficult to come across

communities which retain all their pristine tribal characters. In fact, most such tribal groups show in varying degrees elements of continuity with the larger society of India.[26]

Perhaps this did not matter greatly while the integrationist philosophy evident in the drafting of Convention 107 prevailed: if tribes could not readily be discerned they were not thought to require particular legal protection. But more recent practice has emphasized the rights of tribal peoples to maintain and enhance their distinctive identities, and for these purposes it is more important to know which groups are the intended beneficiaries of the relevant legal instruments.

World Bank Policy

In an Operational Manual Statement introduced as part of World Bank policy in 1982, the bank singled out "tribal peoples" as the category whose members would require special protection when they were likely to be affected by "development" projects. The bank used the term *tribal people* to refer to ethnic groups with stable, low-energy, sustained-yield economic systems such as hunter-gatherers, shifting or semipermanent farmers, herders, or fishermen. These were held to exhibit in varying degrees many of the following characteristics.

(a) geographically isolated or semi-isolated;

(b) unacculturated or only partly acculturated into the societal norms of the dominant society;

(c) nonmonetized, or only partly monetized, production largely for subsistence, and independent of the national economic system;

(d) ethnically distinct from the national society;

(e) nonliterate and without a written language;

(f) linguistically distinct from the wider society;

(g) identifying closely with one particular territory;

(h) having an economic lifestyle largely dependent on the specific natural environment;

(i) possessing indigenous political leadership, but little or no national representation, and few, if any, political rights as individuals or collectively, partly because they do not participate in the political process; and

(j) having loose tenure over their traditional lands, which for the most part is not accepted by the dominant society nor accommodated by its courts, and having weak enforcement capabilities against encroachers, even when tribal areas have been delineated.[27]

Adverse reaction by the World Bank to Brazil's failure to implement agreed-upon measures for the benefit of several Amerindian groups led to the voluntary suspension of certain disbursements of loan financing for the Polonoreste project. Implementation of this policy appears to have had some impact on the conditions of bank financing (for example, for the Narmada River dams project in areas inhabited by scheduled tribes in western India). The bank has been criticized, however, for inadequacies in these projects and for failing to ensure that necessary measures were taken to protect tribal peoples (examples are the Grande Carajás project in Brazil and projects involving transmigration in Indonesia).[28] In these cases, the bank did not deny that tribal peoples were affected. Rather, the controversies centered on the adequacy of the protection provided, on the priority of adequate protection vis-à-vis other project goals, and on the division of responsibility between the bank and the state.

The bank's policy was concerned with ensuring special protection to groups on the basis of their vulnerability and special needs.[29] As such, it was open to allegations of paternalism, and doubts were expressed as to whether the bank was sufficiently concerned with the aspirations or wishes of indigenous and tribal peoples in project appraisal and implementation. Partly in response to general criticisms of its policy and partly in recognition of the fact that its definition was narrower than those employed in ILO Conventions 107 and 169 (narrower, in fact, than those in use in some borrowing countries), the bank in September 1991 promulgated a new Operational Directive.[30] This instrument states that

> The terms "indigenous peoples," "indigenous ethnic minorities," "tribal groups," and "scheduled tribes" describe social groups with a social and cultural identity distinct from the dominant society that makes them vulnerable to being disadvantaged in the development process. For the purposes of this directive, "indigenous peoples" is the term that will be used to refer to these groups.[31]

The reason for choosing *indigenous peoples* as the embracing term is not given but almost certainly it reflects the momentum of international usage. In providing more details about groups to whom the policy applies, the bank states:

> Because of the varied and changing contexts in which indigenous peoples are found, no single definition can capture their diversity. Indigenous

people are commonly among the poorest segments of a population. They engage in economic activities that range from shifting agriculture in or near forests to wage labor or even small-scale market-oriented activities. Indigenous peoples can be identified in particular geographical areas by the presence in varying degrees of the following characteristics:

(a) a close attachment to ancestral territories and to the natural resources in these areas;

(b) self-identification and identification by others as members of a distinct cultural group;

(c) an indigenous language, often different from the national language;

(d) presence of customary social and political institutions; and

(e) primarily subsistence-oriented production.

Task managers (TMs) must exercise judgment in determining the populations to which this directive applies and should make use of specialized anthropological and sociological experts throughout the project cycle.[32]

Categorization as an "indigenous people" for bank purposes has direct operational consequences. A borrowing state, for example, must prepare an "indigenous peoples development plan" if an investment project will affect any group that falls within the category. To be effective, therefore, the Operational Directive must contain definitional criteria which are sufficiently precise to be readily applied by operational staff. Vulnerability and limited capacity to assert rights and interests continue to underlie these criteria, and the 1991 directive remains open to criticism that its references to "local preferences," "indigenous knowledge," and the "informed participation" of indigenous peoples do not go far enough to avoid the imposition of unwelcome development or to facilitate genuine self-development. There is certainly no indication that the absence of informed consent by an affected indigenous people will stop a project from proceeding. In these respects, much will depend on the actual practice of the bank and its borrowers under the 1991 Operational Directive, and other recent policy or process reforms, particularly in the areas of environment and forestry. The bank's withdrawal from further financing of the Narmada project in 1993 reflected both the impact of these new policies within the bank and the political pressure generated by the NGO campaign on the Narmada issue in India, the United States, and Europe.

United Nations Classifications

The first United Nations debate specifically dealing with aboriginal peoples occurred in 1949 over a Bolivian proposal that a subcommission of the UN Economic and Social Council (ECOSOC) be established to study the circumstances of the aboriginal populations of the American continent. The Bolivian delegate in the Ad Hoc Political Committee stated that the aboriginal peoples "could and should be prepared to recover the land which belonged to them and to enjoy self-government." Haiti amended the proposal to encompass the study of colored and other underdeveloped peoples of the American continent as well. Denmark pointed out that the word *aboriginal* does not appear in the UN Charter: "It was an ethnographical term which could hardly be used as a criterion for research within the framework of the United Nations."[33] A diluted version of the resolution was passed by the General Assembly but very little was done to implement it primarily because it had become an issue of East-West contention.[34]

The UN General Assembly has not paid a great deal of attention to questions concerning indigenous peoples outside its important work on European decolonization. In 1990 and 1991, the General Assembly adopted resolutions proclaiming 1993 the International Year *for* the World's Indigenous People. By 1992, indigenous groups had persuaded the UN that this title was patronizing. The General Assembly retained the term *indigenous people* rather than *indigenous peoples*, but the title was changed to the International Year *of* the World's Indigenous People. This compromise precedent was followed in the General Assembly's 1993 proclamation of the International Decade of the World's Indigenous People. The importance attached to terminology in this area is striking, although the elegance of this compromise is not mirrored in all of the UN's six official languages, and political differences continue concerning the proper rendition of these terms in Chinese in particular. Substantive provisions concerning the rights and interests of "indigenous people" were included in the final documents of the 1992 Rio Conference on Environment and Development and the 1993 World Conference on Human Rights held in Vienna. The General Assembly will finally consider substantive general issues relating to indigenous peoples when the Working Group's draft Declaration eventually reaches it.

Much more elaborate was the final report of the UN subcommission's Special Rapporteur on the problem of discrimination against indigenous populations, José Martínez Cobo, which includes a tentative

definition of the term *indigenous populations* "for the purposes of international action that may be taken affecting their future existence."
This definition has been used as a reference in the practice of the UN
Working Group, and it may come to be used as a guide to the scope of
application of the draft Declaration. The Martínez Cobo report states:

> Indigenous communities, peoples and nations are those which, having a
> historical continuity with pre-invasion and pre-colonial societies that
> developed on their territories, consider themselves distinct from other
> sectors of the societies now prevailing in those territories, or parts of them.
> They form at present non-dominant sectors of society and are determined
> to preserve, develop and transmit to future generations their ancestral
> territories, and their ethnic identity, as the basis of their continued exis-
> tence as peoples, in accordance with their own cultural patterns, social
> institutions and legal systems.
>
> This historical continuity may consist of the continuation, for an
> extended period reaching into the present, of one or more of the follow-
> ing factors:
>
> (a) Occupation of ancestral lands, or at least of part of them;
>
> (b) Common ancestry with the original occupants of these lands;
>
> (c) Culture in general, or in specific manifestations (such as religion,
>   living under a tribal system, membership of an indigenous
>   community, dress, means of livelihood, life-style, etc.);
>
> (d) Language (whether used as the only language, as mother-tongue,
>   as the habitual means of communication at home or in the family,
>   or as the main, preferred, habitual, general or normal language);
>
> (e) Residence in certain parts of the country, or in certain regions of
>   the world;
>
> (f) Other relevant factors.[35]

Five definitional criteria receive particular emphasis in the Martínez
Cobo report: self-definition, nondominance, historical continuity with
preinvasion or precolonial societies, ancestral territories, and ethnic identity. The last two, although centrally associated with such vital questions
as land, cultural, and language rights, have not raised as many general
problems of definition as have the first three. These three require further
consideration.

Self-Definition

The report places considerable emphasis on self-definition, insisting that "[t]he right of indigenous peoples themselves to define what and

who is indigenous must be recognized" along with a correlative right to determine what or who is not indigenous.[36] This is part of a tendency in international texts, albeit incomplete and fraught with tensions, to move away from treating indigenous peoples simply as victims who ought to be objects of beneficent protection and toward acceptance of the implications of the ideology of self-determination. However, the issue of self-identification has several dimensions that are not clearly separated in the report.

Although domestic practices are not uniform,[37] states are increasingly inclined to acknowledge the general right of each indigenous people to recognition as a distinct group defined in terms of its conception of itself in relation to other groups. This is important in the case of groups whose historical circumstances have led to difficulties in recognition due to such factors as migration, landlessness, ethnogenesis in the mixing of other communities, division by colonial frontiers, or fractionation of a preexisting group. It also precludes states from requiring distinct groups to amalgamate to secure recognition as a single group, and from denying recognition to a people because fragments of it have been recognized separately.

The applicability of relevant international standards is not determined by self-identification alone (although recognition may be highly relevant), as each international definition also includes objective criteria. This approach is evident in ILO Convention 169. Objective criteria are set out in Article 1(1), but Article 1(2) provides that "Self-identification as indigenous or tribal shall be regarded as a fundamental criterion for determining the groups to which the provisions of this Convention apply." Self-identification may be interpreted as entailing the power to determine at the intergroup or international level which groups are indigenous peoples, either through general rules or specific decisions. It is unlikely at present that states will accept the notion that indigenous peoples are empowered to make general determinations of this sort at the international level, although they certainly have some influence on the practices of the UN and other bodies.[38]

Self-identification may also connote the right of the group to assert and develop rules governing individual membership, raising difficult issues concerning the power to include, exclude, or preclude particular individuals contrary to their own wishes or self-identification. State practice on these questions has been mixed,[39] although there is increasing acceptance that membership is a matter on which legislation and state administration should in general defer either to the wishes of individuals or to the decisions of the groups concerned. Group membership rules must, it appears, be consistent with internationally recognized human rights.[40] Article 8(2) of Convention 169 sets out a controversial further qualification in providing that indigenous and tribal peoples shall have the right to retain their own customs and institutions "where these are not incompatible with fundamental rights defined by the national legal system...."[41]

Self-identification and principles of autonomy suggest that decisions as to self-definition are to be taken by an indigenous people through its own procedures and institutions, subject to international human-rights standards. However, this does not resolve problems that arise when different organizations or individuals make competing claims as to the definition or representation of the group. In such cases, recourse must be had to objective criteria and to other relevant principles. It seems likely that any Declaration on the Rights of Indigenous Peoples ultimately adopted by the UN General Assembly will leave a reasonable margin of appreciation to states with regard to the details of national definitions.[42] Requirements as to consultation and negotiation in the adoption of definitions are likely to be more rigorous.

Nondominance

The criterion of nondominance may require some elaboration in a formal instrument. Certainly the vast majority of indigenous peoples are nondominant within the state polity and the national society. "Nondominance" also covers cases in which they are numerically dominant but politically subordinate. There may, however, be a case for some parallel standard-setting to cover exceptional situations of very small, independent states with traditional social structures and a recent colonial heritage of relocation or resource exhaustion, which may be seen as nondominant either in a subregion or vis-à-vis the former colonial power against which claims may continue to be pursued.[43] Consideration of the situation of the Banabans may illustrate the point. These people are nondominant in relation to both Fiji and Kiribati, and they fit many of the Martínez Cobo criteria in relation to both these states. However, while Banaban grievances include the failure of Kiribati to implement fully Chapters IX and III of its Constitution, their problems are for the most part not of Kiribati's making nor are they within that country's power to remedy without substantial external assistance.[44] They have few claims against Fiji.[45] The despoliation of the island of Banaba, the payment of inadequate royalties and compensation to its people, and their relocation on Rabi, eighteen hundred miles away, were colonial acts. Even if the Banabans had attained the independent statehood they sought at the London Constitutional Conference in 1978, many of their problems would be the same. Their circumstances would still be comparable to those of indigenous peoples in many parts of the world, notwithstanding the formation of their own state.[46] They would have been in a position to bring an international claim before an interstate forum, as the Republic of Nauru has done in bringing a case against Australia to the International Court of Justice, but the reality of their circumstances would have had at least as much in common with those of other indigenous peoples as with those of larger developing countries.[47]

Historical Continuity

The proposed requirement of historical continuity with a preinvasion or precolonial society established on the territory has been at the center of the sharpest difference of views concerning definition. India has argued that scheduled tribes and other tribal groups in Asia are not indigenous peoples within the Martínez Cobo definition because it is often impossible to show which population groups predate others in India.[48] India concedes that the scheduled tribes are covered by ILO Convention 107 but argues that this is because the convention applies to tribal populations independent of indigeneity.[49] Gu Yijie, the former Chinese member of the Working Group, similarly has endorsed the Martínez Cobo definition as supporting her view that "there does not exist any indigenous population in China." She argues that the Han people have been in China for thousands of years and that none of the minority ethnic groups were invaded or conquered. Bangladesh and India likewise have argued that the phenomenon of indigenous peoples only occurs in conjunction with settler colonialism.[50] While there is room to challenge the application of these juridical views to the factual circumstances of many tribal and minority groups in Asia, the possibility of a substantial limitation on the scope of application of UN standards on indigenous peoples is real if historical continuity is introduced as a strict requirement.

Possible Approaches in the UN Draft Declaration

The UN Working Group on Indigenous Populations has not adopted the Martínez Cobo definition, not even as a working definition, although it is referred to from time to time, and the Chairperson-Rapporteur has indicated that it should be applied for purposes of the draft Declaration (United Nations 1993, 15). However, the Working Group has pointedly not sought to include any definition of "indigenous peoples" in the 1993 Draft Declaration on the Rights of Indigenous Peoples. Although some states have criticized this omission, it is probably a political necessity if a Declaration acceptable to indigenous groups and to states is to be adopted by the UN General Assembly in the short or medium term. Such an omission is not without precedent: in several cases important terms have been employed in major human-rights instruments without definition, including the word *peoples* in the various instruments which state that "all peoples have the right to self-determination." The assumption is that if there are active international arrangements for promotion and implementation the functional scope of the instrument can be developed in practice as political circumstances allow. The principal drawback is that in the absence of some definitional criteria it will be possible for states to ignore the Declaration on the basis that it is inapplicable to them. This is particularly significant as, in the absence of wider ratification of the ILO conventions, the Declaration, if adopted, will be the only instrument (albeit without the binding force of a treaty) of general application dealing with indigenous peoples. Several indigenous peoples and governments have drawn attention to the problems that arise when governments simply do not admit that a particular group exists or is in any way distinct.[51]

If the Working Group or another UN body chooses to formulate a definition, several different approaches might be considered. One possibility would be simply to adopt the existing Martínez Cobo definition. This would extend to prior occupants of settler colonies an element of the protection that international law conferred upon colonial territories in which the indigenous populations remained dominant. Thus it appeals to Afro-Asian states and to elements within the "settler" societies concerned. Its inclusion in the final Declaration may lead to objections from many indigenous groups but it would reduce the potential for significant opposition to the more sweeping provisions of that instrument. The ILO conventions thus would establish minimum standards to which all states with indigenous or tribal peoples could choose to adhere, while the UN Declaration would be part of an effort to develop more extensive protection for the narrower group of "indigenous peoples." A second possibility would be for the UN to adopt a definition based on that used in ILO Convention 169. Policy arguments in favor of UN adoption of an ILO-type definition relate to the desirability of consistency in normative development and coverage, the vulnerability and aspirations of many tribal peoples and their need for protection and opportunities comparable to those proposed for indigenous peoples, problems of defining *invasion* or *colonization* in relation to many African and Asian peoples,[52] and the deliberate eschewal of universality entailed in a narrow definition of *indigenous peoples*. Another possibility would be to extend the Martínez Cobo definition, either to expressly include tribal peoples, or to place greater emphasis on ethnic distinctiveness associated with a special and long-standing relationship with a particular land or territory, and less on the subsequent arrival of newcomers.[53] If it is felt necessary to include a definition in the final version of the Declaration, a pragmatic approach might be to adopt a slightly broader and open-ended version of the Martínez Cobo definition, with the understanding that it encompasses peoples on all continents but that its precise application is to be determined by subsequent practice.[54] One proposal for such an indicative definition is offered below.

International practice on the scope of the Working Group's review of developments and other activities, and of any UN Declaration that might finally be adopted without a definition, remains somewhat sketchy. The Working Group takes the position that it is open to any group that may wish to speak. It does not investigate, take positions on the propriety of a participating group, or rule on the credentials of organizations and individuals. The Board of Trustees of the UN Voluntary Fund for Indigenous Populations is mandated by General Assembly Resolution 40/131 (1985) to make grants to enable participation in Working Group meetings of "representatives of indigenous peoples' organizations and communities." It has made grants under this rubric to people from, inter alia, India, Malaysia, and the Philippines. As to state practice, the Latin American states with Amerindian populations, many of which participate in the Inter-American Indian Institute or are parties to ILO Convention 107, have not objected to the evident applicability of the Working Group's activities to them. Several have actively supported the Working Group, as have Norway, Sweden, Finland, Denmark, Canada, the United States, Australia, and New Zealand. Several African and European countries (including France and Senegal) have participated without expressing clear views on definition.[55] The positions taken by Asian states vary appreciably. The Philippines, Japan, and Russia (and previously the USSR) have participated in the Working Group and made several statements about the circumstances of groups within their territories (generally in response to, or in anticipation of, statements by members of these groups) without any indication that they regard the groups as outside the Working Group's mandate. Japan and the Philippines have contributed to the UN Voluntary Fund for Indigenous Populations, although this in itself indicates nothing more than goodwill. The Japanese government welcomed the chairperson-rapporteur of the Working Group and a UN Secretariat official, who visited at the invitation of the Ainu Association of Hokkaido in 1991, without any indication that the visit was inappropriate. The Working Group in 1991 proposed that, subject to budgetary questions, its 1994 meeting would be held in Asia,[56] and the Philippine government informally indicated willingness to hold the session in Manila: however, financial and logistical constraints have prevented the Working Group from acting on this initiative. Indonesia has addressed the Working Group, in response to statements made by groups such as the Homeland Mission 1950 for the South Moluccas and Organisasi Papua Merdeka, without taking an explicit position on its competence.[57] Several other Asian governments have been emphatic in claiming that there are no "indigenous populations [or peoples]" in their countries. Such positions have been taken by Bangladesh, India, and Myanmar.[58]

Although discussions of the question of definition which took place in the early years of the Working Group were inconclusive, there now appears to be agreement on the importance of self-identification, on the right to be different, and on the significance of long and close relationships with land.[59] Working Group members have also reached a consensus that "it is important to continue to distinguish appropriately between indigenous peoples and minorities,"[60] although the nature and significance of such a distinction has not been elaborated,[61] not least because the term *minority* also lacks a generally agreed-upon definition in international human-rights law.[62] Views have differed on the Martínez Cobo definition, however, and the whole question has been deferred for "later consideration." Several governments have stressed that they are not about to abdicate their rights and responsibilities in defining the category so as to transform the definition exclusively into self-definition. Some of these governments favored negotiation of separate definitions for specific purposes.[63]

Requirements and Indicia

It does not appear possible—or indeed desirable—to formulate a rigid list of requirements for use in determining which groups are indigenous peoples. A solution may be to compile a list of indicia, some of which would be requisites, others simply relevant factors to be evaluated and applied in cases of doubt or disagreement. Such a list might resemble the following.

Essential Requirements

- self-identification as a distinct ethnic group
- historical experience of, or contingent vulnerability to, severe disruption, dislocation, or exploitation
- long connection with the region
- the wish to retain a distinct identity

Relevant Indicia

- nondominance in the national (or regional) society
- close cultural affinity with a particular area of land or territories
- historic continuity (especially by descent) with prior occupants of land in the region
- socioeconomic and sociocultural differences from the ambient population
- distinct objective characteristics: language, race, material or spiritual culture, etc.
- regarded as indigenous by the ambient population or treated as such in legal and administrative arrangements

Conclusion

As this review of practice has shown, the term *indigenous peoples* has been used extensively at the international level as part of a remarkable upsurge in international awareness of, and activities relating to, issues with which indigenous peoples are concerned. Many additional examples could be given, including the provisions for the rights of indigenous children in Article 30 of the 1989 UN Convention on the Rights of the Child, the emphasis on the interests and expertise of indigenous peoples in Agenda 21 and other documents adopted by the 1992 UN Conference on Environment and Development in Rio de Janeiro, and the standards concerning rights of indigenous peoples being developed by the Inter-American Commission on Human Rights.

For many of these international purposes a precise definition of the relevant groups is not necessary. The ILO Conventions contain expansive statements as to the scope of the instruments which are indicative in nature: they do not themselves purport to define the concepts of "indigenous" or "tribal." The World Bank criteria are also expansive and indicative rather than precise, although they are more operational in character and more oriented toward the project-related purposes of the Bank. The Martínez Cobo definition is indicative but less expansive, and may potentially exclude certain groups as a result of employing criteria that take some account of the ordinary or dictionary meaning of *indigenous*.[64] The UN Working Group has functioned successfully without adopting a definition. Indeed, this prudent abstention may well have contributed to its work. It is unlikely that any Declaration adopted by the UN General Assembly will contain a definition. If it does, it will almost certainly be indicative and very general.

The scope of the relevant instruments is important in law and policy-making. It affects the impact of these instruments on the groups themselves (through processes of legitimation and empowerment), on states, and on international institutions. The ILO and World Bank definitions are already sufficiently expansive, however, to cover most cases in which (in prevailing political and institutional circumstances) they are likely to be of consequence, and interpretation of the UN Draft Declaration (and the final Declaration should it ever be adopted) is likely to be influenced less by terminology than by a pattern of international institutional practice which already appears expansive. Finally, it must be appreciated that, while the category of "indigenous peoples" may be appealing and important for political and other purposes, as a matter of law many claims by indigenous peoples (or by members of such groups) do not depend for their legal validity upon the group *being* indigenous. Many issues may be addressed under general human-rights law, under prohibitions of discrimination, slavery, genocide, and other abusive practices, under the existing law concerning self-determination or minority rights, or occasionally under applicable treaties, without formal regard as a legal matter to whether or not the group is indigenous.[65] Thus, while certain legal consequences may flow from particular definitional texts or interpretations, at the international level the main impact of the debates about definition is likely to be political rather than legal.

CHAPTER 3

The Indigenous Movement
in Asia

ANDREW GRAY

Over the last twenty years, a social movement has spread throughout the world, drawing together Indian nations, aboriginal peoples,
ethnic groups, and minorities (Moody 1988, xix; International Work
Group for Indigenous Affairs 1988, 13). The basic demands of this
movement are respect for collective rights to land and culture and the
right to self-determination. The word that has gradually come to prominence during the movement's emergence has been the term *indigenous.*

Indigenous is a word that receives criticism from several quarters.
Cynical Europeans claim that "we are all indigenous"; "so are we," cry
the outraged Africans; "indigenous is a paternalistic concept," complain
North Americans; while Asianists retain a stoic skepticism. Yet *indigenous* is now widely used nationally and internationally to refer to
colonized peoples of the world who are prevented from controlling their
own lives, resources, and cultures (see Independent Commission on
International Humanitarian Issues [ICIHI] 1987; Burger 1987; and
International Work Group for Indigenous Affairs 1986a [Introduction],
and 1988 [pt. 1]).

The word *indigenous* is now currently accepted by a sizable body of
international institutions and researchers. The spread of the indigenous
movement, coupled with the establishment of an annual United Nations
Working Group on Indigenous Populations in 1984 (see Eide 1985), has
increasingly stretched the definition of *indigenous* to include peoples
from all over the world.

35

This paper looks at the concept of "indigenous" in Asia. Use of the term has been the subject of discussion for several years. The problems with it stem from two main areas: coherence and application. The meaning varies and there is only a vague consistency among the different definitional interpretations. Furthermore, the application of the term to peoples in Asia is frequently countered by historical data questioning the clear distinction between an indigenous people and other inhabitants of a country.

Heinz (1988, 16–17) describes this difficulty as follows.

> In Asia we note over centuries considerable waves of peoples leaving their country for another, sometimes returning, sometimes not. It might be diffi-cult to define people as "indigenous" because it depends on the one point in time one looks at a certain country. The term could easily be used when there is a homogeneous majority and one or more indigenous minorities.

His examples of indigenous peoples in Asia are the Ainu (Japan), the Meos [sic] (Laos), the Kalinga (Philippines), and the Chakma (Bangladesh). He considers East Timorese to be a "clear-cut" case of an indigenous people.

The Meaning of Indigenous: *A Question of Coherence*

The word *indigenous* has no fixed definition. Although in the sixteenth century the term *indigene* was used as a noun, this use is rarely found nowadays. *Indigenous* is an adjective that refers to a quality. This meaning is carried over into the substantive *indigenousness*. The dictionary defines *indigenous* as meaning someone who is "in-born or a native," one who is born native to a land or region. According to this definition everyone is indigenous to somewhere and nonindigenous to somewhere else. Thus, the term is relative and depends on the geo-graphical context. It has been used in this sense since at least 1646.

The importance of this aspect of the definition is its reference to land or territory. For those people who consider themselves indigenous, a special relationship with the land is a fundamental aspect of their identity. This can be conceptualized in many ways, according to the religion of the people concerned. Yet indigenous peoples are almost invariably those who consider their territorial base under threat from the outside and realize that there is no room for coexistence without their own destruction.

During the period of European colonial expansion the term *indige-nous* was also used to refer to those peoples whose territories were under the control of outsiders. The meaning thus included the idea not just of being indigenous to an area but of being indigenous in relation to someone else. This difference can be expressed in the form of both political and cultural discrimination suffered by the indigenous people. The colonial definition of *indigenous* varies according to the types of colonization. For example, settler colonies of the Americas, Australia, and New Zealand are states controlled by the descendants of the first colonists. On the other hand, in the nonsettler colonies of Asia and Africa, following European rule, those peoples previously termed "indigenous" took power. In many cases, they placed themselves in the positions of their former colonial oppressors.

The breaking of colonial ties involves the concept of "self-determination" (enshrined in the United Nations Declaration of Human Rights), which is the right of peoples to organize their lives on their territories with as little outside interference as they wish. Indigenous peoples use *self-determination* to express most broadly their aim of controlling their political, cultural, and economic lives.

Thus far we can say that *indigenous* refers to that quality of a people relating their identity to a particular area and distinguishing them culturally from other, "alien" peoples who came to the territory subsequently. These indigenous peoples are "colonized" in the sense of being disadvantaged and discriminated against. Their right of self-determination is their way of overcoming these obstacles. The term is coherent on this abstract level but the application is difficult, as it depends on who is seen as the "outsider" and the extent to which the territory is defined. Applying this basic meaning of *indigenous* in Asia, with its waves of migrations, is extremely difficult but by no means impossible.

For example, there are pragmatic approaches for applying the term *indigenous* to Asia (deciding in advance the peoples who are to be so described) but even they encounter difficulties. An example is the veneer of incoherence presented by the report prepared for the Independent Commission on International Humanitarian Issues entitled *Indigenous Peoples: A Global Quest for Justice* (1987). On page xiv, Zia Rizvi says, "Their own perception of themselves combined with the historical fact of being the descendants of the original inhabitants of the lands where they live is enough for anyone to get a fairly precise idea of the subject of this report." The use of the term *original* is the problem.

Out of the nine definitions of *indigenous* consulted for this paper (United Nations 1982–83; International Labour Organisation [ILO] 1957; World Bank 1982; World Council of Indigenous Peoples [WCIP] n.d; Independent Commission on International Humanitarian Issues

1987; Heinz 1988; Stavenhagen 1986; Burger 1987; Gray 1987), *original* as a fundamental criterion is mentioned only in the ICIHI report. It would be misleading, therefore, to see *original* as giving a "fairly precise" idea of the notion of indigenous.[1]

The historical descendants of original inhabitants are termed *aboriginal* or *autochthonous.* This aspect of *indigenous* refers to the inhabitants of areas that were taken over by a settler form of colonization, and in which aboriginal and nonaboriginal peoples are clearly distinguished: namely, the Arctic, the Americas, Australia, New Zealand, and parts of the Pacific such as Hawaii and Kanaky. *Aboriginal* is also a term used in Asia, particularly in reference to the tribal peoples of India and Taiwan.

However, whereas all aboriginal people are indigenous, not all indigenous peoples are aboriginal. Page 6 of the ICIHI report actually demonstrates this distinction in an inconsistent way. There we see a reiteration of Rizvi's definition: "indigenous peoples are the descendants of the original inhabitants of a territory taken over through conquest or settlement by aliens." Yet, among the elements of the definition set out in the preceding paragraph, the first element is "pre-existence (i.e. the population is a descendent of those inhabiting an area prior to the arrival of another population); non-dominance; cultural difference; and self-identification as indigenous."

The incoherent aspect of these definitions is the clash between the word *original,* which is absolute, and the term *prior,* which is relative. When it comes to the application of the term *indigenous* to Asia, the ICIHI report has no real difficulty. It simply translates *indigenous* in Asia as *tribal:*

> In Asia however, where European occupation was the last in a succession of colonial experiences and where there was no major foreign settlement, the question of indigenousness is more complex. In the Indian sub-continent, for example, the continual migration of peoples into the area during the past thousand years has made the question of antecedence too complex to resolve. There, as in other parts of Asia, indigenous refers to tribal and semi-tribal communities, previously threatened with what is sometimes called "internal colonisation." (Rizvi 1987, 6)

Between Coherence and Application

So far we have been able to find examples of general definitions that indicate broadly the peoples who are encompassed by the term *indigenous,* although the application is difficult in specific cases. In contrast, we have seen other, rather incoherent definitions that have tried to resolve any inconsistency by using the existing term in Asia (*tribal*).

Equating *indigenous* with *tribal* is a useful starting point for a pragmatic approach but it does have its problems. In India and elsewhere, *tribal* is an administrative term that links territorial and cultural factors in distinction to the state as a whole. Furthermore, the term in itself does not deal with the colonial factor (indeed, many people consider that the disparaging sense of the term *tribal* is itself an element of colonization).

The principal problem, however, when using the terms *tribal* and *indigenous* interchangeably, is to deal with the absolute nature of the word *original*. There are two ways of dealing with this. One is to distinguish between "original inhabitants" and "prior inhabitants." The Chakma of the Chittagong Hill Tracts in Bangladesh were by no means the first people to enter the Hill Tracts; in fact, they were one of the more recent (eighteenth century). Because of the historical conditions existing at the time, they settled in the Hill Tracts after previous waves of Arakanese and Tripurans. Using the first definition of *indigenous* ("original") only the Kuki peoples can be considered the indigenous peoples of the Hill Tracts.

According to the second definition ("prior"), all the tribal groups of the Hill Tracts would be considered equally indigenous vis-à-vis the later Bengali settlers and the Bangladesh army, which are systematically burning villages and killing the hill peoples (see Anti-Slavery Society 1984, 14). The concept of "prior" is useful because it avoids speculative history as to who are the "original" peoples of an area and instead concentrates on current patterns of colonialism. This position was reinforced by the recent Chittagong Hill Tracts (CHT) Commission report (1991, 119), which stated,

> The Commission is aware of the position of the Bangladesh government that the hill people are not technically "indigenous" peoples. The Commission considers that they are "indigenous" to the CHT, having been in settled occupation and control of the area prior to outside assertions of political authority over the CHT and prior to the relatively recent patterns of outside settlement in the area.

Another approach has been expressed by Gonds in India. In this case *original* is a term applied to those whose ancestry stretches back the farthest.

> The Gonds themselves, both from their mythology and from ruined sites of past civilisations in the area, realise that they are not the first people to have lived here. But the fact remains that they see themselves as the people

who cleared the forests and, although with the other aboriginal groups, have first claim to be the original occupants. (Yorke 1989, 215)

This fits with the view found in India of the *adivasi*, or aboriginal, peoples.

However, the clinching concept in the definition of *indigenous* is "self-determination." This open-ended umbrella term covers self-identification, political and resource control, and free cultural expression. From this we see that indigenousness is a quality or aspect of the identity of peoples who have lived in an area prior to conquest or colonization and who are not empowered to live according to their sociocultural, economic, and political life-styles. The indigenous movement is an assertion of this identity.

Indigenousness is not a thing or a person but an attribute of both personal and collective identity. That some nonindigenous people should find the concept incoherent is not surprising, since they are looking at the term as something substantive rather than something which people identify in themselves. The meaning is bound to shift in terms of the geographical and historical context of the referents.

The Importance of "Indigenous" as a Concept

Like gender, indigenousness is a concept that stimulates debate and skepticism. Its flexibility and somewhat intangible attributes are not readily intellectually identifiable. Indigenousness is something that is experienced. It is actually a self-reflective notion, which means that people have looked at themselves from the outside, identified the problems that face them, and understand why an assertion of their identity is a prerequisite for their survival. Indigenousness is an assertion by people directed against the power of outsiders. This is focused primarily on the nation-state. Whereas people feel skeptical on semantic or pragmatic grounds about the notion of "indigenous," they are less frequently questioning about the notion of "state." For, whereas "indigenous" is a flexible, experiential concept, the "state" sets itself up to be a constant, definable attribute of the world political system as we see it today. Yet, as Andrew Vincent (1987, 3–4) put it,

The State is not something which reveals itself at the first look. Despite its apparent solidity (try not paying taxes or leaving the country without a passport), it is none the less difficult to identify—as an idea or cluster of concepts, values and ideas about social existence.

The "incoherence" of the term *indigenous* reflects the incoherence of the notion of "state," which is bound up with identity and power. As such, the indigenous movement is a challenge to the state because it argues that the existence of a single inflexible entity is not sufficient reason to take control out of the hands of the people who live within its area. Indeed, indigenous peoples argue for the dissipation and distribution of "people power" from the center into other social sectors of the country. Thus, "indigenous" is as much a concept of political action as it is of semantic reflection.

Those who control the state want to control the resources within its boundaries too. However, indigenous peoples live on the land that they consider to be theirs. A struggle for resources is usually the basis on which indigenous peoples first become aware of the threat to their future. It becomes clear very quickly that the agendas of the state and of indigenous peoples are quite distinct. This discrepancy can be illustrated by a recent experience I had in Bangladesh. A government official told me that I must be aware that the term *indigenous* has no relevance in Bangladesh because there are no indigenous peoples there. I mentioned this later to some tribal people who looked at me aghast. "Of course we are indigenous," they said.

The difference in aims is further underlined when we realize that often the problems facing indigenous peoples are part of the national and international systems affecting countries as a whole. The question of indigenous rights in Burma or Bangladesh is just one of several questions concerning the rights of oppressed people in various sectors of the society. The indigenous movement emphasizes the differences between the detailed aims and goals of all these different sectors.

The other concern about the concept of "indigenous" is that it has developed into a global movement. The spread of the indigenous movement throughout the world has caused alarm in some circles. From this perspective, there have been attempts to provide cut-off points intended to prevent the movement from spreading further. By emphasizing the notion of "original" rather than "prior," Asian and African governments might be tempted to deny fundamental rights to the indigenous peoples living in their countries.

The term *indigenous* thus is not simply a matter of analysis. It is a matter of life and death for the millions of people covered by the term in Asia and other parts of the world. Particularly important is the role of the United Nations Working Group on Indigenous Populations. This five-member committee is currently identifying a series of standards on the basis of presentations by indigenous peoples from all over the world. The initial drafts clearly address the needs and problems facing the tribal peoples of Asia. Retaining the term *indigenous* is therefore crucial to ensuring their basic rights. Thus, the discussion of the term *indigenous* is more than an academic debate; it has practical consequences as well. Indigenous peoples frequently say: "We know who we are and don't need anyone else's advice on the matter." In order to understand how this politicization of an analytic concept has taken place, we should review briefly the rise of the indigenous movement.

The Rise of the Indigenous Movement

The indigenous movement can be seen as the heir to a history of anti-imperialism stretching back to prehistoric times. The movement as it stands today received a massive impetus during the 1960s from two sources. First, the decolonization of Asia and Africa brought into the limelight the possibility of peoples controlling their own destinies. Second, the right of self-determination was enshrined in the United Nations Declaration on Human Rights. Indeed, the UN Working Group on Indigenous Populations is seen by some as a continuation of the decolonization process but one occurring within the boundaries of the state (see Erica Daes in International Work Group for Indigenous Affairs 1986b).

Also in the 1960s, the rise of the civil rights movement and antiracism brought to the attention of North American Indians, Aborigines in Australia, and Maori in New Zealand the possibility of fighting for fundamental rights and freedoms. The Black Power movement also contained many elements of consciousness-raising and self-identity that have become a major aspect of the indigenous movement.

The global economic problems of the 1960s also increased the need for Third World states to use the resources of their regions to "develop" their economies. The case of Brazil has been particularly well documented (Davis 1977). This "development" had the effect of causing more problems for indigenous communities. In South America, accounts of massacres of indigenous peoples in Colombia, Brazil, and Paraguay caused considerable activity in anthropological circles. The indigenous movement thus has become an alliance of urban-educated indigenous peoples (who often are the intellectual rationalizers of the movement) and the rural people in the communities who are directly affected by land invasions and massacres.

The late 1960s saw indigenous mobilization springing up throughout the Americas but it was in 1974 and 1975 that the first international indigenous organizations, the International Indian Treaty Council (IITC) and the World Council of Indigenous Peoples were founded in the United States and Canada, respectively. Through the late 1970s, the founding of the Co-ordinating Body of Indian Peoples (CORPI), the Indian Council of South America (CISA), and the Co-ordinating Body of Indigenous Peoples of the Amazon Basin (COICA) in the Amazon shows how the movement spread throughout the continent.

During the 1980s, indigenous affairs have been on the international agenda. With both the IITC and WCIP recognized as nongovernmental organizations (NGOs) by the Economic and Social Council of the United Nations, they have become part of a mass mobilization of indigenous peoples aimed at demanding their rights at the United Nations. The United Nations eventually took the initiative to set up a Working Group on Indigenous Populations in order to discuss the establishment of standards for indigenous peoples with the aim of composing a Declaration, and then a Convention, on indigenous rights. A Draft Declaration is already under discussion (see International Work Group for Indigenous Affairs 1988).

There are various ways of measuring the growth of the indigenous movement, such as the expansion of indigenous organizations, attendance at the United Nations Working Group, and the increasing geographical range of the activities and publications of support groups.

Looking at the attendance at the Working Group, we can see that in 1985 the participants were predominantly from North America and Australia with increasing attendance from Central and South America. Asian representatives came from the Chittagong Hill Tracts and the Philippines. Two years later participation from Asia increased, with large delegations attending from West Papua and the South Moluccas. Also represented were the Karen and the Kachin from Burma, the Nagas and *adivasi* from India, and a regular delegation of Ainu from Japan. Although not always as large, delegations from Asia have become a regular bloc at the Working Group.

During my tenure as director of the International Work Group for Indigenous Affairs, the increase in Asian issues was markedly apparent from 1983 to 1989. Having published little on the area previously, we prepared documents on East Timor (Retbøll 1984), the Chittagong Hill Tracts (Mey 1984), Nagaland (International Work Group for Indigenous Affairs 1986c), and transmigration in Indonesia (Otten 1986). Articles in the newsletters on Asia have become a regular feature, covering the above issues as well as those of the Philippines, West Papua, Burma, Sarawak, India, Tibet, and Japan. The International Work Group for Indigenous Affairs is not unique in this, and similar trends can be seen in the publications of Cultural Survival and Survival International. The Anti-Slavery Society's Indigenous Peoples and Development series has published several documents on the Philippines, the Chittagong Hill Tracts, the Hmong of Thailand, and West Papua. (Strictly speaking, as a part of Melanesia, West Papua ought to be a Pacific matter. It has been brought into Asian affairs because of the Indonesian occupation.)

At the moment, Asian participation in the indigenous movement is a fait accompli. In 1986, the World Council of Indigenous Peoples formed its Pacific and Asian Regional Council. Signed supporters of the WCIP include representatives from West Papua and East Timor, and from among the Karen of Burma and the *adivasi* in India who formed their own National Council in 1986.

The people of the Philippine Cordillera were the first Asians to take part in the international indigenous movement. The Cordillera People's Alliance carried out successful campaigns against the building of the Chico dams in 1981–82, and they have since become one of the best-organized indigenous bodies in the world (see International Work Group for Indigenous Affairs 1988). On 1 May 1992, the Asia Indigenous Peoples Pact (AIPP) was launched with its own charter in Bangkok.

The founding charter of the AIPP explains the rationale behind its establishment.

> We the indigenous peoples organizations and movements in Asia; having come together in mutual trust and respect for each other; having shared, discussed and deeply reflected on the history, present situation, concerns and aspirations of our people. We the indigenous peoples of Asia having affirmed our desire to assert our right to our homeland and ancestral domain; and having declared our right to own as a people our homelands and resources, and to protect, defend, utilize and develop them in ways which are appropriate with our traditions, beliefs, values and culture. We the indigenous peoples in Asia in seeking to assert our just right to self-determination: Hereby establish the Asian Indigenous Peoples Pact.

This pact has provided an opportunity for indigenous peoples from all over Asia (from most of the countries covered in this book) to join together and decide the extent to which they wish to be connected to the indigenous movement.

Asia has not been the last stop in the spread of the indigenous movement around the world. Attention is now on focused on the former Soviet Union where several indigenous organizations sprang up after President Gorbachov made his Murmansk statement in 1988 advocating indigenous cooperation across the Arctic. In 1990, the first elected member of a Soviet indigenous organization attended the United Nations Working Group and made a statement accusing the Soviet government of internal colonizing policies in the north.[2] At the moment, international seminars and meetings are addressing the relevance of the indigenous movement in Africa.

From this it is possible to see the indigenous movement as a cumulative sweep of resistance against the oppression that has encircled the world. We are witnessing the raising of the consciousness of people who decide that they are indigenous or that they want to align themselves with the indigenous movement. It is this aspect of the indigenous movement that makes any universal definition of *indigenous* difficult. The meaning is constantly changing to accommodate new alliances—it is not just a semantic construct but a political strategy for attaining collective rights to territories and cultural respect.

For this reason we should be wary of undue skepticism. "Indigenous" is a notion that challenges the state-centric perspective. Too much skepticism about the notion of "indigenous" could lead to a noncritical stance and the opposite of skepticism itself. The state is not unchanging and indigenous peoples are biding their time.

The Indigenous Movement and Asia

The problems facing the indigenous peoples of Asia are similar to those faced in other parts of the world. The phrases, descriptions, and political positions of representatives from the Chittagong Hill Tracts or the Philippines, for example, are remarkably consistent with statements made by South American Indians and Arctic Inuit. The International Work Group for Indigenous Affairs *Yearbook* regularly gives a summary of some of the main events that have taken place in Asia during the year and provides an update for the background provided by Burger (1987, chap. 8). The following survey provides a rough idea of the problems facing peoples of Asia in common with indigenous peoples in other parts of the world.

Militarization

Militarization is a fundamental problem affecting indigenous peoples throughout Asia. Often these people are not understood, nor do they receive publicity because the areas are closed for reasons of national security. The rationale for militarization is usually counterinsurgency. The main areas where militarization has taken place are the places where indigenous peoples are, or have been, fighting for their existence. Furthermore, from the state perspective, indigenous peoples can be used to destabilize neighboring countries by means of "proxy wars" (Subir Bakesh, personal communication).

Militarization takes forms that are common throughout the area, if not the world. Where the indigenous peoples hold large areas, the military occupation force organizes its attacks in waves or "operations." These are markedly apparent in East Timor, West Papua, and in the annual Burmese army incursions against the Karen in Burma. The immediate effects of these operations are mass killings and detentions; they rarely accomplish more than terrorizing an area until it is time for the next operation.

More long term are the counterinsurgency strategies advocated by Robert Thompson (1974). Based upon the British Malayan experience, these counterinsurgency tactics employ intelligence networks to break popular support for guerrilla fighters. A constant military presence is essential, combining the "stick" of terror with imposed "carrots" that go by the name of development projects. The prime strategy of this form of counterinsurgency is relocation of the indigenous population in strategic hamlets or cluster villages. Tight control of the population ensures a break in communication lines between the people and their guerrilla forces. As Thompson describes it (1974,121):

> The "hold" aspect of operations is undoubtedly the most crucial and the most complex, involving as it does the establishment of a solid security framework covering the whole population; moving in the villages and small towns of a given area. The basis of this security framework is the strategic hamlet.

Relocation for military purposes is in use in the Chittagong Hill Tracts, East Timor, West Papua, and the Philippines. It disregards peoples' rights to land and makes control and terrorization of the population easier.

Militarization and warfare are occurring in several parts of Asia. The effect frequently leads to a high civilian death-rate from the military counterinsurgency operations. Sometimes the level of militarization and oppression is so high that the guerrillas begin to seem more and more like liberators.

According to the Catholic Institute of International Relations, as many as 200,000 East Timorese have died in the war against Indonesian occupation and "90 per cent of the territory's 650,000 people have been forcibly uprooted from their homes" (Tapol 1989, 9). An estimated 2,000 Timorese were killed during 1988 by the Indonesians according to participants at a meeting held in Copenhagen in 1989 (International Work Group for Indigenous Affairs 1989, 57). Accounts of demonstrations, arbitrary detention, and torture continue to come from the country. The situation was vividly brought to international attention by the massacre at Dili on 12 November 1991 of more than 100 people by Indonesian troops.

In West Papua, according to a recent report by the Anti-Slavery Society (1990, 5), it is estimated that the Indonesian occupation has resulted in 300,000 deaths and 15,000 refugees. The report says, "The plight of West Papuans, struggling to survive against an occupying power which is armed with the latest military equipment, is an outrage against humanity" (Anti-Slavery Society 1990, 7).

In the Chittagong Hill Tracts, in spite of initial reports to the contrary, killings continue to occur. The whole of the Hill Tracts is militarized. Between Khagrachari and Dighinala, a distance of less than twenty miles, there are thirty-seven army posts. The government is in the midst of a resettlement program that will eventually force the indigenous tribal population to give up subsistence agriculture to become day laborers on rubber or timber plantations. There were killings at Baghaichari in August 1988, and at Langadu on 4 May 1989. During the Langadu massacre more than seventy local people from the Chittagong Hill Tracts were killed. In October 1990, Batchari village was largely destroyed by the army and 245 families were forced to relocate. On 10 April 1992, a massacre took place at Logang where hundreds of hill people were reportedly killed. Massacre, detention, torture, and rape occur regularly in the Hill Tracts. Today at least 54,000 refugees are living in six camps in Tripura. A recent report from the International Chittagong Hill Tracts Commission analyzes these and other issues affecting the peoples of the Hill Tracts (Chittagong Hill Tracts Commission 1991).

In neighboring Burma, the army is trying to put a stop, "once and for all," to the war with the Karens that has lasted for more than forty years and claimed an estimated 300,000 lives (Burger 1987, 120). Every year in the dry season the Burmese army organizes an operation in Karen territory. The targets and main sufferers are always the civilian village populations. There are currently estimates of more than 50,000 displaced people.

In the Philippines, bombings of communities, which were notorious under the Marcos regime, have resumed with new intensity. Since Aquino came to power, well over sixteen thousand indigenous families from the Cordillera and Mindanao have been displaced by military operations. In 1989, bombings in Mindoro increased the number of refugees in local mission stations to four thousand. In the Cordillera, three hundred families from fourteen villages were forced to flee because of shelling. The attacks increased in 1990 and 1991, and continue now under the new government of Fidel Ramos.[3]

Human-rights organizations quantify violations committed under militarization as far as the information is available. However, statistics ignore the effect on the quality of life of the military occupation, which is even more horrendous than figures can demonstrate. The fear of detention, torture, or death gives rise to a way of life dominated by terror. This qualitative violation of human rights is present throughout the militarized areas of Asia.

Plundering of Resources and Land Incursions

Throughout Asia, resources that lie within the lands of indigenous and tribal peoples are taken without their consent. Land that has belonged to them for hundreds, and sometimes thousands, of years is appropriated for forestry and mining. The most notorious examples of the plundering of indigenous resources in Southeast Asia come from deforestation and logging practices. Sarawak is a particularly bad case. One-third of Sarawak's rain forest already has been logged, primarily by Japanese companies. Three-fifths of the forest has been licensed to companies without any consultation with the indigenous Kayan, Kenyah, Punan, and Penan peoples, among others. Over the last two years the local people have instigated three roadblocks to keep the lorries off their lands. They have been arrested and taken to trial.

Current reports from the area (Pearce 1990, 24) describe twenty-four-hour logging of the forests. The International Tropical Timber Organisation sponsored a Commission, headed by Lord Cranbrook, to review the situation in Sarawak. Its report was published in 1990. Ignoring completely the plight of the native peoples, the report proposes slowing down but not stopping the decimation of the rain forest. Between 1990 and 1991, 18 million cubic meters of timber was logged in Sarawak. At this rate, in eight years the forest will be depleted.

In the Philippines, the government is opening indigenous lands to foreign companies with the active support of the European Community. Logging companies on Palawan Island threaten the remaining four hundred Batak people, while the state oil company threatens the mountain communities of Mt. Apo in Mindanao. One American air base still lies on the land of the Aeta people. In the southern Cordillera, five open-pit mines, already destroying the environment, will be joined by the Grand Antamok Project. The effects will be environmental degradation, pollution, and dislocation of the indigenous Itogon communities residing in the region of the mines. Three thousand Itogon have set up four blockades in an attempt to stop the mining.

South of Sarawak, in Kalimantan (Borneo), the Indonesian company P. T. Astra is planning to develop two hundred thousand hectares for a timber-estate, wood-chipping project, and pulp project. Deforestation, oil prospecting, and mining are all projects attracting outsiders and threatening the land base of people such as the Dayaks. Those living in Sangata are threatened by a massive coal mine proposed by British Petroleum (BP) and CRA (a subsidiary of Rio Tinto Zinc) in Australia (*Down to Earth* 1989a, 11).

West Papua is currently the main focus of Indonesian resource plundering. Logging on the southern coast in the Asmat area continues. Although a Scott Paper Company plan to invest U.S.$650,000 in Merauke for a eucalyptus plantation of about eighty thousand hectares was withdrawn, the Indonesian government has found other partners to continue the project. Meanwhile, to the west, the mangrove regions are under threat from Japanese companies, and the northern area of Mamberamo is threatened by an Australian company.

Transmigration and Relocation

We referred earlier to the difference between settlement colonies in the Americas, Australia, and New Zealand and the colonies of Africa and Asia, which retained a majority of indigenous people throughout the colonial era. Currently in Asia migration to new settler colonies is creating a minority population among the indigenous peoples who already reside there.

The problems facing indigenous peoples who encounter settlers are known throughout the world. Tribal people in India over the last fifty years and more have suffered from a constant stream of settlers moving onto their lands and taking their resources. In his book on the tribes of India, Fürer-Haimendorf (1989, 111) says that "the decline of tribal prosperity is hardly surprising in an area exposed to a development by recent settlers which can only be described as 'colonial'." He contrasts the case of peninsular India with Arunachal Pradesh (p. 297).

> Opponents of any special privileges for tribals, particularly of the exclusion of non-tribal settlers from tribal areas, often put forward the argument that tribals will advance only if they freely mix with other sections of the population. The experience in Arunachal Pradesh demonstrates that this argument is fallacious, for it is precisely the special protection afforded to the tribesmen by the Inner Line Policy which has enabled the Api Taris to achieve within one generation an advancement surpassing any achieved by those Indian tribals whose ancestral homeland has been infiltrated by members of the so-called progressive communities.

In neighboring Nagaland, in northeastern India, there are reports that the Inner Line Regulation preventing internal colonization is under threat. This Inner Line Regulation was a policy of the British administration at the turn of the century and was meant to ensure that hill peoples would not be overrun by the peoples of the plains. Indians have been trying to encourage their fellow citizens to migrate to Nagaland to mix with the local people. Already the town of Dimapur, which is on the border of Nagaland, contains more Indians than Nagas. According to the Nagaland Regulation, only certain categories of people can enter Nagaland.

In the Chittagong Hill Tracts, the 1900 Regulation, similar to that found in northeastern India, has been consistently violated by the Bangladesh government. The most damaging move was the relocation of Bengali settlers from the plains to the Hill Tracts between 1979 and 1983. In all, an estimated four hundred thousand persons have moved there in the last fifteen years. With a delicate carrying capacity, the hills are not able to support such a large population. The result is that indigenous people, particularly Chakma, have been burnt out of their villages and forced to seek refuge in the forest or in refugee camps in Tripura. Today these camps contain more than fifty thousand people from the Chittagong Hill Tracts. Furthermore, as a counterinsurgency measure, both tribal and nontribal peoples are herded into cluster villages without adequate fields, food, or facilities. The tribal people are being told by the military to become day laborers.

The notorious and discredited transmigration program of Indonesia has not stopped. In spite of international criticism and failure within the program itself over many years, the Indonesians are still encouraging people from the inner islands of Java, Madura, and Bali to move to Kalimantan and West Papua. Although targets have not been met, well over 3 million people are estimated to have been moved. The program has been a disaster for both the transmigrants and the indigenous people. In South Kalimantan transmigrants are seeking ways of overcoming the dire hardship they are in. In West Papua, fighting on the border and the Indonesian army's protection and preparation of settlement sites for transmigrants has been a contributing factor in forcing twelve to fourteen thousand refugees to flee over the border to Papua New Guinea.

Cultural Genocide

Nagaland, the Chittagong Hill Tracts, and Indonesia are notorious for the cultural genocide (ethnocide) occurring there. In Nagaland, the Indianization of the country is a gradual but determined process. It operates through the education system, which is tied up with Indian not Naga values (International Work Group for Indigenous Affairs 1986c, 100).

In the Chittagong Hill Tracts, attacks by the armed forces and Bengali settlers on Buddhist monasteries have led to the deaths of monks and the desecration of holy shrines. A recent protest of Buddhist monks in Dakha was denied by the authorities, but a videotape smuggled out of the country shows clearly that the monks consider Buddhism under threat along with other aspects of tribal life such as language, rituals, and social organization. The new District Councils established by the Bangladesh government, although superficially looking like they devolve power, in fact divide the twelve indigenous peoples of the Hill Tracts into arbitrary groups with no means of moving from one area to another.

In Indonesia, Pancasila, with its five principles of nationalism, internationalism, representative government, social justice, and belief in God, has been criticized for its practical emphasis on national identity and lack of respect for indigenous cultures, particularly in occupied West Papua and East Timor. In areas where the assertion of ethnic identity has not been accompanied by insurgency (such as on Sumatra), there have been some examples of bilingual education. The Indonesian government has identified West Papua, Kalimantan, and the Mentawai Islands off Sumatra as areas where indigenous peoples need "civilising" (*Down to Earth* 1989b, 6).

West Papuans face an Indonesian "civilising" policy, which consists of controlling the languages taught at school, providing textbooks that downgrade indigenous life-styles, and prohibiting traditional dress. The Dani uprising of 1977 was a protest at being forced to wear trousers and adopt other western styles of clothing (Anti-Slavery Society 1990, 53–54). In East Timor, where cultural differences are also marked, the military occupation force has been particularly harsh in trying to stamp out indigenous culture and language.

One of the problems facing the Ainu people of Japan is lack of recognition. Whereas one hundred years ago they were a people living on reserved land, since the Former Indigene's Protection Act of 1899 they have been allotted, as happened to some North American Indians, individual plots that make land alienation very easy. With a dwindling land base, loss of ritual life, Japanese-based education, and poverty and disease, the Ainu became very disadvantaged. Recognized as low-ranking members within the state rather than as a distinct ethnic group, they are using tourist centers and their own research to reconstruct aspects of their identity lost during colonization (Sanders 1986; Sjöberg 1990).

Indigenous Resistance and Demands: Self-Determination, Autonomy, and Independence

The historical contexts in which the threats outlined above take place provide specific features in each case. The causes and nature of colonization vary widely in Southeast Asia, and this consequently affects the particular manifestation of self-determination, which each body wants, as well as the strategies they use.

Since East Timor was invaded by Indonesia in December 1975, forced relocations and severe oppression have not deterred the resistance, Fretilin, from carrying on a guerrilla war and maintaining a long struggle within the United Nations to keep the question on the agenda. East Timor is currently on the list of countries recognized as candidates for decolonization at the Committee of 24 in New York.

The Nagas and the West Papuans are not yet on that list. Their positions are slightly different. East Timor was a Portuguese colony invaded by Indonesia, itself a former Dutch colony. Nagaland and India both shared the experience of British domination, while West Papua and

Indonesia were both colonized by the Dutch. The British and the Dutch, respectively, advanced the possibility of independence to the Nagas and the Papuans, only to withdraw it. In neither country was there a real act of self-determination. The inhabitants passed, against their will, from control by a colonial power to control by its successor.

Many of the peoples of Asia were fighting the newly independent nation-states long before the indigenous movement emerged in the late 1970s. The Nagas have been battling the Indians since independence, although the main struggle was an attempt by the Nagas to prevent an army invasion in 1956. Nagaland is still under martial law according to the Armed Forces Special Powers Act of 1958 and 1972. The West Papuans have been resisting the Indonesians since 1965 through the Free Papua Movement (OPM). Like the Nagas, they have been a persistent thorn in the side of the occupying power but have never had the means to take control of their state. Both countries, Nagaland and West Papua, have declared their independence.

In the Chittagong Hill Tracts, the Jana Samhati Samiti Party (JSS) is demanding "provincial autonomy" within Bangladesh and its own legislature. The original intent was to return to the Regulation of 1900 whereby the peoples of the Hill Tracts could control their own affairs. The intransigence of the Bangladesh government has seen a hardening of the JSS line in recent years. Many people of the Hill Tracts now refer to themselves as the Jumma Nation, and the autonomy the people now want is closer to independence.

The nine main minority peoples of Burma formed the National Democratic Front (NDF) in 1976. This coalition has been fighting against Burmese army oppression and to assert their right to semi-autonomous or federal status within the Union of Burma. This status, according to their perspective, was agreed to at the time of decolonization from Britain. The federal claim that the NDF is putting forward is not independence but something to be worked out with the Burmese government. The autonomy demand is similar to that of the hill peoples of Bangladesh.

Philippine indigenous peoples are also demanding autonomy within the country. Because of the great number of indigenous peoples there, this autonomy would be based more on regional criteria. The autonomy measures proposed by the government in 1988 have been heavily criticized by indigenous peoples throughout the country because the structures would be imposed without consultation and provide no protection from the incursions of forestry and mining.

Autonomy can vary in its forms. Provincial autonomy is part of a federal system within a country (this would be similar to the solutions India has found with some of its states). Regional autonomy is more closely tied into the national state but allows some local control, probably without legislative powers. Local autonomy is more like the District Council schemes built up in states of India (such as Mizoram), which are more limited in their scope. The District Councils of the Chittagong Hill Tracts do not even constitute an autonomy, as they are effectively development bodies carrying out central government policy.

In Sarawak, which is a state within Malaysia, the indigenous peoples are seeking a different kind of autonomy. They want the right to control their own affairs but their main concern is the right to land. They want the right to keep logging companies and hydroelectric concerns off their lands so that they can continue to live according to their own needs and desires.

These examples show that self-determination can range from full independence (East Timor, Nagaland, and West Papua) and varying forms of autonomy or federation (Chittagong Hill Tracts, Burma, and the Philippines) to respect for territorial rights (Sarawak). Self-determination is not a specific alternative but an open concept that has to be filled out by a process consisting of the choices, actions, and aims of the people concerned.

All the models of self-determination mentioned above contain provisions for control of territorial resources and free cultural expression. The differences arise from the amount of political autonomy desired and the relationship of each people to the nation-state. Self-determination is the converse of colonization, which, like an empty vessel, is filled according to the historical conditions prevailing at the time.

Indigenous Peoples Movements and Asia

We have seen that the notion of "indigenous" is not just a label given to peoples but also a quality that individuals recognize in themselves. In Asia, as in other parts of the world, these two aspects of indigenousness are clearly apparent. We should look more closely at who considers themselves to be indigenous, why, and why not.

Those who deliberately do not consider themselves to be indigenous, but who see the connection. The Tibetans have discussed the question and on the whole do not wish to be considered indigenous.

Those who recognize the indigenous aspect of their struggle but choose other fora for it. The East Timorese have talked and participated in indigenous fora such as the World Council of Indigenous Peoples. However, they use the United Nations Decolonisation Committee as the body through which to make their complaints heard. They also make great use, as do the Tibetans, of the United Nations Human Rights Commission. This is the highest body in the United Nations in which non-UN members can address human-rights questions.

Those who see themselves as indigenous but do not want to compromise their claim to independence. Both Nagaland and West Papua fit into this category. Nagas participated in the World Council of Indigenous Peoples meeting in 1990 and have also attended the United Nations Working Group as observers. However, as they feel that their case is one of independence as well as human rights, many believe a higher forum such as the Decolonisation Committee would be better for them.

The West Papuans usually make a statement at the Working Group on Indigenous Populations but they also make it clear that their presence at the WGIP should be seen as in respect of human rights. They also feel that as far as independence is concerned, they should be acknowledged at a higher level within the United Nations. This would be particularly appropriate since the UN was responsible for handing the country over to Indonesia in 1969.

Tribal or native people who see that the demands of the indigenous peoples of the world should apply to them. Most of the peoples of Asia would come under this category. People in this forum would use the United Nations Working Group because they seek an autonomy that falls short of independence. Examples range from the tribal people in India suffering the relocation effects of the Narmada dam to the hill peoples of the Chittagong Hill Tracts; the Natives of Sarawak and Peninsular Malaysia; the minority peoples of Burma; the hill peoples of Thailand, Laos, Cambodia, and Vietnam; the Aboriginal peoples of Taiwan; and the Ainu of Japan.

Peoples who are unaware of the indigenous movement but live in circumstances for which the term is appropriate. This paper has concentrated on the emergence of the term *indigenous* throughout Asia and so has not focused on peoples who are not yet consciously involved in the indigenous peoples movement. However, the indigenous phenomenon only makes sense in contexts in which there are peoples with interests opposed to those of the state, with claims to prior occupation, and with a conceptualization of themselves as different from the national society. Peoples of this sort in Nepal have been aptly described by Skar (this volume).

Conclusion

The pragmatic definition of the term *indigenous* could be applied here to all the "tribal," "minority," or "aboriginal" peoples in Asia who suffer from the problems and threats outlined above and who at any moment could find themselves a part of the indigenous movement. Regardless of whether these peoples refer to themselves as indigenous, or are even called indigenous, in the context of human-rights issues, their definition emerges out of the problems they face and the rights for which they are fighting. In each of the above categories the rights and freedoms being discussed at the United Nations clearly apply to all of these peoples. Some will seek redress at the forum of decolonization as independence, whereas the Working Group on Indigenous Peoples is striving to set standards opposing internal colonization. Some will want to use the term *indigenous;* others may want it in the future.

Lack of clarity over the meaning of *indigenous* makes it a chameleon concept that merges into the sociopolitical environment. It is a formula for encapsulating personal and cultural identity within a struggle for territorial decolonization. This is the assertion of the right to self-determination.

The open concept of "indigenous," like self-determination, has the effect of bringing together some of the most disparate and varied peoples of the world by pointing out similarities in their structural positions vis-à-vis the nation-state. Along with *class, ethnicity, culture,* and *gender,* however, the word *indigenous* is somewhat "incoherent" in the sense that it cannot be used in the same way throughout the world. The meaning shifts according to context. The incoherence is only apparent from the perspective of trying to squeeze all cases into one fixed definition. In fact, what could be termed "incoherent" is its very strength because it forces the category to become flexible and to embrace a wide spectrum of decolonization questions.

Indigenousness is not just a semantic issue but one that involves identity and political mobilization. The concept is being created before our eyes in academic meetings and at the United Nations but above all by those peoples who are recognizing daily that the quality of being "indigenous" applies to them. With 300 million indigenous or potentially indigenous people in the world, it is certainly not a development that we can ignore.

I would suggest a way out of the coherence and applicability dilemma inherent in the term *indigenous* (when applied to Asia) by separating the levels of discussion.

On an analytic level, the term *indigenous* presents two related problems. When the definition is fairly coherent its application is difficult. When the application is made broadly pragmatic the definition must be polythetic. It is possible to stretch the meaning of *indigenous* to cover the peoples of Asia but as an analytical category it does not help us understand more than a very general outline of who these peoples are.

On a political level, the term *indigenous* is more an imperative than a descriptive category. It refers to a discussion of the fundamental rights to which peoples in the world who have been colonized are entitled: self-determination, freedom of cultural expression, and control over territories and resources. Indigenousness arises when people recognize these issues as pertaining to their own struggle. As *indigenous* is the principle term used currently to express these issues, the importance of not denying people the means with which to demand these rights becomes critical. When asking peoples in Asia whether they are indigenous in this sense, few will deny it.

On the level of common usage, *indigenous* is not a word encountered frequently in Asia except among leaders who are familiar with international developments. However, the growth of indigenous organizations and the increase in peoples claiming their rights would lead us to expect that the term will become more common in the future.

The term *indigenous peoples* is part of a process that is emerging through history. Governments in Asia (particularly in India, Bangladesh, and Burma) are adamant in claiming that the word does not apply to peoples in their countries. However, the evidence shows that they are markedly out of touch with their own people. The applicability of the term is growing as peoples in Asia come to see the similarities between the problems they face and those threatening indigenous peoples in other parts of the world.

The problem with the term *indigenous* in Asia arises from a gap between coherence and applicability. The way out of this problem is to see the term as a phenomenon to be understood and not as an analytic tool to aid understanding. On an abstract level it may have some value as a general descriptive term of orientation but to apply it we have to understand it as a political tool operating as an imperative term within a growing social movement. The ultimate test of the importance of the word *indigenous* lies not with us but with the millions of people throughout the world who find it an essential element in their political and cultural struggle not only for their rights but for their identities.

CHAPTER 4

Indigenous Peoples' Rights and Sustainable Resource Use in South and Southeast Asia

MARCUS COLCHESTER

> If you have come to help me
> You can go home again
> But if you see my struggle
> As part of your own survival
> Then perhaps we can work together.
> (*Australian aboriginal woman*)[1]

Traditional indigenous systems of land use have proved to be far more environmentally appropriate, resilient, and complex than was initially supposed by outsiders. Indigenous peoples' struggles for their rights, which can be seen at the same time as struggles for "sustainability," have been most obviously expressed in their opposition to socially and environmentally destructive developments imposed from outside. Yet these societies are not resisting all change and the internal dynamic for development also has created social and environmental problems. Numerous examples from the region show how indigenous peoples have surmounted these challenges by creating innovative social, technical, and political institutions.

Who is Indigenous?

Just who is and who is not "indigenous" is a complex question that is answered in very different ways depending upon the views and interests of the proponents. This article focuses on the various ethnic groups in South and Southeast Asia that are officially distinguished from the society of the national majority by a wide range of culturally loaded terms. These include the "scheduled tribes" of India, the "hill tribes" of Thailand, the "minority nationalities" of China, the "cultural minorities" of the Philippines, the "isolated and alien peoples" of Indonesia, the "aboriginal tribes" of Taiwan, the "aborigines" of Peninsular Malaysia, and the "natives" of Borneo.

In recent years, such peoples have begun increasingly to identify themselves as indigenous (Nicholas 1989). In part this is because the term *indigenous* carries fewer pejorative connotations than do other terms commonly applied by outsiders such as *aboriginal* and *tribal*. However, the main reason that they have begun to adopt the term is to demonstrate their common struggle for recognition of their rights. By labeling themselves as indigenous, these ethnic groups at once affirm their solidarity with others using the same term and assert their rights to land and self-determination.

As used by outsiders, the term *indigenous* has come to have a somewhat different emphasis. It is used in order to group together various ethnic peoples with close ties to their lands who are in some way marginalized from the national society within whose boundaries they find themselves (Independent Commission on International Humanitarian Issues 1987; Burger 1987). For example, the World Bank, which used to refer to "tribal peoples" (World Bank 1982a, 1982b), has recently adopted the term *indigenous* in its policy documents. As now used,

> the term indigenous covers indigenous, tribal, low caste and ethnic minority groups. Despite their historical and cultural differences, they often have a limited capacity to participate in the development process because of cultural barriers or low social and political status. (World Bank 1990,1)

This paper explores the implications for natural resources of this tension between local claims to own and control land and a national development policy which, for various reasons, marginalizes indigenous peoples from the process.

Indigenous Peoples' Rights

Across South and Southeast Asia, from Pakistan in the west to the Pacific islands in the east, the claims being made by indigenous peoples show a striking similarity. The three central claims are: the right to ownership and control of their territories, the right of self-determination, and the right to represent themselves through their own institutions.

These claims are not without justification, and to varying degrees they all have a basis in international law. The right of tribal and indigenous peoples to ownership of their lands is accepted in Article 11 of ILO Convention 107. The right of all peoples to self-determination is recognized in the International Covenants of Civil and Political Rights and of Economic, Social and Cultural Rights. The right of tribal and indigenous peoples to be represented through their own institutions is recognized in Article 2 of ILO Convention 169.

Concepts of Sustainability

As made popular by the United Nations' World Commission on Environment and Development (WCED), the phrase *sustainable development* refers to the means by which "development" is made to meet the needs of the present without compromising the ability of future generations to meet their own needs (World Commission on Environment and Development 1987).[2] Since the needs of future generations are undefinable and the future potential for wealth generation of species and ecosystems are equally unknowable, the term apparently implies that total biological assets will not be reduced, in the long term, through use.

In a rural context, sustainable use thus includes not just conserving biological diversity but also maintaining ecological functions such as soil quality, hydrological cycles, climate and weather, river flow, and water quality. It also implies maintaining supplies of natural produce—game, fish, fodder, fruits, nuts, resins, dyes, basts, constructional materials, fuelwood, etc.—essential to the livelihoods of local people.

As the WCED study acknowledges, achieving sustainability implies a radical transformation in present-day economies. It also requires a fundamental change in the way natural resources are owned, controlled, and mobilized. To be sustainable, development must meet the needs of local people; if it does not, people will be obliged by necessity to take from the environment more than was planned. Thus, sustainability is fundamentally linked to concepts of social justice and equity, both within generations and between generations. Achieving sustainability also implies major political changes. As the WCED notes,

> The pursuit of sustainable development requires a political system that secures effective participation in decision-making....This is best secured by decentralizing the management of resources upon which local communities depend, and giving these communities an effective say over the use of these resources. It will also require promoting citizen's initiatives, empowering peoples' organisations, and strengthening local democracy. (Cited in Durning 1989, 54)

There is, thus, a remarkable convergence between what the WCED has set out as the essential conditions for sustainability and the rights demanded by indigenous people. This should come as no surprise, for what indigenous people are demanding is no more than what they should be allowed to sustain their societies from the environments they have always depended on. The WCED study stresses this congruence, noting of indigenous peoples that

> In terms of sheer numbers these isolated, vulnerable groups are small, but their marginalisation is a symptom of a style of development that tends to neglect both human and environmental considerations. Hence a more careful and sensitive consideration of their interests is a touchstone of sustainable development policy....Their traditional rights should be recognised and they should be given a decisive voice in formulating policies about resource development in their areas. (World Commission on Environment and Development 1987, 12, 116)

Indigenous Peoples and Government

The gap between what the WCED has called for and the reality facing indigenous people in South and Southeast Asia could hardly be greater. Even when government policy is notionally designed to discriminate in favor of such peoples, as in China and India, rights to traditional lands and the power to control development are systematically denied (Anonymous 1984, 1987).

Underlying the disenfranchising policies of governments throughout the region lie deeply held prejudices. These have been most explicitly stated in Indonesia, where so-called *suku suku terasing* ("isolated and alien peoples") are defined by the government as

> people who are isolated and have a limited capacity to communicate with other more advanced groups, resulting in their having backward attitudes,

and being left behind in the economic, political, socio-cultural, religious and ideological development process." (*Down to Earth* 1991)

As occurred in the United States at the turn of the century, and in Australia in the 1950s, the Indonesian government pursues a policy of reeducating indigenous people to free them from their "backward" ways. They are also banned from pursuing their traditional religions (Atkinson 1988).

In 1986, the Indonesian government embarked upon a new project, entitled Total Development of Indonesian People, aimed at reeducating West Papuans described as "still living in a Stone-age-like era." In order to bring these peoples "up to a par with the rest of the country," children would be "separated from their parents to keep them from settling into their parents' lifestyle." This was necessary, according to the government, "because changing their parents' lifestyle would be very difficult, and necessitate considerable expenditure and time" (Indonesia 1986).

There have been few local-level studies of the impact of such policies (Persoon 1985; Colchester 1986a). Garna's study in West Java shows how a program of directed development and modernization among the Baduy created a sense of dependency and fatalism with a consequent failure of economic change. He concludes that "given the chance, the Baduy would prefer to be left alone to decide their own future" (1990, 100).

Throughout the region, forced resettlement has been a central plank in government programs designed to "assist" indigenous peoples. Often national security is a paramount consideration. In Malaya, for example, the Department of Aboriginal Affairs embarked upon a hasty program of forced relocation in the 1950s to prevent Orang Asli villages from being used as guerrilla bases. Paternalistic policies still prevail in Peninsular Malaysia where they have proved to be socially destructive, economically unsuccessful, and environmentally imprudent. Today the Orang Asli are still entrusted to the Ministry of Home Affairs whose other charges include administration of the police, armed forces, prisons, and civil defense (Carey 1976; Endicott 1979; Lim and Gomes 1990; Nicholas 1990).

In Thailand, the "hill tribes" face equally severe obstacles. Not only are they subjected to forced resettlement and imposed development programs but they are denied Thai nationality and residence. Thai armed forces have even gone so far as to expel long-settled tribal communities into Burma at gunpoint (Tapp 1986; McKinnon and Bhruksasri 1986; Survival International 1987; Ekachai 1990).

The now-defunct agency PANAMIN (Presidential Assistant [later Assistance] to National Minorities) must bear a large share of responsibility for the breakdown in relations between the indigenous peoples of the Philippines and the national government. The agency came into being under the patronage of President Ferdinand Marcos, and his relative Manuel Elizalde, with the ostensible purpose of protecting indigenous peoples' rights and interests. Far from preventing the pillage of indigenous lands by mining companies, loggers, and hydropower projects, PANAMIN collaborated with Marcos's armed forces to deprive the peoples of their lands. The result was a total breakdown in relations between the government and indigenous peoples, a collapse exacerbated by the heavy handed repression meted out by the Philippine armed forces.

Denied protection by the very institution founded to defend their interests, indigenous people were forced into militant opposition. Many even took up arms against the government, joining the communist insurgency group, the New Peoples Army. During this period PANAMIN consistently failed to defend the indigenous peoples' rights to their ancestral lands. On the contrary, because Elizalde's political base and personal wealth lay in extractive concerns such as mining, logging, and agribusiness, PANAMIN collaborated with the armed forces and industry in dispossessing the indigenous peoples. When PANAMIN was founded, in 1968, the majority of its board members were from wealthy industrialist families. Many had direct financial interests in companies encroaching upon indigenous lands. Elizalde maintained a private army in Cotobato in Mindanao, near the area where the "lost stone-age tribe," the Tasaday, were "discovered." In 1975, PANAMIN created its own counterinsurgency unit; within two years "security" expenses became the single largest item in the PANAMIN budget.

In Mindanao, where the Elizalde family owned several concerns, PANAMIN actively cooperated with agribusinesses in forcing indigenous peoples to give up their lands. Tribal communities such as the Manobo were forced to relocate onto tiny reservations owned by the agency. In all, according to PANAMIN's own claim, some 2.5 million indigenous people were resettled in this fashion (Anti-Slavery Society 1983; Rocamora 1979; Fay 1987).

The Struggle for Land

The most severe problem faced by indigenous people throughout South and Southeast Asia is the lack of recognition of customary rights to their land. With the partial exception of Melanesia (James 1985) and India's northeast (Fürer-Haimendorf 1982), the collective ownership of traditional lands is nowhere legally secure.

In Indonesia recognition of *adat* (customary) law only extends to areas under permanent cultivation or occupancy, and then ambiguously (Colchester 1986b; Brewer 1988). In Peninsular Malaysia areas set aside for aboriginal use are held by the state and may by reallocated at the stroke of a pen (Nicholas 1990). In Sarawak "native customary rights," while tenuously recognized in law, are ignored for practical purposes and can be extinguished by simple gazettement (Colchester 1989, 1991). In Sri Lanka, India, and lowland Bangladesh, although laws have been enacted to protect "tribals" from expropriation and land sales, only individual title is recognized (Colchester 1984; Survival International 1984). In the Philippines, rights to "ancestral domain" are not respected (Anti-Slavery Society 1983), although, after heavy lobbying, the new Constitution has granted them some recognition.

Legal landlessness has not necessarily been the immediate consequence of this lack of recognition of collective land title. Adjusting to the political realities, many indigenous people have used what legal avenues exist to secure individual land rights, usually to small portions of their once-extensive domains. Indeed, during the colonial period in both British and American possessions, registration of individual land title under the Torrens system—whereby individually owned lots had to be registered with the colonial authorities within a prescribed period of time—was strongly promoted, explicitly in order to bring land, labor, and harvests into the market. The Dutch promoted a similar scheme in Indonesia.

The denial of communal land rights, and fragmentation of territory into individually owned plots, undermined traditional systems of resource management. Systems of shifting cultivation, in particular, have suffered (Colchester 1990). On the one hand, confining shifting cultivators to small parts of once extensive territories has reduced or even eliminated periods of fallow, leading to soil exhaustion, accelerated erosion, and poverty. On the other hand, even when access to land has not been physically limited, lack of land security has promoted mismanagement by undermining traditional concepts of custodianship and resource allocation. A good example is Jeffrey Brewer's study of Bima in eastern Indonesia (1988).

Chronic conflict between the state and indigenous peoples has actually promoted the cultivation of ecologically suboptimal crops.

Among the Hmong, for example, the opium poppy, which is very demanding on both soils and labor, is selected because it yields a light-weight, valuable harvest within eight months of sowing. Though illegal, the crop can be taken "on the run" and its considerable cash returns used to pay off army officers and government officials (Geddes 1976; Tapp 1986).

Indigenous economies have been undermined by the creation of a market in land, which many traditionally nonmonetized peoples have found hard to manage. In western Bangladesh, for example, the Santal territories have been progressively reduced so that today the Santal own less land per capita than do the invading Bengalis (Colchester 1984). Fürer-Haimendorf's studies in central India have shown how this process of land transfer accelerates rapidly with the intrusion of markets for new crops (Fürer-Haimendorf 1982). The process also has intensified sharply as a result of the so-called Green Revolution. High-yield, high-input agriculture naturally favors farmers with greater access to land and capital, leading to a growing concentration of land and wealth in the hands of a few (Duyker 1987; Shiva 1989). The process is perhaps fiercest in Thailand where currently a frenzy of land speculation and commoditization is sweeping through provinces once economically isolated (Ekachai 1990). Laments an Akhba from Chiang Rai province, "I don't think we can stay here much longer. Land is most important to our livelihood and there's almost none of it left" (ibid., 181).

State Lands

Whereas the initial aim of the colonial powers in Asia was to gain control of trade, it was only in the eighteenth and nineteenth centuries that western concepts of land ownership and control began to be widely applied. A major force in this process was the demand for timber for the colonial navies, which led to the imposition of new forestry policies over vast areas of Asia (Shiva 1987; Westoby 1989; Peluso 1990). In the process, indigenous people lost control of most of their ancestral lands to newly created government agencies. Reviewing the problems caused by this process in India, Agarwal and Narain note that

> The biggest problem lies in the alienation that the modern state has created amongst village communities towards their commons....The British were the first to nationalise these resources and bring them under the management of government bureaucracies. The laws have totally destroyed the traditional systems of village management...[and] have

started a free for all....Today nearly one third of India's lands and all its water resources are owned by the Government. No less than 22 percent of the national territory is under the control of the forest departments. The result is that village communities have lost all interest in their management and protection....This alienation has led to massive denudation of forests, over-exploitation of grazing lands and neglect of local water systems. (Agarwal and Narain 1989, 13, 27; see also Morris 1982, 1983)

In Southeast Asia the picture is even more startling. Indonesia's Forest Department controls some 74 percent of the national territory, putting it in conflict with the 30 to 40 million people who live in, or derive their livelihood directly from, the forests. The seven-thousand-strong staff of the Royal Forestry Department in Thailand administers 40 percent of the nation's land area, where some 6 million "squatters" reside (Poffenberger 1990). In October 1989, Thailand's newly appointed Forestry Department chief announced that all these people were to be relocated. He drew special attention to the need to expel the 700,000 hill tribespeople living in these areas (*Bangkok Post*, 10 October 1989). In the Philippines, the 55 percent of the country classified as forest reserves is inhabited by some 18 million people, including most of the country's 6 million indigenous people (Poffenberger 1990). Yet forestry policies systematically ignore these peoples' numbers, welfare, and rights (Colchester and Lohmann 1990; Lynch 1990).

One of the main problems with the policy of divesting local people of control of land is that the relatively tiny bureaucracies charged with administering and policing the forests are unable to prevent access by outsiders. Moreover, forest bureaucracies have leased the same areas to private industry in the form of logging concessions. The result of these combined pressures has been environmental devastation on an astounding scale (Repetto 1988; Porter and Ganapin 1988; Myers 1989; Colchester 1990).

In sum, besides replacing previously sustainable systems of resource use with extravagant and destructive practices, forestry has created almost insoluble political conflicts between local people and government. These conflicts have further "limited the ability of both the state and the community to effectively control forest use, and have contributed to uncontrolled exploitation and mismanagement" (Poffenberger 1990, 97).

The policy bias against local people and in favor of timber-based economies has also severely damaged the evolution of democratic institutions in Asian countries. In Sarawak, for example, the corrupting influence of the timber trade has promoted the domination of the economy by nepotistic, patronage politics. This has undermined democratic principles and caused an increasing marginalization of rural people, who find they can no longer rely on their political representatives to defend their interests. The practice of dealing out logging licenses to members of the state legislature in order to secure their allegiance is so commonplace in Sarawak that it has created a class of instant millionaires (Colchester 1989).

The Commission of Enquiry in Papua New Guinea has revealed a similar decay in standards of public service due to the logging industry (Marshall 1990). In fact, the process is very widespread, having formed as well a crucial component of the "crony capitalism" of the Philippines under Ferdinand Marcos (Anderson 1987). In Indonesia, logging concessions continue to be one of the perks enjoyed by the ruling military clique (Hurst 1991).

Ironically, western attempts to promote natural-resource conservation also have foundered on this unresolved conflict between local communities and state administration. Like forestry reserves, national parks established on indigenous lands have denied local rights to resources, transforming the inhabitants practically overnight from hunters and cultivators into "poachers" and "squatters" (Colchester 1989). This problem, too, is very widespread. One example is the Dumoga Bone National Park in Sulawesi, where the indigenous Mongondow people, displaced onto the hillsides from their valley lands by spontaneous and government-sponsored colonization, found themselves persecuted as "encroachers" when the hillsides were declared a national park, created to protect the catchment of a dam constructed to promote irrigation agriculture in the lowlands (*Down to Earth* 1989, 7–8). The last community of forest-dwelling Veddah in Sri Lanka face an identical problem due to the creation of the Madura Oya National Park.

Development as Expropriation

The past forty years have seen a massive acceleration in the rate at which indigenous peoples have been deprived of their lands and livelihoods by imposed development programs (Bodley 1982; Burger 1987). Large-scale projects such as plantations, dams, mines, military installations, nuclear waste dumps, and colonization schemes are the most obvious causes (Anti-Slavery Society 1983; Fiagoy 1987; Tapol 1988; Colchester 1985, 1986c, 1986d, 1987a). In many cases these government-directed development initiatives are justified as being "in the national interest" and the state has thereby exercised its power of "eminent domain" to deny local peoples' rights. In Indonesia, the government feels entitled to invoke this prerogative for any project or program included in its five-year plans (Butcher 1988). In India, it is estimated that as many as two million "tribal" people face eviction from their lands to make way for proposed projects (Colchester 1987b).

Summarizing the experience in India, the Delhi-based Centre for Science and the Environment notes:

> In a country like India, with a high population density and high level of poverty, virtually every ecological niche is occupied by some occupational or cultural human group for its sustenance. Each time an ecological niche is degraded or its resources appropriated by the more powerful in society, the deprived weaker sections become further impoverished. For instance, the steady destruction of our natural forests, pasture lands and coastal water bodies has not only meant an increased economic poverty for millions of tribals, nomads and traditional fisherfolk, but also a slow cultural and social death: a dismal change from rugged self-sufficient human beings to abjectly dependent landless labourers and urban migrants. Current development can, in fact, be described as the process by which the rich and more powerful in society reallocate the nation's natural resources in their favour and modern technology is the tool that subserves this process. (Centre of Science and the Environment 1982)

Traditions of Sustainability

> We hilltribes preserve the forest to protect people and animals against danger, disease, injury, soldiers and bad spirits. Having a forest belt around the village will bring happiness to the community. Big trees are like mothers, and little trees are like children, needing to be encouraged into flower and growth. If no one comes and cuts the little tree, it will grow up to be a big one in place of those there now. The forest belt and the village are things people are not to destroy. (Akha elder, cited in Permpongsacharoen 1990)

For centuries the economic systems of Asia's indigenous peoples have been viewed as backward and irrational. Underlying this prejudice lies a deep mistrust of peoples who are not subject to government control and taxation systems and do not contribute substantially to the market economy (Dove 1985). The Dutch summed up their prejudice against shifting cultivation in Indonesia by referring to it as the "robber economy." As pressure on natural resources has intensified, such systems have been subjected to the added criticism of being wasteful and environmentally destructive (Agarwal and Narain 1989; Colchester 1990).

However, the many detailed studies of these economies made since the 1950s suggest a different conclusion. Hunters and gatherers, such as the Penan of Sarawak, who see themselves as transmitting their lands unharmed to the generations that follow them (Brosius 1986), consciously manage their resources to ensure sustained yield (Langub 1988a, 1988b). The idea that present generations are stewards who hold the lands of the ancestors in trust for future generations is echoed in many indigenous cultures throughout the region, as in New Guinea where the people refer to future generations as "our children who are still in the soil" (Colchester 1986b).

Clear evidence has emerged, too, that these ideas are not just long-cherished ideals but actually inform and influence day-to-day behavior. Studies of shifting cultivation reveal not only their extreme variability and complexity but the enormous reserve of vernacular knowledge on which they are based (Conklin 1954). Practices that function to conserve resources, restore soil fertility, mimic biodiversity, and protect watersheds have been widely documented throughout the region.

Similarly, studies of indigenous systems of irrigation agriculture have revealed both the appropriateness of the technology and the complex social institutions that regulate water rights (Coward 1985). In Thailand, the network of obligations and rights implicit in the traditional institution of the *muang faai* (the community water-management polity) extends the management and protection of resources into the forested watersheds that are essential to the maintenance of water supplies (Project for Ecological Recovery 1990). In this way pragmatic, community-based, management processes secure biodiversity far more effectively than do imposed conservation plans (Lohmann 1991).

Resistance to Destruction

The intimate association between indigenous peoples and their land, and their determination to maintain their ways of life, are most obviously expressed in their opposition to imposed and destructive change. Such opposition may take subtle forms. Von Geusau (1986), for example, sees Akha society in Thailand as fundamentally shaped by centuries of passive resistance to outside interference, creating what might be called a culture of marginalization. Across the region literally hundreds of different indigenous movements have their roots in resistance to cultural, economic, and political oppression (Singh 1982; Worsley 1957).

The most obvious of these are the mass movements of indigenous groups that have mobilized to confront specific threats. One of the most celebrated struggles between indigenous peoples and loggers is still going on in Sarawak where the Dayak peoples, denied legal or political means of defending their lands, have resorted to erecting human barricades across the logging roads to defend the forests around their longhouses. The Malaysian government has responded with mass arrests and passage of a new law making interference on logging roads a criminal offense. Yet, despite the intimidation and threats, the blockades have been re-erected, halting timber extraction on the concessions of such prominent politicians as the minister for environment and tourism. Harrison Ngau, a native activist, who was detained in solitary confinement for sixty days in 1987 without charge or trial, remains defiant. He claims that

> A lot of money is being made from the trees and the Dayaks are not getting anything and they are losing their way of life. The Government says this is development. If this is development, the Dayaks do not want it. (Colchester 1989; see also World Rainforest Movement/Sahabat Alam Malaysia 1990).

In Taiwan, the Malayo-Polynesian Yami fisherfolk of Lan-yu Island have been protesting against the construction of a second nuclear-waste disposal site on their lands, which they claim threatens to poison the fish stocks on which their lives depend. The government has responded by sending in police to beat the demonstrators. In India, mass marches of tribal people protesting resettlement to make way for hydropower projects have resulted in police firings and deaths.

Resistance to imposed development also has been widespread in the Philippines (Anti-Slavery Society 1983; TABAK 1990; Regpala 1990), the most topical example being the Bagobo peoples' resistance to government plans to build geothermal power plants on the forested slopes of Mt. Apo, held sacred by the Bagobo as the domain of the god Sandawa (Fay et al. 1989). Mobilization against the project has linked the indigenous people with local environmental organizations. The protests have been met with intimidatory tactics by the military.

In some areas, relations between the national government and local peoples have become so bad that the affected populations, denied other means of protest, have expressed their opposition through organized armed resistance. The most tragic such case involved the World

Bank–supported Chico dams project in the Philippines, which threatened to displace some eighty thousand Kalinga and Bontoc people from their ancestral lands (Bello et al. 1982). When the locals protested against the project, the Marcos regime responded with brutal violence, leading to an escalating conflict. Many tribals took to the hills and joined the New Peoples Army in defiance of the imposed development program (Drucker 1986; Fay 1987). The conflict endured long after the World Bank pulled out of the project. Villages were repeatedly bombed and subjected to counterinsurgency programs (*Survival International News* 1985, 7:1). North of the Chico, the resistance of the Tinggian people of Abra to the Cellophil Corporation's logging of the pine forests on their watersheds escalated into a similar armed confrontation (Dorrall 1990).

The Philippines is far from the only area in the region where conflicts over natural resources have contributed to armed confrontations between indigenous people and the state. It is no accident that the Naxalite movement in India has thrived in tribal areas (Bannerjee 1984; Duyker 1987). Resistance to exploitation similarly underlies the insurgency in the Chittagong Hill Tracts in Bangladesh (Survival International 1984; Anti-Slavery Society 1984; Mey 1984), in Nagaland and other parts of northeast India (International Work Group for Indigenous Affairs 1986), and in Burma and West Papua (Tapol 1988; Anti-Slavery Society 1991). The recent liberation movement in Bougainville in eastern Papua New Guinea, has its roots in a conflict between indigenous peoples and a mining operation.

Whether violent or not, and successful or not, the most important and enduring outcome of these conflicts over natural resources has been the local, national, and international mobilization that has resulted. For example, opposition to the Chico dams and the Cellophil Corporation in the Cordillera was organized around the revival of the institution of the *bodong*, or "peace pact," by which warring communities can establish peaceful relations. To oppose the dam, the *bodong* was extended over a wide area, even beyond its original extent, so that now it embraces a major part of the Cordillera. Today there are literally hundreds of local organizations in the Cordillera concerned with educational programs, economic development, health, women's rights, marketing, and land. As a consequence, despite the lack of legally secure land rights, the people once more feel in control of their ancestral domains (Regpala 1990).

Change and Sustainability

> Don't mistake us. We are not a backward-looking people. Like others we
> want development and we want to improve our lives and the lives of the
> next generations; we want better education, better health and better
> services. But we want to control this development in our land and over our
> lives. And we demand a share both in decision-making and in the benefits
> of development. (Tinggian statement, cited in Dorrall 1990, 62)

Indigenous peoples and proponents of sustainability assert that
genuine development can only be achieved when local people control
their lands and institutions and have a decisive voice in their future. Far
from reactionary forces resisting all change, most indigenous communities in the region are actively seeking development in the form of better
health, education, and increasing involvement in the cash economy
(Gerritsen et al. 1981).

This raises a crucial question. Can indigenous peoples maintain the
balance between their societies and environments when they have rising
populations and increasing demands for cash and services? Many development planners are skeptical of the ability of indigenous communities
to manage their resources prudently under such changed circumstances,
and they use this as an excuse for maintaining control of indigenous
lands and institutions. The argument is a difficult one to resolve. While,
on the one hand, there is unmistakable evidence of environmental
decline in areas where indigenous peoples are exerting increasing pressure on their resources, on the other hand, this decline has often
occurred when their social institutions and environments are under
heavy pressure from outside.

Papua New Guinea, where collective land rights are strongly
protected by law, forms a crucial testing ground for such arguments: on
the face of it the case is not encouraging. Despite apparently secure land
rights, New Guinea communities have frequently negotiated their rights
away, leasing them to logging and mining companies in exchange for
royalties. Only later have they come to regret the massive damage that
their environments have sustained from such operations. However,
closer examination reveals that the issue is not so simple.

Imprecisions in the law have meant that, while the principle of
collective land ownership is clearly recognized, the law does not make
clear who has the right to negotiate land deals. Outside enterprises have
taken full advantage of this loophole by creating fake landowner

companies, exploiting internal divisions within the local societies, and employing bribery, extortion, and debt leverage (Rainforest Information Centre 1990a; Marshall 1990).

There are also cases in which apparently representative landowner associations have allowed their lands to be exploited (Good 1986; Hughes and Thirlwall 1988). Perhaps the principle reason for this is that many New Guineans are inexperienced in the cash economy and even less aware of the social and environmental implications of inviting in foreign enterprises. There is clear evidence that this situation is changing and much harder bargains are now being struck by local communities than in the past. Another factor is that the rate of social change has been unusually rapid in Papua New Guinea. As a result many New Guineans have unreal expectations about what is achievable. Crucially, many no longer believe that their own future, much less that of their children, lies on the land.

Taxation, schooling, labor-saving technology, new fashions, and consumerism have generated a demand for cash without the corresponding growth of a market for traditional produce. Thus, cashing in natural resources is the only ready option for most communities. New technologies such as *wokabaut somils* (portable sawmills) may provide a solution to this problem (Sargent and Burgess 1988; Rainforest Information Centre 1990b) but the social and political challenges to sustainability in New Guinea are also significant.

Melanesian political processes have traditionally concentrated power and trade in the hands of "big men." Whereas under traditional circumstances such leadership was openly accountable, and, in the context of frequent intertribal war, dependent upon the allegiance of clan members, this is no longer true. Today's community leaders are as likely to be in an office in the local administrative center as in the village men's house, and their wealth is more likely to be stashed in a bank in Port Moresby or Singapore than accumulated as pigs, wives, and cowries. As local leadership becomes less accountable and less responsive to community needs and rights, the opportunities for making land-use decisions that increase personal gain at the expense of the community are widening.

This problem, which I call "lairdism," is very widespread in indigenous societies, and many of them are radically transforming their political institutions to take account of the problem. In Sarawak, for example, the indigenous elite, after a long history of manipulation and co-optation by colonial and postcolonial authorities, often sides with loggers against the local people. To overcome this problem the communities have begun to develop new "longhouse associations." These are run under more democratic principles than are the traditional institutions, and provide more representative leadership (Colchester 1989).

Agarwal and Narain (1989) note a similar situation among rural communities in India. There the leaders of the *panchayats*, made up of several, often large, caste- and class-divided villages, have proved to be wholly unrepresentative. The result has been a disastrous degradation of natural resources. Yet, where communities have managed to create open, accountable, and (crucially) equitable forums for making decisions about resource management, Indian villagers have managed to check and even reverse resource depletion.

Perhaps the best known such example is the Chipko movement, which, along with its derivative, the Appiko, evolved as a community-based response to unsustainable forestry in the foothills of the Himalayas. Having successfully halted the logging of the watersheds and secured control, though not ownership, of their hillsides, women's groups have mobilized effective tree-planting programs, which have begun to spread to other parts of India (Hegde 1988).

In the Philippines, too, the Ikalahan of the eastern Cordillera have developed a successful reforestation program, based on a transfer of resource control from the Department of Energy and Natural Resources to community management, which has restored water quality and brought revenue to the villages involved (Rice and Bugtong 1989; Cornista and Escueta 1990). The project has encouraged the Philippine government to develop a program of leasing state lands under so-called Community Forest Stewardship Agreements, the legal terms of which have been amended so that indigenous signatories are no longer deemed to have waived their ancestral land rights (Gasconia 1989).

In the southern Philippines, on the island of Mindanao, where indigenous communities have lost far more of their lands than in the Cordillera, land reoccupation has become a central part of the struggle. Unproductive state lands and extensive cattle ranches have been taken back by dispossessed tribal people for plough cultivation and subsistence farming (Lumad Mindanaw 1990). Reorganization into novel political institutions has been a critical step in this process, and, as in the Chipko example, women have played a key role in the negotiations (Edtami Mansayagan, personal communication).

Conservation groups also have begun to recognize that effective resource protection is only possible if local communities are both fully involved in protected-area planning and gain direct benefits from the project. The Arfak Mountains Nature Reserve in West Papua, for example, is based, simultaneously, on recognition of the ancestral land rights of the Hatam people and recognition that Indonesian law does not secure those rights. Although the legal definition of the area as a "strict nature reserve" makes indigenous resource use theoretically illegal, the project, which has local government approval, allows the Hatam to continue to use it until the law is changed in their favor. Aware of the benefits, the local people have begun to effectively act as a "guard force" for the reserve (Craven 1990).

Conclusion

Examples such as these provide clear evidence that community-based resource management can be environmentally benign and perhaps even "sustainable." An essential precondition for achieving success is that the state divests itself of control of land and transfers it "into the hands of those whose survival directly depends upon their careful management" (Fay 1989, 8).

Summarizing their studies of community-based resource management in India, Agarwal and Narain (1989, viii) have reached the similar conclusion that to achieve environmental security "each rural settlement of India must have its own clearly and legally defined environment to protect, improve, care for and use."

By itself, land security achieved through communal tenure or collective control may not guarantee prudent resource use. Control and management of the resources must be vested in open, accountable institutions which respect the principle of equity. Moreover, long-term sustainable resource use is only likely to be achieved when the community believes its future does lie on the land.

The barriers to achieving such a transformation in government policies toward indigenous peoples, development, and the environment should not be underestimated (Durning 1989, 53). The promotion of sustainability is by definition political. The assertion of indigenous rights and the transfer of resources back to local communities is being, and will continue to be, resisted by those who benefit most from the present development strategies.

CHAPTER 5

Indigenous People of Asian Russia

JENS DAHL

Until recently the Soviet Union consisted of fifteen Soviet Republics. Of these Union Republics, the Russian Federal Republic was, and is, by far the largest in terms of both number of inhabitants and area. With the exception of Siberia and northern Russia, the republics traditionally have been dominated by their original peoples. The ethnic Ukrainians make up the majority of the population in Ukraine, as do the Armenians in Armenia, and so on. These peoples, numbering millions, speak their own languages and have their own religions, cultures, and histories. All republics had their own parliaments even before the recent political changes in the former Soviet Union.

In all the republics, now independent states, there are a substantial number of immigrant minorities—the Russians in Ukraine, the Armenians in Russia, and so on. The borders of some of these republics originally were drawn so that they included people belonging to the dominant nationalities of neighboring republics. One example is the Armenians in Azerbaijan, now a well-known case.

In Russia, however, there are a large number of aboriginal ethnic groups without their own republics. The majority of these are small indigenous peoples living within the borders of the former Russian Socialist Soviet Republic, mainly in the vast territory of geographical Asia. Most of these peoples live under arctic or subarctic conditions. A large number pursue "traditional" livelihoods such as reindeer herding, hunting, trapping, and fishing. Asian Russia is the vast country stretching from the Ural Mountains in the west to the Pacific Ocean. This

region does not include the Asian republics of the former Soviet Union.
To be absolutely correct, Asian Russia consists of two geographical
regions, Siberia and the Far East, but the term Siberia is usually applied
to the whole of Asian Russia.

The Russian conquest of Siberia was initiated in the sixteenth
century. From then on, the Czars and Russian merchants took the lead
in continuous expansion of Russian domination over the peoples of
Siberia. The Russians, including those of other nationalities such as
Cossacks, Armenians, and Ukrainians, were settlers. Many came to
Siberia in the service of Czarist Russia, and later of the Soviet Union, but
additional thousands immigrated and settled on their own. From the
earliest colonial days the indigenous people were dominated by
merchants, settlers, and representatives of Moscow who treated them as
inferiors, although sometimes recognizing them as indigenous and
aboriginal. Nevertheless, very few of these indigenous people—often
extremely small groups—gave up their distinct identity, which was
rooted in cultures, economies, and languages completely different from
those of the immigrants.

All of these people are indigenous in terms of their relationship to
a distinguished homeland. Even those like the Kamchadals of
Kamchatka,[1] who owe their existence as a distinct ethnic group to mixed
marriages between colonized and colonizers, have claims to a distinguished homeland now controlled by foreign intruders.

The indigenous groups of Siberia are colonized peoples and their
relationship to the state is one of inferiority in cultural as well as
economic terms (see Gray, this volume). Their languages are discriminated against and their social structures are being destroyed by forced
relocation and an economic, legal, and administrative set-up that favors
new trades (such as mining and logging), which compete with or
threaten the indigenous economies. They have lost their land, and their
cultures, economies, and ecological ways of life are discriminated against.
Still, they consider themselves to be distinct indigenous peoples.

Their self-identification as indigenous peoples became obvious
during the Gorbachev era. As soon as the chance came, international
contacts were sought with indigenous peoples like the Saami and the
Inuit. Both the Saami and the Inuit are divided by international borders.
The Saami in Russia are closely related to the Saami in Finland and
Norway, and the Eskimos (Inuit) of Siberia and those of St. Lawrence
Island (Alaska) belong to the same group. The first international poli-
tical appearance by the indigenous peoples of Russia occurred when the

first president of the Association of Small Indigenous People of the Soviet North, Vladimir Sangi, attended the United Nations Working Group on Indigenous Populations in 1990, and their prime international aim was for the USSR to ratify the International Labour Organisation's (ILO) Convention 169, "Concerning Indigenous and Tribal Peoples in Independent Countries."

The indigenous peoples of Asian Russia are a culturally heterogeneous group, united primarily by their common position as indigenous peoples and their assertion of self-determination. When first colonized by European Russia and later dominated by the Soviet power they were forced to orient themselves toward Moscow. This is now changing. The Eskimos orient themselves to fellow tribesmen across the Bering Strait, and the people of southern Siberia undoubtedly will look to the south. The Buryat living southeast of Lake Baikal are a Mongolian-speaking people and the Tuvins are Buddhists who for centuries were under the control of Mongolian and Chinese rulers. But before looking to the outside they wish to reorganize and revitalize their own "traditional" cultures, which for so many years have been dominated and suppressed by the Moscow regimes.

Indigenous Autonomy

In what was usually referred to as the Russian and Soviet North and Far East, two groups, the Komi in European Russia and the Yakut in Siberia, had, and still have, their own autonomous republics. This gave them a certain degree of sovereignty within the Russian Federal Republic. The Komi Autonomous Region was established in 1921 (Mark 1989, 98) and the Yakut Autonomous Republic was founded in 1922. These are also the largest indigenous groups of the North and the Far East (in 1989 there were 382,000 Yakuts and 344,500 Komi). The other indigenous peoples of this northern and eastern region usually have been referred to as Small Peoples of the Soviet North and Far East or simply as the Small Peoples of the North or the Northern Minorities. This concept came into use as early as the 1920s and 1930s. Since then these people have been treated as distinct, and special ordinances have been applied to them. A number of privileges were granted, and institutions were created to protect their interests (Kuoljok 1985, 36).

Students belonging to one of the recognized indigenous groups have priority in access to some types of education, and in today's Russia indigenous students have free education whereas other students have to pay a fee. Among the other preferential rights given to indigenous peoples are specific quotas for subsistence fishing, a practice denied to nonindigenous people. Special benefits are also granted to indigenous people who seek medical assistance.

Table 5.1. The Twenty-Six Officially Recognized "Small Peoples of the North and Far East" and Their Numbers in 1979 and 1989 (earlier names in parentheses).

Names	1979	1989
Aleuts	546	702
Chukchee	14,000	15,184
Chuvans	—	1,511
Dolgans	5,053	6,932
Entsy (Yenisei Samoyeds)	350	209
Eskimos	1,510	1,719
Evenks (Tungus)	27,531	30,163
Evens (Lamuts)	12,286	17,199
Itelmens (Kamchadals)	1,370	2,481
Kets (Yenisei Ostyaks)	1,122	1,113
Khants (Ostyaks)	20,934	22,521
Koryaks	7,879	9,242
Mansi (Voguls)	7,563	8,461
Nanais (Goldi)	10,516	10,023
Negidals	504	622
Nenets (Yurak Samoyeds)	29,894	34,665
Nganasans (Taimyr Samoyeds)	867	1,278
Nivkhi (Gilyaks)	4,397	4,673
Orochi	1,198	915
Oroks	450	190
Saami	1,888	1,890
Selkups (Ostyak Samoyeds)	3,565	3,621
Tofalars (Karagas)	—	731
Udege	1,551	2,011
Ulchi	2,552	3,233
Yukagirs	835	1,142

Note: Besides the "26 Small Peoples" there are a number of other indigenous peoples in Russian Asia. In 1989, there were 421,000 Buryats, 382,000 Yakuts, 207,000 Tuvins, 80,000 Khakass, 71,000 Altays, and 17,000 Shors.

Source: Unpublished official census data, 1979 and 1989.

Twenty-six officially recognized indigenous peoples in Russia lack their own autonomous republics (see table 5.1). Of these, only one does not reside in Asia, the Saami of the Kola Peninsula. The Nenets live in both European Russia and Asian Russia, east of the Ural Mountains. Furthermore, there are small indigenous peoples who are not recognized as distinct ethnic groups and therefore are not accorded the same rights as "the 26." However, two or three of these peoples have been or are now in the process of being recognized.

One of the rights given to several of these peoples in the 1920s and 1930s was the right to have their own National Region (*oblast*), National Area (*okrug*), or, on a lower administrative level, their own National District (*rayon*). The *rayons* were abolished many years ago, and in 1980 the *oblasts* and *okrugs* were changed to "autonomous" regions and areas. Within the autonomous regions and areas the indigenous languages have official status. Nonrecognized indigenous peoples were never conferred such self-governing areas. The authority and power vested in these autonomies reflect their position in the overall Russian administrative hierarchy, from republic at the top, through regions, to districts. Each territorial unit is governed by a council, or *soviet*.

In the mountainous regions bordering Mongolia there are two autonomous republics, the Buryat Autonomous Republic and the Tuva Autonomous Republic (map 5.1). The majority of the 421,000 Buryats live within this republic or within the two autonomous areas east and west of it (Mark 1989). The 207,000 Tuvins have their own autonomous republic west of Lake Baikal and east of the Altai Mountains. In 1921, following the revolution, the Tuvins proclaimed their own independent republic but it was formally incorporated into the USSR in 1944 (ibid., 155). The Tuvins are the only indigenous people numbering a majority (64 percent) within their "own" autonomous republic. The Buryat make up 24 percent within their "own" republic but a bare majority in one of two autonomous areas. To compare, 33 percent of the people living in Yakutia (the Yakut Autonomous Republic) are Yakuts and only about 4 percent in the Yamal-Nenets Autonomous Area are Nenets (table 5.2).

Like the Altays and the Khakass, the Jews have their own autonomous region but very few now live there. The Khakass and the Altais are also far outnumbered by immigrant Russians and others. A large number of people belonging to small indigenous groups live within the Yakut Autonomous Republic, and because of relocation and other population movements the indigenous groups are more spread out than they were before the revolution in 1917. But by far the most important demographic change has been the immigration of such groups as ethnic Russians, Ukrainians, and Armenians. As shown in table 5.2, in all autonomous areas as well as in Yakutia these now outnumber the resi-

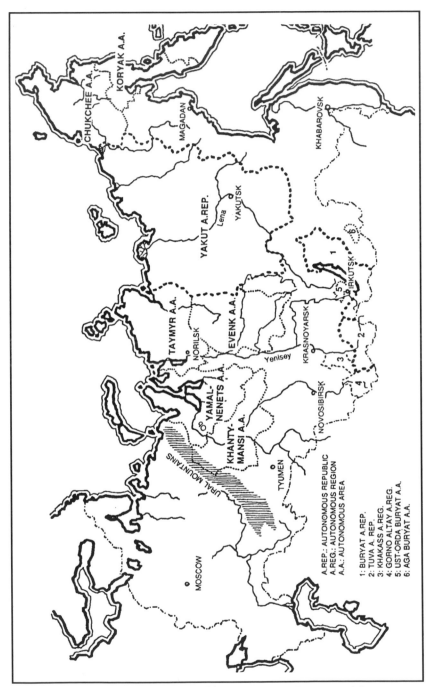

MAP 5.1. *Indigenous Autonomous Republics, Autonomous Regions, and Autonomous Areas of Asian Russia.*

dent indigenous peoples. Although still inhabiting their traditional territory, the small indigenous peoples of the Siberian forest, taiga, and tundra have lost control of their destinies. In the local *soviets* (municipal councils), and in district and regional bodies, the indigenous peoples have lost control to the immigrants.

Table 5.2. Indigenous Autonomous Republics, Autonomous Regions, and Autonomous Areas of Siberia (largest indigenous group in an area, percentage of total population)

Republic/ Region/Area	Indigenous Group	% of Total Population
Tuva Aut. Republic	Tuvins	64.3
Yakut Aut. Republic	Yakuts	33.4
Buryat Aut. Republic	Buryats	24.0
Gorno-Altay Aut. Region (Oblast)	Altays	31.0
Khakass Aut. Region (Oblast)	Khakass	11.1
Aga Buryat Aut. Area (Okrug)	Buryats	54.9
Ust-orda Buryat Aut. Area (Okrug)	Buryats	36.3
Koryak Aut. Area (Okrug)	Koryaks	16.5
Evenki Aut. Area (Okrug)	Evenki	14.0
Taimyr Aut. Area (Okrug)	Dolgans	8.9
Chukotka Aut. Area (Okrug)	Chukchee	7.3
Yamal-Nenets Aut. Area (Okrug)	Nenets	4.2
Khanty-Mansi Aut. Area (Okrug)	Khants	0.9

Source: SUPAR 1991.

These facts should be kept in mind because, even though Armenians are the indigenous people of Armenia, as are the Nenets of the Yamal Peninsula, the former make up a majority in their own republic (now an independent state) while the latter are a minority in their own country, outnumbered by Armenians, Russians, or Ukrainians. Thus, an Armenian construction worker in the Far East may be indigenous to his own home republic but he is not indigenous to the Far East.

Russia is a multiethnic society in which people of many nationalities have moved to all corners of the country. Besides the settlers, many workers have been attracted to the North and Far East by salaries that are two or three times higher than those of the rest of the country. Except for the Russians, most of these people are considered "immigrant minorities" as opposed to "indigenous minorities." As a group they are usually opposed to the granting of preferential rights to indigenous peoples.

In one sense it is easy to define the ethnic affiliation of the peoples of Russia because it is written in every person's passport. In their passports each citizen indicates, by his or her own choice or the choice of the parents, his or her nationality, be it Russian, Ukrainian, Nenets, or Nanais. It has been mentioned that changes in ethnic affiliation from generation to generation can reflect a social strategy by parents who wish their children to belong to a specific ethnic group. Kozlov (1988, 190) writes,

> It turns out that children often adopt the ethnic group of the mother, for example when it has a higher socio-cultural status, when the family lives in the mother's ethnic environment, etc. Children from marriages between Russian women and men of other USSR ethnic groups most often define themselves as Russians, especially in the towns where Russians predominate.

Vitebsky (1991) mentions that many Evens who now speak the Yakut language retain their Even identity. In general, a person of nonrecognized ethnic affiliation is simply registered under another nationality.

Due to the strong Russification policy, some parents may have preferred to have "Russian" written on the passports of their children, and some census fluctuations might be explained by such factors. Today strong opposition to the Russification trend has surfaced. From interviews conducted by the author in Kamchatka and Chukotka in the spring of 1992, it is obvious that an ethnic revitalization process is taking place. One effect seems to be increased registration of people as indigenous.[2]

As mentioned above, in the 1920s and 1930s indigenous territories were established at a lower hierarchical level than the republics. National Areas (*okrugs*) were established and the boundaries drawn with the majority of the inhabitants being indigenous peoples of related cultures (Kuoljok 1985, 80). These included the Chukchee National Area in the Siberian northeast with Chukchee, Evens, and Eskimos as the aboriginal indigenous peoples, and the Yamal-Nenets National Area east of the Ural Mountains established to accommodate the Nenets, the Khants, and the Selkups living on the tundra and taiga of this region.

When, in 1980, the national *okrugs* were changed to autonomous *okrugs,* this only reflected the fact that the indigenous peoples who had given their names to the self-governing areas had lost all political influence. Each autonomous *okrug* was guaranteed a representative in the Chamber of Nationalities of the Supreme Soviet (Bartels and Bartels 1988, 246; Mark 1989, 178). However, for many years a critical factor has been the lack of political representation by the indigenous peoples. Thus, within a system devoid of political democracy, the indigenous people were, in practice, in the most inferior position. In theory the autonomous regions and districts were established to allow all peoples to have their own local governments. To this it should be added that immigration from other parts of the Soviet Union has made most, if not all, small indigenous peoples minorities in their own autonomous regions and districts. Today the indigenous peoples of the North make up from 3 to 23 percent of the total population in the autonomous areas. This led anthropologist Michail Chlenov to say that, from a juridical point of view, the concept of "people" had no meaning in the Soviet North. The term *people* is fiction, Chlenov said, as none of them have their own political representation (Chlenov 1989).

The local *soviets* and the autonomous areas are in principle the *peoples'* representative institutions but in practice they are completely dominated by ethnic Russians and other immigrants who together make up 80 to 90 percent of the inhabitants. The situation in the Yamal-Nenets Autonomous Area illustrates this.

The Yamal-Nenets Autonomous Area: An Example

One of the world's largest reserves of oil and gas has been located under the tundra and taiga of the Yamal-Nenets Autonomous Area. Thus, the Yamal Peninsula is a main candidate for expansion of gas production. That this is reflected in the demographic situation in the Yamal-Nenets Autonomous Area can be seen in table 5.3.

Table 5.3. Inhabitants of the Yamal-Nenets Autonomous Area, 1989 (in numbers and percentages)

Inhabitants	Population in Number	Population in Percent
Total inhabitants	494,844	100
Indigenous peoples of the North	30,203	6.1
Nenets	20,917	4.2
Khants	7,247	1.5
Selkups	1,530	0.3
Russians	292,808	59.2
Ukrainians	85,022	17.2
Tatars	26,431	5.3
Byelorussians	12,609	2.5

Source: Census 1989.

The majority of Russians and "others" live in the larger towns of Salekhard, Labytnangi, and Yamburg. Many are transient laborers who work on the Yamal railway, in the gas fields of the Urengoy area, and in gas exploration sites in Yamal. In the regional center of Salekhard, of a total of thirty thousand inhabitants only fifteen hundred are indigenous, a number that includes many children in boarding schools. On the other hand, indigenous peoples make up the majority in villages and reindeer *sovkhozes* (state farms). Hardly any indigenous persons are employed at the gas exploration sites or among the railway construction teams. There seems to be a significant unemployment rate among indigenous peoples. This is partly explained by the state of affairs related to reindeer herding, hunting, and fishing.

Reindeer herding on Yamal and the areas bordering the peninsula to the south and southeast is dominated by state farms. Reindeer herding on Yamal is still mainly a nomadic activity, the herders moving with the animals every day, summer and winter. On the tundra, people live in small groups and in early winter the herds move south and cross the Ob to pastures south and east of the river.

Today this nomadic way of life is considered very unattractive by young people who prefer life in villages and towns with access to modern comforts. Many young women, in particular, dislike the nomadic way of life. Many reindeer herding families also dislike being separated from their children who are taken away to boarding schools in the towns. One major problem is that very few of these young indigenous persons have the qualifications and the education needed to obtain jobs in the towns or with the construction companies.

In regions occupied by the Nenets (there are Nenets autonomous areas west and east of the Yamal-Nenets Autonomous Area) a more settled way of reindeer herding has developed. Here people move mainly between two places and only the herders move constantly with the animals, working on a rotation basis. In the future this development is expected to take place on Yamal.

Outside the *sovkhozes*, some reindeer are owned privately (according to the journal *Krasny Sever*, Yamal has 180,000 reindeer of which 80,000 are owned privately). "Workers" (the reindeer herders work on a salaried basis) in the *sovkhozes* as well as other people have small herds. Private herds of 10 to 20 animals also exist. Those Nenets not working in *sovkhozes* subsist by hunting during the winter and fishing during the summer.

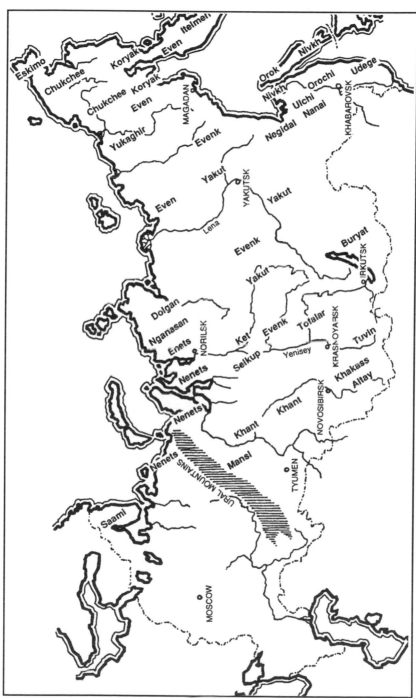

MAP 5.2. Indigenous Peoples of Asian Russia.

In most parts of Russia all reindeer belong to state farms. The small private herds of Yamal are an exception. The privatization process that now affects all state farms thus is expected to be smoother in Yamal than in other reindeer-herding regions. Investigations by the author in Kamchatka and Chukotka show that this process is very complicated. Families are unable to resume their former nomadic lifestyle and the state farms are not easily dissolved.

PHOTO COURTESY OF JENS DAHL

PLATE 5.1. *The Nenets editor Kh. Yaungard addresses the first meeting of the "Association of Small Peoples in the Soviet North," Moscow, 1990.*

Indigenous people in the North and the Far East complain generally of increasingly critical conditions among those living as fishermen, hunters, trappers, and reindeer herders. Today, industrial enclaves, hydroelectric projects, timber operations, mining ventures, and oil and gas wells can be encountered in all corners of the country. Unfortunately, the industrial process has taken no, or very little, consideration of the vulnerable northern ecology. Vast areas have been turned into wasteland. Yamal pastures have been devastated owing to the many exploration activities and the building of a railway north from Labytnangi. Pollution has become a serious problem due to oil spills in the southern parts of the Ob watershed and its tributaries, and because of the pollution of the tundra, lakes, and rivers on Yamal (Aipin 1989; Dahl 1990a; Nordic Yamal Expedition 1989; Pika and Prokhorov 1989; Prokhorov 1989).

The situation of Yamal and the Nenets people is only one example. All the indigenous economies and cultures of Siberia are endangered. After World War II, Moscow followed a policy of resettlement of indigenous people in towns, and indigenous children still spend years in boarding schools forbidden to speak their own language. This Russification policy has had a severe impact on indigenous languages. Some of the twenty-six groups are still without their own written language. Among some of the smaller groups, the native language is on the verge of extinction and children no longer have a command of the vernacular.

With these facts in mind, it is only natural that the question of political representation was raised by indigenous peoples as soon as *glasnost* and *perestroika* reached the taiga and the tundra. In the fluid political situation that has prevailed since 1988, indigenous peoples have put forward demands for self-determination and self-government aiming at a renegotiation of their position within the Russian Republic. Piers Vitebsky (1991) recently has shown that a main demand of an Even community in northeastern Siberia was for the founding of an autonomous district for them. In 1989 this was granted by the authorities in Yakutsk, capital of the Yakut Autonomous Republic. From Yakutsk also came the demand for an upgrade of its autonomous status to that of a union republic, something that would imply secession from the Russian Republic.

On 17 October 1990, the newspaper *Izvestiya* reported that a session of the peoples' deputies of the Yamal-Nenets Autonomous Area had decided to reorganize the area into the Yamal-Nenets Republic. The same newspaper reported six days later that the authorities in Tyumen Region, within which the Yamal-Nenets Autonomous Area is situated, refused to recognize this reorganization.

Also in October 1990, the Koryak Autonomous Area declared itself an Autonomous Republic within Russia. On 19 February 1991, *Izvestiya* announced the foundation of the Chukotka Soviet Autonomous Republic, which would withdraw from the Magadan Region. Similar demands were heard from other autonomous areas. Today most of these demands have been modified. The autonomous areas and republics are now pursuing a higher degree of autonomy but remaining part of Russia.

Anthropologist Igor Krupnik writes that issues of local self-government and autonomy have come to dominate the economic and political climate in Siberia.

> Declarations of sovereignty issued in summer-fall of 1990 by several Siberian autonomies, including the Chukchi autonomous area, now labelled the Chukchi Republic, were followed by claims for a new economic order and new rights to use local mineral and natural resources on behalf of regional populations. For the first time since the 1920's local leaders and legislators are debating the very status of native minorities to ensure their social and cultural protection, and their guaranteed access to certain resources. (Krupnik, in press)

The process goes on and on. Region upon region are declaring themselves as sovereign, as autonomous areas, as autonomous republics, or as union republics. While some of these initiatives apparently have been recognized, others seem to be ineffectual unilateral initiatives ending in a new phase of frustration. Most of these endeavors leave unchanged the fact that indigenous peoples remain minorities and thus without decisive political power within their "own" autonomies. The initiators of these processes are often the nonindigenous immigrants to whom greater autonomy means decentralization without implying the transfer of authority and jurisdiction to indigenous peoples whose names legitimize the autonomies. The overall situation seems to vary from one region to another. Some indigenous peoples are in favor of the process and seem to gain advantage from this; others are against it.

The Turning Point

In 1988 and 1989, an important change in the public's perception of the situation of the Soviet Union's small indigenous peoples occurred. The new openness of the media, and even within the ranks of the Communist Party, revealed an enormous discrepancy between what had been said officially for decades and the documentation then being presented by scientists, authors, and indigenous representatives. The new message was about the destruction of indigenous cultures. People driven away from their land by oil companies were living in utmost poverty. None suffered so much from alcoholism as did the indigenous peoples.

Although the peoples of Siberia live under the harshest climatic conditions in the country, they often have housing of the lowest quality. Health conditions generally are extremely poor with a high incidence of diseases such as tuberculosis. The central organs of the press and the many local and regional newspapers began to write openly about the conditions of the small indigenous peoples. Letters appeared which harshly criticized both the dismal living conditions and the overall Soviet policy in the North.

For the general public, the most significant change came when the ecological state of many areas of the North became known. As Igor Krupnik writes,

> It became clear that unbridled industrial expansion had already ruined the ecological balance in many regions of the Soviet Arctic, and that its continuation would lead to an ecological catastrophe, above all for the native population. Two gigantic industrial projects in particular became symbols of this: the exploitation of the gas deposits in the central part of the Yamal Peninsula and the construction of the Turukhansk hydroelectric dam in the territory of the Evenky people. Both of these were stopped on official instructions as threatening the culture of the indigenous population and their use of the environment. (Krupnik, n.d. [1989])

Krupnik stressed that the significance of industrial expansion and of newly acquired ecological knowledge is that "the fight for clean land and water and for the preservation of hunting grounds and pasture, becomes indistinguishable from cultural, ethnic and even socio-political demands" (ibid.).

Protests against development in the arctic and subarctic regions were first voiced by indigenous people in oil-rich Western Siberia. A political breakthrough came when Vladimir Sangi, a Nivkh writer from Sakhalin, at a meeting of the Writers Association of Russia, suggested the establishment of an association of indigenous peoples of the Soviet North. In late 1989, the idea was supported by the Central Committee of the Communist Party and in March of 1990 the idea became reality. Meanwhile, ethnic associations sprang up in all corners of the Russian Federal Republic.

The First Indigenous Peoples' Meeting

On 30–31 March 1990, more than 350 delegates and observers representing thirty-five nationalities from all over the Russian Republic assembled in the Kremlin in Moscow. Indigenous peoples from "the 26" were represented according to their numbers. In a few months indigenous associations had been established in all regions of the Soviet North and Far East. In the short span of time which followed the meeting of the Central Committee of the Communist Party these associations were organized by political leaders, writers, and intellectuals. So was the meeting in the Kremlin, which was convened by a self-appointed organizing committee. Those indigenous groups "which were removed from the history books during the Stalin era," as one delegate expressed it, were allowed to send observers. They were allowed to speak but not to vote. As a matter of fact, even "indigenous Russians," descendants of Russians who had settled in Siberia and the Far East as hunters and fishermen centuries ago, were represented at the meeting. From abroad the organizers had invited the Inuit Circumpolar Conference, the Saami of the Nordic countries, and a representative of the International Work Group for Indigenous Affairs (Dahl 1990b).

There were very few fishermen, hunters, and reindeer herders among the delegates. A large number were intellectuals and people from the fields of culture and the arts. Although there were many women, men were clearly in the majority. Half of the delegates were members of the Communist Party. The government of the Russian Republic had several observers at the meeting but most significant was the fact that President Mikhail Gorbachev and Prime Minister Nicolai Ryshkov took part in the opening session.

The goal of this first congress of indigenous peoples in the history of the Soviet Union was to establish an Association of Indigenous Peoples of the Soviet North. Chuner Taksami, from the group of organizers, opened the congress. He made a lengthy review of the economic, social, and cultural situation of the indigenous societies (Taksami 1990). In general terms, he outlined the goals and ambitions of a new indigenous association. Although the tone was extremely diplomatic, it was clear that demands for radical change were on the agenda.

After Taksami concluded his summary of the state of affairs, the floor was given to a delegate from each of the twenty-six indigenous groups. Immediately the reality of the North was brought right into the Kremlin. The message, which was reiterated again and again, could not be misunderstood by observers, delegates, or the two leading politicians of the Soviet Union. Speaker after speaker argued that constitutional changes were necessary to ensure the cultural survival of indigenous societies of the Soviet North. The indigenous peoples have to be given positions at all levels of political decision making. The destructive nature of the extractive resource exploitation that has reigned in the North for decades must be changed. A Chukchee reindeer herder talked lengthily in his mother tongue. Although very few of the delegates understood the text, his gestures and his appeals to the listening Gorbachev were unequivocal: no more empty promises while the reindeer die because of diminishing pastures and pollution.

The gloomy picture presented by him and the other twenty-six representatives was repeated in the testimony that followed. Had I not had the opportunity, with my own eyes, to see a corner of this situation I perhaps would have found it exaggerated. But, since March 1990, numerous observers have confirmed the tragic ecological situation of the Russian North. Understandably, "the people of the tundra had been waiting for this day," as a Nenets delegate stated.

"The rivers break up earlier this year than usual," said a Mansi writer. I suppose that he talked in symbolic terms, or did he? In Yakutia the forest is rapidly being cut down and fears were expressed about timber projects organized as joint ventures between the USSR and private companies from Southeast Asia. Gigantic hydroelectric projects like the Turukhan Project will dam rivers, reportedly with enormous ecological consequences. The Nenets people of the Arctic Sea complain of an increased incidence of sickness due to radiation from nuclear testing at Novaya Zemlya carried out in the 1950s and 1960s.

For one and a half days we listened to this testimony. There was much repetition, which only underscored the critical state of affairs for all indigenous peoples of the Soviet North and Far East. From Kola to the Bering Strait, the number of reindeer are on the decrease; so are fish in the large rivers and river systems of Siberia. The state construction companies and the oil, gas, and mining companies show no respect for the vulnerable arctic and subarctic ecology. Even though it takes decades for plants on the permanently frozen subsoil to recover from being trod down, the summers are used for what seems to be completely uncontrolled traffic across the tundra. In Western Siberia, exploitation of one of the world's largest oil and gas reserves has led to cultural ethnocide conducted against the indigenous Khants. They have lost control of their land, and now suffer from unemployment, poverty, and alienation. They want to regain their lost home and native land.

It struck me that, while many of the statements were given in a very resigned manner, now and then the anger of years of suppression came to the surface. Very few believed that the Kremlin, or the international community for that matter, will change policy just because a few indige-

PLATE 5.2. *Forest Nenets, former Soviet Union.*

nous people are "in the red book of endangered species," as one delegate characterized the situation.

After having listened to 96 statements, the speakers' list was closed. We missed listening to 180 registered speakers because there simply was no more time left. It would have been 180 more accounts of alcoholism among the Yukagirs and tuberculosis among the Chuckchee, etc. What impression does it make on the world that tuberculosis in 1990 was one of the most common sicknesses among indigenous people of the Russian North or that the average life expectancy had decreased from sixty-one to forty-seven years within a single decade? Housing standards in the Russian North are inferior to those of the rest of the country—but this holds only for indigenous people not for the Russians and immigrants of other nationalities. The economy has deteriorated to the point at which, as one delegate said, "the consumption of fish to vodka is one fish to two bottles of vodka."

As a matter of fact, the idea of this first congress of indigenous peoples was not to enumerate the existing miserable conditions but to discuss a common political strategy and establish a new country-wide association. The goal is a future in which Evens, Evenks, Nanais, Khants, and all other indigenous peoples are masters of their own land and their own future. A united approach was clearly seen as a precondition to the cultural survival of future generations. Delegate after delegate demanded control of land, and for land management to be returned to the indigenous people. Several speakers demanded that the North be declared a nuclear-free zone while others expressed the wish to have all missiles removed from the area. Nevertheless, one nuclear test has been carried out on Novaya Zemlya since then.

A main claim was ownership of the land in one form or another. The land must be given back to its original owners. So, when the chairman of the State Planning Committee of the Russian Republic said that the peoples of the North should be masters of the land and that they have a right to own their land, this was met with applause.

Some delegates proposed the establishment of reserved ecological areas with priority given to indigenous resource exploitation. Others strongly opposed this type of solution. Since 1990, several initiatives seem to have been taken to adopt this type of ecological-reserve strategy. Thus, on 4 February 1991, *Izvestiya* reported that the Tyumen Region had created a special zone in the Yamal-Nenets Autonomous Area and the Khanty-Mansi Autonomous Area in order to create a place where the native peoples could pursue their traditional life undisturbed. This will keep out the drilling crews, the timber brigades, and the geologists.

Several people stressed the need to redefine the autonomous areas so that indigenous people will regain their majority status. To be in control of their own territory should imply that part of the economic profit created within the territory must be given to the local people. In practical terms this means abolishing fixed prices for furs, fish, and meat. In terms of principles it presupposes the eradication of state monopoly. It also implies that a royalty on timber, oil, gas, and mineral production would be given to the owners of the land, the indigenous people. Changes are underway in this matter and some compensation has been promised to people whose lands have been destroyed by industrial activities. From an indigenous point of view, a major problem concerns to whom the compensation shall be paid. The local councils, or *soviets*, are controlled by nonindigenous persons, and indigenous people have very little influence on the state farms to which many belong. But it seemed as if a delegate from Yakutia had general support when he said, "we wish no material compensation but new legislation which will make us masters of our land."

The political claims put forward at the congress were quite far reaching. As already mentioned, many speakers requested that indigenous peoples be represented at all levels of political decision making, from local *soviets* to national councils. Some delegates spoke in favor of establishing local and regional councils with wide authority under the control of indigenous people. One delegate depicted Russia as a federation of all the peoples of the republic, all with equal rights. He wanted autonomous areas to be represented directly in state parliaments and not through regions as they are today. In their presentations some speakers referred to Greenlandic Home Rule, the Alaska Native Claims Settlement Act, and the Canadian Nunavut as possible models.

When the congress was inaugurated the first day, many decisions were taken (e.g., the appointment of the Presidium) and confirmed unanimously without discussion by a show of hands. After a while this "traditional" Soviet way of decision making was no longer seen to be acceptable and proposals came with alternatives. Voting became more and more exciting, and sometimes confused, such as when one minority delegate refused to accept being voted down.

Shall the new organization develop into a political party or a socio-cultural movement? This is a very important point and emotions ran high on the floor. Should the new organization develop into an association of regional ethnic associations, or should it be a movement elected by direct vote from all over the republic? There was voting on these points but the minority refused to bend to decisions that they thought may have been taken in advance. As an observer, my impression was that people had submitted themselves to the authorities for so many years that they now refused to accept a new authority whose legitimacy was based only on a simple majority vote. Several speakers voiced their distrust of this procedure. The result was that the proposals of the drafting committee were adopted as the preliminary program and preliminary statutes of the new association. An alternative program adopted by five indigenous groups in a Krasnoyarsk meeting in February was also to be incorporated. Further revisions would have to be made on the basis of the many proposed amendments. The final program and statutes would have to be adopted at a new meeting or congress.

The first president of the Association of Small Peoples of the North was elected in a closed meeting without observers. He is the Nivkh writer, Vladimir Sangi, who originated the idea of the organization. The formation of this association signifies that indigenous peoples of Russia, for the first time in history, have the opportunity to speak on their own behalf in a national setting. To gain support they are also looking for help from outside the country. In this they stressed their desire to cooperate with other indigenous organizations, among them those of the Inuit, the Saami, and other northern groups.

Several speakers at the congress called for Soviet ratification of international treaties and conventions, primarily the newly revised and adopted ILO Convention 169, the "Convention Concerning Indigenous and Tribal Peoples in Independent Countries." The view was that, if this treaty is ratified by the state, indigenous peoples then will have a very effective means of fighting for their highest aspiration: to regain their homelands. It is worth noting that, after the disintegration of the Soviet Union following the coup in August 1991 and the declared independence of Russia, the indigenous peoples have kept this as one of their main goals.

Problems and Perspectives

Not only the future political structure of the indigenous autonomies remains precarious and unknown. Just as uncertain is the future political leadership of each indigenous group and the likelihod of their statewide cooperation. As a matter of fact, there seems to be fairly little active indigenous leadership at the community and local levels.

> The highly centralized Soviet system worked for decades to create a new Native elite selected for conformity, obedience, and lack of individual initiative. These people may be very active in personal or official contacts, but they are far less efficient in promoting genuine revival for their respective nations using their new experience acquired in recent years. (Krupnik, in press)

Krupnik also points out the lack of communication between the leadership and people in the communities.

> Slightly influenced by some new political experience of self-determination, the new structure still copied the main Soviet pattern to create umbrella organisations without any real activity on the community level. By this pattern one can easily recruit a new Native elite, but the path to real changes is still hampered by lack of enthusiasm in the Native villages. (Ibid.)

He also makes the interesting observation that the majority of local native activists are well-educated women of the middle generation, mainly teachers and cultural workers. Among other facts, they are Russian-speaking. He writes,

> The "grass-roots" people, like hunters or skilled workers are still too socially passive to form an alternative channel to new leadership. This pattern was evident in the founding meeting of the "Regional Society of

the Eskimos of Chukotka" held in August 1990 in Providenya, which was the first attempt to create a semipolitical umbrella body for all the Siberian Eskimos. All members of the Organising Committee, as well as the main speakers and lobbyists for the most important resolutions were recruited from the same brand of well-educated Native women in their 40's and 50's, while rare male attendants at the meeting had mostly a symbolic role. (Ibid.)

The regional indigenous associations are nonexclusive. Members are drawn from all indigenous groups within a region and even nonindigenous persons can be members. In the interior of Kamchatka, inhabited by reindeer-herding Evens and Koryaks, I learned that the chairman of the area association is Ukrainian and the secretary is Russian. Both are prominent members of the political community. The "Regional Society of the Eskimos of Chukotka" and a similar Even organization in Chukotka are among the few exclusive ethnic organizations.

A final factor mentioned by Krupnik is that information flows from Moscow and Petersburg and not across the tundra and the taiga. There are very few chains of communication across the arctic and subarctic regions to facilitate direct linkages between one indigenous group and another. Even in relation to political development among indigenous peoples the role of the intelligentsia has been noticeable.

At a meeting in Yakutsk held on 16 October 1990, The Association of Small Peoples of the Soviet North agreed upon a political platform called the Convention of the 26 (Association of Small Peoples of the Soviet North 1991). On the local level the future political structure of the North should include the reestablishment of clan councils. The areas in which indigenous peoples live should have legal status as states or republics. Furthermore, the convention calls for the introduction of national electoral constituencies along ethnic lines at all levels. It reveals something about the problems of communication that one year after its adoption the Convention of the 26 had been published in English but not in Russian.

The Convention of the 26 was directed at the Russian Republic. But before the coup in August 1991 the convention was supported by a congress of deputies, the so-called Northern Parliament. This assembly first met in Moscow on 6–7 May. Those taking part were delegates elected to governing bodies at all levels, from local *soviets* far out in the tundra and taiga to the supreme *soviets* of the USSR and the Russian Republic. In all, there were 119 delegates from among the arctic and subarctic peoples.

Although this new initiative was frustrated by the August coup, its ideas seem to have had a significant influence on indigenous politics. Thus, in Chukotka in northeastern Siberia, in the Chukchee Autonomous Area, elected delegates now meet regularly in order to influence decisions to be taken in the *okrug soviet*.

In Moscow it was the deputy from Chukotka, V. M. Etylen, who opened the meeting with suggestions for future political strategies to be followed by the indigenous peoples. He proposed either the election of special quotas of deputies from the small peoples to *soviets* at all levels or a two-chamber system on all levels, wherein one chamber would consist of representatives from the small peoples. There was no general agreement on these alternatives but a majority of delegates supported the idea of a Northern Parliament.

In the last couple of years Russian newspapers have referred to a number of regions that declared themselves to be "autonomous," "independent," "autonomous republics," and so on. The Buryat Autonomous Republic declared itself independent, the Chuckchee Autonomous Area declared itself an autonomous republic, as did the Koryak Autonomous Area, to mention a few examples.

On 31 March 1992, all regions of Russia adopted a federal agreement, which, among other things, stipulates how the rights to resources will be shared between the regions and the center. Furthermore, with the exception of a few autonomous areas, all other regions have accepted the political and administrative structure of Russia, and have agreed to remain part of it. Among those who signed the agreement were, for example, the Chuckchee Autonomous Area (Okrug) and the Koryak Autonomous Area (Okrug).

The Koryak Autonomous Okrug is part of the Kamchatka region and the Chukchee Autonomous Okrug is part of Magadan region. The Okrug councils in both areas have dropped their ambitions to develop into republics on a par with Russia and do not wish to become autonomous republics. Both areas are now trying to secede from the larger regions and are attempting to attain a status similar to that of the Kamchatka and Magadan regions, that is, to acquire the right to deal directly with Moscow. Both have unilaterally declared themselves independent of their regional centers (Magadan and Petropavlovsk, respectively), and this step has de facto been accepted. Public finances, taxes, and supply structures are already being changed, although the new status has not yet been approved de jure.

This decentralization process is an all-Russian phenomenon. However, the question of autonomy is only indirectly linked to the question of the political status of indigenous peoples. As the question of autonomy has been handled by the indigenous peoples of Chukotka and the Koryak Area, it has not directly interfered with the effort to grant political priority rights to indigenous peoples simply because the autonomy question has been treated so as not to imply changes in the existing administrative-political structure of which the autonomous areas and regions are integrated parts.

Being in a legal interregnum, indigenous peoples (and others) have encountered problems in determining just what their rights are. The reindeer herders claim rights to the pastures; but should these rights be vested in the former brigades or in families? The herders also claim the right to fish and hunt; but how can these claims be met in regions in which these rights have already been granted to state farms?

Commercial fishing rights are usually given to large state companies and not to locals. It is ironic that no Aleuts on Bering Island are allowed to fish on a commercial basis, despite the fact that the sea in this part of Russia is the most valuable of all the country's fishing waters. Today not one of the roughly four hundred Aleuts who live on Bering Island fishes for a living. Commercial fishing in the major rivers of the Kamchatka Peninsula is also the preserve of state farms.

Another example of this legal interregnum comes from the mountainous areas north of Vladivostok. Here a small group of Udege people in the Bikin River Valley is being threatened by a major forestry project (see International Work Group for Indigenous Affairs 1992; and Shnirelman 1993). The Udege people stood to have their legal territorial rights to the Upper Bikin Valley annihilated and to lose a substantial portion of their traditional land as the result of a unilateral move by the administrative head of the Promorije Regional administration violating decisions taken by the political authorities. This case was brought to court by the head of the administration. Since the court did not recognize the rights of the indigenous peoples, they took the case to the Russian Supreme Court. The Supreme Court decided in favor of the indigenous peoples and the forestry project has been stopped.

This case provides important evidence of the political and legal uncertainty that reigns during this interim period in which the old Russian system is being abolished while new rules and regulations have not been firmly established. The Supreme Court decision is unique, to my knowledge, and represents the first instance in which indigenous peoples have succeeded in confirming their legal rights at this level. It remains to be seen whether the Supreme Court decision will establish a precedent with lasting practical implications.

CHAPTER 6

"Lost Innocents and the Loss of Innocence": Interpreting Adivasi Movements in South Asia

CRISPIN BATES

In discussing indigenous peoples' movements in South Asia we are concerned with a range of movements that may be subsumed under the title of *adivasi* movements—*adivasi* being a term preferred by the participants in many of the movements themselves.[1] *Adivasi* has been adopted in recent years in India for political reasons similar to those found in Africa, where the term *tribal* is no longer used because of its association with white racial supremacism and the divide-and-rule policies of colonial and postcolonial governments. Nonetheless, this has not prevented the nineteenth-century term *tribal* from continuing in use, especially among anthropologists and ethnographers within India, many of whom employ the term both as an analytical category and simply as a label that can be attached to a variety of social and religious movements. In this there would not be any harm but for the fact that many of the prejudices and misconceptions associated with the origins of the term have persisted as well. It is arguable that *adivasi* leaders and ideologues are not innocent of this, and that the very form of their identification and the trajectory of their political struggle serve to reinforce rather than contradict the prejudices directed against them. The "indigenous peoples" or *adivasi* movements in South Asia may even depend on such prejudices for their survival. Indeed, it is arguable that without such prejudices,

103

recently as well as in the past, the *adivasis* as a community would not exist. The *adivasis* may thus be regarded as not so much the "original" inhabitants of South Asia but the very recent creation of colonial anthropology. Paradoxically, they might be seen as an invention rather than a victim of modernity.[2]

In India as a whole there are supposedly some four hundred different "tribes," which, depending on how you define them, account for more than 50 million of the population, concentrated in the central and northeastern parts of the country—a population now more commonly known not as tribals but as the *adivasis*. The Indian term *adivasi* derives from the Hindi word *adi*, meaning 'beginning' or 'of earliest times', and the word *vasi*, meaning 'resident of'—the Hindi equivalent of the Latin term *aborigine*, meaning 'from the beginning', an equivalence that exists not through coincidence but by design. The epithet in fact was invented by political activists in the area of Chotanagpur in the 1930s, an invention motivated not so much by the idea of abolishing the concept of the "tribal" altogether (as was later attempted by nationalists in Africa) but rather with the aim of forging a new sense of identity among differing "tribal" peoples—a tactic which has enjoyed considerable success, with the term subsequently becoming widely popularized.

It can be seen, however, that there is nothing at all "indigenous" about the term nor about the people which it purports to describe. Indeed, it could be argued that the concept of the *"adivasi"* is a product of orientalism. Orientalism is not just a problem in the western understanding of nonwestern societies but a phenomenon that has deeply affected Indians themselves as they have incorporated into their own understanding of Indian society the statistical, canonical, materialistic, and self-justificatory interpretations purveyed by colonial administrations. As a result, in many aspects, India over the generations has been remade in the image invented for it by European colonialists.[3] In this the *adivasi* shares with other political movements of the nineteenth and twentieth centuries a vital debt to colonial prejudice. However, the consequence has been legitimizing myths that establish claims to political power not in terms of kings, shrines, and the rituals of incorporation, as found in premodern *adivasi* societies, but in terms of very modern notions of property and contract instilled by means of the titles, deeds, and descriptions of Indian society established by the British cartographic and socioeconomic surveys of the mid-nineteenth century.[4] Through their repetitive use as instruments of control by colonial administrators, these ideas came to have a powerful meaning to the subject populations that they affected. It is from these ideas, and the tempering of "rights of conquest" by "rights of occupation" in the British legal framework established in India, that we find the origin of the concept of the "original inhabitant" and of the priority of their claims to landed property—a crucial constitutive development in the birth of the *adivasi* (See Derrett 1968; and Washbrook 1981).

Another important influence on the concept of the *"adivasi"* is the idea of "equality," derived from a quite different direction. It is of premodern European origin, being rooted in Christian belief as well as in the ideals of the eighteenth-century enlightenment, and was brought to India not by colonial administrators directly but more often by Protestant evangelical missionaries. Merged with concepts of possession and ownership, there evolved under this influence a new, contractual notion of the relationship between the rulers and the ruled, and new claims to political representation among the population—claims that were rooted not in status and inherited influence but in terms of universal and natural rights. Such claims issued forth in a number of forms in the late nineteenth and early twentieth centuries. One expression lay in the eruption of a variety of Muslim, Sikh, and Hindu reform movements, anxious to revise and update their respective religions in light of, and in order to meet, the challenge from the West. Among them were a number of low-caste, anti-Brahmin movements, which aimed to restructure Hinduism by abolishing the hierarchies of caste.[5] Later these movements often found a political voice during the nationalist upsurge of the interwar years.[6] More recently still, the same demand for political representation has been expressed by groups that were on the margins of social and political agitation during the colonial period. Asserting rights to property and a share in political power, such political movements are to be seen among so-called indigenous peoples throughout Africa, Asia, and Latin America today. That of the *"adivasis"* of South Asia is one of the oldest of them all.

The Concept of the Adivasi

According to the political activists who coined the word in the 1930s, the *"adivasis"* are the original inhabitants of South Asia. As such, it is claimed that they are are entitled to special privileges. The bulk of the population today, described as Indo-Aryan, are therefore considered as alien interlopers by *adivasi* activists. The term Indo-Aryan itself derives from the popular (though now contentious) belief that Indian civilization as we know it began only after the invasion of Aryan peoples from the north some time around the second millennium B.C.[7] It was the Aryans, supposedly, who originated the Hindu religion, and accordingly in Brahminic ideology the *adivasis,* although having a special status, are often associated with the Untouchables, or Harijans, among the lowliest section of society.[8] In the modern mind the two are also constructed in a similar fashion in that both are regarded as "backward communities" educationally, economically, and socially. Because of this they have been made the beneficiaries of special legislation aimed at raising their status within the society of independent India.

So committed were the founders of modern India to the "uplift-ment" of the *adivasis* that they are specifically mentioned in the Constitution, which singles out the so-called scheduled castes and tribes as in need of special consideration because of their traditionally low status within Indian society. Accordingly, the government since 1951 has instituted a whole series of schemes including, most controversially, the reservation of posts in the government and universities for members of these communities. In many cases it is arguable that these attempts at positive discrimination (as with most "instrumental" efforts at social engineering) have not solved but merely aggravated the problem of caste prejudice within Indian society. The policy recently provoked a ferocious backlash among higher-caste groups and the revival of militant Hindu chauvinist political parties such as the Shiv Sena, Vishwa Hindu Parishad, and the Bharatiya Janata Party.

These failures of reservation ought to have come as no surprise, given the very flimsy rationale upon which the policy was based. In particular, the grouping of *adivasis* and Harijans together as "backward communities" for the purposes of legislation was not only anachronistic but also historically inaccurate. For example, it can easily be shown that many groups within Indian society are highly economically disadvan-taged, although neither *adivasi* or Harijan. Equally, it is the case that many *adivasis* and Harijans have either acquired, or have always had, high status and economic security (it being largely these elite segments among the scheduled groups that have monopolized many of the benefits conferred by discriminatory legislation). In fact, many of the so-called *adivasis* were once regarded as Hindus, and only became known as *adivasis* because of a decline in their economic position in society, or because, more recently, it has actually been to their advantage to call themselves *"adivasis."* A consequence has been that since the introduction of the policy of reservation the number of *adivasis* in India as a proportion of the total population has increased from 5.3 percent in 1951 to 7.3 percent in 1971, a reversal of the steady trend of declining numbers in the preindependence period. This phenomenon suggests very clearly that the category of the *"adivasi,"* or tribal, like so many social categories within Indian society, is highly variable, defined by associations of status and by economic factors that can change considerably over time.

The term *tribal* has been coined at times to describe anyone who practices slash-and-burn cultivation or hunting and gathering, regardless of their culture or for how long they have been doing this. A very good example are the Badaga, inhabitants of the Nilgiri Hills described by the anthropologist Paul Hockings, who were regarded for a long time as "tribals" for their practice of slash and burn, although they were settled peasant cultivators of the Mysore Plain until they were driven into the hills by warfare some time in the sixteenth century (Ross King 1870; Hockings 1980). At the same time, while economics can play a part in defining a community, many settled farmers still call themselves *adivasis,* while there are many hunter-gatherers and slash-and-burn agriculturalists in India today who call themselves Hindus. From this we may conclude that *"adivasi"* communities cannot easily be distinguished from Hindu peasant communities by their way of life. But neither is it easy to describe the *"adivasis"* in terms of their religion since Hinduism itself is so highly eclectic. *"Adivasis"* are often described simply as animists but this does little justice to their religious beliefs, which can be highly complex. Many supposedly Hindu gods, such as Kali (in Bengal) or the supposed incarnation of Vishnu at Jagannath in Puri, were also originally tribal gods, and they are still regarded as such by many today. Discussions with a Brahmin pundit in Benares might give one the impression that Hinduism is a religion with coherent customs and rituals established over many centuries about which the devout are dutiful and precise in their observance (an impression received by many early British scholars of Hinduism). But the reality as one sees it on the margins of Indian society is one of eclecticism, change, and frequent borrowings, which makes it difficult to be certain where one religion ends and another begins.[9]

In this respect Indian religions are like Indian languages, with the boundaries of one frequently merging into another. The main source of consistency in both respects—indeed, often the only source—is politics. More specifically, political power is manifest in the ability of the state, or one ruler or another, to insist on a particular language or a particular religion as the normative language or religion within the boundaries of a certain territory. This can be seen very clearly if one examines the history of particular *"adivasi"* kingdoms such as the central Indian kingdom of Bastar, or even simply by looking at modern South Asia, which has been fiercely divided over what should be the language of government and how the boundaries of states and nations should be drawn.[10]

In the state of Bastar the *lingua franca* among all the *"adivasi"* groups was Halbi, not because this was the most widely spoken, nor even because it was a local *adivasi* dialect, but because it was the language used by the bodyguard hired by the *raja,* or king, of Bastar, who were a group of low-caste Hindus, the Halbas. Likewise, the state religion involved the worship of the *devi* goddess Danteshwari at her shrine in Dantewada, to which human sacrifices allegedly were made. The *raja* could not remain king unless he protected and supported this shrine, while the *adivasis* respected him because he was supposedly an earthly incarnation of the goddess (whose image was in the shrine), a neat conundrum that legitimized all religious and political practices within the state.

Bastar might be regarded as exceptional in its political and religious rituals given that the ruling dynasty was originally Hindu. Nonetheless, the Hinduism of the ruling family was criss-crossed with tribal ritual, in order to render it acceptable to the population, while Hindu ideas were similarly added to local religious customs. The result was that, while the *raja* viewed the *devi* at Dantewada as an incarnation of the Hindu god Vishnu and his subjects as members of the army of the mythical monkey-god Hanuman, the *adivasis* regarded their *raja* as an incarnation of the earth goddess Tallur Mattee, who could be propitiated only by offerings of animal and human blood. This is not as bizarre as it seems, for accommodations and a multiplicity of symbols and meanings in religious ritual are common in South Asia. At the same time, it may be added that the political arrangement in Bastar, although a product of conquest, was by no means uncommon.[11] In this particular kingdom, by necessity, religion was defined by politics, and politics by religion, in such a way that neither could be described as innate or essential. The same can also be said for the category of "the *adivasi.*"

The Adivasis *as a "Backward Community"*

Before continuing with the elusive problem of defining the *adivasi,* it is necessary to go back to the idea of the *"adivasis"* and Harijans as being "backward communities," for this is an important part of modern thinking on the subject. The term *backward community* originated with British legislation, which set up the earliest forms of quasi-representative government in India in the 1920s. Beginning with the Government of India Act of 1918, these early concessions by the British to nationalist opinion in India allowed elected representatives to sit in provincial legislative assemblies which had the power to make laws in certain areas. These assemblies were also crowded with officials and other European nominees, supposedly on the justification that communities from certain "scheduled areas" were either too backward or too oppressed to be able to properly exercise a vote. Their representatives therefore had to be appointed by the administration (a policy frequently resorted to in central India). It was for the same reason that separate seats were established for different religious communities. By asserting that they could never cooperate, the British made the conditions for their cooperation impossible. This was part of what Indian nationalists called the British policy of divide and rule, and it was by using the same arguments and appointing a large number of officials to represent the interests of minorities that the British were able to justify retaining a right of veto over nearly all the affairs of government.

Despite its roots in the political opportunism of a colonial regime, the view that *"adivasis"* were somehow "backward" and unable to represent themselves has stuck to this day, probably because the idea has been opportune and persuasive to more than a few. Indeed, it is arguable that colonial perceptions and policies were not entirely invented *de novo* but were an extension in some cases of Brahminical prejudices.[12] More importantly, since poverty was taken as a mark of "backwardness," colonial anthropologists could readily find evidence of both, since by the time they were writing *"adivasi"* societies were commonly in a state of crisis.

Economic difficulties for many of the so-called *adivasi* communities in fact began in the eighteenth and early nineteenth centuries when the introduction of British conceptions of property rights and a European legal system deprived them of vast areas of land. The stereotype soon developed, as it did of the American Indian, of the *"adivasi"* as an uneducated, landless, and poverty-stricken indigent. In reality the majority of *adivasis* lived comfortable lives, at least until the colonial period, having control over large areas of land, having armies, an aristocracy, tax collection, and judicial systems of one sort or another, and often enjoying lucrative trading relations with merchants (such as the Banjaras) and Hindu cultivators in the plains. Examples include the Ahom kingdom, which flourished in the northeast of India between the thirteenth and the late eighteenth centuries, which had armies and a sophisticated irrigation system (Sinha 1987). In central India there were numerous *"adivasi"* kingdoms, some of which survived from medieval times to the nineteenth century.

Among the *"adivasi"* kingdoms of central India was that of Garha-Mandla, in the area of modern Jubbulpore and Mandla. Garha-Mandla withstood numerous invasions from the north before being defeated by the Mughals in the mid-sixteenth century after a battle in which the queen, Durgavati, commanded an army purported to include several hundred elephants. The account of this army is probably exaggerated since it derives from the *Ain-i-akbari,* the chronicles of the emperor Akbar, which (in common with other Mughal sources) tends to enlarge the opposing odds and hence the scale of the emperor's victories. It is also unlikely that elephants were of much military use in the highlands of central India. But, although there may not have been any war elephants, there were certainly large fortresses and defensive walls constructed by the *adivasis* out of stone, and the remains of these can be seen today. Another *"adivasi"* leader from central India, Bukht Buloond, performed creditably in battles in the mid-seventeenth century with the emperor Aurangzeb, who eventually signed a treaty with him, accepting his conversion to Islam rather than continue with the struggle. He, too, has left forts and other ruins to commemorate his rule.[13]

The "Adivasis" *in History*

The existence in the recent past of organized and powerful *adivasi* kingdoms within India should come as no great surprise since so-called tribal groups have been important in the history of both Europe and Asia since ancient times. There are, indeed, numerous ruling dynasties that originated as invading tribal groups such as the Manchu Ch'ing dynasty (which ruled China up until the beginning of this century) and the Khans in Persia. In India, too, many of the dominant castes, such as the Jats of north India or the Marathas of the west, were originally tribal groupings, and these communities cut across caste associations as well as predating them in many cases.[14] The problem is that most were nonliterate cultures, which, unlike the Mughals, for example, left no written records of their achievements—a problem similar to that faced by students of the predominantly oral civilizations of premodern Africa, Scandinavia, and North America. The temptation has always existed, therefore, to regard these communities as "backward" and to view them as in some way previous rather than parallel to our own or other contemporaneous civilizations. Either that, or historians have simply ignored them.

This temptation was particularly strong to European writers of the nineteenth century. Imbued with a sense of racial and cultural superiority, they were enthusiasts for the new theory of evolution, which seemed to explain the whole of the natural world and to justify their own preeminence (Gould 1979; Huizer and Mannheim 1979; Biddis 1979; Kuper 1991). That tribal peoples might be considered as evolutionary antecedents, as inferior examples of humanity, was confirmed by the ease with which they were conquered. And the impression that they were somehow inferior or previous human specimens legitimized the whole imperial enterprise, making conquest not merely a right of the fittest but a duty, a burden that must be shouldered if the world was to be civilized and the evolution of man advanced.[15]

These ideas persisted for a long time, despite their evident absurdity, and contestation by authors such as Thomas Huxley, mainly because they were very convenient. Apart from justifying a European sense of superiority, the taxonomy of race and culture also made the management of imperial territories easier. In the search for collaborators in imperial rule, or culprits for the failures of the colonial government, the new "science" of anthropology was of particular importance as it seemed to enable entire sections of society to be stigmatized or encouraged without one ever having to determine exactly who they were. In this way theories about supposedly "criminal" tribes and so-called martial races (such as the Sikhs) facilitated the understanding and administration of vast territories that might otherwise have appeared utterly strange, chaotic, and threatening (see Kirk-Greene 1980; Asad 1973; and Stocking 1987). These ideas were used as a basis for such legislation as the Criminal Tribes Act of 1871, which restricted whole sections of the Indian population who were judged to be a threat to peace and order (Nigam 1990; Gunthorpe 1882; Kennedy 1985 [1907]; Somerville 1929).[16] Many of the problems of the people who call themselves *adivasi* therefore originate from their having become just such an *object* of colonial policy. In this context, I have already mentioned the policy of "divide and rule" but many tribal communities were also seriously affected by the range of policies adopted in the late eighteenth and early nineteenth centuries aimed at settling the countryside in the wake of the colonial conquest (see Bayly 1988, chap. 5). By this is meant the new revenue systems, the law courts, and western legal concepts adopted in the administration of land rights, which were introduced at the beginning of the colonial period. Drawn as they were from European experience, where hunting and gathering, pastoral, and other shifting forms of agricultural economy had long since been marginalized or extinguished, these concepts and institutions had the effect in India of destroying *adivasi* economic systems almost overnight. Sometimes this was done deliberately out of a desire to encourage settled systems of agriculture that could be taxed more easily. Often, however, *adivasis* were thrown off their land and prevented from pursuing their traditional occupations simply through ignorance of their importance within the Indian economy. As a consequence, whole communities of *adivasis* were turned into migrants, sometimes almost overnight, being forced to roam the countryside in search of work, many of them ending up employed on the newly established tea plantations in Assam, the coal mines, jute mills, and steel factories of Bengal, or in far-off destinations such as the sugar plantations of Jamaica, Mauritius, and Fiji. These distant overseas destinations absorbed some 2 million of the Indian population between 1860 and 1920, excluding those who migrated to Malaysia and Sri Lanka (Bates and Carter 1992).

A common misconception held by colonial administrators was that, being those of "primitive" societies, the activities of the *"adivasis"* were of little value and unrelated to those of the settled, tax-paying cultivators of the plains. The truth of the matter was that many so-called tribals, such as the Gonds of Deogarh in central India, had been plainsmen themselves until they were driven into the hills by warfare and the growing numbers of Hindu settlers. Even in the early nineteenth century many *adivasis* of central India continued to produce a wide range of valuable products upon which the plains people depended. These included iron ploughshares, made and sold to the peasants of the plains by a tribe called the Agaria (Elwin 1942). The so-called *adivasis* also produced and sold axeheads, *myrabolams* (dyes), wood, *mahua* (an alcoholic drink), cattle, silk, spices, and *tendu* leaves (from which *bidis,* an Indian cigarette, are made). These they exchanged for salt and grain, which they obtained either directly from adjacent peasant communities or by trading with the Banjaras, a trading group whose caravans traversed the length and breadth of India before the advent of railways. The forested highland areas inhabited by the *"adivasis"* were vital for the Banjaras because of the grazing they provided and as a source of young bullocks. Central India was traversed by two such Banjara routes, one beginning in Hyderabad and heading north through Burhanpur, and the other coming from the eastern coast in Orissa and passing north though

Garha-Mandla. Caravans on this second route began loaded with salt, which the Banjaras traded for grain, bullocks, raw silk, iron, etc., in the highlands of central India before heading to Mirzapur in the north. Even as late as the 1820s this trade was substantial, employing as many as one hundred thousand pack bullocks (Blunt 1930; Bates 1987). The impact of colonial policies was such, however, that this trade was completely extinguished by the 1860s, and the once-prosperous Banjaras (who had helped supply the armies of the British during their wars with the Marathas and other Hindu princes) had by the end of the nineteenth century been reduced from their social and economic position on the boundaries between "caste" and *"adivasi"* society to the status of a "criminal tribe" known only for their "vagrancy" and a propensity for thieving (Nigam 1990; Radhakrishna 1989).

The experience of the Banjaras mirrored that of many other *"adivasi"* communities, and it is in this recent experience of impoverishment, and this only, that the conception of many of these communities as "backward" lies. But, even if they were backward, or economically "irrelevant," as far as the British were concerned, within the pattern of the colonial economy, the political and social importance of *"adivasi"* communities continued well into the present century. Although regarded by some British scholars as inferior to caste Hindus, the status of *"adivasis"* in practice most often paralleled that of the Hindus, being regarded by most not so much as inferior as simply outside of the caste system. Nearly every Hindu village in central and northern India depended (and still does) on locally resident tribals (such as the Pardhans in Madhya Pradesh) to perform magic rites at certain times of the year and at marriage ceremonies. They were also called upon to drive out disease or meet the threat of poor crops (Hivale 1946). In areas where they accounted for a large proportion of the population, *adivasis* often wielded considerable ritual and political power, being involved in the investiture of various kings and rulers throughout central India and Rajasthan.

Where such Hindu-tribal associations were broken, as in the nineteenth-century Himalayan kingdom of Garwhal, the *raja* was often no longer able to maintain his authority or his kingdom.[17] Other, originally Hindu *rajas* sometimes had to adopt *adivasi* religions and forms of government completely in order to rule their territories. From this we may conclude that historians ought not to think of *"adivasi"* and "Hindu" kingdoms as being entirely distinct in form and structure. All too often, however, *adivasi* kingdoms are thought of as static and backward societies outside the mainstream of Indian culture. That this is not so I believe to be very clearly illustrated by the case of the kingdom of Bastar, which was itself a relatively recent creation, having been founded by migrants, the family of Annam Deo, who were forced to move northward into the highlands of central India in the early fourteenth century following the Muslim invasion of their homeland at Warangal in Andhra Pradesh.

Looking at "tribal history" more generally, historians such as Christopher Bayly have argued that tribal communities that might be termed *"adivasis"* were involved not only in the downfall of kingdoms but of whole empires, including the Muslim empires of the Ottomans and Safavids, as well as that of the Mughals, who fell prey to tribal incursions in the seventeenth and eighteenth centuries during the periods of their decline (Bayly 1989; Alam 1986). Rebellious tribesmen caused as much trouble for the British as they did for their Mughal predecessors. Throughout central India in the 1820s the British had to battle hordes of raiding horsemen—probably unemployed Afghani tribal mercenaries (Rohillas) known to the British as Pindaris—and they also had to deal with widespread insurrections among the Gonds, Bhils, and Bundela communities. In recent research I have found large numbers of *"adivasis"* to have been involved in fighting during the great uprising of 1857 commonly known as the Indian Mutiny, although they feature little in conventional accounts.[18] Some areas and some tribal communities, in fact, were never effectively pacified, from which one might conclude that the Pax Britannica in India was something of a myth. There were, for example, a total of more than twenty uprisings in Assam between 1826 and 1932 (when the last revolt of the Nagas was put down). There were also a succession of uprisings by the Mal Paharias of Bihar and the Lushais and Daflas of Assam, as well as spectacular insurrections by the Hos of Singhbum and the Konds of Orissa and Andhra Pradesh.

Those who retained some land and some independence usually put up the stiffest resistance, and thus during the Santhal *"hool,"* or insurrection, in Bihar in 1855, fighting continued for many months. Some ten thousand *adivasis* were killed in British reprisals before the movement was effectively suppressed, a fateful struggle that turned the Santhal districts into one of the biggest sources of migrant labor in the second half of the nineteenth century.[19] Other areas such as the Gudem-Rampa region of Andhra Pradesh were a constant source of unrest throughout the nineteenth and early twentieth centuries, the most important and recent of these uprisings being in the Telengana region (an area of sixteen thousand square miles), a communist-led struggle that lasted from 1946 to 1951 and eventually had to be put down by the army of independent India (Arnold 1982; Atlury 1984; Sundarayya 1985).

It was in these struggles against the colonial government, and against the Hindu settlers and moneylenders who came in their wake, that many "tribal" or otherwise marginalized communities for the first time began to forge a common identity, an identity that often conflicted with the ideals of Indian nationalism then being developed by Mahatma Gandhi and the Congress party in the 1920s and 1930s.[20]

During the independence movement itself, the Congress attempted to co-opt many *"adivasi"* movements but, failing to understand what they were about, they were usually unsuccessful, and *adivasi* agitations against the colonial authorities remained largely beyond their control.[21] Sometimes, indeed, they were as much opposed to Congressmen as they were to the British. Examples include the Devi movement in Gujarat in the 1920s, which involved the boycott of Parsi liquor dealers and moneylenders who were supporters of the Congress (Hardiman 1987), and an agitation that took place in the central Indian *zamindari* of Dondi-Lohara over the loss of forest rights. The latter conflict, which began in 1927 and continued until the early 1950s, was actively opposed by the Congress government when it was in power in the province between 1937 and 1939.[22]

The "Adivasis" Today

From the above it should be apparent that relations between the Congress party (which brought India to independence) and the *"adivasis"* have always been somewhat fraught, and since independence the policy of the Indian government has been a curious mixture of inversions and reproductions of the earlier policies of the British. Initially, although perhaps agreeing with the British that the *"adivasis"* were still too "backward" to be allowed responsible government, they rejected altogether the idea that they ought be protected in special reservations. Sardar Patel, the nationalist leader and first home minister of the government of independent India, while answering a question in Parliament posed by Jaipal Singh, the president of the *adivasi* Mahasabha (an important political voice for the *adivasis* by the 1950s), thus described the government's policy as one of "endeavoring to bring the tribal people up to the level of Mr. Jaipal Singh and not keep them as tribes, so that 10 years hence the word 'tribes' may be removed altogether when they should have come up to our level" (Ghurye 1980). As a consequence, although benefiting from the measures of positive discrimination introduced to promote the employment of Harijans and other "backward communities" in government service, the *adivasis* lost much of the protection, such as it was, that had been given to what remained of their land in the later years of colonial rule. Inevitably, a wholesale destruction of forests in the *adivasi* areas ensued, with a million migrant Biharis settling in the *adivasi* areas of Chotanagpur in central India, for example, between 1951 and 1971. This deprived thousands of *"adivasis"* of their land, landlessness among the *adivasis* as a whole increasing from 20 to 33 percent in the ten years between 1961 and 1971 alone (Dubey and Murdia 1977; K. S. Singh 1982b, xii).

Belatedly recognizing the inadequacies of its policy, the government of India has established tribal development blocks, "social forestry programs," and special funds to assist these areas, and it has reintroduced certain restrictions on the sale of tribal lands. This reversal has been ineffective, however, and in both Chotanagpur and Bastar in the 1970s *adivasi* agitators have blocked government forestry programs in protest at the lack of attention paid to their needs and the sacrifice of *"adivasi"* lands to commercial interests (Anderson and Huber 1988).

Resentment among these communities has also encouraged a succession of protest movements, including the Jharkhand agitation calling for a separate *"adivasi"* state in central India; the Chipko movement, a movement of peasants and tribals in the Himalayas that has been campaigning for many years against the degradation of the forests upon which its members depend for a livelihood; and the revolutionary Naxalite movement, which began as a student-led communist insurrection in Bengal in the late 1960s and early 1970s. Following its suppression by the government of India, the Naxalite movement has become established in several of the more isolated and impoverished areas of Bihar, Madhya Pradesh, and Andhra Pradesh (Sengupta 1982; Corbridge 1988; Weber 1985; Ray 1988; Ramchandra Guha 1989; Devalle 1992).

Most recently, furious controversy has blown up over the issue of reservations, and this has encouraged a backlash among high-caste Hindus. The result has been widespread rioting (a virtual caste war) throughout the north of India and the self-immolation of some fifty high school and university students. This problem had been escalating since 1981 but was brought to a head in 1990 by the proposal of the government of Mr V. P. Singh to extend the quotas of government posts and university places allowed to members of the "backward communities" (Engineer 1991). Together with the scheduled castes, the *adivasis* are the main victims of the violence. Like the discrimination that reservation is supposed to combat, one therefore cannot help but conclude that the *"adivasis"* are as much victims of the solution as they were of the problem.

For politicians a way out of this impasse will probably lie in new policies that end the attempt to use countercaste prejudice to deal with caste prejudice, and that see the adoption of primarily economic criteria to assist the advancement of underprivileged communities. For historians and anthropologists the dilemmas are perhaps more acute. It is arguable that in recent times the *adivasis* have taken on many of the characteristics of a superexploited economic class. Their marginalization in the nineteenth century has turned them into a reserve of cheap labor and one of India's most important migratory groups, a phenomenon well illustrated by their presence in large numbers among the annual migration of some 250,000 Biharis from the east of India to the Punjab in the west where they are employed as low-paid agricultural laborers at harvest time (Oberai and Singh 1985, 229).[23] However, this is clearly a feature of *"adivasi"* culture in decline and not a characteristic of these societies.

From a broader perspective one might argue that the search for an "essential" *adivasi* culture and society is itself an illusion, and that both the concept and its object have always been a political construct. Rather than ask "who the *adivasis* were," therefore, it might be better to ask "who wants to define them" since the definition of original or anterior inhabitants is usually a preliminary to the establishment of claims to political or economic power or (alternatively) reflects the power of an existing elite exerting its cultural hegemony.

Claims of this sort perhaps reveal more about the structure of Indian politics and society today than anything else. While governments have viewed them as economic "outlaws," and have treated them as such, most of our definitions of the "tribal" in India (as elsewhere) are derived from the viewpoint of nontribals, and they describe the *"adivasis"* of India in largely negative terms as what is different or "other than" the mainstream of Indian society. Unlike African anthropology, in which the concept has been given real meaning (if only through its persistent use in practice), in India the concept of "the tribal" has been largely a dustbin category into which is thrown all that is unorthodox and non-Hindu. Many anthropologists have also regarded the history of *"adivasi"* societies as a unilineal process, depicting them as merely an early stage in the process of "modernization," as spin-offs from the formation of great states and empires, or as the inevitable victims of Hinduization (as argued by Srinivas 1987; and Bose 1953, 1975). This view is partly conditioned by modern anthropology's experience of *adivasis,* who are normally encountered only when their political authority has vanished and their economies are all but extinct.

These definitions have found their apotheosis in the writings, for example, of Morton Fried (1966), who argued that tribals may only be defined as peoples on the margin of settled kingdoms and empires, and in the early writings of Marshall Sahlins (1968), who has described "tribal societies" as merely an initial phase in the onward march of the conquest of nature by humankind. Generally it may be said that the history of *"adivasi"* peoples has been neglected. At best it has been treated only partially by competing academic disciplines. On the one hand, the existence of ancient *"adivasi"* kingdoms is acknowledged and described by many Indologists but this knowledge is seen as having no connection with the existence of modern nation-states. On the other hand, anthropologists have developed the concept of "the tribe" as an analytical category used to describe kinship patterns in premodern societies. Rarely, however, are these societies seen to have evolved or survived in any substantive form into the present, let alone to have any political or cultural significance. Usually they are judged to have been largely supplanted by more modern social and economic structures: whatever politics and society remain are appropriated by much wider "human-rights" or eco-political concerns.

In this context it is worth mentioning that in central India there are a great variety of *"adivasi"* groups but that a large proportion of them have been subsumed by scholars under the generic title of Gond, a name completely alien to the *adivasis.* In Bastar the tribals of the lowlands most often refer to themselves simply as Koitur, or "the people." Further south and east, in Orissa, the generic name given to a variety of *adivasi* communities is simply Kond, which means 'low hills' in the language of the Telugu-speaking peasants of the plains. It requires little imagination to conceive how this appellation was invented by early colonial explorers. Nonetheless, it became widely used by the *adivasis* for reasons that are simple enough: problems of communication work both ways.

Similar problems of translation and communication lie behind the modern epithets of *"adivasi"* and "indigenous peoples." Both are terms adopted by subordinated groups in order to make themselves understood to the powers that be: the hegemonic classes of towns, cities, and states. These identities are adopted more by necessity than by choice, and they tell us little about the history of those identified as such. They are an adaptation to colonial ideas about castes and tribes based on an epistemology that resolutely refused any understanding of claims to legitimacy and power phrased in terms other than those of property and contract. Rather like the highly inventive *vamshavalis* (genealogies) used by Hindu kings to establish claim to a throne, the claims by certain Indians to be "the original inhabitants" of South Asia are used simply as a means of legitimizing demands for the redress of present-day economic and political inequalities. Such movements of "indigenous peoples" express a desire by subordinate groups to lay claim to their own understanding of the past but the form of this understanding is rooted in the present. The result is fatally flawed. While *"adivasi"* claims often refer to a past golden age of tribal kingdoms and territories, in practice their identity has been forged in a commonality of experience that is very recent in origin. It is arguable, therefore, that the *"adivasis"* are not the "original inhabitants" but merely the recently dispossessed. Not only the signifier but what is signified by the concept of the *"adivasi"* is an invention of colonialism, an essential "other" in the conspectus of modernity. The Independent Commission on International Humanitarian Issues has tried to alleviate doubts by arguing that the Indian *adivasis* are an exceptional case but by conceiving of "indigenous peoples" in less romantic and more practical terms it may be possible to avoid the notional dichotomy between "preservation" and "assimilation" and to move toward a politics that in the long term is more likely to serve the interests of subordinate and marginalized groups. The first step in this direction may be to admit that all Indians are, in one sense, *"adivasis."*

CHAPTER 7

The Invention of the "Jummas": State Formation and Ethnicity in Southeastern Bangladesh

WILLEM VAN SCHENDEL

This paper deals with sociocultural innovation in the hills of south-eastern Bangladesh. Outsiders have always been struck by the ethnic diversity of this area. The literature—written mainly by British civil servants, Bengali men of letters, and European anthropologists—presents a picture of twelve distinct "tribes," all practicing the swidden (or shifting) agriculture locally known as *jhum* cultivation.[1] In addition, there are Bengali immigrants who do not engage in swidden cultivation.

In the following pages I shall review the evidence on the persistence of these groups and argue that the prevalent view is too static and frag-mented; it should be replaced by a more integrated approach to social structure and process in the hills. The need for such a new approach is especially evident if we look at long-term process. I shall reconstruct ethnic persistence and innovation on the basis of documentation cover-ing the last two hundred years. This brings together travelers' accounts, colonial records, anthropological monographs, government publications, statements by political parties, writings by human-rights activists, and press reports. Although this is important in its own right (the informa-tion is scattered and needs to be synthesized), it can also be seen as a small contribution to the integration of anthropological and historical insights. What interests me particularly is the relation between local and

121

regional patterns of change, a theme much broader than that allowed in the present inquiry.

In this paper I use ethnic identity more as a sociocultural than as a psychocultural concept (Royce 1982, 17–33). My interest is in exploring how the self-perceptions of groups are related to their social positions. What is the relationship between changing social circumstances and the emergence of a new group identity? To what extent does a new identity emerge as a spontaneous response to changing external circumstances, and to what extent is it created by a conscious effort? What is the system

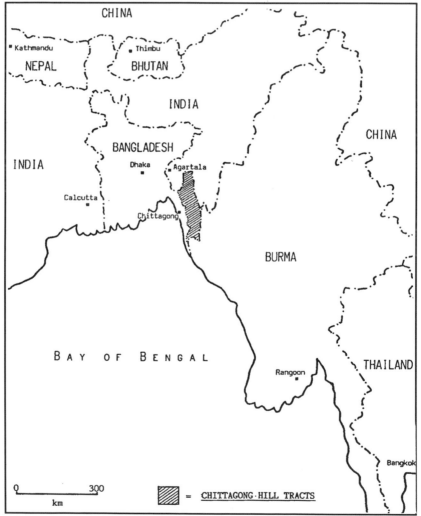

MAP 7.1. *Chittagong Hill Tracts.*

of symbols and interpretations upon which an emerging group identity rests? These are the principal questions addressed.

The hill area of southeastern Bangladesh is known today as the Chittagong Hill Tracts, and it is subdivided into three districts.[2] It forms part of a mountain range that stretches north for some 1,800 km. from western Burma to the point at which it meets the eastern Himalayas in China. Apart from the narrow strip, the Chittagong Hill Tracts (roughly 280 by 60 km.), now administered from the Bangladeshi capital of Dhaka, and the Chinese-administered northern tip, this mountain range is divided almost equally between India and Burma. It is inhabited by a bewildering variety of people speaking a wide range of languages, adhering to various creeds, and organized socially in different ways. Anthropological researchers have established that the Chittagong Hills are the home of people belonging to twelve groups, although there are fewer languages and fewer religions. These groups never developed a particular sense of unity. Lewin reported that "none of them appear to have any general term for all hill dwellers" (1984 [1870], 73). It was only after colonial annexation in 1860 that this section of the mountain range began to take on a separate identity; neighboring parts of the range were colonized at different points in time and were administered separately. In 1947, British rule came to an end. During the Partition that then split British India, the Chittagong Hills were awarded to Pakistan. When Bangladesh seceded from Pakistan in 1971, the hills became part of the new country. They now have a little over half a million inhabitants, less than 1 percent of the total population of Bangladesh. In addition, tens of thousands of people from this area are said to be living in refugee camps in the neighboring Indian state of Tripura. Among the population of the Chittagong Hills, inmigration has made the Bengalis the fastest-growing population in recent years.

Ethnic Identities Before British Rule

Documentation on the Chittagong Hills is fairly rich from the late eighteenth century onward. Before that time, there are scattered references to life in the hills, mostly in relation to events on the coastal plain. For centuries this plain was a battleground between three centers of power that sought to expand their spheres of influence. Arakan to the south, Tripura to the north, and Bengal to the northwest held the plain in turn. From the sixteenth century onward, they had to contend with newcomers, notably Portuguese traders and pirates, Burmese state

PHOTO: H. E. KAUFFMANN

PLATE 7.1. *The Bohmong (Marma chief) and his entourage in Banbardban town. Chittagong Hill Tracts, Bangladesh/East Pakistan, 1955.*

agents, and Mughal emissaries. The expansionism of these newcomers led to an increasingly confused interplay of alliances and counter-alliances. When the Mughals were defeated by the British in the mid-eighteenth century, the Chittagong Plain passed into the British sphere of influence but British hegemony continued to be contested by the Burmese until the early nineteenth century.

References to the adjacent hills, which were beyond any formal state administration until 1860, usually crop up in connection with political refugees from Burmese or British territory seeking shelter there, or in connection with the cotton trade that had taken on the shape of state tribute during the Mughal period.[3] The earliest detailed travel account dates from the 1790s. Surprisingly, this extensive and important manuscript by Francis Buchanan has been ignored by historians of the region; it provides unique insights into ethnic identities in the hills.[4]

During his trip Buchanan interviewed people, asking them about their own "nation" or "tribe" as well as about others in the hills. He came across the Marma (Marama), the Chakma (Saksa), the Mru (Moroo-sa), the Bawm (Bon-zu), the Zo (Zou), the Sak (Thaek), the Mrung (Doing-nak?), and the Tippera, in addition to some Bengalis, Baruas, and Arakanese who were neither swidden cultivators nor permanent residents.[5] He described a complex ethnic situation in the hills and variable ethnic boundaries. There was no question of isolated "tribes" living in distinct territories; on the contrary, there were several "multi-ethnic"

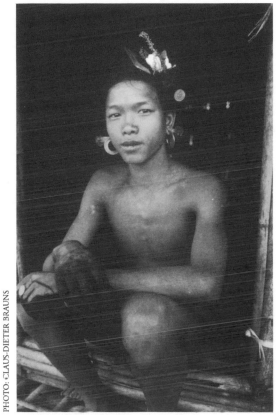

PHOTO: ©CLAUS-DIETER BRAUNS

PLATE 7.2. *Young man (Mru), southern Chittagong Hill Tracts, Bangladesh.*

arrangements (for example, villages inhabited by swidden cultivators belonging to different language groups); villages that were "ethnically stratified," being inhabited by an ethnic group together with its debt peons from different groups; and villages in which the leaders had servants from several other groups.[6] Moreover, "chiefs" often collected tribute from households belonging to an amalgam of ethnic groups.[7] All groups were continually on the move not only because of their style of agriculture but also because of raids and warfare.

What is remarkable about Buchanan's account is that he makes an effort to understand ethnic identities from "within," from the viewpoint of the people concerned. This concern for an "emic" perspective contrasts with the outlook of his contemporaries and many later writers who content themselves with describing the people of the Chittagong Hills in terms of the ethnic categories used by their Bengali neighbors. Thus, John

PHOTO: CLAUS-DIETER BRAUNS

PLATE 7.3. *Young woman (Mru), southern Chittagong Hill Tracts, Bangladesh.*

Macrae makes a distinction between Choomeas, Mugs, and Kookies, or Lunctas (Macrae 1801, 184; Rawlins 1790, 187–93). Lewin (1984 [1870], 73), writing seventy years later, explains that Bengalis distinguish two classes: friendly tribes near the Chittagong Plain, referred to as Joomas; and all others, referred to as Kookies, especially if they are unable to speak Bengali.[8] Mug (also frequently spelled Magh or Mugh) is another blanket term often used by Bengalis to refer to their eastern neighbors.[9]

Two Views of Ethnic Identities Since 1860

The ethnographic map of the Chittagong Hills remains confused well into the twentieth century. Officials such as T. H. Lewin, R. H. Sneyd Hutchinson, and J. P. Mills produced more or less detailed

PHOTOGRAPHER UNKNOWN

PLATE 7.4. *A group of guerrilla fighters of the Shanti Bahini (Peace Troops), Chittagong Hill Tracts, Bangladesh.*

accounts of the different groups living in the area (Lewin 1869, 1984 [1870]; Hutchinson 1906; Mills 1927, 1933; Riebeck 1885), and the colonial censuses attempted to clarify the statistical picture, but it is only with the arrival of professional anthropologists in the 1950s that the "emic" perspective first hinted at by Buchanan reasserts itself strongly. Important insights resulted from studies by a group of German anthropologists (Löffler 1964, 1966; Brauns and Löffler 1986; Spielmann 1968; A. Mey 1979; W. Mey 1980). These studies, begun in the mid-1950s, came to an abrupt end in 1971 when the hills were sealed off by the Bangladesh government.[10] Other studies dating from this period are Lévi-Strauss (1952); Bessaignet (1958); Bernot and Bernot (1958); L. Bernot (1967a, 1967b); and Sopher (1963, 1964). The latest addition is Eva Rosén-Hockersmith's study of the Barua community, which lives on the border of the hill region (Rosén-Hockersmith 1985). It is unfortunate that many of these studies have been published only in European languages that are little understood in the region—German, French, and Swedish. On the other hand, Bangladeshi scholars have done relatively little work in the Chittagong Hills. (It should be realized that until recently the Bangladesh universities lacked departments of anthropology, and that professionals were rare indeed.) Historians, too, have practically ignored the Chittagong Hills, and most of the unpublished records cited in this paper have not been used before.[11]

As a result of these factors, little up-to-date information on the people of the Chittagong Hills has been available to the Bengalis living in the plains that form the rest of Bangladesh, and a remarkably stagnant view of the hill people has prevailed throughout the twentieth century. This view is composed of various elements. First, there are strong echoes of nineteenth-century European views of nonwestern peoples, particularly those formalized in classic anthropological assumptions of unilinear social evolution from a state of savagery or barbarism to that of civilization.[12] Nineteenth-century British writers on the hill people described them as "primitives," "savages," and "wild hill tribes," terms that continue to be encountered frequently in contemporary writings in Bangladesh. Second, these ideas are superimposed on ancient South Asian conceptions of a crucial distinction between civilized society and nature. This distinction, expressed by the terms *grāma* ('village') and *araṇya* ('forest'), implied a complementary but unequal relationship between the inhabitants of the two realms (Heesterman 1985, 118, 170–71). The combination of these two traditions has led to a dominant Bengali view that assumes the Chittagong hill people to be "isolated remnants" of some hoary past who have preserved their culture unchanged from time immemorial. Backward and childlike, they need to be protected, educated, and disciplined by those who are more advanced socially. The relationship between Bengalis and hill people is seen as one of guardianship, and Bengalis assume the responsibility to "uplift" their charges, to bring them into contact with the modern world. This "mission civilisatrice," akin to the colonialist's "white man's burden," is nowadays translated in terms of development policies carried out, or at least nurtured, by the state. This attitude of guardianship over "primitive" people is summed up in the expression "our tribes," which is commonly used. Use of the term *tribe,* an exceedingly vague and confusing term in South Asia (quite apart from the anthropological debate concerning it—see Sahlins [1968]; Fried [1975]; and Béteille [1977]), also reflects the idea that all hill people belong to a single category, and that differences between them are of minor consequence. What is underlined is the wide gulf separating "primitive" tribals from "civilized" Bengalis, and their presumably unchanged symbiosis (see Mazumder 1985; and the quotations in W. Mey 1988, 32–36). These ideas, which might be termed "tribalist," are voiced most clearly by Abdus Sattar, a prolific and influential writer on tribal affairs in Bangladesh in the 1970s.[13]

> The Shendus, Pankhos, Mrus, Murangs, and Bonjugis of the Chittagong Hill Tracts are yet to receive even a peripheral contact with the civilized

world. Their way of life is timeless. Their cultural configuration is still intact, the outlines still hard and sharply drawn against the contrasting background of civilization with no sign of dimming. Their religious beliefs and practices completely insulates [*sic*] them against the demands of modernism. Even their economy is antidiluvian [*sic*]. (Sattar 1975, 6–7)

If there is no education it will further widen the gap between the civilized and the pre–civilized. Isolated and left behind, the tribes will become more inward-looking and aggressive. (Ibid., 4)

The tribals are usually simple, credulous and jovial folks. As long as they have enough to eat they are not much bothered by worries. The elders give themselves up to singing and dancing while children play or frolic. (Ibid., 7)

They are of deep interest to any one who wants to discover man in his raw form. (Sattar 1971, 4)

Juxtaposed against this rather stagnant external image of the people of the Chittagong Hills as tribes lost in time, or "people without history,"[14] is a historic experience and internal images of ethnic relations that are strikingly different. A reconstruction of the historical development of ethnic identities is far from easy and cannot be more than preliminary. Historical records did not concentrate on questions of changing identities to any great extent, the anthropological work done on the area is rather old, and writings by hill people themselves derive mostly from one group, the Chakmas. Nevertheless, the following corrections can be made.

First, the idea of unchangeable tribes frozen in time cannot stand the test of historical scrutiny. There is ample evidence of historical change affecting each group, and for several of them, including the Chakma, Tongchengya, and Mrung, there is information allowing us to suggest how and when they came into being. For example, the Mrung are thought to have developed out of a group of Tippera who were taken to Arakan as prisoners of war and began to return north when the Burmese invaded Arakan, ending up in the southern Chittagong Hills.

Second, the present distribution of different groups in the hills is far from "traditional." Complex patterns of migration into and out of the area have been occurring for centuries. Almost all of these people have been highly mobile not just in the short term and over short distances (as a result of their shifting style of cultivation) but also over long distances and over a long span of time. The main movement into the Chittagong Hills has been from the south, with minor migrations occurring from the east and north. Some of the people who arrived from the south are thought to represent fragments of larger state societies that became separated and, through a process of devolution, turned into "tribal" groups. Others never belonged to state societies and represented the small-scale, mostly acephalous groups that abounded in the mountain range. These different groups certainly did not conceive of themselves as existing in a single social category.

Third, they did not form rigidly bounded units. Even a highly exclusive group like the Mru, which tended to frown on exogamy and usually lived in separate villages, did allow marriage with one other group, the Pangkhua. Moreover, we have seen that many villages were multiethnic, either because two or more "tribes" lived together or because a village dominated by one ethnic group also contained a number of war captives or debt peons from other groups. Finally, "chiefs" and other intermediaries with the state often presided over multiethnic groups of dependents. Therefore, although boundaries did exist, they were often far more blurred than the dominant view presumes.

Finally, the hill people were involved in extensive networks of tribute and trade at least as long as states had been rising and falling in southeastern Bengal, Tripura, and Arakan. For example, they were linked with Bengal's major industry, cotton textiles, as both producers of finished products and providers of raw cotton to the factories around Chittagong town and in Noakhali District. When cotton textiles became precolonial Bengal's foremost export, the Chittagong hill people became tied into an ever denser network of overseas trade, not only as growers of cotton but as providers of timber to Chittagong's shipbuilders. Far from being isolated from the wider world, or survivals from some primeval period, their continual contacts with outsiders, mostly Bengalis, shaped their economic, political, and cultural development. The cultural distinctiveness of the different groups in the Chittagong Hills should be regarded as an outcome of these interactions.

Competing Cultural Models

A crucially important aspect of relations between Bengalis and the inhabitants of the Chittagong Hills was that the hill people had access to two competing models of state society and culture: the South Asian (represented by its Bengali variant) and the Southeast Asian (in the form of its Burmese/Arakanese variant). In this respect they differed fundamentally from many small peoples on either side of this great cultural

divide who had access to one model only. Historically, there are clear
fluctuations in the use that the people of the Chittagong Hills made of
the two models. Some groups leaned toward one more than the other
but all of them changed over time. The Tippera, perhaps, went farthest
in their attempt to emulate the South Asian model. Their leader styled
himself a *raja* ('king', 'ruler') in the Hindu tradition, and Hindu
elements clearly played an important part in Tippera religion. In other
matters (such as dress style) they also followed Bengali examples. But,
despite a degree of Hinduization and Bengalization, they remained
clearly separate. Not only was their language distinct but they also stood
out for their syncretic religion, their kinship system, and their economic
activities. At the other end of the spectrum are the Marma, whose very
name signifies that they perceive themselves as Burmese.[15] The Marma
called their leaders *mang* ('ruler' or 'governor', with the Burmese connotations of that word) or *po mang* ('great captain'; Bohmong),[16] and
village-level leaders were referred to as *rua-sa* (often Bengalized to *roaja*
in the literature), again a reference to the Burmese system of "village
eaters" or local representatives of the state (L. Bernot 1967a, 84, 86–87).
Between these two extremes stand the Chakma in whose history both
models may be seen to vie for dominance. Burmese elements are strong
in their religion, in which Burman-Buddhist elements abound. But their
language is so strongly influenced by the Chittagonian dialect of Bengali
that it has been described as a Bengali dialect rather than a separate
language. Chakma political culture also reflected influences from both
South and Southeast Asian models. Chakma leaders adopted Islamic
names during the Mughal period (although this did not imply any religious change) but they used titles (*mang, khan*) derived from both
Buddhist and Muslim traditions (see Buchanan 1798, 119–21).[17] Only
during the early colonial period did the Bengali cultural model become
dominant among the Chakmas: the chiefly family adopted Bengali titles
(*raja, rani, dewan*) and introduced some Hindu rituals into its religious
observances. At the same time a myth of "western" origin developed,
which linked the Chakmas firmly to South rather than Southeast Asia.[18]

Many more examples could be given of the competing influence of
the Burmese and Bengali models among the hill people and the ways in
which they were combined with the various local cultural traditions.
Historically, the changing influence of these models appears to have been
linked with changing trade routes, which in turn were influenced by the
vagaries of state formation in the plains. Trade between hills and plains
consisted largely of the exchange of cotton yarn, textiles, and forest prod-

ucts for salt, dried fish, and manufactures. Some hill people traded with Bengalis in the Chittagong Plain, others with the Arakanese in the south. Some trade also must have been carried on with the Burmese in the Irrawaddy Valley to the east but that area remained beyond the reach of European travelers till the late nineteenth century and very little is known about eastward trade routes.

Enter the State

The Chittagong Hills had never been incorporated into a state until the British annexed them in 1860. This does not mean that the hill economy was not thoroughly influenced by its contacts with the outside world long before that. The Mughal state extracted a tribute in cotton, and the demand for certain products had led to some economic specialization in the hills. But it is important to realize that before annexation the hill people were free agents feared by the plains people for their independence and military prowess. An uneasy symbiosis between the settled cultivators of the plain and the swidden cultivators in the hills was punctuated by raids that hill people would carry out on plains villages whenever they felt their rights were being encroached upon. Retaliation was extremely difficult because the hill people were seemingly invincible on their own turf.

The British-Indian state was the first that was strong enough to conquer the hills and the first with a reason to do so. The direct cause of annexation was military: retaliation for raids on British territory that had been carried out not by the people of the Chittagong Hills but by hill people living further to the east in the section of the mountain range now known as Mizoram. The aim of formal annexation was to allow the British to station troops on the eastern borders of the new hill district in order to fend off attacks from the east. These attacks had become more frequent as a result of increasing internecine warfare leading to territorial expansion in which Kookies (Koongkies, Kukies, Cucis), now better known as Chin, Lushai, or Mizo, were involved.[19]

Colonial annexation had far-reaching consequences. A small section of the mountain range was parceled off to form a new district, the Chittagong Hill Tracts. It was administered from Calcutta as part of the province of Bengal. This administrative set-up was unique, for the bulk of the mountain range, which the British conquered gradually in the late nineteenth century, was ruled from Assam and Burma.[20] After

1860, the Bengali cultural model suddenly assumed a more prominent position in the Chittagong Hills, and its emergence was linked directly to colonial domination.

From Kin-Ordered to Territorial Authority

Perhaps the most radical change that colonial domination brought about was the abolition of kin-ordered modes of authority. Previously in the Chittagong Hills, surplus extraction had been based largely on personal ties between chiefs and followers. Kinship and fictive kinship was the underlying ideology legitimizing the chiefs' power. This system, which was also important in the precolonial Burmese state, was anathema to the territorial system of surplus extraction that had long been in force in the Bengal plains.[21] When a territorial system was now introduced in the Chittagong Hills, existing chiefs were treated as subordinate territorial lords. The Chakma chief, for example, held some lands in the plains. Here he had the status of a *zamindar* (superior landholder and tax collector) under British-Indian law. The British tended to treat his position in the hills as subsidiary to his status as a *zamindar* (Government of Bengal 1876, 30). After 1860, he and two other leaders (the Bohmong chief in the southern hills and the Mong chief in the north) were made responsible for tax collection in well-defined areas of the Chittagong Hills. Other chiefs were made answerable to them, and taxes were demanded on the basis of territory rather than personal following. Thus, the chiefs became agents of the state with centralized power based on a principle of authority that was new in the hills.[22] Introduction of indirect rule in the Chittagong Hills was advocated but never introduced; although the chiefs were allowed some of the trappings of "native rulers," they were "always treated as tahsildars and rent-collectors" (Government of Bengal 1918).[23]

A Policy of Exclusion

A second crucial change was less apparent at first. Not only did the people of the Chittagong Hills become incorporated in a state for the first time in their history but they also became minorities overnight. The state to which they now belonged was dominated by British and Bengali interests, and the political and social relations between the hills and the plains were reversed. Bengali mores gradually came to be the standard against which the cultural and social life of the people of the hills was judged. A process of legal and commercial "Bengalization" of the hills set in with such force that British officials began to worry about it.[24] Bengali pleaders and moneylenders were particularly successful, and the authorities soon sought to stop their activities on the grounds that they fleeced the "innocent" and "ignorant" hill men. The state decided not to tolerate private accumulation by Bengali entrepreneurs, fearing that this would undermine its new territorial system of surplus extraction, and might also lead to trouble in the hills, as the recent Santal rebellion had revealed forcefully.[25] Consequently, the colonial authorities constituted themselves the protectors of "tribal" rights in the Chittagong Hills.[26]

The Chittagong Hills were proclaimed an excluded area, a policy that was formalized in the Chittagong Hill Tracts Regulation of 1900.[27] This regulation stemmed the tide of Bengalization but also isolated the hill people from the rest of Bengal. Far from being a charter for regional autonomy or a protection of "tribal" rights (as some would have it), it marked the onset of a process of "enclavement" in which the hill people were denied access to power and were subordinated and exploited directly by their British overlords.[28] This was exemplified by various manipulations. First, the colonial state claimed ownership of all land in the hills.

> It appears advisable, as opportunities occur, to make the semi-civilized tribes inhabiting these hills understand more and more that the lands they occupy form an integral portion of Her Majesty's dominion in India, and that the Government alone is the fountain of all honour. (Government of Bengal 1876, 30)[29]

It was entirely in line with this position that the government declared large tracts of hill country to be "reserved forests" and denied hill cultivators access to what they had always considered as common ground.[30] High-quality land was meted out to European entrepreneurs, especially to tea planters, although these enterprises proved relatively unsuccessful.[31]

Second, repeated efforts were made to supplant swidden with settled plough cultivation, as this was expected to yield a higher state revenue and be less "wasteful" of timber resources and land: "Our object should be to put a stop to *jum* culture and induce the people to settle and cultivate by the plough, making land revenue the basis of our district settlement."[32] Swidden cultivation was also prohibited on government estates in the plains district of Chittagong. This led to an influx of swidden cultivators in the hill district and to further physical isolation of hill people from Bengalis.[33]

Third, the authorities began to move groups of hill people to new locations. Although the reason sometimes offered was that the cultivators had "exhausted" the soil, these forced moves were all to the east, serving mainly to strengthen the border against invaders.[34] And, finally, the colonial authorities encouraged outsiders to settle in the Chittagong Hills. Their policy was distinctly anti-Bengali, for, while they continued to forbid Bengalis to migrate to the hills, they made considerable efforts to establish settlements of plough-cultivating Gurkhas and Santals on erstwhile "tribal" land.[35]

The British were not so much interested in preserving the rights of the hill people as in making the Chittagong Hills yield a good revenue for the colonial exchequer. Their interest focused on taxes gathered from the cultivators via the territorial chiefs but also on revenue from trade. The chief items of hill produce were timber, boats, grass, cane, cotton, umbrella leaves, and bamboo.[36]

This colonial policy of excluding Bengalis and isolating the hill people was not entirely successful because the hill people sometimes refused to cooperate. In precolonial days, trade had been carried on by hill people coming down to markets near the foothills and by Bengali tradesmen entering the hills by boat.[37] The British tried to stop the latter entering the hills and encouraged the establishment of permanent hill markets (*bazars*). But this proved impractical, as most hill people preferred bartering with traders at home to walking long distances to one of the thirteen new markets, and the British had to withdraw the prohibition in 1877. So, once again, the trade of the country was "in the hands of a class of men called *Bhasania beparis*, or 'floating traders', who go up the rivers in boats well stocked with articles of all kinds, stopping at the villages to trade" (Government of Bengal 1879, 3; see also Lewin 1984 [1870], 23–24; and Hutchinson 1906, 44–46).

The colonial policy of exclusion meant that only certain economic and ecological niches were open to the hill people. They had no say in administrative affairs and decisions were made for, not with, them. They were not allowed to cultivate outside the Chittagong Hills unless they changed to plough cultivation, which would have required them to relinquish their lifestyle completely.[38] As the local economy became more commercial and external trade grew, hill people played an ever smaller role in it. They became minorities with restricted rights in the territory to which they had been assigned, and they were powerless outside it.

Erosion and the End of Exclusion

A relatively high level of self-sufficiency allowed the hill people to continue enjoying reasonable living conditions. The main articles that they required from outside were salt and dried fish; they produced their own staple foods and clothing long after the people in the plains had become dependent on the market. After 1892, when Mizoram had finally been annexed and the raids had stopped, life in the Chittagong Hills became remarkably peaceful. Isolated and fairly self-sufficient, its population began to grow (Löffler 1963, 179–82). Migration to other parts of the mountain range was still possible in the colonial period but the territorial system of tax collection hampered it. The result was that migration continued to take place mainly within the jurisdictions of territorial chiefs, and population pressure began to rise. Although population densities were far lower than on the plains, the hills began to be overcultivated, leading to lower yields from swidden agriculture, the cultivation of larger fields, shorter periods of fallow, and noticeable erosion from about 1940 (ibid., 179–80, 182). In an attempt to mobilize new resources, some cultivators added plough cultivation in the river valleys to *jhum* cultivation on nearby hill slopes, a move they had resisted earlier when the authorities advocated it.[39] The agrarian system of the Chittagong Hills had become overextended. As the excluded nature of the area had kept nonagricultural employment away, the hill people were now faced with an economic crisis.[40]

In addition to this largely internal development, external changes would deepen the crisis. In 1947, when British India disintegrated into India and Pakistan, the Chittagong Hills, though practically devoid of Muslims, were awarded to (East) Pakistan.[41] While the area continued to have special status, soon attempts were afoot to change it. This was understandable as both land tax and revenues from cotton and forest produce had become much less important. The new power holders were looking for ways to make the Chittagong Hills productive and these made the colonial policy of isolation redundant. The state was no longer interested mainly in the products of hill people's labor (in the form of taxes and cotton); increasingly it was the land on which they lived that interested the state.

The decision to exploit the hills as a source of hydroelectric power turned out to be momentous. East Pakistan had very few other sources of energy, and only the Chittagong Hills offered an opportunity to harness water resources. To this end a huge lake was created north and east of a barrage at Kaptai village between 1959 and 1963. Large tracts were flooded, depriving tens of thousands of cultivators of their best lands and many more of their homesteads. In all, more than one hundred thousand people, "more than one quarter of the total popula- tion of the district," were displaced (*Bangladesh District Gazetteers* 1971, 42). Although some compensation was given to those affected, it proved insufficient.[42] Prospecting for oil and natural gas, which had been under- taken as early as 1908 in the Chittagong region, was resumed after East Pakistan became Bangladesh.[43]

The Bengali nation-state was a relative latecomer in the region but its establishment marked an important change in the hills. From 1971 onward, the dominant Bengali view of ethnic relations in the hills came to inform state policy as never before.[44] It could hardly come as a surprise that the final blow to the colonial policy of exclusion and isolation was dealt in the 1970s when the hills were opened to Bengali settlers. The lowlands of Bangladesh had fallen victim to disastrous poverty, which, despite a large inflow of foreign development aid, showed every sign of increasing. Erroneous conceptions of the "emptiness" and underutilized agrarian wealth of the hills combined with ideas about the superiority of (Bengali) plough cultivation in the presentation of settler migration to the Chittagong Hills as a partial solution to both overpopulation in the plains and underdevelopment in the hills. Considering dominant Bengali conceptions of the hill people's cultural backwardness, it also was assumed that settling Bengali peasants in the hills would contribute to their cultural development.

Resistance and Abandonment of the Bengali Model

It soon became clear that this was not how the people of the Chit- tagong Hills perceived the invasion of their land. Their long history of passive resistance to the state came to an end as open rebellion broke out.[45] When Bangladeshi armed forces moved in, full-scale guerrilla warfare ensued (see Amnesty International 1986; Survival International 1988; Rashid 1980; Roy et al. 1989; S. Chakma [1985–86], and W. Mey 1980, 1984, and 1988). New migrants were brought in under army protection and they could only persevere when they were given arms. By 1990, continuous war had produced thousands of casualties, had led to an exodus of perhaps seventy thousand hill people now languishing in refugee camps in Tripura State (India),[46] and elicited international protests against the government policy, which was branded as genocidal and ethnocidal (W. Mey 1984; Survival International 1988).

It is not my intention to deal with the ongoing conflict in the Chittagong Hills itself; this has been done in detail elsewhere. Here I wish to concentrate on an aspect that has received little attention: the cultural repercussions of the conflict. I have indicated that the Bengali cultural model became dominant from the 1860s onward and that it was linked with state power. The people of the Chittagong Hills had to come to terms with administrative institutions that had been developed in Bengal, they had to learn the Bengali language to communicate with agents of the state, and local cultures developed a relationship with Bengali culture that was distinctly ambiguous. Efforts to adapt to and participate in Bengali culture were counterbalanced by assertions of the worth of each local culture.[47]

Up to 1947, direct interaction between hill people and Bengalis had been somewhat restricted but the end of British rule brought the hill people into closer contact with the Bengali population of the plains. In this period the first organizations intended to unite all the hill people emerged. While earlier organizations had concentrated on single language groups,[48] three new organizations established between 1946 and 1950 opposed the merger of the Chittagong Hills with Pakistan (to various degrees), aimed at "taking care of local needs and complaints," and concerned themselves with minority rights.[49] These organizations failed to attain their aims, however, and in 1957 student protests against political repression in the hills led to the formation of an underground Pahari Chhatro Shomiti (Hill Students' Association). This group formed the organizational core of agitations against the Kaptai hydroelectric project and the abolition of the district's special status. With the establishment of an underground party known as the Chittagong Hill Tracts Welfare Association in 1966, the political organization of the hill people entered a new phase. For the first time proponents of armed struggle against the government came to the fore. After the war between Bangladesh and Pakistan in 1971, the Welfare Association was dissolved. It was supplanted by the Parbotyo Chottogram Jono Shonghoti Shomiti, or Chittagong Hill Tracts People's Solidarity Association (Rashid 1980, 29; A. Chakma 1984, 35–62). This party, usually referred to as the Jana Samhati Samiti, or JSS, has been the main political organization in the Chittagong Hills ever since.[50] It has become best known under the name of its armed wing, the Shanti Bahini (Peace Troops), which has confronted the Bangladeshi army and groups of armed immigrants (known as Village Defence Parties) from 1975 onward (T., C. M. 1988).

Increasing political organization in the Chittagong Hills signalled the progressive abandonment of the Bengali cultural model. The ultimate break came with the mass inmigration of Bengali peasants in the late 1970s. A remarkable cultural innovation then occurred, which was reflected in the emergence of a new term to designate the people of the Chittagong Hills. They were now called *jumma*. An old pejorative term for a swidden cultivator in the Chittagonian dialect of Bengali, it was appropriated by the JSS in an attempt to unify all the hill people under one social umbrella. It is remarkable that this term was adopted at a time when many hill people had been forced to give up swidden cultivation.

The Creation of a People

What are the characteristics of the Jummas? It is difficult to see them as an ethnic group in the traditional, cultural sense since they share neither a single language nor a single religion. The type of collective identity the term *jumma* seeks to create is based more on social than on cultural characteristics, and the fact that the inhabitants of the Chittagong Hills now frequently refer to themselves as "Jumma people" or the "Jumma nation" indicates that a process of "nation building" is under way.[51] The mental construction of a "Jumma nation" shows various aspects, and the ultimate success or failure of this attempt hinges on the future importance of these aspects in the minds of the hill people.

First, the demarcation of cultural boundaries is preeminent in the development of the Jumma identity. Although internally diverse, Jummas highlight their *cultural separateness* from Bengalis. In religion they stress their non-Islamic outlook,[52] and in linguistic terms the fact that Bengali is not their mother tongue. Old negative stereotypes of Bengalis play an important role. Around 1960, Lucien Bernot described Marma perceptions.

> The Bengali is the administration, the police, the greedy merchant, the sometimes unscrupulous money-lender, and so on; the Marmas' list is endless. But the Bengalis are also men who have left behind their wives in the plains...and among them are beggars, coolies, boatmen, and famine. (L. Bernot 1967a, 749–50, my translation)

New negative roles in which the Jummas have cast Bengalis include those of rapist, torturer, killer, extortioner, and arsonist. Older positive images (teacher, friend, partner, patron, protector, broker) are conspicuously absent from the recent literature.

The Jumma identity does not signify a return to the old Burmese cultural model. Rather it is the first serious attempt to develop an indigenous model of state society and culture. English is now often preferred to Bengali, which has served as a lingua franca in the hills since it supplanted Arakanese at the beginning of the colonial period. Attempts to revive the local linguistic heritage also can be observed, for example, in a trend toward giving newborns Jumma names instead of the Bengali names that were fashionable a generation ago. Some efforts are being made as well to resuscitate the old Chakma alphabet, which has been almost forgotten.[53] Cultural purification (the removal of Bengali influences now felt to be "alien") so far is less pronounced than the demarcation of the cultural boundaries between Jummas and Bengalis. Racial overtones also have been weak; the physical differences between "Indic" Bengalis and "Mongoloid" hill people that so preoccupied the British do not appear to figure prominently in the self-image of the Jummas in the 1970s, 1980s, and 1990s.

A second aspect being stressed is the possession of a Jumma *homeland* that must be protected from non-Jumma outsiders. The connection between nation and land is not traditional among swidden cultivators who once considered land as a free gift of nature not the possession of mortals. But territorial thinking developed in reaction to proprietary claims by the British Crown and its successor governments, the introduction of private property rights in land, and exploitation of the region's resources.[54] Among the inhabitants of the Chittagong Hills, whose precolonial forebears did not feel particularly close to each other just because they happened to occupy the same tract of hill land, the possession of a homeland has now become a core element in the construction of a shared identity. Jummas now identify strongly with, and only with, the hills that the British carved out as the Chittagong Hill Tracts and that Bangladesh received as a colonial inheritance.

Third, the creation of the Jumma identity depends crucially upon the perception that the hill people share a unique historical experience. This sets them apart from Bengalis but also from inhabitants of other parts of the mountain range. The emergence of the Jumma identity is accompanied by reinterpretations of that experience. The guerrilla war has intensified the perception among the hill people that they have *always* been beleaguered by outsiders. The invention of a "national" tradition can be observed in attempts to highlight Jumma prosperity and unity in the past and to focus on harmonious historical relations between different hill peoples rather than on conflicts between them. In this way a collective identity that has blossomed as a result of shared experiences in recent times is projected into the more distant past.[55]

Finally, the hill people are striving to develop the "indigenous cultural model" they have begun to adopt. In the 1980s, they established contact with various international organizations of, or concerned with, "indigenous peoples," and they came to see their struggle increasingly in terms of human and minority rights. This was also the period in which they began to participate in new nationwide organizations of minority groups in Bangladesh.[56] The cultural model that is spreading among the inhabitants of the Chittagong Hills emanates from the experiences of minorities as far apart as Australia and Scandinavia. It is couched increasingly in Fourth World terms and stresses their inalienable right to self-determination.[57]

A Successful Identity?

Is it possible to "will" a collective identity into existence? To what extent has the JSS been successful in propagating the new Jumma identity? Is it an ethnic identity in the making, emerging nationalism, or a political pipe dream? JSS documents have embraced the concept whole-heartedly and there are indications that the party enjoys broad support in the Chittagong Hills. But it would seem that there are various obstacles to the acceptance of Jumma ethnicity or Jumma (sub)nationalism by the people to whom it applies. First, the Jumma identity will have to compete with distinct local-group identities that are well established and do not show signs of fading. Of course, no collectivity is homogeneous; it always overlaps with others such as gender, class, kin group, and region. People are capable of having multiple identities, and the different local groups may well adopt the Jumma in addition to their local identity. Second, acceptance of the Jumma identity depends upon the degree to which old intergroup perceptions can be neutralized. For example, some groups consider themselves more "advanced" than others. This is especially clear in the traditional division between "river-valley" groups (such as the Marma and the Chakma) and "hill dwellers" such as the Bawm, Mru, and Khumi (see W. Mey 1980, 226–46; L. Bernot 1967a, 748–50). Third, group size varies from a few hundred to several hundred thousand. If the smaller groups fear that their cultural heritage will be swamped in a Jumma identity that is dominated by the largest groups, they may be tempted to repudiate the Jumma label. Fourth, different ethnic groups have been affected differently by Bengali inmigration and repression, and it is conceivable that allegiance to the Jumma identity will vary accordingly.

At present it is impossible to know to what extent these obstacles operate. Bangladeshi government sources either ignore the Jumma identity or denounce it as a figment of the imagination of some misguided Chakma "miscreants" who are trying to disturb peaceful relations between Bengalis and hill people by means of an illegal organization.[58] It is true that Chakmas are very visible in the JSS. It would be highly surprising if they were not: they are the largest group in the Chittagong Hills, they have an educated elite, and they are among those who have been most severely affected, first by the Kaptai lake and later by immigration and militarization. But the other groups in the Chittagong Hills are not absent from either the JSS or the casualty list. It is certainly too simplistic to dismiss the JSS as a Chakma organization and "Jummaization" as a Chakma ploy. On the other hand, too little is known at present about interethnic relations in or outside the JSS, or the use of symbols of Jumma adherence, to allow us to judge the degree to which the Jumma identity has struck roots in the Chittagong Hills.[59]

So far the resistance movement against the Bangladesh army and Bengali inmigration has been supported by an ideology that leans heavily on ethnic pride and the right to self-determination. Its demands parallel those of the two great nationalist movements in which the hill people have participated to some extent: the independence movement against British rule, and the Bangladesh movement against Pakistan (see S. Chakma [1985–86]; and A. Chakma 1984, 35–62). Both these movements resulted in the formation of national states. Like them the Jumma movement is one of solidarity, endeavoring to achieve self-determination by projecting a clear sociocultural identity and constructing a sharp image of the external enemy. But, unlike them, it cannot fall back upon a well-established "internal" identity. At present its unity within appears to rest squarely upon the awesome opposition without; ultimately its success will depend largely upon the extent to which the people of the Chittagong Hills come to perceive themselves primarily as Jummas.

What an autonomous Jumma region would look like remains vague. At least two factors might undermine the attempt to establish the Jumma identity as a dominant ethnic category in the future. First, there is the old controversy between those who consider the indigenous political tradition of the Chittagong Hills to be one of democratic equality, as exemplified by the "acephalous" political systems of some groups, and those who consider it to be one of hierarchical centralism, as exemplified by chiefly rule. It remains to be seen whether the Jumma identity can survive the competition between these views and the social programs they entail. Second, Jumma self-determination may easily come into conflict with other regional movements in the mountain range. There is, for example, a movement for "Greater Mizoram," which claims parts of the Chittagong Hills.[60]

Conclusion

The emergence of the Jumma identity can be understood as a warning signal, a symbolic response to the calamitous meeting of two incompatible views of ethnic relations in the Chittagong Hills. These views met under conditions of very unequal power, and the creation of the Jummas was an act of defiance. It signalled that after the mid-1970s the hill people increasingly abandoned ideas of ethnic fusion (assimilation to Bengali culture) or ethnic persistence (hanging on to indigenous identity systems) as no longer realistic. Instead, it was a bid for ethnic innovation undertaken in order to cope with the political and economic consequences of loss of power, growing expendability to the state, and cultural marginalization. This makes it an important case for students of ethnicity who have been much concerned with ethnic conflict but have given less attention to ethnic innovation (ethnogenesis) than to other forms of boundary crossing (especially ethnic assimilation, incorporation, and secession).[61]

The Jumma identity turns enclavement upside-down. It signifies the choice for an "ethnic strategy" in politics: the Jummas themselves now seek isolation from the dominant culture and from the state that represents it, and they resist what they consider to be an infringement of their cultural boundaries. Worldwide, ethnic strategies can be seen as thoroughly modern responses to economic and political change.[62] Although such strategies can be observed in several parts of the mountain range, nowhere else have hill people been given so little local autonomy, become so marginalized vis-à-vis the state, and been confronted with so much inmigration. These factors, as well as the cultural diversity of the Chittagong hill people and the peculiarities of the Bangladeshi state, defy easy comparisons with other groups employing ethnic strategies in the region. The Jummas are neither Bangladeshi Nagas nor Bangladeshi Jharkhandis.[63] Their movement is not simply an interethnic alliance; it seeks the creation of a new national collectivity, based on a homeland created by colonialism and decolonization, in the face of extreme adversity.[64] I have indicated that this development can be explained by the unusual combination of factors affecting the Chittagong Hills. The inhabitants of this area did not share a "traditional" sense of unity but nevertheless were ecologically and socioculturally isolated from the plains peasantry. The Bengali majority attained national statehood relatively late and a largely stagnant view of ethnic relations prevailed among those who held state power. In the new state the hills were a small border region with a minute population. An active policy of economic exploitation elicited local protests that went unheeded until armed resistance to inmigration, which hill people regard as an attempt to unload the effects of mass poverty in the plains at least partly onto themselves, led to militarization, warfare, and international attention.

Discussion is clearly possible concerning the extent to which hill people have accepted the Jumma identity in addition to their older ethnic identities. The intensity of the conflict and the clear cultural boundaries between hill people and Bengalis make it likely that the Jumma identity is now more salient than ever.[65] But the focus of this paper is not upon whether the Jumma identity has been universally accepted or whether the old ambivalence toward the Bengali model has turned into complete rejection (which seems unlikely but cannot be verified at present). Rather, this paper has sought to explain why in recent years a new identity has been "invented" at all, and why it has found a measure of acceptance. This in itself is a reflection of important and irreversible change, for "once [ethnic] boundaries have been heavily invested with interpretations and enactments, these acquire a logic and dynamic of their own, and can become...exceedingly difficult to alter" (Fishman 1977, 26). As the most outspoken sociocultural response to the political crisis in the Chittagong Hills, the concept of "Jumma" is here to stay. It will have to be taken into account by anyone planning to resolve that crisis.

CHAPTER 8

Ethnicity and the National Question in Pakistan: The Example of Baluchistan

HÉLÈNE VACHER

All of Pakistan's provinces, with the exception of Sind, are part of wider territories split between Pakistan and its neighbors. Baluchistan is shared with Iran, Pakhtunistan (North West Frontier Province) with Afghanistan, and Kashmir and Punjab with India. As soon as the new state came into being, Urdu became the national language. It was perceived by many to be the Islamic lingua franca of the subcontinent, although only 5 percent of the population were primarily Urdu speakers. Furthermore, Urdu speakers were chiefly immigrants, (*muhajirs*) from northern India who came at the time of Partition. Among the prevailing languages spoken in Pakistan, Baluchi and Pakhtu belong to the Iranian branch of the Indo-Iranian language family, in contrast with Sindi, Punjabi, and Urdu, which are related to Marathi, Gujarati, and Hindi in India and affiliated with the Indic branch. Other linguistic groups are represented by smaller communities. The imposition of Urdu on the nation when independence was achieved has hampered the integration of regional elites who perceive it as a segregative tool of the new state apparatus as well as a threat to their status. Consequently, the framework of federal institutions has been weakened by this handicap.

Pakistani nationhood has been accompanied by the ideology of an ideal community requiring the primacy of individual commitment to the nation instead of relying upon unifying symbols rooted in the identities and loyalties of existing social communities. The stiffening of religious-nationalist values in an ultimate ideological retreat is a relatively new phenomenon, as Muhammad Munir (1980), former president of the High Court, has emphasized. The very concept of the "ideology of Pakistan" was seldom used by politicians after 1947 before it was given a new lease on life by the Islamist parties from the 1960s onward. By doing so they have revived the "two-nations theory," which binds the idea of Pakistan to Islamic unity in opposition to India. The integrative logic of the new state was tested at an early stage when, in the name of the "rule of necessity," the military entered the political scene and eventually seized power in 1958. The army has been overwhelmingly Punjabi since Pakistan's inception, and the other provinces have eventually come to identify Pakistani rule with Punjabi dominance.

Relatively homogeneous sections of the population with different subsistence economies remained on the periphery of the modern national state. Although alliances were forged by the state's apparatus with Pakhtun tribes, Sind *waderas* (landlords) and fractions of the Muhajirs, the provincial elites as a whole had too narrow a base to bargain successfully for significant shares of the state's economic and political development. The process led to a dual economy with a "backward" periphery, especially in Baluchistan and the North West Frontier Province. These provinces provided reserves of manpower and raw-materials extraction, while the bulk of investments were channeled chiefly to Punjab and the cities of Karachi and Hyderabad. One result was that "nation building" became synonymous with the rise of new Punjabi elites who were linked to the old landed ones or to the military hierarchy. That development strongly contributed to growing "subnationalism" in Bengal, Baluchistan, and to some extent in the North West Frontier Province. In the latter the Pakhtuns, who were often supported in their irredentist movement by the Durrani dynasty and the subsequent Pakhtun regimes in Kabul, were much courted by the Pakistani state apparatus. The state agreed to exceptional concessions following previous arrangements made under the British Raj, for example, the free market of Landi Kotal, the tribal tolls at the Khyber Pass, and the "autonomous tribal areas." The integration into the army of high-ranking officers of Pakhtun origin under General Ayub Khan (1958–69), himself a Pakhtun, also undermined the nationalist movement in the North West Frontier Province and its support of other provinces' claims for autonomy.

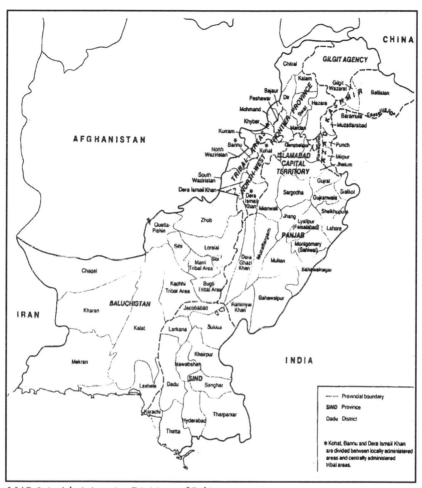

MAP 8.1. Administrative Divisions of Pakistan.

On 14 October 1955, the "One Unit" constitutional scheme merged the four provinces of Western Pakistan into a single unit. That move deeply antagonized provincial elites and triggered sporadic uprisings in Baluchistan, which lasted until the amnesty of 1967. It also laid the groundwork for the partition of Pakistan after General Khan rejected the "six points formula" seeking a confederated Pakistan presented by Sheikh Mujibur Rahman (leader of the Awami League). The Awami League (based in Eastern Bengal) was then supported by 75 percent of the electorate in Eastern Pakistan but Pakistan's military elite proved unable to cope with the situation since it could not abandon its narrow unitarian concepts nor the highly centralized forms of its institutions.

After the conflict ended in military defeat in 1971, the collapse of Pakistan's military machine left a vacuum to be filled by the politicians. The constitution of 1973 restored the federal system and authorized Pakistan's remaining four provinces to administer their own affairs within a somewhat democratic framework until the dismissal of the National Awami Party (NAP) governments in both Baluchistan and the North West Frontier Province in 1973. In Sind the Muhajir hold on urban economic sectors also was challenged by the expression of strong grievances by the indigenous peoples of rural Sind who made up the bulk of the support for Zulfikar Ali Bhutto's Pakistan People Party (PPP). The "language bill" passed by the Sind provincial assembly in July 1972, making Sindi the official language in the province, threw the gates open to widespread "ethnic riots." If the sweeping electoral victory of the PPP in Sind and Punjab in 1970 introduced mass politics in Pakistan, the urban riots in Sind revealed how little room for maneuver the government of Z. A. Bhutto had in appealing to national unity through the honor of "Masawat-i-Muhammadi" above ethno-regional identities.[1] The PPP government could not settle all the interprovincial contradictions that had accumulated since partition, especially during the period following the coercive takeover in October 1958 by Ayub Khan, whose rule lasted until March 1969.

In an apparent paradox, many of the provincial elites chose to support General Zia-ul-Haq's military coup in July 1977 by hailing the end of Bhutto's jacobinism. The martial-law regime of Zia-ul-Haq, who reasserted Islam and "Nizam-i-Mustafa" as the cornerstone of Pakistan's identity, combined pragmatic strategy with rough treatment in dealing with provincial unrest, as in Sind during the uprising initiated by the Movement for Restoration of Democracy in 1983.[2] In 1985, the restoration of the 1973 Constitution in the iron mold of the Islamist polity hardly represented a departure from the strong, centralized power imposed during the decade of Zia-ul-Haq's rule because the many amendments passed during and after the martial-law regime were retained.[3] While provinces' or minorities' political demands were successfully suppressed, new forms of interethnic feuds have materialized, first in Sind and then in the other provinces (Alavi 1991; Ahmed 1986). Neither the weak PPP government of Benazir Bhutto nor the present Islamic Democratic Alliance government, with strong support in Punjab, has responded successfully to the interethnic conflicts that are developing in Pakistan today.

Baluchistan, the Forgotten Province

The Baluch, as they call themselves, inhabit a very large area comprising parts of Pakistan, eastern Iran, and southern Afghanistan. Altogether they probably number less than 7 million, of which at least 70 percent are in Pakistan's province of Baluchistan. Most of the rest are divided between Iranian Baluchistan and the Seistan region of Afghanistan. Population estimates vary considerably, however, and Baluch authors have given figures as high as 30 million (Baluch 1975, 207). However, the lack of comprehensive and up-to-date surveys in both Afghanistan and Iran make reliable estimates highly unlikely. Pakistan's 1961 and 1981 censuses provide statistics according to language spoken that may not correlate with inherently fluid ethnic affiliations (Digard 1988).

The "ethnic minorities" of Pakistan represent one-third of the population and are highly heterogeneous. The majority Punjabi population occupies only 30 percent of the country's area, and most of Pakistan's natural resources are located outside the Punjab. The newly self-proclaimed "fifth nationality" made up of Muhajirs (some 6 to 8 percent of the population), with their strongholds in Karachi and Hyderabad, shifts its alliances to and from the central government and the minorities.

The province of Baluchistan accounts for 5.1 percent of the total population of Pakistan (84,300,000), according to the last census in 1981, but of the province's population only 36.31 and 20.68 percent are Baluchi or Brahui speakers, respectively. The 1981 census lists 4,332,000 inhabitants within the province of Baluchistan. The existence of expatriate communities in other provinces and countries, as well as blurred ethnic definitions, make it impossible to give precise population figures. Pakistani officials refer to Baluchi speakers but the nationalists and many Baluch people regard themselves as belonging to a broader ethnic identity. There are hundreds of thousands of Baluchi speakers in eastern Punjab and possibly 2 million in Sind. A few thousand Baluch also live in the Merv area of Turkmenistan but to what extent they identify themselves as Baluch is open to question.

Taking into consideration the expatriate communities, nearly half of the Baluch people live outside Baluchistan (Government of Pakistan 1991). At the beginning of the twentieth century some Baluch nationalists advocated the idea of a "Great Baluchistan" covering an area equivalent to present-day Pakistan.[4] However, no leader of any major movement since the Second World War has seriously taken up this

PHOTO: PRIVATE COLLECTION OF HÉLÈNE VACHER

PLATE 8.1. *Tribal gathering of Baluch during the Pariri Movement, Pakistan.*

proposal. Social developments, interethnic exchange, submission to different historical situations, Persian domination in Iran, and Punjabi rule in Pakistan have all produced distinct sets of conditions for Baluch living in different areas.

Although under Reza Shah Pahlavi and the Islamic Republic Baluch nationalist movements existed in Iran and received some backing from Baghdad, the center for the development of Baluch political and cultural identity has been chiefly what is known as Pakistani Baluchistan. The province of Baluchistan, at 134,000 square miles, constitutes a little over 40 percent of the total area of Pakistan. The few million Baluch living there are scattered in small fertile niches between wide areas of barren land where river inundation permits the growing of millet, barley, and wheat.

The Baluch keep donkeys, cattle, and camels but goats and sheep are the main source of wealth, and a seminomadic lifestyle is dictated by the need to find sufficient grazing lands (Scholz 1974). On Makran coastal land the tribes concentrate around oases where they trade milk, butter, and grain for dates. Their castelike social structure differs somewhat from that of their neighbors in that the bottom layer consists of descendants of East African slaves. For the inhabitants of Makran, "Baluch" specifically refers to free-born nomads and agriculturalists. In Karachi, people tend to regard all Makrani Baluch as racially distinct. Until the end of the 1970s the majority of the Baluch were seminomadic, with only a few tribes practicing "great camel nomadism," those in the Kheran desert, for example. Less than 5 percent of the land was cultivated, mostly by non-Baluch settlers.

Among the tribal groups that have played a prominent political role during the last few decades are the Marris, the Dombkis, the Mengals, the Bugtis, the Zehris, the Bizenjos, and the Raisanis. Each tribe has a chief, called a *sardar,* whose power and responsibilities used to vary, as did the internal organization of each tribe (Pehrson 1966).[5] Over a long period many tribes have undergone a process of disintegration; today they all are doing so. There are about fifteen "urban centers" in Baluchistan, including pre-British ones such as Kalat and Sibi. Only Quetta, a former British garrison town and now the capital of the province, has a population over three hundred thousand, and this is divided almost equally between the Baluch, Pakhtuns, and Punjabis. Census data (probably overestimated) indicate a literacy rate of 5 to 8 percent, in contrast to the national rate of 16 percent. At the end of the period in which the PPP controlled the central government, in 1976, the per capita income of Baluchistan was the lowest in Pakistan, US$54 per inhabitant per year. Today the per capita income in Punjab is twice as high. Life expectancy in Baluchistan is close to forty-two years, while the national average is sixty years.

After partition, rural Baluchistan remained extremely deprived. The Pakhtuns took control of most of the commercial life, which was previously in the hands of Sindhi Hindus. Then the Punjabis moved in and bought some of the best arable land, for example, in the Pat Feeder tract of Kalat during Ayub Khan's regime. Provincial administration has been predominantly Punjabi, with a few Baluch holding high-ranking positions. Similarly, the majority of the entrepreneurial class is non-Baluch except in a few areas such as marble quarrying and ship breaking. Baluchistan's industries account for only 1 percent of the country's total. Surveys indicate that underground water, as well as mineral resources (copper, gold, silver, pyrite, magnetite), are available in large quantities, and uranium ore also has been detected in the area of Dera Ghazi Khan, but any significant exploitation of these resources has been hindered by the province's underdeveloped infrastructure. The exploitation of natural gas is essentially concentrated around Sui in the Bugti area, accounting for 50 percent of Baluchistan's output. Acccording to the 1989–90 figures, Baluchistan produces two-thirds of Pakistan's gas, as opposed to one-third by Sind Province, which has considerably increased its output in the past decade (Government of Pakistan 1991). For this reason nationalist leaders claim that the royalties returned to the province are minimal in comparison with those redistributed to the regions in neighboring countries. The coal-mining industry is also held by non-Baluch, and most of the coal is used outside the province.

Zia-ul-Haq's period of rule changed the overall picture significantly. Baluch leadership adopted a low profile in order to avoid military confrontation. Maintaining an overinflated military budget and captivated by the arms race with India, the regime of Zia-ul-Haq paid little attention to collaboration with the provincial elites. Its religious dogmatism also was unattractive to the Baluch for whom tribal values have more meaning than do appeals to martial religious bigotry. Although the majority of the Baluch are Sunni Muslims of the Hanafi rite, tribesmen care little for the ritualistic, martial brand of Islam that was promoted in Pakistan under Zia. The five hundred thousand Zikris, a heterodox sect from the Makran coast, often have been suppressed by orthodox Muslims and accordingly have chosen to side with the Baluch nationalists.

Four factors must be considered in assessing Baluch demands for indigenous rights and autonomy: the evolution of minority politics, economic deprivation and government-directed development strategy, population dislocation, and strategic constraints within the region.

Four Decisive Factors

Minority Politics

Whereas the Bengalis were at the forefront of the struggle for national rights during the period preceding the separation of Bangladesh from Pakistan, the Baluch were always in the center of resistance to hegemonist tendencies in the western wing of Pakistan. The two long wars of 1963–67 and 1973–77 fought between separatists and the state during the regimes of Ayub Khan and Z. A. Bhutto bear witness to their determination. Other minorities regard Baluchistan as a symbol of resistance to Punjabi dominance. The Baluch tribal and political leadership escaped almost intact after the four years of severe conflict that ended with the imposition of martial law in July 1977.

Baluch leaders are prone to distrust the politics in which other minorities engage. The Pakhtuns are regarded as kinsmen, sometimes with the aura of common "Aryan" blood, but they are also seen as competitors for grazing land in northern Baluchistan. Today they outnumber the Baluch in the provincial capital Quetta. As a result of the Afghan conflict, which brought successive waves of Pakhtun immigrants from Afghanistan into the crowded North West Frontier Province, friction has increased between the groups competing for scarce resources. The Pakhtuns often have been depicted as uncompromising in their commitment to maintaining their tribal integrity, and the historical role played by leaders such as the "Frontier Gandhi" Abdul Ghaffar Khan and his son Wali Khan has frequently been noted. Today the Awami National Party (ANP), successor of the National Democratic Party, which itself was once called the National Awami Party, commands close to one-fourth of the province's electoral votes and is one of the main proponents of national autonomy in Pakistan. Once branded as "antinational" because of its commitment to a nonaligned foreign policy and its alleged sympathy with successive Afghani regimes, the ANP has emerged nevertheless as a stabilizing force in the North West Frontier Province. It has worked out an alliance with the Islamic Democratic Alliance (IDA) to counter the PPP. Most of the Baluch nationalists are suspicious of ANP leadership, recalling that a broad section of the Pakhtun elite has ranged itself against them and with the center since 1947.

The Sinds constitute the largest "minority" in Pakistan and they maintain strong cultural and tribal ties with the Baluch. In Sind Province many families claim to be of Baluch descent, for example, the Talpur family, which ruled Sind at the turn of the nineteenth century and still plays an important role in provincial and national politics. However, Baluch leaders harbor resentment over the Sinds' silence during Z. A. Bhutto's years. When Sind was subjected to pitiless repression in 1983, the Baluchs adopted a wait-and-see attitude. The nationalist leaders of the other minorities interpreted the Baluch posture as an indication that they did not want to turn their province into a battlefield once again for the defense of the minorities as a whole.

Economic Development and Social Change

Economic deprivation has been one essential factor, though an indirect one, in all the previous insurgencies in tribal areas. The general amnesty of 1977 was followed by implementation of an impressive plan, the Special Development Plan (SDP), which was financed through an American aid package of $2 billion delivered when the war broke out in Afghanistan. The plan was backed by bilateral aid from Japan, Canada, Australia, the EEC (as such), and Persian Gulf countries. The Baluchistan Area Development Program, a project of the U.S. Agency for International Development (USAID), was set up in the meantime.

The flow of money channeled through numerous schemes has introduced some drastic changes in the province. In 1981, Dr. Mahbubul al Haq, a prominent economist who has held important posts in Pakistan (he was Zia-ul-Haq's finance minister) and in international institutions such as the World Bank, described the SDP, as it was mapped out by the United Nations and the World Bank, as aiming to transform the poverty-stricken province "overnight." Fifty percent of the investments were earmarked for infrastructural improvements. Roads, railways, airports, electricity, and irrigation networks, large development projects (including a copper-mining center in Saindak in northwest Baluchistan), and a coal mine near the Afghan border in Chagai were designed. Omara, Pasni, Gwadar, and Jiwani on the coastal Makran were chosen for the development of port installations.

The content and effects of the implementation of this ambitious program for "development and modernization" are still controversial and hard to assess. On the one hand, the population of Quetta doubled in the 1980s as the city experienced a mini-boom. The bazaars are now packed with all kinds of goods and industrial products, and the streets are filled with Japanese motorcycles and cars. On the other hand, it seems that capital and investments were not usefully absorbed in the remote areas. Some argue that widespread corruption combined with insufficient infrastructure and experience were the main obstacles to the success of the SDP. The program's preliminary surveys have been described as overly optimistic, while the lack of impact in inner Baluchistan has led to a greater economic imbalance within the province.

Dislocation

The third factor partially proceeds from the second. Economic imbalance between urbanized and "tribal" areas has aggravated "ethnic" dislocation, although Baluchistan has never contained a single homogeneous people. Hindu merchants have lived side by side with the Baluch even after partition, and the Brahuis, who are said to descend from an earlier Dravidian people, retain distinct characteristics despite the fact that they have been assimilated by the Baluch culture.[6] The majority of the Sinds, Muhajirs, and Punjabis who moved into the province have settled permanently, and more than 1.5 million Pakhtuns are settled mostly in the northern region and in Quetta.

In contrast to movement into the province, there has been an outflow of Baluch, especially as a result of the last war fought there.

During the 1970s, many Baluch migrated to Karachi and the labor-hungry Gulf states. At the beginning of the 1980s, the Baluch living in the Gulf countries numbered three hundred thousand or more. They number at least eight hundred thousand in Karachi, residing mostly in the slum areas, and there are as many scattered throughout inner Sind (these should not be confused with the earlier Baluch settlers who became Sindi speakers). A few hundred thousand Baluch also inhabit the Punjab, chiefly the district of Dera Ghazi Khan, a traditional Baluch stronghold. The accelerated concurrent trends of massive Baluch migration out of Baluchistan and migration of non-Baluch into Baluchistan has led to a paradoxical situation whereby the Baluch are probably a minority in their own province while more than half live outside Baluchistan. Furthermore, this situation has contributed to a new consciousness of identity among the Baluch migrants who are less bound by personal loyalties. The increased activity of the Baluch Ittehad in Karachi, a nonpolitical organization established in the mid-1980s to enhance the welfare of the Baluch community, can also be understood as a sign of growing detribalization.

Regional Constraints

The regional dimension has significantly affected the course of events in the province of Baluchistan. The strategic interest of the United States in Pakistan dates back to the inception of the state. From the late 1970s, two main considerations prompted the United States to work toward strengthening Pakistan and especially the province of Baluchistan. One reason was the loss of the chief ally of America in the Gulf region when Reza Pahlavi's regime in Iran collapsed. Another was the end of an East-West equilibrium that had prevailed under M. K. Daoud in Afghanistan. In 1981, J. Buckley, then an American undersecretary of state, and D. MacPherson, the chief administrator of USAID, declared during a visit to Pakistan that "aid to Baluchistan was essential for the global strength of the country."[7] The Baluch nationalists were quick to point out the geo-strategic dimension of the SDP, and one of their leaders, Sardar Ataullah Mengal, explained that "Baluchistan is already under the U.S. Central Command. The U.S. has bases for the use of its fleets and is in a position to determine the Pakistan government's policy in Baluchistan."[8]

The U.S. Central Command, initiated in January 1983, which was formed out of the Rapid Deployment Force swiftly set up in the wake of events in Afghanistan and Iran by President Jimmy Carter in early 1980, is relying upon the strategic concept of "prepositioning." The U.S. Central Command broadened its geographical zone to nineteen countries bordering on the Indian Ocean. The design of the complex of airfields and roads that was a main component of the SDP was regarded with strong suspicion by the Baluch nationalists. But the Pakistan government has consistently denied charges that there is a formal agreement concerning concessions to the U.S. Central Command. For ten years there have been rumors about a base in Gwadar established to replace the gigantic facilities of Shah Bahar in Iran. Despite speculation, and the fact that the area is closed to most foreigners, no conclusive evidence has been produced.

However, about the existence of formal agreements between the Gulf Cooperation Council (a joint military defense pact grouping Kuwait, Bahrain, Qatar, United Arab Emirates, Saudi Arabia, and Oman) and the Pakistan government there is no doubt. In the early 1980s, two Pakistani army divisions were quartered in Saudi Arabia until the Saudis asked them to remove Shia officers and troops whom the Saudis feared might have ties to, or might show allegiance to, Iran, where the Shia are in the majority.[9] Pakistan has also trained pilots in the Gulf states and maintains a close relationship with Oman, the only country in the region to have officially accepted American bases prior to the 1990–91 Gulf conflict. During the 1980s, a tripartite relationship was consolidated in which the United States provided arms and loans, Saudi Arabia and other Gulf countries provided petrodollars, and Pakistan supplied the technological know-how and military personnel.[10]

Pakistani and western politicians often assessed the Baluch struggle as a cover-up for a "Soviet move towards the warm waters," although the arguments given to substantiate such a "grand theory" were always controversial.[11] One of the serious handicaps the Baluch nationalists had to face was the persistent lack of external support, especially during their armed uprising of 1973–77. They were fighting the Pakistan army with Second World War rifles, with Chinese/U.S. arms captured from the Pakistan forces, and even with nineteenth-century guns. Although Soviet historians long ago recognized the "nationalities" of both Baluchistan and Pakhtunistan (Gankovsky 1971, 1977), their views were confined to the realm of strictly academic interest once the USSR recognized Pakistan as a nation-state. In 1977, the Baluch, led by Mir Hazar Ramkhani and organized in the Baluch People's Liberation Front (BPLF), chose to stay in Afghanistan where three camps had been installed during the 1973–77 war. The group promoted a socialist program while emphasizing the "positive side of nomadic societies" (Jabal 1977). It was backed by Sardar Khair Bux Marri, a former leader of the NAP government who also decided to settle in Kabul.

This "Kabul connection" was neither new nor exceptional. Successive Afghan regimes have granted asylum to Baluch refugees because of the importance of the Pakhtun issue in Afghanistan's national politics and because of the strong and popular affiliations the Pakhtuns have with Baluchistan. Soviet strategists played down the "Baluch question," however, and kept the refugees living at a near-subsistence level (Dastarac and Levent 1981).

Although the bipolar world is gone, the Baluch today are not free of strategic pressures. In the aftermath of the Gulf war, the Gulf Cooperation Council seems almost moribund, and security arrangements yet to come will surely involve the four hundred miles of the Makran coast. Then Riyadh, Washington, and Teheran may have a major say in the new regional political set-up. The Baluch quest for rights and autonomy is fraught with formidable difficulties that need to be put into historical perspective.

From Tribes to Confederacy

Baluchistan has known all the advantages and inconveniences of being a de facto buffer zone. The desolate and inhospitable Baluch territories were not subjected to direct alien domination until recent times. If it did not lie across one of the few East-West transport routes, Baluchistan would have remained a remote, natural fortress. Instead the Baluch have borne the consequences of standing in the path of first the Persian and Mughal empires and then the British Raj. Imperial interest in Baluchistan was limited chiefly to control of the Bolan Pass (which commands access to and from the Helmand and Indus valleys), the recruitment of troops, trade relations, and military expeditions. The many autonomous Baluch tribes took advantage of opportunities to levy tribute from travellers along the highways.

It is difficult to trace the early history of the Baluch tribes as they migrated from the northwest to their present location (possibly from a region south of the Caspian Sea), a process that went on for many centuries.[12] By the fourteenth century the Baluch tribes were moving toward Makran under pressure from Persian rulers. The first recorded account of a Baluch confederacy dates back to the fifteenth century when attempts were made to form a loose political union around the Brahui kingdom of Kalat, the Makran coastal area, and the Dodai confederacy of Derajat. The Baluch then were far from being a homogeneous people, and there is no evidence that they had a unified social system. In their progressive drift toward the southeast, the tribes incorporated or adopted various social customs, which may partially explain the wide range of social organizations and cultural features found in Baluchistan today.

The historical process that produced Baluch identity cannot be explained by reference to ethnic or even linguistic unity. The Brahuis, who still preserve some aspects of their own language, paradoxically have formed the political backbone of the Baluch tribal confederacy (Elfenbein 1960; Swidler 1977). The confederacy was centered in Kalat, in the Jhalawan Range, where it was entangled in endless struggles with the Mughal and Persian empires. Kalat submitted to the emperor Akbar in 1595 but the Safavid, a dynasty of Arab origin that ruled Persia from 1501 to 1736, fought to subdue it and regained control over Kandahar in the middle of the seventeenth century. By the end of that century the Brahui chiefdom had incorporated the Makran area and eventually established the first Baluch *khanate* at the beginning of the eighteenth century. In 1714, Mir Abdullah Khan ruled a domain stretching from the Helmand Valley to Bandar Abbas and from Dera Ismail Khan to Karachi, encompassing an area similar to the one dreamed of by the modern proponents of a "Great Baluchistan."

By the middle of the eighteenth century the Khanate of Kalat was part of a three-sided relationship between the Persian empire, the declining Mughal empire, and the young Afghan state of Ahmad Shah Abdali. For the first years of his long reign, Nasir Khan, the Khan of Kalat, paid tribute to the Afghan ruler for tactical reasons that mainly derived from dynastic difficulties. When he eventually refused to declare allegiance, the ensuing Afghan-Baluch war turned to his advantage. The Treaty of Kalat, of 1758, recognized full sovereignty for the Khanate of Kalat. However, Nasir Khan joined forces with Ahmad Shah Abdali against the Persians, the Hindu Marathas, and the Sikhs. At the same time he annexed the Dodai confederacy of Derajat and tried to raid Sistan. But soon after Nasir Khan's death in 1794, the Baluch Khanate lost its independence, ending the first enduring attempt to forge independent institutions and political unity throughout Baluch territories. The equilibrium of the Kalat state was jeopardized by dynastic feuds and tribal strife. At the turn of the nineteenth century it also faced growing pressure from the British in India, who were gradually overpowering the frail Mughal empire and the fragments of the Maratha confederacy.

The British Raj and the Sandeman System

Sind and Baluchistan played little part in the affairs of the British East India Company until the turn of the nineteenth century when missions were sent by the company to the Talpur Amirs who had ruled the Sind from 1783 and were virtually independent of Afghan tutelage. Besides trade interest and French intrigue, which first attracted the company's concern, the changes affecting the regional scene in northwest India led the British into the so-called forward policy. Once they had gained the neutrality of Ranjit Singh's Sikh Kingdom of Lahore, they drastically revised their strategic position. Turmoil inside Afghanistan resulting from rivalry among Durrani offspring after the death of Ahmad Shah Abdali/Durrani was conducive to British security but also caused them concern about a possible Persian or Russian threat. Direct British involvement in Afghan affairs and the pitiful outcome of the first Anglo-Afghan war (1839–42) led to the abrupt entrance of Sind and Baluchistan into colonial history. The divided Talpur Amirs could not hold out against the British attack. Using the pretext of the Amirs' "malignant neutrality" during the Anglo-Afghan war, the British peremptorily annexed Sind in 1843 in spite of the treaty concluded in 1832. Baluchistan's ruling elite met an even more tragic fate. In order to invade Afghanistan, British troops did not use the Khyber Pass but chose to journey through the Bolan Pass, "the door of Baluchistan." In that venture they stormed Kalat and killed Mehrah Khan in 1839.

The die was cast. Nasir Khan II (1830–57) was appointed by the British in 1841 and signed a treaty that confirmed British dominance over the Kalat state fourteen years later. British political agents were appointed to assist and control the Khan, and in return for his loyalty he received an annual subsidy. The British Raj demarcated the borders between Baluchistan and Sind in 1862.

Baluchistan's history during the nineteenth century reflects its gradual integration into the British status quo of the "three-fold frontier," and the effects are manifest in contemporary Baluchistan. The British perceived the frail tribal structure as both an opportunity and a weakness along the Raj's frontiers. Therefore, Sir Robert Sandeman advocated a policy of reinforcing the authority of the *sardars*, the tribal chiefs, with direct contacts and subsidies (Thornton 1895). The British thereby undermined loyalty to the Khanate in order to control "the dangerous turbulence of tribesmen if they be left to themselves" (Chano 1983, 43). The *sardars* were offered a quick path to wealth through participation in infrastructural projects—for example, by excavating canals. The viceroy received the Khan of Kalat and the prominent *sardars* in Delhi with all the due trappings of honor, including a pretense to feudal bonds of kinship.

On the whole the Sandeman system appears to have succeeded in meeting its major aims: keeping the tribes under control, avoiding polarization, and bolstering a unified pro-British front among many of the tribes. Rather than a restoration of sociopolitical structures that already had begun to disintegrate, the Sandeman arrangement resembled a formal caricature of them. Moreover, it did not affect all the tribes to the same extent, although in some areas it did serve to freeze the tribal social system in the state in which the British found it. A new treaty, concluded in December 1876, extended the 1854 arrangement. One year before the outbreak of the second Anglo-Afghan war the Baluchistan Agency was created, with a garrison town established at Quetta to secure safe passage between Afghanistan and India.

> The century ended in a mold set by the British.

> The Kalat mission might be the father of the Central Asian mission in the future. The agent will reside...chiefly in Quetta....He would have leisure for collecting information for Kandahar, Herat, Kabul, Balk. English rupees would try conclusions with Russians rubles in the Zenana and the diwan.[13]

By 1900, "assigned districts" such as the Pishin and Sibi tracts and the Afghan border region of Chagai and West-Sinjrani had been incorporated into British India as the new province of British Baluchistan.[14] Railway lines were built, including the Bolan-Chaman line to the Afghan border, and telegraph lines installed. Although they remained formally linked to Afghanistan, most of the northern tribes (the Bori, Zhob, and Khetran) were brought under British administration.

Independence and the Rise of Baluch Nationalism

The Khanate of Kalat, surrounded by territories under direct British administration, was given the ambiguous status of an "Indian protected state," which served to maximize the British empire's security while minimizing administrative and welfare costs.[15] But what had been good enough for securing imperial frontiers was inadequate for the needs and aspirations of a people entering the "modern world." With the passing of the first decades of the twentieth century, the Baluchs gave new form to the expression of their political discontent, which they exhibited in sporadic tribal uprisings. The First World War and the 1917 Russian Revolution had repercussions in the remote Baluchistan province. The Marri tribes revolted against the recruitment of soldiers and mercenaries. Rebels fled to the Soviet Union and formed a delegation to the "Baku Congress of the Peoples of the East." Soviet influence in Baluchistan (often overestimated in later years) dated from that time, and Lenin's appeal for the "right of self-determination for all oppressed nations" affected the already developing nationalist resistance.

At the end of the First World War, Baluch secret activities and propaganda chiefly advocated a "traditional" nationalist ideology not averse to the concept of "Great Baluchistan" encompassing the Kalat state, the British-administered territories, and Western Baluchistan in Iran. In the 1930s, an organization known as Anjuman I Ittihad Baluchistan (Baluchistan Unity Association), soon followed by the Kalat State National Party (KSNP), started openly to promote reforms, including representative institutions, in the state of Kalat. The reaction of the Khanate was mixed. Even if Khan Mir Ahmad Yar might personally sympathize with the "modernist" nationalists, he had little room in which to maneuver. On the one hand, the Khans were dependant upon a consensus with the *sardars* on every major issue. On the other, they were under the tight control of British political agents. In this position they had to maintain their historical legitimacy, which was drawn from the tribal confederacy, as well as taking into consideration growing demands for democratic institutions.

The leaders of the Anjuman and its offspring, the KSNP, expressed their loyalty to and acknowledged their roots in the traditional democratic tribal organization, thereby emphasizing the autocratic features of the Khanate and the power of the *sardars* (referred to as "feudal" lords). By the end of the 1930s, the Khan of Kalat made known his willingness to consider representative institutions and a constitutional government. But most of the *sardars* were strongly opposed to the KSNP and put pressure on the Khan to restrict nationalist activities. The leaders of the KSNP were obliged to move their headquarters into the British-administered territories. They went underground shortly afterward, when the Defense of India Act was passed at the outbreak of the Second World War. Despite the prospects for self-rule, and even for complete independence after British withdrawal from India, powerful factors led

Baluchistan down an increasingly ominous path that included frozen social and political structures, pervasive factionalism, and ambiguities in the juridical and administrative situation connected with the British transfer of power in India.

Because Kalat was formally a sovereign and independent state dominated by the British Raj (the Baluchistan case was often compared to that of Nepal), different schemes were solicited for the future of Kalat State and the British leased territories. The Muslim League, as well as the departing British and the Indian National Congress, contemplated independence for Kalat together with the Baluch territories that had been leased to the British.[16] While the British cabinet mission left unresolved the issue of accession to a new status by the autonomous princely states, the cabinet memorandum of 12 May 1946 mentioned the possibility of "entering into a federal relationship with the successor Government or Governments...or failing this, entering into particular political arrangements with it or them" (Mansergh 1977, 516–17). That policy was confirmed as late as June 1947. M. A. Jinnah stated the same day his demand to the cabinet mission: "After the constitutions of the Pakistan Federal Government...it will be open to each Province...to opt out...provided the wishes of the people of that Province are ascertained by a referendum."[17]

On 12 August 1947, in anticipation of the official creation of Pakistan on 14 August, the Khan of Kalat declared Kalat's independence and announced the establishment of two legislatures, with the Upper House reserved to the *sardars*. Elections were held in a short time and gave the majority in the Lower House to Baluch nationalists despite an official ban on the KSNP. Suspicion regarding Pakistan's designs grew during the two sessions of the Kalat Assembly held in September and December 1947. When the Punjab, the Sind, and the North West Frontier Province decided to merge to form Pakistan, the majority in the assembly expressed their preference for full independence by voting against the measure, although the assembly did accept the need for special agreements with Pakistan on such issues as security and foreign policy. Pakistan already had refused to return the former British-administered territories to Kalat and eventually made it clear that it would only accept unconditional accession. The confederation of the Baluch states under the rule of the Khan of Kalat included the states of Las Bela, Makran, and Kharan. The confederation was broken when those three states joined Pakistan in March 1948. General Akbar Khan received the order to move from Quetta to Kalat, and on 1 April 1948 the

Pakistan army occupied the constitutional "vacuum" of Baluchistan. The Khan protested but signed the accession of the state of Kalat and of British Baluchistan to Pakistan. The Baluch nationalist leaders were jailed or exiled.

To justify this blatant intervention, Pakistan claimed that a body of tribal *sardars,* the Shahi Jirga, meeting in Quetta in June 1947, had decided to join the Constituent Assembly of Pakistan. Pakistan did not mention that the electoral college had been appointed by British authorities and that the purpose of the meeting was to discuss British Baluchistan.

The Kalat Lower House unanimously voted for a resolution against the merger with Pakistan but the Khan temporized in fear of the defection of the many *sardars* who had been bewildered by the rise of the nationalist party. Their unassertive policy gave the Muslim League enough time to consolidate, and this ended the Khan's last chance to reestablish his legitimacy. The imposition of accession and the surrender by the Khan triggered the first rebellion under Pakistani rule. Prince Abdul Karim, the Khan's brother and governor of Makran (previously annexed by Pakistan), started an armed movement in the Jhalawan area with the backing of some nationalist leaders and the tacit approval of the Khan, who officially declared him a rebel. Because of poor planning and the lack of expected support from Afghanistan, the prince and his followers were forced to surrender. The door was then shut on rebellion or constitutional struggle within the new state established by the Muslim League.

Suppression and Resistance

During the forty-five years of the existence of Pakistan four conflicts have erupted in Baluchistan in 1948, 1958–60, 1963–67, and 1973–77. The first was almost a symbolic gesture of resistance at the time of the creation of Pakistan. The second began as a reaction to the imposition of the "one unit" scheme and the establishment of the Ayub Khan dictatorship in 1958, and ended in tragedy with the hanging of six nationalist leaders in July 1960.[18] The third was sparked in the main tribal areas of the province and lasted, with sporadic fighting, for more than five years. The last war affected virtually the whole province: from 1973 to 1977 one hundred thousand soldiers were pitted against a few thousand guerrillas. In a thinly populated region, fragile in ecological terms and economically deprived, ten years of fighting have left deep wounds, particularly in tribal areas.

By abolishing in November 1969 the "one-unit outrage," conceived to insure the dominance of the "Western Wing" of Pakistan, General Yahya Khan introduced new ways to broaden a democratic and federal framework. In the aftermath of the traumatic events in Bangladesh during the civil war, which ended in the secession of the Eastern Wing, the Western Wing of Pakistan had to establish some viable institutional accommodation for its minorities if it hoped to survive. The National Awami Party and the Jamiat Ulama-i-Islam (Assembly of Ulama for Islam, or JUI), which won a majority during the 1970–71 provincial assembly elections in the two provinces of Baluchistan and the North West Frontier, were called upon by Z. A. Bhutto to sign a tripartite agreement in March 1972. The understanding provided for lifting martial law and drafting a new constitution, for consultations with majority parties in the provinces before appointing governors, and for guarantees that each province would be allowed to form its own government by parliamentary majority.

The NAP constituted the largest single group in the provincial assemblies of the North West Frontier Province and Baluchistan (eight out of twenty seats in the latter). But to achieve the majority needed to form governments, the NAP had to negotiate with the JUI, which represented the interests of the orthodox Muslims and notables in the North West Frontier Province and in the Pakhtun-dominated districts of Baluchistan. In April 1972, the federal government appointed the Baluch nationalist leader, Ghaus Bux Bizenjo, as governor of Baluchistan. Ataullah Mengal became chief minister, and Khair Bux Marri became the chairman of the NAP parliamentary group in the assembly. A detailed history of the eleven-month NAP government is yet to be written.

The first attempts made by the provincial government to "Baluchistanize" the regional administration and the pressures exerted by tribesmen on the Punjabi landholders antagonized the Punjabis. The NAP government formed a regional guard, established its own press, and launched a program aimed at upgrading Baluch culture. The leaders of the NAP also made statements on foreign issues that stressed their determination to pursue a nonaligned foreign policy. Different interpretations have been made of the sudden decision by Z. A. Bhutto to dismiss the provincial governments on 12 February 1973. The official pretext was that Soviet arms and ammunition ordered by Baluch leaders had been found in the Iraqi embassy in Islamabad, although evidence of the conspiracy was never revealed. Far from pointing to the leaders of the

Baluch provincial government, the few available established facts lead to other conclusions (see Viennot 1973; and Harrison 1981, 34–35).

Apart from Z. A. Bhutto's "hunger for power" and the worries of the Pakistan national leadership about the strengthening of the NAP government's grip in both Baluchistan and the North West Frontier Province, which could undermine their prerogatives, it seems once again that higher regional strategical concerns were overwhelming. In his letter appointing G. B. Bizenjo as governor of Baluchistan, Z. A. Bhutto warned him that "movements such as the Azad Baluchistan [Free Baluchistan] movement, however nebulous, should be firmly put down and not permitted to affect our relations with foreign powers, especially friendly neighboring countries" (Government of Pakistan 1974). The Shah of Iran became concerned that a Baluch provincial government in Pakistan could "contaminate" the Iranian Baluch, and he may have tried to obtain guarantees from G. B. Bizenjo when he visited Teheran in 1973. However, the meeting proved inconclusive.

When the first clashes between guerrillas and army troops occurred in April 1973, Z. A. Bhutto flew to Teheran where he immediately received US$200 million in military aid. The assistance increased when Pakistan's army enlarged its operations in Baluchistan. Islamabad, for example, received thirty Huey Cobra helicopters, sometimes with Iranian pilots (see Harrison 1981). The Baluch soon appreciated that the Persian and Punjabi elites were colluding in order to crush their moves toward self-determination. While there are reliable accounts of some major battles, such as the one that occurred in Chamalang in September 1974, it appears that thousands of Baluch civilian deaths, by bombardment and in various military actions, went unrecorded. At the peak of the war, eight thousand tribesmen (mostly Marri) fled to Afghanistan where they were allowed to settle as refugees. In 1978, some six thousand prisoners were released from the Pakistani jails, and a number of reports testified that torture was common.[19] Nevertheless, because of the scarcity of reliable figures, the magnitude of the devastation caused by the war will only be determined with time.

Among the first actions of the military junta after it took power in July 1977, were the declaration of a cease-fire, the release of NAP leaders jailed in Hyderabad, and the opening of negotiations. Several meetings were held in Islamabad in 1977–78. Although Pakhtun leaders such as Wali Khan, moved by their resentment of Z. A. Bhutto, agreed to discuss a political settlement with the junta, the Baluch leadership made it clear that they were not just fighting individuals. Groups of Baluch who went to Afghanistan declined an amnesty on the grounds that the fighting had been waged against an "illegal government." In 1979, K. B. Marri and A. Mengal, who did not trust a settlement with the martial-law authorities, went quietly into exile. G. B. Bizenjo chose to enter the mainstream of Pakistani politics.

Current Situation and Prospects

The wars fought in Baluchistan since 1947 did not directly challenge the existence of Pakistan's state but they did aim to protect the integrity of major tribal territories. As such they have entered Baluch political mythology. Armed confrontation mostly occurred in the inhospitable *jabals* (mountains) and scarcely extended to the urban milieu or beyond Baluchistan's borders. Revolts and insurgencies erupted every time the central authorities tried to build roads of strategic importance in the highlands, to drill for mineral resources, or to "modernize and disarm the tribals." Most "modernizing" moves directly confront the tribal ethos. For instance, to a Baluch tribesman arms represent a guarantee of security and are strong symbols of identity, hence attempts made by external authorities to take away what is perceived as a natural right are interpreted as a direct assault on personal dignity or *ryvaj* (the traditional code of honor).

Despite dislocation resulting from economic pressure and wars, the tribal system has remained at the core of Baluch society. The last war hastened the decay of traditional sociopolitical forms, and the *jabals* offered the ultimate sanctuary for tribal values and identity. Furthermore, guerrilla activities received the strongest support wherever tribal institutions had resisted "feudalization" (meaning the *sardars'* legal ownership of land and their ability to transfer or sell that property). The persistence of the tribal ethos during the twentieth century helps to explain the ability of tribal leaders to sustain long periods of fighting without external assistance.

In this respect two widespread and recurring assumptions of the Punjabi elites have to be considered: first, that the "troubles" are just the result of the activities of "reactionary" *sardars* manipulating emotions in order to maintain archaic structures; and, second, that the troubles are fomented by foreign agents in order to dismember Pakistan. Such arguments reflect the prejudices evident in Pakistani government statements and the press alike, they served to induce public support for a civilian government that embarked upon a war only two years after the disaster of Bangladesh. Today they are used to render suspicious any move to assert regional autonomy. Z. A. Bhutto emphasized that his policy was aimed at curtailing the "worst remnants of the oppressive feudal system in the form of the sardari system" (Sayeed 1980). But the widely publicized "Bhutto's tour" of Baluchistan in April 1976 and the abolition of *sardar* institutions (enacted in May 1976) were concerned with only some of the features of the *sardar* system, mainly judicial powers, while the pattern of landholding was left untouched.[20] Besides, the NAP government had undertaken a similar move in 1972 by passing a resolution in the provincial assembly. The government's rhetoric succeeded in isolating Baluch leadership from Pakistan's political mainstream but it failed to conceal the collusion between the central government and most of the 108 *sardars*. Only a few *sardars* sided with the Baluch resistance and these were jailed in Hyderabad until the end of the Bhutto regime.

The second argument is even weaker. As already noted, successive governments in Kabul had been lukewarm in their backing of Baluch insurgency. Only the nationalist-minded Afizullah Amin seemed ready to support a pan-Pakhtun policy including the Baluch, and he thereby greatly antagonized his Soviet advisers. The so-called Baluch card was never considered seriously in the Kremlin, as, among other considerations, Pakistan was instrumental in maintaining Moscow's leverage on Indian foreign policy. On the contrary, one specific aspect of the Baluch question is the low degree of internationalization it experienced during the "second cold war."

If the cultural and social deprivation of Baluchistan since its accession to Pakistan has been a determining factor in Baluch nationalism, the more recent development programs can be questioned in the light of their vastly disruptive effects on indigenous social patterns. On the other hand, the viability of a Baluch nation might also be queried in view of persistent divisions within the Baluch leadership. While the Punjabi intelligentsia, be it conservative or liberal, dismisses a viable "Azad Baluchistan," veteran leaders such as A. Mengal point out that no one today questions the viability nor the historical legitimacy of such neighboring entities as the United Arab Emirates, Bahrain, or Qatar. They argue that Baluchistan, with its vast coastline, mineral wealth, and low population, could prove as permanently successful as an isolated and landlocked Pakistan-Punjab, and that an alliance with an urbanized and agriculturally developed Sind should also be given a chance. However abstract and debatable these arguments might appear today, Baluch lead-

ers refuse to be intimidated by yesterday's even more abstract concept—
Pakistan. Despite "the declaration of independence" issued by A. Mengal
in 1983, which made the first full-fledged demand for total independence, nationalist rhetoric is still used by most Baluch politicians only as
an option in a bargaining strategy with the central government. Baluch
politics is highly fluid and its leadership is far from homogeneous or
consistent.

Exiled to Afghanistan since the early 1980s, the main leaders of the
1973–77 rebellion have been successfully marginalized since the Zia-ul-
Haq period. The political vacuum created inside Baluchistan has been
filled by the Baluchistan Student Organisation (BSO), which has been
the cradle of nationalist militancy since 1967. By choosing to reject the
terms of the political amnesty offered by Zia-ul-Haq the hard core of the
guerrilla movement led by Mir Hazar Ramkhani at least had the satis-
faction of denying the right of the Pakistani state to settle the conflict on
its own premises. If not a military force as such, a sanctuary was kept
intact in Baluch politics. But the continuous development of a political
movement inside Baluchistan was not guaranteed.

A decade later, political life in Baluchistan revolves first around
tribal figures. K. B. Marri, whose long, self-imposed exile in Europe and
Afghanistan ended in May 1992, still attracts a significant following and
respect in Baluchistan. But as a *sardar,* his influence does not go far
beyond his tribe, the Marri, and there is no certainty that the reputation
he enjoys all over Pakistan as an incorruptible and steady leader can be
converted into political power. The ascendancy of the aging nationalist
leader A. Mengal, *sardar* of the Mengal tribe, also has been eroded by a
long exile in London. His choice not to settle permanently in Pakistan
since his first return in the summer of 1989 may have been detrimental
to the success of his views within the nationalist movement. Nonetheless,
he has the support of his tribe and is a potent voice within the Baluchistan National Movement (BNM) led by his son Mir Akhtar Mengal.
Maintaining close links since 1979 with K. B. Marri, A. Mengal does not
share the latter's self-styled Marxist leanings and may remain a symbolic,
"pure," nationalist leader following the collapse of "the socialist camp."

The death of G. B. Bizenjo in August 1989 deprived the Baluch,
and probably Pakistan, of their most skillful politician. A moderate, he
always advocated parliamentary politics from the time of the Kalat
assembly when he voted against the accession of Baluchistan to Pakistan.
In 1979, he established the Pakistan National Party (PNP), as a succes-

sor of the NAP, in order to provide an adequate channel for the aspirations of a rising middle class in Baluchistan.

The PNP does not fight for the independence of Baluchistan but advocates a loose federation. Nevertheless, Bizenjo pointed out again and again how artificial are the frontiers of all regional states, having been created as by-products of colonial history. After a congress held by the PNP in November 1989 in Quetta, the party included in its program "the right of self-determination for the nationalities within the framework of Pakistan," complete control over resources by the respective federating units, and a reduction of the federal armed forces. Like his father, the new president of the PNP, Bizen Bizenjo, has no tribal power base as such. But since 1988 the party has been able to enroll powerful tribal chiefs from the Jhalawan and Sarawan areas. This has enlarged its electorate but it has also sparked intense rivalries. Keeping in view the inclusion in the summer of 1989 of both the radical wing of the BSO (known as Zhob) and the Progressive Youth Movement, further conflicts can be foreseen.

The PNP represents neither the bulk of the nationalist forces nor the sole heir of the former NAP, yet other movements may be structurally weaker and more volatile because they are sometimes under the strict patronage of powerful *sardars*. Such is the case with the Baluch National Alliance (BNA) that Nawab Akbar Bugti hastily formed in order to participate in the elections of November 1988. As a nationalist, this *sardar* of the Bugti tribe has a contrasting record, having accepted for one year the position of Baluchistan's chief minister when the NAP was dismissed in 1973. However, in the absence of the prominent NAP leaders, the Baluchistan National Youth Movement (BNYM), which was carved out of the BSO, opted for a marriage of convenience with this towering tribal figure. Though the BNA performed relatively well during the 1988 elections, sending six members to the provincial assembly and allowing Akbar Bugti to form a coalition government with the JUI on 6 February 1989, tensions soon emerged between the BNM (the new name for BNYM) and Akbar Bugti, who increasingly engaged the BNA in confrontation of the federal government of Benazir Bhutto. The majority of the BNM condemned this trend and developed further disagreements with Akbar Bugti, especially over the implementation of social programs and the recurring question of U.S. involvement in Baluchistan. The consequences of the growing rift within the BNA, and within the coalition government, were only prevented by the dissolution of the provincial assembly in the aftermath of the dismissal of the Benazir Bhutto government by President Ghulam Ishaq Khan in August 1990.

The figures for the elections held in 1970, 1988, and 1990 indicate a nationalist comeback after the decline experienced during the Zia-ul-Haq period (1977–88). First, the turnout of 23.8 percent in Baluchistan in 1988 was much lower than the 40.5 percent who voted in 1970. Second, the combined nationalist forces of the PNP, the BNA, and minor groups gathered only 25 percent of the vote in 1988 compared to 45 percent captured by the NAP in 1970. But the turnout in 1990 increased to 28.7 percent and nationalist votes represented 41.75 percent.[21] That development paralleled the fragmentation of Baluch politics. In August 1990, Akbar Bugti launched the Jamhoori Watan (Republican National) Party (JWP) in Quetta, which obtained 18.58 percent of the vote in the elections of the same year. The JWP presents itself as the nucleus of an all-Pakistan party that shall stand for the right of each province to have full control over its own affairs within the framework of the existing Federation of Pakistan. It also demands a new administrative division of the province according to "cultural, linguistic, and ethnic" criteria. Although the JWP allied itself with the IDA in order to win the elections of 1990 in Baluchistan, Akbar Bugti was left out in the cold when Taj Muhammad Jamali forged a new coalition with the JUI under the umbrella of the IDA. The change of alliances got the backing of the PNP. The latter had attracted 13.18 percent of the vote in 1990 but met with strong criticism in nationalist circles, which usually blame Bugti's accommodation with the "remnant of the past regime," namely, Nawaz Sharif.

The third Baluch organized force, the BNM, made a poor electoral showing, with 7.35 percent of the vote in 1990. This reflects a rift between two warring factions that arose after the collapse of the BNA. On one side, Mir Akthar Mengal promoted an electoral alliance with the PNP in order to gather "the progressive Baluch movement." On the other, Dr. Hayee, a former BSO leader, criticized this "opportunist move" solely directed against Akbar Bugti in the tradition of the *sardars'* "tribal politics." It should be underlined here that since 1988 the center has been weakened by ongoing conflicts among the members of the ruling troika (the chief of army staff, the president, and the prime minister), and these have opened new bargaining opportunities for the provincial elites.

Present politics in Baluchistan offer a contrasting picture: the continuity of potent political streams, as demonstrated by the outcome of the elections in 1988 and 1990, aiming at the autonomy of the province; and the political fragmentation that reflects rapid economic and social changes. Since 1947, most Baluch nationalists have avoided raising an open cry for independence with all of its political implications.

All the guerrilla movements also have been ambiguous over this issue. Only hard-core nationalists are convinced that the "Pakistan experience" is already over since the "nation" has been reduced to what they see as a "militaro-bureaucratic" machine. Instead the nationalist streams have focused on goals defending autonomy status within the federation. A vocal group of nationalists also has been advocating a "confederal solution" without making much of a dent in the provincial political process (Bhutto and Pirzada 1987).[22] On the whole, Baluch leaders have mostly made pragmatic moves aimed at carving out a viable niche within the context of recurrent military dictatorships, and they recognize the threat of genocide that hangs over all ethnic minorities in South Asia.[23]

The fragmentation of the Baluch leadership may also be analyzed in the context of ethno-regional fragmentation within the province where the polarization between non-Baluch settlers and the Baluch inhabitants is becoming aggravated. Pakhtun demands to merge parts of the northern districts of Zhob, Loralai, and Pisin with the North West Frontier Province are more and more difficult to dismiss. This could have serious consequences since most of the development projects are situated in the northern districts. The Pakhtunkhwa Milli Awami Party, or PMAP (Pakhtunkhwa National Popular Party, from *Pakhtunkhwa*, meaning "Pakhtun Culture and Society"), a secular and nationalist party with 10 percent of the vote, recently demanded that Baluchistan be declared a "two nations" province after armed clashes broke out between Pakhtun and Baluch militants over the location of a rural college in October 1991. The nomination in the summer of 1991 of the first Pakhtun governor was perceived by influential figures such as the Khan of Kalat as an attempt to reduce Baluch influence in the province's affairs.

Interethnic suspicions are also fueled by the burden of Afghan refugees in Baluchistan. At present they number approximately one million, of which 90 percent are Pakhtuns. A political settlement of the Afghan conflict might not ease the growing tensions since at least 40 percent of the refugees, including those with valuable economic assets, are expected to stay. This ethnic cleavage is reflected by the last elections in which the non-Baluch nationalist contenders garnered approximately 55 percent of the vote in constituencies in which Baluch are a minority. This should be compared to the 55 percent of Baluch and Brahui speakers in the province. The attempt of the NAP to promote a multiethnic policy, at least a Baluch-Pakhtun unity, in order to strengthen the demand for provincial autonomy, seems from that point of view definitively over.

Ethnicization of politics seems to be progressively gaining strength due to actual divisions within the Baluch leadership, and as a result could impede the Baluch movement from full participation in the political and institutional development of the province. The outcome might not be the eventual "dilution" of Baluch identity that Punjabi elites would favor but rather aggressive forms of "little nationalism." Ethno-regional movements can hardly be studied as fixed categories existing per se but as social forces evolving in relation both to the center and to other ethno-regional entities (Digard 1988). On the other hand, the state's institutions cannot stand by themselves; they must accommodate and attempt to unify contradictory social forces within the political process. The negative perception of ethnic demands by the center and, worse, blatant manipulation intended to stir up conflict like that between the Sinds and the Muhajirs, lead the evolution of the dynamic between the center and the peripheries down sectarian paths. This trend can already be recognized in Pakistan as well as throughout South Asia.

CHAPTER 9

Nepal, Indigenous Issues, and Civil Rights: The Plight of the Rana Tharu

HARALD O. SKAR

The focus of this paper will be on the peoples of the Nepali "rain forest," an area known as the Tarai,[1] rather than on those of the traditional tribal hills. As will be explained below, in Nepal the lowlanders bear the reputation of being the most ancient, truly indigenous groups.

Today there are two common approaches to the definition of *indigenous peoples*. One specifies that they were the first inhabitants of an area, while the other stresses that indigenous peoples are generally outside the realm of the state decision-making process, and thus are open to economic, political, social, racial, and religious discrimination (see Independent Commission on International Humanitarian Issues 1987; Burger 1987; International Labour Office 1989; and International Work Group for Indigenous Affairs 1990). While the first definition is based on a clear-cut binary opposition (first inhabitants versus later arrivals), the latter is relative and produces a family resemblance or polythetic category (Needham 1975). Here the question of being indigenous becomes one of degree, dependent upon a group's ties to the nation-state and on whether there is an avenue for participation in democratic national institutions. Thus, the dichotomy between the state and indigenous peoples is far from clear-cut and may divert our interest to internal differences rather than similarities within the indigenous sector. This potentially may be a danger, especially in situations calling for pan-indigenous political action.

The issue of indigenous self-ascription is basic. There is a clear distinction between being aware of material and cultural discrimination, on the one hand, and being aware of the Fourth World Movement's efforts to combat this type of discrimination on the other.

Indigenous groups generally are seen as having been displaced in a colonial process, while in the following I shall maintain that the process of present-day nation building may be just as disruptive as a colonial past. Within the structure of the Nepalese state, the Paharia Hindu are in a controlling position in relation to most other groups, including the indigenous peoples. In some of the examples drawn from the Tarai, one also could argue that one population arrived prior to the others. In the case of the Tharu, whom I shall consider in depth, it is their self-defined cultural uniqueness, and their strong sense of being discriminated against, which is at the core of their status as an indigenous group.

Until approximately 1950, the Nepali lowlands were an untouched frontier on the periphery of national concerns. At that time the Tarai was a wild, malaria-ridden region full of tigers. The indigenous population of different Tharu groups held virtually the whole of the Himalayan rain forest as their exclusive domain, and they were reputed to have the evil eye, fierce dominating women, and a knack for enslaving anyone they could lay their hands on. Only after the eradication of malaria in the 1950s did the Tarai become accessible for settlement by outsiders.[2] Having once covered vast areas from New Delhi to the Himalayan foothills, the forest slowly disappeared until today only patches of virgin forest remain (Bista 1987 [1967], 118; Hamilton 1971 [1819]). During the course of this dramatic change the Tharu peoples have been forced to become sedentary and to relinquish their traditional seminomadic ways based on slash-and-burn agriculture.

Nepal's Multiethnic Composition in Light of Indigenous Issues

Nepal's indigenous issues are very much linked to those found on the Indian subcontinent as a whole.[3] A report for the Independent Commission on International Humanitarian Issues concludes that

> In the Indian sub-continent, the continual migration of peoples into the area during the past thousand years has made the question of antecedence too complex to resolve. There, as in other parts of Asia, indigenous refers

PLATE 9.1. *Tharu people fishing, Nepal.*

to tribal and semi-tribal communities. (Independent Commission on International Humanitarian Issues 1987, 6)

Julian Burger (1987, 6) also stresses that "Many indigenous peoples of the Americas find the terms tribe or tribal derogatory because they claim they are nations, while many peoples in Asia make no objections."

Asian views may differ from region to region on acceptance of the word *tribal,* and we may attribute these differences to variations in colonial experiences. In India and Nepal, the word *tribal* is associated with the British administrative term *scheduled tribes,* which gave recognition and certain rights to special groups due to their cultural separateness and marginalized status. In general, there seems to be a drift in India today toward classifying any group *not* Hindu as tribal. In India, *adavasis* (tribespeople) are assumed to live in isolated communities in hilly or forested areas. In Nepal, the word *adavasis* ('tribal') is rarely used and most groups do live in relative isolation in hilly or forested regions.

Who, then, are the indigenous peoples of Nepal? An answer may be arrived at by looking at the relationship of ethnic groups to state policy and decision making, and by identifying the dominant, and therefore nonindigenous, peoples who control the state apparatus today. As in India, religion plays an important part in this distinction, the dominant population being Brahmin and Chhetri Hindu. The king is still considered by many to be an incarnation of the Hindu god Vishnu. Though there was a move after the recent revolution to desacralize the kingdom, in the minds of many rural inhabitants the king remains divine.

PLATE 9.2. *Tharu woman, Nepal.*

In his comprehensive book on the multiethnic diversity of Nepal, Dor Bahadur Bista (1987 [1967], 1) refers to the Hindu group's role in the process of nation building.

> The Brahmin and Chhetri population of Nepal has had more than any other people, the dominant role in the formation of the modern Kingdom of Nepal in the political realm and in the all-pervading social and religious realms.... However, effective power became limited in fact to one particular Chhetri family, the Rana who gained absolute control over the administration of the country.

The Hindu tradition did not begin with the present Rana dynasty, however. Hindu groups were in the vast majority in Nepal long before the Ranas effectively eliminated their opponents in the Kot massacre of 1856. From approximately the twelfth century onward, a plurality of Hindu traditions were influenced by their local contexts. In Nepal, in contrast to India, this meant considerable influence from Buddhism.

According to tradition, Hindu groups arrived in Nepal after they were driven from India by Moslem invaders.[4] Parallel with this ongoing movement from the south, there was a likely east-west migration along the Himalayan hills when the eastern areas experienced similar unrest.[5]

As Brahminic groups arrived from the south, they must have bypassed the Gangetic inner plains (the Nepali Tarai). The groups that must have come from the east did not linger in this harsh area either. Over the centuries, different groups settled in different regions and local environments. The Brahmins and Chhetris who came to dominate Nepali nation building settled predominantly in the low hills and the warm rice-producing valleys.[6] Today they almost totally dominate the far western hills of Nepal, while in the western and central flatlands they control the best agricultural land, that which can be irrigated by the rivers. In turn, they have forced groups such as the Maggars and the Gurungs into higher altitudes, leaving them little valley-basin lands to work. Thus, the dominant Hindu groups came to live in the fertile valleys of the middle hills of Nepal, while the indigenous inhabitants today are found on the ridges of these hills, in the higher altitudes, and in the remnants of the rain forest, the region we know as the Tarai.

In the 1930s, the population of Nepal, after having been stable for centuries, began to rise dramatically. The territories of indigenous peoples have come under increasing pressure. Since the eradication of malaria,[7] the Tarai has been seriously threatened by Paharia (hill people) who have come down from the hills to settle the formerly uninhabitable plain. Though largely Brahmin and Chhetri, these groups have been transformed from priestly and administrative specialists into a largely agricultural class. The traditional, small, Hindu upper class came to be differentiated; they also came to monopolize much of the agrarian sector. Thus, the Nepali high-caste Hindus stand in contrast to their Indian counterparts who are more likely to avoid such work.

In addition to the politically dominant Hindu people, who constitute about 50 percent of the population, other traditional divisions or groups in the Nepali context are the Newars, the Tibeto-Burmese groups, the Bote (or Tibetan) groups, and the lowlands peoples.[8] All of these groups could make a logical claim to indigenous status in the Nepali context. However, in the continuum between the dominant and the less favored groups, no doubt the traditional rain-forest people of the lowlands would be found at the bottom of the scale.

Nowhere is this more clearly demonstrated than in the Muluki Ain (Muluki Ain 1965), the former law governing the internal affairs of Nepal's many ethnic groups. In this law Nepali society is divided into three ranked categories of pure castes. At the top are the *tagadhaari jat,* or "wearers of the holy cord," then come the "non-enslaved alcohol drinkers," the *namasinya matwali,* and lastly the "enslaved alcohol drinkers," the *masinya matwali.* Generally speaking, we find the Tarai people among the "enslaved alcohol drinkers." Here they were placed together with such groups as the Gharti, the descendants of freed slaves. The Brahmins and the Chhetri, on the other hand, are the two highest-ranked groups in the *tagadhaari jat,* and from 1803 onward these groups could not be enslaved even in cases of incest or crime (for a general discussion of the Muluki Ain, see Höfer 1979).[9]

Having briefly explored the relatively inferior position of the rain-forest people in general power sharing and the hierarchical system of Nepal, let us introduce the traditional inhabitants of the lowlands, or Tarai.

The Lowland Peoples

The lowland peoples are generally considered by other Nepalese to be "the indigenous peoples of Nepal" (Hoftun 1990, 61). They are also thought to be the most "ancient" of the ethnic groups. They have the least share in Nepali development and administration and only a few have any formal education. In the Far West, the area of most concern here, those with secondary education can probably be counted on one hand.[10] Very few have jobs in the state administration; they were generally shifting agriculturalists until twenty or thirty years ago. Due to the increasing pressure on land, they are now basically sedentary. The lowland peoples consist of one large group: the Tharus (with four major divisions, the Dangora Tharu, the Rana Tharu, the Chitwan Tharu, and the Katharia). According to the 1981 census (Nepal 1984), the Tharu in Nepal numbered 407,000, with a similar number estimated for India.

Generally, other ethnically non-Tharu, Tarai groups are smaller, and they are predominantly settled in the east. Groups such as the Rajbansi (in 1961 numbering only 55,803) at one time had a separate kingdom, which, according to Hodgson (1880, 107), "included the western half of Assam on one side and the eastern half of Morang on the other with all the intervening country." This Koch state was overcome by the British in India, and in Nepal they were annexed by the Nepalese king Prithvi Narayan Shah in 1774.

Lowland groups include the Satar who are believed (Bista 1987 [1967], 138) to be the same people as the Santal in Bihar, India (approximately sixty thousand in 1961); and the Dunawar (including the Majhi and Darai), all settled along the rivers toward the mountains. Smaller lowland groups are to be found east of the Nepalese Tarai, while the Tarai from the central region to the west is dominated by the Tharu. In common they share their adaptation to a rain forest and plain savanna. This has made them both increasingly threatened, as the people in the hills have begun to migrate to the plain, and they also have to face the invasion of their homelands by land-hungry Indian peasants from the south.

Tarai Forest Land in National Policy and the Displacement of Indigenous Groups

On the Indian subcontinent in general, two problems seem to be most prevalent in relation to indigenous groups. One relates to the deforestation of tribal lands. Burger (1987, 125) maintains that "most menacing for 'the scheduled tribes' are the national and state policies relating to forest land." The other is the serious ongoing problem of slavery. This last is a problem facing indigenous peoples especially, as latecomers tend to enslave the earlier inhabitants of traditional land. These two themes link Nepal's "last subjugated tribes" to their counter parts on the Indian subcontinent.

As early as 1867, it was noted that "since the advent of British rule, the forest has been disappearing with surprising rapidity, and the Tharus have retired closer than ever to the foot of the Naipal mountains" (Nesfield 1867, 36). Bennet (1878, 3:504–6) describes the indigenous groups as moving northward due to deforestation, and Hamilton (1971 [1819], 4:498) gives us a lively account of the thickness of the jungle cover at that time, mentioning that

> a cordon of elephants was drawn round his camp to keep off the tigers....[It] required a very odious exertion of power to clear so much ground as was sufficient to form a parade, and a kind of breathing hole.

Today, in order to make way for the modern agricultural revolution in the Tarai, the Tharu have been forced into still further restricted areas. As settlement of the region is seen as the solution to almost all of Nepal's problems, some have even proposed moving the capital from the mountains to the Tarai (Gurung 1983).

Objectively viewed, the Nepali Tarai is neither small nor insignificant. It includes twenty of Nepal's seventy-five districts and approximately half the country's total population of 18 million, as well as 57 percent of the total arable land. In 1985–86, the Tarai produced 1.6 metric tons of food-grain, making up 60 percent of the country's total agricultural product, a surplus after consumption of 35 percent. While today approximately 51 percent of the people in Nepal live in the Tarai, in 1954 only 35 percent were settled there. It has been estimated (Himal 1990, 6) that 61 percent of the Nepali people will live in the Tarai by the year 2001, and, as Goldstein predicts, "this shift will transform Nepal from a 'classic' mountain economy into a predominantly flat, subtropical and urban nation" (Goldstein et al. 1983, 62). In the district of Kailali in the Far West, the population increase was 7.1 percent per annum according to the 1981 census (thus, the population doubles approximately every 10 years). Today only half of the agricultural land is in the hands of the traditional Tharu population.

The population increase in the Tarai is not just due to the spontaneous response of land-hungry peasants, for it has been a systematic endeavor of the state to culturally and ethnically transform the Tarai through systematic resettlement of the Paharia (hill people). This process has been termed *paharization* (Shresta 1990, 167; see also Berreman 1985). The strategy has been used by the Nepali state as a means of securing the national structure of the state against the *madhesis* (lowlanders), a colloquial, demeaning term indicating an alien person or an uncivilized immigrant from India. Squeezed between the Paharia and the *madhesis* are the indigenous peoples of the Tarai.

The Nepali government has always been afraid of revolutionary ideas and people from India. In a sense this fear has historical foundations, as India has established trade blockades of Nepal and the Nepali Congress Party has launched political campaigns against the Nepali establishment from its jungle haven, Chitawan, in the Tarai. The links between Congress Party leaders and India are very strong, and this worries other Nepalis. However, as Prithvi Narayan Shah (2016 B.S.) put it in his political testament, *The Dibya Upadesh,* "Nepal is like a little yam nut, between two large rocks" (China and India), and the indigenous peoples of the lowland Tarai are the yam nut between the state policy of *paharization* and *madhesi* Indianization. The indigenous peoples are squashed between nation-states and the policies they formulate.

Early Encroachments on Indigenous Lands, the Quasi-Military Settlements, and the Beginning of *Paharization*

As Nepal was increasingly threatened by the British in India during the eighteenth century, the "ruling elites—both the Shahs and Ranas—believed that the Tarai's development was not in their long-term interest. They feared that such development and full-scale opening of the Tarai would not only attract an avalanche of British colonialism" (Regmi 1988, 26) but they would also increase the chances of revenue leakage through smuggling. Accordingly, the early colonization of the Tarai was not agricultural but military. Few routes were opened through the lowlands and basically only two customs posts and quasi-military settlements were formed, at Heteuda and Makwanpur: "The main duty of the settlers was to maintain only one route through the Churia hills, whichever is the worst one, and close all other routes and tracks....Any person who willfully reopened a closed track was sentenced to death" (Regmi 1984, 2). For the indigenous groups in the Tarai this was a relatively peaceful period.

The policy of maintaining quasi-military settlements has continued until the present day. In a sense it is this militarization, in addition to the 1940 policy of providing free land to increasing numbers of people in Nepal, that has changed the Tarai and now endangers the indigenous population. For example, in the mid-1980s a colonization scheme was initiated along the Nepali-Indian border, which resulted in the forced removal of several indigenous Tharu communities. In this instance, the state settled thousands of Paharia people from the highlands along the border in Kailali so as to form a "human shield" facing India. A belt of forest two to three kilometers wide was cleared. Paharia villages were established at intervals, and each was given a letter of the alphabet as its name.

In 1989, when I visited village H, it was clear that the dust-bowl effect (the blowing of topsoil from dehydrated land) was becoming a problem. Nevertheless, with government encouragement everyone was optimistic about the future. All of the agricultural settlements would depend on ground-water wells for irrigation, an infrastructural feature that the international aid organizations were about to provide. The eventual construction of an east-west highway along the border with India would provide further impetus for colonization. Having been a national priority for centuries, the road nears completion today, with financial cooperation from India and England. There are, in addition, roads leading into the hills financed by the Koreans.[11]

The history of the Nepali government policy of *paharization* may be divided into three historical periods: the immediate postunification period, when the indigenous people essentially were left alone; the postwar period; and the postindependence period (Shresta 1990, 170–86). Some of the ethnic groups and families, as well as the organizational characteristics, that became established during these periods remain in effect today.

The Postwar Period (1814–16)

The 1814–16 war with the British ended the period of expansion for Nepal. In 1792, the Chinese pushed them out of Tibet, establishing the northern border. After the defeat of 1816, Nepal's borders to the east and west also became fixed, depriving it of the Kuaoron and Garhwali Hills and a portion of Sikkhim. Furthermore, it was compelled to accept the presence of the British Resident in Kathmandu. In the period following the war,[12] the state turned to the task of increasing its tax base. Prior to the war, Tarai land tax had been collected on the basis of the unit called *pargamona*, "which comprised a number of villages....A functionary called the *Chaudari* was appointed among local landowners to collect revenue" (Regmi 1976, 104).[13] The Chaudari system gradually changed from one based on "functions traditionally held by village headmen and functionaries" (ibid., 165) to the Jimidar system in which outsiders were given land grants on which to settle. Under the Jimidar system, large estate-holders acted as tax collectors, and, although the earliest Jimidaries were once Chaudaries, most of the later ones were Paharia hill people.[14] Local administrators were encouraged to settle anybody who would come, as long as they could maintain control and pay taxes on behalf of their people.

Hand in hand with establishing estates, forced labor was a means of settling the Tarai. While it remained an alternative for individual Jimidars, it was not a large-scale institution at this time.[15] Some of the bonded laborers, however, were always taken from the indigenous Tharus.

Other settlers who came to replace the indigenous peoples were criminals and runaway slaves. The Rana administration decided that, if they settled in the Tarai and reclaimed waste land, then they would be entitled to a pardon and freedom.

> For the government the Jimidari system was a very important policy with respect to farming development in the Tarai. The system was quite effective in that it minimized land reclamation and settlement costs to the government and maximized its revenue potential as it relied on private enterprising and capital investment. The government was directly involved only in the area of forest clearance which in itself was a very important source of revenue. Such schemes were executed in Morang in 1883 and Nepalganj in 1897. (Regmi 1978, 144)

After World War I, the Nepali government became more directly involved in settlement, especially in the traditional Chitwan Tharu area in Rapti and Makwanpur: "For the first time, the government drew up plans for the government agencies to clear large tracts of forests in these areas directly" (Shresta 1990, 176). New settlements emerged "in forest-areas where Tharus previously grazed their animals" (ibid., 17). As Tharu self-sufficiency was undermined, "landless" households, in particular, seem to have preferred to become what has been termed "permanent farm laborers" (Ghimire 1991, 17), virtually creating the "bonded laborers" who continue to exist today. The incidence of slavery became so excessive that

> even the Rana rulers, who apparently were quite sympathetic to the cause of the landed elites owning slaves and bonded labour, decided to periodically intervene in their attempts to make the most abhorrent institution of slavery a little less inhuman so that slaves would not run away. (Regmi 1978, 133)

When Prime Minister Chandra Shamsher Rana abolished slavery in 1924, colonies for emancipated slaves from other areas were established in the Tarai. These were left free to encroach upon Tharu lands.

Paharization and Displacement of Indigenous Groups
in the Tarai

After Nepali independence in 1951, the government expanded its
Tarai activities in a concentrated effort to conquer the rain-forest slopes.
All was done in the name of progress and with the intent of increasing
revenue. No longer was it considered sufficient to populate the Tarai
with slaves and criminals; now loyal and needy peasantry from the hills
were imported to counter the influence of the Indianized *"madhesis."*

The official program of *paharization* was developed for the "rehabilitation of natural disaster victims and landless hill migrants" (Shresta
1990, 186).[16] The first program was established in the Chitwan Rapti
Valley with the help of the U.S. Operation Mission in Nepal (Elder et al.
1974; Shresta 1990, 186). Nonetheless, landed hill families systematically corrupted the system so as to acquire large tracts in the Tarai.
According to Ojha (1983, 7) more than 50 percent of the Tarai land
went to these "non target groups." Thus, the traditional conflict between
the indigenous peoples and the estate-owning Paharias became well
established. The Paharia

> illegally encroached upon Tharu-held land and claimed ownership
> rights....The largest dispositions occurred between 1968–78, a period
> which was marked by a parallel high level of in-migration of hill
> people....[T]he biggest losses occurred amongst the large [Tharu] farm-
> ers. Since land boundaries were not defined legally [in principle it would
> generally belong to the king], the more powerful elements of hill-migrants
> were permitted to register a great deal of these areas under their own
> names. Moreover, the high productivity of land, especially after the
> construction of an irrigation canal in the 1960's, and easier access to
> market encouraged many wealthier people from the hill-areas...to buy
> land from Tharus....[W]ith respect to the [traditional Tharu] fishing, it
> may also be noted that many of the existing water-sources were diverted
> by migrants [for irrigation purposes] or simply dried up because of the
> large-scale deforestation. (Ghimire 1991, 17)

Aided by the government, Paharia encroachment greatly affected the
Tharu population, and perhaps half of all their traditional land has been
lost to them (Government Land Register, Kailali).

Deforestation and Slavery Among the Rana Tharu

In the Far West, there is a little-known group called the Rana
Tharu.[17] Though they were once shifting cultivators, since around 1970
they have become permanently settled in forest clearings. Their settle-

ments are organized into three-generational households contain-
ing patrilineal family groups. The larger patrilineal unit, called the
kurma, is a wider kin group consisting of up to approximately ten
such households.[18]

Kurma households do not seem to be arranged hierarchically. The
ten different *kurmas* in the village of Urmi, with which we shall be largely
concerned here, have negative marriage rules.[19] A man may not take a
wife from his own *kurma* nor from that of his mother or his maternal
grandparents. Furthermore, he must not take a wife from his own village
nor from the village of his father or grandfather. Finally, the patrilineal
family must not allow two of their daughters to marry men from the same
distant village. As a consequence of these restrictions, daughters tend
to marry within a territory defined by villages located along the river
closest to their natal patrilineage. Thus *kurmas* establish *samdi*, or in-law
relationships, of practical consequence along these vital waterways.

In any given village, then, all the adult women will have married
into the group. They are outsiders who in many ways broaden the village
view of the world. Furthermore, because divorce is relatively frequent
among the Rana Tharu, freedom of movement is considerably greater for
women than for men.[20]

The social horizons of the Rana Tharu people thus extend far
beyond the village itself. Taking into consideration the fact that, prior
to becoming sedentary in the early 1970s, Rana Tharu would abandon
a house after the death of the eldest male (the *mukhia* or *dadu*), it is
obvious that old patterns of territoriality are being severely restricted by
the influx of outsiders today (Srivastava 1958). Mapping the migratory
movements of the past three generations of the Rana Tharu in the Kailali
area also makes it clear that early Rana Tharu territoriality demonstrated
total disregard for the Nepali-Indian border.[21] An important factor in
mobility, however, was the river. In the dry season, rivers became highways of communication as well as geographical markers of traditional
territorial boundaries.

Paharization today has two distinct elements: the influx of modern
Paharia migrants, and the political entrenchment of the earlier Paharia
Jimidars.[22] These old Jimidar families dominate the social life of the
Kailali area not only through monopolization of land but also because of
their total control of the local Congress Party. Through their astuteness,
they have successfully established themselves as sawmill owners, and in
this capacity they have made questionable arrangements with the local
forest rangers.

Modern Forestry Problems

The Private Forest Nationalization Act of 1957 brought all the forests in Nepal under government control, with the result that indigenous peoples lost responsibility for maintaining their own habitat. The Forest Act that followed, in 1961, provided legislation for state administration of the forest, defining the Department of Forests' obligations and prescribing penalties for offenses. From this time on, and particularly after the First Cadastral Survey of the 1970s mapped and registered land ownership, the Forest Department staff acquired the task of policing the forest. This new role posed a threat to the national forests, a point that has only recently been duly recognized (Gunow and Shresta 1989). In giving local forestry officers the responsibility for organizing forestry affairs, the administrators provided the predominantly Brahmin officers with an extraordinary opportunity for corruption.[23]

For an individual landowner to sell a tree he has to have a *kita,* or plot number, for the land on which the tree is growing. The *kita* number is listed in the Lal Purja, or land-registration paper, which most landowning households acquired after the 1961 land reform. The tree owner must write a letter to the Banbi Bhag (forestry registrar) requesting that a ranger be sent to inspect the tree and give permission for its felling. Because most Tharu cannot write, they must ask others for help in writing the application, often the owner of the sawmill. Sometimes the sawmill owner will come to the village and ask if anyone can provide him with trees. The owner generally agrees to pay for the operation if the wood is to be sold to him, and he accepts the responsibility of contacting the ranger. When the ranger arrives, the sawmill owner pays him off. The ranger seldom goes to check the tree but is fed and entertained by the Rana Tharu.

The Tharu receive approximately 200 rupees per tree. The sawmill owner can re-sell the tree for about 1,000 to 2,000 rupees. If he takes the trouble to transport the tree to one of the many sawmills springing up along the Nepali border, it may fetch as much as 3,000 to 6,000 rupees. Prices for wood in the area of Uttarkhand and Uttar Pradesh have soared due to a timber scarcity following the spread of the Chipko ("hug a tree") movement, which was intended to protect the trees from commercial cutters. As the Tharu clear the forest for a pittance, new migrants arrive to settle the clearings. Thus, the Tharu lose twice, once with their trees and then with their land. So far the Tharu have not united against these encroachments but some of the larger villages (for example, Geti) have driven out the rangers, even threatening to kill them. The situation is rapidly moving toward greater violence. Some of the rangers now carry weapons and tyrannize the Tharu by descending upon them in their government jeeps.

Traditionally a villager who felled a tree from the virgin forest, not from land considered to belong to the *kurma,* had to pay the Barra (or Balemansa, the headman) a fixed price of three chickens, today about 300 rupees. The headman was responsible for the forest, both in terms of the villagers and in relation to the outside world. Today the rangers frequently pursue local leaders in order to get a share of the communal income from trees felled but not actually sold. Some powerful Balemansas have gone so far as to legally denounce individual rangers, accusing them of robbery inside the Tharu compounds.

Under the New Master Plan of 1988, the role of the ranger is to be transformed into that of guide or instigator. This does not come easily to most rangers who are trained largely in technical work and policing (Eagle 1990, 4). In order to tackle the grave problems of corruption, a new course in conciousness-raising is being launched by Jane Gunow and Narayan Kaji Shresta of the Ministry of Forestry. The course emphasizes the shift from policing to participation but fails to impose structural barriers to make illegal cutting of trees less profitable. It is said that "the very survival of the nation depends on putting a stop to deforestation" (His Majesty's Government of Nepal 1988, 4), which perhaps means mobilizing the people (in this case the Tharu) rather than the ranger. Local participation means handing over control of forests to the local communities. Gunow and Shresta (1989, 4) note that

> To put two million hectares of forest and tree farms under intensive management is not an easy task....[T]he vast manpower and other resources of the rural communities will have to be mobilized....Still, however, just to stop deforestation will be quite the job as in the 1950s 57 percent of the country was under forest cover and today only 19 per cent remains. Presently then foreign aid donors, especially the Finns, are putting down large sums of money into a Master Forestry Plan (1,5 billion dollars envisioned over the next 25 years), without it seems tackling the basic problem of corruption and control, and furthermore without addressing the question of interaction between forestry and farming practices, as the Kailali district increases its population faster than any other rain-forest area in the world (8 percent a year in some areas). (Ibid., 18)

Though the concept of "community forest" is central to the new law, Nepali foresters agree that this could only apply in the hills and never in the Tarai. From a national point of view, the Tarai continues to be envisioned as "under state control," and thus the exploitation will continue.

Such is also the view of various critics of the Tropical Forestry Action Plan (see Colchester and Lohmann 1990) who complain that community-based organizations generally have been excluded by national plans. The "community forest" concept has been added to the new forestry laws without changing day-to-day realities. With such attitudes prevailing, deforestation will continue and the Tarai will continue to lose its topsoil.[24]

Slavery

Along with territorial alienation and deforestation, slavery stands out as one of the major indigenous issues in Asia today. In Tharu terms, slavery is called *kamaiya/kamlarni* or *gwala/gwalni* (also *halia*). It is widely reported in the districts of Kailali, Banke, Bandia, Dang, Surkhet, Salyan, and Dandedhura (Danish International Development Agency 1991; Gurung and Skar 1988). Furthermore, it should be noted that it is practiced by Tharu and Paharia alike, with the grossest abuses occurring on Paharia estates and in some Dangora Tharu communities in which Rana Tharu people have been enslaved. In a highland Nepali setting (Humla), Nancy Levine (1980, 201) notes that "slaves are the descendants of the first settlers," namely, today's indigenous peoples. As other groups moved into an area, they conquered and enslaved earlier populations.

Along with the gradual decline of prestige associated with owning slaves, today there is increasing mechanization of agriculture. De Ste Croix (1988, 25) argues that today slave ownership is uneconomical. The same argument arose during the Nepali manumission process in the mid-1920s (Rana 1925, 23). Be that as it may, the situation in the Nepali Tarai is distinctive. Although officially slavery has not existed in an institutionalized form since manumission, debt bondage is openly acknowledged. Significantly, the UN declaration on slavery, Supplementary Convention, Article 1 (United Nations 1956), specifically mentions that debt bondage and serfdom *are types of slavery*.[25]

Most slaves in the Nepali Tarai are bonded but some might also be considered serfs.[26] Indeed, the distinction between a person tied to the soil (a serf) and one bound by a debt is crucial in appreciating the specific differences within the slave systems of the Tharu, both within the group and with outsiders. While the few wealthy Rana Tharu slave owners seem to prefer serfs (because the serf is left to marry and live a regular family life), the Paharia, and to some extent the few well-off Dangora Tharu, enslave through debt. The serf is generally considered to be "far better off than the [bonded] slave" (de Ste Croix 1988, 23). His ties to the land mean that he cannot be sold away from the land he works. In the Far West context, the serf is at least assured of being able to harvest his crops, though there remain many abuses, directed especially against young women.[27]

In Nepal, and also in India, there is another distinction to be taken into account, that between agrestic and domestic slaves (Caplan 1980, 169–94). This distinction acquires special meaning due to the "ideas of purity" inherent in the Hindu tradition. The Hindu, or Paharia, groups prefer to use slaves as agrestic workers. For reasons of "purity" they employ few domestic slaves, and they tend to keep slaves separate in a plantation-style setting. The slaves owned by Tharus, on the other hand, almost always have both domestic and agrestic duties. They may even live in the same household or in a lean-to beside the owner's house.[28]

Table 9.1 summarizes the use of slaves in the Far West today and relates this to the ethnic-owner component. The ethnic groups listed in the table are the *owners*, while the slaves themselves are basically Rana Tharu.[29]

Table 9.1. Ethnic Component of Far West Slave Ownership in Nepal

	Owners, Debt Bondage	**Owners of Serfs**
Agrestic	Paharia	Rana Tharu
Domestic	Danghora Tharu	X

Agrestic debt bondage is the form preferred by the Paharia, while the Danghora Tharu use predominately domestic slaves. All forms of slavery are known in Nepal by the same names (*kamaiya*, etc.) but the term takes on different meanings according to the context. Generally we can say that the principle behind the *kamaiya-kisan* relationship (*kamaiya* = 'the slave', *kisan* = 'the owner', or any free, landowning man) is that of *a binding contract in which the rights of the kamaiya as a social "person" are temporarily lost.* Even wage labor with advanced payment in part or whole is described in the same terms as slavery, though UN definitions do not include such temporary bondage. Wage payment in advance creates a debt, which is repaid with work over a stipulated time period. This form of temporary debt falls outside the framework of table 9.1.

An argument frequently heard in the Far West is that slavery is natural to everyone, because it is shared by all.[30] But slaves are *not* all in the same position, and Rana Tharu find themselves in the worst situation in relation to the Paharia.

The *kamaiya* (male worker) or *kamlarni* (female worker) is usually called a "bonded laborer" by the Nepali who insist that there is a great difference between this system and slavery. In Nepal, the argument about the distinction focuses not so much on the work required or the type of debt incurred but on whether people are sold or not. In the *kamaiya* system people are not sold but the debts incurred by one laborer can be transferred from one potential slave owner to another. Contracts negotiating such transfer of debt may only be renewed or changed during the first week of the Nepali new year (approximately 15 January). When a master is able to find someone to pay the *kamaiya's* debt, the difference between selling or buying people (as opposed to selling or buying their indebtedness) becomes rather academic. It seems more worthwhile to focus on the abuses of the system, especially on the estates where for generations the same families continue as debt-bondage slaves (see Sagild 1988). In most of cases with which I am familiar, the *kamaiya* have had several (five to ten) masters over a generation. It should be noted that the transfer of debt may be initiated by either the *kamaiya* (who finds a new master to buy him out) or by the master (who finds someone wishing to take over the *kamaiya* by paying his debt). Some families around Getta, north of Danhardi, have been *kamaiya* for so many generations that they know nothing about the conditions of their original bondage. Though they do not know how their forefathers got into debt, they do know the amount of the debt, a fact that has been impressed upon them from birth.[31]

Traditional contracts on estates generally run for generations, especially because, contrary to the letter of the law, *local interpretation* of Nepali law maintains that sons and daughters automatically acquire the debt responsibilities of their father upon his death. Officially, it would seem, the *kamaiya* do not exist. They hold no citizenship papers nor do they have a say in decision making on the estates or in the villages. When a program to register the disenfranchised was evaluated in 1989, it was reported that only six million of eighteen million Nepali had been awarded citizenship (*Rising Nepal* 1989). From what I know about the Tharu reality, this is hardly surprising, as the selection committees that registered the rights to citizenship were drawn almost exclusively from among the landowners, former military men, and members of the *panchayats* (councils) in official, government-organized villages. One wonders about the long-term prospects of indigenous people on bonded labor contracts.

Besides the problems with registration, even the king's commissioners are unable to "see" the *kamaiya*. In 1989, the king appointed a commission under the Ministry of Social Work and Welfare to look into the problem of slavery in the Far West. Their conclusion, based on interviews with local estate owners and politicians, was that there were no slaves in the Far West. Of course, their interviews were hindered by the fact that no one spoke Tharu, the language of the enslaved. The general insensitivity of the commissioners to the *kamaiya* plight was emphasized when one commissioner scoffingly told me that such people "are ignorant, some are lazy and drunkards. If they want to better their life, they must work harder."

Future Prospects for Indigenous Tharu National Organizations

The indigenous lowland peoples, and especially the Tharu, are today in the process of becoming aware of their common future and their common problems. This awareness can be seen as the first step toward the formation of a political platform.

When the Dangora Tharu attempted to organize themselves by forming the Tharu Educational Committee (Tulsipur Dang) in 1990, they were told by the authorities that no specific interest groups based on ethnic identity would be tolerated in Nepal but that, if the committee was opened up to the other ethnic groups, a local nongovernment organization would be allowed.[32] Subsequently, the Tharu Educational Committee changed its name to the Society for the Education of the Backwards. It was accepted as a Nepali nongovernmental organization (NGO) by the Social Service National Coordination Council.[33]

The educational organization of the Dangora Tharu society has been taken up as a model among the Rana Tharu of the Far West. With the objective of using education as a means of self-determination, adult night schools are set up.[34] The basic purpose of the schools is to make people aware of their fundamental rights, especially the laws that regulate debt and working relations. In the Far West, the law stating that no person will inherit the debt of his father has only recently been translated into Rana Tharu, and it is being disseminated through the regular school system. The rights of the Tharu to learn to read and write, so as "not to be cheated by the *Paharia,* who provides the Tharu with credit and drink," are being given priority (see Gurung and Skar 1988; and Skar 1990). Furthermore, the Rana Tharu women in the Far West are becoming interested in evicting state-licensed alcohol salesmen. In this case, similarities with the Indian Chipko movement are apparent (see Guha 1989).

MacDonaugh has suggested that the rising conciousness of the Tharu resulting from education has the potential of developing into a pan-Tharu movement (MacDonaugh 1989, 191–203). Despite barriers such as dialect and restrictive marriage rules between Tharu groups, efforts are being made to overcome the differences. Some Rana today speak Dangora. In the Dangora language, several important publications have appeared in which the Tharu creation myth of Guru Babak Laulmauti (Badrinath and Chaudari 1959–60) and local legends of Tharu kings have been recorded (MacDonaugh 1989, 200; Krauskopff 1989). The creation of the Tharu journal *Gotcari* and the publication of the *Tharu j-atke dha-rmik itih-as* (Chaudari 1982–83, 3, quoted in MacDonaugh 1989) situate the Tharu as a whole in a larger world. The latter identifies all Tharu as worshippers of Shiva on the grounds that for ages they have done *purja* in the name of Mahadeo and Parbati (Parbati, along with Narangeihei, is the main receiver of ritual attention among the Rana Tharu). Thus, these publications have introduced the idea that all Tharu are members of one group, originally from Assam and of Kiranti heritage, a claim not totally dismissed by my East Nepali Limbu assistant in 1988.

MacDonaugh (ibid.) indicates that the Nepali government may have no objections to such claims as long as these are phrased in mythical and ritual, rather than political or economic, language. He sees the growing sense of national identity in Dang as far overshadowing any claim to Tharu nationhood, while in Kailali the idea of Nepal as a country does not seem to exist in popular awareness.

In Nepal indigenous groups are discriminated against in classical patterns that have become the hallmarks of indigenous issues. However, few local inhabitants seem to consider themselves indigenous (*adivasis*). Due to the systematic discouragement by the authorities of any kind of mobilization along ethnic lines, there seem to be only vague indications of a nascent indigenous movement. Gray, however, concludes that "Regardless of whether these peoples refer to themselves as indigenous, or are even called indigenous, in the context of human-rights issues, their definition emerges out of the problems they face and the rights for which they are fighting" (chap. 3, this volume). As the Tharu become more and more pressured as a group, due to migration, increasing deforestation, and slavery, their time for political mobilization may be drawing near.

CHAPTER 10

Minority Nationality in China: Policy and Practice

NICHOLAS TAPP

Discourse

The notion of anthropology as the study of primitive people is still popular in China today where modernist notions of nationalism have only uncomfortably accommodated the idea of China as a "multinational state." While the rich and unique cultural traditions of those defined as minority nationalities (*shaoshu minzu*) are praised in official discourse, at the same time their economic backwardness is criticized—and this is the more liberal official discourse associated with a tolerant line toward the cultural diversity of minorities. There is more than an element of historical-evolutionalist condescension in these praises, which justify museum reconstructions and tourist-oriented presentations of minority culture in an officially acceptable form. Local governments and institutions sponsor festivals where minority song and dance are staged in a way that often dramatically alters their cultural contexts. The posing of poverty among minorities as a problem, in contrast to China's overall economic progress since 1949, similarly tends to strengthen preexisting prejudices and distaste. In everyday discourse minority people are referred to as backward and dirty. Official doctrine rationalizes these prejudices in the form of the five-stage theory of modes of production associated with Stalin. At the local level it is these prejudices that prevent the implementation of central policies of positive discrimination toward the minority nationalities.

The racism of the dominant Han places minority culture under duress despite the fact that historically minorities have used education and intermarriage to become Han. The Chinese see custom, or *feng su xiguan*, as existing in opposition to the western sense of civilization as "progress" (*fazhan*), and in this form policy since 1949 has wavered between tolerating, manipulating, and attacking custom.[1] The question of culture is not confined to the minorities but is applied to Han peasant society in general, in which lavish wedding and funeral expenditures are frequently criticized in the press for perpetuating economic backwardness. The question of religion is closely related to the question of custom, and the main duties of the United Front Work Department of the Party Central Committee, which works together with the Nationality Affairs Commission in minority regions, concern the issues of "nationality" and "religion." While freedom of religious belief is guaranteed under the terms of the 1982 Constitution, "superstition" (*mixin*) has never been approved, and this antiquated anthropological dichotomy lends itself to arbitrary interpretations and manipulation at the local level (see Feuchtwang 1988; and Heberer 1989).

It is important to clarify the notion of *minzu* (nationality) since it emerged from an attempt to apply Stalin's four stages of social evolution—the clan (*rod*), tribe (*plemya*), nationality (*narodnost*), and nation (*natsiya*)—to the Chinese situation, in which *natsiya* was linked with the emergence of capitalism and *narodnost* referred to a precapitalist formation. *Minzu* from the beginning was taken to mean "nation" but the intermediary formation was problematic and the term *buzu* was coined to designate this posttribal but prenational stage. The historian Fan Wenlan pointed out that the Han people, during the Qin and Han dynasties, had satisfied all the criteria of Stalin's definition of a nation, being a stable community historically constituted by a common language, territory, economic life, and psychological formation expressed in a common culture (Fan Wenlan 1958).[2] It was from this situation, and the difficulties of reserving the term *minzu* for the Han people while referring to other ethnic groups as *buzu*, that the term *minzu*, with its uncertain connotations of nation, nationality, or people, emerged to refer to all the ethnic groups within China at the present time, including the majority Han Chinese. This is why the phrase *minzu wenti* may be translated as the "national problem" as easily as "problems of the (minority) nationalities" (its usual sense).[3]

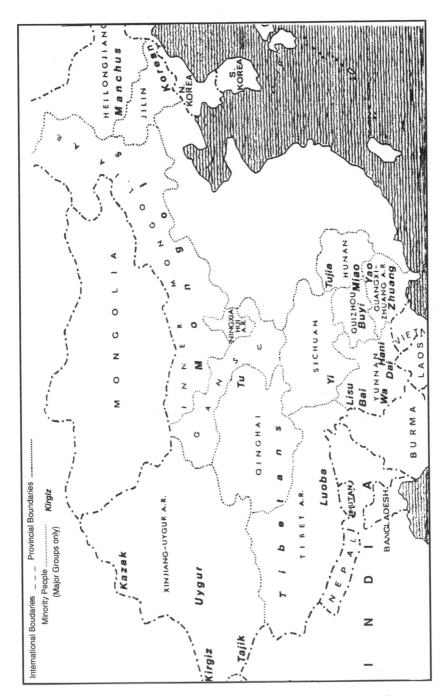

MAP 10.1. *Minority Peoples of China. Source: "China's National Minorities"*
(Briefing Paper) Foreign and Commonwealth Office, U.K., 1987.

The Chinese administration has never lost sight of the political significance of what is known as the "nationalities question." Indeed, it is expressed in the very ambiguity of official rhetoric, which is fundamental to an understanding of the real problems of minority peoples in China today. The Chinese "nation" (as opposed to "people") has itself been designated since the time of Sun Yat-sen as Zhonghua Minzu. This implies that China itself is seen as a great *minzu* composed of fifty-six component *minzu,* including the majority Han people, while if one wishes to specify the plurality of this nation one must resort to the formulation of Zhonghua ge Minzu (the nationalities of China). The implications of this on the ground are breathtakingly clear. Minorities are seen by definition as a political phenomenon, an aspect of the "national question" of direct relevance to issues of international borders and the status of overseas Chinese communities in Hong Kong and Taiwan. Chinese policies toward the nationalities within China therefore take place within the context of the definition of the Chinese state. Chinese research on minorities also has been largely confined to their classification in terms of evolutionary stages. This research views culture as a direct obstacle to the economic advancement that has been China's proudest boast since 1949 and its explicit aim since 1978. Religion itself is a political issue directly challenging the thesis that religious (and eventually national and ethnic) differences will disappear with the "withering away" of the state and the establishment of a fully communist system.

Research on minorities in China therefore has been restricted largely to their classification. This, as Fred Chiu (n.d.) shows for the Taiwanese aborigines, is itself a form of ideological appropriation. It is the reason why such research is termed "nationalities research" (*minzu yanjiu*) rather than "ethnological research," and why, despite the significant emergence in recent years of provincial associations of ethnological research, one finds institutes of the former but not of the latter. Since Chinese society is not seen as primitive, anthropology (*renleixue*) itself is largely limited to the physical variety and restricted to a handful of university departments.

Classification

The arbitrary classification of fifty-six "nationalities" in China on the basis of the preservation of a sense of national unity has led not only to many cases of misclassification (such as the "Miao" of Hainan Island who should be classified as Yao, or the "Pingwu Tibetans" of Sichuan,

classified as Tibetan) and cases in which smaller groups receive no official recognition (such as the Khmu and Lama of Yunnan, the Sherpas of
Tibet, and many others) but it also conceals the obvious and overwhelming differences between the "minority nationalities" themselves.[4]

Most famously, the Tibetans, with a legitimate claim for a separate
state, and a unified history and common language, territory, economy,
religion, and culture, are classified as a *minzu*. Similarly the "Miao," who
include many smaller groups, none of whom traditionally refer to themselves as "Miao," are scattered throughout seven provinces. Internally
distinctions are made, of course, either on an evolutionary basis (as when
Tibet is characterized by the unity of state and religion); or when pragmatic distinctions are drawn between primitive communism, different
forms of slavery, feudal serfdom, and three types of feudal landlord
systems; or between types of economic system; or on the basis of patterns
of settlement. Mixed communities are distinguished from compact
communities, and concentrated settlement from dispersed or scattered
settlement. This leads to a practical four-part distinction between, for
example, mixed communities in dispersed settlements and compact
communities in concentrated settlement areas. Yet the official formulation of *minzu* allows the construction of blanket policies that are applied
to all minorities, and disguises the serious differences between national
and transnational groups, dispersed and enclaved groups, Sinicized
groups, and those that have retained a measure of cultural autonomy, the
large and the small, the powerful and the powerless, the agglomerative
and the integrated, the immigrant and the native.

Indigenous Groups

A closer look at the fifty-five minority nationalities officially recognized in China, numbering more than 80 million or 8.14 percent of the
population,[5] reveals that most of the genuinely indigenous peoples are
largely unheard of outside China owing to their small size, lack of power,
or to the extensive assimilation that many of these groups have undergone.[6] Such groups include the Tai-Kadai–speaking Gelo of Guizhou,
the Maonam and Mulam of Guangxi, the Li of Hainan Island, the
Austronesian "Gaoshan" of Taiwan and Fujian, and the speakers of
Austro-Asiatic languages along the Burmese border such as the Wa and
Dai-influenced Bulang and Deang (Palaung) who largely survive owing
to the maintenance of links with numerically stronger members of the
same groups across the border. Several of these groups (like the Maonam,

Mulam, and Gelo) are partially assimilated, while the others are very weak politically.

Acculturation

Several of the numerically largest minority populations of China have been partially assimilated and acculturated. This is true of the Hui, who are more of a religious than an ethnic minority. While it encompasses some distant descendants of Arab and Central Asian settlers in China, the category also includes descendants of Han Chinese converted to Islam. All are Han-speaking and highly Sinicized today. Sinicization has also proceeded rapidly among China's largest minority nationality, the Zhuang, often held up as a model minority for this reason. The Zhuang are remnants of the populous Tai-speaking people who once dominated much of southern China with their own valley-based principalities. Other Tai-speaking survivors include the numerous Bouyei, closely related to the Zhuang, and the Dong and Shui of Guangxi and Guizhou, whose populations have been enclaved by the slow southward expansion of the Han Chinese. Only the Dai of Xishuangbanna and Dehong in the far south of Yunnan retain some vestige of their traditional autonomy, living in compact communities and occupying a largely unified territory with their own form of wet-rice economy and distinctive religion and culture. This is due in large part to the distance of this area from the center and the strength of the same ethnic group across the borders of Vietnam, Laos, and Burma.

Another huge and largely acculturated population is that of the Manchus, who are in fact a mixed group of Mongolian origin, now largely Han-speaking but having developed and retained a fierce sense of ethnic distinctiveness. Much smaller related groups such as the Ewenki and Oroqen, Xibe, and Hezhen remain powerless and underdeveloped.

Inner Mongolia

The Mongolians themselves are one of the few nationalities numerous, concentrated, and unacculturated enough to have launched serious movements for self-determination in Inner Mongolia. Again, related groups such as the Daur and Mongolian-speaking Yugur, and the Tu, Dongxiang, and Bonan of Gansu, remain relatively powerless and isolated. Certainly Mongolian nationalism has been strengthened by the more than a million Mongolians residing in the Mongolian People's

Republic, in the Buryat, Turinian, and Kalmyk Autonomous Soviet Socialist Republics, and in Afghanistan.

Although the Daur, Hezhen, Oroqen, Ewenki (and Xibe) are also transnational groups (the Ewenki are distributed as far as Siberia), they are not concentrated in sufficiently large numbers to have been able to attain any measure of political power. The Hezhen, traditionally hunters and fishermen, are among the smallest ethnic groups in China, reportedly having a population of only five hundred in 1949. The Oroqen and Ewenki, also traditional hunters and gatherers, were resettled in 1953, 1958, and 1965 but are severely threatened by assimilation and alcoholism. A survey in 1982 showed a mortality rate among newborn babies of 25.4 percent since resettlement (Lin Shengzhong 1984; Lu Guangtian 1986; see also Heberer 1989).

Xinjiang and Tibet

Another nationality sufficiently powerful to have made repeated bids for secession are the Uighur and related Turkic-speaking peoples of Xinjiang. Although the Uighur themselves are most numerous in China, they and related groups of the Uzbek, Kazak and Kirgiz, Tatar and the Iranian-descended Ismaili Muslim Tajik are represented in the former Uzbek, Kazak and Kirgiz, Tatar, and Tajik Autonomous Soviet Socialist Republics and even wider afield in Afghanistan. It may be said, too, that the Tibetans, the third major secessionist group in China, have been encouraged by the presence of an estimated population of two million Tibetans in Bhutan, India, Nepal, and Ladakh, as well as the overseas refugee community.

Tibeto-Burmans

Smaller Tibetan-related groups such as the Qiang of Sichuan, the Moinba and Lhoba of Tibet, and the Nu of Northwest Yunnan, who are far removed from the struggle for Tibetan independence, should be considered separately from other speakers of Tibeto-Burman languages. The latter have not been politically dominated by Tibet, although they may have received considerable cultural influences from it. Chief among these peoples are the Yi, really an agglomerate group including the Nosu people, who comprise the largest component, but also including many smaller groups. Two of these, the Samei and Sani, are aware of no affinities with other Yi groups. For this reason, as well as because of their wide geographical dispersion, they are infinitely less powerful than the large national groups of the Tibetans, Mongolians, and Uighur with their unified histories and common traditions.[7]

The Naxi and Bai people of Yunnan are also Tibeto-Burman groups. They may be seen as indigenous to the area, although the Bai are highly Sinicized and the Naxi of Lijiang are severely threatened by the impact of tourism. The Pumi of Yunnan, Sichuan, and Tibet similarly have been influenced by the Naxi and Lisu. Smaller Tibeto-Burman groups along the Burmese border have been able to retain more of their cultural identity owing to their close association with related people across the border, including the Hani, Jingpo, Achang, Lahu, Lisu, and the Drung of northwest Yunnan.

The Miao-Yao

The Miao are similar to the Yi in being an agglomerate category that includes three major cultural and linguistic groups widely separated by geography and relatively powerless for that reason. Related speakers of Miao-Yao languages are the Yao, branches of whom speak Miao, Han, and Dong, also an agglomerative, widely dispersed group; and the She, scattered along the coasts of Fujian and Guangdong and inland, again largely assimilated. Subgroups of the Miao and Yao, however, are represented by populations outside China, in Southeast Asia, and contacts with these outsiders have led to the emergence of rudimentary nationalist sentiments that consequently are carefully controlled.

Such an overview does not begin to do justice to the complexities of classification and the many anomalies involved.[8] More could be written on the immigrant status of the Russians, the Koreans, and the Vietnamese of Guangxi, who are classified as Jing. Similarly there is room for further consideration of the Tujia, a Yi group assimilated partly by the Miao and partly by the Han, and of the Dongxiang, who are the descendants of Mongolian soldiers who intermarried with Tibetans, Han, and Hui, and who were probably accorded separate minority status because of the anomaly of their Mongolian language and Islamic faith (Dreyer 1976). Also to be considered are the Hani and the Gaoshan. However, we have drawn attention to the some of the distinctions that need to be made.

The notion of indigenous peoples itself warrants further consideration in the light of the very different histories and situations of China's minority peoples. Once one distinguishes between national groups whose territories have been annexed, highly acculturated groups who are nationalities only in name, religious rather than ethnic minority groups, artificially assembled categories (which in fact contain many smaller groups), immigrant populations and transnational groups, one is left with very few groups that can be considered truly indigenous to China. The Miao and Yao are sometimes referred to as the aboriginal Chinese because they undoubtedly preceded the Han in their present locations and were slowly displaced southward, then enclaved, by the expansion of the Han. But the Dai and many Tibeto-Burman groups also have been enclaved. Historically one needs to distinguish between the nomadic pastoral peoples who invaded China from the north, and in some cases dominated the Han, like the Mongols and Manchu, and who then became Sinicized or had their territories annexed by the Han, and the indigenous agrarian populations of the south who have been peripheralized and enclaved by Han expansion in a process that Schafer (1967) termed "internal colonialism."

Yet blanket use of the term *minzu* to describe situations and people as radically different as the Tibetans, Miao, Hui, and Dai allows coherent presentations to be made to the outside world of China as a "unified multinational state" where minorities live together as members of the same "big fraternal and cooperative family." It also allows central policies to be formulated that affect all ethnic groups regardless of local differences and situations. It is to this official policy, rooted in the notion of a unified nationality, which includes and transcends ethnic and subethnic diversity, that we now turn.

Policy

After the Cultural Revolution and the initiation of China's "Open Door" Policy in 1979, the 1982 Constitution restored and elaborated various articles concerning the minority nationalities which had been codified in the 1949 Common Program of the Chinese People's Consultative Conference and the 1952 General Program for the Implementation of Regional Autonomy for Nationalities in the People's Republic of China and which had originally formed part of the 1954 Constitution. The relevant Articles of the Common Program are:

> Article 50: All nationalities within the boundaries of the People's Republic are equal. They shall establish equality and mutual aid among themselves, and shall oppose imperialism and their own public enemies,

so that the People's Republic of China will become a big fraternal and cooperative family composed of all nationalities. Greater nationalism and chauvinism shall be opposed. Acts involving discrimination, oppression, and splitting of the unity of the various nationalities shall be prohibited.

Article 51: Regional autonomy shall be exercised in areas where national minorities are concentrated, and various kinds of autonomous organisations of the different nationalities shall be set up according to the size of the respective populations and regions. In places where different nationalities live together and in the autonomous areas of the national minorities, the different nationalities shall each have an appropriate number of representatives in the local organs of political power.

Article 52: All national minorities within the boundaries of the People's Republic of China shall have the right to join the People's Liberation Army and to organise local people's public security forces in accordance with the unified military system of the state.

Article 53: All national minorities shall have the freedom to develop their dialects and languages, to preserve or reform their traditions, customs, and religious beliefs. The People's Government shall assist the masses of the peoples of all national minorities to develop their political, economic, cultural and educational construction work. (Hsieh 1986)

Regarding the religious question, while Article 88 of the 1954 Constitution stated that "citizens of the People's Republic of China enjoy the freedom of religious belief," Article 28 of the 1975 Constitution added to the "freedom to believe in religion" and the "freedom not to believe in religion," the "right to propagate atheism." It should be noted that a "freedom" does not carry the jural connotations of a "right" (Robert Barnett, personal communication). In the 1982 Constitution the original clause from 1954 is repeated, the phrase about atheism is omitted, and it is further stipulated that "no state organisation, public organisation or individual may force citizens to believe in, or not to believe in, a religion; nor may they discriminate against citizens who believe in, or do not believe in, any religion." However, the state only protects "normal" religion. Using religion to engage in activities that disrupt public order, harm physical health, or undermine the state education system is prohibited, and it is also stated that Chinese religious organizations are not subject to foreign domination.

Section VI of Chapter III in the 1982 Constitution, which addresses the "Organs of Self-Government of National Autonomous Areas" (Articles 112–20), deals specifically with the exercise of autonomous government for the national minorities. Here it is specified that nationalities shall be appropriately represented in the people's congresses on the county, prefectural, and regional levels, and that the administrative heads of autonomous areas must be members of the nationality. Provisions are made for the establishment of organs of self-government and the training of minority cadres, and autonomous governments are given the power to pass specific regulations to administer local finance, to organize local public-security forces, to use and develop their own languages and scripts, and to regulate education and marriage laws. These provisions were endorsed in the 1984 Law on Regional Autonomy for Minority Nationalities (currently under review).

In sum, the law stipulates that the administrative heads of autonomous areas, as well as the chairmen or vice-chairmen of the standing committee of the local people's congresses, shall be members of the nationality enjoying autonomy. The number and proportion of other minority deputies in the people's congresses are to be decided by the standing committees of regional or provincial people's congresses, with due consideration made for numerically small minorities. Minorities also are to be included in the people's governments of autonomous areas. Flexibility in administering central policies is permitted to the autonomous governments, as well as the ability to pass specific regulations dealing with local affairs, as mentioned above. These regulations largely concern local economic construction and planning, including the freedom to make their own arrangements for foreign trade, to manage local funds, subsidies, and budgets, to retain local revenue, and to some extent flexibly administer the state tax laws. Education and the development of local culture are the other main areas in which these bodies enjoy autonomy. They may, for example, amend the Marriage Law, which stipulates twenty-two and twenty as the minimum ages of marriage for men and women, respectively, and forbids marriage between third-degree cousins.

The 1982 Constitution, and the 1984 Law on Regional Autonomy that implemented it, significantly expanded the rights and privileges of autonomous areas over those guaranteed by the Constitutions of 1975 and 1978. Minority nationalities represented 10.9 percent of the 3,947 deputies attending the Fifth National People's Congress in 1979 when an amendment to the Electoral Law was passed stipulating that even the smallest minority should have at least one deputy in the National People's Congress. This and similar provisions for representation of minority nationalities in state organs, general exemption from the most stringent applications of the regulations on birth control, and the lower marks commonly required of members of minority nationalities who apply for admission to universities or colleges add up to a policy of positive discrimination. The provisions generally are implemented at the county, prefectural, and regional (provincial) levels.[9]

In most areas minority couples are allowed two or three children rather than the one child permitted to the Han. In rural areas this is usually quite liberally interpreted, and families with four to five children exist, although they may not be reported. Since massive language-investigation teams were launched in 1956, fourteen Latin-based scripts have been created for the Zhuang, Bouyei, Miao, Yi, Li, Naxi, Lisu, Hani, Wa, and Dong peoples, and attempts have been made to "reform" or standardize the written languages of the Uighur, Kazak, Dai, Jingpo, and Lahu. A total of thirteen Nationalities Colleges have been established, which train minority cadres and technical personnel. These are in addition to the sixty-eight tertiary institutes that had been established in minority-nationality areas by 1982. By that time the minority areas had 14 percent of the national total of medical and health institutes of all types, with 10,700 hospitals and an average of 2.35 beds per 1,000 persons in the minority areas (compared with an overall average for the country of 2.02 beds per 1,000).

Although the 1949 Constitution revoked the "right to complete separation from China" recognized in Article 14 of the Jiangsi Soviet Constitution of 1931, and it replaced the rights of self-determination that repeatedly had been guaranteed for Turkestan (Xinjiang), Tibet, and Mongolia by both the Kuomintang and the Chinese Communist Party with those of a limited form of self-government (Dreyer 1968; Deal 1971), the system of autonomous government was established in accordance with the provisions of the Common Program, starting with the Inner Mongolia Autonomous Region in 1947, at the provincial or regional (*zhou*), the prefectural (*qu*) and the county (*xian*) levels. There are now 5 autonomous regions (Mongolia, Xinjiang, Guangxi, Tibet, and Ningxia), associated with the Mongolians, Uighur, Zhuang, Tibetans, and Hui, respectively, 30 autonomous prefectures, and a total of 113 autonomous counties or banners covering some 63.7 percent of the country. The total population of these regions in 1987 was 142.5 million, including 62.5 million members of minority nationalities. National criteria that require a 30 percent minority population for the establishment of a minority zone are interpreted flexibly by the Nationality Affairs Commission at the provincial or regional levels (in Sichuan, for example, it is 25 percent, while in Inner Mongolia the minority population now stands at only 17.5 percent).

Specific funds for economic construction and subsidies to meet budget shortfalls are channelled to the autonomous areas through the Nationality Affairs Commission and local governments, as are loans and relief funds. Between 1979 and 1983, the state allocated some 24,500 million *yuan* in subsidies to the five autonomous regions and the provinces of Yunnan, Guizhou, and Qinghai, with 5,600 million *yuan* allocated in 1983 (Wang and Bai 1989). Capital goods are also dispatched and technical assistance granted to the autonomous areas, together with tax relief in certain cases. A total of 84 billion *yuan* was allotted for capital investment in state-owned enterprises from 1950 to 1983 (Ma Yin 1989, 31), and the proportion of reserve funds in the budgets of the autonomous areas was said to be higher than that of the nonautonomous areas in 1985 (Xu Yi and Chen Baosen 1984, 492).

I will come to the ways in which these policies are implemented below. Here we are concerned with the policies on paper. Despite the excesses of the Great Leap Forward (1958-60) and the Cultural Revolution (1966-76), there is no doubt that, taken as a whole, national minority policy represents considerable concessions to China's minority population. The provisions outlined above, particularly those providing for educational opportunities and exemptions from birth-control regulations, amount to very considerable advantages for those classified as members of minority nationalities rather than as Han Chinese.

This explains a phenomenon often cited in defense of China's nationality policy: generally the children of mixed marriages between Han and minority members choose (or have chosen for them) minority rather than Han status. There are even attempts to register Han children illegally as the members of national minorities. Such individuals know nothing of the language and culture of the minority concerned but the advantages of minority-nationality membership are felt to be sufficiently attractive to outweigh the benefits of being a member of the dominant majority Han. They may reject their minority status in their personal lives, or they may embrace it all the more eagerly for being unfamiliar with it. I spoke to one child of a Miao mother and a Han father in Sichuan who, although he was officially classified as Miao, initially denied that he was anything but Han. I have spoken with others in Guizhou who are proud of their official identity as Miao, although they have embraced Han culture in all other respects.

This phenomenon occurs not only on an individual but also on a mass scale. Whole counties and districts have applied for autonomous minority status, sometimes on the basis of extremely slender evidence. The discovery of non-Han names in genealogies of several generations' depth or the possession of cultural practices such as a secret form of "women's writing" are presented as evidence of Yao identity by the peasants of Jiangyong and Shangjiangxu counties in Hunan, although judging from their weddings and dialect they are in all other respects entirely Han.[10]

After the launching of the Four Modernizations Policy at the end of 1977, many such claims were put forward. However, the Third National Population Census of China, conducted in 1982, showed what was taken to be an alarming increase in the number of minority nationalities (largely as a result of Han minoritization). The national minority population had increased by 68.4 percent since 1964, compared to an overall Han population increase of 43.8 percent, at an average annual growth rate of 47.7 per thousand since 1978. After 1986, claims began to be rejected.[11] One such was the attempt of a lineage on Hainan Island to register as Hui on the grounds that their remote ancestors had been Muslims (Thoraval 1991).

It can be seen from this that the positive benefits of being the member of a national minority in China are sufficiently institutionalized and attractive to lead to an actual preference for official minority rather than Han ethnic status.

Han-Minority Relations

By emphasizing the unity of China's nationalities, sinologists and specialists such as Fei Xiaotong frequently have stressed the importance of the two-way process of assimilation that occurred between the Han and members of minorities in China's past. For example, Qiu Pu, a former associate director of the Centre for Nationalities Research in the Academy of Social Sciences draws attention to the "long course of historical development" in which "close relations have been established for a long time between the Han nationality and the ethnic minorities" (Qiu Pu 1989). Undoubtedly this was true, particularly in the south and southwest. Not only were members of minorities there Sinicized (Schafer [1967] refers to the entire population of southern China as creoles for this reason) but the descendants of Han settlers were frequently adopted into minority groups, sometimes founding new lineages and clans through intermarriage, as occurred with a number of Miao clans (Tapp 1989). Wu (1989) quotes T'ao (1943) on this.

> A Chinese man arrives in a minority region, becomes an itinerary trader; and after toiling on the road among local villagers and market towns saves enough money to settle down. He either purchases a piece of land or opens a shop at a market town; and this small merchant or landlord acquires a native woman to become his wife. When he prospers and his family grows, he will send one of his mixed sons or grandsons to a school in the regional capital, or even the capital city of Yunnan, to acquire proper Chinese education and eventually to become an official. The idea is that this son, if successful, would carry on the "honorable" Chineseness of his family, while the other sons who stay at home may eventually become natives.

Indeed, I have seen this process occurring myself among Yunnanese Chinese in the Miao villages of northern Thailand.

Processes of direct assimilation occurred simultaneously with this type of "reverse assimilation." Hill (1982) documents cases of Shan (Dai) people in the Tengchong area of Burma who consistently adopted Chinese surnames and burial practices from the sixteenth century onward. Much of this Sinicization was accomplished through the medium of the *tu-si* system of appointing hereditary local administrators from among the indigenous peoples, who adopted Han surnames and received their official titles from the Imperial administration. The *tu-si* system was characteristic of the Ming (1368–1644) and Qing (1644–1911) dynasties, and, although no new *tu-si* were to be appointed after 1931, the practice survived in remote areas up until the founding of the People's Republic in 1949.

The close relations forged by history between the Han and some other nationalities is often given as a major reason why self-determination for minority areas, or Soviet-style federated autonomy, would be untenable in China. Fei Xiaotong, in particular, has recently stressed how the diversity of ethnic groups within historical China contributed to form the "pluralistic yet unified configuration" of the "Chinese people." He refers to these ethnic groups'

> long process of mutual contact, during which many were mixed, aligned or integrated, while others were divided and became extinct...so that many found a part of themselves in others, yet each retained its individual characteristics [*ni zhong you wo, wo zhong you ni.*][12]

Certainly the mass migrations and transmigrations of Han Chinese into minority areas in recent years have added ballast to the argument that it would be impossible to detach areas of China without detaching at the same time large numbers of Han Chinese. Migrations have also reduced the effective autonomy of the minority areas. Besides contributing to closer relations between the Han and other nationalities, Han migration to border and minority areas has been seen as a way of correcting gross population imbalances and disparities of wealth between the more highly developed eastern coastal provinces and the underdeveloped areas of the western region, here taken to include Yunnan and Inner Mongolia (see Cannon 1989, 1990).

To this picture of Han migration into the minority areas should be added the many relocations of minority peoples. These have mainly affected the smaller and more dispersed ethnic groups, or isolated populations among these groups, who have been moved from remote to more "secure" areas, and from mountainous forested zones to valleys. Examples are the Yao villagers of Northwest Guangdong and Guangxi, and the "Miao" of Hainan Island. Twenty thousand Gelo were resettled in Zhunyi County, Guizhou, before the Cultural Revolution. Smaller groups of shifting cultivators have been resettled along the Burmese border, such as the Wa and Nu, as have hunters and gatherers in northern China.

In the late 1950s, many millions of Han were resettled on state farms in minority areas to pioneer virgin land and reclaim forested and desert areas. During the Cultural Revolution many more millions of high school students and graduates were dispatched from the cities to the countryside and minority areas. Even more migration has taken place unofficially. The ratio of Han to Mongolians in the Inner Mongolian Autonomous Region increased from 3 to 1 in 1947 to 12 to 1 by 1968, and the total minority population there stood at only 15.6 percent of the population in 1982. In Xinjiang the Han population increased from 5.5 percent in 1949 to 40.4 percent in 1982, to form the largest group there. It has been said that the past of Inner Mongolia and the present of Xinjiang will be the future of Tibet (Thierry 1989). Han immigration there, concentrated in the towns, has already provoked serious disturbances, although the Tibetan population still officially stands at 95.4 percent of the total and it is claimed that measures have recently been taken to restrict the personnel sent to Tibet to specialized professionals and technicians. Tibetan refugee reports dispute these figures and claim as many as 2 million Han Chinese settlers there, while it is probable that Tibetans have become numerical minorities in Tibetan areas outside

Tibet.[13] Although detailed figures are lacking, Han immigration has affected almost all the minority areas significantly, and for the most part adversely, since Han immigration not only deprives minorities of scarce local resources but the immigrants tend to monopolize the best wage-earning opportunities. The Dai of Xishuangbanna Autonomous Prefecture in Yunnan, for example, made up only 34.7 percent of the population in 1982. In Ningxia Hui Autonomous Region the total minority population was 31.9 percent in 1982, while that of Guangxi Zhuang Autonomous Region was 38.3 percent.

Of course, these figures are not all the result of Han immigration. Natural population increase should be taken into account, as well as the redrawing of provincial and county boundaries and the mass exodus of some minority peoples that has occurred—in particular the flight of Tibetans and Dai to India and Southeast Asia during the Great Leap Forward, and that of Kazakh and Uighur to the Soviet Union in 1962. Yet Han immigration has been a significant factor in reducing the effective autonomy of minority areas.

If anything, then, recent Han settlement in minority areas has exacerbated tensions between minorities and Han rather than proving "beneficial to nationalities solidarity" as the government has officially claimed since the Second Conference of the National Minorities Affairs Commission held in 1951. While the sheer numbers of Han settlers in minority areas, and the long history of dual assimilation that has taken place in some areas, may tend to bolster the argument that the Han and most of the minority nationalities are inseparably bound together by social and economic ties, surely the most important point is that the *boundaries between ethnic groups have been maintained* despite the flow of personnel across them (Barth 1969).

One must ask, I think, whether the policy of positive discrimination toward the members of minority nationalities established by the People's Republic since 1949 has not led to a kind of "majoritarianism," which has reinforced boundaries and barriers between ethnic groups instead of allowing traditional forms of acculturation to continue. The notion of minorities itself, as Kothari (1989) points out, leads to a legalization of authority based on sheer numerical preponderance. Although China's nationality policy has often been criticized as outright assimilationism (Burger 1987, 233), the very enshrinement of national minorities in official policy may have tended to perpetuate the distinctions between them. This will have further strengthened Han dominance as it weakens the possibilities for minority solidarity.

It is at least arguable that the acculturation of certain minorities might have taken place at a greatly accelerated pace had not obvious benefits accrued to those classified as members. Although many of those classified may have become highly Sinicized, owing to their education, it does seem that assimilation has to some extent been prevented by policies of majoritarianism. This is particularly true for the members of dispersed groups such as the Miao and Yao, who have traditionally held Chinese culture, literacy, and wealth in high esteem and have sought to achieve a similar status to that of the Han. In the mixed Miao village in Sichuan where I worked, fifteen households out of a total of ninety-nine belonged to Han Chinese families who had lived in the area for more than five generations. Although some of the Han men spoke Miao (and one had even consulted a Miao shaman), no intermarriage had taken place between the two groups. The reason given for this, by members of both groups, was that "our habits are different." Traditional ethnic barriers remain strong, then, and nationalities policy has if anything reinforced this. Even if intermarriage had taken place, as is more common among other ethnic groups, the boundaries between the groups would have been maintained, since these are the boundaries enshrined in official policy, which consciously formulates special provisions for the members of minority nationalities.

Practice

We have seen that China's nationalities policy is one of positive discrimination—offering tangible benefits to the members of ethnic minorities, which leads to a preference for minority rather than Han status—and that, contrary to popular assumptions (Thierry 1989), it is not a directly assimilationist policy. The policy in practice, however, greatly differs from the policy in theory.

Although the system of autonomous government does allow for a measure of local autonomy, important decisions must still be referred for prior approval to the local party committee and for later endorsement to higher authorities under the principle of "democratic centralism." This ensures that the system of autonomous government remains firmly under the control of the state, since people's congresses must act according to the Constitution and laws.

Autonomous areas are divided into three types: those composed of a single *minzu;* those with a dominant *minzu* and other, smaller ones;

and those based on two or more large *minzu*. Since deputies to the people's congresses at the county, prefectural, and regional levels are "elected" on the basis of population, members of small ethnic groups or groups with dispersed patterns of settlement are clearly at a disadvantage. More than 5 million official members of minorities live outside the autonomous areas altogether, while others live in mixed ethnic areas where they enjoy proportionally insignificant representation (Heberer 1989). As is shown in the ratios of Han to minority populations given above, by locating many autonomous areas in places where there are a number of different ethnic groups, the Han Chinese can in fact become the dominant majority, as has occurred in Xinjiang. In only a third of the autonomous areas does the dominant minority amount to half the population, and Tibet is the only autonomous region in which the "minority" is not also a numerical minority (Cui Jingxiang 1987, 1988; *China News Analysis*, no. 1391, 15 August 1989).

The power of single nationalities also has been diluted through the practice of dispersing them in different autonomous areas. This is the case with the Tibetans who are distributed in Sichuan, Qinghai, Gansu, and Yunnan, as well as in Tibet, forming nine autonomous prefectures, one mixed autonomous prefecture, and two counties besides the Autonomous Region of Tibet. Similarly, the Xinjiang Uighur Autonomous Region is divided into five autonomous prefectures and six autonomous counties under the administration of the Mongolians, Hui, Kazak, Tajik, and Xibe. In several cases the borders of autonomous areas have been changed arbitrarily to reflect political concerns.

The Inner Mongolian Autonomous Region, for example, was reduced to about half its size by the extension of the dominantly Han provinces of Kirin and Heilongjiang to the Soviet border after disputes with the Soviet Union in 1969 (Pye 1975). The Xinjiang Uighur Autonomous Region and the Ningxia Hui Autonomous Region also have been reduced in size, as was Tibet historically by the extension of Sichuan and Qinghai. The Autonomous Li and Miao Prefecture of Hainan was abolished in 1958, later reinstated, and finally abolished in 1988 when the island of Hainan became a province and a Special Economic Region.

The effective autonomy of these areas, then, has been very limited. Moreover, many of the rights and privileges accorded the autonomous governments by the 1984 Law on Regional Autonomy are limited in their actual exercise. Financial planning still must take place within state guidelines. Minorities without their own systems of writing cannot conduct legal proceedings in their own languages. By 1988, only 13 out of 141 autonomous areas had published their own local regulations as they are permitted to do (*China News Analysis*, no. 1391, 15 August 1989).

Nor in the important fields of education and religion is the spirit of the law properly implemented. Illiteracy rates among minority people remain extremely high (42.6 percent in 1982). In most areas primary schools have been established but secondary education remains rare and tertiary opportunities almost nonexistent. The Household Responsibility system introduced after 1978 (in most minority areas not until after 1982), under which households may keep a portion of their produce, has further reduced incentives for education among many minorities. This has particularly affected female students. The nationalities colleges set up across the country (like the universities in minority areas) basically provide a Han education and serve as training centers for minority cadres and technical specialists. A Han education is not seen as leading to particuarly good economic opportunities. And, while the opportunities of economic entrepreneurship outweigh those of becoming a cadre, domestic labor requirements contribute to high drop-out rates among schoolchildren.

In the field of religion, the practice has been to tolerate "normal" religion (as opposed to "superstition") but not its propagation. While temples, mosques, and churches have been rebuilt and restored since the Cultural Revolution, often to attract tourists, restrictions have been placed on the enrollment of new monks, priests, and *imams,* and on establishments of religious education. Since the freedom not to believe in religion is also guaranteed by the Constitution, the teaching of religion is often seen as an attempt to poison the minds of the young. This was the case during both the campaign against spiritual pollution of 1983 and the campaign against bourgeois liberal values of 1987. The reconstruction of Buddhist temples in virtually every Dai village of Xishuangbanna after the Cultural Revolution was a cause for official concern. Later it was claimed that the new economic incentives brought about by the Household Responsibility system had reduced the number of novice monks enrolled in these temples. The arbitrary distinction between religion and superstition also opens the door to local abuses and high-handedness. The shamanism of the Miao, illegal for forty years, still must be practiced secretly, at night, the gong beaten very softly so as not to arouse the neighbors.

In matters of health the picture is no better. While statistics show an enormous improvement in health facilities and the level of health care in minority areas since 1949, wide disparities between Han and minority populations remain. Poor transport coupled with the long distances to most health clinics and centers, as well as language problems and the lack of ready cash, inhibit visits to hospitals. Childbirth generally takes place at home, with families or local traditional experts meeting most health-care needs. Immunization programs have been mounted but they have not reached all minority areas. Although in some villages paramedics remain from the days of the commune, in one Miao village in 1989 the only health specialist was a veterinarian who coped in emergencies. Country hospitals and local clinics can be extremely rudimentary, and worms, rickets, anaemia, and goiter remain particularly common.

Foreign-aid workers in China stress the inadequacy of statistics indicating that every one hundred rural families owns 48 radios, 113 bicycles, 55 sewing machines, and 173 watches. The official yardstick of poverty in minority areas (a per capita income equivalent to 150 to 200 *yuan* per year and grain consumption of less than 200 kilograms) may be too low, local methods of collecting statistics are often dubious, and it is difficult to measure absolute poverty or construct adequate indices of the quality of life. Nevertheless, official statistics clearly show the gross underdevelopment of the five autonomous regions and of Yunnan, Guizhou, and Qinghai, which account for 64 percent of the minority population and 93 percent of the autonomous areas in relation to the rest of the country in terms of the Gross Value of Industrial and Agricultural Output (Wang and Bai 1989). The "backwardness" of the minority-populated western provinces is generally admitted. Yet these figures fail to communicate the reality of poverty. Lack of fuel for fires, insufficient clothing and shoes, several months' shortage of grain each year, and extreme scarcity of animal protein are common conditions in the minority areas.

The minorities suffered particularly during the Great Leap Forward and the Cultural Revolution, when official minorities policy was effectively in abeyance. It was during these periods that the massive Han immigration into minority regions occurred, and radical attempts to change local economies had disastrous results. Collectivization since the mid-1950s already had led to separatist movements among the Uighur, Kazak, and Hui before the Anti-Rightist Campaign of 1957 was converted into a struggle against "local nationalism" in minority areas. Local nationalism continued to be seen as a barrier to the permanent revolution and economic productivity demanded during the Great Leap Forward. The peoples' commune movement brought women into the fields, forced the Hui to eat in communal mess halls, prohibited burials and animal sacrifice, and attacked minority languages, customs, festivals, and costumes.

Direct attacks on minority culture (or the fear of them), social and agricultural experiments, and the famine of 1960–61 fueled rebellion and flight. During the Cultural Revolution the nationalities question was again viewed as an aspect of the class struggle, and again cultural outrages occurred in addition to wholesale killings and the destruction of religious institutions. Thousands of books, including innocent dictionaries of minority languages, were destroyed (Lemoine 1989a). Besides a massacre, the Yao of northwest Guangdong remember not being allowed to speak their own language openly or to sing traditional courting songs. Their customary clothes were confiscated and later burned. As a result, a whole middle generation has grown up deprived of their cultural heritage.

Such atrocities, or the fear of them, led directly to armed uprisings and conflict among the nationalities such as the widely reported Tibetan Rebellion of 1959, followed by the flight of the Dalai Lama and his supporters to India, and a later uprising in 1969. There were other, less publicized uprisings. One occurred in Xinjiang in 1958, and another broke out among the Yi the same year. The Yao of Guangdong and Guangxi arose in 1950, inspired by a female prophet who promised her followers invulnerability to Chinese bullets. The exodus of the Dai to Southeast Asia in 1962 (many groups along the Burmese border also fled into Burma during the Great Leap Forward), and of the Kazak and Uighur to Soviet Central Asia in the same year, have been mentioned. Uighur nationalist uprisings occurred in 1967 and 1968, and among the Kirgiz in 1981.

Although the Great Leap Forward was directly interpreted as an attack on "local nationalism," the "Four Old Things" attacked during the Cultural Revolution (old thinking, culture, customs, and habits) cannot be seen solely in terms of a clash between majority Han and minority cultures. Many of the Red Guards in the Cultural Revolution were members of the minority nationalities whose traditions they were attacking, and the Han, too, suffered unimaginably. But both periods can be seen as a time when official nationalities policy, which insists on special treatment for minorities on the basis of their distinctive characteristics, was temporarily in abeyance. Other lines of rampant assimila-tionism and radical fervor held sway, which allowed local ethnic antagonisms and prejudice to erupt. It is these local ethnic antagonisms and chauvinism that are the main point of this paper.

Chauvinism

Despite a Central Government directive of 1951 that abolished terms of address, place names, and inscriptions on stone tablets and scrolls considered insulting to the minorities—such as the dog, worm, and reptile radicals used in ideograms for the names of minority peoples—ethnic prejudice and antagonism of the type that erupted during the Great Leap Forward and the Cultural Revolution continue to exist at the local level. It has largely been to blame for the failure to implement China's nationality policy. The Chinese themselves have seen "Great Han chauvinism" (*da hanzuzhuyi*) together with "local national-ism" as the two great obstacles (the "two anti's") to the successful implementation of an enlightened policy of positive discrimination toward the minorities. But Han chauvinism is not only great, it is local, and it has existed for a long time.

Tweddell (1978, 315) provides a vignette of everyday attitudes of local discrimination against the Tuli, a Tibeto-Burman group, in West Yunnan in 1948–51.

> Anyone identified as a Tuli was automatically assigned a role of subservience in any situation involving a Chinese. When the market head-man wanted road repairmen, his messengers to the Tuli village bawled and shouted for an immediate labour force. Money earmarked for wages never reached the Tuli. When the Tuli schoolteacher was summoned for [unpaid] duty and travel as a census-taker, he hurriedly donned his long blue gown and went. [A literate Chinese would have been politely asked and paid.] An older Tuli peasant walking through the market was commandeered by a Chinese farmer for several days' forced labour; his reward? a worn-out T-shirt!

Attitudes of discrimination and ethnic prejudice persist at the local level today, although they are subtly expressed, particularly in front of outsiders. When I asked why the local Han never visited the inhabitants of a Yi village in Yunnan, I was told by a Han intellectual that "the customs and traditions of the minority nationalities are so different from our own, we are afraid of making a mistake when we visit them" (Tapp 1986).

An unpublished report from Tibet by Robert Barnett cites the case of an old Tibetan woman whose seat on a bus had been taken by a young Han boy who refused to move or take any notice of her despite her complaints and those of other passengers. Eventually she hit upon the idea of touching his jacket gently. The boy jumped up, furious, and yielded his seat. As the report remarks, "It was an extraordinary episode, because it showed that the Chinese boy assumed the Tibetan to be filthy, and that the woman knew this in advance" (Barnett [n.d.]).

Yet these attitudes and prejudices are part of the coinage of everyday life. When represented in the person of an overzealous, conservative, local party leader who still respects Mao Zedong, and sees religion as a dangerous illusion and local tradition as an impediment to progress, such prejudices tend to become a formidable local force of discrimination against minority status powerful enough to circumvent or overturn favorable official policies. Indeed, I would say that this is a very generalizable picture for most of the smaller or dispersed ethnic groups in China. It is certainly true of the Miao and Yao areas in which I have worked.[14]

My thesis, then, is not only that China's official nationalities policy may have strengthened and reinforced traditional barriers between ethnic groups but also that its provisions favoring the minority nationalities have not been effectively implemented owing to the strength of ethnic prejudice at the local level. Some measure of the strength of this prejudice may be gauged from the atrocities of the Great Leap Forward and the Cultural Revolution.

The argument has been that, while propagating ethnic distinctions, China's minority policy is one of positive discrimination toward minorities but that in practice it has failed to work owing to the strengths of local Han chauvinism and, in the cases of Tibet, Xinjiang, and Inner Mongolia, local nationalism. For, where local prejudice and conservative attitudes are combined with official concerns about China's national identity, as, again, in the cases of Tibet, Xinjiang and Inner Mongolia, a very different situation from that of most of China's ethnic minorities emerges. The Tibetans, Mongolians, and Uighurs, and to a lesser extent the Hui and Kazak, have been the major ethnic groups sufficiently concentrated, powerful, and un-Sinicized to directly challenge the integrity of China's national borders and stress local ethnic identity as a serious alternative to Zhonghua Minzu identity. The roots of the unrest, armed struggle, uprisings, and separatist tendencies that have arisen in recent years must be sought in a variety of causes besides Han chauvinism. Han immigration and widening economic disparities between rich and poor, as well as between Han and minorities, which are exacerbated by the breakdown of the commune system and the recent impact of tourism, have inflamed genuine local nationalism as well as traditional Han discrimination to lead to situations of general international concern. It is also in these arenas that nationalism has been most clearly expressed through the medium of religious identity.

Renewed unrest broke out in Tibet in October 1987 when an unarmed crowd of some two thousand demonstrators was fired upon and about sixty arrests made. Yet further protests took place in March and December of 1988, and major riots in March 1989 led to the imposition of martial law in Lhasa nearly two months before it was declared in Beijing. In October 1988, mounting discontent also led to major demonstrations in Urumqi, the capital of Xinjiang, by Uighurs protesting against racial discrimination. After the suppression of "counterrevolutionary" activity that followed Tianamen in June 1989, a demonstration in February 1990 of more than eight thousand demanding independence and democracy took place in Inner Mongolia. In April, Kirgiz separatists attacked local government offices near Kashgar in Xinjiang, demanding the establishment of a Republic of East Turkestan. In May, when martial law was lifted in Tibet, demonstrations of forty thousand persons took place in Hohhot. Inner Mongolian unrest is said to have been organized by an Inner Mongolian Autonomy Committee and an Asian Mongolian Freedom Front. The Tibet Information Network reported demonstrations and protests in Tibet throughout August and September of 1990, and again in March 1991. Isolated incidents also have occurred. In November 1990, ethnic clashes in Yunnan resulted in the deaths of several Muslims.[15]

But the majority of China's smaller or more dispersed ethnic groups are not in a position to launch serious claims to a separate national identity, and it is for this reason that it is essential to separate their situations from these areas of genuine nationalism and general international concern. These groups, who retain a sense of cultural integrity unlike such acculturated minorities as the Zhuang or Manchu, and yet lack the power of the concentrated settlements of the Tibetans, Mongolians, and Uighur, have mostly failed to benefit from policies of positive discrimination owing to the strength of local ethnic prejudice against them. It is also these groups (such as the Daur, Oroqen, and Ewenki) who are most in danger of complete assimilation, since that trend has certainly continued in China. The formulation of *minzu* disguises the plight of many of these smaller and more dispersed groups who should be the subjects of serious international concern and the focus of future research.

CHAPTER 11

A State of Strife: The Indigenous Peoples of Burma

MARTIN SMITH

Situated between the neighboring powers of India, China, and Thailand, Burma (Myanmar) is a country of colorful ethnic diversity.[1] More than a hundred different languages and dialects have been identified in Burma. The great horseshoe of mountains surrounding the central Irrawaddy Plain plays host to an extraordinary variety of different ethnic subgroups and cultures, many of which have survived well into the late twentieth century. These range from the formerly head-hunting Was and "giraffe-necked" Kayans (Padaungs) of the Shan State to the Salums or sea-gypsies of subtropical Tenasserim. Nor is it correct to describe the ethnic Burman majority, who make up some two-thirds of Burma's estimated 43 million population, as one homogeneous ethnic group. Even today there are Burmese speakers in districts such as Tavoy who, like the Arakanese, claim a separate nationality.

The sheer scale of this diversity in part explains Burma's continuing ethnic problems. But at the same time certain generalizations can be made. For present-day purposes, ethnic groups in Burma can be loosely classified into four major linguistic families—the Tibeto-Burmese, the Mon-Khmer, the Tai (Shan), and the Karen—and it is estimated that 80 percent of the population follows Theravada Buddhism. In more remote mountain areas there are still many people who practice local religions and among minorities such as the Chin, Kachin, and Karen there are large Christian communities. There are also more than 1 million Muslims and an estimated 1.5 million Chinese, Bengalis, and Tamils.

Not for nothing, then, has Burma been described as an "anthropologist's paradise." But beyond this broad picture not many details can safely be added. Few ethnic studies were completed in the brief era of British rule and even fewer have been undertaken since. As the great democracy uprising of 1988 showed, Burma remains a volatile country. Bubbling beneath the surface of the political crisis at the center in Rangoon are crucial ethnic questions that one day will need to be addressed if peace is ever to be found for this deeply troubled land. Many citizens argue that the eventual solution to these problems will come only through free discussion, study, and investigation. But for the moment it is unlikely that any other country in Asia has allowed less self-examination or research on the subject of indigenous peoples. Though since 1988 Burma has appeared to be in a state of transition, it remains handicapped by enormous social and economic problems, all of which have contributed to a desperate state of crisis throughout the country.

There are many complex threads—racial, political, anthropological, and historical—to the present political debate, so the purpose of this paper will be to identify some of these problems, examine how they arose, and look at the steps the Burmese peoples themselves are taking to deal with them. Burma is a highly literate country, with rich cultural and educational traditions, but for many years it has been trapped in a tragic state of political paralysis.

Background to Crisis

Three major reasons can be advanced as to why the study of indigenous peoples in Burma has advanced so little in the past forty years and why the present ethnic crisis is so acute. The first is the continuing state of armed conflict. Little recognized in the world outside, Burma has been beset by near continuous political and ethnic conflict since independence in 1948 in a spiral of insurgency that has reached no final conclusion. Ethnic Rakhine and Mujahid nationalists in Arakan took up arms in 1947 even before the British departure. The Communist Party of Burma (CPB) went underground in March 1948, and the Karen National Union (KNU) in January 1949. Throughout the late 1940s and early 1950s, other ethnic groups, including the Mons, Paos, Chins, and Karennis, all resorted to arms. Finally, in March 1962, as fresh Kachin and Shan separatist movements gained momentum in the northeast, General Ne Win seized power in a military coup and brought to an end the short-lived era of parliamentary democracy.

Ne Win then launched his disastrous twenty-six-year experiment with the Burmese Way to Socialism, which eventually was to bring the country to the brink of social and economic collapse. Renouncing the loosely federalist structure of the 1947 Constitution, Ne Win adopted a simple two-fold strategy to cure all the country's ills: on the one hand turning full attention to defeating the insurgents in the countryside, and on the other building up a centralized one-party system of administration radiating from Rangoon into the ethnic-minority states (Silverstein 1977, 93). To achieve these aims, all political and ethnic opposition was ruthlessly crushed. And yet, by the time of the democracy uprising, which brought about the collapse of Burma Socialist Programme Party (BSPP) rule in 1988, some twenty insurgent forces remained active in more than one-third of the country, controlling vast rural areas, largely in the ethnic-minority states.

Nor is it possible in any analysis of Burma's turbulent history to make a clear distinction between the effects on the country of ethnic insurgent movements such as the KNU and those of political parties such as the CPB. At the time of the mass ethnic mutinies in 1989, which saw the break-up of the CPB's powerful Northeast Command, not only were most recruits to the CPB's fifteen-thousand-strong People's Army from ethnic-minority groups (largely Was, Shans, and Akhas) but the strategy of most armed opposition groups has been to form a "united front." In the late 1960s, for example, the deposed prime minister, U Nu, took to the jungles with Bo Let Ya and other heroes of Burma's national liberation struggle to take up arms with their erstwhile enemies, the KNU. Now joining ethnic insurgent forces in the eastern mountains in the new Democratic Alliance of Burma are thousands of students, monks, and civilian activists who fled underground following the 1988 coup. In December 1990, they were joined by more than a dozen elected members of parliament from the National League for Democracy, which had won a landslide victory in the general election the previous May. Burma's sad cycle of insurgency once again appeared complete.

The causes of endemic insurgency in Burma, which have very particular historical origins, are beyond the scope of this paper.[2] But the consequences have been devastating to a country that at independence in 1948 was still trying to come to terms with the enormity of the death and destruction caused by the Second World War. Casualty figures have rarely been released since independence but an average of ten thousand deaths a

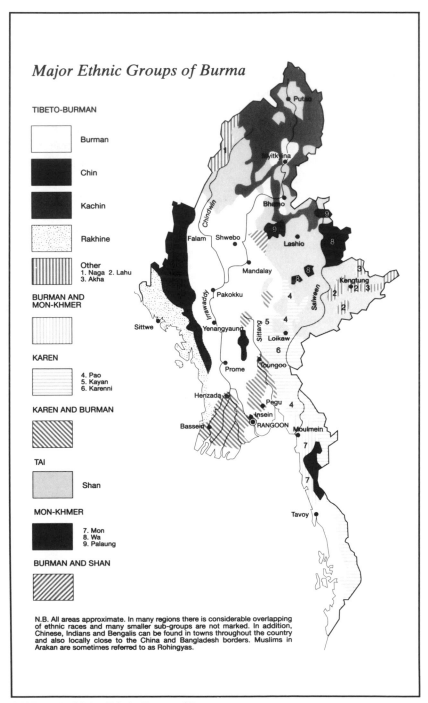

MAP 11.1. *Major Ethnic Groups of Burma.*

year due to insurrection may well be an accurate figure. This was confirmed by Burma's then military front man, General Saw Maung, in a rare public admission in January 1990 when he said he thought the true number of deaths might well be in the "millions" (Saw Maung 1990).

The catastrophe of conflict has impinged upon every aspect of national life. Vast areas have long been officially off limits, and are considered to be virtual free-fire zones by government forces, while in a country with no external enemies an estimated 40 to 50 percent of the national budget goes to defense. In recent years, however, it has been the minorities who have suffered the most. The Kachin Independence Organisation, for example, claims to have recorded the verifiable deaths of 33,336 civilians at the hands of government troops in the years 1961–86 (Smith 1991, 100). Immediately following the anticommunist uprising in Northeast Burma in 1989, the Wa mutineers broadcast a poignant statement on their rebel radio station: "Every year the burden of people has become heavier. The streams, creeks, and rivers have dried up, while the forests are being depleted. At such a time, what can the people of all nationalities do?" (British Broadcasting Corporation 1989).

The second major reason for Burma's political paralysis is closely connected to the insurgencies: the still highly debilitating legacy of the distortions of British colonial rule. American political scientist Josef Silverstein has characterized this as "the dilemma of national unity" (1980). Burma, of course, is hardly alone in facing such a problem. But, as is little recognized by the world outside, in Burma's case the experience has been particularly acute. The casual way in which the present military government, the State Law and Order Restoration Council (SLORC), renamed the country Myanmar in 1989 (in an apparent bid to wipe the historical slate clean) is further evidence of how the country has yet to find a nationwide consensus on an accepted political identity.

To put this into perspective: the land that became modern Burma at independence in 1948 was under British administration for a total of just sixty-two years but it differed greatly from any other nation or state in the recent past. In Central Burma the traditional system of administration under the Burman kings and the royal courts at Ava and Mandalay was destroyed, and, though a limited form of Home Rule was introduced in the 1920s, until 1937 Burma was administered as a province of India. Hindi, not Burmese, was the language of the Post Office. It was thus far from certain that the western-style system of multiparty parliamentary democracy envisaged in the 1947 Constitution would work.

Moreover, it was only at this late stage that the ethnic-minority "Frontier Areas" were fully incorporated into the new union. These hill tracts consisted of thousands of square miles of little-known terrain and loosely independent ministates, comprising some 40 percent of the total land area. During British rule these areas had been administered separately from Burma proper, and in the main they had been left under the control of their traditional rulers and headmen. Nor were any of these regions administered simply on the basis of nationality or ethnicity. The arbitrary divisions of colonial rule, despite a widespread belief today that the minorities were favored by the British, have been as much an impediment to the development of the minority peoples as they have been to the majority Burmans. Though the Karens, Kachins, and Chins were preferred by the British for recruitment into the colonial army and police, all of Burma's ethnic groups, it can be argued, suffered equally in the long run.

The territory of the Karens, for example, was divided into five political regions in British Burma, with different rights granted in each. In the rush to independence, most of these anomalies were written into the 1947 Constitution. This happened despite the repeated objections of the Karen National Union, which boycotted both the 1947 Panglong Conference and the Constituent Assembly where these historic decisions were made (Smith 1991, 82–85). The Shans and Karenni, by contrast, who under the British administration had the strongest legal rights on paper, were left under the rule of their traditional *sawbwas* and granted the unusual right of secession after a ten-year period. The Zos, or Chins, on the other hand, who along with the Was and Nagas were the most neglected peoples under colonial rule, were not even granted a state (Silverstein 1980, 185–205).

Moreover, racial antipathies, which had been strengthened by the nature of British rule, were dangerously heightened by the trauma of the Second World War. The armies of Japan, Britain, the United States, and China had fought their way across Burma's soil. While Aung San and the heroes of Burma's national liberation struggle initially fought on the side of Imperial Japan, many of the hill peoples (especially the Karens and Kachins) joined the British and suffered heavy casualties as a result. There were many bloody communal clashes in which the minorities, for the most part, came off very much the worse.

It is easy for outsiders to forget the compressed time-scale on which Burmese politics still operates today. In the state-controlled press there are constant references to Aung San and the campaigns of the independence struggle. But enmities and suspicions arising from the days of the British live on. Even in the late 1980s, the Burmese army was still accusing the KNU of "craving colonial servitude yearning for their relative over and above their own mother" (Tun Zaw Htwe 1987). The KNU, whose leaders are all veterans of the wartime British army, responded by accusing the Burmese army of seeking to reduce the minorities to the conditions of "slavery" they lived under before the British arrived (British Broadcasting Corporation 1983). Thus, in the restricted political vocabulary of Rangoon, any discussion of federalism or minority rights is immediately equated with the crime of "separatism" and possession of a colonial mind. This stigma, in turn, has been attached to such staunchly nationalist Buddhist groups as the Paos, Mons, and Palaungs, whose influence under colonial rule was rather more slight.

In the twilight of Ne Win's reign, there are some indications that these racial antipathies are slowly dissipating, and within a few years most of the diehards who began these long wars will have passed. But the younger generation now taking up the political baton, despite clear evidence of their desire for change, are enormously handicapped by the consequences of the past five decades of conflict. These issues have never been publicly discussed except in the most highly propagandist terms. Therefore, in 1994, more than ever, the dilemma of national unity remains.

This leads to the third major reason for Burma's continuing political paralysis: the extraordinary character of Ne Win and the Burmese army (or Tatmadaw) who over the past four decades have come to dominate all aspects of national and political life. In the chaos of the early insurrections, much of the political credit for preventing the break-up of the union went to Burma's first prime minister, U Nu. But underpinning his fragile control of the country was the army's chief of staff, Ne Win, backed by the continued loyalty of his old regiment, the Fourth Burma Rifles. Beseiged by rebellion on all sides, the Tatmadaw grew rapidly in the 1950s to become Burma's largest social and financial institution, with interests in shipping, banking, construction, and commerce. In the 1950s, Tatmadaw generals tinkered with a distinctive political philosophy (largely to counter the political challenge of the CPB) and in 1958–60, under the "Military Caretaker administration," temporarily took over the running of the country. But it was only in 1962, with the Ne Win coup, that the Burmese Way to Socialism was formally unveiled.

An idiosyncratic blend of Marxist, nationalist, and Buddhist principles, Ne Win's basic philosophy was never enlarged upon. But it was a

dogma with which the army, dominated by ethnic Burman commanders, maintained a stranglehold on political life for more than a quarter
of a century. At both the national and local levels, virtually all key
administrative positions were staffed by serving or retired army officers,
and only one civilian of any note, Dr. Maung Maung, ever served in the
higher ranks of the BSPP. The BSPP was deeply xenophobic and
frequently anti-intellectual. The chairmanship of the English Department at Rangoon University, for example, was abolished in 1966 (the
teaching of English was only properly restored in the early 1980s) and
universities and schools were always closed down at the first signs of
trouble. The closure of Burma's universities since 1988 thus has clear
antecedents in actions taken by the security forces in 1962–64 and
1974–76 as a third generation of students suffers the disruption of their
academic careers. This is something the young people of Burma deeply
resent, and, with Ne Win still in the wings, the situation has continued
to worsen since 1988. When the universities temporarily reopened in
mid-1991, for example, the SLORC promised many changes. But
following anti-SLORC protests during celebrations at the award of the
1991 Nobel Peace Prize to Daw Aung San Suu Kyi, campuses around the
country were once again shut, more than nine hundred students were
detained, and all of Burma's lecturers and teachers were sent away on
boot-camp "retraining" courses organized by the Military Intelligence
Service. Education officials privately estimated that in a twelve-month
period during 1991–92 alone more than seven thousand teachers and
several hundred university lecturers were sacked, including another two
hundred staff from Rangoon University. The damage thus done to
Burma's education system over the past three decades is incalculable.
There are no Ph.D. programs, and with the lack of trained specialists
many small departments, including anthropology, have virtually
collapsed (Article 19 1992).

However, the main charge by minority parties against Ne Win,
military rule, and the Burmese Way to Socialism is that the latter has just
been a convenient term with which to legalize the process of "Burman-
ization," which, they allege, had already begun under U Nu. All minority
schools and newspapers were nationalized by the BSPP, and the official
usage of minority languages declined dramatically. The university system
continued to be based in Rangoon and Mandalay, in the Burman-major-
ity heartlands. With the later exception of Moulmein College, in the
ethnic-minority states there are still no universities, only state colleges.
The BSPP's one token gesture to the ethnic minorities has been the

Academy for the Development of National Groups, founded in 1965 and located near Sagaing in the heartland of Burman culture. Former students have bitterly criticized its courses (Silverstein 1977, 114). In May 1991, the academy was reformed as a university, under SLORC Law No. 9/91, but its credentials are seriously questioned. There is no provision for research, students must wear uniforms, and it is directly controlled by the SLORC—not by the Ministry of Education (Article 19 1992, 14–16).

With the introduction of a one-party system, there was also an obvious decline in the role of ethnic-minority leaders at all levels of national life. And, though under the BSPP's 1974 Constitution there were clear guarantees for the cultural, religious, and language rights of all minority groups, ethnic leaders allege that there has long been an in-built system of discrimination against minority peoples. The contrast with the days of the British, when there were elected Karen and Rakhine cabinet ministers and Kachins and Karens in the top levels of the army, is extreme.

However, what may be the most serious allegation made by ethnic parties in Burma today concerns not the abuse of political rights but Tatmadaw atrocities, which in the last few years have begun to attract increasing attention abroad. It can be argued that forty years of warfare have had a brutalizing effect on the Burmese army. Many allegations relate to the forced conscription of ethnic-minority villagers to work as porters carrying supplies for the army in the war zones and a particularly ruthless counterinsurgency campaign known as the Four Cuts. In 1988, Amnesty International documented the unlawful killing, torture, or ill-treatment of more than two hundred ethnic-minority villagers but this is just the tip of the iceberg (Amnesty International 1988). All these practices continue today (Amnesty International 1992). This has left a bitter legacy of resentment in many communities, which one day will need to be dispelled, and it has led to the suggestion by ethnic leaders that, rather than being a modern political leader of some consequence, Ne Win has simply been following in the footsteps of Anawrahta, Alaunghpaya, and the other great, all-conquering, Burman monarchs of history who sought to impose control on the ethnic-minority regions by military conquest (Yawnghwe 1987, 120).

To summarize, the consequences of three factors—the continuing civil war, the dilemma of national unity, and the legacy of Ne Win's rule—do much to explain how a country of abundant potential has sunk to such depths. In December 1987, on the eve of the democracy uprising, Burma was given Least Developed Country status at the United Nations. With an estimated average per-capita income of just $200 per annum, this put Burma, in statistical terms, alongside such impoverished nations as Ethiopia, Nepal, and Chad. Undoubtedly one of the most mineral-rich and fertile countries in Asia, Burma was forced to import oil in 1988. Once the world's largest exporter of rice, Burma's rice exports the same year were virtually nil (Kulkarni 1988).

Clearly all the peoples of Burma have suffered in the conflicts of the last five decades, and it is impossible today to find a single Burmese family, from any ethnic background, not deeply touched by the country's political strife. Indeed, since 1988, the incidence of human-rights abuses in Burma has reached a new high (Amnesty International 1990, 1992). But, despite the scale of military repression in the cities, ethnic leaders allege that it is again the minorities who have suffered the heaviest casualties, as the Tatmadaw has gone on an all-out offensive in the war zones. However, before examining the current political crisis in more detail, it is necessary to identify some of the specific problems the minority peoples face as a direct consequence of the political failures of the past forty years.

The Problems of the Minorities

Undoubtedly the most pressing problem is the dearth of reliable data on basic social, economic, cultural, and ethnic issues. Compounding the lack of accurate information from the era of British rule has been the suppression of new studies on ethnicity since independence. The few that have been allowed, such as Lehman's study of the Karenni in the 1950s, have been politically motivated by Rangoon governments, for example, to justify the legal separation of "Kayahs" from "Karens" (Lehman 1967). This situation undoubtedly worsened under the BSPP. Ethnic-minority languages, for example, are rarely taught today beyond fourth grade. Indeed, the few books and magazines that are legally published in minority languages have to go through an exhaustive censorship process before they go to press.

Perhaps the single most controversial issue is that of population statistics. Quite deliberately, there has been no published attempt to take an accurate census of the population of Burma since the last British census of 1931. The British count is itself highly disputed by many minorities. For example, in 1931 the Karen population was calculated at some 1,370,000. But when, during the Second World War, the Japanese conducted their own survey, they came up with a figure of 4.5 million (Smith 1991, 30). Most neutral estimates today put the Karen population of Burma at some 3 to 4 million, with another 200,000 living in Thailand. By contrast, the BSPP usually put the Karen population at just 2 million, while the KNU today claims a figure of 7 million divided into more than twenty subgroups including the Paos, Karennis, and Kayans. As a result, the Karens, like many other minorities, harbor a deep sense of political underrepresentation.

There simply are no reliable statistics. Nationalist leaders from the major ethnic groups claim the following population totals: the Shans and Mons at some 4 million each; the Buddhist Rakhine at 2.5 million; the Muslim Arakanese, or Rohingya, at 1 to 2 million (many of whom are living in exile); the Zos, or Chins, at 2 to 3 million; the Kachin at 1.5 million; and the Palaung-Wa at another 1 to 2 million. However, as these are projections based largely upon ancestral records rather than accurate counts of modern-day communities, they need to be treated with some caution. Complicating the picture even further are the large, intermingled, Chinese and Indian communities. Indeed, many Burmese citizens claim twin nationalities—Mon-Burman, Wa-Shan, or Karen-Muslim, for example—and such prominent figures as Ne Win, Aung Gyi, and San Yu are all believed to be of Sino-Burman ancestry.

This sense of numerical underrepresentation is compounded by the present political map of Burma. Since 1988, SLORC officials have hinted that they are considering alterations to the political regions of Burma in order to take into greater account the aspirations of what they have identified as the 135 ethnic races of Burma.[3] But for the present the seven ethnic-minority states and seven divisions organized under the 1974 Constitution give an unrealistic sense of symmetry to Burma's complex ethnic mosaic. For example, the present-day Karen State, which consists of some of the poorest mountain terrain in Burma, probably does not include even a quarter of the Karen population, while large ethnic groups such as the Paos, Was, Palaungs, and Lahus of the Shan State enjoy no geographic representation at all.

There is also a basic inconsistency in the racial designation of states. The Chin and Kachin, for example, are collective ethnic names that have only become accepted terms of political identity in the last century, while the Shan and Kayah are only the names of the largest ethnic groups within each state. Burmese historian Michael Aung Thwin described the British administration as one of "order without meaning" (Aung Thwin 1985, 245). This excellent expression could be applied equally to the present.

For all these reasons, then, ethnic nationalist leaders claim that a pragmatic redefinition of Burma's political map is vital if the minorities are ever to have representative territories in which they can enjoy the full expression of basic cultural, linguistic, and political rights. Ever since the visionary writings of the Karen leader Dr. San C. Po in the 1920s, "self-determination" has been the main demand of all the nationalist movements (Po 1928, 79–83).

Ethnic leaders contend that the clearest proof of this political underrepresentation can be seen in the economic field. Not only have the country's resources been monopolized by parties at the political center in Rangoon but large areas of territory that the minorities claim they need for their own self-development (such as the Kale-Kabaw Valley formerly in the Chin State and the upper Ledo Road formerly in the Kachin State) have been annexed by Burma proper. One of the key demands of the KNU, for example, has been for a seaport on the Tenasserim coast. What development there has been is located largely in the Burman heartlands, and the few industries still operating in the ethnic-minority states today are for the most part a legacy from the days of the British—for example, the mineral mines at Bawdwin in the Shan State and the sugar mills at Samaw in the Kachin State. One of the few new developments has been the heavily guarded hydroelectric plant at Lawpita in the impoverished Kayah State but this was constructed to supply electricity to Rangoon and Central Burma. As a result it has frequently been the target of insurgent attack. Under the SLORC, in areas where cease-fires with ethnic opposition groups have been agreed upon, an ambitious Border Areas Development program has been mooted with United Nations aid. But suspicions about SLORC motives remain high, and many foreign governments have been reluctant to fund programs such as road building, which may have a counterinsurgency motive, until the real political problems of Burma are resolved. For the moment, other than massive road and rail projects undertaken with conscripted local labor, there are few tangible signs of real development.

The result of this economic and infrastructural neglect is that many ethnic-minority peoples are living at the subsistence level. Often they engage in the unofficial or black-market trading that under the BSPP, at least, was forbidden on pain of the severest penalties, including death. More or less uniquely in Southeast Asia, the jungle has returned to many corners of the country and important highways such as the Ledo Road are no longer passable. The most worrying proof of this economic decline is the steady growth of the opium trade in the northeast, which has reached an estimated two thousand tons per annum, making Burma the world's largest producer of illicit heroin. Equally alarming, AIDS, which is endemic among intravenous drug users, is spreading unpublicized and unresearched into the rest of the community, accelerated by the growing numbers of impoverished young ethnic-minority and Burman girls going into prostitution in neighboring Thailand. Most neutral observers agree that the problems of insurgency and narcotics are inseparable. But, again, it is the minorities who suffer most of the international opprobrium attached to the trade. Indeed, it was not until the bloodshed of 1988 that the United States, which for several years supplied the toxic defoliant 2.4.D to the Burmese army for dumping on remote hill-farm communities, seriously questioned the government commitment to eradicating the trade, despite plentiful evidence over the years of official collusion.[4]

The collective result of more than forty years of political and economic neglect has been the continued marginalization of the minorities. In every field—political, economic, linguistic, cultural, and educational—the minorities have been hugely disadvantaged. Rather than being brought into the mainstream of national life since the British departure, many claim that they have been pushed to the very fringes of Burmese society.

The Present Political Debate

Following the collapse of the BSPP in 1988 and the CPB in 1989, the political situation remains complex. Even if all the different parties could be brought to the same table, finding a common language and an accepted set of definitions with which to discuss the current crisis would be a formidable task. Thus, before examining the recent moves taken by the State Law and Order Restoration Council, the new democracy parties, and the armed nationalist forces, a fourth group needs to be mentioned. For, despite their lack of access to the country, international academics have played an important role in setting the tone of Burma's ethnic debate over the past fifty years, and in the coming decade their work may become even more crucial.

Beginning with Christian missionaries and scholar-adventurers like Sir J. G. Scott, who vainly tried to label peoples on the basis of perceived "differences" in language and culture, there has long been a strong western influence on ethnic studies in Burma (Scott and Hardiman 1900–1901). This in part accounts for the sudden fluctuations in population statistics under the British administration as the criteria for classification of different ethnic groups changed constantly. "Some of the races or tribes in Burma change their language almost as often as they change their clothes," wrote one official in the 1931 census report (Bennison 1933, 245).

The picture changed with the pioneering studies in the Kachin Hills of Edmund Leach, who placed greater emphasis on similarities in language and custom (1954). Using the evidence of intercultural borrowing, one important breakthrough was F. K. Lehman's study of the Kayah (1967), which proved that the distinctive identity of the Karenni subgroup of the Karens developed more by assimilation of the political system of their Shan neighbors than by any ancient historical traditions.

The same line of argument has been taken up by modern historians and political scientists, notably Victor Lieberman and Robert Taylor, who have rejected the previous tendency to write of Burma's precolonial history in terms of Mon, Arakanese, Shan, and even Karen "centuries" (Lieberman 1978; Taylor 1987). Instead they have tried to prove that most political systems were polyethnic and that strictly monoethnic societies probably never existed in Burma.

Though broadly correct, there is a danger in trying to relate such studies too strictly to the current crisis (Taylor 1982, 7). All too frequently parallels to the present, especially inside Burma, have been drawn on the basis of little or no new field research. As a result, while new field studies have been neglected or made impossible, a number of investigations have been caught up in arguments over the incomplete records of earlier writers. An example of this was the heated correspondence between Leach and Nugent in *Man* (Nugent 1982; Leach 1983a, 1983b). Leach, who admits the many gaps in his own research, described Nugent's reinterpretation of his work as "fantasy," claiming that the "Kachin society" about which he wrote no longer existed (1983a, 192). Though leaders of the Kachin Independence Organisation dispute this, any journey into the ethnic-minority regions of Burma would confirm that the last fifty years have wrought enormous changes on traditional societies in Burma. These, however, much to the ethnic-minority populations' detriment, remain largely unrecorded.[5]

There remain huge gaps in our knowledge of Burma's ethnic history and many long-held beliefs about the origins of ethnic groups are highly suspect. For example, contemporary histories continue to identify the Shans with the ancient kingdom of Nanchao in Yunnan Province in China, while other studies suggest that the real rulers were ethnic Lolos

(Yawnghwe 1987, 63; Backus 1981, 44–52). Worst of all, from the minority viewpoint, is the fact that, though they are deprived of access to Burma, western anthropologists continue to develop these theories. The most striking example is Hinton's "Do the Karen Really Exist?" (1983). Such studies, mostly written from the misleading perspective of neighboring Thailand, come nowhere near understanding the dynamism and aspirations of modern nationality movements in Burma.

However unwittingly, the works of many of these writers, by their neglect of contemporary realities, have helped contribute to the marginalization of the minorities. And, with the notable exception of Silverstein, many have fallen into the trap of regarding armed nationalist groups and their leaders as simple terrorists, outlaws, or entities that have somehow "disappeared" from the political stage (Silverstein 1990). Undoubtedly one of the main features of the insurgent movements in Burma has been their isolation, the way they have remained inside their own territories, organizing among their own peoples, unnoticed by the outside world. International perceptions have changed dramatically since 1988 when the Tatmadaw turned its guns on students demonstrating peacefully on the streets of Rangoon. But the fact is that a vibrant and important debate has continued in the jungles of Burma for the past forty years, a debate which, in its causes and solutions, has important implications for the struggles of indigenous peoples around the world. At a time of critical ethnic and political change, there is thus an urgent need for the international academic community to try to rectify many of the serious omissions in recent ethnic-minority studies in Burma.

To give just one example, despite the explosive international nature of the issue, no real field research has been carried out on the ethnic history of the "Rohingya" Muslims from the Rakhine State who have twice in the past two decades fled into neighboring Bangladesh in the hundreds of thousands after the Burmese government, backed by heavy-handed military harassment, appeared to revoke their right to live in Burma. The evidence of a grave ethnic/religious conflict is stark. But for Burma's long-suffering minorities, only dispassionate and neutral studies may now succeed in shedding light where political dogma has failed.

In many parts of the country there are simply no ethnic statistics, histories, or studies for reliable reference. This circumstance is not just a modern impediment, for it continues a neglect begun in the era of British rule. One of the few officials aware of the looming dangers of this neglect was H. N. C. Stevenson, the postwar director of the Frontier Areas. In 1944, while the Second World War still raged, he addressed the

Royal Anthropological Institute in London to call for an immediate program of ethnic field studies. With Burma's independence coming under increasing discussion, his warning on the British failure to institute such studies was clear.

> Books on Burma written by trained social scientists are conspicuous by their absence from the Institute's library. The official files of the past 50 years have disappeared in the defeat of 1942. On what basis then will our future plans be laid? Against what background in recorded knowledge shall we frame our perspective? (Smith 1991, 48)

Today his appeal has equal resonance and urgency.

Of course, it should be stressed that academics from every discipline have faced great difficulties in conducting any new research in Burma since independence. With limits on access, those who have (such as R. Taylor) often have concentrated more on examining the basis for military rule in a united Burma. Not surprisingly, then, with few ethnic-minority studies for contrast, such writings have sometimes been quoted in defense of the BSPP, most recently by SLORC officials. But even the Tatmadaw leaders have recognized that the sheer scale of ethnic diversity in Burma requires that some basic racial differences must be acknowledged. Thus, in a refinement of the theories of polyethnicity, in the standard histories of Rangoon much emphasis is also placed on the shared historical experiences of the different ethnic groups. The SLORC chairman General Saw Maung's speech on independence day in January 1991 is a classic example of this genre.

> The people of all the national races, with a high sense of patriotism, fought with whatever weapons they could lay their hands on against the British imperialists' enslavement of our nation. The patriots from among the various national races, the Kachins, the Kayahs, the Karens, the Burmans, the Mons, the Arakanese, and the Shans, who had taken part in the anti-imperialist and national liberation struggle, must go down in the annals of our history as patriotic heroes so that their memory will last for eternity. (British Broadcasting Corporation 1991)

Word for word, save for the dropped references to socialism, this was the kind of speech produced under the BSPP, and it suggests how little perceptions have changed under the SLORC. Indeed, Saw Maung was the last BSPP minister of defence. But now there does seem to be a new urgency in the government's pronouncements. Recognizing the importance of control of the country's traditions, since 1988 the Tatmadaw leadership have stepped up their efforts to rewrite Burma's history in a new search for political legitimacy. General Ne Win's wife, Daw Ni Ni Myint, author of *Burma's Struggle Against British Imperialism* (1983), has been put in charge of Rangoon University's Historical Research Commission, one of the few departments uninterrupted by the upheavals since 1988. They have been slowly publishing a series of selective books, which, whitewashing the role of Ne Win, present the Tatmadaw as the modern embodiment of all national aspirations. This appears to be one of the reasons why Aung San Suu Kyi, the figurehead of the democracy movement, is seen as such a threat to the SLORC generals. Not only does she deride Ne Win's claims to be the successor of her father, the independence hero Aung San, but she has often said her first move would be to introduce new libraries and a free press. Most other political reforms, she believes, would come naturally in their wake.

Thus, anthropology, history, and education have also become crucial weapons in the political conflict in Burma. Not surprisingly, the military's view of history is completely rejected by the ethnic nationalists. The political aims of the different ethnic fronts and organizations naturally vary but the literature produced by the Karen, Karenni, Kachin, Mon, Pao, Rakhine, Shan, and other nationalist movements over the past forty years consistently confirm that they have always seen themselves as much more than minorities. The term they prefer is *nationalities*. A popular saying of the KNU, for example, accuses the Burmans of practicing what it calls "the three A's" toward the Karens— "annihilation, absorption, and assimilation. The Karens are much more than a national minority. We are a nation" (Smith 1991, 36).

In general, large ethnic groups such as the Mons, Shans, Karens, and Kachins see their situation as comparable to that of the nationalities of the Soviet Union, Yugoslavia, and India, and not as forgotten "tribal" peoples living on the edge of Burman culture and society. The Arakan Independence Organisation (AIO), for example, formerly headed by Kyaw Hlaing, a Rakhine graduate of Rangoon University, describes the ethnic-minority regions as "Hidden Colonies," a situation it equates with that of the Kurds of the Middle East and the Eritreans and Tigreans in Africa. All indigenous peoples, the AIO claims, are regarded as part of the larger, historically recognized nations in the postcolonial world, as though these nations have always been something absolute, yet historically, culturally, and geographically it is something they do not necessarily feel. In line with the new terminology in the international political debate, some nationalist groups have recently begun to use the expression "Fourth World" to describe their plight, though again most nationalist leaders, especially from such ancient civilizations as the Mons and Shans, reject the idea of realigning their struggles with very different ethnic groups like the Amazonian Indians or the Australian Aborigines.

These are claims worth examining seriously. In mainland Southeast Asia, it is, after all, the Karens and Kachins (of the peoples once considered "tribal") who have come closest to their dream of creating independent nation-states. What has always been most striking on visits to the "liberated areas" of insurgent groups such as the Karens, Karennis, Mons, Shans, and Rakhines is how they have kept alive, inside Ne Win's monolithic Burma, a clear sense of their ethnic identity and purpose. Across Burma they have maintained their own armies, schools, hospitals, and administrative systems, and life in their villages and camps is punctuated with a full litany of colorful nationalist days and celebrations. This is not something "bandits" do. It needs, therefore, to be added that with the exception of the Tatmadaw there are no "legal" organizations in Burma today with political traditions more than five years old. By contrast, the outlawed KNU has continued its struggle since 1947, the New Mon State Party since 1958, and the Kachin Independence Organisation (KIO) since 1961.

The Post-1988 Crisis

The situation of all Burma's armed groups has changed considerably since 1988 but in general armed opposition can be divided into two major groups, one headed by the National Democratic Front (NDF), an alliance of eleven ethnic-minority parties, and the other by present or former allies of the CPB, which has struggled to survive since the ethnic mutinies of 1989. The NDF forms the nucleus of another body set up in November 1988, the Democratic Alliance of Burma (DAB), which includes some ten underground democracy groups established in the aftermath of the Saw Maung coup. However, only the All Burma Students' Democratic Front and the All Burma Young Monks Union have any countrywide influence. There are a number of other independent insurgent organizations such as the Tailand Revolutionary Council of Khun Sa in the Shan State, Mujahid groups in Arakan, and Naga factions on the Indian border. But other than the serious opium problem in the Shan State their day-to-day significance can be considered small in the national political context.

For the past decade the NDF has been the main voice for the armed nationalist cause. Formed in 1976, it is in fact the latest in a long line of ethnic coalitions that surfaced after the insurrections began. Over the years its aims and membership have varied slightly but since 1984 all its members have joined in promoting what they call a "genuine federal union" as the solution to Burma's ethnic problems. At its peak in the late 1980s, NDF commanders claimed to have more than twenty-five thousand troops they could call on, although it is unlikely that many more than fifteen thousand regulars could actually have been armed at any one time. Still the two largest groups are the Kachin Independence Organisation (KIO) and the KNU, each of which has several thousand armed supporters. Smaller groups include the New Mon State Party and the Karenni National Progressive Party, both of which have several hundred troops.

Several reasons are given for the demand for a federal union. First, whatever the guarantees in the two constitutions since independence, the ethnic minorities have enjoyed no real political, cultural, or economic autonomy. As they point out, ethnic-minority peoples inhabit at least half the land area of Burma. Yet these areas, as the Tatmadaw's behavior since the 1988 coup has once again shown, are regarded as backwaters to be exploited by selling off their mineral or forest resources as the need arises. There are, of course, many who do not share NDF views (Karens, Kachins, and Mons, for example) but it is undoubtedly true that the first experience for many ethnic-minority villagers of Burman people and the central government has come not through peaceful coexistence or development but through military operations conducted by the Tatmadaw.

A second reason for the idea of a federal Union is the begrudging recognition by groups such as the KNU and the KIO that after more than three decades of armed struggle they are simply not going to make it on their own. Secession, they accept, is no longer practical in the modern political world, and the model they are looking to is a strong federal system, somewhat on the lines of a mix of West Germany, Switzerland, and India, to protect their interests in fields as diverse as education, policing, investment, language, and employment. The example of China, which for many years held some attraction for several ethnic parties, has fallen rapidly from grace in the last few years.

The NDF has put forward two additional ideas; interestingly, these were agreed upon before the seismic events of 1988. The first idea is that ethnic Burmans should also be represented by a nationality state so that the equality of all ethnic groups is clearly demarcated in the legislature. According to the KIO chairman Brang Seng, "Until there is a Burman state, the Burman majority will never really understand or respect ethnic minority rights."[6] But in the 1950s NDF leaders also claimed that the ethnic-minority states were never able to develop their own policies, and as a result they became increasingly subservient to the political intrigues of the mainstream parties in Rangoon.

The second NDF idea is for a nationwide amnesty, the release of all political prisoners, and peace talks. These they want to see completed before the new Constitution is drawn up so that all the minorities can take part in its framing. There were major peace talks with groups currently represented in the NDF in 1949, 1960, and 1963–64. More recently, in 1980–81, talks were conducted with the KIO. But those who took part say they failed because Ne Win and the army leaders, who only see things in terms of law and order, have insisted each time that all armed opposition groups surrender without making any political guarantees. What NDF leaders have been increasingly eager to find is a framework, or at least a neutral environment, in which all of Burma's political problems can be addressed in light of the experiences of the past forty years.

In the late 1980s, this led NDF leaders, frustrated by isolation and their inability to make any impact on Rangoon, to begin to look to the outside world. Initially (before 1988), this took the form of an attempt to find foreign intermediaries to conduct peace talks. Among the governments approached were those of Thailand, the United Kingdom, and West Germany. At first their efforts to come to the West had to be supported by sympathetic nongovernmental organizations (NGOs). The first visit by a representative of the KNU to the Human Rights Sub-Commission of the United Nations in Geneva and to the Foreign Affairs Committee of the House of Commons in London, in March 1987, was made possible by Anti-Slavery International. Somewhat remarkably, the KNU representative, Saw Hsa Ta Nor, was the first KNU representative to visit Britain since the Karen insurrection began in 1949. Later in the year the KIO leader Brang Seng met at the House of Lords with Lord Bottomley, Britain's representative at the Panglong Conference, and Lord Listowel, the last British secretary of state for Burma.

Following this breakthrough, through the continuing efforts of Anti-Slavery International, the World Council of Indigenous Peoples, the International Work Group for Indigenous Affairs, and a number of other western NGOs, representatives of the NDF, and more recently of the DAB, have taken their places at an increasing number of international seminars. Since 1991, NDF representatives have addressed the Working Group on Indigenous Populations and the Working Group on Modern Forms of Slavery at the UN Human Rights Sub-Commission.

And, though travel arrangements remain an acute problem for all the minority groups (representatives from the "liberated zones" are stateless within their own country), more NGOs from countries such as Germany and Thailand have lent their support. Stimulated by these travels and discussions, NDF and DAB lawyers produced their own draft Constitution for debate in late 1990. Federal in principle, it provides for eight states of Burma (including a Burman) with autonomous or special territories for smaller minorities within each state.

Many of these ideas have been accepted by the ethnic-minority parties that won seats in the May 1990 election. Some are even supported by elected members of parliament from the National League for Democracy (NLD) who, since December 1990, have been arriving at the DAB headquarters at Manerplaw. There has been an overwhelming consensus in Burma since the uprising of 1988 that peace and a just settlement of the civil war should be a main priority of the democracy movement in the cities. These sentiments undoubtedly increased after the NDF, in late 1988, provided sanctuary to as many as ten thousand young Burman refugees from the cities. Many students, who previously said they were ignorant of all these minority issues, now say they are committed to staying in the jungles with their new ethnic allies until the wars are finally brought to an end. What is increasingly heard from many different quarters is the need for a new Panglong Conference. Another of the popular ideas of Aung San Suu Kyi is her call for Burma's "second struggle for independence," which all ethnic groups take as an indication of the will to start anew. All can collectively identify with this slogan, and if ever Burma is to emerge from its present state of confrontation some such grand gesture will be needed.

The missing link in all these discussions, of course, is the military government, which for the moment remains very much under the shadow of the aging Ne Win, and in many respects has become very much stronger since 1988. Army leaders were greatly angered by the NDF's appeals to the West. Since 1988, bolstered by massive new purchases of arms and equipment (including a surprise $1.2 billion contract with China), they have launched sustained offensives against the NDF and DAB, resulting in some of the heaviest fighting the country has seen in years. The army was also quick to take advantage of the CPB mutinies in 1989 by offering immediate cease-fires, food, and supplies to the breakaway armies. This allowed the SLORC a vital breathing space in which to concentrate its energies on dealing with the emerging democracy movement in the cities and the DAB in the countryside.

Nonetheless, though the army's grip for the moment appears tighter than ever, something has undoubtedly broken in the mold of Burmese politics. Change is on its way, though its time scale and shape are impossible to predict. Whatever the SLORC's present intentions—and many senior army officers are clearly anxious for change—there will be no real peace or progress without substantive political reform. One of the most striking features of the May 1990 election was that, after twenty-six years of one-party rule, multiethnic politics are definitely back on the political map. Aung San Suu Kyi's NLD, which itself included many minority candidates, won 392 (81 percent) of the 485 available seats, while of the twenty-six other victorious parties no less than nineteen represented the ethnic minorities. In the Shan State, for example, the Shan Nationalities League for Democracy is now the single largest elected party.

This initially encouraged the SLORC to think that, rather like U Nu's governments of the 1950s, they could win a new body of support by playing the ethnic-minority card. The SLORC's first plan after an election result they clearly had not expected (the BSPP's successor, the National Unity Party, won just ten seats) was to call a delay under a new martial-law decree, No. 1/90, and initiate plans for a "National Convention" to draw up the principles of a new Constitution. The convention, it suggested, would be attended by only one or two representatives from each of the twenty-seven victorious parties, which would have completely watered down the NLD majority.

At first this plan was stumped when the nationality parties publicly allied themselves with the NLD, calling for a swift transfer of power. But the SLORC pushed on with the idea of a National Convention, and soon it proved to be a masterstroke. Not only did it allow the army generals (and several insurgent groups) a way back into the political process but it also provided a "legal" basis for their refusal to hand over the government to the NLD.

Throughout these developments, Aung San Suu Kyi (arrested in July 1989) and former prime minister U Nu (arrested in December 1989) were detained along with thousands of other democracy activists. If any doubts still remained, the SLORC's determination to cling to power was signalled in November 1990 by the sentencing to ten years' imprisonment on treason charges of Suu Kyi's successor, former colonel Kyi Maung, and the subsequent arrest of more than fifty of the victorious MPs. Hundreds of Buddhist monks were also imprisoned in October and November during a crackdown on democracy protests in the monasteries.

However, contradicting the SLORC's tough public strategy, behind the scenes the Military Intelligence Service, headed by Major General Khin Nyunt, was playing a classic game of "divide and rule," breaking up the political opposition. One of its most unexpected moves was a series of secret peace talks with several of the ethnic rebel armies. These meetings undoubtedly had been given a new urgency, first by the number of young people who had joined forces with the NDF in the aftermath of the Saw Maung coup, and then by the flight into NDF territory in December 1990 of Aung San Suu Kyi's cousin, Dr. Sein Win, and more than a dozen MPs from the NLD who formed the new National Coalition Government Union of Burma. A number of other MPs went to India, and later to the Kachin-China border.

The situation quickly became confused but a decisive shift in army policy could soon be detected. Following the unannounced cease-fires with the CPB defectors in 1989 (notably the United Wa State Army and Kokang mutineers), while continuing to attack local NDF forces, the SLORC also proposed massive UN-sponsored development programs in the border regions. Beginning in January 1991, at the SLORC's invitation, delegations from various United Nations agencies began visiting the Shan State where they met with veteran insurgent leaders such as Pheung Kya-shin who just two years earlier had been described as warlords in the state press. The carrot the SLORC dangled before the international community was the chance to combat Burma's unrestricted opium trade.

Then in another surprise development following the arrival of Dr. Sein Win and the NLD MPs at the border, the SLORC began secretly offering the same peace terms to carefully selected members of the NDF. Groups supporting the students and the NLD MPs, such as the KNU, remained under attack. Nonetheless, the peace offer produced immediate results. In January 1991, the KIO Fourth Brigade in the Shan State defected, in March the Pao National Organisation in the Taunggyi area declared a cease-fire, and on 23 April the Palaung State Liberation Party also began peace talks. The SLORC quite rightly sensed a difference in day-to-day interests between the ethnic-minority nationalists and the NLD/student opposition. Added to this, in the Shan State, at least, where there was a close link between above-ground and underground parties, ethnic-minority candidates did well in the 1990 election. If multiparty politics are really going to return to Burma, nationalist leaders say they want to seize every opportunity to get on the inside of the political process. This is also the NDF official line because everyone recognizes that any party left outside now, at what may well be the last period of consultative discussions for years, could well spend another four decades in the political wilderness.

This was further brought into focus in January 1993 when the SLORC's carefully managed National Convention finally began in Rangoon, against a backdrop of growing international criticism and condemnation, including an investigation by the UN's Special Rapporteur on Human Rights. With the legally elected political parties now whittled down to just seven (including the NLD, five ethnic-minority parties, and the pro-SLORC National Unity Party), the convention's 702 delegates were packed with co-opted representatives of the peasants, workers, ethnic minorities, and other sectors of Burmese society. All were preselected by the SLORC; their limited brief was to draw up the "principles" for the new Constitution and included the new obligation, under SLORC Order 13/92, to incorporate and guarantee the "leading role" of the Tatmadaw in national political life. Significantly, there was no promise of implementation or a timetable for reform. Nonetheless, the KIO leadership chose this unexpected moment to begin tentative, unilateral talks with the SLORC, apparently breaking the unity of the DAB and NDF, in the hope that at least the the voice of the armed opposition might be heard after so many years of inconclusive struggle.

How these initiatives will translate into a country-wide peace is for the moment unclear, especially while the 1991 Noble Peace Prize laureate, Aung San Suu Kyi, remains in detention and frozen out of the political process. Given the instability of the situation and the continuing repression in the cities, there has been a good deal of international skepticism. Heroin production, it is noted, has actually increased since the cease-fires (Lintner 1991). Leaked documents from these talks show that several "rebel" minority leaders have been promised they can join the National Convention but the SLORC's main intention appears to be to turn these ethnic forces into local police militia similar to the discredited Ka Kwe Ye "home-guards" of the 1960s. The rapid formation of these units did much to take the steam out of the fast-spreading Shan insurrection after Ne Win's 1962 military coup (Smith 1991, 221). This time some observers see an even more cynical ploy behind the SLORC's moves. "While SLORC continues to reject the election result and detains the NLD leaders, every agreement it reaches with any section of the population can be seen to enhance its authority as the *de facto* government of the country," commented one diplomat. But what ethnic leaders have been quick to note is that they have been offered more than the army has ever offered before: the right to keep their weapons and territory. There are also vague promises of autonomy, although SLORC officials seem increasingly interested in the model of Indonesia.

The collective result of all the SLORC's actions since the coup, however, is to ensure that the Tatmadaw remains the only united force in Burmese society. If nothing else, the experience of the last three decades shows that the army cannot solve all of Burma's problems alone. To a certain extent the regime has been bailed out of its financial crisis by foreign "signature money" for oil, teak, gems, and fishery concessions but the overall situation in the country is still desperate. Nowhere is this more obvious than in the chaos of the Shan State, which in early 1993 had a greater variety of political parties, defense militia, and armed ethnic forces than any other place on earth.[7]

The issues facing Burma's indigenous peoples are daunting. There is an increasingly serious refugee problem. Officially more than 70,000 ethnic-minority refugees, mainly Karens, have fled the war zones into Thailand. The true figure is probably five times this amount. Similar numbers of Kachin refugees are living along the Chinese border, while more than 250,000 Muslims fled into Bangladesh from the Rakhine State during late 1991 and early 1992 amid widespread reports of Tatmadaw atrocities and human-rights abuses in one of the least-known corners of Burma. There is also the growing problem of AIDS, prostitution, and semislavery among young hill-tribe girls lured across the border into Thailand. Then there are the growing ecological problems (overfishing, deforestation, and planned dam construction) brought on by the rapid intrusion of foreign companies into Burma. Closely related is the spreading narcotics problem, which is a blight not only for Burma but for its neighbors and the world. Last, but not least, there is the collapse of higher education. Amid Burma's turmoils, yet another generation of students from all ethnic backgrounds has now lost out.

CHAPTER 12

Central Highlanders of Vietnam

GRANT EVANS

Of the two, main, upland minority areas in Vietnam, one is on the northern border, extending to the northwest of the country. Here the highlands are dominated by various "tribal" Tai groups along with Hmong, Yao, and various Mon-Khmer-speaking peoples. Except for the Mon-Khmer, these groups were originally "invaders" from China and in that sense are nonindigenous. Along with considerations of space, this is one reason why I will not deal with the northern highlanders in this paper. The people of the Central Highlands, however, more properly fit the term *indigenous peoples*. They are commonly acknowledged to be the original inhabitants of the southern mountain regions. Generally Austronesian or Mon-Khmer speakers, these are stateless societies whose people live in the forests either as hunter-gatherers, slash-and-burn cultivators, or in some cases sedentary cultivators. They are best known to anthropologists through George Condominas's now classic study of one group, the Mnong Gar, in *We Have Eaten the Forest* (1957, 1977). More recently Gerald C. Hickey has produced an impressive two-volume ethnohistory of the Central Highlands, *Sons of the Mountains* (1982a) and *Free in the Forest* (1982b).

This is not the place to present an outline of the history of the Central Highlands but Hickey makes it clear that these societies have their own dynamic history, are not "living fossils," and have had continuous relations with the lowland states of the Khmer, the Cham, the Lao, and the Vietnamese. These contacts have varied from ritual relations with the Khmer to tributary ones with the Vietnamese—from trading to slave raiding. It was French colonial missionaries who finally established beachheads in the mountains and paved the way for ethnic Vietnamese settlers there. The French also created "montagnard battalions," from which a tiny highland intelligentsia was formed (Hickey 1982b). Once in contact with the ideas of modern nationalism, this group was attracted to the idea of highland independence and established an organization called Le Front Unis pour la Liberation des Races Opprimés (FULRO). During the American intervention in Vietnam, U.S. Special Forces continued the practice of maintaining highland battalions and kept FULRO's hopes alive.

The Vietnam War had a devastating impact on the Central Highlands where some of the most intense fighting, bombing, and use of defoliants occurred. The outcome is best captured by George Condominas who returned to the field during this conflagration and found the Mnong "decimated."

> They were driven from their territory by the Army, and had been further reduced by the consequences of their forcible removal [malnutrition, epidemics, loss of their zest for life]; now they had but two alternatives: they could take to the bush and thereby preserve their liberty, but they would be obliged to endure bombardments and grave consequences should they be captured—all this without being able to lead their traditional way of life; or they could submit to the orders of foreign masters and accede to being penned in the Special Forces camps where, depending on age and sex, they were transformed into beggars or docile hirelings. (Condominas 1977, xv)

Jacques Dournes, who lived among the Central Highlanders for twenty-five years, called this the "era of concentration camps." He wrote:

> I have known a little girl with large, scared eyes; she lay for more than twenty-four hours on the corpse of her mother who had been killed during an operation where the national army used montagnard civilians as a buffer against an attack by the [National Liberation] Front....At the camp of Dam San 6000 Montagnards are without land and have no water. Uprooted, unemployed, dirty, they beg American rice and cover themselves with Western rags. (Dournes 1980, 10)

The disruption of the highlanders' way of life was so extensive that by 1973, according to Hickey, "the existing ethnolinguistic maps were rendered invalid. An estimated 200,000 highlanders died during the Vietnam War, and an estimated 85 percent of the villagers were forced, one way or another, to flee as refugees" (1982b, 290). After the war ended in April 1975, it was hoped that the highlanders would be able to return to their mountain villages and rediscover their dignity and way of life. Sadly, this was not to be.

We know relatively little about what has happened in the Central Highlands since the communists took power in the south. As only Vietnamese ethnographers have been permitted to do research in the region, they are an important source of information about the lives of the indigenous people there. Unfortunately, their narrow theoretical perspective and the concerns of politics influence what they are able to perceive and say (see Evans 1985). The following essay attempts to gather the scattered available information on the Central Highlands. It first examines the impact of internal migration on the highlands. Second, it looks at how Vietnamese anthropologists have interpreted these developments and provides occasional references from their studies to the social and cultural changes induced by the policies of the new regime and the practices of some of its cadres. Finally, this essay briefly surveys what is known of the indigenous peoples' resistance to Vietnamese internal colonialism.

The Central Highlanders

The Central Highland provinces are Gia Lai-Con Tum, Dac Lac (Darlac), and Lam Dong (see maps 12.1, 12.2, 12.3). Naturally, the highland groups in these provinces overlap in neighboring provinces (such as Song Be and Nghia Binh), in Cambodia, or in Laos. Officially there are fifty-four ethnic groups in Vietnam, including ethnic Vietnamese, or Kinh. In the Central Highlands the main groups, in rough order of size of population, are the Jarai (180,000), Ede (129,000), Bahnar (96,000), Kohor (56,000), Sedang (50,000), Hre (data not available), Mnong (40,000), Raglai (n.a.), Stieng (560), Ko Tu (n.a.), Jeh-trieng (11,000), Ma (23,310), Co (n.a.), Cho Ru (7,900), Brau (1,600), and Rmam (137). The Jarai, Ede, Raglai, and Cho Ru are grouped among the Austronesian speakers, while the rest are Mon-Khmer. The population of the Central Highlands in 1979 was 1.5 million, which included 764,600 ethnic Vietnamese, or approximately 50 percent of the highland population. The growth of the Vietnamese population in the highlands in the past thirty years has been dramatic. In 1936, it was around 32,750, by 1970 it was 448,349 (Hickey 1982b, 303), and by 1979 it had nearly doubled again. In 1979, the lowest proportion of Kinh were in Gia Lai-Con Tum Province, accounting for

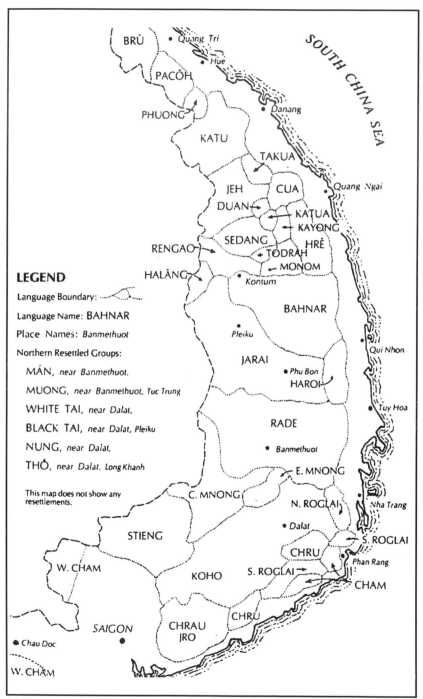

LEGEND

Language Boundary: ⌐‿⌐‿⌐...

Language Name: BAHNAR

Place Names: *Banmethuot*

Northern Resettled Groups:

  MÁN, *near Banmethuot.*

  MUONG, *near Banmethuot, Tuc Trung*

  WHITE TAI, *near Dalat.*

  BLACK TAI, *near Dalat, Pleiku*

  NUNG, *near Dalat.*

  THỔ, *near Dalat. Long Khanh*

This map does not show any
resettlements.

MAP 12.1. *Ethnolinguistic Map of the Vietnamese Central Highlands.*

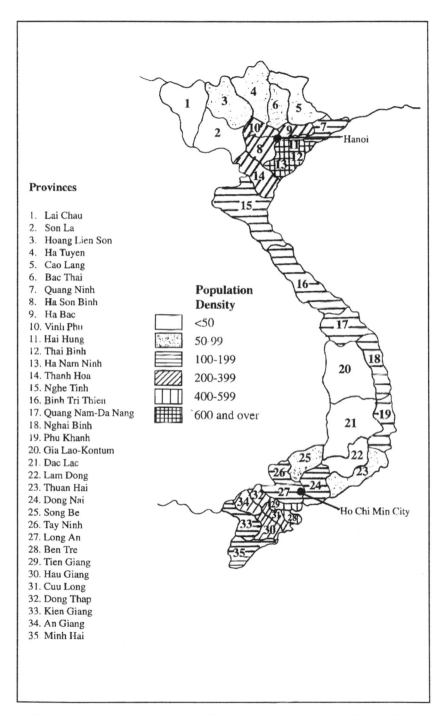

Provinces

1. Lai Chau
2. Son La
3. Hoang Lien Son
4. Ha Tuyen
5. Cao Lang
6. Bac Thai
7. Quang Ninh
8. Ha Son Binh
9. Ha Bac
10. Vinh Phu
11. Hai Hung
12. Thai Binh
13. Ha Nam Ninh
14. Thanh Hoa
15. Nghe Tinh
16. Binh Tri Thien
17. Quang Nam-Da Nang
18. Nghai Binh
19. Phu Khanh
20. Gia Lao-Kontum
21. Dac Lac
22. Lam Dong
23. Thuan Hai
24. Dong Nai
25. Song Be
26. Tay Ninh
27. Long An
28. Ben Tre
29. Tien Giang
30. Hau Giang
31. Cuu Long
32. Dong Thap
33. Kien Giang
34. An Giang
35. Minh Hai

Population Density

	<50
	50-99
	100-199
	200-399
	400-599
	600 and over

MAP 12.2. *Population Distribution in Vietnam, by Province. Source: Jones and Fraser (1984, p. 204).*

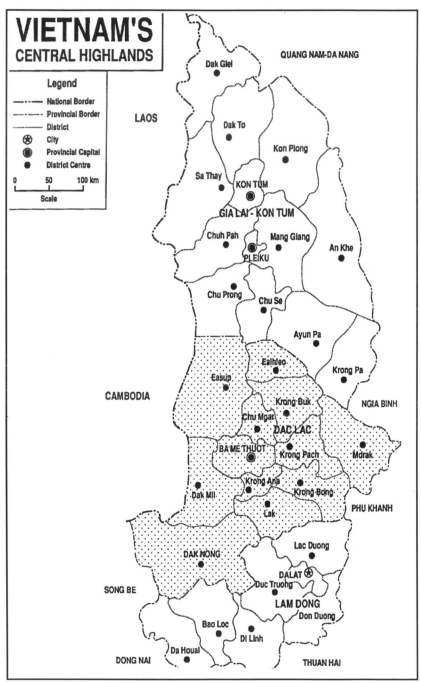

VIETNAM'S
CENTRAL HIGHLANDS

Legend

—·—·—	National Border
—·—·—	Provincial Border
··········	District
⊛	City
◉	Provincial Capital
●	District Centre

0   50   100 km

Scale

QUANG NAM-DA NANG

Dak Glei

LAOS

Dak To

Kon Plong

Sa Thay

KON TUM

GIA LAI - KON TUM

Chuh Pah   Mang Giang

An Khe

PLEIKU

Chu Prong

Chu Se

Ayun Pa

Ealhleo

Krong Pa

CAMBODIA

Easup

NGIA BINH

Krong Buk

Chu Mgar   DAC LAC

BA ME THUOT   Krong Pach

Mdrak

Krong Ana

Dak Mil   Krong Bong

PHU KHANH

Lak

Lac Duong

DAK NONG

DALAT ⊛

Duc Truong

SONG BE

LAM DONG

Don Duong

Bao Loc

Di Linh

Da Houai

DONG NAI

THUAN HAI

MAP 12.3. *Vietnam's Central Highlands, Provinces of Gia Lai-Con Tum, Dac Lac, and Lam Dong.*

40 percent of the population (250,333 persons). In Dac Lac they represented 60.3 percent (290,936 persons), while in Lam Dong they accounted for 69.5 percent (unless indicated, the above figures are taken from Le Duy Dai 1983).

New Economic Zones, Migration, and Resettlement

The Central Highlands' populations have borne the brunt of interprovincial population movements since 1975. This has resulted in occupation of minority peoples' lands by lowland Vietnamese immigrants and has led to tension between the two groups. Three main reasons have been given by Hanoi for population relocation: the return to their home villages of people displaced by the war; the redistribution of peoples from overpopulated rural areas and cities; and the securing of border areas with Vietnamese rather than supposedly less-reliable ethnic minorities. Such policies are not new. During partition the northern regime sent perhaps 1 million people into the Northern Highlands, while the southern regime relocated 58,651 refugees from the north in the Central Highlands after 1954. Many of these were Catholics and included various Tai-Nung groups. Post-1975 plans for spatial "rationalization" of the population, however, were distinguished by their ambitiousness.

Jacqueline Desbarats has analyzed the Vietnamese government's attempts at population relocation for the whole country from 1975 until the early 1980s. The aim of the policy, she points out, was to redeploy labor—or, as Vietnamese official statements put it, to "rationally" distribute labor. It was planned that Vietnam would relocate 10 million people by the end of the century. This involved moving people out of southern cities swollen by the war, relocating people from the overcrowded northern cities and the Red River delta into the south, and the resettlement of "nomadic hill tribes."

> The Second Five-Year Plan (1976–1980) called for the transfer of 4 million people overall: 1.5 million residents of large Southern urban centres to be settled in rural areas, and 2.5 million Northerners from the most over crowded provinces to be transferred South....In addition, the government intended to settle approximately 700,000 members of the Central Highland nomadic hill tribes. (Desbarats 1987, 8)

Desbarats comments that these movements were poorly organized, especially with respect to the virgin New Economic Zones (NEZ). This led to resistance by settlers and the increased use of coercion by the authorities. Many urban dwellers had never been farmers and were unprepared for NEZ life in every way, and the government held a naive view of "empty," territory. As Desbarats drily observes, it was often empty precisely because it was unsuitable for farming.

Resistance did not lead to reappraisal of the policy, only to a revision of its ambitions during the Third Five Year Plan of 1981–86. During 1976–80, the government had hoped to move 4 million people but achieved only 1.3 million. During 1981–85, the plan was scaled back to 1 million persons, and this was barely achieved.

> Under the Third Plan, as under the Second Plan, Southern provinces were the dominant destination of the flows. But in contrast to the previous period, most of the new settlers were now Northerners transferred to state-owned rubber and coffee plantations in the Central Highlands and Southeast Vietnam. (Ibid., 27)

In the period of the fourth plan (1986–90) the target of 3 million persons was reduced to 1.5 million by mid-1988.

As Desbarats points out, compiling statistics for population movements in Vietnam is an extremely tricky exercise. But, while precise figures are illusive, general calculations are possible, and thus a basically accurate picture can be constructed. While her main interest is not the Central Highlands, her calculations show that between 1976 and 1979 the highland province of Dac Lac, and its neighbor Song Be, received the largest number of NEZ settlers (in excess of 55,000), with the other highland provinces of Gia Lai-Con Tum and Lam Dong receiving the next largest number (between 28,000 and 55,000). In the next planning period these provinces swapped places, with Gia Lai-Con Tum and Lam Dong receiving the largest inflows (in excess of 39,000), followed by Dac Lac and Song Be (with 20,000 to 39,000). Like Desbarats, I have used the scattered information contained in radio broadcasts to update her findings, so that in Dac Lac, for example, from 1975 to 1986, 176,000 people were resettled in the province, and from 1985 to 1989 there were a further 31,500 settlers, for a total of 207,500 persons over a period of fifteen years. From 1986 to the end of 1988, another 40,000 people were resettled in Lam Dong, bringing the total to between 110,000 and 130,000 immigrants between 1976 and 1988. It is hard to obtain updated figures for Gia Lai-Con Tum because many of the figures are buried in general statements and statistics. Total figures for the decade 1981–90 are approximately 2 million, including intraprovincial and interprovincial movements, an achievement well short of the government's initial aims. And, while perhaps only a quarter of those ended up in the Central Highlands, they had a major impact on the highland region—mostly unfavorable.

Early on it became clear to the leadership in Hanoi that there were problems with their relocation policy, and, while criticism of the policy has become more vocal over the years, it has not been abandoned. Thus, an appraisal of the program in early 1990 included damning criticism of it while at the same time it spelled out future targets. Information gathered from eleven provinces provide the following far from glowing picture of the NEZs: "Twenty-seven percent of the families which have resettled are much better off than before, 48 percent have a standard of living equal to or a little bit better than before, and 25 percent are worse off than before" (*FBIS Reports*, 3 April 1990). The appraisal goes on to say that the program failed in most of its aims and that "The results obtained do not rationalize the amount of capital invested—equivalent to 67,000 taels of gold—in building NEZs during the period 1981–88" (ibid.). The program has had little impact on heavily populated areas and the lives of those in NEZs have been hard. Furthermore, the "need for self-sufficiency in food grain has resulted in the heavy destruction of forests in various new economic zones" (ibid.). Nevertheless, between 1990 and the year 2000 the government still plans to try to relocate a further 2 to 3 million people.

The Vietnamese ethnographer Le Duy Dai (1983) provides some details of the sociological problems encountered by Vietnamese settlers in the mountains. In particular, he makes special reference to the differences between long-term Vietnamese residents of the highlands, beginning with those who settled prior to the post-1954 influx; those who moved to the Central Highlands after 1954; and those who were relocated in the region after 1975. There has been suspicion and hostility between these groups. Consequently, "marriages between different groups, especially those who came before and after 1975 are extremely rare" (ibid., 32). Different religious affiliations contribute to these difficulties.

> According to the Census of 1976 around 30 percent of the Vietnamese population have no religion (less 15 percent in Gia Lai-Con Tum, over 50 percent in Dac Lac, and less than 30 percent in Lam Dong). Of the remaining population, more than 40 percent are Christians, less than 40 percent are Buddhists, and more than 5 percent are Protestants. Most of the Catholic Christians are migrants from North Vietnam after 1945. Those who hold other religions such as Cao Dai and Hoa Hao [two syncretic, formerly millennial sects] often come from Central Vietnam.

> People with different religious beliefs certainly hold different social view-
> points. This difference creates social barriers between different groups of
> people. (Ibid.)

These differences are expressed in "regionalism." Thus, people from
different areas of Vietnam who were relocated into an NEZ in order to
set up an agro-industrial complex or cooperative would effectively split
into two independent bodies due to economic and political rivalry.

Faced with poor facilities and economic and social deprivation,
many settlers abandoned the NEZs. During a visit to one settlement in
Song Be Province in early 1980, I could not help being struck by the
sense of desolation I found there. People were living in newly
constructed, single-room huts that looked as though they would blow
away with the first strong wind, while the newly cleared land would
require years of labor before becoming fully functioning paddy fields.
The hospitals and schools were rudimentary even by Vietnamese standards—and this was considered one of the better settlements. The people
I spoke with were bewildered and forlorn. Not surprisingly, many abandoned these settlements and illegally slunk back into the cities or their
old villages. Time and again in the reports on population relocation in
Vietnam one comes across descriptions of chaos and mismanagement.
The following account is representative.

> The most difficult problem at present is grain. During this year's first
> quarter, the irrational supply of grain caused a lot of hardship to people
> who had just arrived in the new economic zones. According to state regu-
> lations, the provinces are required to provide three months' supply of grain
> to families leaving for the new economic zones. For the sake of conve-
> nience, some localities have agreed to deliver that grain to the grain
> corporation at the point of departure with the families receiving grain at
> their destination. However, things have not happened like that in reality.
> The grain supply for households leaving Thai Binh Province for the new
> economic zones was delivered to the provincial grain corporation;
> however, on arrival in Dac Lac, those households were told that the
> provincial grain corporation could not sell them any grain at all because
> Dac Lac was facing a grain shortage itself. (*Summary of World Broadcasts*,
> 27 April 1988)

As a solution, some Vietnamese analysts suggested that it would be best
to supply the would-be settlers with grain to take with them. But this
would add a further burden to an already strained transportation system.
Another difficulty was that the receiving provinces and areas rarely
received the money promised by the central government to cover the

expenses of building new settlements, and they could not supply the capital themselves. So, rather than arriving in places with proper roads, housing, and water supplies, settlers sometimes found themselves virtually dumped in the wild. Furthermore, these new areas not only failed to relieve economic pressures elsewhere but they became a burden on the wider economy when they failed to achieve economic self-sufficiency. In late 1990, Dac Lac was still suffering from such serious food shortages that relief had to be provided by the central government (ibid., 29 September 1990).

One serious consequence of the lack of preparation was that settlers resorted to slash-and-burn farming (probably in an improper way, increasing the risk of uncontrolled fires), illegal timber gathering and logging, and hunting of endangered species in order to make ends meet. In other words, the environmental destruction mentioned above was also a consequence of the relocation policy and accelerated a trend that has seen Vietnam's forest cover reduced from 44 percent of the country in 1945 to 22 percent in 1985. Despite its real origin, this degradation is almost invariably blamed on the ethnic minorities. A June 1987 editorial on environmental protection published in the party paper *Nhan Dan* singles out the highlanders for special attention: "The movement to resettle the ethnic minorities for sedentary farming has helped reduce the incidence of bushfires and deforestation" (ibid., 9 June 1987). By comparison, the destruction wrought by anarchic Vietnamese immigrant settlers in the highlands, or by rapacious forestry companies and illegal logging, receives relatively little attention. The following mid-1990 report on "indiscriminate exploitation of forests" is exceptional.

> Many organizations and individuals have felled trees with precious timber for export or for illegal sale in the country. A number of state-run units such as the Song Hieu Union of Agro-Forestry Enterprises, have failed to impose the ban on forest access and have illegally exploited thousands of cubic meters of timber from forest reserves. (*FBIS Reports*, 26 July 1990)

Another feature of uncontrolled logging by large companies, and about which there is no hard information, is that they create roads in the forests, opening them up for more slash-and-burn activity and for the hunting of wild species of animals and rare plants. This no doubt partly accounts for the reports of "unauthorized" people departing for (rather than running away from) the highlands (*Summary of World Broadcasts*, 18 April 1988).

Something like a rough-and-tumble, "Wild West" situation seems to have developed in the mountains. Barry Wain reported in 1988 that ten thousand "freecomers" had poured into Dac Lac, provoking a mixed reaction from local officialdom. They upset "the plan," clashed with residents over land, and

> make a habit of chopping precious forest trees for firewood. But...says Nguyen An Vinh, deputy chairman of Dac Lac "Most of these people are much more determined to build a new life than those who move according to the plan." (Wain 1988)

Ho Xuan Ma, vice chairman of the province's new economic-zone committee is less happy with their arrival. "They're destroying our forests and getting into conflicts with the minorities," he told Murray Hiebert, who reports that "Spontaneous migrants often move into existing villages, settling on land between houses and forcing minority villagers to move because they have no land left for gardens, Ma said." A former Special Forces highlander told Hiebert that "There are many conflicts with ethnic Vietnamese trying to take our land, but the authorities help settle these problems. Usually if an ethnic Vietnamese wants our piece of land, they have to pay us compensation" (Hiebert 1989, 43). One has a right to be slightly skeptical about the claims of compensation made by this ex-inmate of a reeducation camp, and more weight can be placed on his report of "many conflicts with ethnic Vietnamese" (ibid.).

Another example of anarchic population movement is that of highland minorities from the environmentally stressed Northern Highlands. "Since the late 1980s, tens of thousands of Hmong and Dao farmers have moved from areas bordering China to provinces south of Hanoi and to the central highlands, where they have often become embroiled in land disputes with the local population" (Hiebert 1992). A report in *Nhan Dan* spoke of 85,000 northern minority people migrating to Song Be Province alone. Such developments considerably complicate the ethnic map, as these people, whom I referred to in the opening paragraph as "invaders" in northern Vietnam, are now pressing on into southern Vietnam.

A Closer Look at One Highland Province

Once again it is Le Duy Dai (1980) who has provided some details on developments in the province of Gia Lai-Con Tum in an article in the Vietnamese ethnographic journal *Dan Toc Hoc*. This province is the largest in Vietnam (25,542 sq. km.). Central planners are quick to point out that it also is the least inhabited and needs more people. The fact that large parts of the province are inhospitable because of high mountain ranges (averaging 1,500 to 2,500 meters in elevation) does not seem to figure in their calculations. The plain silliness that enters into much command planning can be seen in the fact that planning officials uncritically adopted remarks by the former Communist Party general secretary, Le Duan, to the effect that each district should have a population of at least two hundred thousand persons, regardless, it seems, of the nature of the districts! This is not the place to go into the anomalies produced by central planning but it does give a small indication of the "mind-set" of the planners.

In the 1980s, Gia Lai-Con Tum remained the one province in which the Vietnamese population had not reached an absolute majority (I am unsure of the situation there in the early 1990s). As can be seen in table 12.1, reproduced from Le Duy Dai (1980, 53), the Vietnamese population is situated overwhelming in the capital, Pleiku, and is substantial in three other districts—Con Tum, Chu Prong, and An Khe. Most Vietnamese in the province live in cities, towns, or state-run agro-industrial-forestry complexes, usually in districts sited along the main roads. Few live among local groups and there is little intermarriage. Le gives details on the geographical distribution of the different ethnic groups in the province—the Vietnamese reside on plateaus or in valleys while the various ethnic groups live in "different types of settlement (nomadic, semi-sedentary or sedentary) and different sizes and densities of population" (ibid., 57) as one moves up the mountain.

Le Duy Dai also provides a glimpse of the social consequences of the war by showing how a number of distinct highland groups have been thrown together in single villages. He cites figures from a survey of 147 *xa* (hamlets) in which 10 percent have three or four ethnic or local groups living in them, and 32 percent have two groups. He writes of the Dac Bia area, which was seriously affected by the war:

> The distribution of population in this area is more complex. Within a *xa* there are many local or ethnic groups. For example, *xa* Kroong has the groups Ro-ngao, Jarai, Ha Lang and Vietnamese people; *xa* Ngoc Bay has the groups Bahnar, Ro-ngao, Gio Long, To dra, etc. Other *xa* such as Vinh Quay, Dao La Doam Ket and Gia Chiem have at least two or three ethnic or local groups. (Ibid., 55)

Yet Le suggests that the mixing of groups there is less common than in some other provinces, such as Thanh Hao to the north. The pattern of settlement still tends to be a patchwork of distinct groups, although in the high mountains, which have very low population densities, this pattern is less evident.

Table 12.1. Distribution of Population in Districts and Towns of the Vietnamese Central Highlands

Districts	Viets	Bahar	Ethnic Groups Sedang	Gie-Trieng	Jarai	Brau	Romam
Pleiku	81,616	194	387	57	2,929	—	—
Con Tum	38,230	17,088	5,064	290	3,826	—	—
Dac To	7,820	1,686	19,427	119	66	—	—
Sa Thay	3,633	1,658	4,357	6	6,184	306	158
Dac Glay	623		4,000	14,250	11	—	—
Con Plong	1,032	3,186	12,471	8	7	—	—
Chu Prong	29,252	615	—	—	39,007	—	—
Mang Giang	17,923	38,960	—	—	25,928	—	—
An Khe	45,700	30,213	22	13	910	—	—
Chu Pat	8,796	390	1	2	38,867	—	—
Ayun Pa	13,937	2,379	22	2	37,280	—	—
Krong Pa	1,768	1	—	—	19,060	—	—
TOTAL	250,330	96,370	45,751	14,747	174,075	306	158

Note: Apart from the ethnic groups mentioned in this table there are small groups of Tay, Thai, Muong, Ta Oi, and so on. Le's information was drawn from Census Board of Gia Lai-Con Tum 1979.
Source: Le 1980, 53.

Attitudes of Vietnamese Anthropologists

Generally, anthropologists in Vietnam support and approve of the government's policies in the Central Highlands. There may be differences expressed over implementation but there appears to be agreement over the broad direction of policy. One could, of course, say that under a communist system they have few alternatives, especially if they wish to work in a government-funded institute. It is obvious that the opinions held by Vietnamese ethnographers are seriously constrained by politics but even if they were in a different political environment I doubt whether many would object to the policy of "developing" the highlands. After all, the process of colonizing the Central Highlands began long before 1975 in the noncommunist south. Of course, anthropologists have been largely cut off from debates among westerners concerning the rights of indigenous peoples. Recently, however, some evidence of a more critical attitude among ethnographers has emerged.

Reading the work of Vietnamese ethnographers is a rather strange experience because it often gives the impression of a profound schizophrenia. The ethnographers are much more sympathetic to the minorities than is the society at large, and they attempt to document the ways of life of the indigenous peoples in detail. Yet this documentation is filtered through an inadequate theoretical apparatus that is further burdened by having to find rationalizations for the Communist Party's current policies.

One can see this, for example, in the work of Dang Nghiem Van, the vice-director of the Institute of Ethnography in Hanoi, who is in charge of a research program in the Central Highlands (which the Vietnamese call Tay Nguyen). In 1984, he published an article, "Glimpses of Tay Nguyen on the Road to Socialism," in which he seeks to demonstrate how the traditional social structure in the Central Highlands inhibits development.

> In the old society, food and other products were squandered without any plan, without calculations. This did not serve production and reproduction. Food and wealth were common property and were divided equally among those who lived under same roof. Here the principle "from each according to his ability" was respected, but not the principle "to each according to his work." The wealthy placed their property at the disposal of the village in order to get undeserved reputations. Slaves did not suffer from any discrimination but were regarded as relatives. (Dang 1984, 44)

In addition,

> The people's wealth, the largest part of the food produced, nearly all the fowls and domestic animals, were spent on rituals for the village, family or oneself. Poverty and hunger were partly due to religious rites. Religion, in brief, fascinated the Tay Nguyen people and prevented them from building a life of their own. (Ibid., 46)

What is intriguing about Dang's reflections, and those of others, is how they wrestle with the problem of how "primitive communism" is incompatible with developmental socialism. Thus, another ethnographer, Luu Hung, writes:

> Besides such positive aspects as the sense of equality, mutual assistance and altruism, the communal character with a sense of collectivity inherited from age-old society in the central Highlands has several negative aspects hindering the process of social evolution. In socialist society, the communal relations must be expanded beyond the ties among kinfolk and villagers, and manifestations of sectionalism stemming from the old communal relations must be overcome. Egalitarianism has become obsolete as it is an obstacle to the development of wisdom....The habit of

following the pattern already set by their ancestors and observing old customs fails to give filip to invention, technical innovations and scientific advances in production. On the contrary, it gives rise to self-satisfaction and simplicity. (Luu 1986, 167–68)

And yet, a folklorist from Gia Lai-Con Tum, Trinh Kim Sung, ponders whether traditional culture among the Central Highlanders might help

foster people of a new type and build socialist culture. There is a continuation, to a certain extent, between the primitive communal culture and people of such a community, and the culture and people of a socialist community. (Trinh 1986, 164)

Dang Nghiem Van produces an almost quaint comparison between the "ancient Tay Nguyen man and the socialist man, which the revolution is going to build him into" (1984, 47). The comparison is reproduced in full in table 12.2.

While these views reflect an ambivalence at the heart of the Vietnamese anthropologists' views of "primitive society," there is little ambiguity in their broad support for "socialist development" (in Evans 1990, chaps. 1 and 9, I have discussed this ambivalence in Marxist-inspired anthropology). Dang Nghiem Van, for example, sees development as filling in "the time gap" for highland people who, it is believed, failed to evolve. He writes:

sending people to Tay Nguyen to build this region is not only aimed at redistributing the workforce on a national scale, but also at contributing to filling in the time gap for Tay Nguyen to advance to socialism. (1984, 53)

Or, as the White Tai vice-chairman of the Committee for Nationalities, Cam Ngoan, and his Vietnamese deputy, Hoang Lam, told me in Hanoi in January 1986: "People of a lower civilization follow those of a higher civilization." That is, the people of Tay Nguyen can be helped to make up for the "time gap" by having Vietnamese settlers in their midst.

What is especially interesting is the degree to which, in this patriarchal society, old-style evolutionist-cum-developmental socialist theory has reserved a special hostility for "primitive survivals" like "matriarchy." This emerged clearly during an interview I conducted with Professor Phan Huu Dat at Hanoi University in January 1986. During a discussion that was partly concerned with the curriculum for ethnographers at the university, he informed me that the aim of ethnographic study of the economy is to see how "nomadic" slash-and-burn agriculture can be eradicated among the minorities. By studying the social system, the

Table 12.2. Comparison Between Traditional Man and Socialist Man in Vietnam

Traditional Man	Socialist Man
1. Sincere and honest, selfless. Has a sense of self-respect. Abides by the principle "Each for everybody, everybody for each" on the scale of the village, the area, the ethnic. Has a simple management organization, aimed at defending his own interests and those of the community.	1. Sincere and honest, selfless. Has a sense of self-respect. Abides by the principle "Each for everybody, everybody for each" on national scale, on the scale of Tay Nguyen, of which the village is an organic part. Has a sophisticated management organization and wide cooperation with many people.
2. Engages in collective production; adopts the slash-and-burn and crop rotation method, uses rudimentary implements. Production is unstable, non-specialized. Division of work is done according to the sexes. Pays no attention to improvement of technique; wastes money on spending. Can only meet the requirements of a simple, low living standard.	2. Engages in large-scale collective production, on the basis of sedentary life and farming. Has a high technical level and high productivity. Sets great store by talent and technical advances. Plans his spending to meet the needs of a high living standard, both material and spiritual of an industrial society.
3. Self-sufficient, consumes his products on the spot; advocates egalitarianism in distribution; takes no account of the individual's labor productivity. Takes no account of the cost price and time. Pays no attention to enlarged production.	3. Produces commodities to serve national and local plans. Takes account of cost price, time and labor productivity. Opposes egalitarianism in distribution. Advocates remuneration according to talent and the work done. Accumulates funds with a view to enlarged production.
4. Indulges himself in superstition, which seriously affects the people's material and spiritual life. Is resigned to a life of want and backwardness.	4. Has high knowledge. Advocates coordination in productive labor between manpower and machinery at a high tempo and with a strict sense of labor discipline.
	5. Has self-confidence and confidence in the collectivity. Yearns for a life of plenty and high culture. Has a socialist style of life and thinking.

Source: Dang 1984, 47.

students' aim "is to overcome the vestiges of primitive society, because we know that in our mountains there are still many vestiges of primitive society." Students study the family cycle in order to identify the "bad customs" in need of transformation. For example, "the custom among some minorities where the bridegroom goes to stay and work with the bride's family, in which case the man is not allowed to leave to join the army, for example. This is a bad consequence of this custom." Phan Huu Dat and others have singled out the longhouses of the Ede, Jarai, Sedang, and Ta Oi (in Binh Tri Tien Province) and advocated that they be broken up. Phan argued that "the longhouse is a typical symbol of matriarchy." He went on:

> In each hamlet of these groups there are only three or four houses, each of which contains fifty to one hundred persons. For example, the Ede in Ban Me Thuot. And each of these houses is under the rule of an influential woman, and means of production are held in common. Under the new social and economic conditions in Vietnam this is decadent. This decadence is being rejected by the young in Tay Nguyen who do not want to be tied to the large family group and wish to accumulate and therefore live in small houses. No more longhouses are built, although some people continue to live in the existing ones.

Cam Ngoan, during an interview conducted in February 1987, also spoke of attempts to break up the longhouses in Tay Nguyen.

> People used to live in houses of one hundred families and women brought their husbands to live with them and the young men married out. Now we give people one to two thousand square meters of land to build houses and gardens. By doing that we develop in them a sense of property. In the past these people worked together and distributed the product evenly and no one was responsible for production. There were no private facilities in the longhouses.

A more measured opinion was given by Tran Van Loc, head of the Department of the Central Highlands, an interview conducted in Hanoi in February 1987. He spoke of attempts to break up the "community houses" but said that this was very difficult. Many of the elders resisted, and the Ede continue to live in longhouses. "We have to try to cater to the characteristics of each of the minorities," he said. "We could perhaps begin by building little houses around the big house, and even building them of brick. But if we maintain the longhouse we cannot raise the level of culture and production of these people." He acknowledged that there were differences among some of the ethnographers on this question, however, and soon after I asked Be Viet Dang, director of the Institute of Ethnography, for his opinion. Be felt that attempts to forcibly break up the longhouses were undesirable, and that if they are to dissolve it should occur through a natural process of social evolution. Some ethnographers, according to Tran Van Loc, also oppose mass migration into the highlands.

Recently one sees a new mood being expressed—for example, by Dang Nghiem Van in a lengthy article on socioeconomic development in the Central Highlands published in 1989. While phrased in a politically acceptable manner, his criticism of the population relocation program in the Central Highlands is wide-ranging. He attacks forest destruction, suggesting that the felling of primary (as opposed to secondary) forest has been severe. Both the state and the new settlers have treated the natural environment "as a sort of 'instant noodle,' and an inexhaustible source" (1989, 74). The state and its officials are only interested in narrow economic development and have ignored the social dimension of development. Consequently,

> the solidarity between Kinh [Vietnamese] and the highland people which was handled successfully through two resistance wars has been violated...in some places conditions are worse than during the anti-American wartime. The revolution has appeared to neglect them and religion [meaning Christianity] is now filling the gap instead. (p. 81)

Using the rhetoric of the government concerning "the people's self-mastery," he also criticizes the giving of vast areas of land to state enterprises by central bureaucrats who simply draw lines on maps (pp. 94–95) and ignore the indigenous users of the land. What emerges from Dang's comments on the state takeover of forest land is a problem that has emerged elsewhere as well: the absence of any specific owners of forest land has meant that the groups who use the forest (the indigenous peoples and the settlers) are unable to invest in its long-term conservation. Thus, a main thrust of Dang's article is his recommendation that "mastery" over specific pieces of land be returned to indigenous peoples. With regard to forestry he argues:

> The forests must be returned to the communes [of the indigenous peoples]....Privately owned trees, such as beehive trees, [and] medical trees must be returned to the people, according to their local traditions. The forest products, birds, forest vegetables, wood, etc. must be used by the people according to the law. Forestry enterprises should not be allowed to be a law unto themselves. (p. 137)

Dang draws attention to the peculiarities of land ownership and use among the various minorities of the Central Highlands. For example, among the Ede collective lineage, property was inherited matrilineally. This custom, he suggests, must be respected. In passing he criticizes "ethnocentric" attempts to break up longhouses and force people to build houses on the ground, Vietnamese-style (pp. 111, 120). He also points out that the various minorities have a range of agricultural practices; not all of them engage only in slash-and-burn farming but some have paddy fields. He also argues for a more nuanced understanding of slash-and-burn agriculture. Ethnographers and policymakers must ask why it is so economically and socially attractive to the minorities (p. 108). In other words, he argues that planners must reconsider their generalizations about the way of life of the minorities and the need for "sedentarization." He documents various clashes that have occurred due to misunderstanding of the land-use situation among the minorities. He notes, ironically, that

> people from the plains who used to farm paddy fields now farm dry rice fields, cultivate industrial crops and do forestry, while people who used to do slash and burn have come down to farm wet rice fields, to garden and engage in a sedentary life. (p. 110)

It would have been more rational, he suggests, to incorporate highlanders into forestry and keep the lowlanders in wet rice but the enterprises were a channel for resources for the Vietnamese, and for corruption, so it did not happen.

Dang Nghiem Van also criticizes the bullying of minorities by Vietnamese settlers. He deplores the way the newcomers exploit the minorities by buying their forest products "dirt cheap." The picture he paints of the difference between the two groups in the highlands is undoubtedly an embarrassing one for him.

> Over half the areas of the ethnic groups are short of food for three months a year. In some places hunger is occasionally very serious. These people must sell their forest goods and handicrafts cheaply while having to buy other necessities at a high price. It will take a long time to abolish the contrast that shows the ethnic farmers bending down with baskets on their backs and in tattered clothes in the market crowded with Viets in fine clothes; the shabby *buons* [huts] beside the spacious houses of the Viet state-owned establishments. (p. 119)

The picture of marginalization and impoverishment that emerges is all too familiar to observers of indigenous peoples worldwide.

Within the confines of state policy, Dang Nghiem Van's article is a strong plea for careful consideration of the rights of minority people in the Central Highlands. There are many hints of earlier views expressed throughout his article but it does signal an important shift in the thinking of Vietnamese ethnologists. Unfortunately, one suspects that the views of anthropologists count for little in the central-planning organs of Hanoi's developmental state.

Central Highlands Minority Policy

At its First National Congress in 1935, the Vietnamese Communist Party adopted the standard Comintern line on "national minorities," promising them autonomy: "that is the right to solve local affairs, to use its mother tongue in its political, economic and cultural life, and to choose its own leaders in political and economic affairs" (Viet Chung 1968, 12). This was reiterated in the amended Constitution of North Vietnam in 1960, which stated: "Autonomous zones may be established in areas where people of national minorities live in compact communities. Such autonomous zones are integral and inalienable parts of the Democratic Republic of Vietnam" (ibid., 16). Autonomous zones were established in the northern mountains after the communists came to power in the north. In April 1955, a Thai-Meo Autonomous Region was set up in the northwest and a year later the Viet-Bac Autonomous Region was created in the northeast. In 1957, there was an attempt to create a third autonomous zone between the two others but according to Bernard Fall (1962, 148) the composition of the region was so diverse that it became unmanageable and was dissolved two years later. In establishing these zones the Vietnamese were guided by the policies of the Chinese communists (Dassé 1976).

The existence of these northern autonomous zones was an important propaganda weapon in the hands of communist cadres during the war in the south, especially following the emergence of FULRO and its political leaders among the Central Highlanders, many of whom were attracted by communist promises of autonomy. After the communist victory in April 1975, however, any hopes they had for autonomous zones in the Central Highlands were quickly dashed. Not only were none established there but the existing zones in the north were abolished. The ethnic Nung chairman of the National Assembly Nationality Committee, Chu Van Tan, attempted to assure minorities that "Although the autonomous regions are dissolved, the nationality policy of our State and

Party is still considered important" (*Summary of World Broadcasts*, 19 January 1976). But this reneging on promises of autonomy, combined with the beginnings of mass relocation of Vietnamese into the Central Highlands (which, of course, would dilute the concentration of minorities in the region and reduce their claims for autonomous areas), fueled FULRO opposition and no doubt caused considerable disillusionment among highlander cadres.

The political context already was one of growing regional tensions between Vietnam and China in the north and Vietnam and Pol Pot's Kampuchea in the south. The state wished to gain more control over the border areas in which the minorities overlapped, as they were considered less reliable than ethnic Vietnamese. Naturally, explanations of the change in policy have always been couched in terms of national "unification." As Chu Van Tan suggested, this allows the government to "pay greater attention to the mountainous regions by practically helping the highlands and remote areas along the border" (ibid.). In early 1980, officials in Hanoi told me, with what one suspects was a convenient humility, that their ally Laos had long ago adopted the correct policy of not promising autonomous zones. They, however, had been too much influenced by policies in China (the enemy at that time) and the Soviet Union, when what they needed was a policy that better suited "Vietnamese conditions." They also argued that in the established autonomous regions there were many minorities; giving the Tai or the Hmong the upper hand in them had proven disadvantageous to the smaller groups. They seemed not to recognize that the substitution of Vietnamese control would reproduce this imbalance on a grander scale.

For obvious reasons, the extent of armed FULRO resistance to Vietnamese control in the Central Highlands is unknown. It has never existed on a large scale, although, as Paul Quinn-Judge observed, FULRO

> always had the capability of creating a sense of apprehension disproportionate to either its size or its activities and, at the moment, any insecurity in the Central Highlands upsets Hanoi's plans for extensive development of the area. (1982, 14)

What is clear is that a major Vietnamese attempt to crush the resistance occurred in the wake of the invasion of Cambodia, and that between 1979 and 1981 the back of the resistance was broken through military campaigns and successful maneuvers, which allowed Vietnamese internal security to trap key FULRO leaders ("Asia's Forgotten War" 1986).

According to some FULRO refugees on the Thai-Cambodian border, they had been reduced to stealing food from other highlanders (Ben Kiernan, personal communication) and so could no longer rely on popular support. It also appears that, under pressure, the FULRO leadership turned its guns on itself, carrying out several disastrous purges (Quinn-Judge 1982). It was reported that FULRO received military aid from the Khmer Rouge after 1979 (Chanda 1981), as the Central Highlands border on northern Cambodia and are linked through there to the Thai border. The extent of this assistance has never been made clear. As far as I can ascertain there was little love lost between the Pol Pot regime and the minorities on Cambodia's northern border, mostly Jarai and Rhade. During a mid-1991 trip to parts of Attopeu Province in southern Laos, which borders on the Vietnamese Central Highlands and Cambodia, minority people told me of having to absorb an influx of thousands of minorities from the Cambodian side of the border fleeing the repression and fighting there. Furthermore, reports by FULRO remnants ("Asia's Forgotten War" 1986) indicate that fleeing FULRO personnel were detained, and in some cases executed, by the Khmer Rouge. If, indeed, there was ever an alliance it was purely one of convenience on the Khmer Rouge side.

Despite continued claims of success against FULRO (see, for example, an interview with the Lam Dong provincial military commander [*Summary of World Broadcasts*, 22 February 1988]; or the statement of the chairman of the Council of State, Vo Chi Cong, that Lam Dong Province "was able to solve definitely the problem of FULRO forces in November 1987" [ibid., 2 February 1988]), reports in 1979 from Gia Lai-Con Tum spoke of small-scale engagements with "FULRO bandits" (ibid., 4 August 1979). It would be foolish to argue that these forces are anything more than a nuisance to the Vietnamese, able to upset, at most, only the expansion of tourism in the Central Highlands. But, as we have seen, the highlands have been so flooded with Vietnamese settlers that the ability of FULRO to move among the population has been destroyed and the effectiveness of highland armed resistance with it.

Conclusion

The traditional Vietnamese state laid claim to the Central Highlands as tributary domains, and as such they were incorporated into the modern Vietnamese state under the French. The original impetus for this assertion was part of the traditional court's desire to inflate its stature as a mini–Middle Kingdom. The emperor therefore claimed to have established relations with a "king of fire" and a "king of water" in the highlands—in reality Jarai shamans. The existence of these tributary "states" has formed part of the highlanders' argument for regional autonomy (Hickey 1988, 172–207). Vietnamese anthropologists, however, have allowed themselves to be used to deflate such arguments in the interests of the "unified Vietnamese state." Thus, Nguyen Tan Dac claims that there was no organization or clearly articulated identification among ethnic groups above the village level, stating that the "villages in the central highlands are pre-nation social assemblages" (1986). He rightly criticizes the inflation of the status of the Jarai shamen by the traditional court but asserts that their existence does not imply any supralocal identification. While his argument is debatable, it is unlikely to be seriously debated inside Vietnam itself where it will be used to justify state policies that deny minority rights. Yet, despite his claims, it is clear that many traditional institutions among the highlanders, including that of the "king of fire," operate parallel to the Vietnamese imposed administration. Even Dang Nghiem Van is ambivalent about this, writing that

> reforms imposed from outside are sometimes mistaken and impatient and create a holding place for conservative forces. In fact, throughout the countryside there are parallel family systems, the revolutionary one and the traditional one. So, although the village chief system has been abolished, in fact the "metao" or "potao" are still overseeing traditional activities. The customary courts are still established and perform according to custom. Of 80 cases of divorce and "ma lai" that were brought before the court more than 90 percent had already been tried in a customary way. In Dray Hling collective farm, beside the manager there was a "polan" woman. In 1984, the polan woman died and another woman was immediately elected by the people. In 1987, the King of Fire in Ayun died and people there applied to the authorities to promote a new king. Meanwhile the proposed successor managed operations in the region. The problem is how, with study, to change the customs and conventions of these people slowly in order for them to be more suitable to current conditions and thereby avoid unnecessary confusion. (Dang 1989, 145)

Despite his appeals for tolerance, Dang Nghiem Van shows himself to be set in a mold fashioned by the Vietnamese state and its ideology. But his report does provide some hope concerning the survival capacity of the indigenous cultures that have been swamped by Vietnamese.

The plight of indigenous peoples in Vietnam is no better than elsewhere, and perhaps it is worse given the absence of freedom to organize or to establish contacts with other indigenous peoples. The promises made by the communists to the Central Highlanders have been broken, and the process of Vietnamization and colonization of the mountains, for which they so heavily and opportunistically criticized the southern Vietnamese regime, has been carried forward with a vengeance. It is to be hoped that foreign anthropologists will be able to start fieldwork in the Central Highlands in the coming years. Only then will we begin to get a more accurate (which probably means more depressing) picture of what has been occurring there. And only with an infusion of outside ideas will Vietnamese ethnographers be able to see beyond their present confines and perhaps hazard bolder criticisms of the state's policies.

CHAPTER 13

The Indigenous People of Peninsular Malaysia: It's Now or Too Late

SIGNE HOWELL

The Orang Asli (literally 'original people') are the indigenous people of Peninsular Malaysia. The 1970 census gives a total aboriginal population of 70,937. Significantly, in view of recent Malaysian government policies, they did not appear as a separate category in the 1980 census, but were combined with Malays, so that recent demographic data are available only in Department of Aboriginal Affairs records (Means 1986, 638). The Orang Asli qualify for the designation "indigenous" under most definitions.

Thus, all the criteria listed by Burger (1987, 9) and discussed with reference to Indonesia by Barnes (this volume) can be applied to the Malaysian aboriginal people. Gray (this volume) highlights the important point that *indigenous* is adjectival and refers to a quality; it is relative and depends on the geographical context. Furthermore, and this is apposite with regard to the Malaysian aboriginal people, he points to the significance of

> that quality of a person relating his or her identity to a particular area and distinguishing them culturally from other "alien" people who came to the territory subsequently. These indigenous peoples are "colonized" in the sense of being disadvantaged and discriminated against (Ibid.)

As will become clear in the following, the aboriginal people of Peninsular Malaysia are slowly beginning to think along such lines.

Today the Orang Asli represent approximately 1 percent of the national population but they are only just beginning to develop a conscious concept of collectivity and are, compared to indigenous populations of many other countries in Asia and elsewhere, in their infancy in terms of political awareness and organization. They have not been participating in the major Fourth World fora nor have they developed concerted strategies. This is just beginning to change. There is little doubt that, despite government avowals that it will ensure all Malaysian citizens equal rights and opportunities, the Orang Asli are the losers in the modernization process in Malaysia.

Although physical, cultural, and linguistic boundaries overlap, there are major differences between the various Orang Asli groups. They are usually divided into three major groupings: the Semang (or Negritos), the Senoi, and the Aboriginal (or Proto-) Malays, all of whom are further divided into several social groups, each with a strong sense of separate identity. With the exception of most of the so-called Aboriginal Malay groups who speak Malay dialects, the Orang Asli speak Austro-Asiatic languages belonging to the Mon-Khmer family (Benjamin 1976; Diffloth 1974). The early ancestors of the Orang Asli probably migrated from the north (Burma, Yunnan, Cambodia) through Thailand to the Malay Peninsula as early as ten thousand years ago (Benjamin 1976; Bellwood 1985; Endicott and Bellwood, in press). Current evidence of Hoabinhian occupation in Malayan rock and cave shelters goes back no farther than that. It appears unlikely that they practiced agriculture. According to Bellwood (ibid., 36), the horticultural Senoi are probably the descendants of both the Hoabinhians and the agricultural Austro-Asiatic speakers who arrived in the peninsula in approximately 2000 B.C., whereas the Negritos are likely to be the direct descendants of the foraging Hoabinhians. Today, Orang Asli populations can be found in all the Malaysian states with the exception of Perlis and Penang.

These aboriginal people, living deep inside the rain forest, hunting with blowpipes and poisoned darts, and requiring the minimum of material goods, appealed to the imagination of Europeans in Malaya. Held to represent examples of primitive man, they were the subject of numerous books and papers in the second half of the nineteenth and the early twentieth century (see, for example, Favre 1865; Swettenham 1895; Clifford 1897, 1898; Skeat and Blagden 1906; and Wilkinson 1910). In the postwar period many social anthropologists have carried

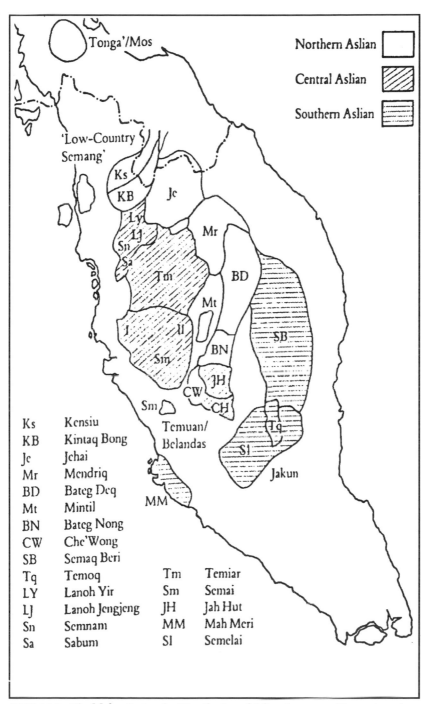

Tonga'/Mos

Northern Aslian
Central Aslian
Southern Aslian

'Low-Country
Semang'

Ks
KB
Je
Ly
LJ
Sn
Sa
Tm
Mr
BD
Mt
J
Il
Sm
BN
SB
JH
CW
CH
Sm
Temuan/
Belandas
Tq
Sl
Jakun
MM

Ks	Kensiu
KB	Kintaq Bong
Je	Jehai
Mr	Mendriq
BD	Bateg Deq
Mt	Mintil
BN	Bateg Nong
CW	Che'Wong
SB	Semaq Beri
Tq	Temoq
LY	Lanoh Yir
LJ	Lanoh Jengjeng
Sn	Semnam
Sa	Sabum

Tm	Temiar
Sm	Semai
JH	Jah Hut
MM	Mah Meri
Sl	Semelai

MAP 13.1. *The Malay Peninsula: Distribution of Aslian Languages (Approximate).*

out intensive fieldwork among the different groups, and, in addition to a large number of essays, several monographs have been published (Dentan 1968; Endicott 1979; Howell 1989a [1984]; Karim 1981; Roseman 1991).

With the arrival (approximately two thousand years ago) and expansion of Malays in the peninsula, the original inhabitants were pushed further and further into the hills and jungles of the interior where they lived relatively undisturbed until World War II and the Emergency (1948–60) when some became pawns in the conflict between insurgents and the colonial power. Traditionally they lived in small mobile groups or impermanent settlements, practicing hunting, gathering, and swidden cultivation. In recent years incursions into their land areas have increased dramatically and the conditions necessary to maintain this way of life, even in a modified form, are rapidly disappearing. This fact is perceived as a major cause for concern by the Orang Asli themselves as well as by those outsiders who take an active interest in them. Sufficient and/or appropriate measures to compensate them for the loss of the means to continue their traditional livelihood, and to ensure an equivalent, or improved, quality of life, are not forthcoming.

During the colonial regime in Malaya, the British—in theory only advisers to the Malay sultans—acknowledged that the aboriginals were "wards" of the sultans while insisting on termination of the practice of slavery. The Malays regarded the aboriginal peoples as wild creatures, more akin to the animals of the jungle than to human beings, and, as such, legitimate objects for the hunt and for enslavement (Endicott 1983). Such practices instilled a terror of outsiders in these people and caused them to withdraw and minimize contact. To the postwar communist guerrillas seeking independence, and operating out of jungle bases, the Orang Asli became an important source for food as well as potential sympathizers. By 1953, an estimated thirty-thousand Orang Asli were under the effective influence of the insurgents (Carey 1976, 311). The exact figure is arguable but to the British at the time the Orang Asli were an important factor in bringing the Emergency to an end.

A Department for the Welfare of the Aborigines was established in 1950 (later renamed the Department of Aborigines) and a policy was embarked upon aiming to resettle the Orang Asli in large areas where they could be controlled. This proved to be a mistake. An estimated seven thousand resettled Orang Asli rapidly died, succumbing to heat, the pressures of overcrowding, disease, and depression. This policy was abandoned by the British in 1953 to be replaced by attempts at winning their support with gifts of such items as food and medical supplies (Carey 1976, 308; Nicholas 1990, 69).

Following independence, the new Malaysian government continued to administer the aboriginal population separately from the dominant populations of the country: Malays, Chinese, and Indians. The official name for them became Orang Asli, supplanting the variety of terms previously used, most of which had derogatory connotations. Consequently, the Department for Aboriginal Affairs (Jabatan Orang Asli, or JOA) was established. It cut across the various ministerial national structures and was given the power to provide such public services as health, housing, education, and agricultural services separately and directly. The ultimate stated aim was the development of these peoples, and their integration into the wider society, while at the same time respecting their desire to maintain their separate cultural traditions.

During the 1960s, the thrust of the JOA's efforts on behalf of the Orang Asli was mainly confined to providing minimal medical services, based in a hospital for the Orang Asli established outside Kuala Lumpur. Primary education of sorts was offered at a few select, and more permanent, villages. Other children had to leave their homes and live in dormitories if they wanted a modern education. Most Orang Asli groups have maintained sporadic trading and labor relations with Malays for centuries. Although from one perspective it could be argued that the relationship was exploitative, the Orang Asli nevertheless obtained what they wanted (mostly iron tools, salt, and some cloth) and were free to interact with the Malays as and when they pleased.

With the rapid and recent loss of forest land in Malaysia, many Orang Asli communities have been forced into more permanent economic relations with nearby Malays and Chinese. With the outsiders dictating unequal and exploitative terms, the Orang Asli are increasingly the losers. Depending upon location and accessibility, many Orang Asli have taken employment at nearby plantations. The commitment to their traditional lifestyle has remained strong, however, embedded in a profound mistrust of the Malays and the Chinese as well as a profound desire to be free to roam the forest. All indications are that the conditions of work, the wages offered, and the prices paid for jungle produce are much worse for Orang Asli than for other ethnic groups in the country. Little has been done by the JOA to ensure equitable and fair conditions in these respects.

The communist incursions from southern Thailand into Peninsular Malaysia, which began in 1973, again led to questions of security in the jungle areas. The government instructed the JOA to draw up a comprehensive plan for development of the Orang Asli in the central mountain chain, with "national security" as a primary aim. The concept of "regroupment schemes" was presented. Instead of moving people, as had been attempted during the Emergency, the idea now was to create development schemes in the jungle areas, close to existing habitats. This involved the establishment of large settled villages where the participants were given the permanent use of land for housing and subsistence gardening, and fruit and/or rubber plantations for generating income. Animal husbandry was introduced and schools were built. It is interesting to look at the JOA's formulation of its policies as expressed by a senior official (Jimin 1983, quoted in Nicholas 1990, 70). These are as follows.

1. Provide for an adequate social service (such as in the fields of health, education, housing and general welfare), so that the Orang Asli may participate effectively in the socio-economic development process.

2. Improve their standard of living through the improvement and modification of their agriculture.

3. Increase their earning capacity and income level by getting them directly involved with the market economy.

However, as Nicholas (1990, 70) points out (with regard to the situation among the Semai but equally applicable to most regrouped peoples), the "twin thrusts of the JHEOA [Jabatan Hal Ehwal Orang Asli, Department for Aboriginal Affairs]—sedentarization and integration—were largely responsible for dissolution of their traditional economy, and in many ways, for the current plight of [the Semai]." In other words, experience today starkly demonstrates that the JOA's official aim of ensuring an improved way of life has not been achieved—leaving aside the question of the desirability of the aim as it was formulated. There are several interconnected reasons for the failure to bring about a fair and positive involvement of the Orang Asli in Malaysian society. I will look at some of those which, to my mind, are the more important. These concern questions of displacement in the face of jungle destruction, of the legal rights (or lack of rights) of the Orang Asli, of the structure of the administration, and of clashes between Orang Asli priorities and those of the government.

The Legal Position of the Orang Asli

The legal position of the Orang Asli is unsatisfactory. The colonial 1939 Enactment, the first attempt at a legal definition, described an aborigine as "a person whose parents were members of an aboriginal tribe and including a descendent through a male line" (Rachagan 1990, 106). The 1954 Ordinance extends the definition: "[The aborigine] speaks an aboriginal language, follows an aboriginal way of life and aboriginal customs and includes a descendent through males of such a person" (ibid.). Also included were the children of "any union between an aborigine female and a male of any race and persons of any race who were adopted by an aborigine as an infant." The 1974 Revised Act maintains this definition. However, according to Rachagan (ibid.) and Hooker (1976), while the term *aborigine* is used in the Constitution of 1957 to distinguish the Orang Asli from the other (arguably) indigenous people of the peninsula, namely the Malays, the Constitution does not further define them either by tribal names or by characteristics. Malays, by contrast, are defined by reference to Islam, Malay language and customs, residence, and lineage.

Use of the term *bumiputera* ('sons of the earth') for Malays confuses the issue of who is and is not indigenous. To uninformed outsiders, and to most Malays, the *bumiputera* constitute the original population of the peninsula, with Chinese and Indians representing the major, more recent, ethnic groups. In political debate about Malaysia's organization and future, the Orang Asli get hardly a mention. By contrast, the indigenous peoples of Sarawak (though not those of Sabah) are listed by tribal names in the Constitution. This further means that, unlike the Malays and the natives of Sarawak, the Orang Asli have no constitutional special privileges or protections. Thus any proposed changes concerning them can be obtained without the otherwise required two-thirds majority vote in Parliament. The minister in charge of the Orang Asli has extensive powers, powers that have been intensified rather than relaxed through the various legislative enactments. He has exclusive power to control and determine the lives of the Orang Asli but there are no provisions obliging him to act. Nor is there any provision allowing the Orang Asli a role in determining their own affairs (Rachagan 1990, 110).

Before pursuing some of the implications of this, let us look briefly at the situation as it is today with regard to land, land holdings, land exploitation, and the Orang Asli. The majority of the Orang Asli live in areas that until very recently were part of the tropical rain forest or, in the case of the Proto-Malays in the southern part of the peninsula, in swampy or semiforested areas—generally those not yet wanted by Malays. This situation is rapidly changing, and like indigenous populations in many other parts of the world, the Orang Asli have defined the

question of land rights as the central issue in the fight for their continued existence. In this regard their position is very weak.

The Malaysian Constitution provides that matters pertaining to
land fall within the legislative and executive purview of the individual
states, and it has frequently been argued that this hinders the establishment of land reserves for the Orang Asli (for example, Hooker 1976).
However, Rachagan argues that, since the Act also allows the federal
government to acquire land, under one interpretation the government
could obtain land for Orang Asli reserves, as well as granting them exclusive rights in other tracts for purposes of fishing, hunting, gathering,
logging, mining, and settlement (1990, 104). Though vested in the
government, these powers are yet to be exercised. A recent High Court
ruling, however, indicates a possible movement toward such an interpretation. Rachagan further states that

> Notwithstanding the Constitutional provisions, the Aboriginal Peoples
> Act, 1954 (revised 1974) empowers "the State Authority" to declare
> aboriginal reserves. This has been held as testimony to the contention that
> it is the state authorities who are the competent authorities to create
> aboriginal reserves. Even if this is the case, there are sufficient provisions
> in the Malaysian Constitution which allow for a Federal Government
> intent on creating aboriginal reserves, securing the compliance of the rele-
> vant state authorities. (Rachagan 1990, 104)

However, there is uncertainty as to the potential scope of the Act.
A. Williams-Hunt, president of the increasingly vocal Orang Asli Asso-
ciation for Peninsular Malaysia (POASAM), argues that, although the
Act allows for the creation of Orang Asli areas and reserves, it

> unfortunately does not provide for the granting to the Orang Asli of
> permanent tenure to their land. The greatest title which they can get,
> either as individual or as a group, is tenant-at-will, and this applies even to
> areas gazetted as Orang Asli reserves. (Williams-Hunt 1990, 4)

All transactions pertaining to the disposal of their land have to be
approved by the director general of the JOA. The fact that they have no
title means, of course, that they can be evicted. In effect, the state executive may grant dispensations for all kinds of exploitation of the forest
areas, and this is being done for logging purposes, for rural development
projects intended to benefit poor and/or landless Malays, and for estate
developments (mainly palm oil and rubber).

The Land (Group Settlement Areas) Act of 1960 concerns the
development of large-scale planned settlements undertaken by various

government agencies. Frequently these are implemented in Orang Asli areas, and in all cases the Orang Asli have been displaced and have lost their traditional means of livelihood (ibid., 8). Even the building of the new campus for the National University of Malaysia in Selangor meant displacing several Orang Asli communities who had lived in the area for centuries. Many Orang Asli view the rural-development schemes for poor Malays with particular bitterness, comparing the relatively large and well-constructed Malay houses with those built in JOA villages and noticing differences in the quality of public services provided in the two types of villages.

Even in jungle areas not yet destroyed or developed, the Orang Asli, without legal title to their land, cannot maintain their rights to fruit trees and other potential sources of income. Malays and Chinese maintain that ungazetted land is public, and so they may exploit it as they see fit. This means in many instances that non–Orang Asli enter the forest to collect for sale rattan and the more popular fruits such as *rambutan, petai,* and *durian.* The fruit trees are usually considered by the Orang Asli to belong to the individuals who planted them in the distant past, and thus as part of their inheritance from their ancestors.

In contrast to the principles underlying modern legal provisions, ownership to the Orang Asli lies not in land but in the fruits of it (see, for example, Benjamin 1966). In recent years, the sale of fruit has represented in many cases a major source of cash income for Orang Asli. This source has now been denied them in many places due to logging, to forest development, and to non–Orang Asli helping themselves. Williams-Hunt cites a case from a Semai community in Perak in which people complained to the authorities that non–Orang Asli had entered their areas and stolen their *petai.* The authorities dismissed the complaints on the grounds that the Orang Asli had no exclusive rights to the trees even though they had planted them (ibid., 6).

Lack of land rights also means that Chinese and Malays come to catch fish and game, frequently using methods not available to the Orang Asli (special nets, poison, and guns). I have seen them demand that the timid Orang Asli tell them where the ripe fruit trees are, where the best rattan is to be found, and the whereabouts of deer and other valuable game. They often ask Orang Asli to act as guides, paying them little or nothing for their trouble. They apparently never think of paying compensation for the fruit, fish, or rattan that they take.

Logging of primary rain forest is another matter affecting the Orang Asli way of life. The legal situation with regard to the forest areas of Malaysia is best described as flexible. State forests are owned by the individual states, which may grant licenses for logging and development despite overall provisions enacted to maintain forested land. Generally, only the designated forest-reserve areas are safe from commercial exploitation, although even this protected status can change extremely quickly (Hurst 1990, 49). The Orang Asli, since they do not have any legal claim to their traditional territories, are pushed aside by the logging companies with no compensation. Although the logging companies have agreed to undertake reforestation, their record of implemention is extremely poor. The overall effect as far as the Orang Asli are concerned is permanent loss of territory, which results in permanent alienation from their traditional ways of life.

Effects of the JOA's Overall Administration

While at first glance the handing over of the administration of the Orang Asli to a special department might seem beneficial, many argue today that the separating of the Orang Asli politically and administratively from the rest of the Malaysian population has had detrimental effects on their lives in the modern world (Hood 1990; Means 1986). The original department was run by British colonial officers who, by and large, had a deep regard for the Orang Asli. This was appreciated by the Orang Asli, accustomed to the contempt of the Malays. The British, however, saw themselves as protectors and their policies were tinged with a strong paternalism. Following independence, several British officials continued to hold senior positions in the JOA but in recent years the leadership has been taken over by Malays. It is an unfortunate fact that even today no Orang Asli occupies a central position in the department, and, despite the increase in middle-level education in some areas, very few Orang Asli are employed by the JOA—centrally or regionally—in capacities other than the lowliest. This is strongly resented by many Orang Asli who feel that the JOA is more concerned with Malay policies than with the plight and priorities of the Orang Asli.

The JOA officials have continued a form of paternalism toward what Nicholas claims they regard as their "client population." The Semai, for instance, were asked to "leave the age of the loincloth and become civilized like the other Malaysians" (Nicholas 1990, 74). Within the constraints of the demands for national security, it is the JOA that has decided what is best for the Orang Asli. Orang Asli involvement in decisions concerning initiatives and projects has been minimal. As a result they feel marginalized by the development process. A strong contributing factor to this alienation is the pressure to convert to Islam. A few have done so. According to Williams-Hunt (1990, 11), many Orang Asli have become Christians or Bahais in direct defiance of the government's efforts at Islamization. The Muslim officials of the JOA do not, despite the constitutional freedom of religion, approve of Christian Orang Asli. A recent incident demonstrates this. On the morning of 27 November 1990, a number of Malays (including, reportedly, JOA officials, officials of the local District Office, and armed members of the Federal Reserve Unit) came in the night to a Semai village with bulldozers and destroyed the recently built church (*Orang Asli News* 1990, 14–16).

Schools built in or near Orang Asli settlements are not subject to Ministry of Education quality controls or standards. The teachers, who tend to be inadequately trained, resent being assigned to the jungle schools. Prior to 1968, not one pupil passed the national exam that would enable him or her to go on to secondary education (Means 1986, 646). Juli Edo, the first professional Orang Asli social anthropologist, was reported in the local press to have stated that Orang Asli schoolchildren have the highest dropout rate in the country; over the past decade it has ranged from 60 to 75 percent of all primary-school children (*Sunday Star*, 5 November 1989). The great bulk of the educational budget is used to pay the salaries of the mostly Malay administrators not to help the Orang Asli. The teachers, who are almost exclusively Malays, receive no special training in Orang Asli cultures and traditions.

In my experience, the Malay teachers who teach Orang Asli children develop a fondness for them but they remain totally unaware of the richness of their culture. They dismiss their way of life as "primitive" and "childlike," defining them as "people without religion." Considering time that has elapsed since the establishment of the JOA, the educational record is extremely poor. There are only a handful of university graduates. Perhaps an even more serious failure on the part of the JOA has been its inability to educate Malaysians about their own minorities. Knowledge about the Orang Asli cultures is minimal even among highly educated Malays, Chinese, and Indians. This ignorance allows the unthinking destruction of the Orang Asli to continue.

Among the earliest initiatives aimed at the Orang Asli was health support. The forts established in the deep jungle during the Emergency were provided with health stations, and the hospital outside Kuala Lumpur continues to be the center for all medical services. However, support for those who do not go to the hospital or do not live in a regroupment area is minimal. The more mobile communities may receive no, or at best sporadic and unannounced, visits from minimally trained JOA medical workers. Even more worrying, those who have settled do not fare any better.

PHOTO: SIGNE HOWELL

PLATE 13.1. *Chewong men with motorcycle and blowpipes, Malaysia.*

It has been estimated that the health of the Orang Asli has not improved and that their nutritional status is lower as a result of "development." Thus, a recent survey of twenty-four settled Orang Asli villages, undertaken by the Faculty of Medicine at the National University, concluded that "Resettlement of the Orang Asli has not improved, or may even retard the nutritional status," and "the prevalence of severe malnutrition is still very high, even higher than the poverty in Malay villages" (Hurst 1990, 55). Endicott estimated recently that "over the last ten years over 20 per cent of babies born among the Aring group [Batek Negritos] died before age 3," and "Most deaths of babies and young children are caused by gastrointestinal and respiratory diseases that are easily cured by modern medicine" (Endicott, n.d., 6). This mirrors my own experience among the Chewong.[1] Such findings are particularly distressing in view of claims that two-thirds of resources allocated for the assistance of Orang Asli are being spent on administration by the JOA (*Sunday Star*, 5 November 1989).

A symposium held in 1984 on development and the future of the Orang Asli, which included several presentations by Orang Asli, overwhelmingly showed how the JOA "is an anachronism today" (Hood 1990, 145). Government plans to abolish the JOA by 1990, when Malaysia's new economic policy was to be reevaluated, have not been implemented. So far, no specific commitments have been made concerning the future of the Orang Asli. The more sophisticated among them are anxious about the protection of their interests.

Orang Asli Priorities in the Shaping of their Future

Anthropologists who have conducted fieldwork with Orang Asli groups stress similar aspects in their social life and ideologies. They live and work in small groupings that are loosely composed and can easily change in composition. They value the freedom of the jungle. Hunting and gathering are important aspects not only of their economic existence but also of their religious and cosmological lives. Their social life is predicated upon a concept of human nature that results in peaceful interaction and egalitarian social institutions—including gender relations—but it also results in timidity and an inability to deal forcefully with outsiders. Their practice in the face of outsiders has been, as it continues to be, to run away. When that is not possible they avoid direct confrontation, espousing to themselves and to each other their fear of contradiction and quarrel (Howell 1989b). Thus, in their dealings with JOA officials they do not complain or comment upon initiatives taken on their behalf nor do they put forward their own preferences and requirements. In my experience, they prefer to remain quiet, nodding anxiously even in the face of undesirable or inappropriate demands or suggestions. Thus, their fundamental social value of peacefulness is detrimental to their fight for survival.

As stated above, many Orang Asli and others concerned with their welfare have been arguing that the Department of Aboriginal Affairs is not the best organization to ensure their welfare. There are charges of paternalism, lack of consultation, and a tendency among the senior officials to be more concerned with government policy than with the special needs of the Orang Asli. When the illegal or incorrect behavior of outsiders is directed at Orang Asli individuals or communities, they usually feel that they get no support from the JOA. This is becoming particularly irksome since, although more and more Orang Asli are obtaining further, if not higher, education, they are excluded from decision-making processes both within and outside the JOA. There is a strong belief among Orang Asli of all groups and categories, by and large well founded, that the main aim of the government—and, by implication, the JOA—is to solve the "Orang Asli problem" by turning them into settled peasants or laborers and converting them to Islam.

Although the expression *orang asli* is of recent origin, and was coined in order to replace derogatory terms for the aboriginal people, more and more of them are beginning to apply it to themselves. One can witness a rapidly increasing awareness of their common heritage and common plight. Dissatisfaction with the JOA led a small group of Orang Asli as long ago as 1977 to form POASAM. That organization now numbers about ten thousand members and is establishing itself as a pressure group, increasingly active in spreading information about the general situation of the Orang Asli as well as reporting transgressions committed against them.

Of particular concern to POASAM is the rapid loss of land, and its members see the question of gazetting land for Orang Asli communities as of immediate and highest priority. The leaders write letters to the press, and have managed from time to time in recent years to interest it sufficiently to publish information about the Orang Asli and their special situation. They have enlisted the support of the active and influential Consumers' Association of Penang, the fortnightly journal of which has on several occasions carried long and detailed reports about the plight of the Orang Asli.

Related to these activities, and partly as a result of them, the first conference of Orang Asli headmen was held in 1982. This resulted in a widely distributed document in which their major grievances and requirements were set out. Their main demands were for secure land titles, effective representation in Parliament (not possible currently due to the electoral system of Malaysia), administration of the JOA by Orang Asli, preservation of Orang Asli languages, and freedom of religion (Means 1986, 649–50).

More recently, the POASAM-associated Centre for Orang Asli Concerns is establishing itself in order to "serve, in part, as a documentation and research centre in Orang Asli matters." As of 1991, it publishes in both English and Malay the quarterly *Orang Asli News.* Although modestly produced and of limited circulation, the newsletter is the only regular source of information about the current situation of the Orang Asli. The editors try, within the constraints of their limited resources, to maintain an overview of events and actions that involve the

Orang Asli, and to ask for information about injustices committed against them by private individuals, companies, the JOA, or other government agencies.

Although these news items make for disturbing reading, the latest issue (June 1991) carries some encouraging news. In a recent case, the High Court ruled in favor of an Orang Asli group against the state government of Perak on the grounds that the latter violated the Aboriginal Peoples Act 1954 (revised 1974) when it allowed a company to log an area that had been approved as an Aboriginal Reserve, although it had not been gazetted. The judge maintained that the tract in question is Orang Asli land and, moreover, that all rights to the produce from it are also theirs. This is the first time such a case has been brought to court, and it represents a major victory for the Orang Asli. It ought to set an important precedent. However, as the correspondent writes, "The decision also highlights the pressing demands for other Orang Asli inhabited areas to be approved and gazetted speedily." These activities represent only a small, although important, start. The Orang Asli continue to be treated as peripheral to Malaysian political and economic life.[2]

CHAPTER 14

Indigenous Peoples and Land Rights in Sarawak, Malaysia: To Be or Not To Be a Bumiputra

VICTOR T. KING

The state of Sarawak within the Federation of Malaysia provides an interesting case study of the relationship between indigenous peoples and rights to land. Usually one of the main elements of indigenous identity is access to or control over land, and in the Sarawak Land Code native customary tenure is accorded a special status. An eminent scholar of Southeast Asian legal systems has remarked that "With one or two exceptions the main legislative initiative in...Sarawak has been in the definition of who was to be considered a member of the native groups and in attempting to regulate land matters" (Hooker 1980, 38).

It is the main purpose of this chapter to examine the divergences between certain politico-legal constructs in Malaysia that define, and in a number of important respects protect, indigenous peoples and their rights, and various political and economic realities that are bound up with interethnic inequalities and discrimination. These divergences are part of a series of interrelated contradictions in Malaysia that revolve around federal-state relations, national development policies of economic growth and poverty alleviation, centralized planning models, and local-level socioeconomic and cultural variations (King 1988a).

First, it is necessary to examine the concept of "native," or "indigene," terms that are equated in Malaysia, since it is the problematical nature of this constitutional artifact that helps to explain the current plight of the non-Muslim native groups of Malaysia, especially the Dayaks of Sarawak.[1] Second, the constitutional position of the natives of Sarawak has to be placed in the context of the politically and economically marginal position of the state in relation to Peninsular Malaysia and the federal authorities. Third, I intend to sketch the historical background of Sarawak's administration of land and the main legal transformations that have occurred in organizing native rights to this key resource. Finally, I present a critique of current land-development policies with regard to natives in Sarawak, while recognizing the inevitability of the processes of agricultural commercialization and the commodization of land.

The Concept of Bumiputra

The special status of the indigenous peoples in Malaysia, including those in Sarawak, is enshrined in the Federal Constitution. It provides for preferential treatment in education and training, employment and business opportunities, and ownership or control of such resources as land (Mohamed Suffian 1972, 249ff). Yet the concept of the native, indigene, or (in Malay) bumiputra (literally 'son of the soil') is not a straightforward one.[2] Furthermore, the native populations of Malaysia do not wholly conform to the definition of "indigenous peoples" put forward in the International Labor Organisation conventions of 1957 and 1987, nor to those of the World Bank and the United Nations Special Rapporteur.

Not all Malaysian bumiputra can be designated as "tribal" or "semi-tribal" peoples. In relation to nonindigenous populations, specifically the immigrant Chinese and Indians, the natives collectively are not a minority. Overall they are not a marginal population; they, or rather their representatives, have been politically dominant in Malaysia since the Federation's independence from Britain in 1957. Finally, indigenous cultural elements such as language and religion are important symbols of national identity and integrity. Rather, it is the nonindigenous groups that can be said to suffer discrimination constitutionally and in practice. Mohamed Suffian (ibid., 276) notes that, in contrast to some countries in which immigrants live in enclaves and require protection, in Malaysia the established indigenous peoples are constitutionally protected.

Nevertheless, there is an important sense in which the bumiputra were disadvantaged on the eve of independence. The immigrant Chinese

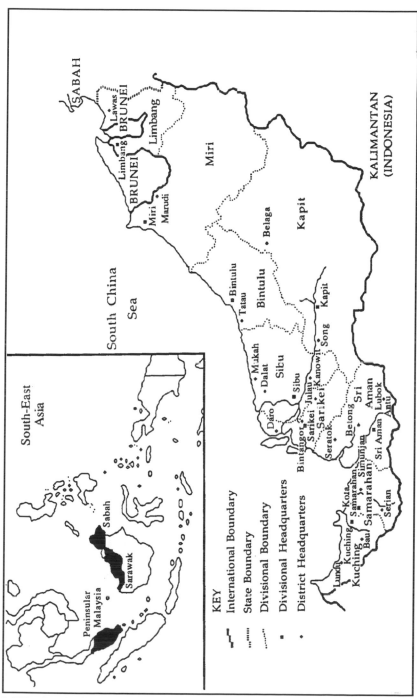

MAP 14.1. *Malaysia (Sarawak).*

and urban Indians to a large extent controlled the key sectors of the economy; they were generally more prosperous, better educated, and economically more advanced than the native peoples. It was precisely to make good these economic deficiencies, and to overcome the problem of large segments of an indigenous majority continuing to constitute a relatively poor, rural-based population, that various constitutional safeguards were granted to them by the British. What is more, although they were not well equipped to compete in economic terms, as the established population the indigenes had political leverage. It was a native-dominated government that, in 1970, specifically promoted Malaysia's New Economic Policy (NEP) in order to restructure society so that economic imbalances, to a large extent coincident with ethnic affiliations, would be redressed in favor of the indigenes.

Yet this is only part of the story. The politico-legal category "native" does not correspond to any definable ethnic grouping in Malaysia. It is in large part a product of British compromises and negotiations arising from the process of decolonization in the 1950s and 1960s in the Malayan and Bornean territories. In other words, the category "native" (or *bumiputra*) covers a complex diversity of peoples and cultures occupying different economic niches with different degrees of political influence.

The concept of "native" has two broad subcategories: the Malays on the one hand, and the natives of Malaysian Borneo (comprising the states of Sarawak and Sabah) on the other.[3] In the Constitution a Malay is defined by Article 160(2) as "a person who professes the Muslim religion, habitually speaks the Malay language [and] conforms to Malay custom" (Malaysia 1964, 103).[4] The definition does not demand that an individual be of Malay ethnic origin, only that he or she assumes the criteria that define "Malayness."

The Malays have an especially advantageous position, both constitutionally and in practice, because Islam is the religion of the Federation, Malay is the national language, and special provisions preserve the sovereignty and prerogatives of the Malay rulers, the various sultans of the constituent states. The monarch of Malaysia (Yang di-Pertuan Agong) is normally elected every five years by the Conference of Rulers from among their number (Groves 1964, 38). Following Article 153 of the original Constitution, the safeguarding of the special status of the Malays is the responsibility of the king, acting on cabinet advice. This is "to ensure the reservation for Malays" of reasonable proportions of positions in the public services, scholarships, exhibitions, and other educational or training privileges or facilities, and trade and business licenses or permits (Malaysia 1964, 97–99). Sheridan and Groves (1967, 213) note that

> This article had its inspiration in the protective discrimination provisions of the Indian constitution; but it is fundamentally different from those provisions, because the class in whose favor the discrimination operates in Malaysia is the class which possesses political control, the Malays.

There are also special arrangements provided in Article 89 for reserving or acquiring land for Malays in Peninsular Malaysia, which in most respects parallels the provisions for the aboriginal populations (Malaysia 1964, 48–49).

The constitutional category "natives of Borneo," however, comprises both Malays and non-Malays, and therefore both Muslims and non-Muslims. It is defined by Clause 6 of Article 161A as "in relation to Sarawak, a person who is a citizen and either belongs to one of the races specified in Clause (7) as indigenous to the state or is of mixed blood deriving exclusively from those races." The Article, in Clause 7, then goes on to specify those groups defined as "native" and "indigenous" to Sarawak. These comprise

> Bukitans, Bisayahs, Dusuns, Sea Dayaks, Land Dayaks, Kadayans, Kalabits, Kayans, Kenyahs (including Sabups and Sipengs), Kajangs (including Sekapans, Kejamans, Lahanans, Punans, Tanjongs and Kanowits), Lugats, Lisums, Malays, Melanos, Muruts, Penans, Sians, Tagals, Tabuns and Ukits. (Ibid., 107).

In the original Constitution of Malaysia, in Article 161A, natives of Borneo to a significant extent were given the same privileges as were the Malays under Article 153: they, too, were to be reserved appropriate numbers of positions in the public services but not "as regards scholarships, exhibitions and other educational or training privileges and facilities" (ibid.). Furthermore, Article 89, covering Malay reserved land, did not apply to Borneo but it was confirmed that it was constitutional under state law in Sarawak and Sabah for special provisions to be made for the reservation of land on behalf of natives, or for alienation to them or for giving them preferential treatment as regards alienation of land by the state (Mohamed Suffian 1972, 148).

Following the serious racial confrontations between Malays and Chinese in the federal capital of Kuala Lumpur on 13 May 1969, and the promulgation of the New Economic Policy in 1970, the Federal Constitution was amended in 1971. Its effect, in relation to the natives of Borneo, was to equate them with the Malays in all respects, and extend to them *all* the special rights and privileges contained in Article 153. To that end, the article was amended so that wherever the word *Malays* appeared it was to be followed by "and natives of any of the Borneo states" (Malaysia 1972, 8). Article 161A, originally covering the special provisions for Borneo natives, was also amended to confirm this parity (ibid., 9). A further clause (8A) was inserted in Article 153 to empower the Yang di-Pertuan Agong to ensure the reservation, given certain conditions, of a reasonable proportion of places in institutions of higher education for Malays and the natives of Borneo. Tun Abdul Razak Hussein, then prime minister, stated in the course of the parliamentary debates on the constitutional amendments that "By these amendments, it can now be clearly seen that the natives of Sabah and Sarawak are placed exactly on [*sic*] the same position as the Malays in the states of West Malaysia" (ibid., 6).

The conclusion is a simple and straightforward one. In constitutional terms, and for the last twenty years, the natives of Sarawak have shared the special rights and privileges enjoyed by the Malays. Yet their general political and economic position in the Federation remains subordinate to that of the Peninsular Malays overall, so much so that it is no exaggeration to refer to the Dayaks of Sarawak collectively as "second-class *bumiputra*." The Dayaks help to provide an indigenous majority in Malaysia that counters the Chinese and Indian populations, and their compliance with the incorporation of British Borneo in the new Federation of Malaysia was essentially secured by granting them special status. But in practice that promise generally has not been translated into real gains for the Dayaks.

Federal-State Relations

As natural resource areas, the Malaysian Borneo territories play an important role in the wider Malaysian economy. Sarawak, for example, is a significant generator of foreign exchange, supplying such valuable exports as oil, natural gas, and timber. It has large volumes of fast-flowing water available for power generation and considerable expanses of land potentially suitable for estate agriculture. Nevertheless, the state is economically backward in terms of a variety of criteria: it has a low level of industrialization and urbanization; inadequate provision of infrastructure and services such as roads, housing, water, electricity, education, and health care; and a high incidence of poverty, especially in rural areas, associated with low-income agricultural activities. There are formidable environmental obstacles to the development of commercial agriculture and the provision of essential services. Population levels are low and communities are generally dispersed, with many of them in relatively inaccessible locations.

These circumstances are the context of a central tension or contradiction between federally generated, national development policies and local-level political, economic, and cultural realities in Sarawak. On the one hand, the Malaysian government addresses itself to problems of poverty and "backward" agriculture in these marginal territories in an attempt to modernize and draw them into the mainstream of national life. On the other hand, the government exploits them, extracting natural resources to generate national development and economic growth. This situation is sustained by another element in federal-state relations. The federal government is dominated by Malays, and, although the Dayaks of Sarawak have equivalent constitutional status, they are remote from the main arenas of political power and have virtually no say in the formulation of development strategies. Advantages generally have gone to Peninsular Malays and a handful of Muslim political clients and brokers in Sarawak who act as intermediaries between the state and senior Peninsular politicians to ensure that the latters' will prevails.

Although Sarawak natives are constitutionally protected and enjoy special advantages and privileges, some have been progressively marginalized, impoverished, and underdeveloped by means of the very process that seeks to transform and modernize them (King 1990a). In particular, models of development have emerged in a West Malaysian context and these, to a large extent, have been applied inappropriately in the different conditions prevailing in Sarawak. This is especially noticeable in the arena of land development where Peninsular strategies of large-scale estate agriculture and resettlement introduced in Sarawak have largely failed. At the heart of this issue of land development is native customary tenure and local forms of agricultural practice such as shifting cultivation. One of the main emphases of government action in Sarawak has been the attempt to move shifting cultivators away from subsistence crops such as hill rice, and low income, low-yield, cash crops like rubber, into the high-yield, cash-crop sector, growing oil palm and cocoa on plantations.

In a special supplement of the *Borneo Post* (26 March 1985), the Sarawak state government's policies and programs in relation to the Fifth Malaysia Plan (1986–90) were clearly enunciated. The article stated (p. 11) that

If the rural sector is to compete properly with the urban sector to keep its population within its own sector then the concept and strategy of rural development must necessarily be one of promoting the growth and development of large scale plantations....While the development of smallholdings can raise the level of income of rural areas, it cannot be expected to do it very satisfactorily.

Unfortunately, in many cases the strategy of public-sector-sponsored estate development as a means of modernizing native economies has had precisely the opposite effect. Schemes that have not lived up to their promises have left their participants economically worse off. Often there have been short-term financial gains for farmers but in the longer term the estates, largely due to poor management and organization, have not proved viable. Local Dayaks, having been pushed into increased dependence upon the marketplace, find themselves with few economic alternatives when the schemes founder and anticipated levels of household income do not materialize. This leads to dissatisfaction and disillusionment. Some Dayak settlers have moved off the estates to eke out a living on small holdings elsewhere, or they have drifted into the towns in search of wage work with which to make ends meet.

Strategies of resettlement and plantation agriculture also must be seen in the context of the accelerating exploitation of the Sarawak rain forests for timber. Shifting cultivation is perceived by officialdom as an obstacle to, and in competition with, commercial logging operations. It is a mode of agriculture to be progressively restricted (or, ideally, eliminated) by moving rural dwellers into cash-crop agriculture. Logging, too, although it provides short-term benefits in wage work, mainly for young males employed in the logging camps, seriously threatens the long-term economic viability of rural communities. It has resulted in severe soil erosion, the diminution of wild animal stocks for hunting, the pollution of drinking water, and the destruction of fish-spawning grounds.

In my view, because of its different historical experiences, Sarawak requires different approaches to development, approaches less heavily committed to large-scale plantation schemes. Yet its incorporation into the Federation of Malaysia in 1963 as a marginal territory subordinate to the politically and economically advanced Peninsula, which had been granted its own independence six years before, has ensured that Sarawak has had little room for maneuver in its development policies and programs. Its land-tenure system was largely inherited from the Brooke Raj and the colonial government. Its small-scale subsistence agriculture, with limited native involvement in cash-crop cultivation, meant that, in contrast to the Peninsula, there was no substantial commodization of land or labor, and very little development of plantation agriculture prior to independence. The issue of customary tenure is vital to my argument and to that I now turn.

Land Tenure in Sarawak: Continuities and Transformations

As we have seen, the Constitution directly confirms that state law in East Malaysia can provide for special treatment of natives with regard to land. The intimate interrelationship between native identity and well being and land has been remarked upon by Evelyn Hong.

> Land has been the Sarawak natives' most important economic resource, and the relationship between land and the community has been the cornerstone of native society. Land has both spiritual and social significance to native people. The community is closely bound to the soil and the land. (1987, 37)

In pre-European Sarawak, land could not be bought or sold. No one had the power to alienate it. It belonged to particular communities, to relatives and ancestors. It was held in trust, and rights in it and responsibilities to it were enshrined in customary law (Weinstock 1979). What the changing system of land tenure since European contact demonstrates is the conflict between a policy intended to maintain a native stake in land, on the one hand, and the demands of an increasingly interventionist state administration and the pressures gradually arising from the commercialization of agriculture on the other.

It is often assumed that the Brooke Raj, established by the first "White Rajah," Sir James Brooke, in 1841, was averse to economic development. Certainly Brooke's rhetoric "emphasized the primacy of Native interests and the dangers of speculative foreign investment" (Reece 1988, 21). Some writers have argued that this was probably a rationalization for the significant obstacles to economic transformation that Sarawak presented. Yet, as Reece suggests, it was also in the interests of the Brookes to encourage only gradual change in order to maintain their own rather precarious rule. They were wary of the threat that large-scale investment and capitalist enterprise might pose to their political position. Thus, the concept of custodianship had an underlying rationale. But it also corresponded to a genuine view held by James and his nephew, Charles Brooke, of the necessity for native protection.

The Brookes promoted controlled and selective development, and it is clear is that, while native rights in land were to some extent accorded special status, they were also progressively circumscribed and regulated. The first land law was promulgated by Rajah James Brooke in 1863. The Land Regulations established the principle that the Raj had rights over all unoccupied and waste lands (Porter 1967, 32). This strategy was continued in the 1875 Land Order and the Fruit Trees Order I of 1899. Lands that were not inhabited and used were firmly established as state lands. For systems of shifting cultivation, in which large tracts of land are left fallow for considerable periods of time, these innovations in land administration meant, in effect, that areas previously governed by customary law were no longer subject to indigenous rights (Colchester 1989, 23).

With the commercialization of agriculture from the latter part of the nineteenth century and the introduction of such cash crops as gambier, pepper, and rubber, land became an increasingly valuable commodity, and hence subject to closer scrutiny and control. A series of ordinances were introduced by the Raj from 1920, the main elements of which were eventually brought together in the 1948 Land Classification Ordinance, introduced by the newly established colonial government, after the third Rajah, Charles Vyner Brooke, ceded Sarawak to the British Crown in 1946.

All land was classified into five categories: Mixed Zone, Native Area, Native Customary, Reserved, and Interior Area Land. Further amendments were introduced in 1952 and 1955, and these and the five-fold categorization of land were incorporated into the 1958 Land Code (Gumis Humen 1981, 7–10). This code continues to form the basis of land administration in the state, although further modifications have been made to the regulations since 1958. In an important sense, natives do enjoy special recognition with regard to land. Only in Mixed Zone Land can nonnatives such as the Chinese, along with natives, specifically and legally acquire rights. These can be titled or, if held by natives, they may be subject to customary tenure. In Native Area Land, in most circumstances, only indigenes may exercise rights under title. Native Customary Land is untitled and defined as land "in which native customary rights whether communal or otherwise have lawfully been created prior to the 1st of January 1958" (Hong 1987, 48). There are procedures available for legally creating additional customary rights over land (in, for example, Interior Area Land) but these are subject to special permission by government officials. Furthermore, native rights can be extinguished by ministerial decision, and government land administrators have wide powers of discretion in deciding claims to customary land, and on whether to extinguish native rights in return for compensation. Customary rights can also be alienated, transformed into a long lease, or granted to an individual in perpetuity, and "decisions of the native courts concerning rights to customary land do not have the force of law" (ibid., 51).

Reserved Land comprises forest reserves, protected forests, national parks, and wildlife sanctuaries, and can be declared as such by the government on state land. Finally, Interior Area Land is that which does not fall into any of the other categories. Much of this is in the deep interior and is covered with primary forest. Parts of it can be reclassified, for example, as customary land, by government decision.

Despite this classification scheme, some categories of which theoretically favor native tenure, and in practice provide some *possibility* of security as well as compensation if rights are removed, native customary rights have little force in law. The overriding legal right, which began to be established from the early days of Brooke rule, is that which is exercised by the state. The area of Native Customary Land has been progressively reduced. Furthermore, native rights are held subject to the will and pleasure of the state since any land not covered by a formal document or title is considered in law to be state land (Cramb and Dixon 1988, 8; Colchester 1989, 23). According to A. F. Porter, this provision "suggests that native customary rights have a legal standing no greater than a bare licence" (1967, 117; Gumis Humen 1981, 66ff). What is more, Native Customary Land has little or no market value, given the fact that it cannot legally be bought or sold on the open market. Thus, natives "can be deprived of equitable compensation" (Hong 1987, 56).

Be that as it may, "The fact remains...that native customary rights to land and their application are a fundamental principle recognized in the Land Code" (ibid., 61). An attempt to abolish native customary tenure by some of Sarawak's political leaders in the mid-1960s, and to categorize all land as either registered or unregistered, provoked fierce local resistance before it was abandoned. Successive state governments have contented themselves with whittling away at customary rights rather than confronting the native population head on. However, politicians, committed to rural development and large-scale agriculture, ultimately desire to remove the perceived encumbrances of customary land.

There is a real dilemma here. The major advantage of the Sarawak

Land Code, despite its limitations, is that it has offered a measure of protection to native rights. Changes until recently generally have been gradual. It has prevented the emergence of a large indigenous landless class, and the substantial alienation of land to nonnatives, private companies, and commercial interests has been avoided. In general, Sarawak natives are not yet short of land. Since most of them living in rural areas have some access to land, there is no large floating labor force looking for work or for land to rent, though this situation is changing under the pressures of modernization. Sarawak is still predominantly a state of small holders who usually combine subsistence and cash-crop production. Many communities have remained in close contact with their land. There are still relatively clearly demarcated areas where native populations may be found dwelling in longhouses, following various of the practices and beliefs authorized by customary law, and farming hill rice using shifting cultivation methods. In this connection, ethnic identity is still strong. Obviously there have been changes, some dramatic, in social, economic, and cultural life. But generally we are able to witness a quite marked resilience of native communities (King 1986a).

However, these circumstances have been produced largely at the expense of the marginalization of these communities. Economic growth and development have taken place in more accessible, coastal and urban locations. There is still much poverty and economic backwardness in rural areas, and during the past decade vociferous protests have been voiced by political representatives of the native populations over the disadvantaged position of their constituencies. They argue that the Dayaks, as *bumiputras* like the Malays with special rights and privileges, should be sharing in the fruits of Malaysia's economic success and generally rising prosperity since the inception of the New Economic Policy. But the concentration on plantation agriculture among those Dayak communities that have managed to attract government attention has also not proved to be an appropriate vehicle of rural development.

There is a further issue, which will probably turn out to be a greater threat to native livelihoods than the gradual undermining of rights to land, and that is commercial logging. In 1988, Sarawak exported approximately 12 million cubic meters of sawlogs, almost double the volume of exports in 1980 (Sarawak 1989, 112). In March 1988, it was reported in the Sarawak government's forestry journal that at current rates sustained logging of the remaining old-growth and virgin forests would result in the "liquidation" of unlogged swamp-forest areas in another five to ten years, and of the of hill forests in fifteen to twenty years (*Simba Newsletter*,

1991). Very roughly, from the early 1960s through the late 1980s, about one-third of Sarawak's rain forests were logged (Hong 1987, 127ff). Because revenues from timber are mainly controlled and used by local politicians to maintain the political status quo and their own clienteles, a blind eye is turned toward many of the deleterious effects of logging.

The clearing of the rain forest obviously endangers the agricultural economies of the Dayaks. Yet the dangers to Sarawak's forest nomads, the Penan, are even more formidable given that they are totally dependent on the resources of the forest for hunting and gathering. Although forest clearance is not my main concern here, it is well to keep this context in mind when considering government land-development strategies in regard to official perceptions of shifting agriculture and rain-forest-based economies.

Land Development in Sarawak: The Problem

The main thrust of land-development policy in Sarawak during the last three decades has been to promote large-scale forms of cash-crop cultivation in order to secure economies of scale, increase agricultural efficiency, raise rural incomes, change the economic practices of farmers (especially in discouraging shifting cultivation), and to concentrate, control, and administer rural settlements. In these respects the Peninsular Malaysian models of land development and resettlement, which draw upon the experiences of such agencies as the Federal Land Development Authority (FELDA) and the Federal Land Consolidation and Rehabilitation Authority (FELCRA), have been especially influential. Sarawak has its own statutory land-development boards, which replicate those of the Peninsula.

Publicly sponsored and managed estates established to "modernize" Sarawak's native farmers have a poor record. Technical and organizational reasons for their lack of success are easily identifiable: poor management, inadequate financial accounting, delays in project implementation, problems of interdepartmental coordination, lack of expertise in estate agriculture, difficulties of access to remote regions, and general environmental obstacles. But a major element has been the continued provisions for native customary tenure, and the prevailing belief among many indigenous peoples that estate agriculture is incompatible with small-holding and shifting cultivation (King 1986b, 1990b). Many delays have been experienced because of the need to survey native land, and negotiate and sometimes litigate over it. Given the fact that natives are often suspicious, and rightly so, of government intentions toward land, the relations between state officials and local farmers are often difficult.

If the government had been determined to make its policy of public-sector plantation development effective, which I personally believe to be a mistaken strategy, as a vital prerequisite it should have confronted the problem of native land and attempted to abolish it. After all, its development policy depends on easy access to land, minimal problems and delays in developing it, and an available labor force willing to work on the estates. Farmers with access to land and a wide range of agricultural alternatives (from subsistence production to small-scale cash-crop cultivation), which can be used to spread economic risks, are very difficult to recruit for plantation work.

What the government now has is the worst of both worlds: a strategy that has failed, and wasted in the process large amounts of public funds; and discontented, disillusioned, rural communities that have been drawn into government schemes but have derived no long-term benefit from them. If anything, the rural dwellers are more economically disadvantaged and marginalized now than they were before the projects were introduced.

In my view, the government would have done better to recognize the socioeconomic and cultural realities of Sarawak agriculture and concentrate on in situ kinds of development using subsidies, credit, extension services, and technical assistance. This would have avoided the need to tackle the problem of native tenure.[5] These gradualist programs can provide a medium-term solution to problems of rural development in native areas. To some extent, the Sarawak Department of Agriculture has pursued this strategy, but not, I think, with total support from the state government. Instead sizeable funds have been diverted to the promotion of public-sector estate development.

In the long term, market forces at work in Sarawak are likely to continue to undermine native land rights. The ultimate aim of government is to register all land, and native customary tenure is generally associated with a system of agriculture (shifting cultivation) that officials wish to replace. Furthermore, because of the lack of land for the Chinese, there is widespread informal use of native land by nonnative farmers. I would argue that a more determined policy of in situ development, coordinating the efforts of small holders, could provide natives with sufficient breathing space to adjust to the transformations that probably will continue.

Native Reservations?

In an attempt to suggest alternative development policies with regard to the native populations and customary tenure in Sarawak, observers such as Evelyn Hong have favored the creation of what, in effect, are native reservations (1987, 215ff). I am critical of Hong's conclusions that we should support, as a general rule, traditional ways of life, shifting agriculture, customary tenure, and longhouse domicile. Her argument must be qualified. In some places, such as in parts of the long-settled, relatively heavily populated, and easily accessible regions of southwestern Sarawak, shifting cultivation is no longer viable and has been replaced by other forms of agriculture. Recognition of this fact is not intended to support the official negative view of shifting agriculture as inherently destructive of the natural environment. Given an appropriate population-land ratio and access to sufficient forest land to permit an adequate fallow period between farming cycles, shifting cultivation is genuinely adaptive of tropical rain-forest environments. However, where there has been population growth or the development of permanent cash cropping, or where farmers have been confined to specific areas by the demarcation of forest reserves, by the official restriction of their movements, or by the allocation of forests to logging concessionaires, shifting agriculturalists frequently have been forced to intensify operations on the land left to them. In some cases this has resulted in environmental deterioration and a fall in rice-production levels, with a consequent increase in poverty. This is not an inevitable consequence of intensification, however, if there are other activities that farmers can undertake to supplement shifting agriculture such as cash cropping, handicraft manufacture, and wage work (Cramb 1989; Padoch 1982).

Where feasible, and certainly in the short and medium term, shifting agriculture can be maintained in various parts of Sarawak if it is integrated with other kinds of cultivation and nonfarming economic activities. This is particularly so where population and other pressures on land are not too great. Nevertheless, it seems unlikely that shifting agriculture can be supported in all cases and in the forms in which it has been practiced in the past. Nor do I agree with Hong that it is "the only form of cultivation suited to their [the Dayak's] physical environment" (1987, 211). Of course, the maintenance of shifting cultivation also depends upon the pace and extent of commercial logging operations in interior areas of Sarawak, given the fact that forest clearance directly impinges on these rural communities (Colchester 1989, 34–44; Insan 1989).

Furthermore, longhouse domicile is no longer as widespread as it once was, and it seems futile to bemoan the demise of longhouse society. Some Dayak households have voluntarily moved out of their longhouses and established single-family dwellings, especially in areas where cash cropping and other processes of modernization have been especially marked. There is certainly evidence that some communities prefer to retain longhouse lifestyles but not all Dayaks wish to do so. In my view, the choice of dwelling must be left to the Dayaks themselves and it should not be prescribed by the government or any other body.

Finally, it is difficult to conceive of what "traditional" Dayak ways of life are, in Hong's terms, and how they might be maintained. Natives have been affected by wider economic and political processes for a considerable period of time, and these pressures will not diminish. Many natives argue that they do not wish to be left alone and protected in defined rural areas. They want the benefits of rural development. They see themselves as marginalized and left behind. When opportunities have been presented, natives have often eagerly grasped them. Generally they are in favor of various in situ forms of agricultural development but they do not approve of resettlement and FELDA-type land-development schemes.

An opinion that I expressed a few years ago has even greater force today given the continued difficulties the Dayaks have in gaining access to real political power at the state level. I proposed that the ability of the Dayaks to control their own destinies depends on them

> obtaining a much stronger political voice than they have hitherto enjoyed, the development of effective, cohesive and unifying political organizations, and the securing of committed and genuinely caring political leaders. This is really the only way to ensure that native land rights, livelihoods and cultural identities are protected. (King 1988b, 28)

It is my view that a reservation policy would leave natives even further behind. It would assign them to a rural sector and limit them to shifting cultivation and subsistence agriculture on land with low market value. From my experience of their communities, the Dayak desire increased incomes from cash crops, assistance in agriculture in the form of extension services, subsidies, and grants, and new crops and technological inputs that they can integrate with their subsistence activities. They want education for their children. Above all, they are demanding that their rights in land be recognized. Some wish their land to be appropriately valued and given a registered title, so that they might realize an adequate return should they wish to sell, mortgage, lease, or rent it.

It is inconceivable that natives can be shielded from economic and political processes that have already transformed their way of life. Ideally, what they have to do is make these forces work for them, so that they can select new opportunities on their own terms. This calls for more effective political representation and a gradualist policy of in situ rural development. I maintain that Hong's proposals are too restrictive. They would not earn the support of all Dayaks nor are they easy to sustain given the level of modernization that has already affected Dayak communities. In any case, no proposal for the safeguarding of native rights in land (be it for the establishment of reservations with some form of communal tenure or for registration of land and protection of individual native titles) will be implemented unless and until Dayaks can secure proper political participation in state government and make their voices heard in decision-making circles.

What is needed as a first step is Dayak empowerment. Once that is achieved there should be a vigorous policy pursued of in situ agricultural development, a gradual withdrawal from public-sector estate schemes, a confirmation of Dayak rights to land (which, I would suggest, requires land surveys, registration, and the granting of titles), and sufficient flexibility so that Dayak communities are not directed into wholly cash-crop forms of production or confined to subsistence agriculture based on shifting cultivation, communal tenure, and longhouse domicile. It is my view that if Dayaks continue to be excluded from the centers of political power in Sarawak, as they have been for the past two decades, then native rights in land will continue to be undermined and the pace of change and its direction will remain largely in the hands of those who have little sympathy with or understanding of Dayak needs, motivations, and ways of life.

CHAPTER 15

Being Indigenous in Eastern Indonesia

R.H. BARNES

The question of who is indigenous in Indonesia is typically both interesting and complex. Even more challenging is the question of who fits into the very special category of the indigenous peoples. The interest in looking at such a problematic category is not to debunk it but to treat it as an object of anthropological appreciation, just like any other product of human activity. Internationally, it is a political category of fairly recent coinage, which is still in the process of taking form. As its history is still in the making, there is no reason to think that it will continue to be defined by the criteria mentioned in contemporary works such as those to be reviewed in this paper. Nevertheless, it is well to pay attention to political and ethnic identities as they are created.

The literature on indigenous peoples in Indonesia focuses on a limited number of regions in which government policy is, or at least has been, in conflict, to put it mildly, with the wishes of the local population. Each case has involved serious loss of life and livelihood, as well as the suspension of political self-determination, but otherwise each example is very different from the others.

The newsletters and annual reports of the International Work Group for Indigenous Affairs (IWGIA), for example, regularly refer to events in East Timor and Irian Jaya (or West Irian), which it prefers to call West Papua. Occasionally they carry articles on the South Moluccas, where a secessionist state was defeated in 1950, and which is now a major destination of Javanese migrants (see also Burger 1987, 141–42). In addition, it has devoted two IWGIA Documents to East Timor (Retbøll 1980, 1984) and one to transmigration (Otten 1986). In recent years the *IWGIA Yearbook* has published a map of Southeast Asia listing a shifting collection of indigenous peoples in Indonesia, including at various times, and among others, East Timor, "Dayaks," Kedung Omo of central Java, Lampung in southern Sumatra, and the peoples of the South Moluccas.

These, of course, are not the only troubled areas in Indonesia and not the only peoples whose suffering is the object of international concern. Logging in Kalimantan receives notoriety in the international press and affects hunting-and-gathering peoples of the kind who are typically classed as indigenous. Of the 1.5 million tribespeople officially recognized by the Indonesian government, most are in Irian Jaya, Kalimantan, Sulawesi, and Sumatra (Burger 1987, 142). None are in eastern Indonesia.[1]

Except occasionally or implicitly, the issue of the status of indigenous peoples has not arisen in the eastern part of the Malay Archipelago other than in East Timor, the South Moluccas, and Irian Jaya. There are, of course, other respects in which issues of indigenousness arise there, and an examination of these may highlight the special status of the indigenous-peoples concept, as well as revealing its limitations even in East Timor.

The IWGIA's rather pragmatic approach toward the definition of indigenousness is shown by the fact that they included among their Documents series a report that I wrote (Barnes 1984) about the people of Lamalera, Lembata, who, except in respect of their hunting whales and porpoise, differ little from their neighbors. They are not tribals, in the way that the Kubu of Sumatra might be said to be,[2] and in general they are "indigenous" only in the ordinary, dictionary sense of the word. Ironically, like many peoples in this part of Indonesia, they regard themselves as *not* being indigenous to the Flores and Timor area in terms of their ancestry.

Definitions of Indigenous Peoples

As Burger (1987, 6) has commented, "the term indigenous peoples has not met with universal acceptance, if only because, taken in its literal sense, most peoples are indigenous to their country." But the alternatives, he says, are even less acceptable. Several publications have

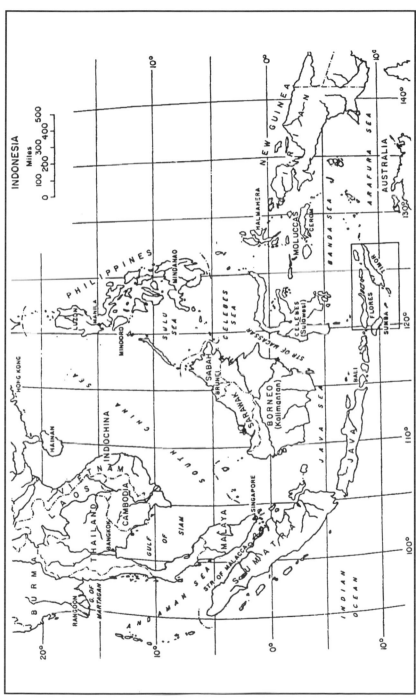

MAP 15.1. *Indonesia.*

attempted to describe or define what it is that distinguishes indigenous peoples from their neighbors, and their authors have often consulted competent anthropologists (see, for example, Independent Commission on International Humanitarian Issues 1987; Goodland 1982; and Beauclerk, Narby, and Townsend 1988; and compare Kingsbury and Gray, chaps. 2 and 3, this volume). After surveying a number of near synonyms, Goodland (1982, vii) comments,

> Four terms—aboriginal, autochthonous, indigenous, and native—apply to those with a traditional culture and with racial origins in the region in which they currently reside. Therefore, these terms also may be broadly applied to the indigenous peasants of a particular area. However, peasants are more a part of the national society than the people addressed in this paper.

The Independent Commission on International Humanitarian Issues, or ICIHI (1987, 5–7) acknowledges that the boundary between ethnic groups and indigenous peoples is difficult to draw. Nevertheless, for the commission (ibid., xiv) indigenous peoples are broadly the same as tribals or semitribals.

> There are four major elements in the definition of indigenous peoples: pre-existence (i.e., the population is descendent of those inhabiting an area prior to the arrival of another population); non-dominance; cultural difference; and self-identification as indigenous. (Ibid., 5–7)

To these criteria apparently should be added the condition that they should be seen to be suffering as the result of domination by others. Crucial here is the relationship to the state and self-definition as indigenous peoples. The recently revised International Labour Organisation Convention Concerning Indigenous and Tribal Peoples in Independent Countries, for example, states that "Self-identification as indigenous or tribal shall be regarded as a fundamental criterion for determining the groups to which the provisions of this Convention apply" (International Work Group for Indigenous Affairs 1990, 162). Although indigenous people strongly objected to other features of this revised convention, self-identification is central to all definitions of the category and to the political process of choosing or rejecting this status.

The phrase *indigenous peoples* seems to pose the least trouble in the Americas, where the dominating group to which the contrast is drawn is Europeans and their descendants. In Asia, the ICIHI acknowledges, European occupation was the last in a succession of colonial experiences, and the question of indigenous peoples is more complex, not to say potentially embarrassing to governments. "In the Indian sub-continent, for example, the continental migration of peoples into the area during the past thousand years has made the question of antecedence too complex to resolve" (Independent Commission on International Humanitarian Issues 1987, 6). Furthermore, there is the problem of "internal colonization." To put it bluntly, if, in the current political sense, indigenous peoples exist in Asia, where there is no longer a significant European presence, then there must be Asian oppressors; and these dominant peoples, no matter how indigenous themselves, must in political terms be denied indigenous-peoples status. In Indonesia the prime target for this unenviable position is, of course, the Javanese.

Burger (1987, 9) has drawn up a list of six criteria defining indigenous peoples for the purpose of his book. He sensibly says that an indigenous people may possess some or all of the traits, which themselves overlap to a degree. He remarks that the peoples discussed in his book do not unequivocally meet his criteria. Anthropologists will recognize the similarity of this approach to Edmund Leach's treatment of marriage as a comparative category (1961, 107–8) and to the literature on polythetic classification. Presumably they will approve. For Burger, indigenous peoples have the following characteristics.

1. They are the descendants of the original inhabitants of a territory that has been overcome by conquest.

2. They are nomadic or seminomadic peoples, such as shifting cultivators, herders, and hunters and gatherers, who practice a labor-intensive form of agriculture that produces little surplus and has low energy needs.

3. They do not have centralized political institutions, they organize at the level of the community, and they make decisions on a consensual basis.

4. They have all the characteristics of a national minority: they share a common language, religion, culture, and other identifying characteristics and a relationship to a particular territory but are subjugated by a dominant culture and society.

5. They have a different world view consisting of a custodial and nonmaterialist attitude toward land and natural resources, and they wish to pursue a development path different from that proffered by the dominant society.

6. They consist of individuals who subjectively consider themselves to be indigenous, and are accepted by the group as such.

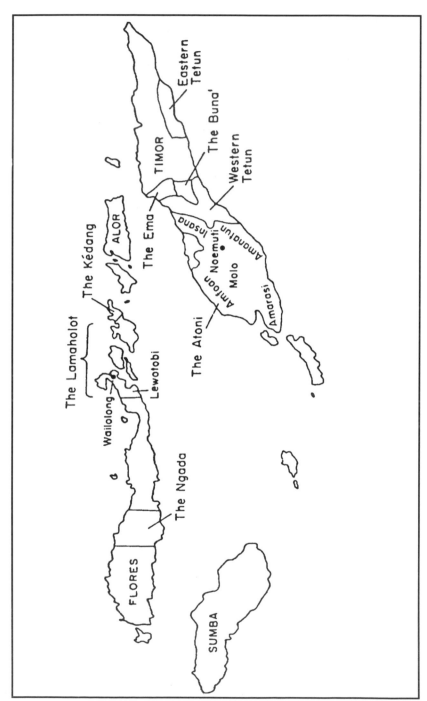

MAP 15.2. *The Flores/Timor Region of Indonesia.*

The Varied Situation in Eastern Indonesia

East Timor has, of course, been conquered, most recently by the Indonesian army in 1975. Continued guerrilla resistance and political and military suppression are the reasons why the inhabitants are given attention by organizations like the IWGIA. To say that the rest of eastern Indonesia also was conquered by the Indonesian government would be to trivialize the East Timor situation, to misinterpret the history of the Republic's struggle against the Dutch after World War II, and above all to seriously underestimate the strength of national feeling among the population. Indeed, one respect in which the occupation of East Timor is not comparable to the way in which Indonesia acquired Irian Jaya is that it represents a major departure from the policy under which, at Mohammed Hatta's urging, the Republic of Indonesia was founded: namely, that it be based on the boundaries of the former Dutch East Indies.

It was this principle which justified the campaign for acquiring Irian Jaya, even though racially, culturally, and linguistically it is predominantly, although not completely, unrelated to the rest of Indonesia. The cultures of East Timor, on the other hand, have "more than a passing resemblance to those of indigenous groups living in Eastern Indonesia" (Gray 1984, 39). What significantly distinguishes them is their different history of European colonialism and the fact that Indonesia has no valid claim to their land in international law.

Although most of the peoples in eastern Indonesia practice a labor-intensive shifting cultivation, which produces at best only small surpluses, none are nomadic or seminomadic. The greater proportion of the population probably would best be described as peasants, and on that ground perhaps they would not be accepted as indigenous peoples. In so far as they are now incorporated into the state of Indonesia, they participate in a centrally organized political organization extending down from the national capital through several levels to the local village government. It is true, of course, that grassroots political activity in rural areas was stamped out by the Suharto government. In the past, communities were governed by local leadership, typically based on diarchic principles, dependent upon (or at least striving for) consensus. There were also princedoms and petty kingdoms of a nonbureaucratic character. Although the historical records for indigenous political life are very incomplete, it is clear that raiding, warfare, and other forms of violence were commonplace. Consensus was, and still is, a typical goal but it is not always achieved.

Indonesia is a nation of more than three hundred languages, and linguistic diversity is also marked in eastern Indonesia. There are some fifteen separate linguistic groups belonging to two unrelated language families alone on both parts of Timor (Hicks 1976, 6). Most people might be able to claim minority status by virtue of speaking a language used by only a small group. Each community has or had its own cultural characteristics, and prior to conversion to Islam or Christianity each had its own local religious particularities. The peoples of eastern Indonesia have precise relationships to territory, although individual ownership of land as an alienable commodity is primarily a recent innovation encouraged by the Indonesian government. The East Timorese are clearly subjugated but that is not how the peoples of Nusa Tenggara Timur normally regard themselves.

In the literature on indigenous peoples, the idea of a custodial attitude toward the land is typically linked to belief in "Mother Earth."

> What is shared by most indigenous peoples is a worldview which incorporates as its dearest principle a custodial concept of land and natural resources: Mother Earth. Indigenous peoples regard the land or earth as sacred. It is a living entity. (Independent Commission on International Humanitarian Issues 1987, 9)

It is true that Traube (1986) has recently identified Mother Earth beliefs in the religious ideas of the Mambai of East Timor, as Hicks did before in the "maternal religion" of those Tetun-speaking peoples who live in Vikeke, East Timor (1976, 21; 1984; 1990). In fact, it is typical of the indigenous religions of eastern Indonesia that they treat the godhead as being dual, comprised of a male figure associated with the sky and a female earth divinity. But these attitudes have not yet assumed the political connotations characteristic of the indigenous-peoples movement.

Gill (1990) has recently argued that the Mother Earth doctrine was an American and European exaggeration, based on thin evidence, which was adopted by some American Indians wishing to preserve their separate identities in the face of the loss of land, political institutions, and language. There is some danger that in translating Indonesian expressions with the phrase "Mother Earth" we will unconsciously and inappropriately bring connotations from the American background into this new context.

The Lamaholot of the Solor Archipelago, in ritual chants recorded by the Catholic priest Paul Arndt in the 1930s, offered invocations to the high god Lera Wulan and his complement Tana Ekan. Lera Wulan is composed of the Lamaholot names for sun and moon. It does not specifically mean the sun and the moon but more likely the firmament or the upper regions. Lera Wulan is said to have power over everything. He is the highest and mightiest. He created the heavens and the earth, the lesser spirits, and the animals. *Tana* means land, ground, field, or the earth. The significance of *ekan* is less certain. Although it is often employed in the same sense as *tana*, Arndt tried to identify it through metathesis with a middle Flores word *gaé* (language unspecified), which he translated rather confusingly as "Earth Mother," "Earth Spirit," or "surface of the earth" (Arndt 1951, 17, 153). The compound Tana Ekan has the general sense of "the earth" and clearly designates the lower world in opposition to the upper.

Arndt often speaks of Lera Wulan and Tana Ekan as though they are a unitary godhead. Normally they are addressed separately but this is due to the dual structure of the ceremonial chants. When they are invoked in the same ceremony they unite a number of oppositions, among them the upper world and the lower, the heavens and the earth, male and female, creation and destruction, kindness and ferocity. However, sometimes in the chants the relative positions are reversed and Lera Wulan is spoken of as below, Tana Ekan above.

Lera Wulan and Tana Ekan are explicitly recognized as male and female, respectively, yet they are frequently addressed in the rituals as Mother Lera Wulan and Father Tana Ekan. Arndt noted that the sexual designations are commonly reversed and mentioned that the custom is not confined to Lamaholot communities but also occurs in neighboring groups (ibid., 1951, 22, 157). When he asked why this custom occurred, he was told that "Tana Ekan is ferocious, because she is a *menaka*, that is a vampire and a corpse eater" (ibid., 247, see also p. 22).

Lera Wulan is a benevolent figure but he is known to eat men, sometimes those guilty of great crimes, more often prisoners taken in warfare or abducted from enemy villages for the purpose of ritual execution. Tana Ekan, through her association with the products of the earth as well as her link with Lera Wulan, is also generally benevolent. Why she is sometimes spoken of as a vampire and corpse eater goes unexplained but one might assume that it has some basis in the fact that the earth receives corpses at burial. It is sometimes mentioned that she satisfies her hunger by drinking the blood of sacrificial animals and of men killed in war.

It is equally easy to overestimate the importance of custodial attitudes toward land and natural resources. The persistent habit of burning vast tracts of land annually to facilitate deer hunting has been outlawed by the Indonesian government and is generally deplored by soil conservationists but it goes unstopped. Attitudes are indeed nonmaterialist in that they are shaped by religious convictions but not in the sense that these peoples are uninterested in exploiting the material world in pursuit of their own well-being. The official political doctrine of the Indonesian government rests on the need to develop the country. Local attitudes, as might be expected, are various and mixed but certainly they are not overwhelmingly negative toward development and material advancement.

This brings us to the first and last criteria, namely, preexistence and self-definition as indigenous. Clearly the Indonesian army is not indigenous to East Timor but the more salient fact is that it is the instrument for denying the national independence that is apparently desired by a majority of East Timorese. I think that, other than in the Moluccas, no one else in eastern Indonesia has claimed indigenousness in the relevant sense, namely, in opposition to a dominating force of external origin.[3] Even if non-Indonesians wished to see them in this light, it is not simply the Javanese who are the dominating group.

The dominating presence is the Indonesian state itself, for, despite its faults, it does have legitimacy outside East Timor and it does represent the nation as a whole rather than just one very substantial part of it. This legitimacy derives in large part from the common (but by no means uniform) experience of Dutch colonialism. The word *Indonesian,* which almost any citizen of this nation would accept as part of his identity, was adopted by nationalists to express their national aspirations. In 1939 and 1940, they requested that the word *Inlander* (native) be replaced by *Indonesian* in government documents (Avé 1976, 229; Pluvier 1974, 140). Although the Dutch government, in exile in London during the Second World War, rejected this request, *Indonesian* of course became the officially correct term after independence. Every Indonesian therefore carries with him a sense of being indigenous in respect of the Dutch colonial past. The tragic irony of the operations in Timor is that all Indonesians, through their government, are implicated as the dominating, colonial power in East Timor.

There are other aspects of self-definition besides belonging to a nation-state and a history of colonialism, and it should be recalled that for parts of this region colonialism was both recent and brief. The peoples of eastern Indonesia have diverse explanations for their origins. Some regard themselves as having local origins, their ancestors having emerged from the earth, from trees or rocks, or from the heavens. Others are conscious of being immigrants, or descendants of immigrants, many of whom who came in ancient times.

It is common for intermarrying clans of the same village to have different stories indicating autochthonous or outside origin. Often the clans identified as "lords of the land," who exercise or once exercised religious supervision over the well-being of the community, claim to be autochthonous. But it is not at all uncommon for the persons or groups who exercise hereditary political leadership to identify themselves as having descended from outsiders.

It is frequently noted that the peoples of the Flores/Timor area are racially and linguistically mixed. The languages belong either to the Austronesian family, as do most in Indonesia, or they are non-Austronesian (Papuan). The latter kind are present in the highlands of central and eastern Timor and on the islands of Alor and Pantar. Melanesian and Proto-Malay elements blended with earlier ethnic groups, though there is no certainty that the Proto-Malays arrived earlier or later than the Melanesians (Schulte Nordholt 1971, 23). As Peter Bellwood (1985, 75) comments, the racial picture in the eastern Lesser Sundas and the Moluccas is markedly clinal, with few sharp boundaries. "This is clearly a situation where races and languages do not match as might be expected."[4]

Bellwood (ibid., 68) concludes that the populations of the Indo-Malaysian Archipelago today derive from the Pleistocene inhabitants, both *Homo erectus* and *Homo sapiens*, of the region extending from central China to Indonesia. "Potential but problematic" examples of stone-tool industries reputed to be associated with *Homo erectus* occur in Flores and Timor (ibid., 56). Bellwood thinks that the *Homo sapiens* who were the true aborigines of the archipelago were the Australoids, ancestral to the Negritos, Melanesians, and Australians. He also believes that the great racial variation in eastern Indonesia is the "result of a gradual Southern Mongoloid settlement, much of it historically recent, over the surviving western boundary of Melanesia" (pp. 72–75). According to archaeologists, the first Austronesian-speaking peoples in Flores and Timor may have been the populations that replaced the hunting-and-collecting economies with ones that include pottery and an expanded agriculture during the third millennium B.C. (Shutler and Marck 1975, 93–95). Local legends describe a continuous movement of groups into the area up to and through the historical period.

Dates are not attached to these stories, and of course their social purpose, hence their accuracy, is open to doubt. Even stories of autochthonous origin may constitute an illegitimate claim to precedence. Leach (1954, 278) wrote that "Myth…is a language of signs in terms of which claims to rights and status are expressed, but it is a language of argument, not a chorus of harmony." What is unexpected, therefore, is the degree to which there can be consensus about whose ancestors arose on the spot and whose traveled from elsewhere.

Many speakers of an Austronesian language, such as the Mambai of East Timor, identify themselves as the original inhabitants of the land and deem themselves its guardians by right of birth. The Mambai even "claim for themselves unique ritual obligations toward the rest of humanity" (Traube 1986, 27). In contrast to this attitude is the account of themselves given by some Belu. The Belu are Tetun speakers of central and southern Timor. A more easterly branch, cut off from the main group by the Mambai, is located in East Timor but the majority live on either side of the border between the two halves of the island. Many Belu speak of themselves as having come from Malacca and claim that they were preceded in Timor by a people whom they called the Melu. Although the Melu were the actual possessors of the soil, they are gone, having been defeated by the Belu who obtained their own right to land through this conquest.

While *belu* is said to mean 'friend' in Tetun, *melu* means 'stingy' or 'greedy'. The Belu gave them this unflattering name because the Melu did not wish to give up the land. The Melu came out of the earth while the Belu came from over the sea. Myths published by Grijzen and Vroklage describe this difference as well as the dispossession of the indigenous predecessors. Among the northern Belu there are still people who claim descent from the Melu. Vroklage found that two hamlets in Lassiolat were inhabited by Melu. These Melu differed from their neighbors not at all in respect of language, culture, or race, and both groups intermarried (Ormeling 1957, 68–70; Vroklage 1953, 13–16).

Not all speakers of Tetun share the tradition of external origin. Like the Melu and Mambai, those who live in the former princedom of Caraubalo in Vikeke, East Timor, believe that the first humans, their ancestors, emerged from womblike depressions in the land of Timor after which they founded the villages of Caraubalo (Hicks 1976, 21–22).

The linguistically distinct, but adjacent, Atoni and Tetun may once have comprised a unified set of semi-independent kingdoms centered on Wehale-Waiwiku (a Tetun district on the south coast of Timor). This structure seems to have been destroyed by a punitive expedition of Portuguese allies coming from Larantuka, Flores, in May 1642. Although physically male, the supreme ruler of Wehale-Waiwiku was symbolically female. This ruler gave away the power to rule, while retain-

PLATE 15.1. *Laba Beda playing a drum, Leuwayang, Kédang, Lembata, Indonesia,* *1979.*

PLATE 15.2. *Pot trader in South Lembata, Indonesia, 1979.*

ing authority, resulting in a form of diarchy in which a female center was opposed to a male periphery.

Legend says that the ancestors of the ruler of Wehale-Waiwiku came from Sina Mutin Malakkan (China White Malacca). A voyage full of misadventures, during which they were shipwrecked at Macassar, eventually brought them to Larantuka, Flores, where some remained. The Raja of Larantuka and the coastal people of Larantuka are descended from this group. The rest continued, via Lamalera, Lembata, and other places, to the south coast of Timor where they founded the kingdom. Various ruling houses of Timor are said to descend from founding fathers sent out by the ruler of Wehale-Waiwika to "grasp the earth," and that ruler claimed to have given everything to them. The legend concerning the founding of the rajadom of Larantuka recounts a similar supplanting of original power, although in this case the transfer is established through intermarriage.

A recurring theme in the indigenous traditions of government in the region of Flores and Timor is the pattern of outsiders taking active leadership while autochthonous authority remains relatively immobile. The ruler of Wehale-Waiwiku was prevented from leaving his palace. Behind the ruler of Larantuka was an autochthonous "lord of the land" whose influence was said to be considerable but whose role is not completely clear. He was of a retiring nature and exercised his influence through intermediaries. In the nineteenth century, the district heads in Horowura, Adonara, were not permitted by customary law to present themselves to strangers nor to travel overseas. Several were not known outside the area, and when they were called to appear in Larantuka, they sent stand-ins. These substitutes were sometimes taken to be the officials they were speaking for, giving rise to confusion.

The legend of the founding of the village of Lamalera, Lembata, relates a long journey by the ancestors, from Sulawesi through the Moluccas, before they settled in south Lembata. There, by means of ceremonial exchange with the local people, they acquired the office of *kakang*, subordinate to the Raja of Larantuka. The "lord of the land" of Lamalera, however, is and was from an autochthonous descent group and today lives just outside the village boundary toward the interior of the island.

An interpretation suitable to both Timor and the Solor Archipelago would be that often spiritual authority is claimed by autochthonous groups subject to political subordination by outsiders.[5] There are, however, pronounced ambiguities about the nature of dominance in these situations. The religious superiority of the lords of the land imposes real limits to temporal power. Where authority is expressed through symbols of reclusiveness, immobility, and inactivity, as opposed to the power of external activity and mobility, there is plenty of scope for divergent views about who is dominant and what dominance means. In fact, one might suspect that in giving away power the rulers of Wehale-Waiwiku were sacrificing their prestige as aristocratic outsiders in order to approximate the religious legitimacy of the truly autochthonous.

Conclusions

It is plain that, leaving East Timor aside, none of Burger's six features fit the peoples of eastern Indonesia very well. The cultural, linguistic, and racial differences among its population do not coincide in a way that would usefully permit a distinction between indigenous peoples and dominant intruders. Nor do these differences distinguish the peoples of East Timor as a group from the rest (see Gray 1984).

What does distinguish East Timor, apart from history, is that it is genuinely dominated by a foreign military power. This situation is not quite the same thing as being descendants of original inhabitants of a territory overcome by conquest. There are important differences in history and international law between the plight of the East Timorese and the peoples of Irian Jaya. Those East Timorese who still desire independence may not think it in their interest to be defined now as indigenous peoples within the Indonesian state. And, of course, the legitimacy of their claims for international support rests on grounds that are not dependent upon whether they are so classified.

If they are to be regarded as indigenous peoples, clearly that will be for political reasons, and will not have much to do with local traditions of origin or the complex and ancient history of how the Timorese peoples came to be where they are. Presumably the self-described newcomers will also be considered members of the category, the Belu no less than the Melu, and the Eurasian political activists of Dili no less than the nobility and peasants of the East Timor mountains.

CHAPTER 16

The Emergence of a Nationalist
Movement in East Timor

JOHN G. TAYLOR

Following the Indonesian invasion of East Timor in December
1975, and the subsequent annexation of the former Portuguese colony,
many commentators were surprised both by the extent of opposition and
by the ability of the population to resist Indonesian incorporation.
While the course of events in East Timor in recent years has been documented in a number of texts (for example, Dunn 1983; Budiardjo and
Lim 1984; Jolliffe 1978, 1989; Ramos-Horta 1985; and Taylor 1990),
several important issues emerging from the conflict remain unanalyzed.

One of the most important of these issues is why, despite such overwhelming superiority, the Indonesian military experienced such
difficulties in quelling resistance to its occupation. Various writers have
tried to answer this question by focusing on issues such as the suitability
of East Timor's terrain to guerrilla warfare (see, for example, Budiardjo
and Lim 1984, chap. 3), the brutal treatment of the population by
Indonesian troops (see Dunn 1983, chap. 10; and Taylor 1991), and the
desire of the military to maintain East Timor as a counterinsurgency
training ground for its forces. While some of these, and notably the
former two, are important in addressing this problem, it seems to me that
we also need to consider other areas. The most notable of these are the
structure of East Timorese society as it emerged in the twentieth century
after a prolonged period of colonial control, and the nature of the independence movement that developed in East Timor in the early 1970s.

Specifically, preliminary consideration seems to suggest that the particular features of East Timorese society that enabled it to contain the spread of Portuguese colonial control have continued to operate during the post-1975 period. Furthermore, the nationalist movement, by addressing these aspects of East Timorese society, was able to develop strategies and policies that resulted in widespread support for its campaign for independence.

What, then, are these aspects of Timorese society, and how are they related to the development of East Timorese nationalism? Answering these questions involves examining briefly a number of features of Timor's recent history.

Settlement and Exchange

Prior to Portuguese and Dutch entry into Southeast Asia, Timor formed a part of the trading networks centered on East Java and the Celebes (Sulawesi). These networks were tied to commercial links with China and India. The commercial value of Timor is highlighted in documents published during the Ming dynasty in 1436. The island is described as one in which "the mountains are covered with sandalwood trees, and the country produces nothing else" (Groeneveldt 1880, 116). Duarte Barbosa, one of the first Portuguese to visit Timor, wrote in 1518 that "There is an abundance of white sanders-wood, which the Moors in India and Persia value greatly, where much of it is used" (Barbosa 1921, 196). Consequently, although other commodities—honey, wax, and slaves—were exported from Timor, its trade was focused primarily on its rich sandalwood reserves.

At first glance, it would seem that Timor's role in the sandalwood trade markedly influenced the structure and development of its political systems. Schulte Nordholt cites early-sixteenth-century reports that seem to indicate that the predominance of coastal kingdoms in the north and south were a direct result of this trade. Each area appeared to be under the control of a chief who supervised all commercial dealings.[1] This illustrates the forms in which Timorese political organization initially appeared to Asian and European traders, with commerce founding a coastal political hierarchy. Colonial history took this form and adopted it as the basis for many of its subsequent analyses. Yet behind it there seems to have been a more complex political organization, which needs to be analyzed if we are to understand the basic structures of Timorese society.

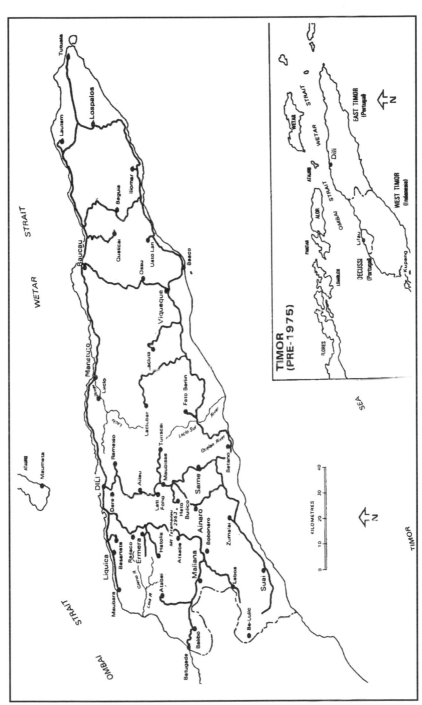

MAP 16.1. *East Timor (pre-1975).*

A Timorese myth recounted to the linguist J. C. G. Jonker in Amabi (western Timor) in the early nineteenth century describes how "A long, long time ago there was one ruler of this island in Babiko-Babali" (the southern coastal plain). The ritual ruler of this realm appears to have had three subordinate rulers (*liurai*) under him, each of whom exercised executive power in his own territory (Middlekoop 1952, 202). The first *liurai* was located in South Belu (on the coastal plain), the second in Sonbai (in the western part of the island), and the third in Suai-Kamanasa (in the south-central part of the island). This triad of heads serving one ruler had its origins in a substantial migration dating perhaps from the early fourteenth century. Myths describe how the original Melanesian inhabitants were displaced in this period by invaders coming from Malacca, via Makassar in the Celebes, and from Larantuka in Eastern Flores. These newcomers, of Malay origin, settled in the southern coastal plain and moved northwest and northeast, displacing the original inhabitants and forming the three kingdoms dominated by "Babiko-Babali."

These kingdoms combined loosely knit, localized, territorial groups in a general hierarchy of clans, each related through exchange (Forman 1978). Each clan paid tribute to the kingdom in which it existed. Consequently, when these localized groups began to trade with the Dutch and Portuguese in the sixteenth century, their encounter with more powerful military systems, which operated economically through exchange, enabled the Europeans to transform the clans' ties with their kingdoms by directing their exchange systems externally. Chiefs who could organize labor to produce and trade in commodities such as sandalwood received from the Portuguese in return trade items such as cloth, guns, and iron tools. These goods enabled coastal groups to assert their identity over their erstwhile rulers. The resultant shifts in political control produced major changes in the distribution of power in the sixteenth and seventeenth centuries. These changes formed the backdrop to the turbulent events of this period—the organization of resistance to European invasion.

Before examining the effects of European intrusions on the reproduction of Timorese society, we need to recount briefly the course of events.

Colonial Interplay

The first Portuguese settlement in the proximity of Timor was established on the island of Solor in 1566. There Dominican friars built a fortress, at Lohayong, which they filled with recent converts from Solor and Flores. At this stage the Portuguese made annual trips to Timor to collect sandalwood and to trade in finished goods. When their trading rivals, the Dutch, managed to capture their fort at Lohayong in 1613, the population of the fortress moved to Larantuka on the neighboring island of Flores. While Solor experienced shifting Dutch and Portuguese rule in the seventeenth century, Larantuka remained firmly within the Portuguese orbit.

This relatively settled period of Dutch rule witnessed the consolidation of a group that was to dominate Timor's development in the seventeenth and eighteenth centuries. The Dutch termed them the "Topasses," and they first appear in colonial history as a "mixed race...the offspring of Portuguese soldiers, sailors, and traders from Malacca and Macao, who intermarried with the local women of Solor" (Boxer 1960, 351; 1947; 1948),[2] and who moved with the Portuguese to Larantuka. After the move, the Topasses, initially with the help of groups of Dominican friars, began to control the trading networks between Solor, Larantuka, and Timor, and particularly the lucrative sandalwood trade. In the process they began to settle in Timor itself, although their presence was not really felt until after 1642.

This mid-seventeenth-century date marked a watershed in Timorese history, since it was during this year that the Portuguese invaded Timor in strength, attempting to extend their influence beyond the coast in order to control the island's internal trade. Justifying their attack by the need to defend recently christened coastal rulers, the Portuguese moved directly against the western kingdom of Sonbai and its parent kingdom, Babali (or Wehale, as they called it). Victory was swift and brutal. An observer described the campaign of the commander, Captain Major Francisco Fernandes, of Solor, in the following words.

> Laying waste the regions through which he marched with his troops, the Captain Major held out in the face of pursuit by the enemy up to the place where Wehale had his residence; after reducing everything to ashes there he withdrew to Batimao. (Cited in Schulte Nordholt 1971, 164)

Topasse migration to Timor increased markedly after this decimation. The Topasse community was centered at Lifau (now Ocussi or Pantai Makasar) on the northern coast. From here the Topasses prepared to quell any internal threat to their position, be it from local communities or from the Dutch. The latter defeated the Portuguese garrison at Kupang in the west of the island in 1653, and landed a substantial military force in 1656. Unlike the earlier Portuguese invasion, the Dutch met with stiff resistance, for Topasse families were provided with military hardware to contain the advance. They routed the Dutch in a short, brutal battle that forced the invaders to move to the neighboring island of Roti, thereby giving effective control of Timor to the Topasses. Opposition to Topasse rule could now come from only three groups— Portuguese merchants, Dominican friars, and the Timorese themselves. The merchants tried to wrest control of the sandalwood trade from the Topasses, with the blessing of the Portuguese crown; the Dominicans attempted to build a power base in their own right; and the Timorese kingdoms rose in periodic revolt against both the "white" and "black" (Topasse) Portuguese. Throughout the late seventeenth and early eighteenth centuries, conflicts between these groups were interspersed with periods during which the combatants united to oppose the spread of Dutch influence.

Thus, after the fall of Kupang the Portuguese embarked upon a campaign of enticing chiefs away from the Topasse sphere. This culminated in attempts to install a governor on the island at Lifau in 1695 and 1702. On both occasions he was forced out by the combined efforts of the Timorese and Topasses. On the occasion of the next attempt, in 1720, the Dominicans were largely responsible for removing the governor. In 1729, another governor and his forces were besieged and defeated in Manatuto, after which the Portuguese withdrew until 1748.

Meanwhile, the Dutch had begun to reassert themselves in the western half of the island. The spread of their influence among local tribes in the 1730s culminated in their rebuilding of Fort Concordia at Kupang by 1746. Unlike earlier conflicts, the campaigns against the Dutch in 1735 and 1746 had only a limited impact; hence the Topasses turned to the Portuguese for assistance, and invaded Dutch areas in 1749. The outcome was a ferocious engagement that came to be known in Timor as the Battle of Penfui. The result was a Dutch victory and a strengthening of their presence in the west of the island. Indeed, with Dutch assistance the kingdom of Serviao was able to rid itself of Topasse control. Penfui laid down a distinct territorial division on the island— the Dutch in the west and the Portuguese in the east. The fact that the Topasses had requested help from the Portuguese ensured the latter a stronger political presence and led to a reduction in Topasse power. The healthy respect engendered by the one for the other meant that neither attempted to extend their influence beyond the kingdom level, thereby leaving Timorese society relatively free from incursion and disruption.

The Structure of Timorese Society

By the end of the eighteenth century, Timorese society had managed to retain many of the features that had characterized its social, political, and cultural systems prior to European contact. Although the island contains as many as eighteen distinct ethnolinguistic groups, these shared common features, which were reproduced through elaborate systems of exchange.[3] The basic structures of these systems can best be illustrated by focusing initially on the features of the Timorese economy.

The organization of production was profoundly influenced by the nature of the Timorese terrain. The main topographical feature of the island is its mountainous backbone, interspersed with fertile valleys and permanent springs. To the north, mountains protrude into the sea, while in the south they give way to a broad coastal plain. Lowland areas are also found in the north and west. In this terrain the flow of water is seasonal. The vegetation produced by the climate and terrain varies from savanna and grassland in the plains areas, to bush land on the hill slopes, and evergreen and tropical forests in the mountainous areas. Under these conditions there could be only a limited amount of land use. Irrigated cultivation could be undertaken only where water supplies were available from flood plains, in the vicinity of springs, or on swamp land. Most cultivation was of the slash-and-burn type, with fields rotated to preserve the soil. Several crops were grown, including rice, maize, cassava, yams, sweet potatoes, and a variety of fruits. Livestock—pigs, goats, sheep, and buffalo—were grazed on the hillslopes. Production was mainly for local subsistence but goods were regularly exchanged at nearby markets. The units in which production occurred were the household garden, the field, and the irrigated *padi*.

Economic organization was based primarily on the extended family, which was responsible for the maintenance of each type of unit. Throughout the agricultural cycle, the low level of technology required extensive cooperation in the use of labor. Production took place in both extended kin and village contexts, each being characterized by distinct sexual divisions and governed by ritual. In the cycle of rice cultivation, for example, planting was generally undertaken by women and harvesting by men. Outside of agriculture, weaving was a female task, while men produced iron implements, and so on.

Economic relations were not influenced solely by divisions in the production process, however. They were also affected by a system of exchange that involved both goods and individuals. Goods were exacted from Timorese communities as tribute due to the chiefs of the various princedoms and kingdoms. In the Wehale kingdom, for example, the *nai boot* ('lord of the land') through his officials granted land to families for their use in return for which they paid a token rent, or *rai teen* (literally, 'excrement of the land'). Goods were also exchanged for women and men in marriage. This exchange was only possible if the goods required could be produced, and villagers had to work beyond the time required to grow their own subsistence crops in order to produce exchange goods. Products of surplus labor-time thus were exchanged for the means of reproduction (marriage partners), and the elders—through their role in exchange—were responsible for distributing these products. Thus, in addition to the economic relations generated by production, there were relations generated by exchange and the consumption of goods exchanged.

The exchange of men and women between groups was channeled through tribal elders who arranged supplies of goods varying from buffaloes and horses to swords and gold ornaments. Consequently, just as the chiefs of the princedoms were able to gain status from their collection of surplus labor through tribute, so also was the status of the elders enhanced through their role in the system of kinship exchange. Although status could accrue to individuals in other ways—such as the amount and fertility of land cultivated, knowledge of tradition, possession of sacred objects, accumulated wealth, and age—the most important hierarchies remained those generated by production and exchange. Thus, in Timor's political systems the predominant positions were occupied by the most elevated individuals in the tribute and exchange systems.

These political systems had three main administrative levels: the village, the princedom, and the kingdom, each with its own head. Other sources of political power resided in clan leadership and in the royal or aristocratic status accorded to some kingdom and princedom leaders. Each village comprised several hamlets spread over a wide area. Each hamlet contained the members of a particular clan, generally tracing itself to six generations. Ruled by a headman in association with a council of elders, the village was part of a princedom (*suco*) headed by a family that was itself subject to the ruler (*liurai*) of the kingdom in which it existed. In kingdoms and princedoms where the ruler and princes possessed royal or aristocratic status, their extended families distinguished themselves from the mass of the population. These were divided into commoners and (at times) slaves, mostly captured in wars between clans, princedoms, and kingdoms. In this system, the men with the greatest political power were those receiving the most tribute and/or those in the most strategic positions within the kinship-exchange system.

Each Timorese kingdom, princedom, and clan possessed value systems whose ideologies highlighted the importance of exchange and justified the hierarchy influenced by this exchange. In the kingdoms of Belu and Serviao, for example, tribute paid to the rulers controlling trade focused particularly on gifts presented at the end of the harvest. These were called *poni pah* (literally, 'rice baskets of the land'). Similarly, gifts of "homage" (*tuthais*) were given to rulers whose political prominence had been established by their success in arranging marital exchanges.

The exchange of gifts in return for access to means of production (land) and reproduction (the creation of new family units) was also expressed in the cultural rites accompanying birth, marriage, and death, all of which were combined in a value system relating them to the place of the tribe in the cosmos. In death rites, for example, the dead person's descent group acted as an intermediary between its wife givers and wife takers, coordinating exchanges between them, and making "death payments" to (in the case of Belu) the deceased's matrilineal kin. Just as marriage was characterized by an exchange of gifts in return for the means of reproduction, so were death rites part of a value system the ethos of which was centered on the notion of exchange. In marriage, food was exchanged for means of reproduction. In death, it was offered to spirits who, in exchange, ensured the fertility of the earth. The products of this fertility were then offered to different spirits who ensured the best climatic conditions for growth, and so on. Life was viewed as a system of interlinked exchanges, the enactment of which was essential for the maintenance of economic and social stability.

Reproduction and Resistance

Bearing in mind these characteristics of the social structure in Timor, and examining the events we have recounted from the history of the sixteenth and seventeenth centuries, we see several trends emerge. While trade in the pre–sixteenth century period led to a gradual increase in the cultivation of goods for export, the political and social effects were minimal and largely confined to a limited increase in the political influence of the heads of coastal kingdoms. Inserting themselves into existing trading patterns, the Portuguese intensified this process, with the long-term aim of undermining the Timorese kingdoms and producing smaller, less powerful units more amenable to European control.

Throughout the sixteenth century, however, Portuguese attempts at divide and rule had only very limited success, and it was not until the mid-seventeenth century, with the defeat of the Wehale kingdom, that the control of kingdoms over their princedoms was lessened.

This decline in the kingdom's powers enabled the invading group of Topasse families to take over the senior positions previously occupied by kingdom and princedom heads in the exchange of tribute, services, and men and women between clans and villages. Through their increasing dominance of this role in the course of the eighteenth century, the Topasses were able to exercise political influence within the Timorese princedoms.

The emphasis on the value of exchange in the early history of Timor was thus reinforced by the Portuguese, who spread the net of exchange economically downward from the kingdom level, and by the Topasses, who reinforced the system of kinship exchange for the purposes of political control. Consequently, although the Timorese economy was directed toward external needs, and control of its political system had shifted to an external group, the effects of these changes were limited. What in other societies might have produced fundamental structural changes resulted in the maintenance of basic aspects of Timorese society. This seems to indicate how Timorese society was able to reproduce its indigenous economic, cultural, and social systems despite foreign control. Once established, this coexistence of external control with indigenous structural reproduction continued throughout the eighteenth and nineteenth centuries. The history of this period is marked by the success of Timorese communities in restricting Topasse and European influence and control to the political sphere of princely kinship alliances.

This resistance took many forms. Throughout the eighteenth century, opposition focused largely on the Portuguese, with attacks on Portuguese troops launched from sheltered mountain areas. One of the most renowned battles took place in the mountains of Cailaco, in 1726, when four thousand troops under Portuguese command were contained by a Timorese army one quarter of its size. As a result of such encounters, by the middle of the eighteenth century the Portuguese had given up their attempts to administer the territory in any meaningful way. In 1769, when they were routed in Lifau, they moved their administrative center eastward to Dili. With the Portuguese threat reduced, the Timorese found themselves defending their territory against the Topasses who tried to extend their political control through kinship agreements. Topasse families tried to entice Timorese kingdom rulers by awarding them Portuguese titles such as Coronel or Brigadeiro, and by providing them with military support in return for tribute exaction. Their success, however, was limited. Resistance continued into the nineteenth century, as is evidenced by eye-witness reports.

In 1825, a Dutch lieutenant visited Dili. In a detailed account of his visit, he described how "The inhabitants of Dili expressed to me their strong desire to be freed from the hateful yoke of the Portuguese" (Kolff 1840, 35). At the end of the 1850s, the English traveler Alfred Wallace spent several months in Timor during a tour of the Malay Archipelago. Witnessing one of the regular attacks on Dili, he concluded that "Timor will for many years to come remain in its present state of chronic insurrection and misgovernment" (Wallace 1869, 1:152). When the naturalist H. O. Forbes traveled in Timor in 1882, he reported that the country was "apportioned out under certain chiefs called Rajahs or Leoreis, each of whom is independent in his own kingdom" (Forbes 1883, 404). Their independence was attested by the fact that Forbes was conducted throughout the country without an escort of any Topasses or Portuguese, except in Dili. He noted that the Timorese had "learnt" many of the customs of the Portuguese in order to "outwit" them more effectively. Forbes's observations on the "independence" of the Timorese kingdoms, and on their ability to control Topasse or Portuguese encroachment, illustrate the constant complaints of Portuguese officials that they were unable to maintain with any degree of success their administrative posts in the interior.

Pacification: The Two Political Systems

At the end of the nineteenth century this situation appeared to change, as the Portuguese tried once again—this time with a greater determination—to exert control over their colony. Colonial history initially recorded this as a reaction to the assassination of a newly appointed governor in 1887 but its causes were rather more fundamental.

Faced with the rapid economic development then occurring in most of Europe, Portugal tried to improve its position by means of more systematic exploitation of its colonies. In Timor this resulted in an expansion of cultivation for export, in campaigns to persuade villagers to increase their yields and diversify into new crops such as cocoa, copra, and rubber, and in the introduction of coffee plantations. Forced labor was used to develop the infrastructure, cultivate crops, and extend the trading system.

The success of these policies would depend upon more widespread political control. Yet the extension of Portuguese authority encountered a barrier, described by the governor of Timor in 1882 in the following terms.

> Marital exchange is our government's major enemy because it produces…an infinity of kin relations which comprise leagues of reaction against the orders of the governors and the dominion of our laws. There has not yet been a single rebellion against the Portuguese flag which is not based in the alliances which result from marital exchange. (Cited in Forman 1978, 105)

Exchange and the kinship system, which had been maintained throughout the years of Portuguese control, were now perceived by the Portuguese as the most important barrier to the extension of its administrative framework. Portuguese policies at the end of the century thus had two objectives: to undermine the indigenous kinship system, and to create a basis for the systematic exploitation of its colony. Thus, between 1884 and 1890, a program of road construction was organized with the use of forced labor. In 1899, a company was set up by the governor, José Celestino da Silva, which introduced coffee plantations into Ermera in the northwest. From 1908, a head tax was levied on all Timorese males between eighteen and sixty. The only way this tax could be paid, of course, was if peasant families cultivated and sold goods over and above their subsistence needs.

The introduction of these measures, and particularly the use of forced labor, produced widespread resentment among the Timorese. The kingdoms united under the leadership of a *liurai* named Dom Boaventura from the southern district of Manufuhi (Same). The rebellion simmered for sixteen years, culminating in a colony-wide uprising, which lasted for two years, until Boaventura's forces were defeated in August 1912 with a reported three thousand Timorese casualties.[4] With resistance quelled, the Portuguese introduced policies intended to undermine the system of political alliances produced by kinship exchanges. The position of the *liurais* was undercut by the abolition of their kingdoms. The colony was divided into administrative units based generally on *suco* boundaries. Thus, a measure of administrative power was given to the unit just below the kingdom level in the indigenous hierarchy. This enhanced the position of the leaders of the *sucos*, although their election as administrators was subject to Portuguese approval. The Portuguese created two additional administrative levels—the *posto*, comprising groups of *sucos*, and the *concelho*, controlling *postos* via a Portuguese administrator. By these means the Portuguese tried to create a new political system, the structure and hierarchy of which would be independent of kinship alliances. Thus, the essence of Portuguese "pacification" was its attempt to destroy a crucial aspect of Timor's social system.

With pacification underway, the Portuguese turned to their Dutch colonial neighbors, completing border discussions with them in 1913. These negotiations resulted in the Sentenca Arbitral, which was signed in 1915, dividing the island equally with the Dutch in the west and the Portuguese in the east. The Portuguese retained the enclave of Oecusse Ambeno on the northwest coast (the site of their former capital of Lifau) and the islands of Atauro and Jaco.

By these measures, the Portuguese hoped finally to be able to exercise more effective control over their colony. It soon became apparent, however, that the impact on the subsistence sector of the economic policies required for cash-crop cultivation was relatively minor. With the exception of the regular demands for forced labor, so were the social effects of these policies. Furthermore, although the kingdoms had been formally abolished, the ideologies legitimizing the traditional political hierarchy and rituals of exchange were perpetuated (*suco* heads, for example, had to ensure that they were supported by the *liurai* and his retinue). Consequently, two political systems—the colonial and the indigenous— coexisted in a rather uneasy truce. While the former was sanctioned through coercion and the use of force, the latter was sanctioned by a powerful cultural tradition.

In contrast to this coexistence in the east, the Dutch implemented different policies, removing the population from the mountains to more accessible locations in the interest of administrative efficiency. Settlements, comprising artificially created villages with colonially appointed heads, were set up along military routes and trunk roads. Most of these heads were Malay speakers who had little affinity for or knowledge of indigenous society. By such means most of the population on the western part of the island was resettled by the end of the 1920s.

Invasion

The Japanese invasion of East Timor in 1941 encountered widespread resistance organized within the framework of the indigenous political system. While history has recorded the gallant campaign of four hundred Dutch and Australian commandos in resisting twenty thousand Japanese troops, little has been written about the participation of the Timorese in this campaign.[5] As several of the commandos subsequently stated, their actions would have been unsustainable without the support and participation of the Timorese who bore the brunt of Japanese reprisals when the commandos withdrew in 1943.[6] By the time the Japanese surrendered in 1945, sixty thousand Timorese had died and most of the towns and villages had been destroyed.

While West Timor became a part of the Indonesian Republic when control was transferred from the Dutch in 1949, East Timor remained under Portuguese rule. The rebuilding of East Timorese society was undertaken mostly within the indigenous system during the 1950s. The Portuguese recruited compulsory labor from the villages to reconstruct government buildings and port facilities but their primary concern in this was to improve the conditions for the cultivation of export crops.

During the 1960s, Portuguese policies favored limited recruitment of East Timorese into the colonial administration. Faced with the success of independence movements in its African colonies, together with an increasingly heavy burden of military expenditure, the Portuguese attempted to create a political elite that could rule East Timor as an "overseas territory" within a federal framework, under Lisbon's benevolent tutelage, as an alternative to independence. Consequently, there occurred a limited extension of education at the secondary and tertiary levels,[7] together with increased recruitment of Timorese into the army, the health service, and the lower echelons of government administration. Although the objective of socializing Timorese into the values of Portuguese culture, as a precursor to federal rule, was modified to some extent after an Armed Forces Movement coup in April 1974, it remained a general aim of decolonization to ensure progress through the inculcation of Portuguese values.[8]

Party Formation

Consequently, several of the early political initiatives undertaken in East Timor after April 1974—notably the creation of the first political party, the Timorese Democratic Union (União Democratica Timorense, or UDT) on 11 May—exhibited the Portuguese idea of progress toward independence through the gradual acquisition of metropolitan culture by elites whose members would be recruited from the indigenous system. The coexistence of the colonial and indigenous systems thus would be superseded by the gradual assimilation of the latter into the former, principally through the recruitment of leading *liurai* and *suco* leaders.

It was in this context that the Timorese Social Democratic Association (Associacão Social Democratica, or ASDT) was formed on 12 May 1974. This party, which subsequently became the Frente Revolucionaria de Timor Leste Independente (Fretilin) on 12 September, differed from the other political groups emerging during this period in its policies, strategy, and attitudes toward East Timorese society.[9] Rather than attempting to incorporate aspects of East Timorese culture, politics, and society within metropolitan culture, it directed its policies toward what it regarded as important areas of indigenous society, taking them as the basis for its organization and strategies. In doing this it began tentatively to create a qualitatively new political culture by combining elements of the indigenous value system into a nationalist ideology. Furthermore, basing elements of its program for political and economic development on the institutions of indigenous society, Fretilin attempted to build upon what its leaders saw as the strengths of this society in resisting colonial control—most notably its system of kinship alliances.

This attempt to take aspects of traditional culture and social organization as a basis for the development of a nationalist movement seems to me to have formed the central part of Fretilin's project. Its support among the population increased steadily, particularly during 1975, in the year leading up to the Indonesian invasion. Initially Fretilin drew most of its support in the countryside from a majority of the central mountain peoples, the Mambai and Makassai, the northern upland Ema, and the Tetum peoples of the south and west. Members of the majorities of East Timor's remaining twelve ethnolinguistic groups tended to be aligned with none of the new political parties, to favor the UDT, or (in the case of some of the northern Tetum in the border villages) to support the minuscule, prointegrationist, Apodeti party. By the end of 1975, however, and particularly during the period when Fretilin administered East Timor after the departure of the Portuguese, support for the movement had increased dramatically, extending to all ethnic groups, even the Fatuluku people at the eastern extremity of the island. This growing support, together with the organization it created, enabled Fretilin to sustain a campaign of resistance to Indonesian incorporation in the years following the invasion.

Fretilin's Programs

These points can best be illustrated by referring briefly to aspects of the development of Fretilin's programs during the period from September 1974 to the Indonesian invasion in December 1975. One of the most important areas of Fretilin's work was its program to tackle illiteracy, a condition experienced by 93 percent of the population. From October 1974, Fretilin members traveled widely, collecting material for a literacy handbook in Tetum, the most widely used of East Timor's many languages. Focusing on words in common use, the handbook, entitled *Rai Timor Rai Ita Niang*, broke these words into syllables and then placed them in different contexts of village life together with associated words. The essence of the handbook was its descriptions of aspects of everyday life in the villages provided by the Timorese themselves.

The way in which this literacy campaign was undertaken illustrates the approach taken by Fretilin: ideas and notions in common use in East Timorese society were adopted as a means of improving the preconditions for development. A similar case was the health program, in which treatment of East Timor's most common diseases—tuberculosis, malaria, and elephantiasis—was introduced in a framework that combined modern methods with the use of traditional cures.[10]

In the early stages of Fretilin's development, the idea was mooted of introducing rural cooperatives as a basis for economic development. As a result, several experimental cooperatives were set up, notably in Bazartete, Alieu, and Bucoli. In these villages, Fretilin members—several of whom had given up jobs in Dili and Baucau to work in their home areas—in consultation with *suco* leaders and villagers, selected areas to be worked collectively. Half the crop was delivered to the cooperative and half to the families involved in cultivation. The cooperative marketed the crop, and, after distributing the income to the families, spent the remainder on expanding output. In Bucoli, cooperation was developed initially at the distributive level. A journalist visiting the cooperative in October 1974 reported that

> Bucoli people were planning a cooperative for next year's harvest. Villagers will pool their surplus crops (after deducting family needs) for sale in Dili for higher prices than they would get through Chinese middlemen. The receipts will be used as the villagers decide, to buy a truck perhaps, or build a cooperative store to buy wholesale basic necessities, or to buy a small tractor. (Evans 1975)

In developing this cooperation, Fretilin adopted methods similar to those employed in its other campaigns: beginning with rather vague, general notions—which were often criticized by villagers in their early formulation—ideas for future development were concretized through the accumulated experiences of their members in working with villagers in areas familiar to them for as long a period as possible.

This stress on developing ideas for programs through work in the villages was accompanied by the creation of an administrative system that emphasized political decentralization. As opposed to the UDT, in which power was held by Dili-based elites, Fretilin devolved a considerable degree of power over decision making to regional committees, particularly in the areas of education and health. This decentralization enabled the regions of East Timor to be involved in the direction of the nationalist movement's development while retaining a considerable degree of autonomy in both organization and the implementation of policies.

Fretilin's Popularity

During the initial phase of party formation and development, from April to June 1974, the Fretlin's precursor, the ASDT, remained much less popular than the UDT, though both attracted far greater support than did the minuscule Indonesian-sponsored party, Apodeti. This remained the case until October and November of 1974 when the ASDT (by now renamed Fretilin) began to be viewed by both East Timorese and foreign commentators as the party with the greatest support—although it was not until the elections for village heads, held in July 1975, that this support was confirmed by a 55 percent vote for Fretilin candidates. Throughout 1975—during a coalition with the UDT from January to May, and after a coup attempt by the UDT in August, followed by the departure of the Portuguese administration to Atauro Island—Fretilin maintained a high degree of support within the population, as attested by a variety of visiting commentators, journalists, and politicians.[11]

The reasons for this popularity owed much to the movement's approach to indigenous society. Unlike the UDT, the leadership base of which resided in the lower echelons of the colonial administration and among coffee-plantation owners and *liurai* in the agriculturally richer areas of Ermera, Maliana, and Maubara, Fretilin moved increasingly into the outer regions. Building regional power by working with existing political alliances based on kinship, and taking concepts and ideas prevalent in traditional society as the bases for the development of its programs, Fretilin emerged as a nationalist movement with extensive support and a decentralized political structure. Despite some support for more centralist notions of political power put forward within Fretilin during the early months of 1975 (when it was involved in its coalition with the UDT) and, more particularly, by a group of Timorese sergeants from the former Portuguese army in the preinvasion period, Fretilin maintained the decentralized approach. Indeed, in recent years this has been reemphasized by the movement's leadership, stressing the importance of ethnic group identities and culture despite the intermixing enforced by the Indonesian military through its resettlement program.

The Indonesian Invasion and its Aftermath

Throughout a series of campaigns initiated in 1975 to "pacify" the territory (1975–77), to "encircle and annihilate" the population outside Indonesian-held areas (1977–78), and to hunt down Fretilin groups through a *pagar betis*, or "fence of legs" (1981 to the present), the Indonesian government has maintained a heavy military presence in East Timor.[12] In actions that have been thoroughly documented by refugees and visitors to the territory, the Indonesian army has exercised a brutal rule, trying to coerce the population through massacres of villages, saturation bombing, and widespread human-rights abuses (see, for example, Amnesty International 1985). The administration installed by the military has attempted a "resocialization" of East Timor through the enforced movement of the population into strategic hamlets, the reorganization of the economy, and systematic outlawing of all aspects of East Timorese culture and society.[13]

East Timorese opposition has been widespread, with a progressive alienation of almost all social groups from the Indonesian project. The nationalist movement resisted the invasion, maintained substantial areas of the territory under its control until the end of 1978, and, after devastating aerial and ground attacks, managed to rebuild a framework for the organization of resistance in the 1980s, which still persists.[14] In this the support of East Timorese society has been crucial. There are many examples, among which a few may be taken for the purpose of illustration.

During late 1976 and the early months of 1977, the resistance movement's national framework began to weaken as Indonesian forces maintained troop concentrations in strategically located villages. In this situation, as many refugee accounts have noted, the movement's success in creating strong, regional, power centers, based on preexisting political alliances, enabled it to maintain influence in its areas despite the weakening links between them.

Similarly, during the "encirclement and annihilation" campaigns the survival of Fretilin, and its rebuilding in the eastern part of the territory, was only possible because party members were protected by villagers (Amnesty International 1985, 29–34). Again, one of the most successful areas of the nationalist movement's strategy has been its development of systematic links with support groups inside the resettlement villages established by the Indonesian military. These groups have organized opposition and supplied the movement with information on Indonesian military intentions. In most cases, the cohesion and organization of these groups has depended to a considerable extent upon kinship ties that have been maintained despite attempts by the military to undermine them by splitting up populations from the same village and settling groups on areas distant from their original villages.

Perhaps some of the most supportive actions, however, came during the "fence of legs" (*pagar betis*) operations in 1981. In these campaigns, according to many refugee accounts, every available male between the ages of sixteen and sixty was recruited to march in line across the territory, in groups five hundred meters apart, in front of Indonesian troops. Despite the extent and duration of these campaigns, few Fretilin troops were captured. Refugees have documented a remarkable process by which Fretilin groups passed through the "fence," unnoticed by the military, with the assistance of East Timorese in the human chain who either hid them or led the military away from their encampments.[15] Such actions illustrate both the strength of support for the nationalist movement within the population and the ability of the East Timorese to frustrate Indonesian objectives by means of their systematic social organization.

Conclusion

The pattern outlined above seems likely to continue, for there is little doubt that East Timor will continue to resist Indonesian incorporation. Its capacity to resist owes much to the way its social structure developed under Portuguese colonialism, which itself resulted from the nature of trading contacts with Portugal, in the ability of the Timorese to "play" one colonial faction against another, and in their capacity to organize resistance through political alliances based upon the kinship system.

In the twentieth century, Portuguese attempts to undermine the reproduction of indigenous society were unsuccessful while the strength of East Timorese resistance to the Japanese invasion and occupation revealed again the ability of indigenous society to contain attempts at incorporation. With the demise of Portuguese colonialism, a nationalist movement emerged, drawing increasingly widespread support by devising policies that were directed toward, and developed aspects of, the indigenous social structure and value system, attempting to form them into strategies for the creation of a national economy and community. This movement was able to mount its campaigns of resistance to the Indonesian occupation, and reorganize itself under the most unfavorable conditions in the late 1970s, due to the popularity of its policies and the strength of its organization within the indigenous society.

It would seem that the Indonesian military had only a limited understanding of the nature of East Timorese society when its troops invaded. It was clearly taken aback by the strength of the opposition. Gradually the military realized that, faced with such strong resistance, its main hope lay in destruction of much of the existing social structure and its replacement by one more amenable to control. Consequently, in the late 1970s, the military launched intensive resocialization and restructuring campaigns involving economic reorganization, control of family life, resettlement, the undermining of East Timorese culture, and the systematic inculcation of state values. These campaigns were carried out brutally and were accompanied by widespread military intimidation. That they have been disastrous for the East Timorese is detailed in many well-documented accounts of the results of the invasion and occupation (see, in particular, Budiardjo and Lim 1984, chap. 5; and Taylor 1991).

Despite its determination, the Indonesian military has not succeeded in fully controlling the territory nor has it established any meaningful support for its annexation among the East Timorese population. In spite of its policies, the social relations and values of the preinvasion period persist, providing a framework for continuing opposition. Indeed, the most vociferous recent opposition to the occupation has come from those raised during Indonesian rule.[16] This has angered military leaders, in particular, many of whom had pinned their hopes on successful socialization of the second generation.

The success of the nationalist movement in maintaining opposition to the occupation, despite overwhelming Indonesian military superiority and under extremely adverse conditions, is a remarkable achievement requiring explanation. The preceding analysis has suggested some preliminary ways in which the reasons for the strength and depth of opposition to Indonesian rule can be analyzed.

CHAPTER 17

Indigenous Peoples of the Philippines: Between Segregation and Integration

CHARLES MACDONALD

Of a total population of 56 million persons in the Philippines (1986 Census),[1] an estimated 4.5 to 7.5 million people (up to 15 percent of the total population) belong to the category of "Indigenous Cultural Communities" (ICC),[2] as they are now officially labeled. These ICC are made up of more than fifty ethno-linguistic groups scattered all over the archipelago.[3] Among them, two main clusters are singled out: the Cordillera peoples, or Kaigorotan, from northern Luzon;[ ] and the Lumad, or non-Muslim tribal groups, from Mindanao in the south. Scattered about the rest of the archipelago are isolated groups of Agtas (Atas, Aytas, Aetas), as well as indigenous groups such as the Palawans and Tagbanuwas of Palawan Island, the "Mangyans" of Mindoro Island, the Sama (Bajaws) of the Sulu Archipelago, and others.

Generally speaking, these peoples share distinctive traits that set them apart from the Filipino mainstream,[4] that is, the Christian, lowland, urban population: they are non Christians; they live in less accessible, marginal, mostly upland areas; they retain a system of self-government not dependent upon the laws of the central administration of the Republic of the Philippines; and they follow ways of life and customs that are perceived as different from those of the rest of the population.[5]

PHOTO: CHARLES MACDONALD

PLATE 17.1. *Traditional Bukidon leader* (datu) *with fellow tribesmen at the seat of the Tribal Datu Association, Mindanao, Philippines.*

PHOTO: CHARLES MACDONALD

PLATE 17.2. *Two families of Tao't Batu (peoples from the caves) sheltering in a cave during the rainy season, Palawan, Philippines.*

PLATE 17.3. *A priest/shaman from Singnapan Valley prepares rice-wine for a ritual, Southern Palawan, Philippines.*

It could be said that these criteria are insufficient to characterize the situation prevailing in the parts of the archipelago where local conditions vary significantly. In a country in which the concept of the nation has emerged only recently, one could argue that every ethnic group—the large and politically dominant Ilocano, for instance—forms a minority with a distinct sense of self-identity and traits that set it apart from the rest of the population. On the other hand, one could dispute the aptness of the label "minority" or "indigenous" when applied to the Muslims of Mindanao and the Sulu Archipelago. Indeed, Islam as a unifying factor, politically and culturally, among a congeries of otherwise distinct ethnic groups (Maranaos, Maguindanaos, Taosugs, Yakans, etc.) does raise a problem of definition distinct from the one raised by the Cordillera peoples who claim that they are "one" people.[6] However, both areas, with their native non-Christian populations, have risen to the status of cohesive political wholes and two autonomous regions have been created to allow them a greater degree of self-determination.

Finally, the ICC do not fit into a single anthropological category. Some groups have a centralized government, some do not; some are wet-rice agriculturalists; some are shifting cultivators; some have a productive hunting-gathering spectrum of activities; and some rely on marine products. Some are traders, some are nearly completely acculturated, some are more resistant to change, and so forth.

In spite of the various conditions prevailing locally, I would argue that a very clear-cut gap sets cultural minorities apart from the major social and historical trends obtaining in the Philippines, and that they are in a very real sense ostracized by the larger society of which they are a part. The separateness of the ICC, and the ways in which these peoples are both rejected and included in national development, are the subject matter of this paper, taking into consideration a few aspects of a picture filled with many different shapes and colors.

Institutions and State Policies

Under the Spanish colonial regime a threefold division of society obtained, with the Spaniards at the top, the "Indios" at the bottom, and the "Mestizos" between them. During the American colonial period something like a twofold division (between "civilized" and "uncivilized" peoples) became ideologically dominant, a situation promoting political and ideological exclusion of the ICC from the national community. Paradoxically, then, the more egalitarian-oriented American rulers introduced an institutional chasm by creating the Bureau of Non-Christian Tribes in 1901 and establishing a policy of reservations for them. This agency, modeled after the bureau dealing with the American Indians, actually took a keen anthropological interest in the Philippine cultural minorities, and it produced a wealth of valuable ethnographic materials about them, but it may have contributed to setting this category of Filipinos even more apart by providing an institutional basis for the notion of a "non-(westernized/Christian)-Filipino" category of people.

After independence in 1946, the Republic of the Philippines followed the scheme set up by the Americans. The Commission on National Integration (CNI) was created in 1957. It was replaced in 1967 by the infamous Office of the Presidential Assistant on National Minorities (PANAMIN), which lasted until 1984. In the meantime, a Ministry of Muslim Affairs had come into existence, and this was merged with PANAMIN, from 1984 to 1987, to form a single agency, the Office of Muslim Affairs and Cultural Communities. The 1986 "revolution" that ousted Ferdinand Marcos, and the resulting 1987 Constitution, created the Office of Muslim Affairs (OMA), the Office for Northern Cultural Communities (ONCC), and the Office for Southern Cultural Communities (OSCC).

From this brief history of the administrative setup, one can draw a few conclusions. First, the American regime created the notion of cultural communities that were not only "non-Christian" but "tribal" as well. The boundary between "Indios" and Spaniards was abolished, and a new dividing line was set within the category of "Filipino." The racial divide became a cultural divide. The concept of social difference, added to that of religious difference, led to the concept of "integration" that the 1946 Republic placed at the forefront of its policy toward the ICC. In turn, this policy met with conditions of emerging political self-awareness among the various peoples concerned, and it had to reckon with the specificity of the resisting federations of Muslim peoples in the south and Cordillera peoples in the north. Dropping the old-fashioned notion of "tribe," the new dispositions highlighted the notion of "minority," soon to be replaced by the more acceptable concept of "cultural community," and reverted (as far as PANAMIN was concerned) to the colonial policy of establishing reservations.

In a way, there has been no radical change in official ideology since the beginning of the century, in the sense that the ICC are to be set apart from the mainstream for political and administrative purposes. The notion of having to deal with these peoples by realigning them on the model of the "Christian" and "civilized" society (integration) is still, or was until recently, the dominant trend in policy-making. Their collective identity, however, has been couched in various terms, some of them derived from the history of American academic anthropology. From being defined in the negative ("non-Christian") at the beginning of the century, the ICC have become the object of a more positive evaluation ("cultural communities"), and the idea of preserving a positively valued identity while bringing them into the fold of the dominant culture has gained ground since 1987. The declaration of policy contained in the Executive Order creating the OSCC (Executive Order 122-C, 1987), for instance, asserts the rights of the southern communities but only in order to "ensure their contribution to national goals . . . and make them active participants in nation-building."

The actual implementation of policies promoted by government agencies dealing with the ICC has met with little success as far as the protection and well-being of these peoples are concerned. To be brief, in its day the CNI had no power to implement integration effectively. It was followed by a very dim era for the ICC under PANAMIN.[7]

PANAMIN was founded in 1968 as a private foundation headed by Manuel Elizalde, Jr., a wealthy scion of a prominent industrial family. Having been appointed a presidential advisor and then a cabinet member by President Marcos, Elizalde concentrated funds and resources on image building, publicity, and impact projects—such as the so-called discovery of the Tasaday, a "stone-age" group of forest dwellers, later exposed as a hoax. In Mindanao the agency resorted to a policy of forced resettlement on reservations, militarization, and intimidation. By herding the natives onto reservations, training them in warfare, and using them as a labor force on PANAMIN land, the agency alienated the native population and widened the gap between them and the lowlanders. Time and again the agency demonstrated that its tactics were aimed at the repression of tribal peoples.

This was followed, between 1984 and 1987, by the complete disappearance of any efforts toward integration. It is also likely that the newly created government agencies (OMA, ONCC, and OSCC) will prove to be relatively powerless in the face of the major issues confronting the ICC in the Philippines in the 1990s.

Issues

The major problem confronting the ICC is the loss of land. In view of the fact that all these groups rely for their subsistence on various forms of agriculture and an extensive use of space, especially in the cases of predominantly shifting agriculturalists and mixed economies that include an important hunting-gathering component, land and space are of vital concern in terms of sheer survival.

In all parts of the country, indigenous groups have suffered loss of ancestral land and displacement. This ongoing process occurs under various conditions.[8] Land is either taken away by violent means or acquired peacefully by individuals or corporations. It has been pointed out repeatedly that legal, peaceful means of taking land from people who have nothing else and are unaccustomed to the ways of modern society amounts to taking unfair advantage of them and results in their ultimate impoverishment.

It should also be noted that in various cultures of the southern Philippines there is no traditional concept of permanent, individual, land ownership. The Palawan people of southern Palawan Island, for instance, say that "Land belongs to Ampu' [God]." This attitude toward land makes the indigenous people more vulnerable to landgrabbing practices since it allows anyone to cultivate land that is not actually being used or cultivated. But settlers from other areas can acquire title to the land, and the plot once used does not revert to the common pool of available land.

In most cases, also, the scarcity of agricultural land, and the fact that its ancestral owners have been pushed back into forested areas, force the indigenous peoples to use land considered to be in the public domain to which they cannot claim ownership. This, of course, is a misconception in legal terms. The "Carino doctrine," based on a U.S. Supreme Court decision of 1909, ensured the constitutional rights of those who inhabited ancestral lands by declaring that members of ICC have a native title derived from their possession of the land since time immemorial. To this day the Carino decision remains a landmark.

> It establishes an important precedent in Philippine jurisprudence: Igorots, and by extension other Tribal Filipinos with comparable customs and long associations, have constitutionally protected native titles to their ancestral lands.[9]

Nevertheless, ICC do face harassment and they are prevented from occupying and cultivating land that is under the jurisdiction of the Bureau of Forestry. It must be pointed out, however, that in a number of instances accommodations have been reached whereby indigenous people have been granted rights over some agricultural land and are protected by certificates of "stewardship" over forested lands.

But, even when there is a sufficient supply of land for agricultural production, various other elements both constrain and disrupt the space wherein traditional productive activities take place. Timber concessions, water projects, plantations, mining, and cattle ranching are five major agents in reducing and destroying the natural environment in which these people once lived. Whether these concerns take away good agricultural land or are peripherally located, they have an adverse effect on the environment (spillage, pollution, deforestation, and so on) while reducing the freedom of movement of people used to hunting and gathering products from all corners of their territory.

Since World War II, a tidal wave of settlers from Luzon and the Visayas has swamped the ICC lands. These settlers, who have been dispossessed themselves, tend to cluster in strategic locations along the roads, near small towns, and along the coastline, thus contributing to the marginalization of the ICC. To take one example of how this affects the indigenous communities, let us consider access to the sea. In a number of cases in Mindoro, Palawan, and Mindanao, hill people and near-coastal communities used to go on short-term expeditions to fish and gather marine products from the reef. The Christian settlers, now located along the coastline, have created a solid barrier of land with a "no trespass" rule attached to it. This, of course, denies the indigenous people access to a source of food upon which they periodically rely.

There are many more effects to be taken into consideration but not all are adverse. In a number of instances groups of migrants and the native people have made arrangements leading to peaceful coexistence, with the natives retaining rights in agricultural land, and keeping very much to their traditional lifestyle, while interacting on a daily basis with their Muslim or Christian neighbors.[10] In other cases, like that of the Buid of Mindoro, native communities have found ways to cope with the economic and social pressures of the encroaching settlers by concentrating their settlement patterns, manipulating patron-client ties, and introducing cash crops.[11] It is my opinion that solutions to nationwide problems of cultural and political integration can be identified at the local level as a result of spontaneous modes of adaptation developed by indigenous peoples and their new neighbors. The settlers are, after all, small farmers sharing the same interests and facing the same threats from corporate agribusiness, mining companies, and multinationals.

Next to land occupation, be it by individual settlers or corporate concerns, a second set of issues affecting the survival of indigenous communities arises from the politico-military situation prevailing in some areas. The counterinsurgency program stepped up by the Marcos administration and pursued by President Aquino caught indigenous peoples in a cross-fire that has led to dramatic cases of murder and displacement. The Chico River dam project in northern Luzon is one of the best-known cases. Military occupation of the site in 1977 led to assassination of the Kalinga leader Macli-ing Dulag the following year.[12] In 1986, military operations were expanded under President Aquino, particularly in the Kalinga-Apayao area of the Cordillera region and in Mindanao where "vigilantes" (officially backed, armed groups of civilians) reportedly caused much suffering among the indigenous communities by forcing them to join in their anticommunist crusade (International Work Group for Indigenous Affairs 1987). In such cases, the ICC do suffer from a common national ailment but it should be emphasized that their isolation and marginality make them even more vulnerable, since the rest of the rural population can avail itself of some connections in the townships and occasional protection from political and military decisions.

Last among all the issues that characterize the situation of the ICC in the Philippines, and the one that points to their structural segregation, is the lack or unavailability of public services. Unequal access to health and sanitation services is an obvious issue. I shall dwell a little longer, however, on the educational problem, since illiteracy is the central obstacle to any policy of integration of indigenous communities in the long run. It is through education, especially elementary education, that indigenous peoples will be able to understand and eventually adapt to or change the rules of a system into which history has thrown them. An ability to master the language and principles of the political, judicial, and administrative mechanisms of the wider social machinery is a precondition of their active participation in the local and supralocal government system and of the defense of their rights. It is in the classroom that both cultures have to meet successfully if there is any chance for them to work out an agreement without prejudice to either. The classroom is also a social milieu in which cultural misunderstandings appear most clearly.

I shall substantiate this point by reviewing the educational problems analyzed by Postma (1989), an experienced educator and anthropologist, in the case of the Hanunoo-Mangyans in Mansalay, Mindoro. First, formal elementary education is delivered according to rules of behavior foreign to the native educational system, namely, coercion and authoritarianism. Second, the subjects taught do not seem relevant to indigenous concerns, and school attendance is viewed by both parents and children as a waste of time and a loss of economic productivity. Third, and most important, young teenagers traditionally engage in an elaborate form of courtship that involves a very high degree of native literacy (for which a pre-Spanish form of writing is used). An education imposed from the outside seems then even less relevant and more redundant. As a result pupils can be expected to show less interest and less eagerness in learning it. Among the external problems are the distance of schools from the concentrations of Mangyan population, and the difficulties of the teachers, who come from non-Mangyan communities, in reaching their schools and adapting physically and psychologically to local conditions.

Other difficulties arise from the educational administration and its program. Teachers are not trained to deal with another culture. Some are poorly trained in general, and sometimes are incompetent. The timetable is entirely unsuited to the seasonal cycle of Mangyan activities, with vacations occurring, for instance, when agricultural activities are minimal. Fees are the same for the Mangyans and for those attending lowland schools, whereas the Mangyans' income is much lower. Teachers are often called back to the district office during the week and schools are left without a teacher for days on end.

There is no lack of good intentions and sound advice, starting with the International Labour Office's Convention 107, which states, for example, that "the formulation of educational programs shall normally be preceded by ethnological surveys." At a seminar held in Manila in 1989, educators, anthropologists, spokesmen for nongovernmental organizations (NGOs) concerned with indigenous rights, and even army officers came up with a wealth of interesting recommendations. Among them were the concepts of a "functional literacy program, that is culture specific," "developmental type of education," "bringing the school to the community," and "interactive type of education." Numerous other "musts" and "shoulds" were added to define a proper approach to education leading to self-determination (Solidarity Seminar 1989). In the field, of course, conditions are far from this ideal state of affairs, and the implementation of such recommendations seems problematic at best. In the realm of education, as in that of land ownership, policies and official directions are simply not implemented, and implementation is the crux of the matter.

Defending the ICC Rights

In spite of the gloomy picture of the state of the ICC, usually drawn on justifiable grounds, and the pessimistic views expressed concerning their survival (for example, in McDonagh 1983), there is real concern about their plight in some government circles and among local leaders, intellectuals, religious congregations, and even various sectors of the business community, as well as in public opinion. Numerous NGOs have taken a prominent place in development work, especially following the 1986 "Revolution" when they were given fuller recognition, and some are now considered legitimate partners in government planning. Among these are the Episcopal Commission on Tribal Filipinos (ECTF) and the National Alliance of Minority Rights Advocates (TABAK). The Consultative Assembly of Minority People of the Philippines (KAMP or CAMMP)—which has sent delegates to the United Nations Subcommittee on Human Rights—is an umbrella organization binding more than ten major tribal Filipino groups, among them the Cordillera People's Alliance (CPA). Several advocacy organizations, like the youth movement Kabataan Tribu ng Pilipino, or Youth for Tribal Filipinos (KATRIBU), and lawyers groups like PANLIPI, are also struggling to promote rights of ICC at the government level and in public opinion.

There is, then, a very prolific surge of collective activity defending and promoting indigenous peoples' rights but not without falling prey to factionalism and political maneuvering. A telling example is that of the various organizations that struggled for overall leadership of the Cordillera peoples liberation movements in 1986–87: the Cordillera People's Liberation Army (CPLA), the Cordillera Bodong ["peace-pact"] Association (CBA), the Cordillera Broad Coalition (CBC), the Cordillera People's Alliance (CPA, itself a federation of 120 cause-oriented groups in the Cordilleras), and the radical-left Cordillera People's Democratic Front, or CPDF (Okamura 1987). One aspect of this situation is the co-optation of indigenous movements by political forces wishing to divert the struggle for indigenous rights toward political goals that have little to do with the real concerns of the people themselves. Likewise, a situation marked by a proliferation of politicized indigenous movements and organizations prevails in the Muslim south, which makes it very difficult for the government to find a broadly accredited interlocutor.

But the defense of indigenous peoples' rights is not solely undertaken by human-rights organizations. Development plans also include provisions pertaining to the ICC. The Palawan Integrated Area Development Plan, for instance, has among its components land titling, stewardship contracts, and agro-forestry projects that are implemented by the Bureau of Forestry and the Department of Agriculture. These are specifically aimed at the improvement of the native population's conditions.

Conclusions

In spite of sound policies, genuine awareness of the ICC plight, and active advocacy of indigenous peoples' rights, implementation of what still remains a blueprint of good intentions lags far behind. In addition, corporate and multinational interests, as well as conditions of extreme violence in some parts of the country, continue to threaten the existence of the ICC.

Unlike what has happened in Indonesia, where mass genocide and ethnocide have been planned and carried out, where the central administration keeps effective dictatorial powers, and where a major historical culture, the Javanese, holds a position of cultural dominance over the rest of the nation, the Philippines has been characterized by a weak administration (although a very centralized one) and by a historical situation that did not give rise to overall cultural dominance by a single ethnic group. Instead, the notion of a large Christian majority pitted against a scattering of small non-Christian groups has been established, the latter being the object of little coherent or systematic policy-making. They have now become the focus of much political attention, with beneficial and adverse effects.

The situation of the ICC is unquestionably marked by extreme vulnerability but there is reason to believe that a number of them will survive in one form or another. This mildly optimistic view is borne out by cases of successful adaptation—usually not spoken of—and by the resilience of traditional cultures in all parts of the country.[13] Paradoxically, it is not always land shortage or violent displacement that causes cultures to die but their own desire to opt for a different way of life.

CHAPTER 18

Report on the Human Rights Situation of Taiwan's Indigenous Peoples

ALLIANCE OF TAIWAN ABORIGINES
I CHIANG, LAVA KAU

I. Demographic Profiles and Distribution of Taiwan's Indigenous Peoples

Taiwan's total area is 35,981 sq. km.: 394 km. in length and 144 km. in width. Surrounded by the Pacific Ocean, its neighbors are China to the west, the Philippines to the south, and Japan to the north.

Evidence from historical sites left by Taiwan's indigenous peoples testifies to a history of at least five thousand years. Before the Han people from China invaded Taiwan in 1624, communities of indigenous peoples were to be found throughout the island. Apart from the Pinpu, who lived on the Western plains—and who have been entirely assimilated by the Han people—the indigenous peoples who still maintain some degree of their traditional culture lived largely in the mountains and on the Eastern plains of Taiwan. The Pinpu, according to early anthropological studies, can be divided into nine groups: Kavalan, Luilang, Taokas, Pazehe, Papora, Bobuza, Hoanya, Siraja, and Ketagalan. Eleven indigenous tribes are in existence in Taiwan today, but the Han Anthropologists of Taiwan recognized only nine tribes.

357

According to the official estimate, there were 337,342 indigenous people in Taiwan in 1989, and the breakdown by tribes shows: 129,220 Amis; 78,957 Taya; 60,434 Paiwan; 38,267 Bunun; 8,132 Puyuma, 8,007 Rukai; 4,194 Saisiat; 5,797 Tsou; and 4,335 Yami people. In addition, Taiwan anthropologists classify the Taroko people, numbering around 30,000, as Taya. Moreover, the anthropologists discount the 248 Thao people as "too few" and classify them as assimilated. The Thao people themselves, however, still identify with their own culture and ethnicity.

The overall population of Taiwan is approximately 20 million; the indigenous peoples represent 1.7 percent of the total population. The Han people who immigrated before 1950 were primarily Minan and Hakka people from Fuchien and Kwangtung provinces in China. After four hundred years of intermarriage with Pinpu and other indigenous peoples, many Han people have come to think of themselves as Taiwanese. The Han people who arrived after 1950 are primarily soldiers who fought for the Nationalist regime, which was defeated by the Chinese Communists during the 1949 Revolution.

II. The History of Taiwan's Colonization

Before 1620, only indigenous peoples occupied Taiwan. What follows is a summary of the colonial governments that have ruled Taiwan from 1624 to 1992.

A. The Dutch and Spanish Colonial Period (1624–1661)

While the Han Chinese who lived along the Chinese coast had already made contact with Taiwan in the thirteenth century, those early contacts were sporadic, isolated, temporary, unplanned, and undertaken without government participation. They did not, therefore, constitute a decisive force of oppression; the indigenous people were still the sole masters of the island of Taiwan. In 1624 and 1626, respectively, Holland and Spain invaded Taiwan with government-backed forces. They sought to subjugate the indigenous peoples with their superior material power and their fervor of religious indoctrination. During this time, some of the Pinpu people lost their autonomy, but the vast majority of other indigenous communities remained unaffected.

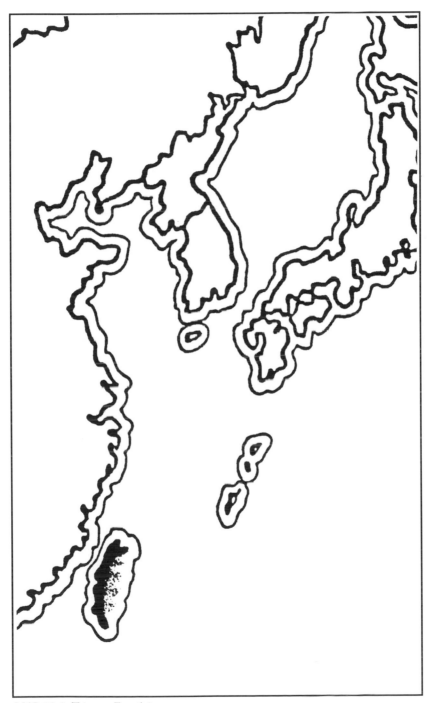

MAP 18.1. Taiwan, East Asia.

B. The Cheng Rule and Manchu Colonial Period (1661–1895)

The son of a pirate, Cheng Chen-kong waged war against the Dutch in a struggle to lay claim to Taiwan, and his subsequent victory ensured his position as colonizer. At the same time, the Chinese rulers were non-Han Manchus, another ethnic minority within China. During Cheng's rule, his forces occupied the Western plains of Taiwan and a small part of the mountainous areas. Attempting to protect their lands and tribal territorial lines, the indigenous peoples had countless conflicts with the Han, who were gradually invading the territory of the indigenous peoples and assimilating them. In 1885, without obtaining the consent of the people of Taiwan, the Manchu regime annexed Taiwan. This period witnessed the first massive influx of Han people, who took control of Taiwan's natural resources and land. However, even in 1895, the mountains and the Eastern plains were still under the effective control of the indigenous peoples.

C. The Japanese Colonial Period (1895–1945)

In 1895, the Manchu government lost the Sino-Japanese War and signed the Treaty of Shimonoseki, ceding Taiwan to Japan. The Japanese government began to exploit Taiwan's economic resources through a systematic, capitalistic style of management. It was during this period that the subsistence lifestyle of the indigenous peoples began to crumble. In order to obtain control over Taiwan's forests, mineral resources, water, and tourism potential, the Japanese rulers contained indigenous peoples in "Mountain Reservations," thus slashing the traditional territory of 2 million hectares down to 24,000 hectares, to which the indigenous peoples had utilization rights but could not claim permanent possession. In order to squash resistance from the indigenous peoples, the Japanese colonial government launched a large number of massacres. During the "Five-Year Expedition," between 1910 and 1914, ten thousand Taroko people were massacred. In the Wushe Rebellion, in 1930, the Japanese attacked six Taya villages with airplanes, cannons, machine guns, and chemical weapons, and massacred all the men, women, and children of the villages. In order to assimilate the indigenous peoples, the Japanese government encouraged the indigenous peoples to use Japanese names and forced the children to speak Japanese under their compulsory elementary-school program. It was during this period that the traditional political, economic, cultural, and social systems of the indigenous peoples began to collapse.

D. The Nationalist (KMT) Colonial Period (1949-Present)

After its defeat in World War II, Japan accepted the San Francisco Treaty and its stipulation that Japan renounce its right to "Formosa and the Pescadores" on September 8, 1951, ending fifty years of colonial occupation. In 1949, the Nationalist (KMT) militarist regime, after its defeat by the Communist government, fled to Taiwan. In order to consolidate its rule, the Nationalist government massacred thousands of indigenous, Minan, and Hakka intellectuals in the early 1950s and imposed martial law, which was not lifted until 1987. In its policies toward the indigenous peoples, the KMT is the direct heir of its totalitarian and colonial Japanese predecessor, and indeed surpasses the latter in planning and implementing its policies. More discussion will be devoted to this subject in the next section.

After this short introduction to the history of Taiwan's colonial governments, and before proceeding, we, as members of Taiwan's indigenous peoples, have the obligation to inform the governments and indigenous peoples' representatives who are attending this United Nations conference, as well as members of the United Nations, of the fact that, as the government of the People's Republic of China (PRC) has never ruled Taiwan, Taiwan belongs to the 20 million of the island. Taiwan does not belong to China.

III. The Current Human-Rights Situation of the Indigenous Peoples in Taiwan

The government that rules Taiwan today is named the "Republic of China," known as the KMT regime by both indigenous activists and the opposition party. Ever since its exile in 1949, the KMT has advocated the military "recovery" of mainland China. The proposal of unification between Taiwan and China by peaceful negotiation is a recent development.

Decades of this goal of "recovering China" on the part of the ruling government of Taiwan has meant, then, an attitude of "passing through" toward both the people and the natural environment of Taiwan. At the same time, the PRC government has always maintained that Taiwan is Chinese territory, periodically seeking to intimidate the Taiwanese people with slogans such as "solving the Taiwan problem with force." On the other hand, the biggest opposition party in Taiwan, the Democratic Progressive Party, advocates Taiwanese independence. Taiwan's indige-

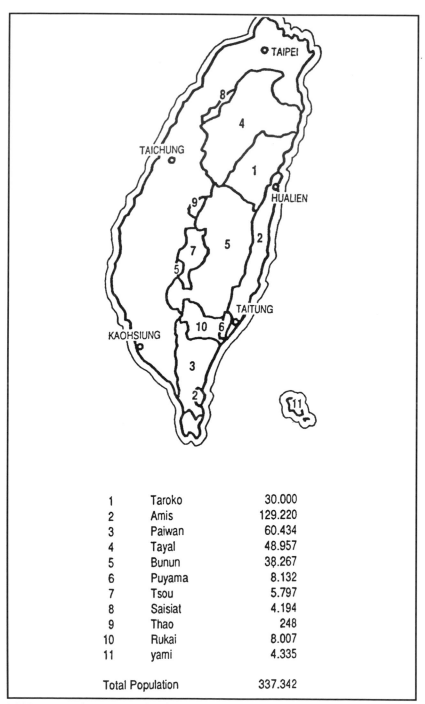

1	Taroko	30.000
2	Amis	129.220
3	Paiwan	60.434
4	Tayal	48.957
5	Bunun	38.267
6	Puyama	8.132
7	Tsou	5.797
8	Saisiat	4.194
9	Thao	248
10	Rukai	8.007
11	yami	4.335
	Total Population	337.342

MAP 18.2. *Indigenous Peoples of Taiwan.*

nous peoples, carrying on their struggle for survival, are caught in the middle of a political environment where the contenders differ in political perspective but share the same Han ethnicity.

According to the United Nations Declaration of Human Rights, no people can be denied their human rights on the basis of race and ethnicity. However, the crisis in basic human rights that the indigenous peoples have to confront in Taiwan today is different from that of the Han people. Not only do the indigenous peoples have to suffer the same oppression as the Han people but we must also bear the persecution of the indigenous policies and Han cultural chauvinism of the present government. In other words, the deprivation of our human rights is twofold—we believe that this scheme is a familiar one for the indigenous peoples all over the world.

An exploration and assessment of the human-rights situation of the Taiwanese indigenous peoples should not be undertaken by simply examining the greater context of the Taiwanese peoples' human-rights situation; such an assessment must also take into account the inferior position to which indigenous peoples have been relegated, based on the cultural differences and economic development of their communities. The first aspect of such an assessment is already addressed in the Report on Taiwan's Current Human Rights Situation. The account that follows is grounded in the perspective of Taiwan's indigenous minorities. We sincerely hope that it will facilitate the world community's understanding of the human-rights situation of Taiwan today.

A. Human Rights and KMT Policies

The KMT Constitution, implemented in 1947, was legislated in China and is therefore unsuitable for Taiwan. It contains no laws that directly describe or protect the rights of Taiwan's indigenous peoples; therefore, we have no right to self-determination and no collective rights as a group. While the KMT government was a co-signer of the Convention Concerning the Protection and Integration of Indigenous and Other Tribal and Semi-Tribal Populations in Independent Countries passed by the International Labour Organisation of the UN, it has not abided by the regulations of that agreement. The basic policy of the KMT government toward the indigenous peoples is one of artificial assimilation, aiming at the complete effacement of the indigenous peoples' consciousness of their own history, culture, and language. The first "Summary of Policies Toward the Mountain Brothers," issued in

1951, already stated clearly that all provisions pertaining to indigenous peoples were to be temporary and were to be gradually abolished. The formulation of basic policy from this point on has been based upon this insistence. Taiwan's government does not recognize the ethnic status of the tribes and our historical position in Taiwan; it has deprived us of our traditional right to the land and our traditional territorial sovereignty.

B. Political Rights

Taiwan's government has deprived the indigenous peoples of our political, cultural, economic, educational, and social autonomy. In terms of political participation, it has designed a system of "protective quotas," symbolically handing the indigenous peoples a few seats in Taiwan's legislative bodies. In the parliament, where the majority rules, the rights and welfare of the indigenous peoples are completely at the mercy of the Han majority, a fact that renders our quotas little more than political ornament. Indeed, as the Taiwanese people did not have the right to form a political party before 1988, the KMT has enjoyed decades of one-party rule among the indigenous peoples, a monopoly it has maintained to this very day. Party intervention in the areas of predominantly indigenous population is highly organized and pervasive; elections at all levels always yield results that conform to the will of the Party. The parliament can give no real expression to the will of the indigenous peoples. In a word, the rights of political participation for the indigenous peoples are manipulated by the KMT regime in particular and the Han people in general.

On April 2, 1991, Taiwan's indigenous peoples put forth our demand for autonomy as an organized group. The official answer was, however, that an autonomous region for the indigenous peoples is out of the question. The administrative sector responsible for handling indigenous affairs is subordinated to the larger administrative bureaucracy. In the central government, this sector is represented with a third-level office (the Mountainous Regions Desk) under the Human Affairs Division of the Ministry of Internal Affairs, employing a total of three people and budgeted with US$12 million annually. At the provincial level, there is also a third-level office (expanded only in 1990), the Office for the Mountainous Regions, a subdivision of the Human Affairs Bureau. With twenty workers and headed by a person of Han descent, this office is responsible for formulating most of the policies concerning indigenous peoples. It is unreasonable to expect a Han executive to be able to transcend the values and interests of his own ethnic group. He is certainly unable to solve the indigenous peoples' problems and promote their interests in ways that are grounded in their perspective and compatible with their values. Yet he is entrusted with overseeing indigenous peoples' affairs. The same principle of personnel choice is to be found everywhere else in the bureaucracy. While each local government in areas of predominantly indigenous population has an Office of Mountainous Areas, the office head is almost always Han. The political unit that is most directly relevant to the indigenous peoples is the so-called mountainous county, of which there are thirty. At first glance, it may appear that the counties can be taken as burgeoning forms of indigenous autonomy, as the KMT government ordains that the county head must be chosen through local elections. However, in reality the county heads have virtually no executive power, not to mention that candidates other than KMT nominees have little chance of winning. Consequently, most indigenous people who are elected are funded by the local Han and/or involved in a local Han patronage system. Even those who are elected with the genuine support of the indigenous population find their powers curbed by the chairpersons of the County Representative Committee who are, again, overwhelmingly Han. Therefore, Taiwan's political system is entirely under the control of the KMT and the Han people; indigenous peoples have absolutely no voice, let alone autonomy, in such a political system.

C. Legal Rights

Historically, Taiwan's colonial governments have found it most expedient to subjugate the island's indigenous population by use of direct physical force; treaties and agreements have been virtually absent from the colonial relationship. However, when indigenous peoples have asserted their original rights, colonial governments have always been quick to negate these rights with the laws that they themselves have created. To this day, indigenous peoples have no legal status; whatever protection our rights may enjoy has resulted from executive orders. As this process is not subject to the scrutiny of the parliament, it is never exempt from frequent and ill-considered revisions. At the same time, the attacks on indigenous peoples' rights are also launched in the form of executive orders. Many laws claim to protect the interests of indigenous peoples when, in reality, they are wielded to destroy the indigenous peoples as ethnic groups and take away our rights.

A national census that includes an accurate ethnicity count is, needless to say, of the utmost importance to the indigenous peoples; not only is it crucial to our very survival as a group, but the population count is also crucial in determining the political strength of a group in a certain locale. Such an important and fundamental human right, however, has only been delineated and protected by a provincial executive order in Taiwan whose main purpose is to assimilate the indigenous peoples. The "Identification Standards for the Mountain Natives of the Taiwan Province" divides indigenous peoples into "mountain brothers of the mountainous areas" and "mountain brothers of the plains," representing a flat refusal to recognize us as the indigenous peoples of Taiwan. The former term refers to those who were registered in the mountain areas during the Japanese rule, who number about 182,718, while the latter term refers to those who were registered in the plains during Japanese rule, who number 155,938. The laws that call for a national ethnicity count are fraught with contradictions and injustice for Taiwan's indigenous peoples. Upon marriage with a Han man, an indigenous woman loses her legal ethnic identity automatically. On the other hand, a Han woman who marries an indigenous man remains Han legally. In a matrilocal marriage in which the husband is Han and the wife indigenous, the woman retains her ethnic identity and so does the man. However, if an indigenous man were to enter into a matrilocal marriage with a Han woman, he would automatically become Han. More absurd than anything else, perhaps, is the fact that an indigenous person can legally discard his or her own ethnic identity but can never reclaim it. In addition, there are many other discriminatory and unjust regulations in the "Identification Standards." This executive order is an important factor in the failure of the indigenous populations to grow at a normal rate.

Also, the executive order "Regulations Regarding the Development and Management of the Reservations of Mountain Brothers in Taiwan Province" seems to provide important protection of the land-ownership rights of the indigenous peoples. However, this order has proven in practice rather to affirm our loss of these rights. It declares the nationalization of our traditional territories, hunting grounds, and ritual sites. The order declares the privatization of land already inhabited by individuals but this privatization entails only rights of use and not rights of ownership. Ownership management belongs to the government. Even more outrageously, this order grants any Han person who chooses to take up residence in the areas of the indigenous peoples .03 hectares of land for construction. Both public and private industries, as well as individuals, can obtain the rights to develop the mineral, quarry, industrial, or tourism resources located in mountain reservations, if they follow the specified procedures. What this means in practice is that all the land with development potential has already been wolfed up by either the government or by Han capitalists. In 1987, the KMT government lifted martial law and put in its place the "National Security Law," which continues to impose many restrictions upon the mountain areas inhabited by indigenous peoples. In other words, martial law continues to rule these areas. Nothing illustrates the pervasive ignorance and oppression prevalent in this legal system more accurately than the complete absence of any multicultural consideration in Han law. All the laws of Taiwan are legislated according to the values of the Han people. The common laws of the indigenous peoples are neither incorporated into nor acknowledged by the laws of this land. The legal system, then, only serves the Han people at the expense of the indigenous peoples.

D. Land Ownership and Economic Rights

With a total area of only 35,981 sq. km., and a population of 20 million, Taiwan is a country of staggering population density. Land is, therefore, one of the most precious and coveted resources in Taiwan. History reveals generations of colonial governments and immigrants who obtained land by means of force; almost no contractual arrangement or effort at obtaining the consent of the indigenous peoples was ever made. Even when such arrangements did take place, they inevitably were couched in a language foreign to the indigenous peoples and designed to deceive and swindle.

After their ancestral lands were appropriated as national property, the indigenous peoples lost their claim to the very land on which their private homes were built. In recent years, under the current government's policy of massive development of the areas in question, demand and exploitation have occurred on several fronts: forested land has been assigned to the management of the Bureau of Forestry, land with mining potential has been claimed as national property, areas noted for their natural beauty and tourism potential have been designated national parks, and the Ministry of Defense has appropriated vast tracts of land from the indigenous peoples under the pretext of national security. The last pieces of land upon which the aborigines rely for their survival have been taken away, and their consent was never sought in the process.

In order to build national parks, industrial zones, and reservoirs, the government forcibly relocated aboriginal tribes such as Fu-shih Village of Shou-lin County; Hua-lian, in the case of the Tai Lu-ke National Park; and Mei-shan Village of Tao-yuan County, Kaohsiung, in the case of the

Yu-shan National Park. They also moved the ancestral graves of the Bunun tribe in Tong-pu Village, Shin-yi County, Nanto; the villages within the Ho-ping cement industrial district in Shou-lin County, Hualien; and the Hao-cha Village in Wu-tai County, Pin-tung, in order to build the Wu-tai Reservoir, just to give a few examples.

After government policy is formulated, the indigenous people involved have absolutely no channel through which to express their opinions; indeed, they lack the very right to do so. There has been some monetary remuneration but the amount is negligible in view of the losses sustained. In addition, land belonging to indigenous peoples was awarded to army veterans who came over from China after 1950, while other plots were designated university property. The KMT's local organizations, such as the People's Service Station in each county and the activity center of the National Salvation Group, all occupy land that belongs to indigenous peoples. In a word, virtually all land with development value has been occupied and exploited.

Traditionally, indigenous societies have thrived upon subsistence economies, wherein each tribe makes its livelihood as dictated by its geographical environment. However, under laws that were legislated in accordance with the Chinese value system, all hunting, fishing, lumbering, and agricultural activities undertaken by indigenous peoples on their own ancestral lands are now strictly forbidden. Every year indigenous peoples from various parts of the island, uninformed of or unable to obey these laws, are punished legally and often must serve two-to-three-year prison sentences. Deprived of their resources and lands, indigenous peoples can no longer eke out a living in their traditional tribal villages. Large numbers of those who are capable of physical labor have flowed toward the industrial towns and cities to become laborers.

According to the official statistics in 1989, 48.8 percent of the indigenous people are agricultural workers, while the rest work in nonagricultural professions. In reality, however, the majority of peasants go to neighboring cities to take temporary jobs requiring intense physical labor during the off-season, as the income from their land can no longer support a household. According to a 1986 survey, the annual income of indigenous peasants is 54.3 percent of that of Han peasants. At that time the annual agricultural income of indigenous peasants was US$1,457, and their nonagricultural income was $2,478, giving a total income of $3,935. The average agricultural and nonagricultural incomes of Han peasants, on the other hand, were $2,638 and $4,607, respectively, yielding a total of $7,935.

The vast majority of the indigenous peoples who become city dwellers enter labor-intensive jobs that require little or no technical training and tend to be low in both status and pay. The men are primarily workers in wood and steel manufacturing, truck drivers, miners, and deep-sea fishermen, while most women become electronics and textile workers. These industries are among the most labor-exploitive in Taiwan. Many indigenous workers frequently find that their pay is withheld without reason. They have neither labor insurance nor a pension and are constantly threatened with unemployment.

Taiwan's international image may be that of an economically prosperous and wealthy nation, boasting foreign exchange reserves of US$80 billion dollars and an annual individual income of $8,000. However, these figures are, as far as indigenous peoples are concerned, legerdemain figures that have little meaning. Indeed, Taiwan's economic development has been attained at the expense of the rights of workers and of the environment. The wealth is concentrated in the hands of a few capitalists, and the gap between rich and poor is very wide.

Most urban aborigines live in illegal constructions or construction-site shacks. An indigenous person cannot afford to buy a house of his or her own with his or her life savings. According to data from 1983, more than 35 percent of the aborigines are at least NT$80,000, or US$3,000, in debt, and the main reasons for this debt are a fast-rising cost of living and an increasing incidence of illness. The individual annual income surveys conducted by the Taiwan government each year never isolate the incomes of indigenous people, which means that the official statistics entirely fail to describe the economic situation of the aborigines. In the meantime, both the international and the Taiwanese communities, including the indigenous community itself, continue to be deceived by the high income figures produced by the Taiwanese government.

E. Cultural and Educational Rights

In 1945, the KMT regime issued "Regulations Regarding the Recovery of Ancestral Names," under which all Han people can discard the Japanese names imposed upon them by the colonial regime and reclaim their family lines. However, not only were the indigenous peoples unable to reclaim their ancestral names but under the assimilationist policy of the Taiwan government they were denied even the right to register their citizen identification with their traditional names. The family organization of each indigenous people, once perfectly described by our traditional system of names, has completely disappeared. This has resulted in both difference between family names within a lineage and differences between lateral relations. This confusion in familial names leads to a corresponding chaos in familial relations. Tragic incest cases constantly occur.

The KMT shows equal disregard for the cultural sites of the indigenous peoples. For example, the designated site for the new train station in Tai-tung happens to be a thousand-year-old historical site, while the sewage processing plant currently under construction in Taipei will lead to the irreversible devastation of the two-thousand-year-old Pinpu site of She-san. The Cultural Gardens of the Indigenous Peoples, designed as a museum, is being built and managed by the KMT government. It is being built upon land bought at a price far below market value from the local indigenous population, and its commercial attraction is to put existing indigenous cultures on display for tourist consumption.

For the last forty years, children have been forbidden to speak their own language in the schools, let alone learn that language as part of their education. All the textbooks for elementary and middle schools are homogenized and edited by the government, and thus are devoid of any reference to the culture, history, and ethnic consciousness of the indigenous peoples. Only .3 percent of the indigenous peoples had received a college education in 1989, while 5.8 percent of the Han population already had college degrees in 1978. Part of this discrepancy may be attributed to the fact that the qualifications of teachers in the mountainous areas are on average lower than teachers in other districts, not to mention that the facilities are far below average as well. All in all, the educational system systematically discriminates against the children of the indigenous peoples.

F. Social Rights

In 1978, the government, in a blatant deception of the Yami people of the island of Lan-yu, announced the construction of a military harbor and widely publicized the employment opportunities such a project would bring. The unsuspecting Yamis joined the construction project willingly, only to find out after its completion that the project was actually a nuclear waste dump. Currently Taiwan has three nuclear plants, with the construction of a fourth pending, and all of Taiwan's nuclear waste is dumped on Lan-yu. Since this site has reached full capacity, the government is now planning expansion of the site. The Yami, however, are putting up stiff opposition, and the conflict is still unresolved. Without garnering the benefits of nuclear power, the Yami nevertheless have been tricked into shouldering the immense risk of a nuclear disaster. This is a classic case of racial discrimination and deserves international censure.

Another example of social discrimination can be found in the housing problems that urban indigenous peoples confront. While Taipei has tens of thousands of illegally constructed buildings, the government very rarely enforces construction codes. However, when indigenous peoples put up temporary housing on government-owned lots or alongside rivers, the government frequently sends out bulldozers. No corresponding interest was ever taken in the housing problems of the indigenous peoples. Due to the need to move frequently, many school-age children could not receive formal education on a continuous basis.

Last of all, a significant portion of indigenous girls and young women have absolutely no human rights whatsoever. Bought and sold as child prostitutes, they are in every sense the victims of an established system of slavery with which the entire Han society is complicitous. Aged from nine to eighteen, these girls are estimated to account for 20 percent of the child and adolescent prostitutes in Taiwan, a prosperous market that is part of the vast and ubiquitous Taiwan industry that thrives upon sexual exploitation of women. Given hormone shots, beaten, tortured, and repeatedly raped on a daily basis, these girls live entirely outside modern society and the rudiments of human rights by which such a society supposedly defines itself. The very survival of our ethnic groups is jeopardized as the daughters and future mothers of our race are reduced to commodities and denied their very right to existence as human beings.

IV. Our Expectations of the United Nations

Even though Taiwan is currently not a member of the United Nations, the indigenous peoples are part of the world community. This report is aimed at providing the governments and the indigenous peoples of the world a preliminary understanding of the human-rights situation of the indigenous peoples in Taiwan. This is the first time Taiwan's indigenous peoples have had the chance to report the human-rights problems we confront.

We have always taken a deep interest in the human rights of indigenous peoples all around the world, and we hope that this interest will prove mutual. We also sincerely hope that the United Nations and other

PLATE 18.1. *Representatives from Alliance of Taiwan Aborigines, Geneva, Switzerland, 1991.*

concerned international organizations will scrutinize the human rights of Taiwan's indigenous peoples based on the principles of international justice that you uphold. All the indigenous peoples of Taiwan, including our organization, Alliance of Taiwan Aborigines, will welcome you with all our hearts if you can come to Taiwan to obtain first-hand understanding of our situation. Last of all, we are very happy to have the opportunity to participate in the discussion of the draft of the International Human Rights Declaration of Indigenous Peoples, as this is a document long overdue. We look forward to its completion and hope that it will offer indigenous peoples all over the world substantial protection of our human rights.

CHAPTER 19

Practicing Ethnicity in a Hierarchical Culture: The Ainu Case

KATARINA SJÖBERG

It has often been argued that Japan is inhabited by one homogeneous people, known in colloquial language as the Japanese. This claim
is so often made that one tends to slide into unthinking acceptance. In
fact, the population of Japan consists of several groups of people who
differ culturally, linguistically, and biologically from the dominant ethnic
group, the Wajin. One of these groups, the Ainu, Japan's indigenous
people, is the subject of this article. Official statistics on the Ainu are
based upon free choice, that is, a person can choose whether he or she
wants to register as Ainu or not. A person registering as Ainu must have
been either born Ainu, raised among the Ainu since childhood, or
married to an Ainu. In 1988, the official number of the Ainu amounted
to 24,381 (Hokkaido Registration Office, Sapporo). This figure can
hardly be said to represent their true numbers. It is conjectured that
some 50,000 to 60,000 Ainu live in Japan proper, Honshu, under various names and identities.

Challenging the preestablished social and cultural context of Japan,
the Ainu are demanding official recognition as a unique ethnic group
with its own customs and values.[1] The presentation below is an attempt
to show how the Ainu develop and articulate an identity based on what
they perceive as their cultural distinctiveness.

PLATE 19.1. *Ainu, Hokkaido, Japan.*

PLATE 19.2. *Ainu woman, Hokkaido, Japan.*

PHOTO: KATARINA SJÖBERG

PLATE 19.3. *Ainu women, Hokkaido, Japan.*

Although Japan recognizes the Ainu as a religious and cultural minority, Ainu efforts to celebrate, revive, and preserve the customs of the past are severely circumscribed. Arguing that the Ainu of today have forgotten most of their former customs and practices, due to a previously positive attitude toward the assimilation policy of the Japanese government, Japan considers practicable maintenance of Ainu customs outside the tourist arena unrealistic.

This presentation is based on archival material, written and taped sources, and field material. Fieldwork was conducted in Hokkaido, the main territory of the Ainu, for a period of twelve months, extending from 1985 to 1988.

Background

The Ainu, who primarily inhabit the northern island of Hokkaido, are traditionally assigned by anthropological literature to the general category of hunters and gatherers (Sugiura and Befu 1962; Ohnuki-Tierney 1976; Watanabe 1972), although, of course, they are no longer hunters and gatherers. Since 1868, they have been officially incorporated into the Japanese nation. The incorporation of Hokkaido, which took place without negotiation with the Ainu, was in effect a colonization. The government of Japan assumed direct administrative and juridical control over the Ainu and initiated an official policy of assimilation. This included legislation forbidding the maintenance of Ainu customs, religious beliefs, and language. From then on the land and natural resources

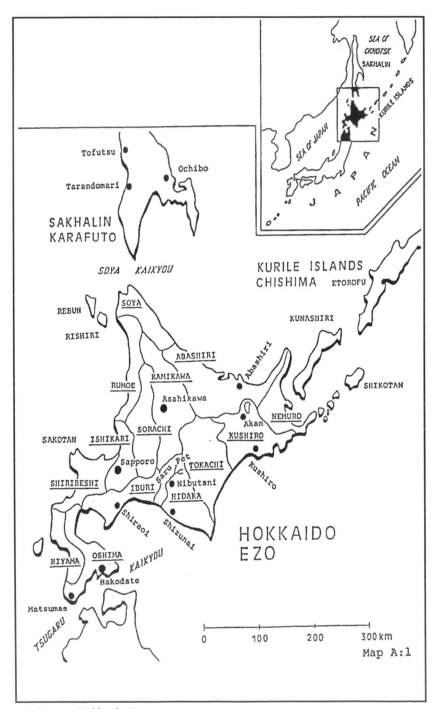

MAP 19.1. *Hokkaido Ezo.*

of the Ainu were to be used in conformity with the purposes of the Japanese nation.

Since the early days of colonization, Hokkaido has been developed to receive immigrants, to defend Japanese territory, and to provide a base for food supplies, not only for Hokkaido but for the nation as a whole. Today the better part of Hokkaido's land and natural resources is used for bean, corn, and rice cultivation, cattle and race-horse breeding, and other economic activities brought in from the main islands of Japan. Hokkaido is also Japan's leading producer of rice (Hokkaido Government 1988).

The attitude of the authorities toward the Ainu as part of the larger society is based on the assumption that the Ainu reject their ethnic status and wish to adapt to the nonethnic premises of state ideology as defined by the highest authority. According to this definition, all peoples native to Japan are to be addressed by the term Nihonjin (Japanese). "Nihonjin" is a nonethnic concept linked to the ideology of the Meiji Restoration (established in 1868). Introducing foreign, western ideas such as the rights of the governed and constitutional limitations on the power of the government, the Restoration aimed at forming a nation out of the Japanese islands and uniting its various peoples.

Previously the Ainu had no objection to the Japanese way of handling Hokkaido affairs nor did they object to a view of themselves as Japanese. On the contrary, they devoted much time to becoming properly assimilated and much effort to forgetting their Ainu heritage (Cornell 1964; Baba 1980; Refsing 1980; Sanders 1985; Sjöberg 1991).

The Ainu have only recently come to "realize" that what was good for the nation was not necessarily good for them. While the nation to which they belong flourished, they became a marginal minority on the outskirts of the larger society. Discrimination against Ainu, manifested in Wajin reluctance to marry or employ an Ainu, is a common feature; even if officially the Ainu are as Wajin as any Japanese, they are nonetheless outcasts. In other words, their social position, their aboriginal status, functions as effectively as any ethnic stigmatization. Today there is resistance both to the policy of assimilation and to the way in which Ainu land and natural resources are being used. This does not imply a general wish to seek departure from the nation but rather the desire to secure a place for themselves as a distinct component of Japanese society. They have plans to create national parks in the forests and mountains, which formerly were both famous and revered. There are also plans to use part of their land to grow Ainu crops and vegetables and to establish centers for the study of Ainu history, material culture, language, and religious beliefs. These studies are to be supervised by the Ainu themselves.

In interviews, government officials have argued that the essence of Ainu self-identification is "folklore," that is, a mere display of cultural artifacts. Even if there is a desire among the Ainu to function politically and economically within the larger society, this is a serious misinterpretation by those who fail to see the relationship between culture and identity. While there is a clear desire to remain part of the nation, they wish to do so as a political unit rather than as isolated individuals. In this sense their emphasis on culture implies a degree of political autonomy as well. This might appear simple but, in a system in which multiethnicity is seen as a threat to the very existence of society, it is a serious problem. For the Wajin, the commercial aspect of Ainu customs has come to overshadow their cultural content. Accordingly, substance has been deemphasized, while the display of their customs for tourists and the larger public has become dominant. According to this view, museums, exhibition halls, and the like will become the only possible forum for the survival of Ainu customs and beliefs.

Even though it is generally agreed that the Ainu are indigenous to Hokkaido, their indigenous status has not been scientifically established and is still open to debate. Recognition by the Japanese government in 1988 of the Ainu as a religious and cultural minority does not indicate that Japan has reconsidered the view that it is inhabited by one homogeneous people. Yet, while Japan pursues this view, it hesitates to recognize the link between the Ainu and the dominant ethnic group.

According to Wajin myths, Japan's indigenous peoples are of unknown origin. The Yamato people conquered them and "mixed their blood" with theirs. Speculation has it that the Ainu descend from one of these peoples and that some of these "supposed" Ainu descendants mixed their blood with the conquerors while others escaped to Ezo where they remained relatively pure (see Munro 1911). Hence the concept of Kyuudojin (aborigines).

The position of the Ainu is apparently somewhat different from that of other indigenous peoples and, as has been pointed out by Cornell (1964, 24), "The colonization of Hokkaido has little in common with for instance the European colonization of America." Hokkaido was not an unknown country to the colonizers. Interaction between the Ainu and the colonizers had been going on for several hundred years, implying that the Ainu were not isolated from their intruders in the same way that the American Indians were. As Giichi Nomura points out, the Ainu never sold or lent their land to the lords of Japan, and they were never defeated in battle (Ueda 1991, 2).

Yet it cannot be argued that the circumstances that led to the Ainus' loss of land, forests, fishing and hunting rights, religious customs, and language differ from those of other indigenous groups altogether. One important argument is that the Ainu relationship to their territory does not differ from that of the Indians, and that the intruders did not recognize this but imposed their own system on the native peoples. The Ainu view is that they are the victims of shrewd manipulators who lured them into thinking that they would benefit from the system imposed upon them, guaranteeing them equality under the Japanese Constitution. Naturally Japan does not agree. Its position is that the nation rescued both itself and the Ainu from falling victim to Russia, and thereby secured its status as a nation and the place of the Ainu within it.

Although the Ainu are regular United Nations attenders, participants in International Labour Organisation meetings, and have links to the World Council of Indigenous Peoples, their primary concern is not to promote external status but to eradicate the stigma of being "outcasts" and gain a cultural status equal to that of the Wajin.

Japanese national identity presupposes a political symbiosis between the concept of state and the concept of nation. Its practice is notably political, since it is dictated by the highest authority. Japanese nationalism, Koka-Shugi, as the name indicates, is closely tied to the concept of the state, Koka, and the sign for *koka* denotes both nation and state. The guidelines made up by the state classify the Wajin with respect to their function in a hierarchical system, originally referred to as the Si-nou-koushou system, dividing the people of Wajin descent into four social strata. The ideology of the system connects to the concept of *giri*, which literally means 'burden', a sense of moral obligation to one's superior. The system leaves no room for social mobility nor does it allow people outside the mainstream (that is, Japan's minority groups) to enter it.

These peoples are classified with respect to place of birth, leaving them outside the Wajin social strata. In practice, neither intermarriage (which results in loss of Wajin status) nor wealth and education gives a person who is outside these strata access to an identity as a Japanese national in Wajin eyes. Self-identification as Japanese nationals by minorities is recognized only by other minorities. Although Japan now recognizes the Ainu as a cultural and religious minority, Ainu prospects of becoming accepted as Japanese nationals of Ainu descent on the same terms as Japanese nationals of Wajin descent are severely limited.

Problems with Respect to the Identification of the Ainu

The scholarly problems of the identity of the Ainu are considerable. Although research into their origins has played a central part in studies of the Ainu, the mystery remains largely unsolved. The strategy of early research intended to solve the problem of Ainu identity was undertaken from the standpoint of the Ainu relationship to the aboriginal population of the Japanese archipelago. A primary goal was to prove that the Ainu were not the aboriginal population of Japan. This concern was of considerable political import, for, if evidence was found that the Ainu were in fact Japan's aboriginal population, they must also be regarded as the rightful owners of the land. However, the theoretical and methodological positions taken by early scholars shed no light on the origins of the Ainu nor do they clarify the confused picture of a joint Ainu-Wajin ethnic and territorial past. Although arguments about the origins of the Ainu do not go beyond hypotheses and speculation, the view that they are of Caucasoid origin was until recently generally accepted (Naert 1958; Kodama 1970). Recent research favors Ainu affinity with other Mongoloid peoples (Ohnuki-Tierney 1981).

The Ainu view themselves as having the same origin as the Koropok-un-guru, a "mythical" people who once inhabited the Japanese archipelago and are considered to be its earliest population. This theory is in line with the views of early researchers. Yet, according to them, the Ainu and the Koropok-un-guru are not one and the same people (Munro 1911).

> We know that we are the earliest settlers in Japan. Why is this not accepted? I myself think that they already know this in their hearts, but with their minds they cannot accept it. That is why they go on and on with this question and present "results" of which the one is more confusing than the other. (Interview with Ainu male, 1988)

Another problem with the identification of the Ainu relates to the Wajin approach to "history." A common feature of their historiography is that only selected parts of the historical record are presented, painting a picture of the Yamato people (the ancestors of the Wajin) as conquerors and heroes while all other peoples were assimilated or driven away (Munro 1911). In their attempts to trace this image as far back in time as possible, they have even managed to provide a mythological charter for their position.

For the Ainu this has serious consequences, since their verbal accounts have been molded to fit the dominant ideology. According to the Ainu version of their history and ethnography, their former lifestyle was more elaborate than previous researchers assert. In the opinion of the Ainu they were neither conquered nor assimilated in a general sense. Their present situation is of their own doing: either their ancestors chose to abandon their Honshu territories or they chose to take up the customs and practices of neighboring tribes.

Major Strategies Used by the Ainu for Identification

Speaking in general terms, we may discern among the Ainu today at least two major strategies for identification. One is used by those Ainu who put strong emphasis on themselves as a distinct cultural entity. The other is used by Ainu who put strong emphasis on the similarities between their own cultural tradition and that of the Wajin. In a national context the latter identify themselves as Japanese, whereas in regional and local contexts they identify themselves as Japanese of Ainu descent. These people employ what we might call double identities used in a hier-archical sense. They use their identity in a chameleonlike way; the two concepts are not interchangeable but are used according to the purposes they best serve. The people who manipulate their identity in this way are to be found among those Ainu who seek their livelihood in the rural sector or in other sectors connected with the industries of the big cities.

Those who are more consistent identify themselves as Ainu in a national context and in the regional and local contexts as *un-guru*, mean-ing 'person' or 'man' belonging—for example, to a group or a place (Batchelor 1938). These people use their identity for "clarification" purposes. The use they make of their identity therefore must be inter-preted in a strictly horizontal sense. The two concepts are interchangeable, with neither providing any advantage the other does not. Ainu who manipulate their identity in this way are occupationally engaged in various Ainu activities and they are to be found both in the countryside and in the cities.

We also have examples of Ainu who reject their identity in words but reveal it in practice. This is best exemplified by the way Ainu engaged in the rural sector seek recognition as farmers, peasants, and the like, yet in Ainu festivities or other activities many of them dress in Ainu clothes. Further, among the Ainu who have migrated to the metropolis, we have examples of some who suppress their Ainu identity. These people seek recognition as Japanese, claiming to have lost contact with their Ainu relatives. Their relatives, on the other hand, claim to have close contact with them, identifying them either as Ainu, the term used by the Wajin, or as *un-guru*, the term used by the Ainu.

The Ainus' varying attitudes toward their inheritance should be seen as responses to the reality in which they live. Both the Ainu who choose to base their identity on ethnic features and those who do not are aware that their official status as Japanese is not accepted by the dominant ethnic group, which identifies them as Ainu or Kyuudojin (aborigines).

At present the concepts of Wajin and Japanese have identical status, although the Wajin is an ethnic concept and Japanese is not. This state of affairs is linked to the fact that national identity is not considered to be separate from the cosmological order. It is constructed out of myths of history and deeds of heroes. According to this model, national identity originates with the ancestors of the Wajin who, according to historians and archaeologists, are defined as the people who founded the empire of Japan in contradistinction to the primitive inhabitants (Munro 1911, 11). These latter people (the Ainu) are described by the same historians and archaeologists as simple-minded, kind, stupid, and so forth.

Although the Ainu, as they are "written" about, are seen as marginal and indigenous (Cornell 1964; Newell 1967; DeVos 1975), this is not the way they look upon themselves. The Ainu do not refer to themselves as indigenous, nor do they think of themselves as marginal. To the Ainu, the Ainu are "central," as are their land and natural resources, their activities, and their ways of handling their situation. It is in this light that their emphasis on culture must be analyzed.

Neither the various peasant communities in which the Ainu live nor the villages in which the Ainu tourist centers are located can be said to represent Ainu society, not even the village of Nibutani, located in the southeastern part of Hokkaido, where the majority population is of Ainu descent and the village's Ainu profile is strongly emphasized. Instead of comprising more or less homogeneous groups, Ainu "society" is made up of people who register and identify themselves as Ainu and those who do not. Some are actively engaged in activities and practices that belong to the Ainu, whereas others are occasionally or seasonally so engaged. Some participate as individuals, others on a group level. Some conceal their Ainu identity among Wajin but display it among Ainu. Some wish to be identified as Ainu, while others are only interested in becoming familiar with Ainu material culture.

From an Ainu Angle

Since the Ainu do not constitute a society in the "traditional" anthropological sense, the best approach to understanding their situation is one that focuses on strategies rather than structures. This perspective allows the incorporation of individuals and their actions in the dialogue between the Ainu, the larger Japanese society, and its authorities. Focusing on strategies best suits the analysis of a multivocal reality.

If we wish to understand the situation of the Ainu as it actually appears to the Ainu, we have to make use of the conceptual and explanatory tools of the Ainu themselves. Their present-day engagement in activities and practices tied to old beliefs, and the consequent change in their attitude toward the policy of assimilation, are best understood if we take a closer look at the role they themselves, their land and their natural resources play(ed) in interaction with the majority population. As for their present situation, we have to consider that their land and resources are essential to the nation as a whole whereas their skills and knowledge are of minor importance. Of particular interest is, of course, the holistic and hierarchical identity of the dominant ethnic group. Within this group it is denied that there are, or that there could be, ethnic minorities in Japan (Nakane 1970; Smith 1983).

Finding themselves part of the process of change, the Ainu react to and interpret the events around them. The actions they take relate as much to the interaction situation as to values rooted in their own customs. Within this framework, Ainu contact with the larger society teaches them not only how to go about restoring these values but also which niches they can successfully exploit. It must be remembered, however, that their actions relate to the restrictions imposed upon them by the larger society. They feel that their land and natural resources are properly integrated but that they have been left with a circumscribed ability to enjoy the fruits of their resources.

Interaction with the larger society provides alternative or new ways of displaying and strengthening their ethnicity. An example of this is the way tourist production and display have become central in their conscious reconstruction of their identity. In several areas they have established village structures for the express purpose of producing hand-crafted goods. They have also built Ainu-style houses, *chise*, where important village activities such as the teaching of history, language, and Ainu dances, weaving, and wood carving occur on a weekly basis. For the Ainu, the stressing of cultural factors has become an indispensable means of defining their own position within the larger society unequivocally.

By employing an Ainu perspective, we may find other causes of the Ainus' previous attempts to become "even more Japanese than the Japanese" (Refsing 1980, 87) and why these attempts failed. In this way we are given an opportunity to explore their cultural tradition from an Ainu angle. There is also a possibility for us to add an alternative explanation both of the present change in the relationship between the Ainu and the Wajin and of its contemporary direction. The fact that the Ainu at the time of the annexation of their land were left in extreme poverty seems to have been as obvious to the emperor as it was to the Ainu themselves. The cause of the conditions, however, was differently interpreted.

To the emperor (the Tenno), "the immigrants and the innocence of the Ainu" (Hokkaido Government 1899) caused this effect, whereas to the Ainu it resulted from bad relations with "nature." They felt that nature had deserted them and their own explanation was that they had not fulfilled their obligations toward nature. Due to their "disgrace" and the favorable position of the conquerors, the Ainu chose to abandon their own beliefs and customs. After all, the gods of the invaders had turned out to be the most powerful ones. This strategy did not fulfill the promises of a future ideal life, nor, for that matter, did they involve the mere copying of the customs of the invaders.

The Ainu do not look upon themselves in the same way today as they did a hundred years ago. Few people would connect their contemporary efforts to revive their customs and beliefs with the realization that their own gods, perhaps, were not so powerless after all. Today their attempts to become accepted as Ainu, to get to know their own customs, and to reconsider values and beliefs that belong to the past relate to other factors. Thus they need to be looked upon in a different light.

Today the Ainu make use of information gathered about them not only to reconstruct, reorganize, and reinvent their values and beliefs but to gain an understanding of why their ancestors acted as they did and how they became marginal in their own domains. They try to understand how the minds of the historic Ainu operated by questioning the conceptual tools of those who have interpreted their history.

Interpreting Tourism

Ironically, Ainu tourist centers have come to constitute the basis for their cultural redress. The irony in this lies in the fact that these centers were initially more in accordance with commercial Japanese interests than with the interests of the Ainu. The centers were initiated by Japanese authorities to increase the profits of tourism, and as such they had very little to do with the customs of the Ainu. They were arranged according to a pattern that was supposed to have existed at the dawn of history and presented as "the contemporary Ainu way of life." Naturally the Ainu felt humiliated by the ways in which their former lifestyle was exposed in these centers.

The change of profile of the tourist centers took place when Japanese "intellectuals" (journalists and students), in connection with the centenary of Hokkaido's incorporation into the Japanese nation, initiated a series of destructive acts (the bombing of historic Japanese monuments, the attempted murder of the Japanese mayor of Shiraoi, the setting alight of a tourist bureau) in professed sympathy with the Ainu (Refsing 1980; Sanders 1985). It was obvious that the Ainu had nothing to do with these acts and those among them who were initially blamed and sent to prison were soon released. This obviously unfair treatment affected the Ainu in several ways, which prompted them to take a stand against both "misguided sympathy" (as expressed by the Japanese in the acts of violence) and Japanese involvement in Ainu affairs.

After the violence the tourist centers began to play another, and for the survival of Ainu customs a more important, role. The Ainu began to organize studies for those Ainu who were interested in understanding their past. The movement took up studies of former place-names, oral literature and recitations, the teaching of old-time knowledge of nature, the manufacturing of Ainu cultural items, and so forth. Equipped with this knowledge, the people working in the tourist centers began to present a different picture of their customs to the public. Hence, the centers and the people working in them are now regarded in a new light by the Ainu.

Today the centers also function as places where Ainu feelings of common understanding and mutual belonging can be displayed. In 1988, during one of my visits to the Akan tourist center in the eastern part of Hokkaido, I overheard the following conversation between two Ainu women.

> Can you imagine, the other day a Shamo [Wajin] asked me if the *chise* [pointing at the house where she works, which consists of a big room with a fireplace at its center] was my dwelling house. I said "Yes, my family, our six children, and I live there." Thinking of it, I should have added our grandparents. How come the Shamo are so ignorant? We thought they were smart. *Wen guru* [stupid people].

For the Ainu the main purpose of the tourist centers today is to foster an awareness of Ainu identity and to function as information centers. If we consider the time and effort that the Ainu spend on increasing their knowledge about their own customs we will also realize the contribution of the centers to an increased knowledge of their cultural tradition.

Those who work in the tourist centers are Ainu from all over Hokkaido. The centers offer a manifold picture because the Ainu who work there add local and regional variants of their language, beliefs, and customs. Ainu who visit the centers recognize products coming from their own areas, and they discuss and compare them with those of other areas. This is demonstrated by a converstion between two Ainu women overheard at the Shiraoi tourist center, situated in the southern part of Hokkaido, in 1988.

> I see you are using the same technique as a person from our village. Did she teach you how to weave *saranip* [an Ainu-style bag]? [Answer:] No, I was taught this technique by one of her pupils. My mother and the person you are referring to came from the same village. It took a great deal of time to learn but now I am glad I did not give up. You are not the first person to ask me this question.

The manifold quality of Ainu activities and practices reveals itself in the different ways in which the Ainu approach their own culture. This in turn makes up the network of interest in cultural heritage among contemporary Ainu communities. The basis of knowledge obtained in this way allows for the assignment of specific tasks and activities that can be orchestrated in various ways. In some Ainu areas the emphasis is put on the natural environment, and these areas may function as national parks where local fauna and flora can be preserved. Areas where powerful Ainu leaders (*ekashi*) once lived may serve as "historic" meeting places. One example of this is Shizunai village in southern Hokkaido. In Shizunai, Ainu from all over Japan have gathered once a year since 1976 to take part in the celebration of Shakushain. Other areas may function as "knowledge centers." An example is Nibutani village, in the Hidaka area, situated in the southeast. Nibutani is perhaps the best-known Ainu village in Hokkaido. John Batchelor, the missionary from Great Britain, lived here once, as did Neil Munro, the doctor and archaeologist from the United States, and Pierre Naert, the French linguist.

The violent Japanese "sympathy acts" resulted in the Ainu themselves making an effort to alter their situation and place the emphasis on

ethnic issues. As the Ainu are different, and feel themselves to be different, so they also express a desire that their problems be treated in
accordance with their own views and in ways they feel to be most appropriate. This was expressed by their Kyokai representative in the
following way.[2]

> Their problems should be treated as the ethnic problems of ethnic minori-
> ties. This viewpoint must be firmly established and efforts must be
> directed in such a way that their ethnic uniqueness and potentials will be
> exercised to the full. (Utari Kyokai 1987)

Their criticism addresses the assimilation policy of the government,
noting that "The government policy has been an assimilation policy.
This policy was aimed to extinguish the Ainu, under the pretext of
equality under the law" (ibid).

The official stance of the Japanese government is exemplified by its
declaration to the United Nations in 1980.

> There are no minorities in Nihon to which Article 27 of section III [the
> article defining minorities and guaranteeing them freedom to practice
> their own religion and speak their own language] of the international
> Covenant on Human Rights refers. (Quoted in ibid.)

As pointed out by Kingsbury (1990, 106), this statement provoked
some controversy in Japan (including questions in the National Diet)
and deliberations on Article 27 contributed to a delay in the submission
of Japan's second declaration to the United Nations on the International
Covenant on Human Rights. This declaration eventually included a delicate formulation that recognized the Ainu as a religious and cultural
minority. Such recognition could be a great step forward for the Ainu.
But, given Japan's contention that the Ainu have forgotten most of their
customs, and that maintenance of them on a large scale is unrealistic, it
is unlikely that much will come of this concession. Thus, as Davis argues:

> If the Japanese government recognizes the Ainu as a people, then it will
> have to come up with a cultural definition which would mean a doubling
> or tripling of the financial support it would have to pay to these people.
> Instead, the Japanese government would rather ignore the Ainu hoping
> they'll be culturally assimilated. (Davis 1987, 19)

Under the present official definition of the Ainu, their distinct
culture can still be defined as a variant of Japanese culture (Cornell 1964;
Newell 1967; DeVos 1975; Peng and Geiser 1977). This is a condition
the Ainu do not accept. To make this absolutely clear, their strategy is

now to give a face to their culture, to put themselves on show, so to speak. The problem, as the Ainu encounter it today, is that in Japan cultures are ranked rather than analyzed.

Conclusion

What makes the case of the Ainu different from others is that the government of Japan and its Wajin functionaries relentlessly deny what is taken as the basis for contemporary state policies vis-à-vis aboriginal peoples. This denial by the state not only makes Ainu attempts to revive and preserve their cultural heritage extremely difficult but it also makes them seem different to other minorities. Other minorities stress political and economic factors and are less concerned with how the majority evaluate their beliefs and customs. The Ainu stress the latter factors and are more concerned with the judgment of the Wajin than with their own. Although, as the revised version of Article 27 indicates, Japan now recognizes the Ainu as a cultural and religious minority, Ainu prospects of becoming accepted as Japanese on the same level as Wajin are severely limited. They will remain so until Japan decides to bring its minority groups into the mainstream.

Contributors

R. H. BARNES is University Lecturer in Social Anthropology at the University of Oxford and a Fellow of St. Antony's College. He is a former Director of the Asian Studies Centre at St. Antony's College (1988–91). His publications include *Kédang: A Study of the Collective Thought of an Eastern Indonesian People* (Oxford: Clarendon Press, 1974); and *Two Crows Denies It: A History of Controversy in Omaha Sociology* (Lincoln and London: University of Nebraska Press, 1984). As the anthropological adviser, he was involved in making the television documentary *The Whale Hunters of Lamalera, Indonesia* (Disappearing World, Granada Television, 1988).

CRISPIN BATES is Lecturer in South Asian History, Department of History, University of Edinburgh, Scotland, where he was appointed in 1989. He studied history at Sidney Sussex College, Cambridge, where he completed his Ph.D. on the social and economic history of colonial central India in 1984. He subsequently held a research fellowship at Churchill College, Cambridge, and has been a Visiting Professor at the Écoles des Hautes Études en Sciences Sociales, Paris. He has travelled widely in India and conducted more than two years of research in colonial archives in the subcontinent, mostly in Madhya Pradesh. He has published a number of articles on the social and economic history of central India, with particular reference to the *adivasis*, or tribals, of this region. His first book, *A Political Economic History of Central India, 1820–1950*, is to be published soon.

MARCUS COLCHESTER is the Director of the Forest Peoples Programme of the World Rainforest Movement, an international network of citizens' groups concerned about tropical deforestation based in Malaysia. He received his D.Phil. in anthropology at the University of Oxford for his studies of the social ecology of the Sanema, the northern Yanomami Indians of Amazonia. For many years he worked for the human-rights organization Survival International, focusing on the problems faced by indigenous peoples, from forced resettlement to colonization, especially in South and Southeast Asia. His published books include *Pirates, Squatters and Poachers: The Political Ecology of Dispossession of the Native Peoples of Sarawak* (Selangor, Malaysia: Survival International in association with the Institute of Social Analysis [INSAN], 1989); and *The Tropical Forestry Action Plan: What Progress?* with Larry Lohman (Penang, Malaysia: World Rainforest Movement; Sturminister Newton, Dorset, England: *The Ecologist*, 1990). He is at present completing another book with Larry Lohman entitled *The Struggle for Land and the Fate of the Forests: The Case for Agrarian Reform.*

JENS DAHL is an Associate Professor at the Institute of Eskimology, University of Copenhagen, Denmark. Since 1989, he has been on leave from the university, serving as Director of the International Work Group for Indigenous Affairs, Copenhagen. His publications include articles on indigenous peoples of the Soviet north published in the yearbooks and documents of the IWGIA.

GRANT EVANS is Reader in Anthropology, Department of Sociology, University of Hong Kong. His main field of research has been Laos, and his latest book is *Lao Peasants Under Socialism* (New Haven: Yale University Press, 1990). Currently he is researching upland Thai in Indochina. He is the editor of *Asia's Cultural Mosaic: An Anthropological Introduction* (New York: Prentice Hall, 1992). He is Chairman of the Hong Kong Anthropological Society and Associate Editor of the *Journal of Oriental Studies.*

ANDREW GRAY has served as a Researcher and Director of the International Work Group for Indigenous Affairs since 1983, and is a member of its International Board. He earned a D.Phil. in Social Anthropology at the University of Oxford in 1983 with a thesis on "The Amarakaeri: An Ethnographic Account of Harakmbut People from South Eastern Peru." His publications include "The People of East Timor and their Struggle for Survival," in Torben Retbøll, ed., *East Timor: The Struggle Continues*, IWGIA Document 50 (Copenhagen: International Work Group for Indigenous Affairs, 1984); "Indigenous Affairs and Anthropology," in H. Skar and F. Salomon, eds., *Natives and Neighbors in South America: Anthropological Essays*, Goteborgs Etnografiska Museum Studier, no. 38 (Goteborg: Etnografiska Museum, 1987); and *Between the Spice of Life and the Melting Pot: Biodiversity Conservation and its Impact on Indigenous Peoples*, IWGIA Document 70 (Copenhagen: International Work Group for Indigenous Affairs, 1991). Among his many contributions to the IWGIA, he wrote and compiled the *IWGIA Yearbook* for the years 1986–88. In 1991 and 1992, he returned to Peru to conduct further research.

SIGNE HOWELL is Professor of Anthropology, Department and Museum of Anthropology, Universitetet i Oslo, Norway. She obtained her M.Litt. and D.Phil. at the University of Oxford and was previously Lecturer in the Department of Social Anthropology, University of Edinburgh. She has published *Chewong Myths and Legends*, Malaysian Branch of the Royal Asiatic Society, Monograph No. 11 (Kuala Lumpur: Council of the MBRAS, 1982); *Society and Cosmos: Chewong of Peninsular Malaysia* (Singapore: Oxford University Press, 1984; Chicago: University of Chicago Press, 1984); and *Societies at Peace* (London: Routledge, 1989), edited with Roy Willis.

VICTOR T. KING is Professor of South-East Asian Studies and Director of the Centre for South-East Asian Studies, University of Hull. His publications include *Essays on Borneo Societies*, Hull Monographs on South-East Asia, no. 7 (Oxford: Oxford University Press, 1978); and *The Maloh of West Kalimantan*, Verhandelingen van het Koninklijk Instituut voor Taal-, Land- en Volkenkunde, no. 108 (Dordrecht, Holland, and Cinnaminson, N.J.: Foris Publications, 1985).

BENEDICT KINGSBURY is Professor of Law at the Duke University School of Law, North Carolina. He was formerly University Lecturer in Law at the University of Oxford, and Fellow and Tutor in Law at Exeter College, Oxford. A specialist in international law, he jointly edited and contributed to *United Nations, Divided World* (Oxford: Clarendon, 2d ed., 1993); *Hugo Grotius and International Relations* (Oxford: Clarendon, 1990); and *The International Politics of the Environment* (Oxford: Clarendon, 1992). A New Zealander, he has been extensively involved with legal aspects of indigenous peoples' issues, and is working on a book on indigenous peoples and international law (Oxford: Clarendon, forthcoming).

CHARLES MACDONALD is a Researcher at the Centre National de la Recherche Scientifique, Paris, where he is director of the team working on a comparative ethnology of Southeast Asia. He is the author of *Une société simple: Parenté et résidence chez les Palawan (Philippines)* (Paris: Institute d'Ethnologie, 1977); *L'éloignement du ciel: Invention et mémoire des mythes chez les Palawan du sud des Philippines* (Paris: Editions de la Maison des Sciences de l'Homme, 1988); and *Sinsin: Le théâtre des génies, le cycle rituel féminin de Punang-Iräräj, Palawan, Philippines* (Paris: Editions du Centre National de la Recherche Scientifique, 1990). He is editor of *De la hutte au palais: Sociétés "à maison" en Asie du Sud-Est insulaire* (Paris: Editions du Centre National de la Recherche Scientifique, 1987).

WILLEM VAN SCHENDEL studied sociology and anthropology at the University of Amsterdam. He is Professor of Comparative History at the Department of History, Erasmus University, Rotterdam, the Netherlands. His publications include *Peasant Mobility: The Odds of Life in Rural Bangladesh* (Assen: van Gorcum and Manohar, 1982); *Three Deltas: Accumulation and Poverty in Rural Burma, Bengal and South India* (New Delhi: Sage, 1991); and *Francis Buchanan in Southeastern Bengal: His Journey to Chittagong, the Chittagong Hill Tracts, Comilla and Noakhali (1783)* (Dhaka: University Press, 1992).

KATARINA SJÖBERG lectures at the Department of Social Anthropology, Sociological Institute, University of Lund, Sweden. She also lectures in Medical Anthropology at the Biological Institute at the University of Lund. She specializes in the construction of strategies of adaptation to larger systems by minority and indigenous peoples. Her doctoral thesis was entitled "Mr. Ainu: Cultural Mobilization and the Practice of Ethnicity in a Hierarchical Culture" (University of Lund, 1991). She is the author of a number of articles and reports on the Ainu. She is now working on the situation of native peoples of Canada and of refugees and immigrants in Sweden.

HARALD O. SKAR is Director of Research at the Norwegian Institute of International Affairs, Oslo, Norway. He served as Associate Professor in the Department of Social Anthropology, University of Gothenburg, Sweden, from 1981 to 1986, and as a Development Expert with the United Nations (International Labour Organisation) at the Latin American Regional Headquarters in Peru in 1979–80. His publications include *Anthropological Contributions Towards Planned Change and*

Development (Gothenburg: Acta Universitatis Gothenburgensis, 1985); *The Warm Valley People* (Gothenburg: Gothenburg Ethnographic Museum, 1988); and *Natives and Neighbors in South America* (Gothenburg: Gothenburg Ethnographic Museum, 1987), edited with Frank Salomon. He has undertaken field research in Latin America and Nepal and is currently preparing a monograph on the Rana Tharu people of Nepal and India.

MARTIN SMITH is a journalist specializing in Burmese affairs. He has made several television documentaries on Burma, including *Burma: Dying for Democracy* (Channel Four, Granada Television, 1989) and *Forty Million Hostages* (British Broadcasting Service, 1991), and has reported for many news and human-rights organizations, including the *Guardian*, Anti-Slavery Society, and Article 19.

NICHOLAS TAPP completed his Ph.D. in Social Anthropology at the School of Oriental and African Studies in London in 1986, and has served as a Lecturer in Anthropology at the Chinese University of Hong Kong. Currently he is a Lecturer in the Department of Social Anthropology, Edinburgh University. His original research was among the Hmong people of northern Thailand where he spent eighteen months in 1981–82. Since 1986, he has undertaken extensive research on the Hmong and Yao peoples of southern China. His publications include *The Hmong of North Thailand* (London: Anti-Slavery Society, 1986); *Sovereignty and Rebellion: The White Hmong of Northern Thailand* (Singapore and Oxford: Oxford University Press, 1989). With Chien Chiao he coedited *Ethnicity and Ethnic Groups in China* (Hong Kong: New Asia College, 1989).

JOHN TAYLOR was educated at Sussex University, the School of Oriental and African Studies, and the City University, London. He has held a variety of teaching appointments in universities and polytechnics, most recently as Principal Lecturer at the South Bank Polytechnic, London, where he is also Director of the Centre for Chinese Studies. For many years he has been associated with the Open University as a tutor and academic adviser in development studies. His main areas of research have been Southeast Asia and China. He is the author of *From Modernisation to Modes of Production* (New York: Macmillan, 1979); and coeditor (with Andrew Turton) of *The Sociology of Developing Societies: Southeast Asia* (Basingstoke: Macmillan, 1988). On East Timor, he has published

The Indonesian Occupation of East Timor: A Chronology, 1974–1989
(Oxford and London: Refugees Studies Programme, Oxford University,
and Catholic Institute for International Relations, 1990); and *Indonesia's
Forgotten War: The Hidden History of East Timor* (London and Leichard,
N.S.W, Australia: Zed Books and Pluto Press, 1991). He currently coed-
its *Timor Link* for the Catholic Institute for International Relations, on
whose Education Committee he serves as an adviser.

HÉLÈNE VACHER lectures at the Aalborg University Center, Denmark,
while working on her doctoral thesis on the nationalist movement in
Punjab between the two world wars. She has been a free-lance journalist
for various newspapers and magazines and has worked as a consultant for
UNESCO and UNDP on programs for the safeguarding of the cities of
Fez and Sana'a. She is a collaborator of the journal *Le Monde Diplomatique* and a correspondent for *Le Journal de Geneve-Gazette de Lausanne.*
Her recent publications include a contribution on Pakistan to the review
HERODOTE (Paris), a paper on urbanization in the Third World for
the Finnish Association for Development Geography (Helsinki); a paper
on symbols of identity in Pakistan and India for the *Working Papers of
International Studies* (Aalborg); and a series on Lahore, Sana'a, and Fez
for *Arkitekten.*

Notes

Notes to Chapter 2

1. The 1991 United Nations Working Group Report (United Nations 1991b, 3–4) lists the following Asian "indigenous peoples' nations and organizations" as participating that year: the Aetas' Association in Western Luzon (Philippines), Ainu Association of Hokkaido (Japan), Alliance of Taiwan Aborigines, Asia Indigenous Peoples' Pact, Association of Minority Peoples of the Soviet North, Bougainville Republic, Cordillera People's Alliance of the Philippines, Hmong People, Jumma, Kamp IP (Philippines), Kamp LM (Philippines), Karen National Union, Naga Peoples Movement for Human Rights, and the Sarawak Indigenous Peoples Alliance (Malaysia, Sarawak, Kelabit). It also includes, in a separate list of "other organizations and groups," the Ambedkor Centre for Justice and Peace, Bonded Labour Liberation Front, Centre of Concern for Child Labour (India), Gerakan Revolutioner Rajat Nanusaka (Maluku), Homeland Mission 1950 for the South Moluccas, Papuan Peoples Federation, Shimin Gaikou Centre (Japan), and the West Papuan Peoples Front.

2. The People's Republic of China was a participant in previous years. Sri Lanka has also been a frequent participant.

3. The text of the Draft Declaration proposed by the Working Group after a second reading is reproduced in United Nations (1993). The earlier version adopted after a first reading is in United Nations (1992, 44–52). The 1993 text includes a sweeping provision on self-determination (Article 3), strongly supported by indigenous peoples' organizations but highly contentious for many state governments: "Indigenous peoples have the right to self-determination. By virtue of that right they freely determine their political status and freely pursue their economic, social and cultural development" (United Nations 1993, 52).

4. The Asian Development Bank is not known to have adopted a comparable policy.

5. Convention Providing for Creation of the Inter-American Indian Institute 1940 (United States Treaties Series No. 978 1942). In the preamble the

395

states that are parties to the convention recognize "that it is highly desirable to clarify, stimulate and coordinate the Indian policies of the various nations, such policies being construed as the aggregation of desiderata, standards and measures that should be applied for integral improvement of the living standards of the Indian groups of the Americas."

6. The Special Commission was established in 1989 by the Third (Quito) Meeting of Foreign Ministers of parties to the Treaty for Amazonian Co-operation 1978 (Bolivia, Brazil, Colombia, Ecuador, Guyana, Peru, Suriname, and Venezuela). For the text of its declaration and resolutions, see United Nations (1989c).

7. Some claims expressed in such language have aroused international political controversy, as, for instance, that surrounding the two coups in Fiji in 1987 and subsequent proposals for revision of the Fijian Constitution (see Islam 1988). Claims based on the priority of "first occupants" or "sons [or children] of the soil" have attracted considerable domestic support when advanced by dominant groups at the national, state, or provincial levels. For examples concerning Maharashtrian preferences in India and the *bumiputra* policy in Malaysia, see Weiner (1978); Katzenstein (1979); and Lee (1986).

8. See Kingsbury (1992b); Brownlie (1988, 6); Hannum (1990, 473–77); and Sacerdoti (1983, 116). Scelle (1936, 258) took a similar position in the 1930s: "Le régime minoritaire est, avons-nous dit, un succédané du droit des peuples a disposer d'eux-mêmes."

9. For background, see Sanders (1983); Independent Commission on International Humanitarian Issues (1987); and Hannum (1990, 74–103). Further complications arise in that interpretations of particular definitions, or of the classification of particular peoples or groups, differ among and between organizations, indigenous peoples, and governments. Inconsistencies may arise between different departments of the same government, and the national practice of a particular state may not be consistent with the position it takes internationally.

10. See International Labour Office (1951); and International Labour Office (1954). Indigenous peoples scarcely participated.

11. See International Labour Office (1953, 584–90).

12. Gamio 1966 [1948], 1949. Manuel Gamio was then director of the Inter-American Indian Institute.

13. See International Labour Office (1953, 17).

14. See, for instance, Caso (1948, 244).

15. International Labour Conference 1956b, 13. This definition is strikingly similar to the one proposed by UN Special Rapporteur, José Martínez Cobo in 1983. However, there has been a marked change in the tenor of ILO and UN texts with regard to the implication in Brazil's formulation that "territory" appertains to the state and not to indigenous peoples. The UN Working Group has taken a sharply different position in the 1993 Draft Declaration, which provides: "Indigenous peoples have the right to own, develop, control and use the lands and territories which they have traditionally owned or otherwise occupied or used" (United Nations 1993, 56). This issue has long been one of great controversy in international fora, and implementation of the Working Group's formulation would require dramatic changes in the law and practice of many states.

16. International Labour Conference 1956b, 13. The United Kingdom made a substantially similar proposal in International Labour Conference (1957, 10).

17. International Labour Office 1953, 26.

18. International Labour Conference 1956a.

19. International Labour Conference 1988, 4.

20. International Labour Conference 1956b, 11.

21. In 1977, the World Council of Indigenous Peoples condemned ILO Convention 107 because of its "integrationist" emphasis (Resolution B.1 of the Second General Assembly, Kiruna). Many states held similar views. Norway and Australia, among others, were reluctant to consider accession to the Convention in the 1980s for this reason, as was the Office itself. See, generally, Norwegian Sami Rights Committee (1984, 18, 301–13); the 1982 statement by Australia's minister of foreign affairs (Street 1982, 487); and International Labour Office (1986).

22. This text closely follows that suggested by the International Labour Office in a 1987 questionnaire to governments—see International Labour Conference (1988, 94). The principal differences are the substitution of *own* for *traditional* as the qualifier for the institutions referred to in (b), and the addition of the reference to the establishment of present state boundaries.

23. Brazil has stipulated that Convention 107 applies only to forest-dwelling Indians, not to those in agricultural or urban areas. Bolivia considers it applicable to all persons of Indian descent if they retain ties to their traditional cultures. Mexico regards the Convention as applying in Mexico only to persons who speak an indigenous language (Swepston 1978, 715, 718–19, citing reports by these countries to the ILO). See also International Labour Conference (1956b, 9 [Brazil]). In a direct request to Ecuador in 1984, the Committee of Experts specifically asked for information on

indigenous groups in the Sierra and coastal regions to supplement information provided by the government on forest-dwelling indigenous people in the Amazon region (ILO files). El Salvador reported that the indigenous sector of the population was less than 2 percent of the total, and so well integrated as not to trigger obligations under the Convention. The Committee of Experts was not willing to accept this, pointing to the guarantees for indigenous languages in Article 62 of El Salvador's 1983 Political Constitution, to special measures for indigenous culture and traditions taken by the Ministry of Education and the National Indigenous Association, and to other estimates placing the indigenous population as high as 9 percent (Report of El Salvador, and Committee of Experts Direct Request, 1986, in ILO files). The Committee of Experts previously had accepted the government's position that there were no populations in El Salvador to whom the Convention applied (Swepston 1978, 715, 756). See also International Labour Office (1984, 17).

24. Swepston 1978, 755–56.

25. African groups were not represented at the UN Working Group until 1989. The first statement by such a participant was that of Tanzanian MP Moringe Parkipuny at the 1989 meeting, published under the title "The Indigenous Peoples' Rights Question in Africa" (Parkipuny 1989). From 1991 onward, participants have included representatives of groups from several African countries.

26. Béteille 1977 [1960]. See also Fried (1975), especially chapter 1, "Do Tribes Exist?"

27. Quoted from the World Bank's Operational Manual Statement "Tribal People in Bank-Financed Projects" (World Bank 1982).

28. See, for example, Treece (1987); *The Ecologist* (1986); Survival International (1985); and Otten (1986). On the World Bank and human-rights issues generally, see Paul (1988, 67); and Shihata (1988, 39).

29. As one bank official enthusiastically put it, while under India's domestic law the chief secretary of a state may happen to have additional privileges on account of descent as a member of a scheduled tribe, the bank confines its special protection to persons whose current circumstances are felt to require it (statement by Carlos Escudero in International Labour Office 1986. See also Escudero [1988, 10–13]).

30. It appears that the bank's 1982 policy was adopted primarily in light of its experience with projects in Brazil.

31. World Bank 1991, 1.

32. Ibid.

33. United Nations General Assembly Official Records 1949a.

34. See the General Assembly debate, in ibid.; and that in United Nations Economic and Social Council Official Records 1949. The resolution passed was GA Res. 275 (III), 11 May 1949.

35. E/CN.4/Sub.2/1986/7/Add.4 (Martínez Cobo 1986), paras. 378–80. This definition, like much of the report, was drafted by A. Willemsen-Diaz, then with the UN Secretariat and subsequently chairman of the Board of Trustees of the UN Voluntary Fund for Indigenous Populations. Martínez Cobo's report was prepared for the UN Sub-Commission on the Prevention of Discrimination and Protection of Minorities over a period of about ten years beginning in 1973. For the working definition used during the study, see Martínez Cobo (1983, paras. 24–45).

36. Martínez Cobo (1986, paras. 369–70).

37. See the survey in chapter 5 of ibid. It has been suggested, for instance, that the recognition by the People's Republic of China of fifty-five minority nationalities has had the effect of lumping together separate groups with distinct self-identities. See, for example, Gladney (1989).

38. Norway, for instance, has consulted Sami bodies before allocating aid to indigenous-peoples groups abroad. The UN Working Group on Indigenous Populations (WGIP) has avoided becoming involved in determining whether participating groups are or are not indigenous peoples, or in issues of representativity or credentials beyond those normally required for groups having status with ECOSOC. The Board of Trustees of the UN Voluntary Fund for Indigenous Populations (the five members of which are appointed by the Secretary-General and currently include a Maori and a Saami) of necessity makes decisions about status in deciding which representatives will receive grants to travel to Geneva for Working Group meetings. It has not, however, adopted formal definitional criteria beyond some apparent reference to the Martínez Cobo proposals. The World Council of Indigenous Peoples, which does make decisions on classification, after initial reticence has extended participation beyond its five established regions (North, Central, and South America, Northern Europe, and the South Pacific) to Asia through a Pacific-Asia Council of Indigenous Peoples.

39. See the national legislation surveyed in Martínez Cobo (1986, chap. 5, esp. paras. 210–374).

40. See, for example, UN Human Rights Committee (1981) for the decision in *Lovelace v Canada*; and ibid. (1988) for the decision in *Kitok v Sweden*. One government urged in the Working Group that "the individual choice to identify or not to identify with the rights and responsibilities of indige-

nous group membership should be explicitly recognized in the [draft UN] Declaration"(United Nations 1989a, 18).

41. Article 3(1) of Convention 169 provides that "The provisions of the Convention shall be applied without discrimination to male and female members of these peoples." Taken in conjunction with Article 8(2), the Convention would appear to preclude many forms of sex discrimination in membership rules and procedures.

42. The World Bank's Operational Directive 4.20, p. 1, advises bank staff: "Within their national constitutions, statutes, and relevant legislation, many of the Bank's borrower countries include specific definitional clauses and legal frameworks that provide a preliminary basis for identifying indigenous peoples."

43. The United Nations Conference on Trade and Development seeks to develop special programs for "island developing countries" (see, for example, UNCTAD 1983) and the (British) Commonwealth has a category of Island Developing and Other Specially Disadvantaged States. See also Dumenge (1983).

44. This is the reality of the matter, without entering upon questions of legal responsibility.

45. The fact that Fijian law does not allow for dual nationality, thus effectively negating the possibility of joint citizenship, is scarcely a violation of the rights of one of Fiji's indigenous peoples.

46. See, generally, *Tito v Waddell* (English High Court of Justice 1977). The Independent Commission of Inquiry into the Provisions of the Constitution of Kiribati Relating to the Banabans reported to the government of Kiribati in September 1985.

47. The Nauru application instituting proceedings in *Certain Phosphate Lands in Nauru (Nauru v. Australia)* was filed on 19 May 1989 (International Court of Justice 1989). The Ilois, who were relocated from the island of Diego Garcia raise somewhat similar issues. In this case the excision and relocation were also accepted by key members of the Mauritian delegation to the independence negotiations with the United Kingdom. The Mauritian government has established a trust fund for the Ilois to which the UK made an *ex gratia* contribution while insisting on renunciation of and indemnification by Mauritius against all past and future Ilois claims. See the 1982 UK-Mauritius Agreement Concerning the Ilois (United Kingdom Treaty Series 1983). See also *Pirmal v. The Ilois Trust Fund* (Mauritius High Court 1985).

48. Puri 1983. This contention is often reiterated by India, which has proposed that indigenous populations be defined as "the existing descendants of the

peoples who *originally* inhabited the present territory of a country wholly or partially at the time when persons of a different culture or ethnic origin arrived there from other parts of the world, and in the course of the last two centuries, overcame them" (United Nations 1984, 8). Myanmar has proposed that the forthcoming UN Draft Declaration use the definition in Article 1(b) of ILO Convention 107 (United Nations 1989b, 4). The Philippines expressly recognizes in its 1987 Constitution that its population includes "indigenous cultural communities" that fall within the ambit of the WGIP (see Philippines Government 1988).

49. A reply by the International Labour Office points out that India participated actively in discussions on early drafts of Convention 107 with no reservations about terminology, even though those drafts referred only to indigenous populations (Report of the UN Working Group on its Second Session, 1983, para. 116). During the revision of Convention 169, the government representative from India maintained the position "that the tribal peoples in India were not comparable in terms of their problems, interests and rights, to the indigenous populations of certain other countries. For this reason, attempts to set international standards on some of the complex and sensitive issues involved might prove to be counter-productive." Further, "he did not consider the term 'peoples' to be relevant to the tribal situation in his country" (International Labour Conference 1989, 3).

50. In general, see Barsh (1986, 369, 373–76). The quote by Gu Yijie is from her statement to the Working Group, 6 August 1987 (Gu 1987). The Chinese Mission privately indicated that its government takes the same view.

51. See, for example, the common statement made to the Working Group on 2 August 1991 by members of the West Papuan Peoples' Front, Karen National Union, Jumma Network in Europe, Indian Council of Indigenous and Tribal Peoples, Alliance of Taiwan Aborigines, National Federation of Indigenous Peoples of the Philippines (KAMP), Lumad-Mindanao, Cordillera People's Alliance, Ainu Association of Hokkaido, Asia Indigenous Peoples Pact, Naga Peoples Movement for Human Rights, Homeland Mission 1950 for South Moluccas, and Hmong People (UN files). The statement read: "First and foremost, we want to bring to your attention the denial of some Asian governments of the existence of indigenous peoples in our part of the world. This denial presents a significant obstacle to the participation of many indigenous peoples from our region in the Working Group's deliberations. The denial also seeks to withhold the benefits of the Declaration from the indigenous, tribal, and aboriginal peoples of Asia. We hereby urgently request that peoples who are denied the rights to govern themselves, and are called tribal, and/or aboriginal in our region, be recognized, for purpose of this Declaration, and in accordance with I.L.O. practice, as equivalent to indigenous peoples." Canada

has urged the Working Group to consider "how the principles might address the very real problem of indigenous populations or tribal groups that live in States that refuse to recognize their very existence. The impact of the principles will be considerably diminished if their applicability can be negated simply by a State asserting that it has no indigenous populations or tribal groups within its territory" (United Nations 1987b, 2–3). This raises serious issues concerning implementation, and emphasizes the desirability of either an explicit and coherent definition or, failing that, of a clear body of practice concerning definition. As a matter of international law, municipal nonrecognition or alternative classification has little bearing on the applicability of relevant obligations. Examples of the abusive use of definitions in national law are given in Gros (1985).

52. The report itself foreshadows a shift in the latter direction, commenting that "the special position of indigenous populations within the society of nation-States existing today derives from their historical rights to their lands, as well as from their right to be different and to be considered as different" (Martínez Cobo 1986, chap. 21, para. 373). Note also Norway's view that "In the efforts to protect the rights of indigenous populations…it is natural to take as a point of departure the need to preserve cultural identity" (United Nations 1987b, 2). Czechoslovakia was one of several states to affirm the importance of the rights of indigenous peoples to their traditional lands and waters and the resources of these as the basis for protection of their other rights (United Nations 1987a, 4).

53. See Hannum (1990, 89), who argues that Asian "hill tribes" and Arab and African nomadic tribes "should be included in a common-sense understanding of 'indigenous'. Less certain would be the inclusion of central Asian peoples…or survivors of overland invasions by peoples of similar race."

54. Compare this with the definition proposed by Canada (United Nations 1988, 3).

55. Japan chose not to make a substantive reply to ILO questionnaires concerning revisions to Convention 107, as a domestic debate was then in progress concerning the government's policy of describing Japan as ethnically homogeneous.

56. United Nations, 1991b, 24.

57. See the statement by the Indonesian Delegation to the Working Group (Indonesia 1991). The statement did note that "Indonesia comprises more than 300 ethnic groups, indigenous to our various regions."

58. See the statement by Deputy Permanent Representative U Win Mra (Win Mra 1991). For reiteration of India's position, see the statement by Prabhu Dayal on behalf of the Delegation of India to the Working Group (Dayal

1991), commenting that most of the tribes in India share ethnic, racial, and linguistic characteristics with other people in India, and that 300 to 400 million people there are distinct in some way from other categories of people in India. A further complication was introduced by a statement at the 1991 Working Group meeting by a representative of an organization of members of "scheduled castes," in which scheduled castes were described as indigenous peoples.

59. See the 1991 version of the Draft Universal Declaration on the Rights of Indigenous Peoples (United Nations 1991b, 30). In particular, operative paragraph 5 provides that "Indigenous peoples have the collective and individual right to maintain and develop their distinct ethnic and cultural characteristics and identities, including the right to self-identification."

60. Ibid., 29. During the 1985 session of the Working Group, one member, Mr. Tosevski from Yugoslavia, stated that "Most indigenous peoples could be treated as minorities, and any attempted distinction between the two was nothing more than an artificial dilemma" (United Nations 1985, para. 66). For a further statement stressing the importance of maintaining the distinction, see the preliminary report of the Special Rapporteur on Treaties, Agreements and Other Constructive Arrangements between States and Indigenous Peoples (Alfonso Martínez 1991, para. 98).

61. Gudmundur Alfredsson, a UN Secretariat official familiar with the subject (although writing in his personal capacity), suggests bluntly that "The crucial factor in the definition of indigenous peoples is their original inhabitation of land on which, unlike the minorities, they have lived from time immemorial." By contrast, he suggests that "most [presumably nonindigenous] tribal peoples are likely to be classified as minorities" (1990, 15). Such an approach might well suggest, depending upon detailed facts, that some groups in Asia that have participated in the Working Group meetings would be regarded as minorities rather than indigenous peoples. However, there is no indication that the Working Group intends to take such a position.

62. The Declaration on the Rights of Minorities finally adopted by the UN General Assembly refers simply to national, ethnic, religious, and linguistic minorities without further definition (United Nations 1991a). See also the preliminary report of the UN Sub-Commission's Special Rapporteur on possible ways and means of facilitating the peaceful and constructive solution of problems involving minorities, Asbjorn Eide, in which he uses the term *minorities* "in a very broad sense, meaning nationalities, ethnic, linguistic or cultural groups which in significant respects are different from other groups in a sovereign state" (Eide 1991, 2). It is difficult to envisage any definition of *indigenous peoples* that would not be entirely subsumed within this definition of *minorities*.

63. United Nations 1984b, paras. 99–110. See also United Nations (1982, 1983). The matter was discussed again briefly in 1989, with some governments suggesting that it would be necessary to include a definition in the draft principles before they were finalized (United Nations 1989a, 18). As the drafting progressed, several states insisted that, even if "indigenous peoples" was not defined, there must be clear statements about the term *peoples* and the limits of the right to self-determination (see, for example, United Nations 1992, 13–19; and United Nations 1993, 19–20). Some states, including the United States, argued that a disclaimer of international-law implications of the term *peoples* should be included, as was done in ILO Convention 169. Several states argued that, where the right to self-determination applied to indigenous peoples, this right did not extend to a right to form separate states. In response to these concerns the chair of the Working Group sought to clarify that use of the term *peoples* in the Draft Declaration did not itself confer a right to "external" self-determination (see United Nations 1992, 17; and United Nations 1993, 18–19).

64. For criticism by the ILO official chiefly responsible for Convention 169 of the focus on historical precedence in the Martínez Cobo definition, see Swepston (1990, 667, 695).

65. See Kingsbury 1992a.

Notes to Chapter 3

1. The eight other "definitions" of indigenous peoples can be divided into two types: those that emphasize particular features of what constitutes being "indigenous," and others that set out multiple criteria that need not all be present in any one example. In this way these definitions use a polythetic method of classifying the notion.

   The definition of *indigenous* by the World Bank (1981) is tied up with the notion of "tribal." The four-fold definition is based on distinctions between "isolated," "semi-isolated," "permanent contact," and "integrated" peoples. The criteria are fundamentally socioeconomic and relate to the respective distance from the nation-state. In contrast, the World Council of Indigenous Peoples' definition (see Burger 1987, 8) links prior residence on territory with culture and self-definition (belonging).

   The International Labour Organisation, in Article 1 of its old Convention 107 (1957), has a double definition. Tribal peoples are socioeconomically less advanced than other sectors of the nation-state (clause a), while indigenous peoples are "pre-conquest or pre-colonial." According to Bennet (1978, 17), the first part of the definition is meant to cover Africa and Asia and the second part the Americas. The implication is that *indigenous* refers only to "original" inhabitants of settler colonies, whereas the others are tribal societies. This is implied in the definition but not stated explicitly.

The United Nations, in both of its definitions, which are reproduced in the ICIHI report (1987, 7–8), tries to cover aspects of the World Bank, ILO, and WCIP definitions. Its main emphasis is on indigenous peoples as colonized but it does not say whether this is external or internal, thereby collapsing the ILO distinction between the Americas and the rest of the world. Distinct social, economic, and cultural features are mentioned but without the "tribalism" of the World Bank and the ILO. Finally, the UN definition adds the concepts of "nondominance" and "self-identification."

The four individual definitions vary in emphasis in a way that parallels the definitions mentioned above. Heinz (1988) follows the World Bank's emphasis on the "backwardness" of indigenous peoples vis-à-vis the nation-state while Stavenhagen (1986), following the UN, looks at the exploitation, nondominance, and colonized aspects of the relationship. Burger (1987) and Gray (1987) share Stavenhagen's preoccupation but emphasize the culture and self-identification features of the WCIP definition.

2. African peoples are also taking note of the indigenous movement. In 1989, a Maasai and a Hazda made the first African presentation to the UN Working Group on Indigenous Populations. The question of whether there are indigenous peoples in Africa is now under discussion among Africanists and Africans and some of the issues raised in the Asia debate are similar.

3. Alejandro Parrillada, of the International Work Group for Indigenous Affairs, saw clear evidence of bombing on a trip to the Philippines in November 1992 (personal communication).

Notes to Chapter 4

1. Cited in Asian NGO Coalition (1989, 4).

2. The term *development* is rendered in quotation marks because it is the author's opinion that the WCED definition of *sustainable development* is actually a definition of *sustainable resource use*. Whether or not this use allows "development" to occur is highly arguable.

Notes to Chapter 5

1. For many years travellers, administrators, and scientists used the term Kamchadals to describe the aboriginal inhabitants of Kamchatka. Today these people are known as Itelmens. The term Kamchadals is only applied to a group descended from mixed marriages between Itelmens, Russians,

and Cossacks. The Kamchadals were not recognized by the Soviet regime as a legal indigenous entity but after being recognized by the Kamchatka regional authorities in 1991 they have acquired certain privileges as a small indigenous group.

2. Concerning ethnic territory it is important to note that it was a constitutional principle in the Soviet Union (Vitebsky 1991, 4) and that ethnic affiliation is an officially recognized means of classification.

Notes to Chapter 6

This chapter is a modified and shortened version of a seminar presented at the Centre d'Études de l'Inde et de l'Asie du Sud in the Écoles des Hautes Études en Sciences Sociales, Paris, in March 1992. I am extremely grateful to the Écoles des Hautes Études en Sciences Sociales and Professor J.-C. Galey for making it possible for me to visit the Centre and to enjoy the rare opportunity to write and discuss in such stimulating company. I am especially grateful for his comments, and for those of Prof. Nicholas Dirks, Denis Vidal, and Prof. Burton Stein.

1. For an outline of the large number of movements, otherwise known as "tribal movements," with which we are concerned, see K. S. Singh (1982a). The word *adivasi* is used in a dual sense in this paper. First, the concept as used by contemporary writers is deconstructed; second, I use it myself as a purely descriptive category in the context of a discussion of the multiplicity of tribal societies and kingdoms to be found in premodern South Asia. Tribal kingdoms are the sites of political process, and therefore may be a valid object of historical enquiry, but the term *adivasi,* I would argue, has no essential, ontological, or analytical value.

2. This point has been acknowledged in respect of the worldwide indigenous peoples' movement in the report of the Independent Commission on International Humanitarian Issues. This report admits there to be an "overlap" between indigenous peoples and ethnic and minority groups but argues that "indigenous refers to peoples affected by the past 500 years of colonialism," describing them as "an unresolved part of the legacy of colonialism." Also cited in this report is the definition of the UN Working Group on Indigenous Populations, which insists upon two further criteria: nondominance and self-definition. In other words, they must still be the victims of colonialism in some shape or form, and regard themselves principally in the light of this experience, if they are to qualify as "indigenous peoples." The significance and ahistoricism of these definitions are far more profound than the authors themselves may have imagined (see Independent Commission on International Humanitarian Issues 1987, 6–9). For a much broader view of

the *adivasi*, rooted in both an historical and anthropological understanding of the subject with which I am more sympathetic, see K. S. Singh (1985), and also the now more dated account in Ghurye (1980).

3. A useful discussion of the concept of "orientalism" and how it has affected understanding of Indian society is to be found in Inden (1990). The connections between racial theory and ideas of caste and tribe were also discussed at a conference on the Concept of Race in South Asia, convened by Dr. Peter Robb at the School of Oriental and African Studies at London University in December 1992. Papers from this conference are to be published.

4. On the nature of colonial epistemology and the mechanisms of colonial governance, see Cohn (1983, 1985).

5. For an overview, see Jones (1989). An account of the creation of a lower-caste identity, influenced by the activity of Christian missionaries in nineteenth-century western India, is to be found in O'Hanlon (1985).

6. For the Untouchables, or Dalits (meaning 'oppressed ones'), as they are now known, the principal spokesman in the 1920s was B. R. Ambedkar. Later, in the 1930s, Mahatma Gandhi himself invented the somewhat patronizing title of Harijans, or children of God, for members of this community.

7. A contestation of this theory may be found in Renfrew (1987). The idea originated in the writings of the eighteenth-century Indologist, Sir William Jones (see Leopold 1970).

8. The idea of a "pre-Aryan" golden age formed a basis for the rejection of caste among low-caste Hindus, as well as among the so-called *adivasis*. For the former, see O'Hanlon (1985, chaps. 8 and 9).

9. To argue so is not "orientalist," as the same can be said of early western Christian society as well.

10. This phenomenon is by no means exclusive to South Asia. Examples of similarly constructed identities found elsewhere are given in Anderson (1983).

11. The impact of colonialism, the nature of political and religious practice in Bastar, and its implications for understanding Hindu kingship and the relations between caste and tribe elsewhere in India, I have addressed in two as yet unpublished papers: "'The Invention of Perdition': Human Sacrifice and British Relations with the Indian Kingdom of Bastar in the 19th Century," and "Dasehra and Revolt: Problems of Legitimacy in 20th Century Bastar," presented at the Centre d'Études de l'Inde et de l'Asie du Sud in the Maison des Sciences de l'Homme in Paris, April 1992.

12. See Saha (1986). Saha has a rather conventional view of history but gives perceptive examples of the types of prejudice directed toward *adivasis* by

Indians (predominantly Brahmins) as well as by anthropologists and officials in more recent times.

13. The ruins of these forts are highly inaccessible today but photographs of them may be found in nineteenth-century and early-twentieth-century gazetteers—for example, that for the Chhindwara district, published in 1907, which illustrates the ruins of "Deogurh" fort, to be found near the modern village of Deogarh. The keep of the Garha fortress, known as the Madan Mahal, also still crowns the range of hills along the foot of which the town of Jabalpur is built.

14. The classic text on this is Fox (1971). See also Zaid (1989); and C. Singh (1988).

15. A classic of this school is J. Peggs's *India's Cries to British Humanity: An Historical Account of Suttee, Infanticide, Ghat Murders and Slavery in India* (1832). This influential book, which brought the term *juggernaut,* among others, into the English language, was originally published as a series of pamphlets by the Coventry Society for the Suppression of Human Sacrifice in India.

16. What was convenient in India was also convenient in Africa, where the policy of "indirect rule" produced very similar results (see Vail 1989; and Ranger 1983).

17. Galey (1989, 166–85) discusses the status of the *gaddi* (throne) both in general and in the kingdom of Garhwal.

18. See also Baker (1991). It is probable that unemployed mercenaries and nomadic and newly landless tribesmen were also an important part of the bandit problem in central India, which became known from the 1830s onward as the criminal and religious conspiracy of Thuggee.

19. An account of this insurrection is given in Ranajit Guha (1983).

20. An example of the invention of a form of *"adivasi"* identity in the Chittagong Hill Tracts that began long before the advent of the anticolonial movement in India and was largely unaffected by it is given in van Schendel (this volume). See also Attwood (1989), an account of the invention of an "aboriginal" identity among the indigenous peoples of southern Australia.

21. For a summary of the issues involved here, see Sarkar (1983).

22. A coauthored paper on Dondi Lohara (C. Bates and S. Dube) will be published in the near future.

23. For a case study of *adivasi* migrant labor in western India, see Breman (1985).

Notes to Chapter 7

1. These groups, with rough estimates of their numbers in 1981, are the Chakma (260,000), Marma (120,000), Tippera (40,000), Tongchengya (25,000), Mru (22,000), Mrung/Riang (10,000), Bawm (7,000), Khumi (3,000), Sak (2,000), Pangkhua (2,000), Khyang (1,500), and Lushai (500). In 1951, there were 26,000 Bengalis in the Chittagong Hill Tracts (10 percent of the total population, up from 2.5 percent in August 1947). By 1981, there were about 260,000 (35 percent of the total). Recent reports assert that Bengalis now make up about 45 percent of the population. For an older but most detailed count by mother tongue and religion, see *Census of India*, 1931 (1933, 5:194, 197); *Bedrohte Zukunft* (1988, 13); Bessaignet (1958, 4); P. Chakma (1986, 45–46); and "Fresh Influx in Tripura" (1989, 15).

2. For more than 120 years the area was administered as the Chittagong Hill Tracts District. In 1983, it was split into the Khagrachari Hill District, the Rangamati Hill District, and the Bandarban Hill District.

3. In the precolonial period both raw cotton and hill textiles were exported from the port of Chittagong (Qanungo 1988, 615; see also Serajuddin 1971, 51–60).

4. Buchanan (1798). Entitled "An account of a Journey undertaken by Order of the Board of Trade through the Provinces of Chittagong and Tiperah, in order to look out for the places most proper for the cultivation of Spices, by Francis Buchanan, M.D.," the manuscript is in the collections of the British Library. I am grateful to Richard Eaton for drawing my attention to it, and to Francis Rolt for providing me with a copy. All page references to Buchanan in this chapter refer to the original manuscript, which has now been published (van Schendel 1992).

5. Ibid. The Marma were commonly known as Joomea (Mogs) to the Bengalis of the plain but their leader, Kaung-la Pru [Kong Hla Phru], explained to Buchanan that "the proper name of the Joomeas is Ma-ra-ma, and that they have resided in this Country from time immemorial" [p. 91]. Of the Chakma, he wrote,

> I found that the men, except a few words, understood no other language [than Bengali]. They say that they are the same with the Sak of Roang or Arakan: that originally they came from that country; and that on account of their having lost their native language, and not having properly acquired the Bengalese, they are commonly called in ridicule Doobadse. They call themselves Saksa, which word corrupted has, I suppose, given rise to their Bengalese name Sagma or Chakma. From the few words of their native language, which they retain, it is evidently

a dialect of the Burma, nearly the same with that of Arakan. Their religion is that of Godama, corrupted by their having adopted many Brahmanical superstitions, and especially bloody sacrifices to the Devtas [p. 114]....A priest, who assumed the name of Poun-do-gye or Great royal virtue, informed me, that the Chakmas have in general forgot the Roang language: but that it is the dialect spoken by the Sak-mee, who still live in Arakan. The books, which this priest has, are written both in the Roang character and dialect. (p. 121)

Buchanan wrote that the Mru "call themselves Mo-roo-sa....They said they knew no God (Takoor), and that they never prayed to Maha-moony, Ram, nor Khooda...their native tongue has some affinity to that of the Burmas" (pp. 67–68; see also p. 97). He was unable to interview the Bawm and had only second-hand information on them:

[T]he Bonjoogies are by the Rakain [= Arakanese] and the Joomeas [= Marma] called Bon-zu....They have a number of slaves, originally prisoners of war: and many Lan-ga have settled among them, and are subject to their Prince [pp. 91, 92]....The chief of the Bonjoogies, as I am told here, is by the Chakmas called Tai-koup. His subjects are said to be numerous, and to consist of two tribes, the Bon-zu, and Loo-sai. From the head of every family in his dominions Tai-koup receives an annual tribute of one basket of rice, and one piece of cotton cloth. (p. 123)

The language of the Zo

has some affinity to the Burma: but they did not seem to understand the Ma-ra-ma dialect, a proof perhaps of their not having been long dependent on Kaung-la-pru. They name their own tribe Zou. By the Ma-ra-mas they are named Lang-ga, which by the Bengalese is corrupted into Lingta. By the Bengalese they are commonly called Koongky, which we have corrupted into Kooky, or as it is written in the Asiatic Researches Cuci. (pp. 98–99)

Other "rude tribes" of which Buchanan heard were the Khumi (Hkwe-myi), the Shein-du, Hkyaw, and Kaung-me (pp. 41, 68; see also pp. 123, 139a). He did not meet any Sak personally but wrote about

a people, whom they [= the Chakma] name Sak, and the Bengalese name Chak. These people are evidently the Thaek of the Burmas....In order to distinguish the Sak settled here, from those called Sak-mee, who still live in Arakan, the [Chakma] priest calls them Moishang Sak. (pp. 56, 121)

Buchanan's references to the Mrung, whom he could not meet, are confusing in the light of later reports. Although he is evidently talking about the Mrung, a group closely related to the Tippera, he also refers to Deinea, apparently a form of Doingnak, which was later applied to a group in Arakan as well as to the Tongchengya of the Chittagong Hills. The latter, according to later reports, split off from the Chakmas in 1782 (Lewin 1984 [1870], 164–65; see also pp. 182–83). There is no mention of Tongchengya in Buchanan's manuscript. Were the Doingnak and Mroung a single group or did Buchanan lump the two together? He was told that

> The Tiperah and the Mroung…dress alike, and speak the same language. From some circumstance in collecting the revenue these Mroungs are frequently called Wa-thé Mroo. From some similar circumstance the Mroo proper [Mru] are called Lay Mroo….It is to be observed that both Mroo and Mroung are by the Bengalese called Moroong. To distinguish the last mentioned tribe from the Mroo they are often called Deinea Moroong [Buchanan 1798, 78, 79; see also p. 81)….[The Marma leader, Kaung-la Pru, said that] the Mroung and Tiperah dress in the same manner, and speak Dialects of the same language, having to each other as great an affinity as the Burmas and the Rakain [= Arakanese] have [p. 91]….The Mroung wear their hair tied in a knot on the nape of the neck, by which they may easily be distinguished from the Mo-roo [Mru], who wear their knot of hair on the forehead. (p. 70; see also pp. 68, 75)

Of the tribe named "Tiperah, Tipperah, or Teura," the Dewan, or Minister, of the Tippera Raja told Buchanan "that the Tiperah, Reang, and Alynagur, are of the same nation, and speak dialects of the same language. The different names arise from the places they inhabit" (pp. 35, 164).

6. Examples of swidden villages composed of different language groups are the Marma and Sak, the Marma and Bawm, and the Mru and Arakanese (ibid., 62, 67, 90, 104). The Chakma kept Tippera debt peons, and the Bawm kept Lang-ga debt peons and prisoners of war (pp. 98, 115). The Marma leader Kaung-la Pru had "about twenty Hindoo Servants, and still more Mohammedans, his Dewan or Minister being of that Religion. The domestic who takes care of his table is a Rajbunjee [= Barua, a Buddhist Bengali]" (p. 63). Even a minor Marma chief, named Umpry Palong, had two Bengali servants. Taubboka (Tabar Khan), the Chakma leader, also had Bengali servants, and a Tippera boy was reported to serve a Chakma monk (pp. 63, 93, 120, 122).

7. Kaung-la Pru, the Po-mang-gre ('great captain') of the Marma, ruled over Marma, Mru, Mroung, Tipera, and Lang-ga subjects who paid him tribute (ibid., 34–35, 39, 67–68, 70, 75 [insert], 81, 98, 101). The minor Marma chief Umpry Palong received tribute from Marma and Sak (p. 62). The independent Marma chief Agunnea (Bunnea) received tribute from Marma and Bawm (p. 90). Taubboka (Tabar Khan), the Chakma *mang* (which Buchanan translates in English as "prince" and in Bengali as *"raja"*—and

renders in Burmese script as *min* (= *'min,* 'ruler')—had Chakma, Koongky, and Bengali subjects in the Chittagong Hills. He was also a *zamindar* (superior landholder and tax collector) in parts of the Rangunia region in the plains where he had his main residence and received tribute from Bengali and Barua subjects (pp. 108–9, 120–21, 142–43, 144–45). The Ta-kang ('prince'; also *mang* or *raja*) of the Bawm received tribute from Bawm, Lushai, and Lang-ga (pp. 69, 90–92, 123, 136–37).

8. Forty years later, R. H. Sneyd Hutchinson, who described the inhabitants of the Chittagong Hills as "more or less savages," concurred: "The Bengali of the plain divides the inhabitants into two classes. Those able to understand the vernacular of Bengal are designated as Jumiyas, while the others are distinguished as Kukies" (Hutchinson 1909, 14). The Kookies, whose ethnic identities long remained a puzzle to British and Bengalis alike, were sometimes subdivided on practical grounds. According to a report of 1862, they "are locally known and divided by two general names, as 'Mela' (friendly) and 'Ghyr Mela' (unfriendly). The former may be roughly said to live to the West of a line drawn North and South from Burkal: the latter live to the East of that line" (Government of Bengal 1862a).

9. See also Francis Buchanan's remark: "I find, that the appellation of Mug is given by the people of this province [= Bengal] to all the Tribes, and nations, east from Bengal, who as differing from the Hindoos, and Mussulmans, are considered as having no Cast, and as therefore being highly contemptible" (Buchanan 1798, 28, see also p. 56). The term also was, and continues to be, used more specifically but confusingly to refer to the following distinct groups: Arakanese (or Rahkain or Rakhine), Marma, and Barua. Sometimes these were distinguished by labels such as Jhumia Mughs, Roang Mughs, Inland Mughs, Hill Mughs, and Barua Mughs but these labels were not used consistently (see Lewin 1984 [1870]; and *East Pakistan District Gazetteers: Chittagong* 1970). The derivation of the name Mug is unknown, and various explanations have been put forward, the most fanciful no doubt being Pogson's suggestion that Maghs are Magi, hence Jews. For other conjectures, see Lewin (1984 [1870], 95–96, 302); *East Pakistan District Gazetteers: Chittagong* (1970, 114–17); Pogson (1831, 70); Risley (1981 [1891], 1:28–29); Ghosh (1960, 17–25); and L. Bernot (1967a, 1:49–54).

10. The special status of the Chittagong Hills was abolished in 1964. The hills were officially closed to outsiders in that year but some anthropological research could be carried on until 1971 (see Brauns and Löffler 1986, introduction).

11. Bangladeshi historians who have done work on the eighteenth century are Serajuddin (1971, 1984); Chakraborty (1977); and Islam (1983). The most

extensive work on the nineteenth and twentieth centuries was done by Wolfgang Mey who based his work on annual administration reports and published selections of records (W. Mey 1980, 5). For an overview of anthropological studies, see Qureshi (1984). The first Department of Anthropology was established at Jahangirnagar University in the early 1980s.

12. For example, in 1879 the area beyond the eastern boundary of British India was described as "a large area of mountainous and forest land inhabited by tribes who, paying no tribute to, and independent of, the British Government, revel in a state of almost unrestrained barbarism" *(Administration Report on the Hill Tracts* 1879).

13. Such representations of the "tribe" are based on the presumption that all tribes share characteristics that are fundamentally different from, even opposite to, those of civilized people. Principal among these are "childish" qualities that betray a lack of socialization: immoderately emotional behavior (revelry, sensuality, extravagance, cruelty, and fear of the supernatural) and naivety (credulity and the incapacity to plan for the future). This discourse may be referred to as "tribalist" because of its similarities to the orientalist representation of "the Orient" (see Said 1979).

14. The term is taken from Wolf (1982). It goes without saying that other views also are expressed among Bengalis in Bangladesh but these are rarely heard, have little or no influence on national policy, and appear to be restricted largely to the academic community. Even in the most vocal collection of these counterviews to date (Qureshi 1984), the "dominant view" manages to reassert itself occasionally. See Mazumder's (1985) and Mey's experience in 1968: "Again and again I was told, even by educated Bengalis: 'They are savages; they are still living in the stone age. They do not know plough cultivation and are underdeveloped'" (W. Mey 1988, 35 [my translation]).

15. But see Bernot's critical remarks about this popular notion (L. Bernot 1967a, 41–42).

16. Buchanan, who translates *mang* as 'prince', states that the titles Ta-kang and Po-mang, too, "are titles analogous to our term Prince: and are the Rakain [Arakanese] pronunciation of သာကြင် [*tha-hkyin*] and မင် [*min*], the Burma titles for the Sons of their King, and bestowed also upon Officers of high rank" (Buchanan 1798, 91). *Bohmong,* a transliteration of *po-mang,* is a title still used to refer to one of the three territorial chiefs in the Chittagong Hill Tracts.

17. Use of the suffix *-khan* is usually interpreted as an attempt on the part of the local chiefs to adapt to Mughal practices. It is more likely that the term

derived from Muslims immigrating from Arakan (see Serajuddin 1971).

18. Many Bengalis claim roots in more westerly parts of South Asia, or even in West Asia, because such "western" connections are considered prestigious. The Chakma claim that they are descendants of Ksattriya migrants from "Champa(k)nagar," thought to be in north India, can be interpreted as an effort to invent a tradition that might lead to both Sanskritization and Bengalization. As we have seen, Buchanan (1798, 114) recorded the story of an Arakanese origin, which was also suggested by the Chittagong Qanungo's report in Government of Bengal, Proceedings of the Committee of Revenue, 6 May 1784, cited in Serajuddin (1971, 52ff); and partly quoted in Serajuddin (1984, 95–97). The Champanagar story was first recorded in Lewin (1869, 62–63). See also Lewin (1984 [1870], 170); Mills (1933); Bessaignet (1958, 88ff); and Ali (1962, 227–28). For critiques, see W. Mey (1980, 38–43); and Serajuddin (1984, 90–98).

19. This development on the borders of British-controlled areas in Bengal and Lower Burma probably was related to dislocations of old trade routes. Standard explanations refer mostly to possible population expansion in the Chin-Lushai Hills but the connection with colonial state formation and trade should not be overlooked. For a capsule history of the Chins, see Bernot and Bernot (1958, 7–14, 74n).

20. Only "Hill Tippera," present-day Tripura, was an exception. It was given a special status as a Princely State in communication with the Government of Bengal.

21. The precolonial Burmese state relied heavily on surplus extraction by means of nonterritorial "crown service groups" (*ahmudan*). See Furnivall (1957, 28–41).

22. W. Mey (1980) analyzes this change at length. In addition to the three chiefs, there were initially "several petty Chiefs holding settlements in the Hills of new settlers, chiefly consisting of deserters from Independent Tipperah, under the local name of Noabad Kapass Mehals" (Government of Bengal 1862a, Proceeding 226).

23. A most eloquent advocate of indirect rule was Lewin (1869), who wrote, "They [the chiefs] are on the spot, and have enormous local influence, and in my humble opinion they are the legitimate instruments of rule placed ready to our hand. I would subordinate them in every way to our authority. *Let them be guided or checked as need be, but within their own limits I would have their authority paramount*" (T. H. Lewin, quoted in Government of Bengal 1917, 100–101, appendix A [emphasis in original]; see also the instructions of the Government of Bengal in 1860, quoted in Lewin 1984 [1870], 63). In 1874, the government decided to confer on the new

Chakma chief, Harish Chandra (ruled 1873–85), the title of *raja* in order to underline his dependence on "the pleasure of the paramount authority" (Government of Bengal 1874a). But it was not deemed "desirable that any representative of Government should take part in the ceremonies incident on installation to the guddi [throne]; that would, I think, be assigning undue importance to the matter" (Government of Bengal 1874b). In the event, the deputy commissioner at Rangamati presented the Chakma chief with a *sanad* (deed of grant) and a *khilat* (dress of investiture) in return for a *nazar* (ceremonial present) but he did not take part in other ceremonies. The *sanad* read "Fort William 24-3-1874—In recognition of your position as the head of the Chukma tribe in the Chittagong Hill Tracts, I hereby confer upon you the title of 'Raja' for your life, —Northbrook" (Government of Bengal 1874a, 1874b). On the history of the Chakma chief's family, see Lewin (1984 [1870], 162–63); Ali (1962, 229); and W. Mey (1980).

24. As early as 1866 this was voiced strongly.

> I think it is unadvisable that Bengallees of all descriptions should be allowed ingress at will into the hills. Several cases of extortion have come to my own notice where Bengallees have forced hill men to give them money by the threat of a false complaint, and on the other hand murders of Bengallees for reasons unknown are by no means uncommon, and the authors of the crime have to the best of my knowledge in no one instance been ascertained. (Government of Bengal 1866)

See also Lewin 1984 (1870), 62–68; Hutchinson 1906, 42; and Mills 1933, 514.

25. In 1855, the Santal rebellion had erupted in hill country some four hundred km. to the west, across the deltaic plains of Bengal, and the area still had not been "pacified" by the time the Chittagong Hills were annexed (see, e.g., Ray 1983; Baske 1976; and Guha 1983).

26. The appointment of a "superintendent of hill tribes" ostensibly was to "administer justice to the Hill people in our jurisdiction, and to prevent that oppression and plunder of poor and ignorant savages by the crafty Bengallee moneylender which may lead, as in the case of the Sonthals, to violence and bloodshed" (Government of Bengal 1862b). This policy was also followed in the adjacent portion of the mountain range which the British annexed as the Hill Tracts of Arakan. Here a superintendent was appointed in 1866. His job was described in equally high-minded terms: "The Superintendent—a specially selected officer—has brought justice, administered in the simplest and most paternal form, to their doors" ("Report on the Progress made in the Arakan Division from 1826 to 1869," in *Report on the Progress of Arakan* 1873, 19).

27. The excluded status of the Chittagong Hills was confirmed during administrative changes in 1935 (Hutchinson 1906, appendix A; S. Chakma 1985–86, 149–62). Both sources include the text of the Resolution.

28. For example, Hutchinson (1906, 32): "The policy of the Government is to interfere as little as possible with tribal customs." For applications of the concept of "enclavement," developed by Edward H. Spicer, see Castile and Kushner (1981).

29. This principle determined not only the position of common cultivators but equally that of the chiefs in the eyes of the colonial state: "The Chiefs of the Chittagong Hill Tracts have no title to the ownership of the land which is vested exclusively in the Crown: they exercise only the delegated right of collecting taxes and rents on behalf of Government" (Government of Bengal 1918).

30. In 1871, almost all forest area was designated "government forest." A few years later, five reserved forests were created in which no cultivation was allowed; together they covered an area of 3,500 sq. km. (26 percent of the total area, which encompasses 13,000 sq. km.). The District Gazetteer of 1971 states that the total area of reserved forests was 2,600 sq. km. and that of unclassed state forests was 8,800 sq. km. (20 percent and 67 percent of total area, respectively) before the Kaptai lake was created. Afterward the figures were 2,400 sq. km. (18 percent) and 8,200 sq. km. (62 percent), with the lake taking up 663 sq. km. (5 percent). See Hutchinson (1906, 29–31, 51); W. Mey (1980, 120–22); and *Bangladesh District Gazetteers* (1971, 99). See also Anti-Slavery Society (1984, appendix 4).

31. Tea, coffee, and orange plantations were established in the 1860s, as were teak plantations in the 1870s, but only tea was successful over the long term. The main problem was the labor supply (see *Administration Reports* for various years; and W. Mey 1980, 121–24).

32. T. H. Lewin, letter to the Government of Bengal (1872), quoted in Hutchinson (1906, 49–50). The idea had been voiced a century earlier, in 1784, and again in 1798 and 1829. After 1860, a considerable correspondence developed on the topic of plough cultivation in the Chittagong Hills. The general feeling was that it should be encouraged.

> The advantages of this scheme would be—1st, that we would spur the hillmen into getting civilized and settling down; there would be no danger of being [*sic*] any scarcity of land, or the hill people being ejected by outsiders, or of the immigrants oppressing or disagreeing with them; 2nd, we would get the country cleared and opened out to the rest of India; 3rd, we would have a population which would serve as a barrier against the wild tribes to the east; 4th, in ten or fifteen years the state

would begin to draw a large revenue from this district; 5th, the district from the clearing of the jungle would become healthy. (Government of Bengal 1872b, letter by A. W. Cochrane)

See also the letter of 6 May 1784, from Govt. to Mr. Irwin, Chief of Chittagong, and the letter of 21 April 1829, from Mr. Halhed, Commissioner, both quoted in Lewin (1984 [1870], 58–60); and Buchanan (1798, 103). For a dissenting view, see Hutchinson (1906, 47–54), and for a modern contribution, Ahmad (1976, 111–13).

33. In 1798, Buchanan had observed large communities of swidden cultivators in the hilly parts of the Chittagong Plain. Chakma, Marma, Bawm, and Tippera were found in such places as the low hills between Mirsarai and Sitakund; Chattarua in the north; the Songu Valley as far west as Dohazari; around Rangunia, Harbang, and Chakaria; on Maheshkhali Island in the Bay of Bengal; and down the coast south of Cox's Bazar (Buchanan 1798, 13, 15, 19–20, 32, 46–50, 54, 69, 86, 89–90, 147, 152). On the prohibition of swidden cultivation on government lands in the plains district, see Government of Bengal (1876, 21); and Kindersley (1939, 6).

34. "As the lands in the vicinity of Bunderban have become exhausted by repeated jhooming, it was found necessary that the Mugh [Marma] population of the Sungoo valley should be moved eastward, where virgin soil was available along the right bank of the river. The movement, however, was checked by the fear of raiders" (Government of Bengal 1876, 2). Similarly, Khumis and Bawm (Bunjoogies) were to be moved to the frontier to protect the "weaker tribes behind," and Tipperas entering the Chittagong Hills from Hill Tipperah (now Tripura) were induced to settle in the far east, north of Barkal (Government of Bengal 1873).

35. It is interesting to see how selective this policy was, and how changeable official views of Bengalis. In the Hill Tracts of neighboring Arakan, Bengalis were welcome immigrants. Here the authorities did not perceive them as rapacious fleecers of ignorant tribals but as "timid." According to the Administration Report of 1877–78, plough cultivation should be stimulated at the foot of the hills around Myouktoung, and it should be carried out by "the timid Chittagonian immigrants who are commencing to arrive here" (*Administration Report, 1877–78*, 1879, 14). In the Chittagong Tracts, the Gurkhas were allowed to *jhum* for the first few years but then had to switch to plough cultivation. Lewin argued that "The introduction of Goorkha colonists into our scantily peopled Hill Tracts would, I think, be productive of unmixed good" (Government of Bengal 1872a). Other groups also were welcomed (Banthallees, Dangurs, and Assamese, for example) but "Bengallees are the only race which I would exclude; they have an unhappy bias at least. The classes of them that would be likely to

come in here have to [*sic*] usury litigation and fraud; they would be of no use in frontier protection, and they would worry the hillmen as they do so far as they are allowed at present" (Government of Bengal 1872b).

36. These and other products and the rates levied on them were itemized in a highly detailed manner (e.g., thirteen different kinds of timber were listed) in Revenue Department (1862). See also the annual reports of the Chittagong Hill Tracts (e.g., the one for 1878–79) in Government of Bengal (1879, 2–3).

37. One of these foothill markets, Bajalia on the Songu River, was described by Buchanan (1798, 88–89) as a "market place made by [Marma chief] Kaung-la-pru for the convenience of his people, who here exchange their Commodities for those of the Bengalese. A Mussulman attends here, and procures all the luxuries of Bengal, that are wanted by the Chief." During his trip Buchanan reported extensively on Bengali trade in the Chittagong Hills. See his observations in ibid., 34, 117, 118–19, and 134–35.

38. In the words of the Report on the Administration of the Chittagong Hill Tracts for 1875–76, "Hillmen dislike cultivation by the plough alone, because they cannot under that system grow cotton and the vegetables and fruits produced in jhooms....It is no light thing to change the method of life of an intensely conservative people" (Government of Bengal 1876, 29).

39. In 1869, Lewin remarked (p. 13) that "Throughout the whole of the Hill Tracts, I know no single instance of a hill man cultivating with the plough; indeed, it is rare to find a man earning his livelihood in any other way save by joom cultivation." Three years later, A. W. Cochrane, the officiating deputy commissioner of the Chittagong Hill Tracts, wrote: "I do not believe that the hill men will ever devote themselves to it [= plough cultivation] unless urged by emulation, and having the advantages brought clearly before them." He attributed this reluctance to the "dislike to change characteristic of them and other half or quarter civilized people" (Government of Bengal 1872b). For the later shift to plough cultivation, see Löffler (n.d.); and Sopher (1964).

40. The one sizeable factory in the Chittagong Hill Tracts was the Karnafuli Paper Mills, at Chandraghona, on the border with the plains. Although the mill used bamboo cut in the hills, employment there was a predominantly Bengali affair. According to the district gazetteer, hill people constituted less than .5 percent of the labor force of 3,920 "at one stage of its normal operation" (*Bangladesh District Gazetteers* 1971, 139; see also W. Mey 1980, appendix, iv).

41. The anomalous nature of this decision and the confusion surrounding the "Radcliffe Award" in the Chittagong Hills in August 1947 are discussed in

S. Chakma (1985–1986). See also Talukdar (1988, 47–58).

42. According to various sources, 650 sq. km. were flooded (5 percent of the total area of the Chittagong Hill Tracts), destroying 40 percent of the arable land. The gazetteer states that compensation was adequate but Almut and Wolfgang Mey disagree (see *Bangladesh District Gazetteers* 1971, 42–44, 99; *Population Census of Bangladesh 1974* 1979, 12; A. Mey 1979, 280–87; W. Mey 1980, 210–18; and Ahmad 1976, 123).

43. The national oil company, Petrobangla, reached a twenty-five-year agreement with Shell Petroleum Development for oil exploration in the Chittagong Hills and plains in 1981 (W. Mey 1984, 120–22).

44. In 1972, a delegation from the Chittagong Hills met with Bangladesh's new leader, Sheikh Mujibur Rahman. They demanded regional autonomy, retention of the Regulation of 1900, continuation of tribal chiefs' offices, and a ban on inmigration. Mujibur Rahman replied that fulfilling such demands would encourage ethnic feelings. According to Kazi Montu, he advised the delegation to go home and "do away with their ethnic identities." In 1975, during a visit to Rangamati, the district headquarters, he "addressed the tribals as brethren and told them to become Bengalis, to forget the colonial past and join the mainstream of Bengali culture. At this, the tribal people left the meeting." Successive governments in Bangladesh have not departed from this basic position, despite occasional gestures toward preserving "tribal culture" (Montu 1980, 1511; A. Chakma 1984, 58).

45. There had been one sizeable rebellion against British expansion between 1776 and 1787 (see Buchanan 1798; Serajuddin 1971, 54–55; Chakraborty 1977; and Islam 1983; see also Lewin 1984 [1870], 57). In 1864, a short-lived revolt by the minor chief, "Ougyphroo," broke out against the Marma chief. Ougyphroo thought that he was to be the new Marma chief "and that his dominion was to extend all over the Hill Tracts and from Cox's Bazaar to the Mugh Bazaar at Dacca" (Government of Bengal 1865).

46. The Bangladeshi government estimates the number of refugees to be much lower. In 1987, at a time when Indian officials talked of 50,000 refugees, the foreign secretary of Bangladesh claimed that there were only 29,920. Since then there have been various estimates, from 24,000 according to Bangladeshi officials (June 1989) and 45,380 according to an Indian observer (June 1988), to a figure of 70,000 claimed by the Jana Samhati Samiti party (JSS) in May 1989 (Bangladesh Groep Nederland 1988, 35; Kamaluddin 1989, 24; Survival International 1988, 3; Dewan 1989, 5; and "Fresh Influx in Tripura" 1989).

47. Bengali disdain for the people of the Chittagong Hills has been amply documented, beginning with Buchanan in 1798. By contrast, hill people's

feelings of superiority toward each other and toward Bengalis have rarely been recorded. See, however, Bernot's analysis of the ambivalent sentiments of Marmas toward their Bengali and Mru neighbors (L. Bernot 1967a, 748–50; see also the discussion in W. Mey 1980, 232–33).

48. In 1915, Rajmohon Dewan founded the Chakma Jubok Shomiti (Chakma Youth Association), and in 1928 this was followed by Ghonoshyam Dewan's Chakma Jubok Shongho (Chakma Youth Society). See S. Chakma [1985–86], 5–6).

49. These were the Hill Men Association (1946?), the Barbotyo Chottogram Jono Shomiti (People's Association of the Chittagong Hill Tracts, founded in 1947), and the Hill Tracts People's Organization (1950). See Rashid (1980, 28); and S. Chakma ([1985–86], 6–22).

50. Other organizations exist but appear to be much weaker or inactive. These organizations, most of which the JSS considers to be creatures of the Bangladeshi government, include the Pahari Jono Kolyan Shomiti (Hill People's Welfare Association), Tribal Convention, Marma Unnoyon Shongshod (Marma Development Council), Tripura Unnoyon Shongshod (Tripura Development Council), Hill District Co-ordination Committees, and the Headmen's Association. It is significant, however, that a recent protest against killings in Longodu, signed by representatives of several of these organizations "on behalf of the tribal people," also spoke of "genocidal attacks" and demanded the removal of all Bengali settlers from the Chittagong Hills (see *An Urgent Statement* 1989, 3; and Roy et al. 1989).

51. *An Urgent Statement* (1989, 1) speaks of the "national entity of the Jumma people" and claims: "The Jumma national unity and solidarity has been jeopardised dividing ten linguistically different Jumma national minorities into three Zilla Parishads." The third use of *national* apparently refers to Bangladesh. In 1985, the JSS had spoken of Juma *peoples* ("the Jumma Peoples were compelled to organize a Movement for ensuring their National Identity and the integrity of their Motherland") but significantly the plural was later dropped (Central Executive 1985, 2).

52. In the 1970s, Jummas were often equated with Buddhists because the majority of the hill people consider themselves to be Buddhists. More recently this has been played down in deference to non-Buddhist influences among them: for example, Hinduism among the Tippera, Christianity among the Lushai and Bawm-Zo, and local religions such as that of the Mru.

53. Although the Chakmas now speak a language closely akin to Chittagonian Bengali, they once spoke an Arakanese dialect that was already largely lost

when Buchanan visited them. Lewin (1984 [1870], 307) reported, however, that Arakanese was the lingua franca in the Chittagong Hills, "spoken and understood by every one," as late as the 1860s. The Chakma language was written in a script closely related to that of Burmese. During the twentieth century this was gradually replaced by Bengali script. The best introduction to the history of the Chakma language is in Löffler (1964). See also C. Chakma ([1984–85]); C. Chakma ([1987], 13); Choudhuri (1980); and Maniruzzaman (1984).

54. JSS resistance led to the discontinuation or suspension of various development projects in which the Bangladeshi government was involved (e.g., a Swedish-funded forestry project, an Australian-funded road-building project, and oil prospecting by Shell). An overview of the government development program can be found in Anti-Slavery Society (1984, 37–41); "Shantibahini Activities" (1986); Ali (1986, 5,7); and "Chittagong Hill Tracts" (1985).

55. For a general analysis of "invented traditions" and attendant reinterpretations of the past, see Hobsbawm and Ranger (1983, 1–14).

56. Several ethnic minorities live elsewhere in Bangladesh, though their numbers are smaller and they live more dispersed than do the Chittagong hill people. National organizations called the Bangladesh Adibashi Upojati Kolyan Federation (Bangladesh Aboriginal-Tribal Welfare Federation) and the Aboriginal Development Services of Bangladesh were established around 1980. Information can be found in their journals, *Matir Manush* (People of the Soil) and *Aronyok* (Forest People).

57. "But circumstances so led them [the Jumma peoples] that at last, a full decade ago, they had to take to Arms in demand of SELFDETERMINA-TION....The War of Selfdetermination shall run unabated" (Central Executive 1985, 2).

58. Amnesty International reports that the term *miscreant* is "officially used for *Shanti Bahini* forces." Though they also are frequently called "terrorists," the authorities no longer dismiss them as simple criminals. In the words of Major General Abdus Salam, area commander of the Chittagong Hill Tracts, as reported in the Bangladesh press, "We are not fighting just a bandit group. The insurgents are really quite deep into their mission and they are organized and motivated" (Amnesty International 1988, 5; Naser 1990, 8).

59. The cultural and political problems surrounding the search for an acceptable generic name for all the "Chin-Kuki-Mizo-Zoumi" groups inhabiting the area east of the Chittagong Hills should alert us to the potential limitations of the use of "Jumma" in the Chittagong Hills (see Kamkhenthang 1988, esp. 1–11).

60. "A part of Zoram lies in the eastern part of the Chittagong Hill Tracts of Bangladesh....The Zo clans in Bangladesh are Bawmzo, Asho (Khyang), Khami, Lusei, Masho (Mru), and Pankhu" (Vumson 1986, 316). See also Bhaumik and Vanlalruata (1988, 64); and Menon (1988, 63–77).

61. Similarly, the ethnic consequences of migration are usually studied among inmigrants; the Chittagong Hills case reveals that this is insufficient, for it may result in critical ethnic change among the "receiving" population (Fishman 1977, 15–57; Royce 1982, 108–41).

62. Anthony Smith mentions six main strategies. In the Jumma movement the dominant one is "autonomism" but "separatism" is a second option (Smith 1981, 15–17). See also Fishman (1977, 35–38).

63. The cultural diversity of the Chittagong hill groups (with their separate links to Arakan, Chin country, Tripura, and Bengal) is greater than elsewhere in the mountain range, where overarching collective identities were usually available for diverse cultural groups from an early age. The Naga identity is a case in point; it helped overcome local antagonisms and organize resistance in the far north from a much earlier date, first against the British and then against the independent Indian and Burmese states. Similarly, the Jharkhand identity was first used in Chhota Nagpur and Santal Parganas in 1938, and followed the much older concept of *diku* ('alien oppressor'), which had fired earlier rebellions. However, the Jharkhandi identity is even now "an extremely amorphous concept." There are many historical, political, and economic differences between the Jharkand and Jumma movements (e.g., the role of the Jharkand urban middle class, the activities of Christian missionaries, extensive "nontribal" support, and close links with all-India political parties from the 1930s). See Dubey (1982); *Naga Nation* (1986); Singh (1982); and Sengupta (1982).

64. The distinction between *ethnic group* and *nation* becomes rather arbitrary in acute conflicts: "when nations stand in a conflictive relationship with one another, the confrontation bears many of the earmarks of ethnic conflict" (Royce 1982, 84).

65. On the "saliency" of ethnicity, see Fishman (1977, 32–34).

Notes to Chapter 8

1. "Masawat-i-Muhammadi" is "equality" as preached by the prophet, the basis of the slogan "Islamic Socialism."

2. "Nizam-i-Mustafa" is the ideal order established by the prophet Muhammad and the four Caliphs.

3. For instance, the Eighth Amendment of 1985 gave wide powers to the president and made valid all actions and legislative measures undertaken under martial law.

4. The Islamic Republic of Pakistan covers 310,403 square miles according to the *Pakistan Statistical Yearbook, 1990* (Government of Pakistan 1991).

5. *Sardar* is a term, possibly of Persian origin, meaning 'chief' or 'commander'. It was used in the British Indian army as a title for Indian officers.

6. Brahui syntax is supposed to be Dravidian in origin but most of the vocabulary is borrowed from Baluchi (Moore 1980).

7. See *Pakistan Times* (Lahore), 20–21 September 1981; and Dastarac and Levent (1984).

8. See Baluchistan Cover Story (1986); and Lifschultz (1983).

9. At that time about forty thousand military personnel were serving in the Middle East on six- to twelve-month rotations. It is estimated that from 1977 to 1985 almost 60 percent of the Pakistan armed forces received increased allowances for serving abroad.

10. See *The MERIP* (Middle East Research and Information Project, New York), July-September 1984; and Dastarac and Levent (1985).

11. The "warm-waters theory" has been used to interpret all of the various Baluch insurrections. A research memo by T. L. Hughes (November 1964, for the U.S. Department of State—Director of Intelligence and Research, III E-4 [INRI]), concluded that "There is no evidence that the USSR intends to supply [Baluchistan] with Soviet arms in the near future, reports of arms shipments remain unconfirmed."

12. See *Enzyklopaedia des Islām*, (1913–36).

13. See Letter of Lord Salisbury to Lytton (22 August 1876) in Dodwell (1964, 414–15).

14. In 1877, the Baluchistan Agency was established with headquarters at Quetta. It included Kalat State and its dependencies. In 1879, the British Crown assumed direct administration of the Sibi and Pishin assigned districts. In 1887, the Treaty of Gandammak incorporated the assigned districts into British India as the province of British Baluchistan. In 1890, Bori, Zhob, and Khetran (nominally linked to Afghanistan) were brought under British administration within the Baluchistan Agency, as were Chagai and West Sinjrani in 1896.

15. In 1893, the Mortimer Durand Line was accepted by Abdur Rahman as the Indo-Afghan boundary in return for subsidies. The Quetta railways were

extended to Nuski in order to protect the border.

16. On Baluchistan and the British cabinet mission, see Jalal (1985, 190, 196–97).

17. See Memorandum on States' Treaties and Paramountcy presented by the Cabinet Mission to the Nawab of Bhopal, reproduced in Mansergh (1977, 522–24). See also letter of Mr. Jinnah to Lord Pettrick-Lawrence, in Principles to be Agreed as Our Offer (ibid., 516–17). In the summer of 1947, Jinnah declared the right of the states to choose their own future, although the case of Baluchistan was not specifically mentioned (Rafique 1973, 427).

18. On 14 October 1955, the "one unit" constitutional scheme merged the four provinces of western Pakistan into a single unit. This triggered a nationalist uprising in Baluchistan, which lasted until the amnesty of 1967.

19. See "Pakistan's Civil War" (1975); and Dastarac and Dersen (1976).

20. On the Baluch nationalists and the *sardari* system, see a special section in *The War in Baluchistan: Strategies for Liberation* (Baluch People's Liberation Front 1976).

21. The results of the October 1990 elections for the provincial assembly in Baluchistan were JWP, nine members; IDA, seven members; JUI, six members; PNP, five members; PMAP, two members; and PDA (PPP), one member. A few seats were postponed. The results for the national assembly were JWP, two members; IDA, two members; JUI, two members; PNP, two members; PMAP, one member; and PPP, two members.

22. Mumtaz Bhutto and Hafiz Pirzada founded the Sindi Baloch and Pushtoon Front with the initial backing of Ataullah Mengal. See their manifesto, *A Confederal Constitution for Pakistan: An Outline* (1987).

23. See an interview with Akbar Bugti published in *The Herald* (Karachi), February 1989, 127–29.

Notes to Chapter 9

1. The celebrated spy for the British East India Company, Kirkpatrick (1975 [1811], 50), who arrived in Nepal in 1791 in the guise of an intemediary during the Nepal China war, defined the Tarai as "marshy lands, and tarai is sometimes applied to the flat lying below the hills in the interior parts of Nepal, as well as to the low tract bordering immediately on the Company's northern frontier." Today the general meaning of the word *tarai,* or *tarrai,* is "land at the foot of the mountain, often wet and swampy land" (Gaige 1970).

2. It has been assumed that the aboriginal groups had some resistance to this malady (Nesfield 1867). Following Bista (1987 [1967], 118), the Tarai was described as "tropical malaria areas, infested with wild animals such as elephants, rhinoceros, bears, tigers and poisonous snakes." Of all these threats, malaria was considered the most serious.

3. There are some important distinctions between general Indian and Nepali conditions, the major ones being that the Gorkhali regime of Nepal successfully kept the British at bay, and the fact that there was a large Buddhist influence in Nepal.

4. This is the general tradition claimed by many ethnic groups in Nepal. Some Brahmin and Tharu groups claim that they came from Chittore in India. Such claims may be useful in caste climbing, and Nesfield (1867, 5) writes that "there is scarcely any hunting tribe or caste in Upper India which has not set up a similar claim." It is still an open question whether the groups actually migrated northward, as they claim, or whether only cultural traditions shifted as the northerners made higher status claims. Both real migration, as described in nineteenth-century sources, and cultural "acquisitions" or borrowings may have taken place simultaneously (see Allen 1969).

5. Local tradition as to the names of gods (i.e., Parbati) and certain cultural and linguistic traits can be taken as substantiating this claim (see ibid.)

6. Tucci (1956, 60–61) found that from the eleventh to the thirteenth centuries the Brahmins founded an empire of their own in the west. This Khas empire may have included a large part of western Tibet and extended as far as Dullu and Kaskikot in western Nepal.

7. The World Health Organisation, in cooperation with His Majesty's Government and other international agencies, eliminated malaria with an antimalaria campaign begun in the Tarai in 1958.

8. The Newars are the original inhabitants of the Kathmandu Valley. Tourists often come to Nepal to see the magnificent ruins of Newari culture, as well as the living trade cultures of Baktapur and Kirtipur. Despite having been conquered by the Gorkhali in 1769, they have retained much influence in the new Nepali state. In the eighteenth century, the Newars asked the British East India Company for help in their struggle against the Gorkha people and their expansive king, Prithvi Narayan Shah. However, General Kinlock was taught a lesson, as the malaria in the Tarai took a large toll among his men, and the Gorkhas further reduced his forces to under a third before his retreat. While this event changed the history of Nepal, the Newars held onto their power by monopolizing modern trade (especially with the British and other foreigners). The Gorkhas also united Nepal as one kingdom and effectively kept the British out until the war of 1814.

As the first group to arrive in an area later conquered, the Newars must be classified as indigenous in the original sense of the word. However, as the Newars today are among the educated elite and play an important economic part in the development of Nepal, it is doubtful that they would accept this identification.

The Tibeto-Burmese groups traditionally monopolized the middle hills but they were displaced by the invasion of the Brahminic groups. A few groups, such as the Limbu, however, succeeded in acquiring what must be considered something close to reservation status through separate land agreements concluded with the Nepali state. Such *kipat* (communal land ownership) systems were, according to Regmi (1976, 87),

> a relic of the former form of land control which communities of Mongoloid or autochthonous tribal origin established in areas occupied by them before the immigration of racial groups of Indo-Aryan origin.

Regmi further refers to similarities, in this instance to the Mundu Community Revenue agreement in Chhotangpur in India (1869–1908), the gist of it being that individual or feudal rights were granted to newcomers, while traditional rights were only respected when they could be considered communal. Today the Tibeto-Burmese peoples still retain a majority in the middle hill region of Nepal, where they constitute five large ethnic divisions (the Tamang, the Kiranti [Limbu, Rai], the Maggars, the Gurung, and the Thakali) in addition to several smaller groups.

The Tamang, located in the Kathmandu Valley, is the largest Tibeto-Burmese group in Nepal. Probably it is also one of the most oppressed, as it is located close to the center of the state system and Brahminic influence. The Maggars and the Gurung, who traditionally have been conscripted as "Gurkha" soldiers, have fared better and are today rapidly becoming the Nepali middle class. They also share with the Thakali an adaptive and rather pragmatic view of religion. The northern Gurung call themselves Buddhist, while the southern are Hindu. The Thakali is a rather well-off group, which to a large degree monopolizes the trade with Tibet and today lives off the tourists who make the "round the Anapurna trek." Today neither of these latter groups seem to be especially exploited nor are they excluded from the decision-making realm in relation to the state apparatus. In this respect they have also recently begun to cultivate the rich and fertile Tarai area and thus dominate the indigenous inhabitants of these regions.

The same problem of self-identification applies to the Bote people. Today, as well as traditionally, several of these groups, which live along the Tibetan border, consider themselves part of the large Buddhist tradition of the north. However, after the border between China and Nepal was closed in the early

1960s, and following the invasion of Tibet by the Chinese, their traditional focus was eliminated, resulting in severe marginalization. Today one may say that the total Buddhist-Tibetan population constitutes a very important indigenous element in Asia. In this context it will suffice to mention such groups as the Sherpas, the Lopas, the Manangba, and the Dolpo people, and suggest that they should be the focus of separate discussions.

9. Below these pure castes were legally placed the so-called impure castes (untouchables), or "water unacceptable castes," the *pani na calne jat*. In the Tarai of the Far West, these groups were often economically better off than the indigenous Tharu groups (see Gurung and Skar 1988).

10. Nepal is divided into five regions: the Central, Eastern, Western, Mid-Western, and Far Western. The Far Western region consists of the two zones (counties) of Mahakali and Seti.

11. The military advantage, as well as the social value, of such a road is obvious. Today the drive to Delhi is seven hours from Danghardi in the Far West, and the area is without connection to Kathmandu in the rainy season (i.e., without going by land via Indian territories, a journey of two days). The value of the road to indigenous groups will be rather a different matter, however, as large strips of land have been cleared and much virgin forest has disappeared forever.

12. In this war the Nepali-Gorkha kingdom lost much Tarai land but it regained those portions in the West and Far West in the negotiations led by Prime Minister Bhinsen Thapa. Since 1816, the Nepali-Indian borders have remained the same.

13. Today all Dangora Tharu people bear the family name of Chaudary.

14. The Jimidari can be compared to the *encomiendas* of the Spanish in South America. In both cases, those holding land grants from the king had specially defined responsibilities in relation to the indigenous inhabitants.

15. For a discussion of the relation between Indian Zamidars and the Nepali Jimidars, see Regmi (1976). Foreign workers were encouraged to come as sharecroppers under the Jimidars. Thus, many Indian peasants came, especially from the province of Bihar, "which suffered from severe land shortages and the aftermath of a serious famine in the late 1760's and early 1770's" (Shresta 1990, 173). Settlers were also attracted from Bengal, after the British in 1793 introduced the system of revenue collection called "permanent settlements," with land ownership vested in the Zamidars and no land rights for tenants. The system of the Nepali Jimidars seemed better to the Indians, as basically they only saw the Jimidari (or his messenger, the Potwari) once a year.

16. In the colonization process a person should first register with the CDO (chief district officer) and then with the zonal commissioner. After this, the application would be forwarded to the ministry and finally it would be sent for implementation to the Nepal Punarvaas (Resettlement) Company (NRC), a national agency established in 1964. Fewer and fewer settlers today bother to register with this corrupt entity. As a 1980 NRC document states (quoted in Shresta 1990, 191),

> In many districts of Terai reckless felling of the trees for disorganised settlement began to extend everywhere. Such encroachment led to the rapid deterioration of the valuable forests of the Terai. The government realized that if such process continued for some years it would disturb even the ecological balance of the country.

17. I shall at this point turn directly to material I gathered in Nepal, during short periods of fieldwork in 1989 and 1990, among the Rana Tharu of the Nepali Tarai. This study was made possible by a grant from the Norwegian Research Council.

18. The *kurmas* usually are not referred to by specific names but are differentiated on sight by the arrangement of god constellations and by door arrangement on the east side of the main house. Each house god receives a special bump in front of the kitchen door, and by differentiating between square and round bumps, and by their frequency and numbers, anyone can see which households are related in the village context. The *kurmas* function as reference groups for marriage, and the most able-bodied men in the different *kurmas* represent the village in the village council.

19. Note the debate on Crow-Omaha systems in Barnes (1984).

20. The men do go out for short hunting trips, to make "expeditions" to the mountains for thatching grass and the white chalk stones used for coloring houses, or when they work for a *kisan* (landlord) somewhere else. With regard to divorce, a woman may leave her husband with any man who can repay the husband the brideprice.

21. Such institutions as wife capture basically functioned better across national borders than within one jurisdiction.

22. Today these latter families own approximately 25 percent of all land in Kailali but the land ratio is better than that found in Nepalganj, further west, where five families own approximately 75 percent of the land.

23. Currently the Forestry Department is running a program under the New Forestry Master Plan (1988) to "reorient its staff," which is seen by many as too corrupt. However, in this reorientation program the central issue may still be hedged.

24. Today Nepal is a raw exporter of topsoil, as the monsoon rains sweep away approximately 240 million cubic meters of earth every year, creating increasingly worse floods along the Ganges. This also contributes to the problems of Bangladesh, as the Indian dam at the Farakh Barrage redistributes the water to the progressively silted-up Calcutta harbor.

25. Slavery, according to the first convention (League of Nations 1926), is defined as "the status or the condition of a person over whom any or all the powers attaching to the right of ownership are exercised." This convention and the later amendments to it (United Nations 1956) have been ratified by Nepal. Debt bondage, according to the conventions, is "the status or condition arising from a pledge by a debtor of his personal services or those of a third person under his control as security for debt, *where the value reasonably assessed of those services rendered is not applied toward the liquidation of the debt and the nature of those services are not respectively limited and defined*" (ibid., Article 1; my emphasis).

26. Serfdom, according to the UN declaration, is "the tenure of land whereby the tenant is by law, custom or agreement bound to live and labor on land belonging to another person and render some determinate services to such other person, whether for reward or not, and is not free to change his status" (ibid.).

27. Indeed, as Tharu domestic slaves live in the same Tharu household and have close contact with other family members, there seems to be a pattern of sexual abuse.

28. A rich Tharu family may have two or three *kamaiya* working for them. But this also depends on the developmental cycle of the "host" household. In the first stages of a rich family's cycle (i.e., just after marriage and the establishment of the household), there will be more unproductive than productive young members of the household. This is especially true since relatively rich, landholding Tharus today tend to have two wives of approximately the same age (or with an age difference of only five to ten years). At this stage the household traditionally will acquire *kamaiya* from others but as their own sons and daughters grow they will "sell off" a family or two. As the host household ages, labor is needed from the outside again, and new *kamaiya* contracts are acquired. Today fewer *kamaiya* contracts are being made between the Tharu, and there is a tendency for the new ones to be more temporary than those of previous times.

29. As the number of members of untouchable castes are low in the Far West, and as these generally have a specialty skill, they are in a better position to negotiate trade agreements with the dominant population.

30. In this respect, we are reminded of Aristotle's treatise on the "natural slave" (Politics i. 1253), which states that "from the hour of their birth some are

marked out for subjection, others for rule," analogous to the subordination of the body to the soul and of animals to men (1254a-b).

31. On the Paharia estates a local overseer, the Agua, watches the Tharu workers. The Agua is traditionally a Dangora Tharu who was brought from Dang in the Western Zone to the Far West by the estate owner. Under land reform, the Aguas were given part of the estate land in name, but the slave practices continued as before. Sagild (1988) reports from the Getta area that people turn up blind at the missionary hospital because estate owners do not let them take a day off to have their medical problems treated.

32. The prohibition of parties and organizations with possible political intentions was an integral policy of the now-defunct *panchayat* system. Even in the election of May 1991, the principle of abolishing ethnic parties was adhered to, as the nation feared an outbreak of ethnically linked riots.

33. The Tharu educational venture was for a time considered to be aligned with the Communist Party, as people saw it in the Tulsipur context. The leaders of the movement refused to be backed by any political party. As the old *panchayat* party would basically not be an option, and as the Paharia in the rural area all vote Congress, one choice for the Tharu would seem to lie with the Communist Party. However, by making such a choice the ethnic and cultural component in their struggle could run the risk of becoming blurred in favor of the general class-oriented categories. One interesting new formation is "The Sadhlawa Party," a Tarai-based party catering primarily to the Indian emigrant. This party may in the future widen its base to include other Tarai dwellers such as the Tharu.

34. In Dang there are now 37 night schools with 2,500 students located in different Tharu villages. Of this number, according to a conversation with a local organizer, Dilli Bahadur Chaudary, female students comprise more than 60 percent.

Notes to Chapter 10

My main research in China was conducted between June and December of 1989 on a Hmong (Miao) village in Sichuan, although research visits to other minority areas in southern China were also conducted in 1986–91. For assistance with the research in Sichuan, I should like to thank the British Academy, as well as the Centre of South-East Asian Studies at the School of Oriental and African Studies (University of London) and the Sichuan Minorities Research Institute as affiliating agencies. For comments on this paper, I am most grateful to Robbie Barnett and John Dolfin.

1. On the ambiguity of the Chinese notion of culture (*wenhua*) in also refer-

ring to "progress," see Lemoine (1989b).

2. See Fan Wenlan (1953). These points are also discussed by Moseley (1965); Hsieh Jiann (1986). For a recent discussion, see Thoraval (forthcoming). Also, on the notion of *minzu,* see Harrell (1989); and Wu (1989).

3. This point came up in discussions at a conference on *minzu wenti* convened in Beijing, 16–20 May 1990, by the Central Minority Affairs Commission, which I attended.

4. Four hundred ethnonyms were originally submitted for recognition, of which 260 came from Yunnan.

5. Figures and statistics are from the 1982 National Census unless otherwise specified ([National Census] 1985).

6. Nongovernmental organizations of indigenous peoples in China (where the category of "indigenous peoples" is not recognized) are not permitted, and even academic societies for the study of minority peoples are discouraged for fear of potentially damaging political consequences. This means that international representation of Chinese minorities in China can only take place through official channels. China has sent observers to the United Nations Working Group on Indigenous Populations, and has participated in the Independent Commission on International Humanitarian Issues, established in 1983. But, while formal complaints have been made regarding China's treatment of minorities before such international bodies such as the U.S. Congress, the UN General Assembly, and the European Parliament, given current sensitivities within China on the issue of human rights, it is unlikely that any more direct representation of minorities will be permitted, either at the United Nations or within other organizations such as the World Council of Indigenous Peoples.

Religious and cultural fora provide better opportunities for minority participation than do those the Chinese government sees as purely political. Catholic and Protestant organizations provide channels of communication with the minorities of China, although their scope for political activity is limited. Islamic organizations provide still more functional links. A Haj committee is allowed to travel overseas, and delegates from the China Islamic Association have attended meetings of the Islamic Affairs Grand Council. Now that China may become a member of the World Council of Churches, it remains to be seen what place will be accorded to the representation of Chinese minorities by this organization. It is reported that a delegation from the Tibet Autonomous Region government is to visit the United States, and this may mark a major shift toward increasing cultural and ethnic representation overseas (Robert Barnett, personal communication, 15 August 1991).

7. See Harrell (1989) on the Yi, and Hsieh Jiann (1984) on the Samei.

8. The classic account of these is Fei Xiaotong (1981), following Lin Yaohua (1956).

9. On China's Constitution as it affects the national minorities, see Hsieh Jiann (1986); and Heberer (1989).

10. I visited this area in December 1987 and November 1988 with the assistance of the Hunan Minorities Research Institute, the International Association for Yao Studies, the Department of Anthropology at the Chinese University of Hong Kong, and the Centre d'Anthropologie de l'Asie du Sud-est et le Monde Insulindien. Currently, 50 to 80 percent of Jiangyong *xian* (peasants) are applying for national minority status on the basis of the womens' script and the dialect spoken in ten surrounding counties, although the dialect appears to be a Han Chinese one. See Gong Zhebing (1986a, 1986b); and Chiang Wei (1989).

11. A total of 879,200 persons are listed as not yet officially classified but this figure does not include all of those who have applied for recognition in recent years. Recent figures suggest a 35.5 percent increase in the national minority population since the 1982 census (*China Now* no. 135, Winter 1990).

12. Fei Xiaotong 1988, 1. The notion of cultural autonomy familiar in UN pronouncements also merits further consideration here, since it partly implies an idealized image of isolated ethnic groups enacting their distinct cultural traditions in a unique and necessarily remote solitude. Not only is it true that there has been a great deal of cultural interchange between most of the ethnic groups in China, as official publications are at pains to point out, but the notion fails to account for the many cases in which cultural and ethnic identity do not coincide (as with the Dong-speaking Yao, the Bouyei-influenced Miao, or the Miao-speaking Tujia) just as the Stalinist criteria of a "nationality" (in which the notion of *minzu* is rooted) fail to account for such cases (Wu 1989; Harrell 1989). I prefer to refer to cultural integrity rather than autonomy for this reason, defined as the means and ability of a group to determine its own future in accordance with its preferred cultural traditions, which implies a measure of group self-consciousness. To their credit, Chinese nationality experts do add the criterion of self-consciousness to the other Stalinist criteria of "nationalities."

13. Troops (of which there may be up to a quarter of a million in Tibet), political prisoners, and those classified as temporary workers are not included in the Chinese statistical data. According to Robert Barnett (personal communication, 1991), the Chinese population in the Tibet Autonomous Region is generally an urban not a rural phenomenon.

14. Conflicts between what may be seen as a relatively enlightened minorities policy and the strengths of local nationalism, conservatism, and prejudice are particularly acute among those cadres who are also members of minority groups. Often highly Sinicized and committed to Maoist ideals, yet with lingering loyalties to the culture of their own ethnic group, the distance between minority cadres and those of the same nationality who work manually for a living can be as great as those between minority and Han cadres. Yet it is often in their hands that the implementation of local policy lies. Much has been written about the ability of culture brokers to exploit the boundaries of different cultures to their own advantage. Yet often the more Sinicized members of local ethnic groups, who may include rich farmers and entrepreneurs as well as cadres, are at the mercy of a double set of cultural obligations. The minority cadre who takes part in a local funeral may experience an agony of role conflict.

15. *Cultural Survival Quarterly,* 12 January 1988; *The Independent,* 14 January 1988; *The Observer,* 12 August 1990; *China News Analysis,* 1 November 1990; *South China Morning Post,* 26 November 1990, 5 April 1991, 6 April 1991, 21 May 1991.

Notes to Chapter 11

1. Adoption of the historic name Myanmar by the present government in 1989 has yet to become widely accepted, and the name is not used hereafter. For similar reasons, the new transliteration of many indigenous words, e.g., "Bamars" for "Burmans" or "Kayins" for "Karens," is not employed.

2. Many of the arguments advanced in this paper are developed more fully in *Burma: Insurgency and the Politics of Ethnicity* (Smith 1991), which examines the roots of insurgency and ethnic conflict in Burma.

3. SLORC Press Release, 19 October 1990.

4. For a summary of the opium problem in Burma, see U.S. General Accounting Office (1989).

5. For recent eyewitness accounts of travels in the minority war zones, see Falla (1991) in Karen territory; and Linter (1990).

6. Brang Seng, interview with the author, 17 July 1990, Manerplaw, Burma.

7. These include Tatmadaw, MPs of the NLD and other newly elected parties, four remnant allied forces from the CPB, six armed forces from the DAB (some of which signed peace treaties with the SLORC in early 1991), the

Tailand Revolutionary Council of Khun Sa, and four breakaway defector armies from the CPB headed by the ten-thousand-strong United Wa State Army, which, with the SLORC's apparent encouragement, was trying to seize control of the opium trade from Khun Sa.

Note to Chapter 12

I would like to thank Hoang Ti Lee and Tran Van Duy for their help with translations from Vietnamese.

Note to Chapter 13

1. Initial fieldwork among the Chewong was carried out during eighteen months in 1977–79. It was funded by the Social Science Research Council (UK) and undertaken under the auspices of the Jabatan Hal Ehwal Orang Asli. Return visits were made in 1981, 1990, and 1991. The present paper has been read and commented upon by Kirk Endicott and Hood Moham-mad Salleh. Much of the recent literature on the current state of the Orang Asli was made available to me by Colin Nicholas and Tony Williams-Hunt.

2. Recently (in 1994), the Malaysian government has set up a commission to look into the situation of the Orang Asli. Its brief is to make suggestions for legislation and other concrete measures that will help to protect their rights and improve the quality of their lives. It is to be hoped that this represents a first step in the right direction.

Notes to Chapter 14

1. Dayak is a general term for the non-Muslim, non-Malay indigenes of Borneo. It covers a large number of separately named ethnic groups. The derivation of the term is uncertain, although in various indigenous Bornean languages it is used to refer to people of the upstream or interior regions of the island. Terms such as Daya, Dayeh, Dayuh, and other variants occur in several Bornean ethnonyms, including Kedayan, Kendayan, Bidayuh, and Lun Dayeh. Certainly it was commonly used in a pejorative sense by coastal populations such as the Malays, and by Europeans, to denote the "tribal" peoples of the interior who were considered to be culturally, economically, and politically backward. However, as a general referent to distinguish themselves, from the Malays in particular, the term has gained acceptance among the non-Muslim indigenes, so much so that it is now used as a means of forging new political identities. In the 1980s, for example, a new indigenous political party was established in Sarawak and given the name

Parti Bansa Dayak Sarawak (Sarawak Dayak Peoples' Party). Sometimes the general term Dayak is extended to the small groups of forest nomads in interior Borneo. But commonly these hunter-gatherers are distinguished from settled Dayak agriculturalists and are referred to by the cover name Punan, or in Sarawak usually Penan.

2. There is no constitutional definition of *bumiputra*. Yet the word is used widely in political and public discourse. The relevant constitutional terms are Malay, *native*, and *aborigine*.

3. The complexity of the definition of *native* and the special arrangements implemented to protect them is further illustrated by the non-Muslim, non-Malay, aboriginal populations (Orang Asli) of the Peninsula. Like the Malays and the natives of Borneo, they can claim a long-established association with territories in what is now Malaysia. But they are classified separately in the Constitution as "aborigines" (Groves 1964, 201; Sheridan and Groves 1967, 92). In practice, the Orang Asli, a general term that also covers a number of differently named groups, are gradually being assimilated into the category "*bumiputra*" but constitutionally they are dealt with independently under Article 8, Clause 5(c). Article 8 makes a general provision that all persons are equal before the law but Clause 5(c) states that this does not invalidate or prohibit "any provision for the protection, wellbeing or advancement of the aboriginal peoples of the Malay Peninsula (including the reservation of land) or the reservation to aborigines of a reasonable proportion of suitable positions in the public service" (Malaysia 1964, 4; Hooker n.d., 28-29; Mohamed Suffian 1972, 246).

4. There are some definitional variations in different state enactments dealing with Malay reserved land. For example, in Kedah and Perlis the category "Malay" can specifically include Arabs (ibid., 248).

5. The only state land-development board that pursues this strategy, in part, is the Sarawak Land Consolidation and Rehabilitation Authority (SALCRA). For legal purposes this body is treated like a "native" and can deal in and develop native land in situ without changing the status of the land rights. However, while I believe that the SALCRA concept is a more appropriate one than resettlement strategies, the authority has been plagued by problems of implementation. Again, as a large-scale enterprise, there are problems of coordination, local management, and relations with local farmers (King 1986c).

Notes to Chapter 15

1. For purposes of this paper, the phrase "eastern Indonesia" is best construed loosely as the eastern part of the Republic of Indonesia. There are two

important exceptions. The paper needs to distinguish from time to time between the reasonably normal political situation in eastern Indonesia and the exceptional situation in East Timor and Irian Jaya. The fact that there are independence movements in the latter two areas is also sufficient reason not to include them. The paper also explains that the colonial history of East Timor and the cultural history of Irian Jaya distinguish them from eastern Indonesia. "Eastern Indonesia" coincides essentially with the provinces of Nusa Tenggara Timur (the eastern Lesser Sundas) and Maluku (the Moluccas), especially in the latter case the southern Moluccas. Because of the author's familiarity with the area, most examples are taken from Flores and Timor. Because East Timor is linguistically and culturally part of eastern Indonesia, but not so in terms of political history, it assumes an awkward position in this paper, for which the author requests the indulgence of readers.

2. Kubu is a pejorative Malay name resented by those to whom it is applied—remnant nomadic peoples, calling themselves by various ethnic names, residing along the east coast of Sumatra (LeBar 1972, 46).

3. A recent *IWGIA Newsletter* contains a statement by the Organisasi Papua Merdeka seeking recognition for the Indigenous Peoples of West Papua (Irian Jaya) and restitution under the terms of the Universal Declaration on Rights of Indigenous Peoples (Organisasi Papua Merdeka 1990). Clearly it is less difficult to apply this category to the peoples of Irian Jaya than to those of eastern Indonesia.

4. Cultural differences also fail to correspond to racial and language boundaries. The Fataluku at the eastern end of East Timor speak a non-Austronesian language but their social organization (involving generalized exchange of women or asymmetric marriage alliance) has the same form as that found among speakers of the Austronesian languages Lamaholot and Kédang in the Solor Archipelago (Campagnolo 1979, 30–31).

5. The Portuguese and Dutch colonial powers sometimes must have conformed to this pattern, without knowing it.

Notes to Chapter 16

1. In a similar vein, Groeneveldt cites a Chinese report of 1618, which claims that trading could not begin until a figure he calls "the king" appeared: "When they see their king, they (the Timorese) sit down on the ground with folded hands," prior to the commencement of transactions (Groeneveldt 1880, 116).

2. The term *Topasse* originates either from the group's role as interpreters (from the Dravidian word *tuppasi*, meaning 'interpreter') or from their mode of dress (from the Indian *topee walas*, meaning 'hat-men'). See Boxer (1947, 1).

3. Several ethnolinguistic groups in East Timor were studied by anthropologists during the ten- to fifteen-year period preceding the Indonesian invasion. Their work has provided rich, detailed, contemporary and historical knowledge of the organization and cultures of the Fatuluku, Mambai, Ema, Bunaq, Makassai, and Tetum groups. These supplement the excellent study of the Atoni of West Timor conducted by Schulte Nordholt (1971). See, in particular, the writings of Traube (1980, 1986); Berthe (1961, 1972); Friedberg (1980); Campagnolo (1973, 1979); Clamagirand (1980); Renard-Clamagirand (1982); Françillon (1967, 1980); Forman (1978, 1980); Hicks (1972a, 1972b, 1976); Lazarowitz (1980); Metzner (1977); Ormeling (1956); and Cowan (1963). For a survey of some of these authors' findings, see Barnes (1980). In my descriptions of Timorese society I have tried to outline what I consider to be the significant shared features of these groups despite the diversity of many of their economic, social, political, and cultural characteristics (see also Gray 1984). Concerning the economic structure of Portuguese Timor, see Telkamp (1979). For the linguistic picture and recent linguistic develpments, see Capell (1944, 1972); and Thomaz (1981).

4. This figure is taken from a report published in the *Argus* (Melbourne), August 1912.

5. A notable exception to this is found in Dunn (1983, 22–27).

6. See, for example, Callinan (1953).

7. For analyses and data on this process, see Hill (1978, 43–51).

8. Despite its modification, this "socialization" remained a general aim for some months after the coup. Elements of it were retained in General Antonio de Spinola's notion of a Lusitanian Federation to which the governor of East Timor, Colonel Lemos Pires, appointed in November 1974, subscribed. Pires was given instructions to the effect that, no matter what the political outcome, he should try to preserve the legacy of Portuguese culture and traditions in East Timor.

9. Concerning Fretilin, see Capizzi, Hill, and Macey (1976). In addition to the ASDT and the UDT, there were four other parties: the Indonesian-sponsored Associacão Popular Democratica Timorense (Apodeti), the Klibur Oan Timor Aswan (or KOTA, literally, 'The Sons of the Mountain Warrior Dogs'), the Partido Trabalhista (Labor Party), and the Associacão Democratica Integracão Timor-Leste Australia (ADLITA). Apart from

Apodeti, which drew support from the border villages of a *liurai* named Guilherme Goncalves; from a small number of administrators, all of whom came from Dili; and from the capital's small Moslem community, the other parties never had more than minuscule support.

10. Knowledge obtained in developing these treatments was used widely in Fretilin-held areas after the invasion, particularly from 1975 to 1978, as refugees subsequently testified (see Taylor 1991).

11. Apart from visiting journalists, detailed reports were published following visits by delegations from the Australian Trades Union Movement and the Australian Parliament, in May and September of 1975, respectively. The International Red Cross (IRC) also visited before and after the UDT coup attempt and produced a report.

12. Numbers of Indonesian troops in East Timor during this period varied from thirty to eighty thousand men.

13. For detailed discussions and refugee testimonies on this issue, see ibid.

14. For the most recent reports on the condition of Fretilin, see articles written by Robert Domm following his meeting with Fretilin leader Kay Rala Xanana Gusmao in September 1990. In particular, see *Sydney Morning Herald*, 25 October 1990; and *Indonesian News Service* (Maryland, USA), 1 November 1990.

15. This, of course, did not prevent these *pagar betis* campaigns from being accompanied by the most brutal actions committed by Indonesian troops (see, for example, Anonymous 1988).

16. During the visits of the Pope (October 1989) and U.S. Ambassador to Indonesia, John Monjo (January, 1990), demonstrations against integration were led by young people in Dili. A similar pattern could be observed recently during a demonstration held at the end of a Catholic Mass commemorating the fiftieth anniversary of the founding of the Dili diocese. The Mass, attended by Monsignor Canalini, the Apostolic Nuncio in Jakarta, and the governor of East Timor, Mario Carrascalao, took place on 4 September 1990.

Notes to Chapter 17

1. This figure will likely be updated to around 60 million in the 1991 census report.

2. These groups are otherwise referred to as "Ethnic Minorities," "Tribal

Filipinos," and "Native Citizens" (Katutubong Mamamayan), among others.

3. Fifty-nine "better-known minority ethno-linguistic groups" are listed in Tribal Forum (1983).

4. "Filipino" refers to the status of a "citizen of the Republic of the Philippines." Cultural and linguistic affiliation is specified by ethnonyms such as "Ilokano," "Tagalog," "Cebuano," and the like. Nine percent of the population belongs to eight major cultural-linguistic groups: Tagalog, Ilokano, Pampangan, Pangasinan, Bikol, Cebuano, Hiligaynon, and Samar-Leyte (Evangelista 1983, 161). The word "Pilipino," instead of "Tagalog," has been coined to give a politically neutral name to the national language.

5. This can mean "quaint," "primitive," "uncivilized," and "uneducated." The perception of the ICC by the lowland Christians is more complex than these terms indicate, however, and not purely negative. Indigenous peoples are also viewed by some (urban intellectuals or simple farmers, as the case may be) as retaining some ancient wisdom, and, as such, conserving useful knowledge about the natural or supernatural environment. Thus, they can also be positively perceived as "genuine," "good," "honest," "peaceful," etc.

6. The word "Moro" is applied traditionally to the Muslims of the Sulu Archipelago, with a heavy connotation of piracy and fierceness. The Muslims of the southern Philippines today constitute an organized force, or a complex set of militarily and politically organized forces, which are contending for the status of nation-state.

7. See, for example, Episcopal Commission on Tribal Filipinos (1979).

8. See Lynch (1984).

9. Lynch 1984, 2. See also pages 9, 17, and *passim.*

10. This picture is drawn from a case I have personally documented of Punang and Iräräj communities on the east coast of southern Palawan (Macdonald 1990).

11. See Gibson (1986, chap. 5).

12. See Neumann (1981).

13. I have witnessed this myself in Palawan, Mindoro, northern Luzon, and Mindanao, among the Palawan, Hanunoo, Kalinga and Ifugao, T'boli, and many other peoples.

Note to Chapter 18

This chapter was originally submitted as a report to the United Nations

Working Group on Indigenous Populations, Ninth Session, Geneva, 1991. It is reproduced (with minor alterations) from *IWGIA Newsletter*, no. 2 (November-December 1991):42–47.

Notes to Chapter 19

1. The Ainu interpretation of culture is equivalent to that of an ethnic group. To them, "ethnic group" is a concept that derives from or relates to a human group having racial (anthropomorphic), religious, linguistic, and historical traits in common. People sharing these basic features also share a common identity.

2. Kyokai is an Ainu association established in 1930 by the authorities in Japan to prevent further exploitation of the Ainu by the unscrupulous mainland profiteers who were numerous at the time. The Kyokai's first purpose was to make sure that the regulations and restrictions of the protectionist law, Hokkaido Kyuudojin Hogoho, were not violated. Today the Kyokai gives priority to ethnic issues. Yet the Kyokai does not have the confidence of the majority of the Ainu. Some are discontent with the fact that the Kyokai places Ainu affairs in the hands of the Wajin, pointing to the fact that people of Wajin descent are employed by Kyokai, allowing them to represent the Ainu. Some are unhappy with the Kyokai's protectionist policy. Not denying the importance of the rights to practice their customs and to have their identity as Ainu firmly established, they would rather see these rights based on choice than on protectionist laws.

References

References to Chapter 1

Southeast Asian Tribal Groups and Ethnic Minorities: Prospects for the Eighties and Beyond. 1987. Proceedings of a conference cosponsored by Cultural Survival, Inc., and the Department of Anthropology, Harvard University. Cultural Survival Report, no. 22. Cambridge, Mass.: Cultural Survival.

Government of Indonesia. 1991. Statement by the Indonesian Delegation to the Working Group on Indigenous Populations, Ninth Session of the Working Group on Indigenous Populations, Geneva, July-August 1991. Unpublished.

Lim Teck Ghee and Alberto G. Gomes. 1990. *Tribal Peoples and Development in Southeast Asia.* Special issue of *Manusia & Masyarakat.* Kuala Lumpur: Department of Anthropology and Sociology, University of Malaya.

Wijeyewardene, Gehan, ed. 1990. *Ethnic Groups Across National Boundaries in Mainland Southeast Asia.* Singapore: Institute of Southeast Asian Studies.

Win Mra, U. 1991. Statement by Deputy Permanent Representative U Win Mra, member of the Observer Delegation of the Union of Myanmar, Ninth Session of the Working Group on Indigenous Populations, Geneva, July–August 1991. Unpublished.

References to Chapter 2

Alfonso Martínez, Miguel. 1991. *Preliminary Report of the Special Rapporteur on Treaties, Agreements and Other Constructive Arrangements Between States and Indigenous Peoples.* Geneva: United Nations. Doc. E/CN.4/Sub.2/1991/33.

Alfredsson, Gudmundur. 1990. *Report on 'Equality and Non-Discrimination: Minority Rights'.* Strasbourg: Council of Europe. Paper H/Coll(90) 6.

Barsh, Russel L. 1986. Indigenous Peoples: An Emerging Object of International Law. *American Journal of International Law* 80:369–86.

Béteille, André. 1977 [1960]. The Definition of Tribe. In *Tribe, Caste and Religion in India*, ed. R. Thapar. Delhi: Macmillan.

Bramble, Barbara J., and Gareth Porter. 1992. Non-Governmental Organizations and the Making of U.S. International Environmental Policy. In *The International Politics of the Environment*, ed. A. Hurrell and B. Kingsbury, 313–53. Oxford: Oxford University Press.

Brownlie, Ian. 1988. The Rights of Peoples in Modern International Law. In *The Rights of Peoples*, ed. James Crawford, 1–16. Oxford: Oxford University Press.

Caso, Alfonso. 1948. Definición del indio y lo indio. *América Indígena* 8:239–47.

Dayal, Prabhu. 1991. *Statement on Behalf of the Delegation of India to the United Nations Working Group on Indigenous Populations, 31 July 1991*. Geneva: United Nations. Mimeo.

Dumenge, Francois. 1983. *Viability of Small Island States (A Descriptive Study)*. Geneva: United Nations Conference on Trade and Development. Doc. TB/B/950.

Eide, Asbjorn. 1991. *Preliminary Report of the Special Rapporteur on Possible Ways and Means of Facilitating the Peaceful and Constructive Solution of Problems Involving Minorities*. Geneva: United Nations. Doc. E/CN.4/Sub.2/1991/43.

English High Court of Justice, Chancery Division. 1977. *Tito v. Waddell (No 2)*. *All England Reports* 3 [1977]:129.

The Ecologist. 1986. Banking on Disaster, Indonesia's Transmigration Programme: A Special Report in Collaboration with Survival International and Tapol. *The Ecologist* 16:2/3:58–117.

Escudero, Carlos. 1988. *Involuntary Resettlement in Bank-Assisted Projects: An Introduction to Legal Issues*. Washington, D.C.: World Bank.

Fried, Morton. 1975. *The Notion of Tribe*. Menlo Park, Calif.: Cummings.

Gamio, Manuel. 1949. El Congreso de Cuzco y las actividades contra el indigenismo. *América Indígena* 9:91–103.

———. 1966 [1946]. La identificación del indio. In *Consideraciones sobre el problema indígena*, 2d ed. Mexico City: Instituto Indigenista Interamericano.

Gladney, Dru. 1989. Identifying the Hui in China: Self-Definition, Ethno-Religious Identity and the State. Paper presented at The Legacy of Islam in China, an International Symposium in Memory of Joseph F. Fletcher, Harvard University, April.

Gros, Christian. 1985. Vous avez dit indien? L'Etat et les criteres d'indianité en Colombie et au Brésil. *Cahier des Ameriques Latines*, n.s., 1:29.

Gu Yijie. 1987. *Statement to the United Nations Working Group on Indigenous Populations, 6 August 1987*. Geneva: United Nations. Mimeo.

Hannum, Hurst. 1990. *Autonomy, Sovereignty, and Self-Determination: The Accommodation of Conflicting Rights*. Philadelphia: University of Pennsylvania Press.

Independent Commission on International Humanitarian Issues. 1987. *Indigenous Peoples: A Global Quest for Justice*. London: Zed.

Indonesia, Government of. 1991. *Statement to the United Nations Working Group on Indigenous Populations, 1 August 1991*. Geneva: United Nations. Mimeo.

International Court of Justice. 1989. *Certain Phosphate Lands in Nauru (Nauru v. Australia)*. The Hague: International Court of Justice.

International Labour Conference. 1956a. Report VIII (1), 39th session. Geneva: ILO.

————. 1956b. Report VIII (2), 39th session. Geneva: ILO.

————. 1957. Report VI (2), 40th session. Geneva: ILO.

————. 1988. Report VI (1), 75th session. Geneva: ILO.

————. 1989. *Report of the Committee on Convention 107*. Geneva: International Labour Organisation. Doc. ILC/76th session/PR.25.

International Labour Office. 1951. First Session of the ILO Committee of Experts on Indigenous Labour. *International Labour Review* 64:61–84.

————. 1953. *Indigenous Peoples: Living and Working Conditions of Aboriginal Populations in Independent Countries*. Geneva: International Labour Organisation.

————. 1954. The Second Session of the ILO Committee of Experts on Indigenous Labour. *International Labour Review* 70:418–41.

————. 1984. *Indigenous and Tribal Populations and Land Rights*. Geneva: ILO. Mimeo.

International Labour Organisation. 1986. Report of the ILO Meeting of Experts on the Revision of ILO Convention 107. Geneva: ILO, Doc. APPL/MER/107/1986/D.7.

Islam, M. Rafiqul. 1988. The Proposed Constitutional Guarantee of Indigenous Governmental Power in Fiji: An International Legal Appraisal. *California Western International Law Journal* 19:107–28.

Katzenstein, Mary Fainsod. 1979. *Ethnicity and Equality: The Shiv Sena Party and Preferential Policies in Bombay*. Ithaca: Cornell University Press.

Kingsbury, Benedict. 1992a. Claims by Non-State Groups in International Law. *Cornell International Law Journal* 25:481–513.

————. 1992b. Self-Determination and "Indigenous Peoples." *Proceedings of the American Society of International Law* 86:383–94.

Lee, Raymond, ed. 1986. *Ethnicity and Ethnic Relations in Malaysia*. DeKalb: Center for Southeast Asian Studies, Northern Illinois University.

Martínez Cobo, José. 1983. *Tentative Proposals Concerning the Definition of Indigenous Populations.* Geneva: United Nations. Doc. E/CN.4/Sub.2/L.566.

———. 1986. *Study of the Problem of Discrimination Against Indigenous Populations.* Geneva: United Nations. Doc. E/CN.4/Sub.2/1986/7.

Mauritius High Court. 1985. *Pirmal v. The Ilois Trust Fund. Law Reports of the Commonwealth (Constitutional Law)* (1985): 514.

Norwegian Sami Rights Committee (Samerettsutvalget). 1984. *Om Samenes rettsstilling.* Oslo: Universitetsforlaget, 1984.

Otten, Mariël. 1986. *Transmigrasi: Indonesian Resettlement Policy, 1965–1985.* Copenhagen: International Work Group on Indigenous Affairs.

Parkipuny, Moringe. 1989. The Indigenous Peoples' Rights Question in Africa. *IWGIA Newsletter* 59:92–94.

Paul, James C. N. 1988. International Development Agencies, Human Rights and Humane Development Projects. *Denver Journal of International Law and Policy* 17:67–120.

Philippines, Government of. 1988. *Statement to the United Nations Working Group on Indigenous Populations, 2 August 1988.* Geneva: United Nations. Mimeo.

Piddington, Kenneth. 1992. The Role of the World Bank. In *The International Politics of the Environment,* ed. A. Hurrell and B. Kingsbury, 212–27. Oxford: Oxford University Press.

Puri, Lakshmi. 1983. *Statement on Behalf of the Delegation of India to the United Nations Working Group on Indigenous Populations, 12 August 1983.* Geneva: United Nations. Mimeo.

Sacerdoti, Giorgio. 1983. New Developments in Group Consciousness and the International Protection of the Rights of Minorities. *Israel Yearbook on Human Rights* 13:116–46.

Sanders, Douglas E. 1983. The Re-emergence of Indigenous Questions in International Law. *Canadian Human Rights Yearbook* 1:3–30.

Scelle, Georges. 1936. *Précis du droit des gens.* Vol. 2. Paris: Sirey.

Shihata, Ibrahim. 1988. The World Bank and Human Rights: An Analysis of the Legal Issues and the Record of Achievements. *Denver Journal of International Law and Policy* 17:39.

Street, Harry. 1982. Answer to Parliamentary Questions Concerning the Possibility of Ratifying ILO Convention 107. *Australian Yearbook of International Law* 10:487.

Survival International. 1985. An End To Laughter? Tribal Peoples and Economic Development. *Survival International Review,* no. 44.

Swepston, Lee. 1978. The Indian in Latin America: Approaches to Administration, Integration and Protection. *Buffalo Law Review* 27:715–56.

————. 1990. A New Step in the International Law on Indigenous and Tribal Peoples: ILO Convention No. 169 of 1989. *Oklahoma City University Law Review* 15:677–714.

Treece, Dave. 1987. *Bound in Misery and Iron: The Impact of the Grande Cara-jás Programme on the Indians of Brazil.* London: Survival International.

United Kingdom Treaty Series. 1983. *UK-Mauritius Agreement Concerning the Ilois, 1982.* United Kingdom Treaty Series, no. 6. London: Her Majesty's Stationery Office.

United Nations. 1982. *Report of the Working Group on Indigenous Populations on its First Session.* Geneva: United Nations. Doc. E/CN.4/Sub.2/1982/33.

————. 1983. *Report of the Working Group on Indigenous Populations on its Second Session.* Geneva: United Nations. Doc. E/CN.4/Sub.2/1983/22.

————. 1984a. *United Nations Working Group on Indigenous Populations: Infor-mation Submitted by Governments (India).* Geneva: United Nations. Doc. E/CN.4/Sub.2/AC.4/1984/2/Add.2.

————. 1984b. *Report of the Working Group on Indigenous Populations on its Third Session.* Geneva: United Nations. Doc. E/CN.4/Sub.2/1984/20.

————. 1987a. *United Nations Working Group on Indigenous Populations: Infor-mation Submitted by Governments (Norway and Czechoslovakia).* Geneva: United Nations. Doc. E/CN.4/Sub.2/AC.4/1987/WP.1.

————. 1987b. *United Nations Working Group on Indigenous Populations: Infor-mation Submitted by Governments (Canada).* Geneva: United Nations. Doc. E/CN.4/Sub.2/AC.4/1987/WP.1/Add.2.

————. 1988. *United Nations Working Group on Indigenous Populations: Infor-mation Submitted by Governments (Canada).* Geneva: United Nations. Doc. E/CN.4/Sub.2/1988/2/Add.1.

————. 1989a. *Report of the Working Group on Indigenous Populations on its Seventh Session.* Geneva: United Nations. Doc. E/CN.4/Sub.2/1989/36.

————. 1989b. *United Nations Working Group on Indigenous Populations: Infor-mation Submitted by Governments (Myanmar).* Geneva: United Nations. Doc. E/CN.4/Sub.2/1989/33/Add.1.

————. 1989c. United Nations. Doc. A/44/188/1989.

————. 1991a. *Human Rights Commission: Report of the Working Group on the Rights of Minorities.* Geneva: United Nations. Doc. E/CN.4/1991/53.

————. 1991b. *Report of the Working Group on Indigenous Populations on its Ninth Session.* Geneva: United Nations. Doc. E/CN.4/Sub.2/1991/40.

————. 1992. *Report of the Working Group on Indigenous Populations on its Tenth Session.* Geneva: United Nations. Doc. E/CN.4/Sub.2/1992/33.

————. 1993. *Report of the Working Group on Indigenous Populations on its Eleventh Session.* Geneva: United Nations. Doc. E/CN.4/Sub.2/1993/29.

United Nations Conference on Trade and Development 1983. UNCTAD Resolution 137(VI). *Report of the United Nations Conference on Trade and Development on its Sixth Session Held at the Sava Centa, Belgrade from 6 June to 2 July 1982.* Geneva: United Nations, Doc. TD/325.

United Nations Economic and Social Council Official Records. 1949. *Summary Records of the Economic and Social Council, 11th Session, 397th Meeting.* New York: United Nations.

United Nations General Assembly Official Records. 1949a. *Summary Records of the Ad Hoc Political Committee, 53rd Meeting, 10 May 1949.* New York: United Nations.

———. 1949b. *Summary Records of the General Assembly, 208th Meeting.* New York: United Nations.

United Nations Human Rights Committee. 1981. *Lovelace v. Canada (Final Views). International Law Reports* 68:17.

———. 1988. *Kitok v. Sweden (Final Views).* New York: United Nations. Doc. A/43/40, 221.

United States Treaty Series. 1942. *Convention Providing for Creation of the Inter-American Indian Institute, 1940.* United States Treaty Series, no. 978. Washington, D.C.: Government Printing Office.

Weiner, Myron. 1978. *Sons of the Soil: Migration and Ethnic Conflict in India.* Princeton, N.J.: Princeton University Press.

West Papuan Peoples' Front et al. 1991. *Common Statement by Indigenous and Tribal Peoples of Asia to United Nations Working Group on Indigenous Populations, 2 August 1991.* Geneva: United Nations. Mimeo.

Win Mra, U. 1991. *Statement on Behalf of the Delegation of Myanmar to the United Nations Working Group on Indigenous Populations, 31 July 1991.* Geneva: United Nations. Mimeo.

World Bank. 1982. *Tribal People in Bank-Financed Projects.* Operational Manual Statement, no. 2.34. Washington, D.C.: World Bank. Mimeo.

———. 1991. *Indigenous Peoples.* Operational Directive, no. 4.20. Washington, D.C.: World Bank. Mimeo.

References to Chapter 3

Anti-Slavery Society. 1984. *The Chittagong Hill Tracts: Militarization, Oppression and the Hill Tribes.* Indigenous Peoples and Development Series, no. 2. London: Anti-Slavery Society.

———. 1990. *West Papua: Plunder in Paradise.* Indigenous Peoples and Development Series, no. 6. London: Anti-Slavery Society.

Bennet, R. 1978. *Aboriginal Populations and the Law.* London: Survival International and the Royal Anthropological Institute.

Burger, Julian. 1987. *Report from the Frontier: The State of the World's Indigenous Peoples.* London: Zed.

Chittagong Hill Tracts Commission. 1991. *Life is not Ours: Land and Human Rights in the Chittagong Hill Tracts, Bangladesh.* London: Calverts.

Davis, S. H. 1977. *Victims of the Miracle: Development and the Indians of Brazil.* Cambridge: Cambridge University Press.

Down to Earth. 1989a. *Down to Earth,* no. 3.

Down to Earth. 1989b. *Down to Earth,* no. 5.

Eide, A. 1985. Indigenous Populations and Human Rights: The United Nations Efforts at Mid-Way. In *Native Power,* ed. Jens Brøsted et al. Bergen: Universitetsforlaget.

Fürer-Haimendorf, Christoph von. 1989. *Tribes of India: The Struggle for Survival.* Delhi: Oxford University Press.

Gray, Andrew. 1987. Indigenous Affairs and Anthropology. In *Natives and Neighbors in South America: Anthropological Essays,* ed. H. Skar and F. Salomon. Goteborgs Etnografiska Museum Studier, no. 38. Goteborg: Etnografiska Museum.

Heinz, Wolfgang. 1988. *Indigenous Populations, Ethnic Minorities and Human Rights.* Berliner Studien zur Internationalen Politik, no. 10. Berlin: Quorum Verlag.

Independent Commission on International Humanitarian Issues. 1987. *Indigenous Peoples: A Global Quest for Justice.* London: Zed.

International Labour Organisation. 1957. Convention 107. Geneva: International Labour Organisation.

International Work Group for Indigenous Affairs. 1986a. *IWGIA Yearbook, 1986: Indigenous Peoples and Human Rights,* written and compiled by Andrew Gray. Copenhagen: IWGIA.

————. 1986b. Chairwoman of the Working Group on Indigenous Populations—Erica Daes—visits IWGIA. *IWGIA Newsletter* 46:78–87.

————. 1986c. *The Naga Nation and its Struggle against Genocide: A Report Compiled by IWGIA.* IWGIA Documents, no. 56. Copenhagen: IWGIA.

————. 1988. *IWGIA Yearbook, 1988: IWGIA 20 Years,* written and compiled by Andrew Gray. Copenhagen: IWGIA.

————. 1989. East Timor: "No Improvement in Human Rights Says Copenhagen Conference." *IWGIA Newsletter* 57:57–59.

Mey, Wolfgang, ed. 1984. *Genocide in the Chittagong Hill Tracts, Bangladesh: They are Now Burning Village After Village.* IWGIA Documents, no. 51. Copenhagen: IWGIA.

Moody, R. 1988. *The Indigenous Voice: Visions and Realities.* 2 vols. London: IWGIA and Zed.

Otten, Mariël. 1986. *Transmigrasi: Indonesian Resettlement Policy, 1965–1985, Myths and Realities*. IWGIA Documents, no. 57. Copenhagen: IWGIA.

Pearce, F. 1990. Hit and Run in Sarawak. *New Scientist*, 12 May, 24–27.

Retbøll, Torben, ed. 1980. *East Timor, Indonesia and the Western Democracies*. IWGIA Documents, no. 40. Copenhagen: IWGIA.

——. 1984. *East Timor: The Struggle Continues*. IWGIA Documents, no. 50. Copenhagen: IWGIA.

Rizvi, Zia. 1987. An Editorial Note. In *Indigenous Peoples: A Global Quest for Justice*, comp. Independent Commission on International Humanitarian Issues. London: Zed.

Sanders, Douglas. 1986. The Ainu as an Indigenous People. *IWGIA Newsletter* 45:118–49.

Sjöberg, Katarina. 1990. "Mr. Ainu" in the Japanese Culture. *IWGIA Newsletter* 60–61:79–101.

Stavenhagen, R. 1986. Human Rights and Peoples' Rights: The Question of Minorities. Paper presented at the International Labour Organisation Meeting of Experts, Geneva.

Tapol (Tahanan Politik [Political Prisoner]). 1989. *TAPOL Bulletin*, no. 95.

Thompson, R. 1974. *Defeating Communist Insurgency: Experiences from Malaya and Vietnam*. London: Chatto and Windus.

United Nations Economic and Social Council, Commission on Human Rights. 1982–83. Preliminary Report on the Study of the Problem of Discrimination against Indigenous Populations. UN doc. E/CN.4/Sub.2/L.566.

Vincent, A. 1987. *Theories of the State*. Oxford: Blackwell.

Yorke, Michael. 1989. The Situation of the Gonds of Asifabad and Lakshetipet Taluks, Adilabad District. In *Tribes of India: The Struggle for Survival*, ed. Christoph von Fürer-Haimendorf. Delhi: Oxford University Press.

World Bank. 1982. *Tribal Peoples and Economic Development: Human Ecological Considerations*. Washington, D.C.: World Bank.

World Council of Indigenous Peoples. N.d. Definition of Indigenous Peoples. Typescript.

References to Chapter 4

Agarwal, Anil, and Sunita Narain. 1989. *Towards Green Villages*. Delhi: Centre for Science and the Environment.

Anderson, James N. 1987. Lands at Risk, People at Risk: Perspectives on Tropical Forest Transformations in the Philippines. In Little et al. 1987.

Anonymous. 1984. *China's Minority Nationalists*. Beijing: Great Wall.

Anonymous. 1987. *Minority Peoples in China*. Beijing: China Pictorial.

Anti-Slavery Society. 1983. *The Philippines: Authoritarian Government, Multi-nationals and Ancestral Lands.* London: Anti-Slavery Society.

———. 1984. *The Chittagong Hill Tracts: Militarization, Oppression and the Hill Tribes.* London: Anti-Slavery Society.

———. 1991. *West Papua: Plunder in Paradise.* London: Anti-Slavery Society.

Asian NGO Coalition. 1989. *People's Participation and Environmentally Sustainable Development.* Manila: Asian NGO Coalition for Agrarian Reform and Rural Development.

Atkinson, Jane M. 1988. Religion and the Wana of Sulawesi. In Dove 1988.

Bannerjee, Sumanta. 1984. *India's Simmering Revolution.* London: Zed.

Bello, W., D. Kinley, and E. Elison. 1982. *Development Debacle: The World Bank in the Philippines.* San Francisco: Institute for Food and Development Policy.

Bodley, John H. 1982. *Victims of Progress,* 2d ed. Menlo Park: Benjamin/Cummings.

Brewer, Jeffrey D. 1988. Traditional Land Use and Government Policy in Bima, East Sumbawa. In Dove 1988.

Brosius, J. Peter. 1986. River, Forest, and Mountain: The Penan Gang Landscape. *Sarawak Museum Journal* 36, no. 57:173–84.

Burger, Julian. 1987. *Report from the Frontier: The State of the World's Indigenous Peoples.* London: Zed.

Butcher, David. 1988. *A Review of Land-Acquisition and Resettlement under Four World Bank Financed Projects in Indonesia.* Washington, D.C.: World Bank.

Carey, Iskander. 1976. *Orang Asli: the Aboriginal Tribes of Peninsular Malaysia.* Oxford: Oxford University Press.

Centre for Science and the Environment. 1982. *The State of India's Environment.* New Delhi: Centre for Science and the Environment.

Cernea, Michael M., ed. 1985. *Putting People First: Sociological Variables in Rural Development.* New York: Oxford University Press.

Colchester, Marcus. 1984. The Crisis of Ownership: The Plight of the Tribal Populations of Northern Bangladesh. *Survival International Review* 43:29–35.

———. 1985. An End to Laughter? The Bhopalpatnam and Godavari Projects. In Goldsmith and Hilyard 1985.

———. 1986a. Unity and Diversity: Indonesian Policy Towards Tribal Peoples. *The Ecologist* 16, nos. 2/3:61–70.

———. 1986b. The Struggle for Land: Tribal Peoples in the Face of the Transmigration Programme. *The Ecologist* 16, nos. 2/3:89–98.

———. 1986c. Banking on Disaster: International Support for the Transmigration Programme. *The Ecologist* 16, nos. 2/3:99–110.

————. 1986d. Wereldbankprojekt in India: Ramp voor Tribalen. *Derde Wereld* 5, no. 2:31–39.

————. 1987a. The Tribal Peoples of the Narmada Valley: Damned by the World Bank. In *Forest Resources Crisis in the Third World*. Penang: Sahabat Alam Malaysia.

————. 1987b. The Social Dimensions of Government-Sponsored Migration and Involuntary Resettlement: Policies and Practice. Paper prepared for the Independent Commission on International Humanitarian Issues, Geneva, January.

————. 1989. *Pirates, Squatters and Poachers: the Political Ecology of Dispossession of the Native Peoples of Sarawak*. Kuala Lumpur: Survival International and Institute of Social Analysis.

————. 1990. Shifting Cultivation: Rational Resource Use or Robber Economy? Paper presented to the Third World Network and Asia-Pacific Peoples Environment Network Conference on the Destruction of Asian Agriculture, Penang, Malaysia, 10–13 January.

————. 1991. A Future on the Land? Logging and the Status of Native Customary Land in Sarawak. *Ilmu Masyarakat* 19 (April-June):36–45.

Colchester, Marcus, and Larry Lohmann. 1990. *The Tropical Forestry Action Plan: What Progress*. 2d ed. Penang: World Rainforest Movement.

Conklin, Harold. 1954. The Relation of Hanunóo Culture to the Plant World. Ph.D. diss., Yale University.

Cornista, Luzviminda B., and Eva F. Esćueta. 1990. Communal Forest Leases as a Tenurial Option in the Philippines Uplands. In Poffenberger 1990.

Coward, E. Walter, Jr. 1985. Technical and Social Change in Currently Irrigated Regions: Rules, Roles and Rehabilitation. In Cernea 1985.

Craven, Ian. 1990. Community Involvement in Management of the Arfak Mountains Nature Reserve. World Wide Fund for Nature (Indonesia). Typescript.

Dorrall, Richard. 1990. The Dialectic of Development: Tribal Responses to Development Capital in the Cordillera Central, Northern Luzon, Philippines. In Lim and Gomes 1990.

Dove, Michael R. 1985. The Agroecological Mythology of the Javanese and the Political Economy of Indonesia. *Indonesia* 39:1–30.

Dove, Michael R., ed. 1988. *The Real and Imagined Role of Culture in Development: Case Studies from Indonesia*. Honolulu: University of Hawaii Press.

Down to Earth. 1989. *Down to Earth* no. 5:7–8.

————. 1991. *Down to Earth,* no. 12:8.

Drucker, Charles. 1986. Dam the Chico: Hydro Development and Tribal Resistance. In Goldsmith and Hilyard 1986.

Durning, Alan B. 1989. *Action at the Grassroots: Fighting Poverty and Environmental Decline*. Worldwatch Papers, no. 88. Washington, D.C.: Worldwatch.

Duyker, Edward. 1987. *Tribal Guerrillas: The Santals of West Bengal and the Naxalite Movement.* Delhi: Oxford University Press.

Ekachai, Sanitsuda. 1990. *Behind the Smile: Voices of Thailand.* Bangkok: Thai Development Support Committee.

Endicott, Kirk M. 1979. The Impact of Modernisation on the Orang Asli (Aborigines) of Northern Peninsular Malaysia. In *Issues in Malaysian Development,* ed. James C. Jackson and Martin Rudner. Singapore: Heinemann.

Fay, Chip. 1987. *Counter-Insurgency and Tribal Peoples in the Philippines.* Washington, D.C.: Survival International.

Fay, Chip, ed. 1989. *Our Threatened Heritage.* Seminar Series, vol. 124. Manila: Solidarity Foundation.

Fay, Chip, Nonette Royo, and Gus Gatmayan. 1989. The Destruction of Mt. Apo: In Defense of Bagobo Ancestral Domain. In Fay 1989.

Fiagoy, Geraldine. 1987. *Death Stalks the Isneg: Report of Three Fact-Finding Missions to Lower Kalinga-Apayao, Northern Philippines.* Baguio, Philippines: Cordillera Resources Center.

Fürer-Haimendorf, Christoph von. 1982. The Tribes of India: The Struggle for Survival. Berkeley: University of California Press.

Garna, Judistira. 1990. The Baduy of Java: A Case Study of Tribal Peoples' Adaptation to Development. In Lim and Gomes 1990.

Gasconia, Donna Z. 1989. Breaking the Minority Myth: A Step Towards Resource Transfer. In Fay 1989.

Geddes, William Robert. 1976. *Migrants of the Mountains: The Cultural Ecology of the Blue Miao (Hmong Njua) of Thailand.* Oxford: Clarendon.

Gerritsen, R., R. J. May, and M. Walter, eds. 1981. *Road Belong Development: Cargo Cults, Community Groups and Self-Help Movements in Papua New Guinea.* Working Papers, no. 3. Canberra: Department of Political and Social Change, Australian National University.

Geusau, Leo Alting von. 1986. Dialectics of Akhazang: The Interiorization of a Perennial Minority Group. In McKinnon and Bhruksasri 1986.

Goldsmith, Edward, and Nicholas Hilyard, eds. 1985. *The Social and Environmental Impact of Large Dams.* Vol. 2. Wadebridge: Wadebridge Ecological Centre.

Good, Kenneth. 1986. *Papua New Guinea: A False Economy.* London: Anti-Slavery Society.

Hegde, Pandurang. 1988. *Chinko and Anniko: How the People Save the Trees.* London: Quaker Peace and Service.

Hughes, Philip J., and Charmina Thirlwall, eds. 1988. *The Ethics of Development: Choices in Development Planning.* Waigani, New Guinea: University of Papua New Guinea Press.

Hurst, Philip. 1991. *Rainforest Politics.* London: Zed.

Indonesia. 1986. *Indonesia: News and Views* 6, no. 21. Published by the Indonesian Embassy, Washington, D.C., cyclostyled.

Independent Commission on International Issues. 1987. *Indigenous Peoples: A Global Quest for Justice. A Report for the Independent Commission on International Humanitarian Issues.* London: Zed.

International Work Group. 1986. *The Naga Nation and its Struggle against Genocide.* Copenhagen: International Work Group for Indigenous Affairs.

James, R. W. 1985. *Land Law and Policy in Papua New Guinea.* Law Reform Commission Monographs, no. 5. Port Moresby, New Guinea: Law Reform Commission.

Langub, Jayl. 1988a. Some Aspects of Life of the Penan. Paper presented to the Orang Ulu Cultural Heritage Seminar, Miri, Malaysia, 21–23 June.

————. 1988b. The Penan Strategy. In *People of the Rain Forest*, ed. Julie Sloane Denslow and Christine Padoch. Berkeley: University of California Press.

Lim Teck Ghee and Alberto G. Gomes, eds. 1990. *Tribal Peoples and Development in Southeast Asia.* Selangor: University of Malaya.

Little, Peter D., Michael M. Horowitz, and A. Endre Nyerges, eds. 1987. *Lands at Risk in the Third World: Local Level Perspectives.* Boulder: Westview.

Lohmann, Larry. 1991. Who Defends Biological Diversity? Conservation Strategies and the Case of Thailand. *The Ecologist* 21, no. 1:5–13.

Lumad Mindanaw. 1990. Land Reoccupation: A Significant Step Towards Self-Determination. Davao City, Philippines: Suwara.

Lynch, Owen. 1990. *Whither the People? Demographic, Tenurial and Agricultural Aspects of the Tropical Forestry Action Plan.* Washington, D.C.: World Resources Institute.

McKinnon, John, and Wanat Bhruksasri, eds. 1986. *Highlanders of Thailand.* Singapore: Oxford University Press.

Marshall, George. 1990. The Political Economy of Logging: The Barnett Enquiry into Corruption in the Papua New Guinea Timber Industry. *The Ecologist* 20, no. 5:174–81.

May, R. J., ed. 1982. *Micronationalist Movements in Papua New Guinea.* Political and Social Change Monographs, no. 1. Canberra: Australian National University.

Mey, Wolfgang. 1984. *Genocide in the Chittagong Hill Tracts, Bangladesh.* Copenhagen: International Work Group for Indigenous Affairs.

Morris, Brian. 1982. *Forest Traders: A Socio-Economic Study of the Hill Pandaram.* London: Athlone.

————. 1983. Forest Tribes and Deforestation in India. Paper presented to the Fauna and Flora Preservation Society, London, 1 October.

Myers, Norman. 1989. *Deforestation Rates in Tropical Forests and Their Climate Implications.* London: Friends of the Earth.

Nicholas, Colin. 1989. *Towards Self-Determination: Indigenous Peoples in Asia.* Bombay: Asia Indigenous Peoples Pact.

———. 1990. In the Name of the Semai? The State and Semai Society in Peninsular Malaysia. In Lim and Gomes 1990.

Peluso, Nancy Lee. 1990. A History of State Forest Management in Java. In Poffenberger 1990.

Permpongsacharoen, Witoon. 1990. Tropical Forests Movements: Some Lessons from Thailand. Project for Ecological Recovery. Typescript.

Persoon, Gerard. 1985. From Affluence to Poverty: The "Development" of Tribal and Isolated Peoples. In *Poverty and Interventions: Cases from Developing Countries,* ed. Leen Boer, Dieke Bujis, and Benno Gljart. Development Studies, no. 6. Leiden: Institute of Cultural and Social Studies, University of Leiden.

Poffenberger, Mark, ed. 1990. *Keepers of the Forest: Land Management Alternatives in Southeast Asia.* West Hartwood, Conn.: Kumarian.

Porter, Gareth, and Delfin J. Ganapin, Jr. 1988. *Resources, Population and the Philippines' Future: A Case Study.* Washington, D.C.: World Resources Institute.

Project for Ecological Recovery. 1990. *The Muang Faai Irrigation System of Northern Thailand.* Bangkok: Project for Ecological Recovery.

Rainforest Information Centre. 1990a. *The World Bank Tropical Forestry Action Plan for Papua New Guinea: A Critique.* Lismore, Australia: Rainforest Information Centre.

———. 1990b. *Pacific Eco-Forestry Project, Papua New Guinea and Solomon Islands.* Year One Report for the Australian International Development Assistance Bureau. Lismore, Australia: Rainforest Information Centre.

Regpala, Maria Elena. 1990. *Resistance in the Cordillera: A Philippines Tribal People's Historical Response to Invasion and Change Imposed from Outside.* In Lim and Gomes 1990.

Repetto, Robert. 1988. *The Forest for the Trees? Government Policies and the Misuse of Forest Resources.* Washington, D.C.: World Resources Institute.

Rice, Delbert, and Nonoy Bugtong. 1989. Democratization of Resources: The Kalahan Experience. In Fay 1989.

Rocamora, Joel. 1979. The Political Uses of PANAMIN. *Southeast Asia Chronicle,* no. 67 (October):11–21.

Sargent, Caroline, and Peter Burgess. 1988. The Wokabaut Somil: Some Issues in Small-Scale Sawmilling in Papua New Guinea. International Institute for Environment and Development, London. Typescript.

Shiva, Vandana. 1987. *Forestry Crisis and Forestry Myths.* Penang, Malaysia: World Rainforest Movement.

———. 1989. *The Violence of the Green Revolution: Ecological Degradation and Political Violence in the Punjab.* Dehra Dun, India: Shiva.

Singh, K. S. 1982. *Tribal Movements in India.* 2 vols. Delhi: Manohar.

Survival International. 1984. *Genocide in Bangladesh.* London: Survival International.

———. 1987. *Thailand: Akha Expelled.* London: Survival International.

TABAK (Tunay na Alyansa ng Bayan Alay sa Katutubo [Indigenous Peoples Support Group]). 1990. *Struggle Against Development Aggression: Tribal Filipinos and Ancestral Domain.* Manila: TABAK.

Tapol (Tahanan Politik [Political Prisoner]). 1988. West Papua: The Obliteration of a People. 3d ed. London: Tapol.

Tapp, Nicholas. 1986. *The Hmong of Thailand: Opium People of the Golden Triangle.* London: Anti-Slavery Society.

Westoby, Jack. 1989. *Introduction to World Forestry.* Oxford: Basil Blackwell.

World Bank. 1982a. *Tribal Peoples in Bank Financed Projects.* Operational Manual Statement, no. 2.34. Washington, D.C.: World Bank.

———. 1982b. *Tribal Peoples and Economic Development: Human Ecologic Considerations.* Washington, D.C.: World Bank.

———. 1990. *Indigenous Peoples in Bank-Financed Projects.* Operational Directive, no. 4.40. Washington, D.C.: World Bank.

World Commission on Environment and Development. 1987. *Our Common Future.* Oxford: Oxford University Press.

Worsley, Peter. 1957. *The Trumpet Shall Sound: A Study of 'Cargo' Cults in Melanesia.* London: MacGibbon and Kee.

World Rainforest Movement/Sahabat Alam Malaysia. 1990. *The Battle for Sarawak's Forests.* Penang, Malaysia: World Rainforest Movement/Sahabat Alam Malaysia.

References to Chapter 5

Aipin, Y. 1989. Not by Oil Alone. *IWGIA Newsletter* 57:137–43.

Association of Small Peoples of the Soviet North. 1991. Convention of the 26. *IWGIA Newsletter,* no. 2 (November-December):17–18.

Bartels, D., and A. Bartels. 1988. Are Siberian Native People Part of a "Fourth World"? *Dialectical Anthropology* 12:245–52.

Chlenov, M. 1989. [The Murder of All Living Things.] *Sovetska Kultura,* 11 February 1989. Cited from *Novosti Presse-nyt* (Copenhagen), no. 49, 10.

Dahl, J. 1990a. Indigenous Peoples of the Soviet North. In *IWGIA Yearbook, 1989,* 215–29. Copenhagen: International Work Group for Indigenous Affairs.

———. 1990b. Introduction. In *Indigenous Peoples of the Soviet North,* 11–22. IWGIA Documents, no. 67. Copenhagen: International Work Group for Indigenous Affairs.

International Work Group for Indigenous Affairs. 1992. Ethnocide Against the Udege. *IWGIA Newsletter,* no. 4 (October-November-December):31–32.

Kozlov, V. 1988. *The Peoples of the Soviet Union.* London: Hutchinson.

Krupnik, I. N.d. [1989]. "Arctic Ethno-Ecology": The Current State of Environmentalist Debate in the Soviet North. Typescript.

————. In press. East Meets West in the North: New Circumpolar Experience Influencing the Siberian Natives. Typescript.

Kuoljok, K. E. 1985. *The Revolution in the North: Soviet Ethnography and Nationality Policy.* Uppsala: Almqvist and Wiksell.

Mark, R. A. 1989. *Die Völker der Sowjetunion.* Opladen: Westdeutscher Verlag.

Nordic Yamal Expedition. 1989. *Yamal Augusti 1989: A Report from the Nordic Yamal Expedition.* Uppsala: Nordic Yamal Expedition.

Pika, A., and B. Prokhorov. 1989. The Big Problems of Small Ethnic Groups. *IWGIA Newsletter* 57:123–36.

Prokhorov, B. 1989. How to Save Yamal. *IWGIA Newsletter* 58:113–28.

Shnirelman, V. A. 1993. Are the Udege People Once Again Faced with the Threat of Disappearance? *IWGIA Newsletter,* no. 1 (January-February-March):31–35.

SUPAR. 1991. *Report 11.* Honolulu: Center for the Soviet Union in the Pacific-Asian Region, School of Hawaiian, Asian, and Pacific Studies, University of Hawaii, Manoa.

Taksami, C. 1990. Opening Speech at the Congress of Small Indigenous Peoples of the Soviet North. In *Indigenous Peoples of the Soviet North,* 23–44. IWGIA Documents, no. 67. Copenhagen: International Work Group for Indigenous Affairs.

Vitebsky, P. 1991. Culture and Environment: The Quest for Self-Determination among Siberian Reindeer Herders Today. Paper presented at the Association of Social Anthropologists of the Commonwealth Conference, Cambridge, England, 1991.

References to Chapter 6

Alam, M. 1986. *The Crisis of Empire in Mughal North India: Awadh and the Punjab, 1707–1748.* Delhi: Oxford University Press.

Anderson, Benedict. 1983. *Imagined Communities: Reflections on the Origin and Spread of Nationalism.* London: Verso.

Anderson, R. S., and Walter Huber. 1988. *The Hour of the Fox: Tropical Forests, the World Bank, and Indigenous People in Central India.* Delhi: Vistar.

Arnold, D. 1982. *Rebellious Hill-Men: The Gudem-Rampa Risings, 1839–1924.* In *Subaltern Studies I,* ed. R. Guha. Delhi: Oxford University Press.

Asad, Talal, ed. 1973. *Anthropology and the Colonial Encounter.* London: Ithaca.

Atlury, M. 1984. Alluri Sitarama Raju and the Manyam Rebellion of 1922–24. *Social Scientist* 131:1–33.

Attwood, Bain. 1989. *The Making of the Aborigines.* Sydney: Allen and Unwin.

Baker, D. 1991. Colonial Beginnings and the Indian Response: The Revolts of 1857–58 in Madhya Pradesh. *Modern Asian Studies* 25, no. 3:511–43.

Bates, C. 1987. Tribalism, Dependency and the Sub-Regional Dynamics of Economic Change in Central India. In *The State and the Market: Studies in the Economic and Social History of the Third World,* ed. C. J. Dewey. Riverdale, Md.: Riverdale.

Bates, C., and M. Carter. 1992. Tribal Migration in India and Beyond. In *The World of the Rural Labourer in Colonial India,* ed. G. Prakash. New Delhi: Oxford University Press.

Bayly, C. A. 1988. *The New Cambridge History of India.* Vol. 2.1: *Indian Society and the Making of the British Empire.* Cambridge: Cambridge University Press.

———. 1989. *Imperial Meridian: The British Empire and the World, 1780–1830.* London: Longmans.

Biddis, M. D., ed. 1979. *Images of Race.* Leicester: Leicester University Press.

Blunt, J. T. 1930. Narrative of a Route from Chinargur to Yentragoodum... 1795. In *Early European Travellers in the Nagpur Territories.* Nagpur: Government Press.

Bose, N. K. 1953. The Hindu Mode of Tribal Absorbtion. In *Cultural Anthropology and Other Essays.* Calcutta: Indian Associated Publishers.

———. 1975. *The Structure of Hindu Society.* Delhi: Orient Longmans.

Breman, Jan. 1985. *Of Peasants, Migrants and Paupers: Rural Labour Circulation and Capitalist Production in West India.* Delhi: Oxford University Press.

Cohn, B. 1983. The Invention of Authority in Victorian India. In *The Invention of Tradition,* ed. E. Hobsbawm and T. Ranger. Cambridge: Cambridge University Press.

———. 1985. The Command of Language and the Language of Command. In *Subaltern Studies IV,* ed. R. Guha. Delhi: Oxford University Press.

Corbridge, S. 1988. The Ideology of Tribal Economy and Society: Politics in the Jharkhand, 1950–1980. *Modern Asian Studies* 22:1–42.

Derrett, J. D. M. 1968. *Religion, Law and the State in India.* London: Faber and Faber.

Devalle, S. 1992. *Discourses of Ethnicity: Culture and Protest in Jharkhand.* Delhi: Sage.

Dubey, S. N., and R. Murdia. 1977. *Land Alienation and Restoration in Tribal Communities in India.* Bombay: Himalaya.

Elwin, V. 1942. *The Agaria.* Bombay: Oxford University Press.

Engineer, Asghar Ali. 1991. *The Mandal Commission Controversy.* Delhi: Ajanta.

Fox, R. G. 1971. *Kin, Clan, Raja and Rule: State-Hinterland Relations in Pre-Industrial India.* Berkeley: University of California Press.

Fried, Morton H. 1966. On the Concepts of "Tribe" and "Tribal Society." *Transactions of the New York Academy of Sciences* 28, no. 4:527–40.

Galey, J.-C. 1989. Reconsidering Kingship in India: An Ethnological Perspective. In *Kingship and the Kings,* ed. J.-C. Galey. New York: Harwood Academic Publishers.

Ghurye, G. S. 1980. *The Scheduled Tribes of India.* New Brunswick, N.J.: Transaction.

Gould, Stephen Jay. 1984. *The Mismeasure of Man.* New York: Pelican.

Guha, Ramchandra. 1989. *The Unquiet Woods: Ecological Change and Peasant Resistance in the Himalaya.* Delhi: Oxford University Press.

Guha, Ranajit. 1983. *Elementary Aspects of Peasant Insurgency in Colonial India.* Delhi: Oxford University Press.

Gunthorpe, E. J. 1882. *Notes on Criminal Tribes Residing in or Frequenting the Bombay Presidency, Berar and the Central Provinces.* Bombay: Government Press.

Hardiman, D. 1987. *The Devi Movement: Adivasi Assertion in Western India.* Delhi: Oxford University Press.

Hivale, Samrau. 1946. *The Pardhans of the Upper Narbada Valley.* Bombay: Oxford University Press.

Hockings, Paul. 1980. *Ancient Hindu Refugees: Badaga Social History, 1550–1975.* The Hague: Mouton.

Huizer, G., and B. Mannheim, eds. 1979. *The Politics of Anthropology: From Colonialism and Sexism Toward a View from Below.* The Hague: Mouton.

Inden, R. 1990. *Imagining India.* Oxford: Basil Blackwell.

Independent Commission on International Humanitarian Issues. 1987. *Indigenous Peoples: A Global Quest for Justice.* London: Zed.

Jones, K. W. 1989. *The New Cambridge History of India.* Vol. 3.1: *Socio-Religious Reform Movements in British India.* Cambridge: Cambridge University Press.

Kennedy, J. 1985 [1907]. *The Criminal Classes of India.* Delhi: Mittal.

Kirk-Greene, A. 1980. "Damnosa Hereditas": Ethnic Ranking and the Martial Races Imperative in Africa. *Ethnic and Racial Studies* 3, no. 4:393–414.

Kuper, A. 1991. *The Invention of Primitive Society: Transformations of an Illusion.* London: Routledge.

Leopold, J. 1970. The Aryan Theory of Race. *Indian Economic and Social History Review* 7, no. 2:271–97.

Nigam, S. 1990. Disciplining and Policing the "Criminals by Birth." Parts 1, 2. *Indian Economic and Social History Review* 27, nos. 2, 3:131–65, 257–88.

Oberai, A. S., and H. K. Manmohan Singh. 1985. *Causes and Consequences of Internal Migration: A Study in the Indian Punjab.* Delhi: Oxford University Press.

O'Hanlon, R. 1985. *Caste, Conflict and Ideology.* Cambridge: Cambridge University Press.

Peggs, J. 1832. *India's Cries to British Humanity: An Historical Account of Suttee, Infanticide, Ghat Murders and Slavery in India.* 3d ed. London: Simpkin and Marshall.

Radhakrishna, M. 1989. The Criminal Tribes Act in Madras Presidency: Implications for Itinerant Trading Communities. *Indian Economic and Social History Review* 26, no. 3:269–96.

Ranger, T. 1983. The Invention of Tradition in Colonial Africa. In *The Invention of Tradition,* ed. E. Hobsbawm and T. Ranger. Cambridge: Cambridge University Press.

Ray, Rabindra. 1988. *The Naxalites and Their Ideology.* Delhi: Oxford University Press.

Renfrew, C. 1987. *Archaeology and Language: The Puzzle of Indo-European Origins.* London: Penguin.

Ross King, W. 1870. *The Aboriginal Tribes of the Nilgiri Hills.* London: Longmans.

Saha, Suranjit. 1986. Historical Premises of India's Tribal Problem: A Study of the Political Economy of Exploitation and Exclusion. *Journal of Contemporary Asia* 16, no. 3:274–319.

Sahlins, M. D. 1968. *Tribesmen.* Englewood Cliffs, N.J.: Prentice Hall.

Sarkar, S. 1983. *"Popular" Movements and "Middle Class" Leadership in Late Colonial India: Perspectives and Problems of a "History from Below."* Calcutta: Centre for Social Studies.

Sengupta, N., ed. 1982. *Fourth World Dynamics: Jharkhand.* Delhi: Authors Guild.

Singh, Chetan. 1988. Conformity and Conflict: Tribes in the "Agrarian System" of Mughal India. *Indian Economic and Social History Review* 25, no. 3:319–40.

Singh, K. S., ed. 1982a. *Tribal Movements in India.* Vols. 1, 2. Delhi: Manohar.

———. 1982b. *Economies of the Tribes and Their Transformation.* Delhi: Concept.

———. 1985. *Tribal Society in India: An Anthropo-Historical Perspective.* Delhi: Manohar.

Sinha, Surajit, ed. 1987. *Tribal Polities and State Systems in Pre-Colonial Eastern and North Eastern India.* Calcutta: K. P. Bagchi.

Somerville, Augustus. 1929. *Crime and Religious Beliefs in India.* Calcutta: The Criminologist.

Srinivas, M. N. 1987. *The Dominant Caste and Other Essays.* Delhi: Oxford University Press.

Stocking, G. W. 1987. *Victorian Anthropology.* London: Macmillan.

Sundarayya, P. 1985. *Telengana People's Armed Struggle, 1946–1951.* Delhi: National Book Centre.

Vail, L. 1989. *The Creation of Tribalism in Southern Africa.* London: James Currey.

Washbrook, D. A. 1981. Law, State and Agrarian Society. *Modern Asian Studies* 15, no. 3:649–721.

Weber, Thomas. 1985. *Hugging the Trees: The Story of the Chipko Movement.* Delhi: Viking.

Zaid, Sunita. 1989. The Mughal State and Tribes in Seventeenth Century Sind. *Indian Economic and Social History Review* 26, no. 3:343–62.

References to Chapter 7

Administration Report on the Hill Tracts, Northern Arakan, for the Year 1877–78. 1879. Rangoon: Government Press.

Ahmad, Nafis. 1976. *A New Economic Geography of Bangladesh.* Delhi: Vikas.

Ali, Syed Murtaza. 1962. Hill Tribes of Chittagong. In *East Pakistan: A Profile.* Dacca: Orient Longmans.

———. 1986. Hill Tracts Solution in Sight? *Holiday* (12 September).

Amnesty International. 1986. *Unlawful Killings in the Chittagong Hill Tracts.* London: Amnesty International.

———. 1988. *Bangladesh: Report of a Mission Concerning Reported Human Rights Violations in the Chittagong Hill Tracts, 24–30 January 1988.* London: Amnesty International.

Anti-Slavery Society. 1984. *The Chittagong Hill Tracts: Militarization, Oppression and the Hill Tribes.* London: Anti-Slavery Society.

An Urgent Statement of the Jana Samhati Samiti on the Parbatya Zilla Parishad Bills Placed in the Jatiya Sangsad (Parliament) by Bangladesh Government. 1989. N.p.: Department of Information and Publicity, Parbatya Chattagram Jana Samhati Samiti, 18 February.

Bangladesh District Gazetteers: Chittagong Hill Tracts. Dacca: Government Press. Various years.

Bangladesh Groep Nederland. 1988. Bangladesh: Refugees from an Unknown War: Bangladeshi Tribals in India. *IWGIA Newsletter,* nos. 53, 54 (May/August):33–51.

Baske, Dhirendronath. 1976. *Shaontal Gonoshongramer Itihash* [History of the mass struggle of the Santals]. Calcutta: Pearl.

Bedrohte Zukunft: Bergvölker in Bangladesh [Threatened future: Mountain people in Bangladesh]. 1988. Zurich: Völkerkundemuseum der Universität Zürich, IWGIA-Lokalgruppe Zürich.

Bernot, Denise, and Lucien Bernot. 1958. *Les Khyang des collines de Chittagong (Pakistan oriental): Matériaux pour l'étude linguistique des Chin* [The Khyang of the Chittagong Hills (East Pakistan): Material for the linguistic study of the Chin]. Paris: Mouton.

Bernot, Lucien. 1967a. *Les paysans arakanais du Pakistan Oriental: L'histoire, le monde végétal et l'organisation sociale des réfugiés Marma (Mog)* [Arakanese peasants of East Pakistan: The history, vegetative world, and social organization of Marma (Mog) refugees]. 2 vols. Paris and The Hague: Mouton.

————. 1967b. *Les Cak: Contribution à l'étude ethnographique d'une population de langue loi* [The Cak: Contribution to the ethnography of a Loi-speaking people]. Paris and The Hague: Mouton.

Bessaignet, Pierre. 1958. *Tribesmen of the Chittagong Hill Tracts.* Dacca: Asiatic Society of Pakistan.

Béteille, André. 1977. The Definition of Tribe. In *Tribe, Caste and Religion in India,* ed. Romesh Thapar. Delhi: Macmillan.

Bhaumik, Subir, and H. C. Vanlalruata. 1988. Sailo's Grand Strategy: The Former CM Has Picked Up the Greater Mizoram Cause to Come Out of the Political Wilderness. *Sunday* (19–25 June):64.

Brauns, Claus-Dieter, and Lorenz G. Löffler. 1986. *Mru: Bergbewohner im Grenzgebiet von Bangladesh* [Mru: Mountain people in a border area of Bangladesh]. Basel and Stuttgart: Birkhäuser.

Buchanan, Francis. 1798. An Account of a Journey Undertaken by Order of the Board of Trade through the Provinces of Chittagong and Tiperah, in Order to Look Out for the Places Most Proper for the Cultivation of Spices, by Francis Buchanan, M.D. Manuscript, British Library, ADD 19286.

Castile, George P., and Gilbert Kushner, eds. 1981. *Persistent Peoples: Cultural Enclaves in Perspective.* Tucson: University of Arizona Press.

Census of India, 1931. 1933. Vol. V: *Bengal & Sikkim,* Pt. 2, tables (by A. E. Porter). Calcutta: Central Publication Branch.

Central Executive. 1985. Jana Samhati Samity, An Open Letter to Lt. General Ershad, Chief Martial-Law Administrator of Bangladesh, on his October 3 Proclamation. Printed leaflet dated 25 November.

Chakma, A. B. 1984. Look Back from Exile: A Chakma Experience. In *They Are Now Burning Village After Village: Genocide in the Chittagong Hill Tracts, Bangladesh,* ed. Wolfgang Mey. Copenhagen: International Work Group for Indigenous Affairs.

Chakma, C. R. [1984–85]. *Changma Kodha Bhandal/Chakma Bhashar Obhidhan* [Dictionary of the Chakma language]. Calcutta: Pustok Biponi, 1391 B.E.

————. [1987]. *Jug-Bibortone Chakma-Jati (Prachin Jug)* [The Chakma nation through the ages (ancient period)]. Calcutta: Pustok Biponi, 1394 B.E.

Chakma, P. B. 1986. Chittagong Hill Tracts and its Development. *Bangladesh Journal of Buddhist Studies* 3, no. 1:45–46.

Chakma, Siddhartha. [1985–86]. *Proshongo: Parbotyo Chottogram* [On the topic of the Chittagong Hill Tracts]. Calcutta: Nath Brothers, 1392 B.E.

Chakraborty, Ratan Lal. 1977. Chakma Resistance to Early British Rule. *Bangladesh Historical Studies* 2:133–56.

Chittagong Hill Tracts: An Observer Supplement. 1985. *Bangladesh Observer* (12 November).

Choudhuri, Dulal. 1980. *Chakma Probad* [Chakma proverbs]. Calcutta: Pustok Biponi.

Dewan, R. S. 1989. The Jumma Representative's Statement on the Systematic Genocide of the Helpless Jumma People of the Chittagong Hill Tracts being Carried Out by the Bangladesh Armed Forces. Geneva: Working Group on Indigenous Populations, United Nations Economic and Social Council.

Dubey, S. M. 1982. Inter-Ethnic Alliance, Tribal Movements and Integration in Northeast India. In *Tribal Movements in India,* ed. K. S. Singh. Vol. 1. Delhi: Manohar.

East Pakistan District Gazetteers: Chittagong. 1970. Dacca: East Pakistan Government Press.

Fishman, J. A. 1977. Language and Ethnicity. In *Language, Ethnicity and Intergroup Relations,* ed. Howard Giles. London, etc.: Academic.

Fresh Influx in Tripura. 1989. *Times of India* (June 23).

Fried, M. H. 1975. *The Notion of Tribe.* Menlo Park, Calif.: Cummings.

Furnivall, John S. 1957. *An Introduction to the Political Economy of Burma.* Rangoon: People's Literature Committee and House.

Ghosh, Jamini Mohan. 1960. *Magh Raiders in Bengal.* Calcutta, etc.: Bookland.

Government of Bengal. 1862a. *Government of Bengal, Judicial Department, Political Branch, Proceedings 226–227* (April 1862).

————. 1862b. *Government of Bengal, Judicial Proceedings 142–143* (December 1862).

————. 1865. *Government of Bengal, Judicial Department, Political Proceeding 187* (June 1865).

————. 1866. *Government of Bengal, Judicial Proceedings 83–84* (July 1866).

————. 1872a. *Government of Bengal, Revenue Department, Land Revenue Branch, Proceeding 53* (May 1872).

————. 1872b. *Government of Bengal, Revenue Department, Land Revenue Branch, Proceeding 54* (May 1872).

————. 1873. *Government of Bengal, Revenue Department, Land Revenue Branch, Proceeding 15* (September 1873).

————. 1874a. *Government of Bengal, Judicial Department, Political Branch, Proceedings 15–17* (February 1874).

————. 1874b. *Government of Bengal, Judicial Department, Political Branch, Proceeding 3* (April 1874).

————. 1876. Report on the Administration of the Chittagong Hill Tracts for 1875–76. *Government of Bengal, Judicial Department, Political Branch, Proceedings 22–23* (September 1876).

————. 1879. Annual Report of the Chittagong Hill Tracts for 1878–79. *Government of Bengal, Judicial Department, Political Branch, Proceeding 11* (September 1879).

————. 1917. Appendix A: References regarding the position of the Hill Tracts Chiefs. *Government of Bengal, Political Department, Political Branch, Proceedings 100–101* (May 1917).

————. 1918. Issue of a Warning to the Mong Chief, Chittagong Hill Tracts, for Dereliction of Duty. *Government of Bengal, Political Department, Political Branch, Proceedings 1–2* (June 1918).

Guha, Ranajit. 1983. *Elementary Aspects of Peasant Insurgency in Colonial India.* Delhi: Oxford University Press.

Heesterman, J. C. 1985. *The Inner Conflict of Tradition: Essays in Indian Ritual, Kingship, and Society.* Chicago and London: University of Chicago Press.

Hobsbawm, Eric, and Terence Ranger, eds. 1983. *The Invention of Tradition.* Cambridge: Cambridge University Press.

Hutchinson, R. H. Sneyd. 1906. *An Account of the Chittagong Hill Tracts.* Calcutta: Bengal Secretariat Book Depot.

————. 1909. *Eastern Bengal and Assam District Gazetteers: Chittagong Hill Tracts.* Allahabad: Pioneer.

Islam, Sirajul. 1983. Tribal Resistance in Chittagong Hill Tracts (1776–1787). In *Saga of Freedom,* ed. Nishit Ranjan Ray. Delhi: People's Publishing.

Kamaluddin, S. 1989. Bangladesh—Tribal Insurgents Try to Disrupt Hill Council Polls: Intimidatory Tactics. *Far Eastern Economic Review* (29 June):24.

Kamkhenthang, H. 1988. *The Paite: A Transborder Tribe of India and Burma.* Delhi: Mittal.

Kindersley, J. B. 1939. *Final Report on the Survey and Settlement Operations in the District of Chittagong, 1923–1933.* Alipore: Bengal Government Press.

Lévi-Strauss, Claude. 1952. Le syncrétisme religieux dans un village mog du territoire de Chittagong [Religious syncretism in a Mog village in the Chittagong region]. *Revue de l'Histoire des Religions* 141, no. 2, 202–37.

Lewin, T. H. 1869. *The Hill Tracts of Chittagong and the Dwellers Therein, with Comparative Vocabularies of the Hill Dialects.* Calcutta: Bengal Printing.

————. 1984 [1870]. *Wild Races of the Eastern Frontier of India.* Delhi: Mittal.

Löffler, Lorenz G. 1963. Carrying Capacity, Schwendbauproblem in Südostasien [Carrying capacity, a problem of shifting cultivation in Southeast Asia]. In *VIe Congrès International des Sciences Anthropologiques et Ethnologiques, Paris 1960* 2, no. 1:179–82.

————. 1964. Chakma und Sak: Ethnolinguistische Beiträge zur Geschichte eines Kulturvolkes [Chakma and Sak: Ethno-linguistic Contributions to the history of a "cultured" people]. *Internationales Archiv der Ethnographie* 50:72–115.

————. 1966. L'Alliance asymétrique chez les Mru (Pakistan oriental) [Asymmetrical alliance among the Mru (East Pakistan)]. *L'Homme* 6, no. 3:68–80.

————. N.d. Der Uebergang vom Schwendbau zum Ackerbau im Chittagong-Gebiet [The transition from shifting cultivation to plough cultivation in the Chittagong region]. Manuscript.

Macrae, John. 1801. Account of the Kookies or Lunctas. *Asiatick Researches* 8:5.

Maniruzzaman. 1984. Notes on Chakma Phonology. In *Tribal Cultures in Bangladesh,* ed. M. Qureshi. Rajshahi: Institute of Bangladesh Studies, Rajshahi University.

Mazumder, Begum Ismat Ara. 1985. Kaptai—Coexistence of Civilized and Tribal People. In Chittagong Hill Tracts: An Observer Supplement, *Bangladesh Observer* (12 November):7–8.

Menon, Ramesh. 1988. Mizoram—Wild Dreams: Plans to Carve a New State. *India Today* (30 June):63–67.

Mey, Almut. 1979. *Untersuchungen zur Wirtschaft in den Chittagong Hill Tracts (Bangladesh)* [Research into the economy of the Chittagong Hill Tracts (Bangladesh)]. Bremen: Uebersee-Museum.

Mey, Wolfgang. 1980. *Politische Systeme in den Chittagong Hill Tracts, Bangla Desh* [Political systems in the Chittagong Hill Tracts, Bangladesh]. Bremen: Uebersee-Museum.

————, ed. 1984. *They Are Now Burning Village After Village: Genocide in the Chittagong Hill Tracts, Bangladesh.* Copenhagen: International Work Group for Indigenous Affairs.

————. 1988. "Es ist verboten, die Chittagong Hill Tracts zu betreten": Siedlungsgebiete der CHT-Völker ["Entry into the Chittagong Hill Tracts prohibited": Settlement areas of the CHT peoples]. In *"Wir wollen nicht euch—Wir wollen euer Land": Macht und Menschenrechte in den Chittagong Hill Tracts/Bangladesch* ["We do not want you, we want your land": Power and human rights in the Chittagong Hill Tracts, Bangladesh], ed. Wolfgang Mey. Göttingen and Vienna: Pogrom Taschenbücher.

Mills, J. P. 1927. "Report on the Chiefs of the Chittagong Hill Tracts" and "Proposals Regarding the Chiefs." 2 vols. Manuscript report.

————. 1933. Notes on a Tour in the Chittagong Hill Tracts in 1926. *Census of India, 1931.* Vol. 5, Appendix 2, 514–21. Calcutta: Central Publications Branch.

Montu, Kazi. 1980. Tribal Insurgency in Chittagong Hill Tracts. *Economic and Political Weekly* (6 September).

Naga Nation. 1986. *The Naga Nation and its Struggle against Genocide.* IWGIA Documents, no. 56. Copenhagen: International Work Group for Indigenous Affairs.

Naser, Moinuddin. 1990. Shantibahini Now Uses Remote Control Explosives. *Holiday* 25, no. 24 (12 January):1, 8.

Pogson, Captain. 1831. *Captain Pogson's Narrative During a Tour to Chateegaon, 1831.* Serampore: Serampore Press.

Population Census of Bangladesh, 1974: District Census Report, Chittagong Hill Tracts. 1979. Dacca: Bangladesh Bureau of Statistics.

Qanungo, Suniti Bhushan. 1988. *A History of Chittagong.* Vol. 1: *From Ancient Times Down to 1761.* Chittagong: Signet.

Qureshi, Mahmud Shah, ed. 1984. *Tribal Cultures in Bangladesh.* Rajshahi: Institute of Bangladesh Studies, Rajshahi University.

Rashid, Kazi Mahmudar. 1980. A Study on Administration of Indigenous People of the Chittagong Hill Tracts. Typescript.

Rawlins, John. 1790. On the Manners, Religion, and Laws of the Cúcì's, or Mountaineers of Tipra. *Asiatick Researches* 2, no. 12:187–93.

Ray, Tarapada, comp. 1983. *Santal Rebellion: Documents.* Calcutta: Subarnarekha.

Report on the Progress of Arakan under British Rule from 1826 to 1875. 1873. Rangoon: Government Press.

Revenue Department. 1862. *Revenue Department, Land Revenue Branch, Proceedings 120–122* (March 1862).

Riebeck, Emil. 1885. *Die Hügelstämme von Chittagong: Ergebnisse einer Reise im Jahre 1882* [The hill tribes of Chittagong: Results of a journey in 1882]. Berlin: Verlag von A. Asher and Company.

Risley, H. H. 1981 [1891]. *The Tribes and Castes of Bengal: Ethnographic Glossary.* Calcutta: Firma Mukhopadhyay.

Rosén-Hockersmith, Eva. 1985. *Buddhismen i Bangladesh: En studie av en minoritetsreligion.* [Buddhism in Bangladesh: A study of a minority religion]. Uppsala: Religionshistoriska Institutionen vid Uppsala Universitet.

Roy, Devasish (Chakma Raja) et al. 1989. *04/05/89 Ing roj brihospotibar Rangamati Parbotyo Zelar Longodu Upozelar upojatiyoder biruddhe shonghotito shohingsho ghotonar protibade smaroklipi* [A memorandum in protest against the genocidal attacks on tribals in Langadu Upazilla, Rangamati Hill District, on Thursday, 4 May 1989]. Typescript petition presented in Rangamati, 1989.

Royce, Anya Peterson. 1982. *Ethnic Identity: Strategies of Diversity.* Bloomington: Indiana University Press.

Sahlins, Marshall. 1968. *Tribesmen.* Englewood Cliffs, N.J.: Prentice Hall.

Said, Edward. 1979. *Orientalism.* New York: Vintage.

Sattar, Abdus. 1971. *In the Sylvan Shadows.* Dacca: Saquib Brothers.

————. 1975. *Tribal Culture in Bangladesh.* Dacca: Muktadhara.

Schendel, Willem van, ed. 1992. *Francis Buchanan in Southeast Bengal (1798): His Journey to Chittagong Hill Tracts, Noakhali, and Comilla.* Dhaka: University Press.

Sengupta, Nirmal. 1982. Background to the Jharkhand Question. In *Fourth World Dynamics: Jharkhand,* ed. Nirmal Sengupta. Delhi: Authors Guild.

Serajuddin, A. M. 1971. The Origin of the Rajas of the Chittagong Hill Tracts and their Relations with the Mughuls and the East India Company in the Eighteenth Century. *Journal of the Pakistan Historical Society* 19, no. 1 (January):51–60.

————. 1984. The Chakma Tribe of the Chittagong Hill Tracts in the 18th Century. *Journal of the Royal Asiatic Society of Great Britain and Ireland,* no. 1:90–98.

Shantibahini Activities Hinder Road Works in Ctg Hill Tracts. 1986. *New Nation* (13 February).

Singh, K. S. 1982. Tribal Autonomy Movements in Chotanagpur. In *Tribal Movements in India,* ed. K. S. Singh. Vol. 2. Delhi: Manohar.

Smith, Anthony D. 1981. *The Ethnic Revival in the Modern World.* Cambridge: Cambridge University Press.

Sopher, David E. 1963. Population Dislocation in the Chittagong Hills. *Geographical Review* 53:337–62.

————. 1964. The Swidden/Wet-Rice Transition Zone in the Chittagong Hills. *Annals of the Association of American Geographers* 54, no. 1:107–26.

Spielmann, Hans-Jürgen. 1968. *Die Bawm-Zo: Eine Chin-Gruppe in den Chittagong Hill Tracts (Ostpakistan)* [The Bawm-Zo: A Chin group in the Chittagong Hill Tracts (East Pakistan)]. Ph.D. thesis, University of Heidelberg.

Survival International. 1988. *Bangladesh—Chittagong Hill Tracts Report for 1988: No End to Human Rights Abuses.* London: Survival International.

T., C. M. 1988. Beleaguered Tribals. *Far Eastern Economic Review* (6 October).

Talukdar, S. P. 1988. *The Chakmas: Life and Struggle.* Delhi: Gian Publishing House.

Urgent Statement of the Jana Samhati Samiti on the Parbatya Zilla Parishad Bills Placed in the Jatiya Sangsad (Parliament) by Bangladesh Government, An 1989. N.p.: Department of Information and Publicity, Parbatya Chattagram Jana Samhati Samiti (18 February).

Vumson. 1986. *Zo History, With an Introduction to Zo Culture, Economy, Religion and their Status as an Ethnic Minority in India, Burma, and Bangladesh.* Aizawl, Mizoram: Vumson.

Wolf, Eric R. 1982. *Europe and the People without History.* Berkeley: University of California Press.

References to Chapter 8

Ahmed, Akbar S. 1986. *Pakistan Society: Islam, Ethnicity and Leadership in South Asia.* Karachi: Oxford University Press.

Alavi, Hamza. 1991. Nationhood and Communal Violence in Pakistan. *Journal of Contemporary Asia* (Adelaide, Australia) 21, no. 2:152–78.

Baluch, Mir Ahmed Yar Khan. 1975. *Inside Baluchistan.* Karachi: Royal Book Company.

Baluch People's Liberation Front. 1976. *The War in Baluchistan: Strategies for Liberation.* London: Baluch People's Liberation Front.

Baluchistan Cover Story: Ataullah Mengal Interview. 1986. *The Herald* (Karachi), July.

Bhutto, Mumtaz, and Hafiz Pirzada. 1987. *A Confederal Constitution for Pakistan: An Outline.* London: Bhutto and Pirzada.

Chano, Sahib Khan. 1983. Baluchistan, 1867–1877: Sind and Punjab British Officers' Differences. *Sind Quarterly* 11, no. 4:41–45.

Dastarac A., and R. Dersen. 1976. Baloutchistan la guerre oubliée. *Le Monde Diplomatique* (August):38–39.

Dastarac, A., and M. Levent. 1981. Le Pakistan, fragile bastion de la strategie occidentale. *Le Monde Diplomatique* (March):1, 4–5.

———. 1984. Pakistan, le verrouillage. *Le Monde Diplomatique* (August):12–13.

———. 1985. Le golfe sous surveillance. *Le Monde Diplomatique* (July):14–15.

Digard, J. P., ed. 1988. *Le fait ethnique en Iran et en Afghanistan.* Paris: Editions du CNRS.

Dodwell, H. H. 1964. *The Cambridge History of India.* Vol. 6: *The Indian Empire, 1858–1918.* New Delhi: Chand.

Elfenbein, J. H. 1960. Balūčistān. *Encyclopedia of Islam.* Leiden and London: Brill and Luzac.

Enzyklopaeda des Islām. 1913–36. Leiden and Leipzig: Brill and Otto Harrassowitz.

Gankovski, Yuri V. 1971. *The Peoples of Pakistan: An Ethnic History,* trans. I. Gavrilov. Lahore: People's Publishing House.

———. 1977. *Natsional'nyi Vopros i National'nye Dvizheniia v Pakistane.* Moscow: Nauka Publishing House.

Government of Pakistan. 1974. *White Paper on Baluchistan*. Islamabad: Government of Pakistan.

————. 1991. *Pakistan Statistical Yearbook, 1990*. Karachi: Federal Bureau of Statistics.

Harrison, Selig S. 1981. *In Afghanistan Shadows: Baluch Nationalism and Soviet Temptations*. New York: Carnegie Endowment for International Peace.

"Jabal": Bulletin of the Baluchistan People's Liberation Front. [1977]. N.p., n.d.

Jalal, Ayesha. 1985. *The Sole Spokesman: Jinnah, the Muslim League and the Demand for Pakistan*. Cambridge: Cambridge University Press.

Lifschultz, L. 1983. Ataullah Mengal's Declaration of Independence. *Economic Political Weekly* (Bombay), (19 May):735–52.

Mansergh, Nicholas, ed. 1977. *The Transfer of Power, 1942–47*. Vol. 7. London: Her Majesty's Stationery Office.

Moore, Alvin, Jr. 1980. Publishing in Pushto, Baluchi, Brahui, and Other Minor Languages of Pakistan. Chicago: South Asia Reference Center, University of Chicago.

Munir, Muhammad. 1980. *From Jinnah to Zia*. Lahore: Vanguard Book.

Pakistan's Civil War. 1975. *Manchester Guardian*, 24 January.

Pehrson, Robert N. 1966. *The Social Organisation of the Marri Baluch*. Viking Fund Publications in Anthropology, no. 43. Chicago: Aldine.

Rafique, Afzal M., ed. 1973. *Selected Speeches and Statements of Quaid-i-Azam*. Lahore: M. A. Jinnah.

Sayeed, Khalid B. 1980. *Politics in Pakistan: The Nature and Direction of Change*. New York: Praeger.

Scholz, Fred. 1974. *Belutchistan (Pakistan): Eine Socialgeographische Studie des Wandels in einem Nomadenland Seit Beginn der Kolonialzeit*. Göttingen: Verlag Erich Goltze.

Swidler, Nina. 1977. Brahui Political Organization and the National State. In *Pakistan's Western Borderlands*, ed. Ainslie T. Embree. Durham, N.C.: Carolina Academy Press.

Thornton, Thomas Henry. 1895. *Colonel Sir Robert Sandeman*. London: John Murray.

Viennot, J. P. 1973. Baloutchistan, Vers un nouveau Bengladesh? *Le Monde Diplomatique* (October):24–25.

References to Chapter 9

Allen, N. J. 1969. Some Problems in the Ethnography of the Peoples of Nepal and their Neighbors. D.Phil. thesis, University of Oxford.

Badrinath, Yogi, and Ruplal Mahatau Chaudari. 1959–60. *Dangiśaran Kathā-Barkimār Dang*, Nepal: Badrinath and Chaudari.

Barnes, R. H. 1984. *Two Crows Denies It: A History of Controversy in Omaha Sociology.* Lincoln and London: University of Nebraska Press.

Bennet, W. C. 1878. Introduction: Province of Oudh. *Oudh Gazetteer* 3, no. 504:6.

Berreman, Gerald D. 1985. Internal Colonialism and Fourth-World Movements in the Indian Himalayas. In *Native Power,* ed. Jens Brøsted et al. Oslo: Universtietsforlaget.

Bista, Dor Bahadur. 1987 [1967]. *The Peoples of Nepal.* Kathmandu: Ratna Pustak Bhandar.

Burger, Julian. 1987. *Report from the Frontier: The State of the World's Indigenous Peoples.* London: Zed.

Caplan, Lionel. 1980. Power and Status in South Asian Slavery. In *Asian and African Systems of Slavery,* ed. James L. Watson. Oxford: Basil Blackwell.

Chaudari, M. 1982–83. *Guru Bābak Jalmauti.* Dang, Nepal: M. Chaudari.

Colchester, M., and L. Lohmann. 1990. *The Tropical Forestry Action Plan: What Progress?* Dorset: World Rainforest Movement.

Danish International Development Agency. 1991. *Internal Report on Bonded Labour.* Kathmandu: DANIDA.

De Ste Croix, G. E. M. 1988. Slavery and Other Forms of Unfree Labour. In *Slavery and Other Forms of Unfree Labour,* ed. Leonie Archer. London: Routledge.

Eagle, S. 1990. Viewpoint of a Man on the Ground in the Far West of Nepal. Typescript.

Elder, Joseph W., Mahabir Ale, Mary A. Evans, David P. Gillespie, Rohit Kumar Nepali, Sitaram P. Pondyal, and Bruce P. Smith. 1974. *Planned Resettlement in Nepal.* Kathmandu: Institute of Nepal and Asian Studies, Tribhuvan University.

Gaige, F. H. 1970. A National Integration in Nepal: A Study of Nepal Tarai. Ph.D. diss., University of Pennsylvania.

Ghimire, Krishna B. 1991. The Victims of Development. *Development and Cooperation* 1:16–18.

Goldstein, Melvyn C., J. L. Ross, and S. Schuler. 1983. From Mountain-Rural to Plains-Urban Society: Implications of the 1981 Nepalese Census. *Mountain Research and Development* 3:61–64.

Guha, Ramachandra. 1989. *The Unquiet Woods: Ecological Change and Peasant Resistance in the Himalayas.* Delhi: Oxford University Press.

Gunow, Jane, and Narayan Kaji Shresta. 1989. *From Policing to Participation: The Reorientation of Forest Department Field Staff in Nepal.* Manual prepared for the National Workshop on Planning for Community Forestry Projects, FAO/RWEDP, State Planning Institute and Forest Department of Uttar Pradesh, Luchnow, India, 17–21 October.

Gurung, Harka. 1983. *Internal and International Migration in Nepal.* Kathmandu: National Commission on Population, Task Force on Migration.

Gurung, Ganesh M., and Harald O. Skar. 1988. *Social Life in Urma and Urmi.* Kathmandu: Kathmandu University and the Norwegian Institute of International Affairs.

Hamilton, Francis Buchanan. 1971 [1819]. *An Account of the Kingdom of Nepal and of the Territories Annexed to this Domain by the House of Gorkha.* New Delhi: Manjushri [Edinburgh: Archibald Constable].

Himal. 1990. Nepal's Tarai: Backwater or New Frontier? *Himal* 3, no. 3:5–8.

His Majesty's Government of Nepal. 1988. *Master Plan for the Forestry Sector, Nepal.* Kathmandu: Ministry of Forests and Soil Conservation. Sector Project HMGN/ADB/FIMNIDA.

Hodgson, Brian H. 1880. *Papers Relative to the Colonization, Commerce, Physical Geography, Etc., of the Himalaya Mountains and Nepal.* Selections from the Record of the Government of Bengal, no. 27. Calcutta: Calcutta Gazette Office.

Höfer, Andras. 1979. *The Caste Hierarchy and the State in Nepal: a Study of the Muluki Ain of 1854.* Khumbu Himal, Band 13/2. Innsbruck: Universitätsverlag Wagner.

Hoftun, Martin, ed., 1990. *Nepal: et land i omveltning.* Oslo: Cappelen.

Independent Commission on International Humanitarian Issues. 1987. *Indigenous Peoples: A Global Quest for Justice.* Report for the Independent Commission on International Humanitarian Issues. London: Zed.

International Labour Office. 1989. *ILO Convention 169, Concerning Indigenous and Tribal Peoples in Independent Countries.* Geneva: ILO.

International Work Group for Indigenous Affairs. 1990. First Revised Text of the Draft Universal Declaration on the Rights of Indigenous Peoples. In *IWGIA Yearbook, 1989.* Copenhagen: International Work Group for Indigenous Affairs.

Kirkpatrick, William. 1975 [1811]. *An Account of the Kingdom of Nepal.* New Delhi: Asian Publications Services.

Krauskopff, Gisele. 1989. *Maitres et Possedes.* Paris: Center National de la Recherche Scientifique.

League of Nations. 1926. *Convention on the Abolition of Slavery.* Geneva: League of Nations.

Levine, Nancy E. 1980. Opposition and Interdependence: Demographic and Economic Perspectives on Nyinba Slavery. In *Asian and African Systems of Slavery,* ed. James L. Watson. Oxford: Basil Blackwell.

MacDonaugh, Christian. 1989. The Mythology of the Tharu: Aspects of Cultural Identity in Dang, West Nepal. *Kailash* 15, nos. 3–4:191–206.

Muluki Ain. 1965. *Sri Panc Suendra Vikram Sahdecka Sasankalma Baneko Muluki Ain.* Reprint. Kathmandu: Law and Justice Ministry.

Needham, R. 1975. Polythetic Classification, Convergence and Consequences. *Man* 10:348–69.

Nepal. 1984. *Population Census, 1981*. Kathmandu: National Planning Commission, Central Bureau of Statistics.

Nesfield, John C. 1867. The Tharus and Bogshas of Upper India. *Calcutta Review* 159:1–46.

Ojha, D. P. 1983. History of Land Settlement in Nepal Terai. *Contribution to Nepalese Studies* 11, no. 2:93–96.

Privi Narayan Shah. 2016 B.S. *Dilya Upadesh*, ed. Yogi Narhari Nath. Kathmandu: Ratna Pustak Bhandar.

Rana, Chandra Shamsher. 1925. *Appeal to the People of Nepal for the Emancipation of Slaves and Abolition of Slavery in the Country*. Kathmandu: Subba Rama Mani.

Regmi, M. C. 1976. *Landownership in Nepal*. Berkeley: University of California Press.

———. 1978. *Thatched Huts and Stucco Palaces: Peasants and Landlords in 19th Century Nepal*. New Delhi: Vikas.

———. 1984. *The State and Economic Surplus: Production, Trade and Resource Mobilization in Early 19th Century Nepal*. Varanasi: Nath.

———. 1988. *An Economic History of Nepal, 1846–1901*. Varanasi: Nath.

Rising Nepal. 1989. Work Continues on Citizenship Issue. *Rising Nepal* (10 May):1.

Sagild, Inge Kirstine. 1988. *Internal Report, Greta Eye Hospital*. Report of Norwegian Church Aid, Nepal, October.

Shresta, Nanda R. 1990. *Landlessness and Migration in Nepal*. Boulder: Westview.

Skar, Harald O. 1990. *Norwegian Non-Governmental Involvement in Nepal*. NUPI Reports, no. 148. Oslo: Norwegian Institute of International Affairs.

Srivastava, S. K. 1958. *The Tharus: A Study in Culture Dynamics*. Agra: Agra University Press.

Tucci, Giuseppe. 1956. *Preliminary Report on Two Scientific Expeditions in Nepal*. Rome: Instituto Italiano per il Studio del Medio ed Estreme Oriente.

United Nations. 1956. *Supplementary Convention on the Abolition of Slavery, the Slave Trade and Institutions and Practices Similar to Slavery*. Geneva: United Nations.

References to Chapter 10

Barnett, Robert. N.d. General Impressions: Emotions, Repression, and Propaganda. Typescript.

Barth, F. 1969. *Ethnic Groups and Boundaries*. Boston: Little, Brown.

Burger, J. 1987. *Report from the Frontier: The State of the World's Indigenous Peoples.* London and Cambridge, Mass.: Zed and Cultural Survival.

Cannon, T. 1989. National Minorities and the Internal Frontier. In *China's Regional Development,* ed. D. S. G. Goodman. London; Routledge.

―――. 1990. Regions: Spatial Inequality and Regional Policy. In *The Geography of Contemporary China: The Impact of Deng Xiaoping's Decade,* ed. T. Cannon and A. Jenkins. London and New York: Routledge.

Chiang Wei. 1989. The Womens' Script: Introduction, Preliminary Catalogue and Analysis of Extant Documents. *Hong Kong Anthropology Bulletin,* no. 3:26–30.

Chiu, Yen Liang (Fred). N.d. Some Observations on Social Discourse Regarding Taiwan's "Primordial Inhabitants." Typescript.

Cui Jinxiang. 1987. Preliminary Exploration of the Legislative Principles of the Self-Regulations for the Autonomous Regions of the Nationalities. *Zhongguo faxue,* no. 5:8–20.

―――. 1988. An Important Way to Implement the Law of Regional Autonomy for Minority Nationalities in Multi-Ethnic Provinces. *Minzu yanjiu,* no. 1:1–11.

Deal, M. 1971. National Minority Policy in Southwest China, 1911–1965. Ph.D. diss., University of Washington.

Dreyer, J. 1968. China's Minority Nationalities in the Cultural Revolution. *China Quarterly,* no. 35 (July-September):96–109.

―――. 1976. *China's Forty Millions.* Cambridge and London: Harvard University Press.

Fan Wenlan. 1958. Zi Han Qin qi zhongguo cheng wei yige tongyi guojia de yuanyin. In *Han minzu xingcheng wenti taolunji,* by Fan Wenlan et al. Beijing: Sanlian shudian.

Fei Xiaotong. 1981. Ethnic Identification in China. In *Towards a People's Anthropology.* Beijing: New World Press.

―――. 1988. Plurality and Unity in the Configuration of the Chinese People. Hong Kong: N.p. Tanner Lecture, 15 November, Chinese University of Hong Kong.

Feuchtwang, S. 1988. The Problem of "Superstition" in the People's Republic of China. In *Religion and Political Power,* ed. G. Benavides. New York: Oxford University Press.

Gong Zhebing, ed. 1986a. *Funu Wenzi he Yaozu Qianjiadong.* Beijing: Zhanwang.

―――. 1986b. Hunan Jiangyong Shangjiangxu de Nushu. *New Asia Academic Bulletin* (Hong Kong) 6:291–303.

Harrell, S. 1989. Ethnicity and Kin Terms among Two Kinds of Yi. In *Ethnic-*

ity and Ethnic Groups in China, ed. Chiao Chien and Nicholas Tapp. Hong Kong: New Asia College, Chinese University of Hong Kong.

Heberer, T. 1989. *China and its National Minorities: Autonomy or Assimilation?* New York and London: M. E. Sharpe.

Hill, A. 1982. Familiar Strangers: The Yunnanese Chinese in Northern Thailand. Ph.D. diss., University of Illinois, Urbana-Champaign.

Hsieh Jiann. 1984. Population Structure and Family Pattern under Directed Social-Cultural Change: The Samei Case in Yunnan, P.R.C. *International Review of Modern Sociology* 14:1–22.

———. 1986. China's Nationalities Policy: Its Development and Problems. *Anthropos* 81:1–20.

Kothari, Rajni. 1989. Ethnicity. In *Ethnicity: Identity, Conflict, Crisis,* ed. Kumar David and Santisalan Kadirgamir. Hong Kong: ARENA Press.

Lemoine, J. 1989a. Ethnologues en Chine. *Diogène,* no. 133 (January-March):82–112.

———. 1989b. Ethnicity, Culture and Development among Some Minorities of the People's Republic of China. In *Ethnicity and Ethnic Groups in China,* ed. Chiao Chien and Nicholas Tapp. Hong Kong: New Asia College, Chinese University of Hong Kong.

Lin Shengzhong. 1984. The Present Demographical Situation of the Olunchun Nationality in Heihe Prefecture and the Causes of its Slow Growth. *Renkou Xuekan,* no. 1 (cited in Lu Guangtian 1986).

Lin Yaohua. 1956. Problems Concerning Chinese Ethnographers in Connection with Solving the Nationalities Question in the CPR. *Sovietskaya etnografia,* no. 3:79–91. Translated in *Ethnography and National Minorities in Communist China,* 1–32. Joint Publications Research Service. Washington, D.C.: U.S. Department of Commerce, 1962.

Lu Guangtian. 1986. A Review of Demographic Studies of China's National Minorities. *Social Sciences in China* 7, no. 3:89–109.

Ma Yin, ed. 1989. *China's Minority Nationalities.* Beijing: Foreign Language Press.

Moseley, G. 1965. China's Fresh Approach to the National Minority Question. *China Quarterly* 24:15–27.

[National Census]. 1985. *Zhongguo 1982 nian renkou pucha ziliao* [1982 population census of China]. Beijing: Zhongguo tongji chubanshe.

Pye, L. 1975. China: Ethnic Minorities and National Security. In *Ethnicity: Theory and Experience,* ed. Nathan Glazer and Daniel Moynihan. Cambridge: Harvard University Press.

Qiu Pu. 1989. On the Trend of the Development of the Relations among the Nationalities in China. In *Ethnicity and Ethnic Groups in China,* ed. Chiao Chien and Nicholas Tapp. Hong Kong: New Asia College, Chinese University of Hong Kong.

Schafer, E. 1967. *The Vermilion Bird: T'ang Images of the South*. Berkeley: University of California Press.

T'ao Yun-kun. 1943. Lun Bianjiang-di Han-ren Ji Qi Yu bian-jiang Jian-she Zhi Guan-shi. *Bian-zheng Gong-Lun*, no. 2:34–38.

Tapp, N. 1986. The Minorities of Southern China: A General Overview. *Journal of the Hong Kong Branch of the Royal Asiatic Society* 26:102–14.

———. 1989. *Sovereignty and Rebellion: The White Hmong of Northern Thailand*. Kuala Lumpur: Oxford University Press.

Thierry, F. 1989. Empire and Minority in China. *Minority People in the Age of Nation-States*, ed. G. Chaliand. London: Pluto Press.

Thoraval, Joël. 1991. "Religion ethnique, religion lignagère: Sur la tentative d'islamisation d'une lignage Han en Hainan. *Études Chinoises: Bulletin de l'Association Française d'Études Chinoises* 10, nos. 1–2:9–75.

———. Forthcoming. Le Concept Chinois de Nation—est-il "Obscur"? In *Pactes de la Recherche en Science Sociale*, ed. P. Bourdieu. Paris: École des Hautes Études en Sciences Sociale.

Tweddell, C. 1978. The Tuli-Chinese Balk Line: Minimal Group Self-Identity. In *Perspectives on Ethnicity*, ed. R. Holloman and S. Arutionov. The Hague: Mouton.

Wang Xiaoqiang and Bai Nanfeng. 1989. *The Poverty of Plenty*. London and New York. Macmillan.

Wu, David Y. H. 1989. Culture Change and Ethnic Identity among Minorities in China. In *Ethnicity and Ethnic Groups in China*, ed. Chiao Chien and Nicholas Tapp. Hong Kong: New Asia College, Chinese University of Hong Kong.

Xu Yi and Chen Baosen. 1984. Finance. In *China's Socialist Modernization*, ed. Yu Guangyuan. Beijing: Foreign Language Press.

References to Chapter 11

Amnesty International. 1988. *Burma: Extrajudicial Execution and Torture of Members of Ethnic Minorities*. London: Amnesty International (May).

———. 1990. *Myanmar: "In the National Interest."* London: Amnesty International (November).

———. 1992. *Myanmar: "No Law at All": Human Rights Violations under Military Rule*. London: Amnesty International.

Article 19. 1992. *"Our Heads are Bloody but Unbowed": Suppression of Educational Freedom in Burma*. London: Article 19.

Aung Thwin, M. 1985. British "Pacification" of Burma: Order Without Meaning. *Journal of South East Asian Studies* 16, no. 2:245–61.

Backus, C. 1981. *The Nan-chao Kingdom and T'ang China's Southwestern Frontier.* Cambridge: Cambridge University Press.

Bennison, J. J. 1933. *Burma, Part 1—Report: Census of India, 1931.* Vol. 11. Rangoon: Government Printing and Stationery Office.

British Broadcasting Corporation. 1983. *Summary of World Broadcasts,* 4 August.

————. 1989. *Summary of World Broadcasts,* 2 May.

————. 1991. *Summary of World Broadcasts,* 7 January.

Falla, J. 1991. *True Love and Bartholomew: Rebels on the Burmese Border.* Cambridge: Cambridge University Press.

Hinton, P. 1983. Do the Karen Really Exist? In *Highlanders of Thailand,* ed. J. McKinnon and W. Bhruksasri. Kuala Lumpur: Oxford University Press.

Kulkarni, V. G. 1988. Straining at the Seams. *Far Eastern Economic Review* 7 (July):18–19.

Leach, E. R. 1954. *Political Systems of Highland Burma.* London: Bell.

————. 1983a. Correspondence: Imaginary Kachin. *Man* 18, no. 1:191–99.

————. 1983b. Correspondence: Imaginary Kachin. *Man* 18, no. 3:787–88.

Lehman, F. K. 1967. Burma: Kayah Society as a Function of the Shan-Burman-Karen Context. In *Contemporary Change in Traditional Societies,* ed. J. Steward. Urbana: University of Illinois Press.

Lieberman, V. B. 1978. Ethnic Politics in 18th Century Burma. *Modern Asian Studies* 12, no. 2:455–82.

Linter, Bertil. 1990. *Land of Jade.* Edinburgh: Kiscadale.

————. 1991. Triangular Ties. *Far Eastern Economic Review* (28 March):26.

Ni Ni Myint, Daw. 1983. *Burma's Struggle Against British Imperialism.* Rangoon: Universities Press.

Nugent, D. 1982. Closed Systems and Contradiction: The Kachin In and Out of History. *Man* 17, no. 3:508–27.

————. 1983. Correspondence: Imaginary Kachin. *Man* 18, no. 1:199–204.

Po, San C. 1928. *Burma and the Karens.* London: Elliot Stock.

Saw Maung. 1990. Address by Gen. Saw Maung to Co-ordination Meeting of SLORC and State/Division LORCs. *Working People's Daily* (10 January).

Scott, Sir J. G., and J. T. P. Hardiman. 1900–1901. *The Gazetteer of Upper Burma and the Shan States.* Rangoon: Government Printing and Stationery Office.

Silverstein, J. 1977. *Burma: Military Rule and the Politics of Stagnation.* Ithaca: Cornell University Press.

————. 1980. *Burmese Politics: The Dilemma of National Unity.* New Brunswick, N.J.: Rutgers University Press.

————. 1990. Civil War and Rebellion in Burma. *Journal of Southeast Asian Studies* 21, no. 1:114–34.

Smith, M. 1991. *Burma: Insurgency and the Politics of Ethnicity.* London: Zed.

Taylor, R. H. 1982. Perceptions of Ethnicity in the Politics of Burma. *Southeast Asian Journal of Social Science* 10, no.1:7–22.

———. 1987. *The State in Burma.* London: C. Hurst.

Tun Zaw Htwe. 1987. Those Craving for Colonial Servitude. *The Guardian* (Rangoon), 19 September.

United States General Accounting Office. 1989. *Drug Control: Enforcement Efforts in Burma are Not Effective.* Washington, D.C.: USGAO.

Yawnghwe, Chao Tzang. 1987. *The Shan of Burma: Memoirs of an Exile.* Singapore: Institute of Southeast Asian Studies.

References to Chapter 12

"Asia's Forgotten War." 1986. *Asiaweek,* 7 December, 35–36.

Chanda, Nayan. 1981. The Enemies Within. *Far Eastern Economic Review,* 30 October, 9–10.

Condominas, Georges. 1957. *Nous avons mangé la forêt: De la pierre-génie Gôo.* Paris: Mercure de France.

———. 1977. *We Have Eaten the Forest: The Story of a Montagnard Village in the Central Highlands of Vietnam.* New York: Hill and Wang.

Dang Nghiem Van. 1984. Glimpses of Tay Nguyen on the Road to Socialism. *Vietnam Social Sciences* (Hanoi) 2:40–54.

———. 1989. Nhung van de xa hoi hien nay o Tay Nguyen [The social problems at present in Tay Nguyen]. In *Tay Nguyen Tren Duong Phat Trien.* Hanoi: Nha Xuat Ban Khoa Hoc Xa Hoi.

Dassé, Martial. 1976. Montagnards revoltes et guerres revolutionnaires en Asie du Sud-Est continentale. Bangkok: DK Books.

Desbarats, Jacqueline. 1987. Population Relocation Programs in Socialist Vietnam: Economic Rationale or Class Struggle? *Indochina Report* 11 (April–June).

Dournes, Jacques. 1980. *Minorities of Central Vietnam: Autochthonous Indochinese Peoples.* Minority Rights Group Reports, no. 18. London: Minority Rights Group.

Evans, Grant. 1985. Vietnamese Communist Anthropology. *Canberra Anthropology* 8, nos. 1, 2:116–47.

———. 1990. *Lao Peasants Under Socialism.* New Haven: Yale University Press.

Fall, Bernard. 1962. Problèmes politiques des Etats poly-ethniques en Indochine. *France-Asie* 18, no. 172:129–52.

FBIS Reports. Foreign Broadcast Information Service, Far East. Various dates.

Gregerson, Marilyn, and Dorothy Thomas, eds. 1980. *Notes From Indochina on*

Ethnic Minority Cultures. Dallas, Tex.: Summer Institute of Linguistics, Museum of Anthropology.

Hickey, Gerald Cannon. 1982a. *Sons of the Mountains: Ethnohistory of the Vietnamese Central Highlands to 1954*. New Haven: Yale University Press.

————. 1982b. *Free in the Forest: Ethnohistory of the Vietnamese Central Highlands, 1954–1976*. New Haven: Yale University Press.

————. 1988. *Kingdom in the Morning Mist*. New Haven: Yale University Press.

Hiebert, Murray. 1989. Taking to the Hills. *Far Eastern Economic Review*, 25 May, 42–43.

————. 1992. Vietnam Dynamics of Despair: Poverty Condemns Minorities to Margins of Society. *Far Eastern Economic Review*, 23 April, 26–30.

Jones, Gavin W. 1984. *Demographic Transition in Asia*. Singapore: Maruzen.

Le Duy Dai. 1980. Mot vai dac diem phan bo dan cu tinh Gia Lai-Con Tum [Some significant aspects of population distribution in Gia Lai-Con Tum]. *Dan Toc Hoc*, no. 3:52–61.

————. 1983. Nhung van de dat ra xung quanh viec bo sung them lao dong de phat trien kinh te-xa hoi o Tay Nguyen hien nay [Problems relating to the additional labor destined for socioeconomic development of the present-day Central Highlands]. *Dan Toc Hoc*, no. 3:30–37.

Luu Hung. 1986. Forum: Vietnam's Central Highlands. *Vietnam Social Sciences*, nos. 1, 2:146–68.

Nguyen Tan Dac. 1986. The Village as the Highest Level of Social Organization in the Central Highlands. Typescript.

Quinn-Judge, Paul. 1982. Flushing Out Fulro. *Far Eastern Economic Review*, 8 October, 14.

Summary of World Broadcasts, Far East. British Broadcasting Service. Various dates.

Trinh Kim Sung. 1986. Forum: Vietnam's Central Highlands. *Vietnam Social Sciences*, nos. 1, 2:146–68.

Viet Chung. 1968. National Minorities and Nationality Policy in the D.R.V. *Vietnamese Studies*, no. 15:4–23.

Wain, Barry. 1988. Vietnam Keeps its People on the Move. *Asian Wall Street Journal*, 20 July, 1, 8.

References to Chapter 13

Bellwood, P. 1985. *Prehistory of the Indo-Malaysian Archipelago*. Sydney: Academic Press.

Benjamin, G. 1966. Temiar Social Groupings. *Federation Museums Journal* 11:1–25.

————. 1976. Austroasiatic Subgroupings and Prehistory in the Malay Peninsula. In *Austroasiatic Studies,* ed. P. N. Jenner. Honolulu: University of Hawaii Press.

Burger, Julian. 1987. *Report from the Frontier: The State of the World's Indigenous Peoples.* London: Zed.

Carey, I. 1976. *Orang Asli: The Aboriginal Tribes of Peninsular Malaysia.* Kuala Lumpur: Oxford University Press.

Clifford, Hugh. 1897. In *Court and Kampong.* London: Grant Richards.

————. 1898. *Studies in Brown Humanity.* London: Grant Richards.

Dentan, R. K. 1968. *The Semai: A Non-Violent People of Malaya.* New York: Holt, Rinehart and Winston.

Diffloth, G. F. 1974. Austroasiatic Languages. In *Encyclopaedia Britannica, Macropedia.* Chicago: Encyclopedia Britannica.

Endicott, K. M. 1979. *Batek Negrito Religion.* Oxford: Clarendon.

————. 1983. The Effects of Slave Raiding on the Aborigines of the Malay Peninsula. In *Slavery, Bondage, and Dependency in Southeast Asia,* ed. A. Reid. New York: St. Martin's.

————. N.d. Social Change among the Batek of Malaysia: Preliminary Findings. Typescript.

Endicott, K. M., and P. Bellwood. In press. The Possibility of Independent Foraging in the Rain Forest of Peninsular Malaysia. *Human Ecology.*

Favre, the Rev. [Pierre Étienne]. 1865. *An Account of the Wild Tribes Inhabiting the Malayan Peninsula, Sumatra and a Few Neighbouring Islands.* Paris: Imperial Printing Office.

Hood, Salleh. 1990. Orang Asli of Malaysia: An Overview of Recent Development Policy and its Impact. In *Tribal Peoples and the Development in Southeast Asia,* ed. Lim Teck Ghee and Alberto G. Gomes. Special issue of *Manusia & Masyarakat.* Kuala Lumpur: University of Malaya.

Hooker, M. B. 1976. *The Personal Laws of Malaysia: An Introduction.* Kuala Lumpur: Oxford University Press.

Howell, Signe. 1989a [1984]. *Society and Cosmos: Chewong of Peninsular Malaysia.* Chicago: University of Chicago Press.

————. 1989b. To Be Angry is Not to Be Human, but to Be Fearful is: Chewong Concepts of Human Nature. In *Societies at Peace: Anthropological Perspectives,* ed. Signe Howell and Roy Willis. London: Routledge.

Hurst, P. 1990. *Rainforest Politics: Ecological Destruction in South-East Asia.* London: Zed.

Jimin Idnis. 1983. Planning and Administration of Development Programmes for Tribal Peoples: The Malaysian Setting. *Country Report, Center for Integrated Rural Development for Asia and the Pacific.* Kuala Lumpur, Malaysia: JHEOA.

Karim, Wazir-Jahan. 1981. *Ma' Betisek Concepts of Living Things*. London: Athlone.

Means, G. P. 1986. The Orang Asli: Aboriginal Policies in Malaysia. *Public Affairs* 58, no. 4:637–52.

Nicholas, C. 1990. In the Name of the Semai? The State and Semai Society in Malaysia. In *Tribal Peoples and the Development in Southeast Asia*, ed. Lim Teck Ghee and Alberto G. Gomes. Special issue of *Manusia & Masyarakat*. Kuala Lumpur: University of Malaya.

Orang Asli News. 1990. Bulldozed: Orang Asli Church in Selangor. *Pernloi Gah: Orang Asli News* 1:8–10.

Rachagan, S. S. 1990. Constitutional and Statutory Provisions Governing the Orang Asli. In *Tribal Peoples and the Development in Southeast Asia*, ed. Lim Teck Ghee and Alberto G. Gomes. Special issue of *Manusia & Masyarakat*. Kuala Lumpur: University of Malaya.

Roseman, M. 1991. *Healing Sounds from the Malaysian Rain Forest: Temiar Music and Medicine*. Berkeley: University of California Press.

Skeat, W. W., and C. O. Blagden. 1906. *Pagan Races of the Malay Peninsula*. London: Macmillan.

Swettenham, F. A. 1895. *Malay Sketches*. London: Macmillan.

Wilkinson, R. J. 1910. Supplement: The Aboriginal Tribes. In *Papers on Malay Subjects*, ed. R. J. Wilkinson. Kuala Lumpur: F.M.S. Government Press.

Williams-Hunt, A. 1990. Law and Poverty: The Case of the Orang Asli. Typescript.

References to Chapter 14

Colchester, M. 1989. *Pirates, Squatters and Poachers: The Political Ecology of Dispossession of the Native Peoples of Sarawak*, London and Petaling Jaya: Survival International and Insan.

Cramb, R. A. 1989. Shifting Cultivation and Resource Degradation in Sarawak: Perceptions and Policies. *Borneo Research Bulletin* 21:22–49.

Cramb, R. A, and G. Dixon. 1988. Development in Sarawak: An Overview. In *Development in Sarawak*, ed. R. A. Cramb and R. H. W. Reece. Monash Papers on Southeast Asia, no. 17. Clayton, Australia: Monash University, Centre of Southeast Asian Studies.

Groves, H. E. 1964. *The Constitution of Malaysia*. Singapore: Malaysia Publications.

Gumis Humen, G. 1981. Native Land Tenure Protection in Sarawak. M.A. thesis, University of Malaya.

Hong, E. 1987. *Natives of Sarawak: Survival in Borneo's Vanishing Forests*. Pulau Pinang: Institut Masyarakat.

Hooker, M. B. 1980. *Native Law in Sabah and Sarawak.* Singapore: *Malayan Law Journal.*

———. N.d. The Orang Asli and the Laws of Malaysia: With Special Reference to Land. Typescript.

Insan and authors. 1989. *Logging Against the Natives of Sarawak.* Petaling Jaya: Institute of Social Analysis.

King, V. T. 1986a. Anthropology and Rural Development in Sarawak. *Sarawak Museum Journal* 36:13–42.

———. 1986b. Land Settlement Schemes and the Alleviation of Rural Poverty in Sarawak, East Malaysia: A Critical Commentary. *Southeast Asian Journal of Social Science* 14:71–99.

———. 1986c. Land Development in Sarawak, Malaysia: A Case Study. *Land Reform, Land Settlement and Cooperatives,* nos. 1, 2:53–60.

———. 1988a. Models and Realities: Malaysian National Planning and East Malaysian Development Problems. *Modern Asian Studies* 22:263–98.

———. 1988b. The Costs of Development in Sarawak. *Borneo Research Bulletin* 20:15–28.

———. 1990a. Why is Sarawak Peripheral? In *Margins and Minorities: The Peripheral Areas and Peoples of Malaysia,* ed. V. T. King and M. J. G. Parnwell. Hull: Hull University Press.

———. 1990b. Land Settlement Programmes in Sarawak: A Mistaken Strategy? In *Margins and Minorities: The Peripheral Areas and Peoples of Malaysia,* ed. V. T. King and M. J. G. Parnwell. Hull: Hull University Press.

Malaysia. 1964. *The Federal Constitution.* Kuala Lumpur: Government Printers.

———. 1972. *Parliamentary Debates on the Constitution Amendment Bill, 1971.* Kuala Lumpur: Government Printers.

Mohamed Suffian bin Hashim, Tan Sri. 1972. *An Introduction to the Constitution of Malaysia.* Kuala Lumpur: Government Printers.

Padoch, C. 1982. *Migration and its Alternatives Among the Ibans of Sarawak.* Verhandelingen van het KITLV, no. 98. The Hague: Martinus Nijhoff.

Porter, A. F. 1967. *The Development of Land Administration in Sarawak from the Rule of Rajah James Brooke to the Present Time (1841–1965).* Kuching: Land and Survey Department.

Reece, R. H. W. 1988. Economic Development under the Brookes. In *Development in Sarawak,* ed. R. A. Cramb and R. H. W. Reece. Monash Papers on Southeast Asia, no. 17. Clayton, Australia: Monash University, Centre of Southeast Asian Studies.

Sarawak. 1989. *Annual Statistical Bulletin, 1988.* Kuching: Department of Statistics Malaysia, Sarawak Branch.

Sheridan, L. A., and H. E. Groves. 1967. *The Constitution of Malaysia.* Dobbs Ferry, N.Y.: Oceana.

Simba Newsletter. 1991. Sarawak: The Disposable Forest. *Simba Newsletter,* no. 3.1 (June).

Weinstock, J. A. 1979. Land Tenure Practices of the Swidden Cultivators of Borneo. M.A. thesis, Cornell University.

References to Chapter 15

Arndt, Paul. 1951. *Religion auf Ostflores, Adonare und Solor.* Studia Instituti Anthropos, no. 1. Wien-Mödling, Missionsdruckerei St. Gabriel.

Avé, Jan B. 1976. Supplementary Remarks on Russell Jones's Article on "Indonesia." *Archipel* 12:227–30.

Barnes, R. H. 1984. Whaling Off Lembata: The Effects of a Development Project on an Indonesian Community. IWGIA Documents, no. 48. Copenhagen: International Work Group for Indigenous Affairs.

Beauclerk, John, and Jeremy Narby, with Janet Townsend. 1988. *Indigenous Peoples: A Fieldguide for Development.* Development Guidelines, no. 2. Oxford: Oxfam.

Bellwood, Peter. 1985. *Prehistory of the Indo-Malaysian Archipelago.* Sydney: Academic.

Burger, Julian. 1987. *Report from the Frontier: The State of the World's Indigenous Peoples.* London: Zed.

Campagnolo, Henri. 1979. *Fataluku I. Relations et Choix: Introduction méthodologique à la description d'une langue «non austronésienne» de Timor Oriental.* Langues et Civilizations de L'Asie du Sud-Est et du Monde Insulindien, no. 5. Paris: Société d'Études Linguistiques et Anthropologiques de France.

Gill, Sam. 1990. Mother Earth: An American Myth. In *The Invented Indian: Cultural Fictions and Government Policies,* ed. James A. Clifton. New Brunswick, N.J.: Transaction.

Glover, Ian C. 1977. The Late Stone Age in Eastern Indonesia. *World Archaeology* 9:42–61.

Goodland, Robert. 1982. *Tribal Peoples and Economic Development: Human Ecologic Considerations.* Washington, D.C.: World Bank.

Gray, Andrew. 1984. The People of East Timor and their Struggle for Survival. In *East Timor: The Struggle Continues,* ed. Torben Retbøll. IWGIA Documents, no. 50. Copenhagen: International Work Group for Indigenous Affairs.

Hicks, David. 1976. *Tetum Ghosts and Kin: Fieldwork in an Indonesian Community.* Palo Alto, Calif.: Mayfield.

———. 1984. *A Maternal Religion: The Role of Women in Tetum Myth and Ritual.* Special Reports, no. 22. DeKalb: Center For Southeast Asian Studies, Northern Illinois University.

————. 1990. *Kinship and Religion in Eastern Indonesia.* Gothenburg Studies in Social Anthropology, no. 12. Gothenburg, Sweden: Acta Universitatis Gothoburgensis.

Independent Commission on International Humanitarian Issues. 1987. *Indigenous Peoples: A Global Quest for Justice.* Report prepared for the Independent Commission on International Humanitarian Issues. London: Zed.

International Work Group for Indigenous Affairs. 1990. *IWGIA Yearbook, 1989.* Copenhagen: International Work Group for Indigenous Affairs.

Leach, E. R. 1954. *Political Systems of Highland Burma: A Study of Kachin Social Structure.* London: Bell.

————. 1961. Polyandry, Inheritance and the Definition of Marriage: With Particular Reference to Sinhalese Customary Law. In *Rethinking Anthropology.* London School of Economics Monographs on Social Anthropology, no. 22. London: Athlone.

LeBar, Frank M. 1972. *Ethnic Groups of Insular Southeast Asia.* Vol. 1: *Indonesia, Andaman Islands, and Madagascar.* New Haven: Human Relations Area Files Press.

Organisasi Papua Merdeka [West Papua Peoples Front]. 1990. Indonesia: 20 Years of Denial of the Right to Self-Determination of the Peoples of West Papua. *IWGIA Newsletter,* nos. 60–61 (April–September):55–60.

Ormeling, F. J. 1957. *The Timor Problem: A Geographical Interpretation of an Underdeveloped Island, Second Impression.* The Hague: Nijhoff.

Otten, Mariël. 1986. *Transmigrasi. Indonesian Resettlement Policy, 1965–1985, Myths and Realities.* IWGIA Documents, no. 57. Copenhagen: International Work Group for Indigenous Affairs.

Pluvier, J. M. 1974. *South-East Asia from Colonialism to Independence.* Kuala Lumpur: Oxford University Press.

Retbøll, Torben, ed. 1980. *East Timor, Indonesia and the Western Democracies: A Collection of Documents.* IWGIA Documents, no. 40. Copenhagen: International Work Group for Indigenous Affairs.

————, ed. 1984. *East Timor: The Struggle Continues.* IWGIA Documents, no. 50. Copenhagen: International Work Group for Indigenous Affairs.

Schulte Nordholt, H. G. 1971. *The Political System of the Atoni of Timor.* Verhandelingen van het Koninklijk Instituut voor Taal-, Land- en Volkenkunde, no. 60. The Hague: Nijhoff.

Shutler, R., and J. C. Marck. 1975. On the Dispersal of the Austronesian Horticulturalists. *Archaeology and Physical Anthropology in Oceania* 10:81–113.

Traube, Elizabeth G. 1986. *Cosmology and Social Life: Ritual Exchange among the Mambai of East Timor.* Chicago and London: University of Chicago Press.

Vroklage, B. A. G. 1953. *Ethnographie der Belu in Zentral-Timor, erster Teil.* Leiden: Brill.

References to Chapter 16

Amnesty International. 1985. *East Timor: Violations of Human Rights.* London: Amnesty International.

Anonymous. 1988. Timorese Refugee on Indonesian Operations since 1975: The Aitana Massacre. *Tapol: The Indonesia Human Rights Campaign Bulletin,* no. 87 (June):9–11.

Barbosa, Duarte. 1921. *The Book of Duarte Barbosa: An Account of the Countries Bordering on the Indian Ocean and their Inhabitants, Written by Duarte Barbosa and Completed about the Year 1518 A.D.,* trans. Mansel Longworth Dames. Vol. 2. London: Hakluyt Society.

Barnes, R. H. 1980. Marriage, Exchange and the Meaning of Corporations in Eastern Indonesia. In *The Meaning of Marriage Payments,* ed. J. L. Comaroff. London: Academic.

Berthe, Louis. 1961. Le marriage par achat et la captation des gendres dans une société sémi-feodale: les Bunaq de Timor Central. *L'Homme* 1, no. 3:5–31.

———. 1972. *Bei Gua: Itinéraire des ancêtres, mythes des Bunaq de Timor.* Paris: Centre National de la Recherche Scientifique.

Boxer, C. R. 1947. The Topasses of Timor. *Koninklijke Vereeniging Indisch Instituut, Mededeling* 73, no. 24:1–22..

———. 1948. *Fidalgos in the Far East, 1550–1770: Fact and Fancy in the History of Macao.* The Hague: Nijhoff.

———. 1960. Portuguese Timor: A Rough Island Story, 1515–1960. *History Today* 10, no. 5 (May):349–55.

Budiardjo, C., and Lim Soei Liong. 1984. *The War against East Timor.* London: Zed.

Callinan, Bernard J. 1953. *Independent Company: The 2/2 and 2/4 Australian Independent Companies in Portuguese Timor, 1941–3.* London: Heineman.

Campagnolo, Henri. 1973. *La langue des Fataluku de Lórehe (Timor Portugais).* Thèse de doctorat de 3ème cycle. Paris: Université René Descartes, Sorbonne.

———. 1979. *Fataluku I: Relations et chois, introduction méthodologique à la description d'une langue «non austronésienne» de Timor Oriental.* Langues et Civilizations de l'Asie du Sud-est et du Monde Insulindien, no. 5. Paris: Société d'Études Linguistiques et Anthropologiques de France.

Capell, Arthur. 1944. Peoples and Languages of Timor. *Oceania* 14, no. 3:191–219; 14, no. 4:311–37; 15, no. 1:19–48.

————. 1972. Portuguese Timor: Two More Non-Austronesian Languages. In *Linguistic Papers, I: General; II: Indonesia and New Guinea,* ed. Arthur Capell. Oceania Linguistic Monographs, no. 15. Sydney: University of Sydney.

Capizzi, Elaine, Helen Hill, and Dave Macey. 1976. FRETILIN and the Struggle for Independence in East Timor. *Race and Class* 17, no. 4:381–95.

Clamagirand, Brigitte. 1980. The Social Organization of the Ema of Timor. In *The Flow of Life: Essays on Eastern Indonesia,* ed. James J. Fox. Cambridge: Harvard University Press.

Cowan, H. J. K. 1963. Le Buna' de Timor: Une langue "Oueste Papoue." *Bijdragen tot de Taal-, Land- en Volkenkunde* 119, no. 4:387–400.

Dunn, J. S. 1983. *Timor: A People Betrayed.* Milton, Queensland: Jacaranda.

Evans, Grant. 1975. *Eastern (Portuguese) Timor: Independence or Oppression?* Melbourne: Australian Union of Students. Reprinted as "Portuguese Timor," *New Left Review* 91 (May-June):67–79.

Forbes, Henry O. 1883. On Some Tribes of the Island of Timor. *Journal of the Anthropological Institute* 13:402–30.

Forman, Shepard. 1978. East Timor: Exchange and Political Hierarchy at the Time of European Discoveries. In *Economic Exchange and Social Interaction in Southeast Asia,* ed. Karl Hutterer. Michigan Papers on South and Southeast Asia, no. 13. Ann Arbor: Center for South and Southeast Asian Studies, University of Michigan.

————. 1980. Descent, Alliance and Exchange Ideology among the Makassae of East Timor. In *The Flow of Life: Essays on Eastern Indonesia,* ed. James J. Fox. Cambridge: Harvard University Press.

Françillon, Gerard. 1967. Some Matriarchal Aspects of the Social System of the Southern Tetum. Ph.D. thesis, Australian National University.

————. 1980. Incursions upon Wehali: A Modern History of an Ancient Empire. In *The Flow of Life: Essays on Eastern Indonesia,* ed. James J. Fox. Cambridge: Harvard University Press.

Friedberg, Claudine. 1980. Boiled Woman and Broiled Man: Myths and Agricultural Rituals of the Bunaq of Central Timor. In *The Flow of Life: Essays on Eastern Indonesia,* ed. James J. Fox. Cambridge: Harvard University Press.

Gray, Andrew. 1984. The People of East Timor and their Struggle for Survival. In *East Timor: The Struggle Continues,* ed. Torben Retbøll. IWGIA Documents, no. 50. Copenhagen: International Work Group for Indigenous Affairs.

Groeneveldt, William Pieter. 1880. Notes on the Malay Archipelago and Malacca, Compiled from Chinese Sources. *Verhandelingen van het Bataviaasch Genootschap van Kunsten en Wetenschappen* 39:1–144.

Hicks, David. 1972a. Timor-Roti. In *Ethnic Groups of Insular Southeast Asia,* ed. Frank M. LeBar. Vol. 1. New Haven: Human Relations Area Files Press.

————. 1972b. Eastern Tetum. In *Ethnic Groups of Insular Southeast Asia,* ed. Frank M. LeBar. Vol. 1. New Haven: Human Relations Area Files Press.

————. 1976. *Tetum Ghosts and Kin.* Palo Alto, Calif.: Mayfield.

Hill, Helen. 1978. Fretilin: The Origins, Ideologies and Strategies of a Nationalist Movement in East Timor. M.A. thesis, Monash University.

Jolliffe, Jill. 1978. East Timor: Nationalism and Colonialism. St. Lucia: University of Queensland Press.

————. 1989. *Timor, Terra Sengrenta.* Lisbon: Editora O Jornal.

Kolff, D. H. 1840. *Voyages through the Southern and Little Known Parts of the Moluccan Archipelago, and along The Previously Unknown Southern Coast of New Guinea, 1825–26,* ed. G. W. Earl. London: Madden.

Lazarowitz, Toby. 1980. The Makassai: Complementary Dualism in Timor. Ph.D. diss., State University of New York, Stony Brook.

Metzner, Joachim K. 1977. *Man and Environment in Eastern Indonesia: A Geoecological Analysis of the Baucau-Viqueque Area as a Possible Basis for Regional Planning.* Development Studies Center Monographs, no. 8. Canberra: Australian National University.

Middelkoop, Pieter. 1952. Trektochten van Timorese Groepen; Amabi-Tekst uit de Verzameling van wijlen Prof. J. C. G. Jonker, verhaald door Jun Talan. *Tijdschrift voor Indische Taal-, Land- en Volkenkunde* 85, no. 2:173–272.

Nicol, Bill. 1978. *Timor: The Stillborn Nation.* Melbourne: Visa.

Ormeling, Ferdinand Jan. 1956. *The Timor Problem: A Geographical Interpretation of an Underdeveloped Island.* The Hague: Nijhoff.

Ramos-Horta, José. 1985. *Funu: the Unfinished Saga of East Timor.* Trenton, N.J.: Red Sea Press.

Renard-Clamagirand, Brigitte. 1982. *Marobo: Une société ema de Timor.* Langues et Civilisations de l'Asie du Sud-est et du Monde Insulindien, No. 12. Paris: Société d'Etudes Linguistiques et Anthropologiques de France.

Schulte Nordholt, H. B. 1971. *The Political System of the Atoni of Timor.* Verhandelingen van het Koninklijk Instituut voor Taal-, Land- en Volkenkunde, no. 60. The Hague: Nijhoff.

Taylor, John G. 1990. *The Indonesian Occupation of East Timor, 1974–1989: A Chronology.* London: Catholic Institute for International Relations, in association with the Refugee Studies Programme, University of Oxford.

————. 1991. *Indonesia's Forgotten War: The Hidden History of East Timor.* London: Zed.

Telkamp, Gerard J. 1979. The Economic Structure of an Outpost in the Outer Islands in the Indonesian Achipelago: Portuguese Timor, 1850–1975. In *Between People and Statistics: Essays on Modern Indonesian History, presented to P. Creutzberg.* The Hague: Nijhoff.

Thomaz, F. R. Luis Filipe. 1981. The Formation of Tetun-Praca, Vehicular Language of East Timor. In *Papers on Indonesian Language and Literature,* ed. N. Phillips and K. Anwar. Cahiers d'Archipel, no. 13. Paris: Archipel.

Traube, Elisabeth. 1980. Mambai Rituals of Black and White. In *The Flow of Life: Essays on Eastern Indonesia,* ed. James J. Fox. Cambridge: Harvard University Press.

————. 1986. *Cosmology and Social Life: Ritual Exchange among the Mambai of East Timor.* Chicago: University of Chicago Press.

Wallace, Alfred Russel. 1869. *The Malay Archipelago: The Land of the Orang-Utan, and the Bird of Paradise, A Narrative of Travel, With Studies of Man and Nature.* 2 vols. London: Macmillan.

References to Chapter 17

Episcopal Commission on Tribal Filipinos. 1979. A Report on Tribal Minorities in Mindanao, Part 1: A Report on PANAMIN in Mindanao. Manila: ICL Research Team.

Evangelista, A. E. 1983. Indigenous Cultural Minorities of the Philippines. In *Filipino Tradition and Acculturation: Reports on Changing Societies.* Philippine Studies Program, Research Reports, no. 2. Tokyo: Institute of Social Sciences, Waseda University.

Gibson, Thomas. 1986. *Sacrifice and Sharing in the Philippine Highlands: Religion and Society among the Buid of Mindoro.* London School of Economics, Monographs on Social Anthropology, no. 57. London and Dover: Athlone.

International Work Group for Indigenous Affairs. 1987. Statement of the Delegation of the Philippine Indigenous Organizations to the UN Working Group on Indigenous Populations. *IWGIA Newsletter,* nos. 51/52:81–84.

Lynch, O. J. 1984. Native Title, Private Right and Tribal Land Law: An Introductory Survey. *ECTF Research Series* 4, no. 2:1–29.

Macdonald, C. 1990. Sinsin, le théâtre des génies, Paris: Paris: Ed. du Centre National de la Recherche Scientifique.

McDonagh, S. 1983. Modernization, Multinationals and the Tribal Filipino. *Solidarity* 4, no. 97:73–82.

Neumann, L. 1981. Philippines: Tribal Leader Murdered. *IWGIA Newsletter,* nos. 25/26:62–64.

Okamura, J. Y. 1987. The Politics of Neglect. *Tribal Forum* 8, no. 4:18–23.

Postma, A. 1989. Formal Education Among the Mangyans: Suggestions Toward Improvement and Implementation. *Solidarity,* no. 122 (April-June):54–60.

Solidarity Seminar Series on Public Issues. 1989. Ethnic Minorities: Education Toward Self-determination. *Solidarity,* no. 122 (April-June):4–39.

Tribal Forum. 1983. Better-Known Minority Ethno-Linguistic Groups in the

Philippines. In *Indigenous Peoples in Crisis.* Tribal Filipino Lecture Series, Collated Papers. Manila: Episcopal Commission on Tribal Filipinos.

References to Chapter 19

Baba, Y. 1980. Study of Minority-Majority Relations: The Ainu and the Japanese in Hokkaido. *The Japanese Interpreter* 13:60–92.

Batchelor, J. 1938. *An Ainu-English-Japanese Dictionary.* Tokyo: Iwanami-Syoten.

Cornell, J. 1964. Ainu Assimilation and Cultural Extinction. *Ethnology* 3:287–304.

Davis, G. 1987. Japan's Indigenous Indians the Ainu. *Tokyo Journal* (October): 7–13, 18–19.

DeVos, G. 1975. Ethnic Pluralism: Conflict and Accommodation. In *Ethnic Identity,* ed. G. Devos and L. Romanucci-Ross. Palo Alto: Mayfield.

Hokkaido Government. 1899. *Hokkaido Kyuudojin Hogoho* (Law for the Protection of Native Hokkaido Aborigines). Hokkaido: Hokkaido Government.

———. *Passport to Hokkaido.* Hokkaido: Hokkaido Government.

Kingsbury, Benedict. 1990. Indigenous Peoples in International Law. D.Phil. thesis, University of Oxford.

Kodama, S. 1970. *Ainu Historical and Anthropological Studies.* Sapporo: Hokudai University Press.

Munro, N. 1911. *Prehistoric Japan.* Tokyo: Daiichi Shobo.

Naert, P. 1958. La Situation Linguistique de l'Ainou et Indoeuropeen. *Luã* 53, no. 4:1–234.

Nakane, C. 1970. *Japanese Society.* Berkeley: University of California Press.

Newell, W. 1967. Some Problems of Integrating Minorities into Japanese Society. *Journal of Asian and African Studies* 2:212–29.

Ohnuki-Tierney, E. 1976. Regional Variation in Ainu Culture. *American Ethnologist* 3, no. 2:297–329.

———. 1981. *Illness and Healing among the Sakhalin Ainu: A Symbolic Interpretation.* Cambridge: Cambridge University Press.

Peng, F. C. C., and P. Geiser. 1977. *The Ainu: The Past in the Present.* Hiroshima: Bunka Hyoron.

Refsing, K. 1980. The Ainu People of Japan. *IWGIA Newsletter,* no. 24:79–92.

Sanders, D. 1985. The Ainu as an Indigenous Population. *IWGIA Newsletter,* no. 45:119–50.

Sjöberg, K. 1991. *Mr. Ainu: Cultural Mobilization and the Practice of Ethnicity in a Hierarchical Culture.* Lund: Lund University Press.

Smith, R. J. 1983. *Japanese Society: Traditional Self and the Social Order.*

I

N

Z

MONOGRAPHS OF THE ASSOCIATION FOR ASIAN STUDIES

1. *Money Economy of Medieval Japan: A Study in the Use of Coins*, by Delmer M. Brown. 1951
2. *China's Management of the American Barbarians: A Study of Sino-American Relations, 1841–1861, with Documents*, by Earl Swisher. 1951.
3. *Leadership and Power in the Chinese Community of Thailand*, by G. William Skinner. 1958.
4. *Siam Under Rama III, 1824–1851*, by Walter F. Vella. 1957.
5. *The Rise of the Merchant Class in Tokugawa Japan: 1600–1868*, by Charles David Sheldon. 1958.
6. *Chinese Secret Societies in Malaya*, by L. F. Comber. 1959.
7. *The Traditional Chinese Clan Rules*, by Hui-Chen Wang Liu. 1959.
8. *A Comparative Analysis of the Jajmani System*, by Thomas O. Beidelman. 1959.
9. *Colonial Labour Policy and Administration 1910–1941*, by J. Norman Parmer. 1959.
10. *Bankguad—A Community Study in Thailand*, by Howard Keva Kaufman. 1959.
11. *Agricultural Involution: The Processes of Ecological Change in Indonesia*, by Clifford Geertz. 1963.
12. *Maharashta Purana*, By Edward C. Dimock, Jr. and Pratul Chandra Gupta. 1964.
13. *Conciliation in Japanese Legal Practice*, by Dan Fenno Henderson. 1964.
14. *The Malayan Tin Industry to 1914*, by Wong Lin Ken. 1965.
15. *Reform, Rebellion, and the Heavenly Way*, by Benjamin F. Weems. 1964.
16. *Korean Literature: Topics and Themes*, by Peter H. Lee. 1965.
17. *Ch'oe Pu's Diary: A Record of Drifting Across the Sea*, by John Meskill. 1965.
18. *The British in Malaya: The First Forty Years*, by K. G. Tregonning. 1965.
19. *Chiaraijima Village: Land Tenure, Taxation, and Local Trade*, by William Chambliss. 1965.
* 20. *Shinran's Gospel of Pure Grace*, by Alfred Bloom. 1965.
21. *Before Aggression: Europeans Prepare the Japanese Army*, by Ernst L. Presseisen. 1965.
* 22. *A Documentary Chronicle of Sino-Western Relations: 1644–1820*, by Lo-shu Fu. 1966.
23. *K'ang Yu-wei: A Biography and a Symposium*, trans. and ed. by Jung-pang Lo. 1967
24. *The Restoration of Thailand Under Rama I: 1782–1809*, by Klaus Wenk. 1968.
* 25. *Political Centers and Cultural Regions in Early Bengal*, by Barrie M. Morrison. 1969.
* 26. *The Peasant Rebellions of the Late Ming Dynasty*, by James Bunyan Parsons. 1969.
27. *Politics and Nationalist Awakening in South India: 1852–1891*, by R. Suntharalingam. 1974.

* Indicates publication is available.